ADVANCES IN EQUINE NUTRITION

Advances in Equine Nutrition

Edited by Joe D. Pagan Ph.D
Kentucky Equine Research Inc., Versailles, Kentucky, USA

NOTTINGHAM
University Press

Nottingham University Press
Manor Farm, Main Street
Thrumpton, Nottingham, NG11 0AX, UK

NOTTINGHAM

First published 1998
Reprinted 2000
© Kentucky Equine Research, Inc. 1998

British Library Cataloguing in Publication Data
A catalogue record for this book is available from the British Library

ISBN   1-897676-83-2

Typeset by Nottingham University Press, Nottingham
Printed and bound by Redwood Books, Trowbridge

ACKNOWLEDGEMENTS

The editor gratefully thanks Catherine Bishop for her assistance in the prepartion of this text.

Dedicated to the memory of my father,

JOHN F. PAGAN
1920-1998

CONTENTS

General Nutrition

The Digestive Tract of the Horse - Practical Considerations 1
Forages for Horses: More Than Just Filler 13
Carbohydrates in Equine Nutrition 29
Protein Requirements and Digestibility: A Review 43
Mineral Requirements in the Horse: A Historical Perspective 51
Cereal Grains and Byproducts: What's in Them and How are
    They Processed? 57
Measuring the Digestible Energy Content of Horse Feeds 71
Nutrient Digestibility in Horses 77
Effect of Feeding Frequency on Digestion in Ponies 85
Effects of Meal Feeding Frequency and Roughage on Behaviors
    of Stabled Horses 89
Responses of Blood Glucose, Lactate and Insulin in Horses Fed
    Equal Amounts of Grain With or Without Added Soybean Oil 93
Selenium Supplementation for Horse Feed 97
What Does Your Horse Weigh? 105
Computing Horse Nutrition: How to Properly Conduct an
    Equine Nutrition Evaluation 111

The Performance Horse

Choke Points:What Factors Limit Performance in the Equine Athlete? 125
Form Follows Function? How Does Conformation Affect
    the Performance Horse? 129
Energy and the Performance Horse 141
The Gut During Exercise 149
Protein Requirements of Equine Athletes 161
Blood Analysis and its Relationship to Feeding the Performance Horse 167
Skeletal Muscle Function and Metabolism 181
The Use of Nutritional Ergogenic Aids in Horses 191
Electrolytes and the Performance Horse 201

Trace Minerals for the Performance Horse: Known Biochemical
   Roles and Estimates of Requirements   205
Fat Soluble Vitamins and the Performance Horse   215
Testing for Drugs, Medications and Other Substances in Racing Horses   229
Recent Developments in Equine Nutrition Research   251
The Effect of Pre-exercise B-vitamin Supplementation on Metabolic
   Response to Exercise in Thoroughbred Horses   259
Effect of Dietary Vitamin E Supplementation on the Exercising Horse   261
The Effect of Chromium Supplementation on Metabolic Response
   to Exercise in Throroughbred Horses   263
The Effects of Niacin Supplementation on Niacin Status and Exercise
   Metabolism in Horses   271
The Influence of Trimethylglycine on the Untrained and Trained Horse
   Exercising to Fatigue   275
The Effect of Feeding Restricted Diets on Thyroid Hormone
   Concentrations and Metabolic Responses in the Exercising Horse   277
The Long-term Effects of Feeding Fat to Two Year Old Thoroughbreds
   in Training   281
The Influence of Time of Feeding on Exercise Response in
   Thoroughreds Fed a Fat Supplemented or High Carbohydrate Diet   289
The Effect of Feeding After Exercise on Glucose and Glycogen
   Responses in the Horse   293
Effect of Diet on Weight Loss and Plasma Variables in Endurance
   Exercised Horses   297
Effect of Exercise Conditioning and Type on Serum Creatine Kinase
   and Aspartate Amino-Transferase Activity   299
The Effect of Warming-up on Response to Exercise   303

Feeding Management

Myths and Wives' Tales of Feeding Horses: "some truth, some fiction"   307
Feeding the Three-Day Event and Dressage Horse   319
Feeding Practices in Australia and New Zealand   331
Some Aspects of Feeding the Endurance Horse   341
Feeding The Endurance Horse   351
Feeding and Fitting: The Halter and Sales Horse   365
Feeding the Western Performance Horse   373

Growth and Broodmare Nutrition

The Equine Skeleton: How Does Bone Grow and how do
   Abnormalities in the Developmental Process Affect Soundness?   383
Protein and Energy Requirements of Growing Horses   407
Energy Requirements of Lactating Mares and Suckling Foals   415
Delivering Essential Nutrients to Young, Growing Horses   421
Growth Management of Young Horses to Achieve Different
   Commercial Endpoints   437
Effects of Yeast Culture Supplementation on Growth of
   Thoroughbred Foals at Weaning   447
A Summary of Growth Rates of Thoroughbreds in Kentucky   449
The Effect of Weaning Age on Foal Growth and Bone Density   457
Investigation of Farm Wide Incidence of Bone Formation Problems
   in the Horse   461
The Incidence of Developmental Orthopedic Disease (DOD)
   on a Kentucky Thoroughbred Farm   469

Pathological Conditions

Nutrition Related Pathological Conditions of the Performance Horse   477
Colic   483
Nutrition and Productivity Practical Problems Related to Nutrition   489
Exertional Rhabdomyolysis in The Horse   507
Tied Up With Electrolytes - Or Not?   513
Mycotoxins: A Nationwide Problem   531
Implications of Mycotoxins   535
Small Airway Disease and Equine Respiratory Health   539

Index   555
Contributing Authors   563
Team Members   565

GENERAL NUTRITION

THE DIGESTIVE TRACT OF THE HORSE - PRACTICAL CONSIDERATIONS

STEPHEN G. JACKSON

Kentucky Equine Research, Inc., Versailles, Kentucky, USA

The horse is classified, based on the anatomy of the digestive tract, as a non-ruminant herbivore. More specifically the horse is a hindgut fermenter and as such combines some of the advantages of the strict monogastric animal and the ruminant. Failure to understand the anatomy of the gastro-intestinal (GI) tract and basic digestive physiology is the root of many feeding errors involving both nutritional management and feed formulation.

Basic anatomy

The digestive process begins with prehension of food. Feed is supplied as fresh pasture, long hay or variations of stored forage and as concentrate feed containing processed or unprocessed cereal grains. In order to properly start the digestive process, the horse needs a sound, functional mouth. This means the teeth should be in good condition with functional occlusive surfaces. The mature horse has 18 upper and 18 lower teeth consisting of six upper and six lower incisors and 12 upper and lower molars. The function of the teeth is prehension (gathering) and chewing of food. The teeth participate in the digestive process primarily by reducing the particle size of food. Chewing also stimulates the flow of saliva which may initiate chemical digestion of feed and lubricates feed prior to its passage to the remainder of the tract. Dental problems resulting from wear and genetic defects such as parrot mouth interfere with dental function. Many times horses that waste feed, bolt their feed or are finicky eaters have dental anomalies which once corrected allow the horse to utilize feed more efficiently. Horses should have annual dental exams and should have their teeth floated should sharp edges be detected on the upper (outside) or lower (inside) molar arcades. Older horses which through normal wear have lost functional dentition or younger horses with dental problems may benefit from use of pelleted concentrate rations since the particle size has been mechanically reduced in the pelleting process. Certainly examination of the teeth should be an integral part of the nutritional management program on a farm.

The esophagus is a muscular tube connecting the mouth and the stomach. Food is forced down the esophagus by peristaltic waves or muscle contractions. Saliva produced by secretory glands in the mouth lubricates the feed and prevents the feed from becoming lodged in the esophagus. Although there is a great deal of discussion about choke in the horse, it is actually quite rare for the horse to choke or for esophageal obstruction to occur.

The stomach of the horse is relatively small when compared to the capacity of the entire tract. The horse really evolved as a continuous grazer and is better equipped to utilize small frequent meals rather than large meals of concentrates. Rate of passage through the stomach is such that ingesta remains in the stomach only a very short time. Figure 1 shows the relative size of the stomach when compared to the other segments of the GI tract. The pH of the stomach is quite acidic. Kern (1974) measured pH in various segments of the horse's GI tract and these values are shown in Table 1. Although the major impact of the stomach on ingesta is acid hydrolysis and enzymatic digestion of protein, there is a significant amount of lactic acid produced from the fermentation of soluble sugars by microbes located in the fundic region of the stomach.

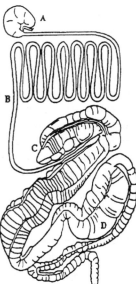

A   Stomach
B   Small intestine
C   Cecum
D   Colon

Figure 1. The horse's digestive tract

The chyme (ingesta) passes from the stomach into the small intestine. The small intestine is composed of the duodenum, the jejunum and the ileum (figure 1). The small intestine is 21 meters long and has a capacity of about 56 liters of ingesta. The small intestine receives a continuous flow of pancreatic juice which increases due to nervous or hormonal factors associated with a meal. The small intestine is, or should be if the feeding program is properly designed, the major zone of absorption for simple sugars derived from starch digestion, of amino acids from protein digestion, of free fatty acids resulting from digestion of the lipid component of the diet, of fat soluble vitamins A, D & E and of some minerals.

Material not digested in the foregut passes through the ileo-cecal orifice into the cecum. The cecum and large colon are analogous to the rumen and reticulum of the cow and sheep, and house billions of bacteria and protozoa which serve in a symbiotic relationship with the horse enabling the digestion of cellulose and other fibrous fractions of the feed. Additionally, the cecal and colonic microbes synthesize B vitamins and vitamin K which are available to the horse to help meet the requirements for these nutrients.

Table 1. pH IN VARIOUS REGIONS OF THE EQUINE DIGESTIVE TRACT

Region	*pH*
Stomach-fundic	5.4
Stomach-pyloric	2.6
Ileum	7.4
Cecum	6.6
Terminal Colon	6.6

(Kern, 1974, JAS)

There is a significant amount of microbial protein synthesized in the horse's hindgut. Whether the microbial protein is available to the horse to contribute to meeting amino acid requirements is still somewhat controversial.

The rectum is the posterior part of the digestive tract and serves primarily as a storage area for fecal products which have not been digested. Material is held in the rectum until sufficient material accumulates which then results in nervous stimulation and voiding of feces through the anus.

Effects of feed processing on digestion

The aim of feed processing is to change the physical or chemical form of ingredients resulting in greater nutrient availability to the target animal while preserving the quality of the nutrients in the raw material for as long as possible. The most frequently used method of feed processing is the mechanical reduction of particle size. This is done by cracking, crimping or grinding ingredients.

There are pros and cons associated with this reduction of particle size. The major disadvantage is the reduction of storage life of cereal grains by exposing the starchy endosperm and seed lipids to oxidation once the seed coat is broken. This disadvantage is for many ingredients far outweighed by the advantages of reducing preconsumption particle size. For horses, crimping or rolling of oats results in about a 5% increase in digestibility and may or may not be worth the increased milling cost, either to the feed manufacturers or to the consumer. On the other hand, some kind of mechanical milling of barley, wheat, milo and corn is a must in horse diets. Meyer (1993) has shown, for instance, that prececal digestibility of corn starch is significantly altered by feed processing (Table 2). The increase in prececal digestibility of starch is a result of increasing the surface area exposed to digestive enzymes, and in the case of popping, gelatinization of the starch molecule which increases digestibility. It is important to note that cracking corn resulted in no increase in prececal digestibility whereas corn starch that was heat treated was nearly entirely digested prececally (90.1%). These data would indicate that milling of corn is important if the site of digestion of the starch is of concern (later we will see that it is).

Hintz and Loy (1966) compared the digestibility of a pelleted or loose ration fed to horses. The loose diet consisted of rolled barley, ground alfalfa, wheat, molasses and tallow (2%). The pelleted ration was of the same composition but ground and pelleted. There was no difference between the two diets in terms of total tract digestibility of protein, crude fiber or nitrogen free extract. However, rate of passage was significantly greater for the pelleted diet at 33 hours post feeding. By 45 hours post feeding, 95.6 and 95.8% of a digestibility marker (Styrofoam beads) had been recovered in the feces for the loose and pelleted diets respectively.

Table 2. PREILEAL STARCH DIGESTIBILITY IN THE HORSE AND EFFECT OF GRAIN PROCESSING (MEYER, 1993)

Ingredient	Preileal digestibility %
Whole Oats	83.5
Rolled Oats	85.2
Rolled Barley	21.4
Whole Corn	28.9
Cracked Corn	29.9
Ground Corn	45.6
Popped Corn	90.1

More recently, Freeman, *et al* (1991) have reported little difference in intake of pellets ranging in size from 0.4-1.9 cm but that intake was greater 20 minutes post-feeding with pellets of lower density when compared with harder, more dense pellets.

Little research has been done to determine the utilization of extruded feeds by horses. Hintz *et al* (1985) compared the digestibility of pelleted, extruded or unprocessed diets fed to horses. The concentrate diets consisted of 36% oats, 34% corn, 20% soybean meal, 6% molasses, and 4% vitamin-mineral premix. Rate of intake of the three forms of the ration was significantly different with rate of intake being significantly (P<0.01) slower for the extruded diet for both ponies and horses (Table 3). Digestibility of energy, protein and dry matter for the three diets is shown in table 4.

Table 3. RATE OF INTAKE OF THREE FORMS OF A GRAIN MIXTURE DURING THE FIRST 20 MINUTES POST-FEEDING

	Control	(g/min) Pelleted	Extruded
Horses	97[a]	109[a]	67[b]
Ponies	60[a]	68[a]	45[b]

Each value is a mean of 6 animals
[a,b]Values in the same row bearing unlike superscripts are significantly different (P<0.01). (Hintz *et al.*, 1985)

The increase in digestibility for extruded feed seen in this experiment suggests that extruded feeds are efficiently utilized by the horse, but cost is still a major obstacle in the way of wide-spread acceptance of extruded feeds by consumers.

Table 4. DIGESTIBILITY (%) OF DIETS FED IN PELLETED, TEXTURED OR EXTRUDED FORM TO HORSES

	Control	Pelleted	Extruded
Energy (%)	73.5[ab]	72.0[a]	75.5[b]
Dry Matter (%)	73.3[ab]	72.1[a]	75.3[b]
Protein (%)	84.7[a]	86.0[a,b]	87.7[b]

[a,b]Values in the same row with unlike superscripts are significantly different (P<0.05)

Effect of diets on the digestive tract

The end effect that consumption of a diet has on the gastro-intestinal tract is a function of physical form of the diet, percent concentrate vs percent forage in the diet, chemical composition of the diet and feeding rate. These factors govern both the utilization of feeds as well as chemical and microbiological changes which occur in the tract in response to feeding. Obviously, the closer a feeding program is to the natural manner in which the horse evolved to eat, the smaller the effect on gut homeostasis. Radical departures from small continuous meals consisting of predominantly forage result in the largest effects on gut function and stability.

Willard *et al* (1977) compared cecal pH and volatile fatty acid production in cecal fistulated horses fed either an all hay or all concentrate diet. Horses fed a diet of 8 kg of mixed hay showed smaller changes in cecal pH than seen in horses consuming 6 kg of a "sweet feed" (Table 5). In addition to the noted difference in cecal pH, the molar percentages of volatile fatty acids were different between the two diets. Horses consuming the all hay diet had higher molar percentages of acetic and lower molar percentages of propionic acid in the cecal fluid when compared with horses on an all concentrate diet. Willard *et al* (1977) further reported that the horses consuming all concentrate diets spent more time chewing wood and practicing coprophagy (eating of manure) than did horses on the all hay diet. Interestingly, both wood chewing behavior and coprophagy were reduced when 62.5 ml of 20% Na_2CO_3 was infused hourly into the cecum of the all concentrate fed horses.

Table 5. MEAN CECAL pH FOLLOWING THE FEEDING OF AN ALL HAY OR ALL CONCENTRATE DIET TO CECAL FISTULATED HORSES.

Hours post feeding	Hay	Concentrate
0	7.14	7.22
2	7.04	7.14
4	6.92[a]	6.43[b]
6	6.87[c]	6.12[d]

[a,b,c,d]Values in the same row with unlike superscripts are significantly different (P<0.05). (Willard *et al.*, 1977)

Hintz *et al* (1971) compared digestion coefficients, blood glucose levels and volatile fatty acid production in ponies fed varying forage:grain ratios. They reported that as concentrate intake increased from 0 (1:0 forage:grain ratio) to a 1:4 forage:grain ratio, molar percentages of acetate decreased and propionate increased (Table 6). However, they failed to see any associative effects on the digestibility of fiber as forage:grain ratio changed. Digestibility of dry matter, crude protein, neutral detergent fiber and available carbohydrate was greater for higher concentrate diets than for the all forage diet.

Radicke *et al* (1991) reported the response of cecal pH to the feeding of graded levels of starch from oats and corn. Figure 2 shows cecal pH response to either oat or corn starch at graded levels of intake. Radicke *et al* (1991) reported that a cecal pH of 6.0 represented sub-clinical cecal acidosis and that cecal pH below 6.0 represented significant risk to the stability of cecal fermentation and to precipitation of clinical problems such as colic or laminitis. Chronic exposure to low pH in the cecum also predisposes the horse to anorexia and other metabolic disturbances. pH response typical of concentrate feeding is not similar to that seen with the feeding of a more fibrous diet. Data from Radicke *et al* (1991) characterizing cecal pH response to meals of hay, corn, or oats are shown in figure 3.

Table 6. EFFECT OF FORAGE:GRAIN RATIO ON MOLAR PERCENTAGE OF VOLATILE FATTY ACIDS IN THE CECUM.

Forage:grain ratio	Acetate	Propionate	Butyrate
1:0	76.2	14.8	8.0
3:2	70.4	21.2	7.2
1:4	61.2	26.0	10.2

(Hintz *et al.*, 1971)

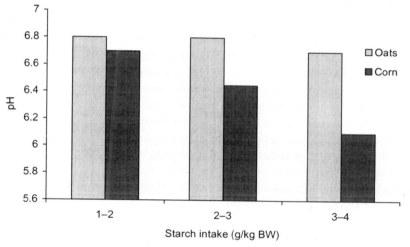

Figure 2. Minimum cecal pH as a function of starch intake g/kg bw/meal (Radicke *et al.*, 1991)

The above described physiologic responses to dietary constituents are of critical importance when viewed in the context of normal feeding management practices. Due to space, employment and labor constraints, many horses are confined to stalls and fed relatively high concentrate, low forage diets which varies dramatically from the normal manner in which horses eat. Gastro-intestinal tract disturbances such as colic, rapid cecal fermentation, radical changes in the cecal micro-flora and pH, and endocrine anomalies result from episodic rather than continuous ingestion of nutrients.

Plasma volume has been shown to decrease as much as 24% in response to large meals and was accompanied by hyperproteinemia or an increase in plasma

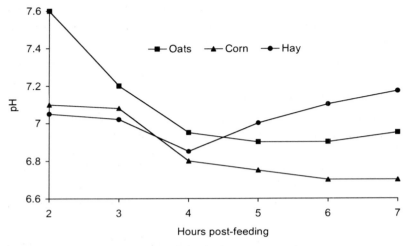

Figure 3. Postprandial cecal pH change after feeding oats, corn or hay

protein (Clarke *et al.*, 1990). Large, infrequently fed meals also increase rate of passage of ingesta through the gastro intestinal tract, which may lead to a greater amount of very fermentable carbohydrate entering the large bowel. The physiologic consequences of soluble carbohydrate in the large intestine are increased microbial fermentation, which leads to decreased cecal and colonic pH, and increased production of gases derived from fermentation. Decreased cecal pH may initiate a serious and detrimental chain of events including alteration of the microbial flora, lysis of bacteria allowing the release of endotoxins, damage to the mucosa of the cecum and colon allowing for absorption of endotoxin and various gastro-intestinal tract pathologies including acute colitis, flatulence, colic and laminitis.

As such, the producer must be aware of the physiologic consequences of meal feeding rather than continuous feeding.

Management to prevent gut pathology

FEEDING MANAGEMENT

A crucial question is the relationship between feed and pathology involving the gastro-intestinal tract. Besides cases involving accidental inclusion of ionophores (rumensin & lasalocid) and antimicrobials (esp. linkomycin) far more problems associated with gut dysfunction and pathology are the result of poor feeding management than of the feed *per se*. The following are important:

1.   Horsemen (educated by feed producers, nutritionists and veterinarians) must realize that horses were not designed to eat large meals of readily fermentable

carbohydrate and must ensure adequate fiber intake which more closely mimics the horse's evolutionary adaption to alimentation. More frequent, smaller meals always decrease feeding related problems.

2. Regularity of feeding is crucial. Many times horses appear to do well on a feeding program that should be risky until the normal feeding routine is upset, at which time problems begin to occur.

3. Ingredients-Are there optimum inclusion rates? The cited work of Meyer and Radicke suggests that there is a practical maximum inclusion rate for corn. At KER we rarely would use corn at greater than 23% of the concentrate mix. Certainly there are practical maximums for other ingredients as well.

4. Feed to maintain hindgut function, maximize the contribution of forage, reduce carbohydrate overload of the cecum, manage the feeding program to promote gut homeostasis.

5. Eliminate the possibility of bad feed. Storage and procurement of feed is crucial to the prevention of mold, rancidity and loss of feed quality.

6. Maintain ingredient quality (especially critical is fusarium in corn, i.e., leukoencephalomalacia or moldy corn disease).

7. Feed by weight not volume. The bulk densities of feeds vary significantly and feeding by the "coffee can" is not appropriate.

8. Encourage adequate exercise and manage to prevent all classes of horses from becoming too fat.

9. Maintain functional dentition and routinely deworm. Immunization for botulism may be considered. Starting with a healthy, parasite "free" horse aids in allowing maximum feed utilization and decreased feed usage.

On the horizon

There are nutritional tools being developed, or that are already here, that may have real advantages.

1. Yeast Cultures - Already well accepted as a valid ingredient, yeast culture has a role in designing horse feeds. Pagan (1989), Glade (1991), Krusic (1991), Corujeira and Scipioni (1992) have reported increases in the digestibility of horse rations as a result of the addition of live yeast culture (Yea-Sacc[1026]). More recently Newman (1993) has shown that yeast may have a stabilizing effect on in vitro cecal fermentation. Cultures of cecal microbes were challenged with amounts of starch that might be equivalent to a starch overload. Lactic acid production and pH decrease in the cultures containing yeast were less than for those cultures without added yeast culture (Yea- Sacc[1026]).

Pagan's (1990) work showed an increase in the digestibility of fiber and phosphorus indicating a positive effect on cecal fermentation. The exact role of yeast in reducing lactate production in the cecum and on stabilizing the cecal environment is not clear but it is likely that similar modes of action to those in the rumen of the cow are present in the hindgut of the horse.

2.   Enzymes - The use of enzymes such as cellulase, beta-gluconase, amylase and lipase is becoming more wide spread in the feed industry and more accepted by the scientific community. It is thought that some of the mode of action of yeast culture is due to enhanced activity of phytase, and Meyer (1993) has reported enhanced preileal digestion of starch when exogenous amylase is added to the diet. Meyer's work as well as the work of Radicke (1991) suggests that for starches of intermediate small intestinal digestibility, amylase is a limiting factor in digestibility. Recently Simon (1992) reported that the addition of phytase to pig diets resulted in a 20-30% increase in the digestibility of total phosphorus as well as an increase in the digestibility of dry matter and some amino acids. Pointillart (1987) has reported that there was an increase in the density of the tibia, fibula and third metatarsal in pigs receiving phytase supplementation when compared to controls. At this time there is a significant body of evidence to suggest that the utilization of barley based diets by broilers is significantly greater in betagluconase supplemented diets than in control diets (Raudati, 1991). As we explore new methods of enhancing the utilization of feed for growth, reproduction and performance, enzymes will play an increasingly greater role.

References

Arnold, F.F., G.D. Potter, J.L. Kreider, G.T. Schelling and W.L. Jenkins. 1981. Carbohydrate Digestion in the Small and Large Intestine of the Equine. Proc. 7th Equine Nutr. Physiol. Symp.: p. 19.

Clarke, L.L., M.C. Roberts and R.A. Argenzio. 1990. Feeding and Digestive Problems in Horses: Responses to a Concentrated Meal. In Clinical Nutrition (H.F. Hintz: ed) Veterinary Clinics of North America. WB Saunders. Philadelphia.

Corujeira, M. and A. Scipioni. 1992. Eficacia Terapeutica de los Probioticos in Patologias Malasimilativas y Desordenes Nutricionales: Estudis Preliminar. Proc. Vet. Conf. of Chile.

Freeman, D.W., D.L. Wall and D.R. Topliff. 1991. Intake Response of Horses Consuming a Concentrate Varying in Pellet Size.

Glade, M.J. 1991. Dietary Yeast Culture Supplementation of Mares During Late Gestation and Early Lactation. J. Eq. Vet. Sci. 11(3): 167.

Hintz, H.F. and R.G. Loy. 1966. Effect of Pelleting on the Nutritive Value of Horse Rations. J. Anim. Sci. 25:1059.

Hintz, H.F., R.A. Argenzio and H.F. Schryver. 1971. Digestion Coefficients, Blood Glucose Levels and Molar Percentage of Volatile Fatty Acids in Intestinal Fluid of Ponies Fed Varying Forage:Grain Ratios. J. Anim. Sci. 33:992.

Hintz, H.F., J. Scott, L.V. Soderholm and J. Williams. 1985. Extruded Feeds for Horses. Proc 9th Equine Nutr. Physiol Symp. Lansing MI.: 174.

Kern, D.L., L.L. Slyter, E.C. Leffel, J.M. Weaver and R.R. Oltjen. 1974. Ponies vs. Steers: Microbial and Chemical Characteristics of Intestinal Micro Flora. J. Anim. Sci. 38:559.

Meyer, H., A. Radicke, E. Kienzle, S. Wilke and D. Kleffken.1993. Investigations of Preileal Digestion of Oats, Corn and Barley Starch in Relation to Grain Processing. Proc. 13th Equine Nutr. Physiol Symp. Gainesville, Fla: p. 92.

Pagan, J.D. 1989. Calcium, Hindgut Function Affect Phosphorus Needs. Feed Stuffs 61 (No. 35):1.

Pagan, J.D. 1990. Effect of Yeast Culture Supplementation on Nutrient Digestibility in Mature Horses. J. Anim. Sci. 68(Suppl.1):371.

Pointillart, A., A. Fourdin and N. Fontaine. 1987. Importance of Cereal Phytase Activity for Phytate Phosphorus Utilization by Growing Pigs Fed Diets Containing Triticale or Corn. J. Nutr. 117:907.

Radicke, S., E. Kienzle and H. Meyer. 1991. Preileal Apparent Digestibility of Oats and Corn Starch and Consequences for Cecal Metabolism. Proc. 12th Equine Nutr. Physiol. Symp. Calgary Canada: p. 43.

Raudati, E., A.H. Cantor, F. Rutz and M.L. Straw. 1991. Effect of Betagluconase Supplements to Barley and Wheat-Based Diets on Performance of Broiler Chicks. In Biotechnology in the Feed Industry (T.P. Lyons, Ed.), Alltech Technical Publications.

Simon, R.C. 1992. Georgia Nutrition Conference. Personal Communication.

Willard, J.G., J.C. Willard, S.A. Wolfram and J.P. Baker. 1977. Effect of Diet on Cecal pH and Feeding Behavior of Horses. J. Anim. Sci. 45:87.

This paper was first published in "Feeding the Performance Horse," Proceedings for the 1993 Short Course for Feed Manufacturers

FORAGES FOR HORSES: MORE THAN JUST FILLER

JOE D. PAGAN

Kentucky Equine Research, Inc., Versailles, Kentucky, USA

Horses have evolved over millions of years as grazers, with specialized digestive tracts adapted to digest and utilize diets containing high levels of plant fiber. They are capable of processing large quantities of forage to meet their nutrient demands. In an attempt to maximize growth or productivity, horses are often fed diets which also contain high levels of grains and supplements. Unfortunately, this type of grain supplementation often overshadows the significant contribution that forages make in satisfying the horse's nutrient demands.

Digestive function

Horses are classified anatomically as nonruminant herbivores or hindgut fermenters. The large intestine of the horse holds about 21 to 24 gallons of liquid and houses billions of bacteria and protozoa that produce enzymes which break down (ferment) plant fiber. These microbes are absolutely essential to the horse, since the horse itself cannot produce these enzymes. The by-products of this microbial fermentation provide the horse with a source of energy and micro-nutrients.

The equine digestive tract is designed in this fashion to allow the horse to ingest large quantities of forage in a continuous fashion. The small capacity of the upper part of the tract is not well suited for large single meals, a fact which is often ignored by horsemen. Large single meals of grain overwhelm the digestive capacity of the stomach and small intestine resulting in rapid fermentation of the grain carbohydrates by the microflora in the hindgut. These fermentations may result in a wide range of problems including colic and laminitis.

The fact that horses are hindgut fermenters has several implications for the person feeding the horse. First, since horses are designed to live on forages, any feeding program that neglects fiber will result in undesirable physical and mental consequences. Horses have a psychological need for the full feeling that fiber provides. Horses fed fiber deficient diets will in extreme cases become chronic woodchewers, 1000 pound termites that can destroy a good deal of fencing or stall front. It is also important to maintain a constant food source for the beneficial bacteria in the hindgut. Not only does their fermentation of the fiber provide a great deal of energy for the horse, but their presence prevents the proliferation of other, potentially pathogenic bacteria. Horses, like man, need a certain amount of bulk to sustain normal digestive function. Horses have an immense digestive system designed to process a large volume of feed at all times. Deprived of that bulk, the many loops of the bowel are more likely to kink or twist, and serious colic can result.

Forage should remain the foundation of a horse's feeding program, regardless of where it is raised or how it is used. Additional grains or protein and mineral supplements should only be used to supply essential nutrients not contained in the forage. This is the most logical and economical way to approach feeding horses, because it eliminates the needless duplication or dangerous excess of fortification. The problem with this method of ration balancing is that the quantity and quality of forage eaten by most horses is not precisely known. Horsemen pay close attention to a difference of a few percentage points of protein in a grain mix, but rarely assay hay or pasture for nutrient content. To compound the problem, intakes of hay and pasture are difficult to measure. This does not mean, however, that reasonable estimates of forage intake cannot be made. The following guidelines should help horsemen evaluate their forage programs and assist them in the selection of proper fortification for each class of horse that they are feeding.

Forage composition

Forages are composed of two components, cell contents and cell walls. Cell contents contain most of the protein, and all of the starch, sugars, lipids, organic acids and soluble ash found in the plant. These components are degraded by enzymes produced by the horse and are highly digestible. The cell wall contains the fibrous portion of the plant which is resistant to digestive enzymes produced by the horse. The primary components of the cell wall are cellulose, hemicellulose and lignin. The nutritive value of forages is determined by two factors:

1)   Fiber content (the proportion of the plant that is composed of cell wall)

2)   Fiber quality (the degree of lignification)

These factors are important because the horse can digest practically all of the cell contents contained in forages, but bacterial fermentation can only digest 50% or less of the plant cell wall. The degree to which plant cell wall is digestible is largely dependent on the amount of lignin that it contains. Therefore, it's important to understand how much of these components various forages contain and what factors affect their nutrient content.

Forage analysis

A great deal can be learned about the nutritive value of a forage by having it chemically analyzed. A number of commercial labs do a good job analyzing forage, but we regularly use the Northeast DHIA Forage Testing Laboratory in Ithaca, New York. This lab is fast and economical and they can conduct the majority of assays necessary to fully evaluate the nutritional value of a forage. Contact them at: Northeast DHIA, Forage Analysis Laboratory, 730 Warren Rd., Ithaca, NY 14850-9877 for postage paid mailers.

Of course, forage analysis is fairly useless if you don't know how to interpret the results. Below are listed many of the components often measured in forages with an explanation of why they are or aren't important for horses.

DRY MATTER

Dry matter, or % moisture, measures how much of the forage is water. Hays are typically 85-95% dry matter, but pastures contain much more water and can contain as little as 15- 20% dry matter. This water dilutes the other components of the forage, so for more of an "apples to apples" comparison, the composition of forages should be compared on a 100% dry matter basis. For example, a hay that is 90% dry matter may be 14.4% protein on an as fed basis. This is equivalent to 16% protein on a 100% dry matter basis. The difference between as fed and dry matter for this hay is not great. Compare this to a pasture sample that is 25% dry matter. If it contained 4% protein on an as fed basis, then this would equal 16% protein on a 100% dry matter basis. The hay and pasture actually have identical protein contents when the water is removed. Of course, be sure and express forage intake in the same terms as forage composition.

CRUDE PROTEIN

Crude protein is called "crude" because the assay used in its determination doesn't actually measure protein at all. Instead, the Kjeldahl analysis used by most labs measures nitrogen. Protein is calculated by multiplying nitrogen by 6.25. There are other substances in forages that contain nitrogen, so this analysis is subject to some error.

Most of the protein in forages is in the cell contents. This protein is readily digested by the horse's proteolytic enzymes. The digestibility of protein found in the cell contents is 80% or higher (table 1). Some protein in forages, however, is incorporated into the cell wall. This protein is called unavailable protein because it is completely indigestible. Unavailable protein is measured by running a Kjeldahl nitrogen analysis on the acid detergent fiber (ADF) of the forage. It can be expressed as ADIN (acid detergent insoluble nitrogen) and figure 2 shows how it affects protein digestibility in horses. In this study (Pagan and Jackson, 1991), the ADIN was primarily from distillers dried grains. ADIN is usually produced from heat damage in a chemical reaction between carbohydrate and protein called a Maillard reaction.

CRUDE FAT

Crude fat measures the lipids in forages that are soluble in ether. These lipids are contained in the cell contents of forages and have a true digestibility in horses of about 75% (table 1).

Table 1. ESTIMATED TRUE DIGESTIBILITY OF DIFFERENT CHEMICAL FRACTIONS OF FORAGE (ADAPTED FROM FONNESBECK, 1969)

Chemical fraction	Estimated true digestibility (%)
CELL WALL	
Cellulose	43.4%
Hemicellulose	49.5%
Lignin	0%
CELL CONTENTS	
Protein	81.7%
Soluble carbohydrate	100%
Ether extract	75.1%
Ash	90.5%

ACID DETERGENT FIBER (ADF)

Acid detergent fiber (ADF) contains cellulose, lignin, and any of the insoluble nitrogen produced by a Maillard reaction. These are cell wall components and are therefore indigestible by the horse's digestive enzymes. Lignin and ADIN are also indigestible by the bacteria in the horse's hindgut, and lignin will decrease the digestibility of other cell wall components as well. ADF digestibility by horses averages 35-45% and is largely dependent on the level of lignification. We will discuss what affects lignin content later.

LIGNIN

Lignin is not usually assayed individually in a standard forage analysis, but the DHIA laboratory will perform lignin assays for an additional charge. If both ADF and lignin are determined, then cellulose can be calculated by subtraction. [ADF (%) - lignin (%) = cellulose (%)].

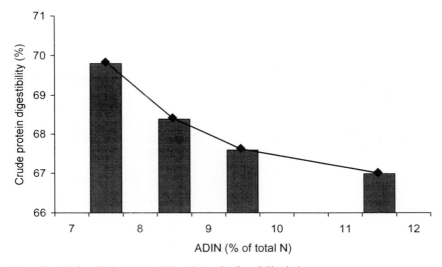

Figure 2. The relationship between ADIN and protein digestibility in horses

NEUTRAL DETERGENT FIBER (NDF)

Neutral detergent fiber (NDF) measures the entire cell wall content of a forage. It consists of lignin and cellulose like ADF as well as hemicellulose. NDF (%) -ADF (%) = hemicellulose (%). The overall digestibility of NDF in forages by horses varies from 40-50%. Hemicellulose is usually more digestible than cellulose, but its digestibility is also more depressed by lignin.

CRUDE FIBER (%)

Crude fiber is a very old and imprecise assay that is unfortunately part of our labelling requirements for animal feeds. This is a particularly bad assay because it doesn't really measure anything in particular. Table 2 shows what cell wall components crude fiber does not measure in different types of forages. For example, mature alfalfa hay contains 45% cell wall, but only 27% crude fiber. Even worse, beet pulp contains 47% cell wall but only 17% crude fiber. Crude fiber always underestimates the actual fiber content of a forage and its use for anything but to satisfy a government regulation should be avoided.

Table 2. THE PERCENTAGE OF ORIGINAL FEED LIGNIN, HEMICELLULOSE AND CELLULOSE DISSOLVED IN CRUDE FIBER DETERMINATION. (ADAPTED FROM VAN SOEST, 1982)

Class		Lignin %	Hemicellulose %	Cellulose %
Legumes	Range	8-62	21-86	12-30
	Average	30	63	28
Grasses	Range	53-90	64-89	5-29
	Average	82	76	21

ASH

Ash is what is left after the forage is burned at a high temperature in a furnace. Ash contains all of the inorganic components of the forage. Included in the ash portion are all of the minerals normally considered important for horses (calcium, phosphorus, potassium, magnesium, copper, zinc, manganese, iron, etc.) and minerals that are not usually considered as nutrients (mostly silica, but also traces of aluminum, fluoride, boron, etc.). Ash is not usually performed on forage samples, but it can provide valuable information in certain circumstances.

INDIVIDUAL MINERALS

The DHIA forage report includes calcium (%), phosphorus (%), magnesium (%), potassium (%), sodium (%), iron (ppm), zinc (ppm), copper (ppm), manganese (ppm), and molybdenum (ppm). Other labs also perform additional assays for selenium, cobalt, iodine, and sulfur.

CALCULATED VALUES

There are two values that can be calculated from a forage analysis that are very useful in evaluating its quality. First, the amount of soluble carbohydrate or sugar can be calculated. The original way to calculate this was as nitrogen free extract (NFE) = 100 - crude protein - crude fat - crude fiber - ash. This is not a good way to estimate soluble sugar because a lot of the cell wall components end up in the NFE estimate since they aren't recovered in the crude fiber fraction. True cell soluble sugars are completely digestible by horses, so any of the cell wall that escapes crude fiber detection is falsely estimated to be completely digestible. A much better way to estimate this fraction is to substitute neutral detergent fiber (NDF) for crude fiber. By doing this, what is left by subtraction is likely to be readily digestible by the horse.

The second value that is often calculated for forages is energy content. This is expressed as either digestible energy (DE) in calories or joules per kilogram or pound or as percent total digestible nutrients (TDN %). For all practical purposes, these various expressions of dietary energy are interchangeable. TDN% X 4.4 = DE (Mcal/kg) or TDN% X 2 = DE (Mcal/lb). What is important to realize is that both DE and TDN are only estimates of the actual digestible energy content of forages. They are calculated based on the relationship between some of the assays mentioned above to the digestible energy content of feeds determined in actual digestion trials with animals. Be sure you know which equations are used to calculate DE or TDN by a laboratory. DHIA uses equations developed with horses, but some labs still use equations developed with cattle or hogs.

Factors affecting forage quality

There are a number of factors which can affect the quality of a forage. Most important of these are the species of plant, stage of maturity, location where the plant was grown and content of inhibitory substances. All of these factors should be considered when assessing the suitability of a particular forage for horses.

SPECIES

Most plants that serve as forage for horses can be divided into two different categories, grasses and legumes. Grasses contain much structural matter in their leaves and leaf sheaths and these can be as important or more important than the stem in holding the plant erect. Examples of grass forages used for horses include temperate species such as timothy, orchard grass, brome grass and fescue and tropical species like pangola, guinea, bermuda and kikuyu. Legumes, on the other hand, tend to be tree-like on a miniature scale. Their leaves have very little structural function and tend to be on the ends of woody stems. The primary legumes used as horse forage are alfalfa and clover.

At a similar stage of maturity, legumes tend to be higher in protein, energy and calcium than grasses. Tables 3 and 4 describe the composition of legume and grass hays according to market grade. ADF (lignin plus cellulose) does not vary that much between grasses and legumes at the same stage of maturity. NDF (lignin + cellulose + hemicellulose), however, is much higher in grasses than legumes (figure 3). This is because grasses contain a great deal more hemicellulose than legumes. Therefore, evaluating the fiber content of forages based on ADF alone underestimates the total cell wall content and overestimates the total energy content of a grass.

Table 3. MARKET HAY GRADES FOR LEGUME HAYS (ADAPTED FROM HAY MARKETING TASK FORCE)

Grade	Stage of maturity	Physical description	CP %[a]	ADF %[a]	NDF %[a]
1	Pre bloom	40-50% leaves	>19%	31%	<40%
2	Early bloom	35-45% leaves	17-19%	31-35%	40-46%
3	Mid bloom	25-40% leaves	13-16%	36-41%	47-51%
4	Full bloom	<30% leaves	<13%	>41%	>51%

[a] 100 % DM basis

Table 4. MARKET GRADES FOR GRASS HAY (ADAPTED FROM HAY MARKETING TASK FORCE)

Grade	Stage of maturity	Physical description	CP %[a]	ADF %[a]	NDF %[a]
2	Pre head	50% or more leaves	>18	<33	<55
3	Early head	40% or more leaves	13-18	33-38	55-60
4	Head	30% or more leaves	8-12	39-41	61-65
5	Post head	20% or more leaves	<8	>41	>65

[a] 100 % DM basis

Remember, hemicellulose is only 50% digested in the horse and cell soulubles are almost completely digested. By only considering ADF, the assumption is that the rest of the forage (besides protein, fat and ash) is soluble sugar. This is truer in legumes which only contain around 10% hemicellulose than in grasses which can have hemicellulose contents of 30% or more. The fiber that is in legumes tends to be less digestible than the fiber in grasses, largely because legumes tend to have a higher lignin content per unit of total fiber. This means that the digestible fiber content of grasses is much higher than it is in legumes of similar maturity.

Because of the factors mentioned above, legumes contain 20-25% more digestible energy than grasses at the same maturity. In certain instances, the amount of legume hay fed may be limited so that the horse doesn't get too fat. This can result in intakes of digestible fiber that are below optimal levels, particularly in extremely high quality hays.

STAGE OF MATURITY

Generally, as plants mature they become less digestible. This is because a greater proportion of their mass becomes structural and less metabolic. Legumes tend to mature by decreasing leafiness and increasing the stem-to-leaf ratio. Alfalfa leaves maintain the same level of digestibility throughout their growth. Their stems, however, decrease dramatically in digestibility as they mature. This is because they become highly lignified to support the extra weight of the plant. The ultimate example of lignification for support is the oak tree. The wood of the oak tree is highly lignified and practically indigestible. When pulp wood is processed to make paper, the lignin is removed using harsh chemicals such as sulfuric acid (hence the sulfur smell around paper mills).

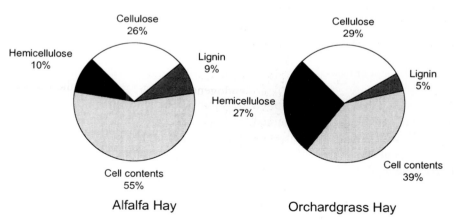

Figure 3. A comparison of the fiber content of early bloom alfalfa and orchard grass hay

The leaves of grasses serve more of a structural function than in legumes. As they mature, these leaves become more lignified and less digestible. Since the stems of certain grasses serve a reserve function, they may actually be more digestible than the leaves of these grasses at a later stage of maturity. Table 5 illustrates the effect that stage of maturity has on protein and fiber content of a temperate grass (timothy), temperate legume (alfalfa) and a tropical grass (pangola grass). When forage is grazed as pasture, its nutrient quality is almost always higher than when it is harvested as hay unless the pasture is the dead aftermath leftover from the previous growing season. New spring pasture can be quite low in fiber content and high in soluble carbohydrates. At this time of year, it is often a good management practice to continue to offer horses on pasture additional hay even if the pasture appears thick and lush. If the horses are getting adequate fiber from the pasture, then they will ignore the hay.

Table 5. THE EFFECT OF STAGE OF MATURITY ON PROTEIN AND FIBER CONTENT OF LEGUMES AND GRASSES

Forage/stage of maturity	Crude protein %[a]	ADF%[a]	NDF%[a]
Timothy Hay early bloom	12.0	35.2	61.4
Timothy Hay mid bloom	9.7	36.4	63.7
Timothy Hay late bloom	8.1	37.5	64.2
Alfalfa Hay early bloom	19.9	31.9	39.3
Alfalfa Hay mid bloom	18.7	36.7	47.1
Alfalfa Hay late bloom	17.0	38.7	48.8
Pangola Hay 15-28 days growth	10.1	40.8	70.0
Pangola Hay 29-42 days growth	7.4	41.8	72.7
Pangola Hay 43-56 days growth	6.3	46.0	77.0

[a] 100 % dry matter basis

Table 6 compares digestibility of an early cut alfalfa hay with a more mature alfalfa hay. The less mature hay contained 37% cell wall while the mature hay was almost 52% cell wall. These differences were reflected in a 15% higher energy content in the early cut hay. This illustrates how stage of maturity and fiber content can impact the quality of alfalfa hay.

Table 6. NUTRIENT COMPOSITION AND DIGESTIBILITY OF EARLY AND LATE CUT ALFALFA HAY (KENTUCKY EQUINE RESEARCH DATA)

Nutrient	Early cut composition	Early cut digestibility	Late cut composition	Late cut digestibility
Digestible energy[a]	2.60 Mcal/kg	59.2%	2.27 Mcal/kg	51.6%
Dry matter[a]	90.4%	65.9%	92.4%	56.0%
Crude protein[a]	19.8%	79.8%	17.2%	69.5%
ADF[a]	32.3%	41.6%	40.7%	39.2%
NDF[a]	36.6%	38.8%	52.0%	41.5%
Soluble carbohydrate[A]	28.5%	92.2%	18.6%	93.9%

[a] 100% dry matter basis

LATITUDINAL EFFECTS

Dr. Peter Van Soest has reported that the digestibility of tropic forages averages on the order of 15 units of digestibility lower than temperate forages. Plants that grow in the tropics have been genetically selected for a larger proportion of protective structures such as lignin to avoid predation. At the other extreme are the perennial plants in the far northern regions of the world. These plants have very short growing seasons and need to store energy in reserves rather than in irretrievable substances such as lignin and cellulose.

INHIBITORY SUBSTANCES

Besides lignin, a number of other substances in forages can reduce digestibility of fiber and minerals. Silica is used as a structural element complementing lignin to strengthen and add rigidity to cell walls. Alfalfa and other temperate legumes restrict absorption of silica and never contain more than a few hundred ppm in their tissue (Van Soest, 1982). Table 7 shows how the cumulative effect of silica and lignin can depress forage digestibility in ruminants. Cereal straws are quite high in silica. This gives the straw a clean, glassy appearance and it also depresses its digestibility. Rice hulls are extremely high in silica and indigestible by horses.

There are also substances contained in forages that can inhibit mineral digestibility. Two that are particularly important are phytate and oxalate. Phytates contain phosphorus in a bound form that is unavailable to the horse. Phytate may also inhibit the digestibility of other minerals such as calcium, zinc and iodine. Research from our laboratory (Pagan, 1989) suggests that the addition of yeast culture (Yea Sacc[1026]) may improve the utilization of phytate phosphorus by the horse. The digestibility of phosphorus was 23% from a control ration and 28% from the same ration containing Yea Sacc[1026]. Zinc digestibility was also improved.

Oxalates can reduce the digestibility of calcium in forages if the calcium-to-oxalate ratio in the forage is 0.5 or less on a weight-to-weight basis (Hintz, 1990). This is a common problem in tropical forages which tend to be high in oxalates and low in calcium (table 8). Hintz (1990) cited data from Blaney *et al* (1981) showing how oxalate affected calcium digestibility in horses (table 9). Calcium from forages with high Ca:oxalate ratios (>1) had very high calcium digestibility, while those with low ratios had very poor digestibility. Low calcium availability in tropical forages can lead to nutritional secondary hyperparathyroidism (NSH) or "big head" disease. Therefore, when tropical forages are fed to horses, supplemental sources of calcium should be available.

Table 7. CUMULATIVE EFFECTS OF SILICA AND LIGNIN ON FORAGE DIGESTIBILITY IN RUMINANTS (ADAPTED FROM VAN SOEST, 1982)

Forage	Source	Silica %DM	Lignin %DM	Lignin + silica	Apparent digestibility
Bermuda	Tex	2.2	4.7	6.9	56%
Bermuda	Ark	2.3	6.0	8.3	50%
Bermuda	S.C.	0.7	8.5	9.2	53%
Bermuda	Ariz	4.1	4.9	9.0	55%
Bermuda	Ariz	6.2	4.8	11.0	47%
Bermuda	La	6.7	5.5	12.2	42%
Rice straw	Ark	13.1	3.1	16.23	7%
Rice hulls	Tex	22.9	15.6	38.5	8%

There is a common misconception that oxalates reduce calcium digestibility in alfalfa hay. This is not true because the Ca:oxalate ratio is much higher than 0.5, even in alfalfas that contain high levels of oxalates. Hintz *et al* (1984) demonstrated this in an experiment in which no difference was found in the absorption of calcium from alfalfa containing 0.5% and 0.9% oxalic acid in which the calcium:oxalate ratios were 3 and 1.7, respectively. The true digestibility of the calcium from both hays was estimated to be >75 %.

Table 8. CALCIUM AND OXALATE CONTENTS OF FORAGES FROM COLOMBIA, SOUTH AMERICA (ADAPTED FROM HINTZ, 1990)

Name	Calcium %	Oxalate %	Ca:oxalate
Napiergrass	0.21	1.6	0.13
Napiergrass	0.41	1.5	0.24
Kikuyu	0.37	1.6	0.23
Kikuyu	0.32	1.2	0.27
Guineagrass	0.54	2.0	0.27

Table 9. EFFECT OF CALCIUM:OXALATE RATIO ON DIGESTIBILITY OF CALCIUM (ADAPTED FROM HINTZ, 1990)

Name	Calcium %	Oxalate %	Ca:oxalate	True digestibility
Flinders	0.49	0.25	1.92	99%
Spear-blue	0.33	0.18	1.81	78%
Rhodes	0.80	0.45	1.79	76%
Oaten Chaff	0.11	0.08	1.36	100%
Buffel	0.40	1.06	0.38	17%
Pangola	0.34	0.92	0.37	39%
Green panic	0.26	0.81	0.32	42%
Para	0.22	0.75	0.29	24%
Kikuyu	0.28	1.30	0.23	20%
Narok setaria	0.27	1.60	0.13	0%
Kanzunguki setaria	0.21	3.37	0.10	0%

FORAGE SAMPLING

Knowing what your horses are actually eating is not always easy. Sampling forages presents a challenge, especially when sampling fresh forage or pasture. A hay core should be used to get a meaningful hay sample for analysis. Hay cores are available that may be attached to a hand-held (brace and bit) or electric drill. Square bales of hay should be sampled diagonally across the long axis of the bale rather than directly through the center. This direction is more critical for sampling legume or mixed grass-legume hays than for single-species grass hays. During the baling process leaves are shattered and may fall to the bottom of the baling chamber. Thus, the diagonal sampling technique should provide an artificial remixing of the stem and leaf, and a more representative sample of the material actually available to the horse. Many times, multiple cores must be taken to obtain an adequate sample for analysis. To get the most accurate mean analysis when sampling hay, one should sample four to six bales taken from different parts of the stack. Pasture analysis is even more perplexing than the sampling of other feedstuffs. The basic question that must first be addressed is whether the entire pasture should be systematically sampled or if only those areas heavily grazed should be sampled. As horses are spot grazers, tending to graze in the lawns and defecate in the roughs, it is probably more accurate to sample the forage actually eaten to get an assessment of the forage quality that contributes significantly to the nutrient intake of the horse. Additionally, unless the sward is a monoculture (one species of forage present) one must try to make sure that the species of forages sampled are those that the horse selects when grazing. This attempt is best done by examining the pasture, observing the grazing behavior, and then sampling the turf as a horse appears to graze. Because of the high moisture level in many fresh forages (50-85%), a sample of at least 1 lb of fresh forage must be taken to ensure that adequate dry matter is available for analysis.

SELECTING HAYS

When selecting hays, the appearance can tell a great deal about the quality of the forage. If it is a predominantly grass hay, remember that as these hays mature and go to seed, their relative energy value goes down. This means that more will have to be fed than a hay cut at a younger time. However, being less energy dense may be an advantage in some instances. For horses on a restricted diet, this type of hay would be ideal to keep the horse happy and its gut full without providing unneeded energy.

FORAGE INTAKE

To accurately calculate the contribution that forage makes to the horse's overall feeding program, forage intake as well as composition must be known. Hay intake can be determined by simply recording the total weight of hay offered minus any hay wasted or refused. This record does not take into account the differences in composition between hay that is offered and that consumed, but is accurate enough to do a good evaluation in the field.

Table 10 gives a range of forage and concentrate intakes for various classes of horses based on their body weight. High forage intakes will occur where there is an abundance of forage available, such as with Kentucky pasture or Washington state alfalfa hay. Low forage intakes will occur where forage is sparse and of poorer quality such as in the tropics. These estimates illustrate how much forage quality and level of intake can affect a horse's overall feeding program. Not taking into account the contribution that forage makes to a horse's overall nutrient intake can result in some serious errors in feeding. At the very least, underestimating a forage's nutrient contribution will result in unnecessary and expensive supplementation. In extreme cases, this may cause nutrient imbalances or toxicities to occur. At the other extreme, overestimating what a horse gets from its forage will result in nutrient deficiencies. Therefore, it is very important that forage's role in supplying nutrients to the horse be accurately assessed. Hopefully, the guidelines presented here will make that evaluation easier and more meaningful.

Table 10. EXPECTED FEED CONSUMPTION BY HORSES

Horse	% of body weight		% of diet	
	Forage	Concentrate	Forage	Concentrate
Maintenance	1.0-2.0	0-1.0	50-100	0-50
Pregnant mare	1.0-2.0	0.3-1.0	50-85	15-50
Lactating mare (early)	1.0-2.5	0.5-2.0	33-85	15-66
Lactating mare (late)	1.0-2.0	0.5-1.5	40-80	20-60
Weanling	0.5-1.8	1.0-3.0	30-65	35-70
Yearling	1.0-2.5	0.5-2.0	33-80	20-66
Performance horse	1.0-2.0	0.5-2.0	33-80	20-66

References

Blaney, B.J., R.J. Gartner and R.A. McKenzie, 1981. The inability of horses to absorb calcium oxalate. J. Agr. Sci. Camb. 97:639-645. (as cited by Hintz, 1990).

Fonnesbeck, P.V. 1969. Partitioning of the nutrients of forages for horses. J. Anim. Sci. 26:1030.

Hintz, H.F., H.F. Schryver, J. Doty, C. Lakin, and R.A. Zimmerman. 1984. Oxalic acid content of alfalfa hays and its influence on the availability of calcium, phosphorus and magnesium to ponies. J. Anim. Sci. 58:939-942.

Hintz, H.F. 1990. Factors affecting nutrient availability in the horse. In: Proceedings 1990 Georgia Nutrition Conference, 182-193.

Pagan, J. 1989. Calcium, hindgut function affect phosphorus needs. Feedstuffs 61(35) 10-11.

Pagan, J.D. and S.G. Jackson. 1991. Distillers grains as a feed ingredient for horse rations: a palatibility and digestibility study. In: Proceedings of the 12th ENPS Symposium, Calgary Alberta.

Van Soest, P.J. 1982. Nutritional Ecology of the Ruminant. O&B Books, Inc., Covallis, Oregon.

This paper was first published in "Feeding the Performance Horse," Proceedings for the 1994 Short Course for Feed Manufacturers

CARBOHYDRATES IN EQUINE NUTRITION

JOE D. PAGAN

Kentucky Equine Research, Inc., Versailles, Kentucky, USA

Carbohydrates are an extremely important part of a horse's diet since about 75% of all plant matter is comprised of carbohydrates. There are a number of different types of carbohydrates in horse feed and they vary considerably in how well horses digest and utilize each one. In nutritional terms, carbohydrates can be divided into two broad categories:

Non-structural carbohydrates (NSC)

Non-structural carbohydrates are those that occur either as simple sugars in the horse's feed or that can be broken down by enzymes produced by the horse. Included in this category are glucose and fructose, lactose, sucrose and starch. They range from being almost non-existent in a grass hay diet to comprising a high percentage of the total diet in a high grain-low fiber ration.

Structural carbohydrates (cell wall)

Structural carbohydrates are those that are resistant to the horse's digestive enzymes. These carbohydrates occur in the cell wall portion of the plant and they must be fermented by bacteria living in the horse's gut before they can be utilized by the horse. As a group, these carbohydrates are called plant fiber and they consist primarily of cellulose and hemicellulose.

The various types of non-structural carbohydrates that appear in horse feed are summarized in table 1. Only these types of carbohydrates will be considered in depth in this paper.

Carbohydrate chemistry

Carbohydrates got their name from the fact that they contain carbon combined with hydrogen and oxygen which are usually in the same ratio as in water. The basic repeating unit of a carbohydrate is called a monosaccharide and these usually have either 5 carbons (pentoses) or six carbons (hexoses). Hexoses have the empirical formula $C_6H_{12}O_6$ and are the most important types of carbohydrates for horses. Hexoses that appear naturally as single sugars (monosaccharides) are fairly rare. Glucose and fructose are the only ones that appear free in nature. When glucose appears as a single sugar, it is called dextrose. Small amounts of dextrose are found in fruits and fruit juices and also in honey. It is obtained commercially by the hydrolysis of cornstarch. Glucose is of special interest in horse nutrition because the digestion of many more complex carbohydrates yields glucose as the end product of digestion and it is the form of carbohydrate which circulates in the blood. Glucose has a sweet taste, but it is not as sweet as cane sugar.

Table 1. NON-STRUCTURAL CARBOHYDRATES IN HORSE FEEDS

Substance	Type of sugar	Digestive enzyme	Approximate digestibility	Digestive products
Dextrose	monosaccharide	–	complete	glucose
Fructose	monosaccharide	–	complete	fructose[a]
Maltose	disaccharide	maltase	complete	glucose
Sucrose	disaccharide	sucrase	complete	glucose, fructose
Lactose	disaccharide	lactase	complete[b]	glucose, galactose
Starch	polysaccharide	amylase	complete[c]	glucose

[a]fructose is converted to glucose in the liver
[b]lactase activity diminishes after weaning
[c]total tract starch digestibility is complete, but prececal digestibility varies

Fructose occurs freely along with glucose in fruits and honey and in combined forms in higher carbohydrates. It is sweeter than sucrose which is a two sugar molecule (disaccharide) composed of one glucose and one fructose. Sucrose is the sugar obtained from sugar cane or sugar beets and it is the type used on the table and in cooking. It also occurs in ripe fruits and in tree sap (maple syrup). On hydrolysis with the enzyme sucrase or dilute acids, sucrose is split into mixtures of glucose and fructose which are called invert sugars. Cane molasses also contains sucrose, glucose and fructose. After sugar cane juice is boiled down and as much sugar as possible has been crystallized from it, the remainder is known as cane molasses. It contains about 55% invert sugar.

   Lactose is another disaccharide, composed of one glucose molecule and one molecule of galactose, another hexose monosaccharide. Lactose is the sugar of milk and it is only about one-sixth as sweet as sucrose. It is broken down by the enzyme lactase and it is less likely than glucose or sucrose to undergo acid fermentation in the stomach, a process which may result in irritation. It also promotes the development of acidophilic organisms in the intestine and opposes the growth of undesirable putrefactive bacteria in foals. Lactose also has been shown to favor calcium and phosphorus assimilation, so it is the sugar of choice for the suckling foal. As horses age, their ability to digest lactose decreases, so large intakes of lactose in the adult horse may lead to diarrhea.

Polysaccharides are complex carbohydrates that are long strings of simple sugars of varying lengths. They are of high molecular weight and are usually insoluble in water. Upon hydrolysis by enzymes and acids, they are broken down into various intermediate products and finally to their constituent monosaccharides. The most important form of polysaccharide for horses is starch. Starches are long strings of glucose molecules in both straight chains (amylose) and branched chain structures (amylopectin).

Carbohydrate digestibility

Since monosaccharides are the only form of carbohydrates that can be absorbed from the intestine, more complex carbohydrates must be broken down into simple sugars before they can be utilized by the animal. Starches are broken down into the disaccharide maltose (two glucoses) by the enzyme amylase. Maltose, sucrose and lactose are split into their two monosaccharide units by the disaccharide enzymes maltase, sucrase and lactase which are produced in the intestinal brush border. These disaccharides are completely digested in the small intestine of the healthy horse. This is not the case, however, for starch. The horse's ability to produce amylase is limited. Horses only produce about 8-10% as much amylase as the pig. Therefore, a great deal of the starch in a horse's diet escapes digestion in the small intestine.

Meyer *et al* (1993) summarized five factors which affect prececal starch digestibility in horses:

1. Source of starch
2. Processing of starch
3. Amount of starch intake
4. Source and timing of forage feeding
5. Individual differences between horses

Each of these factors will be discussed below.

SOURCE OF STARCH

Although all starch is made up of chains of glucoses, how the starch molecule is constructed is very different in different types of grain. This difference in the architecture of different starches has a large impact on how well they are digested in the horse's small intestine. Of the grains most commonly fed to horses, oats contain the most digestible form of starch followed by sorghum, corn and barley.

Dr. Meyer in Germany has conducted a large number of experiments evaluating the digestibility of different starch sources. In one study (Meyer *et al.*, 1993) either corn or oats was fed to horses and the concentration of starch was measured in the jejunal chyme. Jejunal chyme is a mixture of digestive juices and undigested feed material at the end of the small intestine. The concentration of corn starch remained high for 11 hours after feeding while oat starch concentration dropped rapidly and was very low after five hours (figure 1). Prececal digestibility of the two starch sources averaged 84% and 29% for oats and corn, respectively.

In another experiment from Dr. Meyer's laboratory, Radicke *et al* (1992) measured amylase activity in the jejunum of horses fed either hay, corn or oats. The amylase activity increased in the jejunal chyme with all rations, with low values after feeding hay, moderate values after feeding corn and high values after feeding oats. Thus, the type of grain appears to affect the amount of amylase produced by the horse.

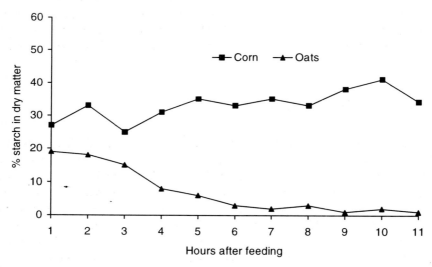

Figure 1. Starch content in the small intestine of horses fed either corn or oats.

At KER's laboratory, we measured blood glucose concentration for four hours after feeding four horses either 1 kg of cracked corn or 1 kg of oats. Peak blood glucose and the overall shape of the glucose curve were similar for the oats and corn even though 1 kg of corn provides much more starch (~700 grams) than 1 kg of oats (~500 grams). This demonstrates that the horse's ability to digest starch in the small intestine is different for different grains.

If starch is not digested in the small intestine, it travels to the large intestine. Here bacteria that normally make up only a small portion of the intestinal flora undergo a population explosion as they feed on the starch. These bacteria are quite efficient at breaking down starch, so that the total tract digestibility of starch is very high

(>95%) regardless of the source. One of the end products of microbial starch fermentation is lactic acid, which irritates the gut lining as well as changing the pH of the intestine. This causes other formerly more prevalent bacteria to die, releasing endotoxins into the gut which are absorbed into the bloodstream. These circulating endotoxins can lead to laminitis.

PROCESSING OF STARCH

Since oat starch is already extremely digestible in the horse's small intestine, processing has little effect on prececal starch digestibility. Corn starch digestibility, on the other hand, benefits greatly from processing. Dr. Meyer showed that grinding corn increased its prececal digestibility from 29% to 45%. Cooking the corn starch by either steam rolling, extruding or micronizing will result in an even higher degree of digestibility. Popping corn increased prececal digestibility to 90%.

Barley also benefits greatly from some type of heat or steam processing. Simply dry rolling or crushing grain does not increase prececal starch digestibility, probably because by chewing the whole grain, the horse grinds the starch finer than does the rolling or grinding. Of course, if your horse has bad teeth, then any type of grinding will help.

AMOUNT OF STARCH INTAKE

The amount of starch intake will also affect prececal starch digestibility. Radicke *et al* (1991) measured pH in the large intestine after feeding ponies corn or oat starch at three different levels of intake (figure 2). The pH in the large intestine was unaffected by the level of oat intake. Higher levels of corn intake (3-4 g/kg BW), however, resulted in a drop in cecal pH indicating that starch escaped digestion in the small intestine. This level of corn intake would be comparable to feeding a 500 kg horse between 2 and 3 kg of corn in a single meal. Both the corn and oats in this experiment were coarsely ground and had not undergone heat treatment. Potter *et al* (1992) reported that research at Texas A&M suggests that the upper limit to starch digestion in the small intestine of the meal-fed equine may be an amount of starch in the range of 0.35-0.4% of body weight per feeding. This would equal about 2.5 to 2.85 kg of corn and is in agreement with the German findings.

SOURCE AND TIMING OF FORAGE FEEDING

Surprisingly, the type of forage and time that it is fed relative to grain can have a large effect on prececal starch digestibility. Meyer et al (1993) showed that substituting grass hay for ground alfalfa meal resulted in a decrease in the prececal starch digestibility of ground corn from 45% to 16%. He attributed this drop to changes in rate of passage and dilution of substrates and enzymes in the chyme by increased secretion of digestive juices.

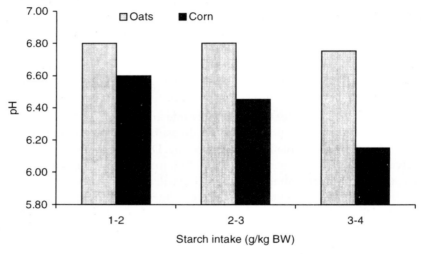

Figure 2. pH in the large intestine of ponies fed three different levels of corn or oat starch.

At the KER laboratory we have studied the effect of time of hay feeding on starch digestibility using glycemic response to feeding as an indication of prececal starch digestibility. Six Thoroughbreds were fed 2.26 kg of sweet feed (a mixture of oats, corn, molasses and a supplement pellet) as a morning meal. The grain was fed either alone (Grain Only), with 2.26 kg of hay (Hay + Grain), or 2 hours after the horses received 2.26 kg of hay (Hay 2 hrs before grain). There was a large difference in glycemic response between the Grain Only treatment and the two treatments where hay was fed either before or with grain (figure3).

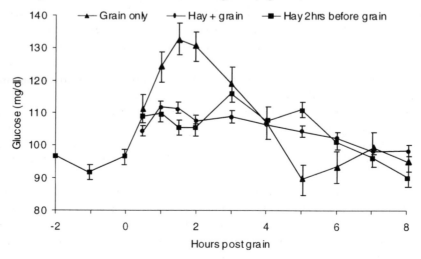

Figure 3. Effect of time of hay feeding on glycemic response.

The horses were offered water each hour during the experiment. They consumed the highest amount of water 2-3 hours after being fed hay. This increased water intake coincided with an increased total plasma protein (TPP). TPP is an indirect measure of plasma volume where a higher TPP correlates with a reduced plasma volume. Eating hay stimulated saliva production and an increase in the secretion of digestive juices into the intestines. Much of the fluid in these secretions came from blood plasma, resulting in a drop in plasma volume. Decreased plasma volume stimulated a thirst response and the horses drank more water. All of these factors, combined, increased the dilution of the intestinal contents and increased rate of passage. Starch digestibility in the small intestine was reduced and glycemic response diminished.

INDIVIDUAL DIFFERENCES BETWEEN HORSES

There can be large differences in individuals' ability to digest starch. These may be due to differences in rate of intake, rate of passage, or the amount of digestive enzymes produced by an individual.

Measuring carbohydrates in horse feed

Directly measuring the amount of sugar in the horse's ration is not easy to do and can be quite expensive. Instead, it is preferable to indirectly estimate the sugar content of feeds and forages by measuring several components of a feed and calculating non-structural carbohydrate (NSC) content. The equation to calculate NSC on an as fed basis is: NSC (%) = 100 - moisture (%) - crude protein (%) - crude fat (%) - neutral detergent fiber (NDF) - ash (%).

This calculation will measure all forms of sugar in the feed including simple sugars as well as polysaccharides such as starch. All of these carbohydrates will be absorbed as simple sugars if they are digested by the horse's digestive enzymes, so nutritionally speaking they can be lumped into this single category.

Table 2 shows the NSC composition of some common feedstuffs along with their digestible energy contents.

As you can see, there is a wide range in DE and NSC among common horse feeds. Typically, the NSC content is lowest in straw and mature hays. Legume hays are usually higher in NSC than grass hays and cereal grains have the highest concentration of NSC. Molasses is also high in NSC, containing a level between corn and barley, but its overall DE content is lower because it contains 25% water. As a rule, the lower the cell wall content of a feed, the higher the NSC and energy density. This is because horses digest over 95% of the NSC and typically only about 40-50% of the cell wall. There are certain feedstuffs, however, that contain much more digestible cell wall such as beet pulp and soy hulls. These have digestible energy values that are intermediate between hays and cereal grains.

Table 2. NUTRIENT COMPOSITION OF COMMON EQUINE FEEDS ON AN AS FED BASIS (%)

Feedstuff	DE (MJ/kg)	Moisture (%)	Protein (%)	Fat (%)	NDF[1]	Ash (%)	NSC[2] (%)
Timothy hay	7.40	10.0	8.6	2.3	56.6	5.4	17.1
Alfalfa hay	8.65	90.0	17.0	2.4	42.9	7.8	21.9
Wheat straw	6.19	90.0	3.2	1.8	72.1	7.1	6.8
Sweet feed	13.52	14.0	12.6	6.0	14.0	4.3	49.0
Oats	12.00	10.8	11.5	4.6	24.4	3.1	45.6
Corn	14.71	12.0	9.1	3.6	9.5	1.3	64.5
Barley	13.06	10.4	11.7	1.8	16.8	2.4	56.9
Molasses	10.27	25.7	4.3	0.2	0.4	9.9	59.5
Beet pulp	10.86	9.0	8.9	0.5	40.5	4.90	36.2

[1]neutral detergent fiber
[2]non-structural carbohydrate

What about molasses?

Many horse owners are concerned about feeding their horses molasses. As discussed earlier, molasses has about the same amount of NSC as barley or corn. Most of this is in the form of either sucrose (glucose + fructose) or as free glucose and fructose. Both fructose and glucose are readily absorbed from the digestive tract and fructose is converted into glucose by the liver. Therefore, molasses would result in an increase in blood glucose in a similar fashion to the digestion of starch. We recently conducted an experiment where we fed four Thoroughbred horses one of four meals:

1.   1 kg of whole oats

2.   1 kg of cracked corn

3.   0.9 kg of oats + 0.1 kg of molasses

4.   0.9 kg of corn + 0.1 kg of molasses

Blood glucose was measured in these horses for 4 hours after feeding. The glycemic response of the horses when fed 1 kg of oats was nearly the same as when they were fed 1 kg of corn even though corn has 40% more NSC than oats. This is because the starch in oats is much more digestible than the starch in cracked corn.

Adding molasses to oats had little effect on glycemic response. Until 3 hours after feeding, the glucose curves were about the same for the two treatments. After 3 hours, glucose remained slightly elevated in the horses fed only oats. When molasses was added to corn, there was a large difference in glycemic response. Adding molasses to corn caused a large increase in glycemic response which was particularly pronounced in one horse. Why adding molasses affected corn and oats differently may be explained by the rate with which they consumed each diet. When fed straight oats and corn, the horse's average rate of intake was equal to 107 and 105 grams/minute, respectively. When molasses was added to oats, intake rose to 122 grams/minute, a 14% increase. When molasses was added to corn, rate of intake rose to 156 grams/minute, an increase of 49%! At this high rate of intake, the sugar in the molasses was digested rapidly, resulting in a large increase in blood glucose. Combining molasses with a more digestible starch source (oats) with a lower rate of intake buffered the glycemic response of the molasses. Therefore, it appears that the way that molasses affects blood glucose in horses will depend to a large degree on what other NSC sources are in the feed and how quickly the horse eats its grain.

Time of feeding before competition

The most common question that is asked about feeding the performance horse is when to feed before a competition. Theoretically, feeding should be timed so that all of the nutrients from a meal have been digested, absorbed and stored before starting exercise, but not so long before exercise that the horse begins to mobilize fuels just to maintain its resting body functions. To test this hypothesis, KER conducted an exercise experiment in conjunction with the Waltham Centre for Equine Nutrition and Care (Pagan *et al.*, 1996). Six trained Thoroughbreds performed a Standardized Exercise Test (SET) at three different times after eating a grain based meal. The exercise was performed either 1) 8 hours after eating, 2) 3 hours after eating, or 3) after an overnight fast. This SET, carried out on the high speed treadmill, consisted of a 2 minute warm-up walk, 1/2 mile trot, 1/2 mile slow gallop, 1 mile fast gallop (25 miles per hour) and a warm-down trot and walk. Heart rate was monitored throughout exercise and blood samples were taken before feeding, hourly until the beginning of the SET, throughout exercise and 15 and 30 minutes post exercise. Blood was analyzed for glucose, insulin and lactate.

Heart rate was higher at the slow gallop and during the warm-down trot when the horses were exercised 3 hours after feeding. Insulin was significantly higher in the 3 hour fed horses at the beginning and throughout exercise. Blood glucose was also higher after the 3 hour feeding at the beginning of exercise. During exercise, however, blood glucose dropped in the horses exercised 3 hours after eating while it increased in the horses fasted overnight or fed 8 hours before work. Lactate increased with exercise, but was unaffected by time of feeding.

The large drop in blood glucose experienced by the horses worked 3 hours after feeding is not desirable. Basically, the horse has three sources of energy to fuel muscle contraction during exercise. It can use fat, either from the diet or from body stores, it can use muscle glycogen, or it can use blood glucose. Fat stores are plentiful and are good sources of energy during slow work. As exercise intensity increases, faster fuel is needed and glucose is oxidized. If this glucose originates from muscle glycogen, stores are fairly plentiful and depletion is unlikely at distances shorter than endurance rides. Blood glucose is the most limited fuel available to the horse. Blood glucose is maintained primarily from mobilization of liver glycogen and these stores are small compared to the amount of glycogen stored in the muscle. If blood glucose is used extensively by the muscle, then blood glucose will fall and this may lead to a central nervous system fatigue since glucose is the primary fuel used by the nervous system.

The horses exercised three hours after feeding experienced a large drop in blood glucose because insulin was elevated at the onset of exercise. This caused an increased uptake of glucose by the working muscle. The horses exercised after an overnight fast or 8 hours post feeding began work with resting levels of both glucose and insulin. During exercise, blood glucose actually increased, indicating that the horses were mobilizing liver glycogen at a faster rate than the glucose was being cleared from the blood.

Time of feeding had no effect on lactic acid accumulation during exercise, suggesting that time of feeding only affected how fuels were used for aerobic exercise. Anaerobic energy generation was unaffected. This means that during really intense exercise of short duration such as a Thoroughbred race, time of feeding is not nearly as important as strenuous exercise of longer duration such as the cross country phase of a Three-day Event.

All of the parameters measured responded basically the same whether the horses were fed 8 hours before work or fasted overnight. It is probably better to exercise horses 8 hours after feeding rather than fasting them overnight, since an overnight fast may disrupt digestive function and there is evidence that fasting horses may lead to stomach ulcers.

Feeding and behavior

There is certainly a great deal of controversy about whether the type of feed you give your horse will affect its behavior. There are two schools of thought about whether feed affects behavior. The more traditional one held by many scientists is that the only important factor governing feeding and behavior is caloric intake. If a horse is underfed and in negative energy balance, then it will not be as active or aggressive as when it is well nourished. Advocates of this point of view insist that when a horse's behavior changes when it is on full feed, all the owner is really seeing is an expression of that individual's "true colors." They are more likely to suggest that the horse simply needs more training to become controllable when it is well fed. They would further insist that all you will get when you overfeed your horse grain is a fat horse.

A second school of thought acknowledges that what so many horseman believe is indeed real. Certain types of feed may affect some behaviors in some horses. As of yet there is not concrete proof that this happens, but I would like to propose a mechanism of how feed might affect behavior. I must emphasize, however, that at this point this is only a theory and much more research is needed before it can be stated as fact.

I have been involved in a couple of experiments that suggest that feed may affect behavior. The first one was with Standardbred horses at the veterinary college in Sweden (Pagan *et al.*, 1987). When horses were fed a high carbohydrate diet, they appeared subjectively to be more excitable and their heart rates were higher during an exercise test than when the same horses were fed a high fat diet. In more recent studies at KER's research facility using more objective measures of behavior, a difference was detected when horses were fed the same number of calories from different sources.

Why would grain affect behavior? As we have already shown, when a grain meal is fed, blood glucose levels increase. The extent of increase depends on the type of diet and some horses have much higher blood glucose peaks than others. This much is fact. Now for the theory. In humans, it has been suggested that many mental disorders such as schizophrenia, mania and depression are the result of uncontrollable fluctuations of brain glucose levels acting in conjunction with insulin resistance (Holden *et al.*, 1995). These fluctuations affect the production of the neurotransmitter serotonin. The behavioral disorder mania has been associated with hyperglycemia (high blood sugar) and hyperserotonergia (too much serotonin). Mania is defined as excitement of psychotic proportions manifested by mental and physical hyperactivity, disorganization of behavior and elevation of mood. Does that sound like a horse you know?

Horses evolved eating diets that were fairly low in NSC, so in the wild they would not experience wide fluctuations in blood glucose and insulin. Insulin resistance is also common in certain horses, so it is conceivable that these horses may experience high levels of glucose and insulin in the brain. In rats, injection of insulin caused an increase in 5-HT (the major metabolite of serotonin) (Vahabzadeh *et al.*, 1995). KER has conducted research demonstrating that supplemental trivalent chromium (from chromium yeast) increased the sensitivity of tissue to insulin so that less insulin was produced in response to a grain meal (Pagan *et al.*, 1995). Blood glucose was also lower indicating that it was more efficiently cleared from the blood. Interestingly, there have been numerous reports from the field that horses given supplemental chromium appeared calmer and experienced a lower incidence of tying up. Since nervousness is associated with many cases of tying up, it is intriguing to speculate whether these two problems (nervousness and tying-up) are related to insulin resistance in certain horses.

Again, it should be emphasized that the connection between behavior and feeding is only a theory, but if we assume that it is true, then what should we feed to reduce the high peaks in blood glucose seen in certain horses?

1.   Keep meal sizes small. Blood glucose increases in response to the size of the meal.

2.   Feed plenty of forage. Feed at least 1% of body weight to all horses and increase that to at least 1.5% in horses that are particularly excitable. If nothing else, they will spend more time eating and less time being bored.

3.   Add fat to the diet. Substituting fat for carbohydrates will reduce glycemic response. Fat (usually vegetable oil) contains about 3 times as much digestible energy (DE) as oats and 2.5 times as much DE as corn. Also, research at KER (Pagan *et al.*, 1995) has shown that adding fat will actually reduce glycemic response of the NSC fraction of the diet, possibly by slowing gastric emptying.

4.   Substitute fermentable fiber for NSC. Certain fiber sources (beet pulp, soy hulls) can replace part of the grain in a horse's concentrate.

5.   Feed supplemental chromium. Unfortunately, chromium has not yet been approved for inclusion in horse feeds, so you must get it from your health food store (it is approved for humans) or from your veterinarian.

Even if feeding doesn't affect behavior, guidelines 1-4 listed above will result in a healthy digestive system and reduce the danger of starch overload in the large intestine.

Conclusions

Carbohydrates are an essential part of a horse's diet, making up around 75% of the total ration. Much of this carbohydrate is made of cell wall which is only digestible by bacteria living in the hindgut. Every equine diet should include at least 25% cell wall (NDF). The non-structural carbohydrate (NSC) content of the horse's diet can vary tremendously depending on the class of horse and energy requirement. Mature idle horses need little added NSC in their diets while the diets of high performance horses should contain 32-36% NSC.

It is probably preferable to wait several hours after feeding the horse before it is strenuously exercised. This will allow blood glucose and insulin to return to a resting level and prevent a rapid drop in blood glucose at the onset of exercise. Feeding hay with grain may decrease the digestibility of starch in the small intestine. Horses should have free choice access to hay so that they will eat small amounts continually. If this is not possible, it may be best to feed grain a few hours before hay to allow complete digestion of the grain's starch in the small intestine.

Large fluctuations in blood glucose and insulin may affect behavior in horses. If this is true, then meal size should be small and a portion of the concentrate's DE should come from fat and fermentable fiber. A single meal should never supply over 0.3-0.35% of the horse's body weight as non-structural carbohydrate (NSC) since higher levels of grain intake will result in starch overload which may lead to colic and laminitis.

References

Holden, R.J. (1995) Schizophrenia, suicide and the serotonin story. Med Hypotheses, 44: 5, 379-91.

Meyer, H., S. Radicke, E. Kiengle, S. Wilke and D. Kleffken (1993) Investigations on preileal digestion of oats, corn and barley starch in relation to grain processing. In: Proceedings of 13th ENPS, Gainesville, FL, pp. 92-97.

Pagan, J.D., B. Essen-Gustavsson, A. Lindholm and J. Thornton (1987) The effect of dietary energy source on exercise performance in Standardbred horses. Equine Exercise Physiology 2, ICEEP, San Diego, CA, 686-700.

Pagan, J.D., T. Rotmensen and S.G. Jackson (1995) Responses of blood glucose, lactate and insulin in horses fed equal amounts of grain with and without added soybean oil. In: Proceedings 14th ENPS, Ontario, CA, 13-14.

Pagan, J.D., T. Rotmensen and S.G. Jackson (1995) The effect of chromium supplementation on metabolic response to exercise in Thoroughbred horses. In: Proceedings 14th ENPS, Ontario, CA, 96-101.

Pagan, J.D., I. Burger and S.G. Jackson (1996) The influence of time of feeding on exercise response in Thoroughbreds fed a fat supplemented or high carbohydrate diet. World Equine Vet Review, 1: 2, 43-44.

Potter, G.D., F.F. Arnold, D.D. Householder, D.H. Hansen and K.M. Brown (1992) Digestion of starch in the small or large intestine of the equine. Pferdeheilkunde, pp. 107-111.

Radicke, S., E. Kienzle and H. Meyer (1991) Preileal apparent digestibility of oats and corn starch and consequences for cecal metabolism. In: Proceedings of 12th ENPS, pp. 43-48.

Vahabzadeh, A., M.G. Boutelle and M. Fillenz (1995) Effects of changes in rat brain glucose on serotonergic and noradrenergic neurons. Eur J. Neurosci., 7:2, 175-179.

This paper was first published in Proceedings, Kentucky Equine Research 1997 Equine Nutrition Conference

PROTEIN REQUIREMENTS AND DIGESTIBILITY: A REVIEW

JOE D. PAGAN

Kentucky Equine Research Inc., Versailles, Kentucky, USA

After water, the major constituent of the horse's body is protein. Eighty percent of the horse's fat-free, moisture-free body composition is protein (Robb *et al.*, 1972). Protein is a predominant component of blood, muscles, organs and enzymes and it is a critical part of the horse's diet throughout its life. The age and use of the horse are the most important considerations in determining protein requirements. In addition, there are several other important factors concerning protein which should be evaluated when selecting a ration for a particular phase of a horse's life. Among the most important of these factors are the digestibility of the protein, the amino acid content of the protein, and the protein to energy ratio (PER) of the ration. These factors are especially important when considering the requirement of the young growing horse.

Protein digestibility

The first factor to consider when evaluating a source of protein for a horse ration is the digestibility of its protein. Unfortunately, the digestibility of the protein in many ingredients commonly used in horse feeds has not been adequately determined. The National Academy of Sciences (NRC 1989) recommended three regression equations for estimating the apparent digestibility of the crude protein content of horse diets. These equations take the form $Y = (b)X + (a)$ where Y = digestible protein content; X = crude protein content; (b) estimates the true digestibility of protein; and (a) estimates the metabolic (obligatory) fecal excretion of protein from that source. The equation to be used for estimating protein digestibility of hay/concentrate diets was taken from a study by Slade *et al* (1970) in which four different concentrations of protein were fed to horses. In this experiment, the diets consisted of fish meal, almond hulls, and oat hay. The resulting regression equation: DP% = 0.80 CP% - 3.3 had a large metabolic fecal component and only an 80% estimated true protein digestibility. These diets are hardly representative of what is commonly fed to horses and their low protein digestibility may have been due to the high level of poorly fermentable fiber which these formulations contained (Glade, 1984).

In a series of studies using rations consisting of from 35 to 50% forage and 50 to 65% grain (Pagan, 1982; Pagan et al., 1986), protein digestibility was best described by the equation DP% = 0.86 CP% - 1.06. This equation has a much lower metabolic fecal component than the equations published by the NRC, but these diets were also fairly low in fiber (15-30% NDF). In a separate study using a diet which consisted of 75% alfalfa meal and 25% oats, Pagan (1985) measured nitrogen balance at various levels of protein intake. The crude protein requirement for mature geldings was calculated to be 1.30 g CP/kg BW/day. This would equal a requirement of 650 grams (1.44 lb) of CP per day for a 500 kg horse which is very close to the current NRC requirement for mature horses of this weight (656 g CP/day). The calculated digestible protein requirement, however, was 1.05 g CP/kg BW/day or 1.16 lb of digestible protein per day which was 0.52 lb/day higher than estimated by the NRC. The diet used in this experiment contained 17.0% CP and its digestible protein content averaged 13.0% in 12 digestion trials. The regression equation determined by Pagan (Pagan, 1982; Pagan et al., 1986) would estimate the DP% of this diet to be 13.6% while the regression equations listed by the NRC would have resulted in DP% estimates of 10 to 12%.

Other investigators have reported estimates for the DP% of grains of 94 to 96% (Glade, 1984) and of mixed hay-grain diets of 87 to 95% (Prior et al., 1974; Glade, 1984). A "working average" of 93% has been suggested (Glade, 1984). In any case, it appears that the NRC equations may underestimate the horse's ability to digest protein in common equine rations.

Protein quality

Many of the amino acids which make up the body protein of horses must be supplied in their diets. These amino acids are classified as being essential for growth and reproduction. Sources of feed protein which contain an assortment of amino acids which approximate the needs of the animal are considered of high quality (high biological value), while those which do not are considered low quality.

The amino acid most likely to be deficient in the diets of growing horses is lysine. A great deal of research has been done on the requirement for lysine by growing horses (Hintz, et al., 1971; Potter and Huchton, 1975; Ott et al., 1979; Ott et al., 1981). This research has shown that horses fed diets deficient in lysine will grow more slowly than horses fed a diet high in lysine, even if the crude protein percentages of the diets are identical.

Research at the University of Florida (Graham et al., 1993) suggest that the second limiting amino acid for growing horses may be threonine. Yearlings fed corn/oats/soybean meal diets along with coastal bermudagrass hay grew faster with additional muscle gain when threonine was added to the concentrate at a level of 0.1% of the grain mix.

There are a number of different sources of supplemental protein which are commonly used in horse feeds. These include milk proteins, alfalfa meal, and a number of by-product meals made from the production of oils such as soybean meal, linseed meal, cottonseed meal, safflower meal, and sunflower meal. What is often overlooked, however, is the amount of protein and lysine which is supplied by the grain portion of a horse ration. Typically, the grain portion (corn, barley, oats, etc.) contributes about 40 to 50% of the total protein of a feed for growing horses. The amount of lysine supplied from these cereal grains, however, is only about 30 to 40% of the total, since cereal grains are fairly low in lysine. Therefore, the supplemental source of protein used in horse feeds should be high quality. Alfalfa, milk proteins, and soybean meal are all good sources of quality protein for growing horses. Protein supplements which are deficient in lysine include linseed meal, cottonseed meal, and peanut meal.

Protein to energy ratio

In addition to protein, the young growing horse has a requirement for energy in its diet. These requirements are closely linked and a deficiency of either will result in a reduced growth rate. In fact, protein and energy are so closely linked that one should not be considered without the other in rations for growing horses. In other words, it is the ratio of protein to energy that is important for growth rather than either the protein percentage in a ration or even the daily intake of protein, because it is the energy that provides the potential to grow new tissue that will then require protein.

If there is an excess of protein supplied with an inadequate amount of energy, the protein will be oxidized to produce energy. This is a very expensive way to supply energy, however, and it should be avoided whenever possible. Therefore, knowing the ideal protein to energy ratio will greatly increase the precision with which a horse ration can be balanced.

Growing horses

Weanling horses require 50 g CP/Mcal DE (NRC, 1989). The lysine content of weanling diets should be at least 2.1 g/Mcal DE. Yearling and long yearling horses require 45 g CP/Mcal DE and 1.9 g lysine/Mcal DE. Two year olds require 42.5 g CP/Mcal DE and 1.7 g lysine/Mcal DE.

The protein to energy ratio and lysine to energy ratio are only indirectly related to growth rate. It is the total energy intake which will influence how fast the young horse will grow. Ott (1988) proposed an equation for calculating the DE requirements of yearling horses. This equation incorporates a maintenance energy requirement from the work of Pagan and Hintz (1986) and takes the form: DE (Mcal/day) = 1.4 + 0.03 (BW kg) + 16 (average daily gain (ADG) in kg). According to this equation, a 340 kg yearling would require 11.6 Mcal DE plus an additional 16 Mcal DE for each kg of body weight gained per day. An average Thoroughbred yearling would gain about 0.5 kg BW/day and would therefore require 11.6 + 8 = 19.6 Mcal DE per day. Similar equations can be developed for other ages by taking into account the efficiency of utilization of DE for gain by each age group. Energy requirements for weanlings can be calculated as: DE (Mcal/day) = 1.4 + 0.03 (BW kg) + 10 (ADG kg); and for long yearlings: DE (Mcal/day) = 1.4 + 0.03 (BW kg) + 20 (ADG kg).

A ration for yearlings might consist of 50% timothy hay and 50% grain mix. Since the protein to energy ratio of timothy equals 42.7 g CP/Mcal DE, the grain mix must contain 47.3 g CP/Mcal DE in order to average 45 CP/Mcal DE. Also, the grain must provide 1.93 g lysine/Mcal DE. A mix of 92% oats and 8% soybean meal will provide 47.3 g CP/Mcal DE and 1.97 g lysine/Mcal DE. Of course, this mix would also have to be balanced with the proper amount of minerals and vitamins, but it would provide the proper balance of protein and energy. The ration would contain 2.39 Mcal DE/kg and a yearling would therefore have to eat 8.2 kg (18 lb) per day in order to gain at a rate of 0.5 kg/day.

This method of formulation is superior to using a table listing the protein percentage required by each age group. Basing calculations of the protein requirement of young growing animals on the protein percentage in the diet assumes that the energy concentration of the total diet is constant. For example, the 1989 NRC states that a yearling would require a diet which contains 11.3% protein. This requirement assumes that the total diet contains 2.6 Mcal DE/kg. If the energy density of this diet were greatly different from this, then this concentration of protein would not be appropriate. Rations which are based largely on roughage have much lower energy densities and would therefore require a lower concentration of protein. At the other end of the spectrum are the high fat diets which are becoming more and more popular as diets for young growing horses. These diets have much higher energy densities than common horse rations, and would therefore require a greater protein percentage to obtain similar protein to energy ratios.

It has already been stated that if a diet has a higher than optimal protein to energy ratio then the extra protein will be broken down and used as an inefficient and expensive source of energy. But what happens if the diet has too low a protein to energy ratio? This type of ration will also be used inefficiently by the growing horse and result in a reduced feed to gain ratio. If the protein to energy ratio is a great deal lower than optimal, the young horse will quit eating altogether. Schryver *et al* (1987) fed twenty-four weanling horses one of three diets which contained either 23.7 g CP/Mcal DE, 40.6 g CP/Mcal DE or 63.8 g CP/Mcal DE. The weanlings fed the low protein diet gained only .06 kg/day during the first five months of the experiment compared to 0.63 and 0.69 kg/day on the middle and high protein diets. The foals on the low protein diet ate an average of only 2.7 kg/day compared to 4.4

and 4.7 kg/day on the middle and high protein diets, respectively. When these foals were faced with a very low protein to energy ratio they simply decreased feed intake and essentially quit growing altogether.

Often when veterinarians are faced with a case of epiphysitis or some other metabolic bone disease in young growing horses, they recommend that the foals be placed on a total hay diet or grass hay plus a 10% protein grain mix (Rossdale and Ricketts, 1980). The intention is to slow down growth rate which often will help the problem. However, this type of approach is probably not the best one to use. It would be preferable to feed less of a feed with a proper protein to energy ratio which has been balanced with the correct amounts of vitamins and minerals for a foal of that age.

Broodmares

One of the most important nutrients to consider when feeding the broodmare is protein. Both during pregnancy and lactation, the broodmare uses a large amount of protein for either fetal growth or milk production. Why does the broodmare require protein and how is the best way to supply it?

During pregnancy, fetal growth is very slow during the early months. By the end of the seventh month of pregnancy the fetus has only deposited 10% of its protein content at birth. In the last four months of pregnancy the fetus will deposit about 18 lb of protein as it grows to a birth weight of 120 lb. During the last month of pregnancy alone, the fetus will deposit over 6 lb of protein into its body. Since birth weight is dependent to a large degree on protein deposition, it is critically important that the pregnant mare be fed so that she can supply the growing fetus with an ample supply of protein.

Besides supplying the demand for fetal growth, the mare needs additional protein for other body functions and for the growth of the placenta and amniotic tissues surrounding the fetus. This protein must also be of high quality.

Usually a 13-16% concentrate feed is offered to pregnant mares. When this type of feed is fed at rates from 6 to 10 lb/day, it supplies plenty of protein for fetal growth, providing that it is made using quality sources of protein. Sometimes, however, pregnant mares don't need this much grain. In this case, it is best to feed the mare a more concentrated source of both protein and minerals. A 25-30% protein supplement pellet is excellent for this type of application. It should contain quality sources of protein along with plenty of vitamins and minerals to ensure optimal fetal growth and the birth of a big strong foal. 2 lb of this type of supplement can be fed in place of a regular broodmare feed when the mare doesn't need a bunch of extra calories.

Some people worry that a 25-30% protein supplement supplies too much protein for the mare. In reality, 2 lb of this type of supplement supplies the same amount of protein as 4 lb of a 15% protein feed. The protein from the supplement is of higher quality since about 2/3 of the protein in the 15% concentrate comes from cereal grain and this protein is low in lysine. Substituting 2 lb of supplement for 6-8 lb of a grain mix actually supplies less total protein, but a similar amount of quality protein.

Lactating mares also require large amounts of quality protein. A lactating mare needs twice as much protein as a barren or early pregnant mare. She needs this much protein because mare's milk is high in protein, typically containing about 20-25% protein on a dry basis. A mare during peak lactation will secrete over 1 lb/day of protein in her milk. This milk protein is very high in lysine and the mare requires high quality protein in her diet to produce it. In fact, the surest way to decrease milk production in a mare is to restrict her protein intake. If energy only is restricted, the mare will use her body fat reserves to produce milk. Restricting protein in the diet will cause a decrease in milk production and foal growth.

Performance horses

The protein requirement of the mature performance horse is fairly low. The 1989 NRC estimated the requirement to be equal to 40 g CP/Mcal DE. This recommendation is probably too generous, since protein requirements don't increase as quickly as energy requirements in the performance horse. Lawrence (1992), however, suggested that higher quality protein in the equine athlete's diet may improve performance.

If the protein requirement of a performance horse exceeds its requirement, then the extra protein can used as a source of energy. The amino acids from this extra protein are broken down by the liver, and the nitrogen from the protein is excreted as ammonia. The carbon "skeletons" that are left can be oxidized to produce ATP or used to make glucose or fat.

Excessive protein intake should be avoided in the exercised horse for a number of reasons:

1)   Water requirements increase with increased protein intake.

2)   Urea levels increase in the blood leading to greater urea excretion into the gut, which may increase the risk of intestinal disturbances such as enterotoxemia.

3)   Blood ammonia increases causing a number of problems such as nerve irritability and disturbances in carbohydrate metabolism.

Increased ammonia excretion in the urine may also lead to respiratory problems because of ammonia buildup in the stall.

Summary

Protein is required by all ages of horses, but the amount and quality required depends on the horse's age and physiological status. Young growing horses and broodmares need the most and best protein while performance horses require less protein. An evaluation of protein supplied from the horse's forage is necessary before correct protein supplementation is possible.

References

Glade, M.J. (1984) The influence of dietary fiber digestibility on the nitrogen requirements of mature horses. J. Anim Sci. 58:638.

Graham, P.M., E.A. Ott, J.H. Brendemuhl and S.H. TenBroeck (1993) The effect of supplemental lysine and threonine on growth and development of yearling horses. Proc. 13th ENPS, Gainesville, FL.

Hintz, H.F., H.F. Schryver and J.E. Lowe (1971) Comparison of a blend of milk products and linseed meal as protein supplements for young growing horses. J. Anim. Sci. 33:1274 Lawrence, L.M. 1992. Protein Requirements of Equine Athletes. Proc. for the 1992 Short Course: Feedings the Performance Horse. Kentucky Equine Research, Inc., Lexington, Ky.

NRC. (1989) Nutrient Requirements of Horses. No. 6. (5th ed.). National Academy of Sciences. National Research Council, Wash. D.C.

Ott, E.A., R.L. Asquith, J.P. Feaster and F.G. Martin (1979) Influence of protein level and quality on the growth and development of yearling foals. J. Anim. Sci. 49:620

Ott, E.A., R.L. Asquith, and J.P. Feaster (1981) Lysine supplementation of diets for yearling horses. J. Anim. Sci. 53:1496

Ott, E.A. (1988) Protein and amino acid requirements of the young horse. Horse Research Reports, Univ. of Florida, Gainesville. pp. 20-26.

Pagan, J.D. (1982) The digestible energy requirements of lactating pony mares. M.S. Thesis, Cornell University, Ithaca, New York.

Pagan, J.D. (1985) Equine Energetics: The relationship between energy requirements and body size in horses and energy expenditure in horses during submaximal exercise. Ph.D. Thesis, Cornell University, Ithaca, New York.

Pagan, J.D. and H.F. Hintz (1986) Equine Energetics. I. Relationship between body weight and energy requirements in horses. J. Anim. Sci. 63:815.

Pagan, J.D., B. Essen-Gustavsson, A. Lindholm and J. Thornton (1986) (unpublished data).

Potter, G.D., and J.D. Huchton (1975) Growth of yearling horses fed different sources of protein with supplemental lysine. In: Proc. Fourth ENPS, Calif. State Polytech. U., Pomona, pp 19.

Prior, R.L., H.F. Hintz, J.E. Lowe and W.J. Visek (1974) Urea recycling and metabolism of ponies. J. Anim. Sci. 38:565

Robb, J., R.B. Harper, H.F. Hintz, J.E. Lowe, J.T. Reid, and H.F. Schryver (1972) Body composition of the horse: Interrelationships among proximate components, energy content, liver and kidney size, and body size and energy content, liver and kidney size, and body size and energy value of protein and fat. Anim. Prod. 14:25.

Rossdale, P.D. and S.W. Ricketts (1980) Equine Stud Farm Medicine. Bailliere Tindall, London.

Schryver, H.F., D.W. Meakim, J.E. Lowe, J. Williams, L.V. Sonderholm and H.F. Hintz (1987) Growth and calcium metabolism in horses fed varying levels of protein. Equine Vet. J. 19(4): 280. Slade, L.M., D.W. Robinson and K.E. Casey. 1970. Nitrogen metabolism in nonruminant herbivores. I. The influence of nonprotein nitrogen and protein quality on the nitrogen retention of adult mares. J. Anim. Sci. 30:753.

This paper was first published in "Feeding the Performance Horse," Proceedings for the 1992 Short Course for Feed Manufacturers

MINERAL REQUIREMENTS IN THE HORSE: A HISTORICAL PERSPECTIVE

HAROLD F. HINTZ
Cornell University, Ithaca, New York, USA

Equine mineral nutrition has long been of great interest to me. In fact, I have been fascinated by mineral nutrition of the horse ever since my days as a graduate student at Cornell University where I observed the animals in the studies of Krook and Lowe (1964). It was demonstrated that an imbalance of calcium and phosphorus could cause lameness in growing horses within 12 weeks after being fed the imbalanced diet. The lameness was described as being "insidious shifting." Because the entire skeleton was affected, the lameness shifted from one leg to another . When the horse favored the lame leg, the other three became more stressed. Inevitably, one of the three would then show signs of lameness. The horses also demonstrated a rabbit hopping gait, which I assumed was to decrease stress on the hind legs. Repletion with calcium was effective in treating the lameness.

Of course, calcium deficiency had been demonstrated in horses long before the studies of Krook and Lowe. Many case histories of "big head disease," or osteoporosis, can be found in the horse and veterinary literature of the 1800's and early 1900's (Hornbrook, 1826 and James, 1886). Berns (1890) reported that hundreds of horses were lost annually in New York City to osteoporosis. The disease was named "big head" because of the increase in head size. When horses are fed a diet lacking in calcium, the concentration of blood calcium drops which is a trigger to release parathyroid hormone. This hormone releases calcium from the bone in an attempt to maintain the needed concentration of blood calcium. The blood level of calcium needs to remain within certain limits because calcium is necessary to maintain normal nervous and muscle tissue activity. In the horse, when extensive calcium is removed from the head, the fibrous connective tissue content increases and the head actually increases in size, the head appears puffed or swollen, hence the name "big head disease."

Many theories ranging from poor ventilation (Berns, 1890) to infectious disease (Jasme, 1891) were proposed as to the etiology of "big head." Many severe treatments such as burning the enlarged area with a hot iron (Hornbrook, 1826), puncturing the enlarged area with an awl and pouring arsenic into the opening were used without success (Stowell, 1858). In the late 1800's limestone and other calcium supplements were found to be beneficial (Marshall, 1899). The incidence of the disease gradually decreased but information was not spread as rapidly then as it is now, hence, the calcium treatment was not immediately accepted. Even as late as 1901, the famous Cornell veterinarian James Law wrote "Faulty food - a lack of lime - has been a favorite explanation ... but there is a growing tendency to suspect a microbial origin." Although the severe cases of calcium deficiency that result in big head are not common today, the condition still appears from time to time. We also believe marginal cases of calcium deficiency resulting in predisposition of lameness are not a rarity.

In 1967 the Equine Nutrition Program was formed at Cornell University, thanks largely to the efforts of Dr. Steve Roberts of the College of Veterinary Medicine. The program was a joint effort between the College of Veterinary Medicine and the College of Agriculture and Life Sciences. Dr. Herbert Schryver and I were first to be hired with Dr. Jack Lowe soon joining the team. Our first goal was to study the effect of nutrition on the skeleton of the horse. We decided that the first step to reach the goal was to learn more about basic mineral metabolism of the horse. Because of the obvious relationship of calcium to the skeleton, the decision was made to study calcium nutrition.

First we studied the maintenance requirements (Schryver *et al.*, 1970, and Hintz *et al.*, 1973). Several methods can be used to estimate maintenance requirements. One approach is the balance study. Calcium intakes above and below the estimated requirement are fed to mature animals in metabolism stalls. Calcium intake, fecal and urinary calcium losses are determined. Intake is plotted against retention. The intake of calcium needed for zero calcium retention (maintenance) can then be calculated. Another approach is to measure obligatory (endogenous) losses in urine and feces. Endogenous losses are those that the body loses regardless of intake and can be measured with isotope studies or with balance studies in which losses are extrapolated at zero nutrient intake. Knowledge of endogenous losses is useful not only in the estimation of maintenance requirements, but also for the factorial method to measure requirements above maintenance. Endogenous losses are also needed to determine true digestibility of nutrients. For example, if the endogenous fecal loss of calcium is 2 g/100 kg of body weight, a 500 kg horse would excrete 10 g of endogenous calcium in the feces daily, even when the diet provided no calcium. If calcium was fed at a rate of 20 g per day and 20 g of calcium appeared in the feces, the apparent digestibility would be zero. However, if the fecal loss is corrected for endogenous loss (20-10=10), the true digestibility would be 50% (10 g in feces ÷ 20 g of intake). True digestibility is particularly valuable when comparing sources of calcium or when studying the effect of level of calcium intake on calcium metabolism.

Our estimates of maintenance requirements obtained by the balance study method and by the use of endogenous losses were similar. We calculated that horses lost 20 to 25 mg of endogenous calcium/kg of body weight/day. The calcium in a typical ration had an efficiency of absorption of around 50 percent in mature animals fed at a reasonable rate. Thus the horse would need 40 to 50 mg of dietary calcium/kg of body weight/day.

If the calcium intake was excessive, the efficiency of absorption was decreased (Schryver *et al.*, 1970). Ca:P ratio, oxalate and source of calcium could also influence efficiency (Whitlock *et al.*, 1970, Schryver *et al.*, 1971a, Hintz *et al.*, 1972, Swartzmann *et al.*, 1978, and Hintz *et al.*, 1984). Nevertheless, it seemed reasonable to estimate that horses weighing 500 to 600 kg needed about 20-24 grams of calcium per day for maintenance. Pagan (1994) recently reported similar values from his balance studies. Our estimates for maintenance were used in the 1973, 1978 and 1989 NRC publications of Nutrient Requirements of the Horse. Similar values were used in the 1982 and 1994 German standards (Meyer *et al.*, 1994) and the 1990 French standards (INRA. 1990).

Calcium requirements of pregnant mares were calculated by adding the amount deposited in the fetus during late gestation, with an assumed efficiency of 50%. The values for the mineral content of new born were obtained from body composition studies conducted in Germany. We estimated that a 500 kg mare would need 35-37 grams of calcium daily during late gestation. The German estimate was 38 g per day, the French estimate was 39 g per day.

Calcium requirements of the lactating mare were calculated by adding the amount of calcium in milk to the maintenance requirement, again corrected for efficiency of utilization. Milk production and milk composition were estimated in several studies including those at Cornell University (Schryver *et al.*, 1986). The estimates of milk composition are probably more accurate that the ones for milk production. Our estimates of calcium needs are 50 to 56 g per day for a 500 kg mare in early lactation and 36 to 41 g per day for a mare in late lactation. German estimates are 52 g per day for early lactation and the French estimates are 47-61 g per day.

We estimated calcium requirements for growing horses by adding the amount of calcium deposited in body gain corrected for efficiency of utilization to the maintenance requirement (Schryver *et al.*, 1974). Horses 4 to 12 months of age with an expected mature weight of 500 kg would need 29 to 36 g of calcium per day. German estimates are 20 to 33 g per day, French estimates are 28 to 39 g. However, the optimal composition for bone has not yet been determined and more studies on the effect of calcium intake on bone integrity in the horse should be conducted.

Phosphorus requirements were estimated by the same methods used to estimate calcium (Schryver *et al.*, 1971b). The values were 15-18 g per day for 500-600 kg horses. Pagan (1994) reported values of 18.5 g per day. German and French values are 15 g per day. Our values for pregnant mares (23 - 28 g daily) are similar to the French and German estimates. Mares in early lactation need 34 to 36 g per day. German estimates are 35 g, French estimates are 40 to 55 g. We suggest that growing horses need 16 to 20 g of phosphorus daily while French values are 16 to 22 g and German values, 18 to 23 g per day.

There has been considerable discussion concerning the copper requirements of growing horses since Knight and co-workers (1985) reported a negative correlation between the copper concentrations in the diets for weanlings and incidence of skeletal problems. These findings resulted from a survey of horse farms. They suggested that the copper requirement might be 30 to 50 mg/kg of diet. There is no doubt that copper deficiency can induce skeletal problems. Osteochondrosis has been produced experimentally in foals fed a diet containing 1.7 mg of copper per kg of feed (Bridges and Harris. 1988). Hutrig *et al* (1993) fed 18 foals diets containing 8 or 25 ppm copper. They concluded there was a relationship between low copper intake in fast growing horses and inferior collagen quality, biomechanically weak cartilage and osteochondrosis lesions. All nine foals fed the low copper diet had histological lesions but only 5 developed clinical lesions. It was concluded that factors other than nutrition, such as individual variation in growth or genetic potential, influence the expression of osteochondrosis.

We estimated copper and zinc maintenance requirements with balance studies (Cymbaluk *et al.* 1981). We found it difficult to measure endogenous zinc losses with isotope studies. Our studies with copper indicate the maintenance requirement may be slightly less that the 10 ppm suggested by NRC. In 1989, NRC considered that the studies which Knight et al used to suggest the necessity for high levels of copper to be inconclusive and decided not to increase their estimates of requirement but to keep it at the concentration of 10 mg/kg of diet. Meyer (1994) recently suggested a requirement of 10-12 mg per kg of diet but he also pointed out that attention should be paid to copper status of weaned foals that graze pastures that contain low copper concentrations. In our studies, the factorial method using body composition to estimate copper requirements in growing horses failed to provide data to suggest a diet containing 10 ppm copper to be inadequate for growing horses.

References

Berns, G.H. 1898. Osteoporosis. J. Comp. Med. Surg. 19:651-654.

Bridges, C.H. and E.D. Harris. 1988. Cartilaginous fractures ("osteochondritis dissecans") induced experimentally in foals with low copper diets. J. Am. Vet. Med. Assoc. 193, 215-221.

Cymbaluk, N.F., H.F. Schryver and H.F. Hintz. 1981. Copper metabolism in mature ponies. J. Nutr. 111:87.

Hintz, H.F. and H.F. Schryver. 1972. Magnesium metabolism in the horse. J. Anim. Sci. 35:755.

Hintz, H.F. and H.F. Schryver. 1973. Magnesium, calcium and phosphorus metabolism in ponies fed varying levels of magnesium. J. Anim. Sci. 37:927.

Hintz, H.F., H.F. Schryver, J. Doty, C. Lakin and R.A. Zimmerman. 1984. Oxalic acid content of alfalfa hays and its influence on the availability of calcium, phosphorus, and magnesium to ponies. J. Anim. Sci. 58:939.

Hornbrook, S. 1826. Big head. New England Farmer. 5:150-151.

Hutrig, M., S. Green, H. Dobson, Y. Mikuni-Takagaki and J. Choi. 1993. Correlative study of defective cartilage and bone growth in foals fed a low-copper diet. Equine Vet. J., Supplement 16. 66-73.

INRA. 1990. L'alimentation des chevaux. W. Martin-Rosset, ed. Paris. 277.

James, H.F. 1886. Osteo-porosis. J. Comp. Med. Surg. 7:293-196.

Jasme, A. 1891. Osteo-porosis. J. Comp. Med. Surg. 12:404-407.

Knight, D.A., A.A. Gabel, S.M. Reed, R.M. Embertson, W.J. Tyznik and L.R. Bramlage. 1985. Correlation of dietary mineral to incidence and severity of metabolic bone disease in Ohio and Kentucky. Proc. Am. Assoc. Equine Practitioners. 445-461.

Krook, L. and J.E. Lowe. 1964. Nutritional secondary hyperparathyroidism in the horse. Pathol. Vet. Supplement 1. 1-98.

Law, J. 1901. Osteoporosis. Veterinary Med. 3:579.

Marshall, C.J. 1899. Osteoporosis. J. Comp. Med. Surg. 20:346-350.

Meyer, H. 1994. Cu-stoffwechsel und-bedarf des Pferdes. Übers. Tierenährg. 22. 363-394.

Meyer, H., M. Kirchgessner, K. Bronsch, H.H. Freese, H. Jeroch, J. Pallauf, E. Pfeffer and E. Schulz. 1994. Energi- und nährstoffvedarf landwirtschaftlicher nutztiere. Empfehlungen zue Energie- und Nährstoffversorgung der Pferde. 48.

National Research Council. 1973. Nutrient requirements of horses. 3rd Edition NRC-NAS. Washington, DC.

National Research Council. 1978. Nutrient requirements of horses. 4th Edition NRC-NAS. Washington, DC.

National Research Council. 1989. Nutrient requirements of horses. 5th Edition NRC-NAS. Washington, DC.

Pagan, J.D. 1994. Nutrient digestibility in horses. Proc. Feeding the Performance Horse:127.

Schryver, H.F., P.H. Craig and H.F. Hintz. 1970. Calcium metabolism in ponies fed varying levels of calcium. J. Nutr. 100:955.

Schryver, H.F., H.F. Hintz and P.H. Craig. 1971a. Calcium metabolism in ponies fed high phosphorus diet. J. Nutr. 101:259.

Schryver, H.F., H.F. Hintz and P.H. Craig. 1971b. Phosphorus metabolism in ponies fed varying levels of phosphorus. J. Nutr. 101:1257.

Schryver, H.F., H.F. Hintz, J.E. Lowe, R.L. Hintz, R.B. Harper and J.T. Reid. 1974. Mineral composition of the whole body, liver, and bone of young horses. J. Nutr. 104:126.

Schryver, H.F., O.T. Oftedal, J. Williams and H.F. Hintz. 1986. Lactation in the horse: The mineral composition of mare's milk. J. Nutr. 116:2142.

Stowell, S. 1858. Big head. Amer. Vet. J. 3:85-86.

Swartzmann, J.A., H.F. Hintz and H.F. Schryver. 1978. Inhibition of calcium absorption in ponies containing oxalic acid. Am. J. Vet . Res. 3:1621.

Whitlock, R.H., H.F. Schryver, L. Krook, H.F. Hintz and P.H. Craig. 1970. The effects of high dietary calcium for horses. P 127 in Proc. 16th Am. Assoc. Eq. Pract., F.J. Milne, ed. Lexington, Ky.

This paper was first published in "Focus on Equine Nutrition," Proceedings for the 1996 Short Course for Feed Manufacturers

CEREAL GRAINS AND BYPRODUCTS: WHAT'S IN THEM AND HOW ARE THEY PROCESSED ?

CHARLES FAHRENHOLZ

SmithKline Beecham, West Chester, Pennsylvania, USA

When you go into a feed store and purchase a bag of feed, the label gives you certain information. Law requires that labels include net weight, product name, guaranteed analysis, ingredient listing, and manufacturer's name. Medicated feed must also list the active ingredient along with any precautionary statements and adequate directions for use. For formula feeds, guarantees must be listed for minimum crude protein, minimum crude fat, maximum crude fiber, minimum and maximum calcium, minimum phosphorus, minimum and maximum salt. There should be a list of ingredients used to make the feed; however, today many of the ingredients are listed as "collective terms" (groupings of feed ingredients) rather than individual ingredients. This allows the manufacturer to substitute ingredients, within a defined group such as grain by-products, without having to change labels every time there is a reformulation. These changes are most often due to changes in supply or costs.

Although the guarantees and other information provided on a label aid us in comparing products and making purchasing decisions, these guarantees tell us nothing about the quality of the feed.

Grains such as oats, corn, and barley and grain byproducts such as wheat bran, wheat middlings, and wheat mill run are used primarily as energy sources in horse feeds. Soybean meal is the primary source of protein used in North America. Nearly all cereal grains and any number of byproducts from the food and feed industry can be, and are fed to horses to supply digestible energy (DE). Several other protein sources are also available when formulating diets. This paper will discuss the nutrient composition of these ingredients and how processing affects their quality. I will also briefly describe some of the processing techniques used in manufacturing horse feeds, again focusing on areas where feed quality may be affected.

Grain is marketed by grade according to certain quality characteristics. Some of the criteria used to determine the grade are bushel test weight, foreign material, damaged kernels, and moisture. As test weight decreases and the other factors increase, the grade goes down and the price usually decreases accordingly. Generally, as bushel test weight goes down, the protein content increases and starch content decreases. Although the protein content increases, protein quality generally decreases. The berries are often more shriveled and seed coats are harder. Often times the grain can still be used, but the nutritional profile has changed and must be accounted for. If molds or mycotoxins are detected, however, the grain should not be used in horse feeds.

Soybean meal

Soybean meal was once merely the by-product of the soybean oil processing industry. Today it is a major protein source in livestock feeding. There are two main types of meal produced in the US, 44% protein solvent extracted and 48% protein dehulled solvent extracted meal. The difference in protein content is because hulls are added back to the extracted meal of the solvent extracted type. The dehulled, solvent extracted meal can be fed to all classes of livestock and poultry. The solvent extracted meal can also be fed to all types of livestock; however, it is better utilized by animals, such as mature ruminants, having the ability to digest higher concentrations of fiber.

The process of extracting oil from beans, thus producing soybean meal is as follows:

1.   Raw beans are cleaned and then dried, hulls are separated.

2.   Beans are passed through cracking rolls and then heated to 165°F to 175°F for 10 minutes.

3.   Beans are then flaked and passed through the extraction tower. Solvents such as hexane or other hydrocarbons are used to extract the oil from the flakes. The oil level is reduced to less than 1%. Temperature is 113°F.

4.   The extracted flakes are dried at 208°F for 10 minutes, toasted at 220°F for 90 minutes and ground into meal. This meal is generally 48% to 50% protein. Hulls are then added back to produce the 44% protein meal.

Good quality soybean meal (defined by AFIA, 1992) should have the following physical characteristics:

Color: light tan to light brown.
Odor: fresh, typical of the product, not sour, musty, or burned.
Taste: Bland and free of any "bean" or burned taste.
Texture: homogeneous, free flowing, without coarse particles or excessive fines.
Bulk density: 36 - 40 lbs per cubic foot.
Screen analysis: 95 - 100% through US Standard Sieve No. 10, 40 -60% through US Standard Sieve No. 20, and a maximum 6% through US Standard Sieve No. 80.
Moisture: 12% or less improves flowability and reduces incidence of mycotic growth.

The final product must not contain more than 3.5% crude fiber. It may contain an inert nontoxic conditioning agent, either nutritive or non-nutritive, to reduce caking and improve flowability. The conditioning agent may not exceed 0.5% and the name must be shown on the label as an added ingredient. Frequently calcium carbonate is used as the conditioning agent.

Soybean meal must be properly cooked during processing to provide optimum protein nutrition for animals. These antinutritional factors are primarily digestive enzyme (protease) inhibitors. Soy hemagglutinin and trypsin inhibitor are the greatest concern to producers.

The aim of heat processing is to reduce the inhibitors to acceptable levels, not to totally destroy them. Underheating soybean meal fails to reduce the effects of growth inhibitors, resulting in low protein efficiency, reduced growth and feed efficiency in monogastric and young ruminant animals. It has been shown in turkey poults that underheated soybean meal greatly increases the need for vitamin D to prevent rickets.

Overheating soybean meal tends to inactivate or destroy essential amino acids such as lysine, cystine, methionine, and possibly others. Overprocessed soybean meal is seldom a problem with commercial vendors because of the energy required to process soybean meal. However, soybeans processed on the farm or at smaller crushing plants are likely to be over or underprocessed if the operator does not carefully monitor the temperature.

The two main assays for determining soybean meal quality are urease activity and protein solubility. Feed manufacturers tend to prefer the urease method because it is easy, quick and relatively inexpensive. It indirectly determines the amount of inactivation of trypsin inhibitor by measuring urease activity, an enzyme present in soybeans similarly destroyed by heating. A major limitation of the urease assay is it cannot measure overheated soybean meal. Protein solubility can measure both over and under processed meal, but the assay is more complex and requires an analytical laboratory. Numerous studies have shown decreases in weight gain and feed efficiency when bean meal has been overprocessed.

We normally think of soybean meal strictly as a protein source; however, there is a significant amount of carbohydrate in soybeans (Table 1.). After the oil is removed, the remaining constituents are predominantly protein, ash, and carbohydrate. The carbohydrate fraction is approximately 42%. Since hulls are removed during processing and, by definition, dehulled meal can have a maximum of 3.5% fiber, that leaves 38% - 40% available carbohydrates. These are primarily oligosaccharides or complex sugars, raffinose, and stachyose.

Table 1. CHEMICAL COMPOSITION OF SOYBEAN PRODUCTS

Product	Protein %	Fat %	Ash %	Crude fiber %	Cell wall (NDF%)	Carbohydrate %
Whole beans	40	21	4.9	5.3	–	34
Flakes/Meal	47.5-49	1	6	3.5	12	40
Hulls	8	1	4.0	36	65	4.3

Corn

Corn is the leading crop in America in terms of volume and value. It is a major cereal grain used in horse feeds. Chemical composition is shown in Table 2. As in most cereal grains, corn is used primarily for its energy, thus its carbohydrate components are usually considered to be most important. The starch, found mainly in the endosperm, comprises 70-72% of the corn kernel. The type of starch may be horny or floury, depending on variety. The starch in dent corn, the type normally used for feed, is approximately 74% amylopectin or branched glucose and 26% amylose, or long chain glucose. These starch granules are readily available to enzymatic digestion by amylases and amyloglucosidases.

Table 2. CHEMICAL COMPOSITION OF CORN AND CORN PRODUCTS

Product	Protein %	Fat %	Ash %	Crude fiber %	Cell wall (NDF%)	Carbohydrate %
Grain	10.0	4.3	1.5	2.9	9	71.7
Hominy feed	11.5	7.7	3.1	6.7	55	78.2
Gluten meal	47	2.4	3.4	4.8	14	19.5
Gluten feed	25.6	2.4	7.2	9.7	41	48.7
Germ meal	22.3	4.1	4.2	13.1	–	49.6

Corn is considered to be low in protein, generally averaging 8% - 10%. Because of the high incorporation rate in feeds, however, substantial amounts of protein are supplied by corn. Corn protein is especially deficient in lysine, 0.25% as opposed to 0.40% for oats and barley, 0.6% for wheat mill run, and 3.1% for soybean meal.

Most of the corn used in the feed industry is No. 2, sometimes No. 3, with the following general specifications for grinding and use in feed:

Test weight: 50 lbs/bu. (No. 1 corn is 56 lbs/bu)
Maximum foreign material: 4%
Maximum damaged kernels: 10%
Maximum moisture: 15.5%
Color: bright to golden yellow
Odor: no moldy, sour, or musty smell should exist.

Grains are routinely stored for long periods of time, thus the quality factors often revolve around proper storage conditions and the adverse effects resulting from improper storage. In general, particular attention must be paid to moisture and temperature. Microbe growth is minimized when grains are stored at less than 13%

moisture. Corn is normally harvested at 22-28% moisture to maximize efficiency of harvesting and reduce the amount of broken kernels. The corn must be dried for proper storage. Corn dried at temperatures greater than 140°F often becomes cracked or damaged, making it more susceptible to insect or microbial damage. Studies have shown that corn stored at 14.5% moisture at 55°F retained condition for 1.5 years. The same corn stored at 68°F changed only slightly after 1.5 years. At 15.2% moisture, corn stored at 77°F deteriorated rapidly. Corn that is stored too wet may begin to mold, and in some extreme instances may heat up enough to cause severe damage to the kernels.

Moldy or musty smelling corn should not be used in horse feed. If a moldy or musty odor can be detected, the corn has been severely damaged, since changes take place long before the odor is detectable. Certainly the possibility exists that toxins have been produced by the infestation. These toxins are, for the most part, very heat stable and even if the feed is pelleted or extruded, the toxins will not be destroyed.

Oats

Because the average oat grain is about 30% hull (fiber), and oats contain sufficient protein, calcium and phosphorus to meet the requirements of mature horses, oats have traditionally been the predominant grain used by horsemen. Oats once made up nearly 31% of all equine feed consumed. Horses digest oats easily in comparison with heavier whole grains like wheat and corn (Coffman, 1961).

During the mid 1950's, over 40 million acres of oats were harvested in the US, but more recently production has dropped below 10 million acres. The decline has been mainly due to poor yields. Genetic gains have been only 9-14% compared to 35-100% increases in other crops.

In spite of the poor yields, the quality of the oat groat cannot be denied. Oats are the most balanced cereal grain, from an amino acid standpoint. Generally, as the protein quantity in cereal grains increases, the quality decreases. This does not occur in oats. A ranking of protein quality among cereal grains lists oats first followed by barley, corn, and wheat.

Nutrient composition of oats and oat products appears in Table 3. As mentioned earlier, approximately 30% of the whole oat is hull. Oat hulls are relatively low in energy and nutritive value. The majority of the protein is found in the groat. Protein content averages 12% but ranges from 11.5% - 24%. Lysine in the same test cultivars ranged from 3.2% - 5.2%. This points out one of the precautions that must be taken when formulating a ration with oats, as nutrient composition varies greatly between cultivars and is very susceptible to environmental factors.

Starch is the major carbohydrate in oats, averaging 52.8% and ranging from 43.7% to 61%. The carbohydrate fraction is low in free sugars, amylose content is

19% - 28%. Starch level varies inversely with protein content. Carbohydrate, reported as NFE in the proximate analysis scheme, is 71.8% in rolled oats, 72.1% in oat groats and 64.2% in whole oats.

Table 3. CHEMICAL COMPOSITION OF OATS

Product	Test weight lb/bu.	Protein %	Fat %	Crude fiber %	Cell wall (% NDF)	Ash %	NFE %
Whole oats	38.5	12.1	5.1	12.1	32	3.4	61.4
Groats	52.0	15.8	7.2	2.8	7.0	1.9	66.6

Fiber content is as follows:

Oat fraction	Crude fiber %	Cell wall (NDF%)	Hemicellulose %	Cellulose %	Lignin %
Whole oat	10.7	24.4	10.4	11	3
Rolled oat	1.7	–	–	–	–
Hull	33.2	78	28.8	39.2	10.0

General specifications of oats for grinding and use in feed are:

Test weight: 27 lbs/bu. (No. 1 32 lbs/bu.)
Maximum foreign material: 5%
Maximum heat damaged kernels: 3%
Color: soft yellow or buff, may vary from almost white to dark yellow or gray.
Odor: no moldy, sour, or musty smell should exist.

Quality of oats usually relates to the deterioration or oxidation of the lipid. Lipid content is low in hulls, higher in groats and varies widely with cultivars. Average content ranges between 5% - 9%. Approximately 95% of the fatty acids are palmitic (C16:0), oleic (C18:1) and linoleic (C18:2). Whole oats and intact groats can be stored successfully at 10% moisture and normal temperatures; however, free fatty acids increase rapidly in ground oats at normal temperatures and the deterioration rate increases rapidly at storage temperatures of 85°F. Quality is determined by measuring the free fatty acid levels.

Barley

Barley is used as a feed grain, for malting and brewing of beer and for distillation of liquors. In the US, barley ranks only behind corn and sorghum in terms of feed grain production, and constitutes 4% of the total grain used in livestock feed (Feed Management, 1985). Barley must be differentiated in terms of the desired end use; cultivars are developed for specific purposes. Malting and feed barley are distinctly different; high protein content is desirable in feed grain but not for malting. In general, barley has a feeding value of 95% that of corn.

Table 4 lists the nutritive profile of barley. Barley is generally categorized as Pacific coast and non-Pacific coast, with the Pacific coast being lower in protein. Barley is relatively high in crude protein for a feed grain, ranging from 8% to 13%, but is relatively low in lysine and methionine. Because most feed barley contains the hull, fiber content is relatively high, 5% - 7%. Starch makes up nearly 65% of the kernel. Additionally, the kernel has approximately 1% simple sugars and 2% sucrose.

Table 4. CHEMICAL COMPOSITION OF BARLEY

Product	Sugars %	Protein %	Fat %	Crude fiber %	Cell wall (%NDF)	Ash %	Others %
Grain	2-3	8-13	2-3	5.6	28	2-2.5	5-6

General specifications of barley for grinding and use in feed are:

Test weight: 40 lbs/bu. (No.1 48 lbs/bu.)
Maximum foreign material: 6%
Maximum heat damaged kernels: 3%
Color: yellow to golden yellow, should be free of excessive dustiness with no evidence of seed treatment.
Odor: no moldy or musty smell should exist.

The grain tends to be hard and requires some type of processing to make the nutrients more available to the animal. The most common types of processing include rolling and steam flaking. Concerns for barley quality, again, surround storage issues. Improper storage will allow fungus, molds and insects to enter the grain and alter the nutrient profile.

Wheat byproducts

Wheat byproducts were part of the beginning of the feed industry. Many of the earliest feed companies were flour milling companies looking for an outlet for their byproducts. Since wheat byproducts are so important to the feed industry, it is essential that proper terminology be used to differentiate between the fractions, particularly between wheat bran, wheat middlings and wheat mill run. AAFCO (Association of American Feed Control Officials) official definitions for these products are:

<u>Wheat bran</u> - the coarse outer covering of the wheat kernel as separated from cleaned and scoured in the usual process of commercial milling.

<u>Wheat middlings</u> - fine particles of wheat bran, wheat shorts, wheat germ, wheat flour, and some of the offal from the "tail of the mill." This product must be obtained in the usual process of commercial milling and must contain not more than 9.5% crude fiber.

<u>Wheat mill run</u> - coarse wheat bran, fine particles of wheat bran, wheat shorts, wheat germ, wheat flour, and offal from the "tail of the mill." This product must be obtained in the usual process of commercial milling and must contain not more than 9.5% crude fiber.

All too often these terms are used interchangeably and, as the above definitions indicate, they are not the same. When flour is milled from wheat, the amount of the outer layers of the kernel that are removed are determined by the quality of the flour desired. As flour purity goes up, yield goes down. The amount of milling that occurs is dictated by the marketplace, both the price of grades of flour and the price of byproducts. For example, if the market price for bran is high and the demand for midds is low or the price is low, the milling process will be adjusted such that more of the starchy endosperm will be diverted into the bran fraction.

The nutrient composition of wheat and wheat byproducts appear in Table 5. Wheat is generally classified by agronomic and utilization criteria. Hard wheats are generally grown in medium temperate zones, low rainfall, small hard berries, and moderately strong gluten (wheat protein). Soft wheats are found in milder climates, more rainfall, larger kernels. Hard wheats are generally higher in protein. Winter wheats are planted in the fall, spring wheats are planted in the spring. The resulting varieties, then, are numerous, i.e. hard red spring, hard red winter, soft white spring, etc.

The nutrient composition of wheat grain, because of varietal differences, tends to be more variable than any other grain, especially with respect to protein content. Protein content of hard red winter wheat ranges from 13% to 15%, soft white winter from 10% to 12%. The endosperm makes up almost 83% of the kernel and contains 73% of the total protein. Bran is about 14% of the kernel and contains 19% of the total protein. The germ makes up the remaining 3% of the kernel and contains 8 % of the total protein. The majority of the vitamins are in the bran. Perhaps the most attractive aspect of wheat byproducts as a feedstuff is the relatively high protein content, 17.5% in bran, 18.5% in midds and 17.3% in mill run.

Table 5. CHEMICAL COMPOSITION OF WHEAT AND MILLED WHEAT PRODUCTS

Product	Wheat %	Protein %	Fat %	Crude fiber %	Cell wall (%NDF)	Ash %	Starch %	Total sugars %
Wheat	100.0	15.3	1.9	2.9	14	1.8	53.0	2.6
Bran	16.4	16.7	4.6	11.3	51	6.5	11.7	5.5
Midds	8.4	18.5	5.2	8.2	37	5.0	19.3	6.7
Mill run	–	15.6	4.1	9.1	–	5.1	16.9	5.9

Moisture is one of the major considerations in maintaining the quality of wheat byproducts. Wheat is tempered to between 17% and 19% moisture prior to milling to improve the efficiency of the milling process. Byproducts are often stored at this higher moisture content and if not properly managed, will heat up and begin to sour and mold rather quickly. Some flour mills are pelleting their midds and mill run to help stabilize the byproduct and to improve storage, shipping, and handling characteristics.

From a practical standpoint, is there really anything we, the feed customer just stopping in at the local feed store to buy our week's supply of horse feed, can do to check or evaluate the quality of the feed? Certainly most of us have neither the expertise or wherewithal to go back into the mill and "check" the quality of the soybean meal or grain being used in our feed. We certainly should use our sense of smell and sight to detect musty or moldy odors or changes in colors that may indicate overprocessing. We might be able to detect burned soybean meal if we are feeding a mash. There are a few things we should be aware of that may help in making purchasing decisions. Most major feed manufacturers have Quality Control (QC) programs that include establishing ingredient specifications with vendors along with checks of incoming ingredients. If a supplier has a load of "off spec" meal, he knows he cannot sell it to a mill that has a good QC program. Likewise, vendors also know who does not check, and thus where that particular load can be sold. One cannot assume that buying from one of the large feed manufacturers assures that only good quality ingredients are used. Although the size of the mill does not necessarily correlate with a good QC program, it is often the small, local mills where no one checks ingredients that receive poor quality ingredients. We, as consumers, must decide if the place we buy feed is reputable, if they appear knowledgeable, and if they seem to be conscientious about their work. If you are buying from a local manufacturer, ask where they purchase ingredients and if the quality of the soybean meal and other ingredients is ever checked; this will at least let them know you are aware and care about the quality of the horse feed you are buying.

Feed processing

Most of today's feeds are processed in some manner before being fed. Although some grains can be fed whole, processing, even if it is only grinding, usually makes the nutrients more available to the animal, thus improving digestibility and feed efficiency.

GRINDING

Grinding is done using either a hammermill or roller mill. Hammermills are the most abundant type in the feed industry, although roller mills have been gaining in popularity in recent years. Hammermills grind primarily by the impact of free swinging hammers on the grain as it falls through the grinding chamber. Screens with specific size holes surround the grinding chamber and, as the grain particles become small enough, they pass out through the holes. Roller mills have pairs of rolls, often two or three pairs per mill, that essentially crush the grain as it passes between the rolls. The space between rolls can be adjusted to give various particle sizes.

Dry heat processing

MICRONIZING

Micronizing is the heating of grain with infrared heaters. The grain is heated to approximately 300°F for 25 to 50 seconds causing kernel swelling and cell rupturing. The grain is slightly expanded and the moisture content is reduced to about 7% . This product can be stored in conventional units without spoiling. Micronized corn generally has a bulk density of 25 lb/cu. ft. compared to the normal 45 lb/cu. ft. Micronizing improves both rate of gain and feed efficiency in ruminant animals.

POPPING

Popping is achieved by rapid, intense heating of grain. Rapid heating with 700 to 800°F hot air makes the water expand all at once, thereby expanding the grain.

Most feed grain does not pop like popcorn, but grain does expand and starch is gelatinized, resulting in the grain being much more available to digestive enzymes or organisms.

Bulk densities, in pounds per cubic foot, are: oats 22, barley 19, wheat 34, and corn 32. (Normal bulk densities are: oats 25-35, barley 38-43, wheat 45-52, corn 45). The low bulk density causes two problems: (1) feed is often blown from feeders causing waste, (2) the animal cannot consume sufficient feed resulting in reduced gains. Many users of popped grain roll the popped grain to increase the bulk density and to help flatten the grain for easier handling.

ROASTING

Roasted grain is similar to popped grain except the grain is heated at a much slower rate. Grain is passed through a rotating drum which lifts the grain through a flame. Grain temperatures reach 260 to 300°F. Water is lost without the expansion. Depending on the rate of heating, the starch may be gelatinized and some puffing may occur. This leads to improved rate of gain, 6% - 14% and improved feed efficiencies 10% - 14% in feedlot cattle.

In dry heat processing, because of the dry heat sources and the limited amount of water available within the grain, there is very little nutritional damage that occurs during normal processing. Obviously, if the grain is overprocessed (overheated) during any of these processes, damage will occur. This is normally not a problem as each process requires a large amount of energy; thus expense limits overprocessing. The more frequent problem is underprocessing, again due to energy costs. Although this does not harm the grain, it is wasteful because there are no added benefits if it not done correctly.

Wet processing

STEAM FLAKING

Steam flaking has become a very well defined process. It is the most popular method of processing feedlot grains. Steam flaking differs from steam rolling in the amount of time used to steam the grain. Flaking calls for longer conditioning times, sufficient to gelatinize some of the starch. Grain is conditioned at atmospheric pressure for 15 to 30 minutes. Grain temperatures should reach 200 to 210°F with moisture around 17 - 18%. The amount of starch gelatinization depends on heat, moisture and roll pressure. Studies conducted on steamed grain before and after rolling show most of the changes in starch occurred after the rolls. Properly flaked grain results in improved feed efficiency and rate of gain.

If the grain is not properly flaked, starch will not be gelatinized and there will be no benefits that could not have been achieved by dry rolling. Steam flaked grain must be fed relatively soon after flaking or it must be dried. In most operations, the added expense of drying the flakes makes it impractical. Steam flaked grains are often used in textured horse feeds and it is critical that the grain be properly dried or it will begin to mold almost immediately. Frequently when corn is flaked, the germ is dislodged from the remainder of the kernel. Often, if dryers are not properly adjusted, this material goes out with the air being passed through the drier and is lost. If this happens, the energy content of the flaked grain drops somewhat due to the loss of oil and protein.

PELLETING

Pelleting is the most common form of thermal processing used in feed manufacturing. Feed is heated by steam in a conditioning chamber, raising the temperature and moisture content. The temperature and moisture reached depend on the length of time spent in the conditioner. Temperature may range from slightly above ambient, if little steam is added, to nearly 200°F. Moisture may also range from that normally present in the grain to approximately 17%. Once the moisture gets above 17%, rolls begin to slip and the pellet mill plugs.

There are too many variables of the pelleting process to discuss the effects of all of them here. There are, however, some basic aspects that affect the quality of the feed. Pellets are hot when they leave the pellet die, the heat coming from the steam conditioning and/or the friction of being extruded through the die. Pellets should be properly cooled. As they are cooled, moisture content is also reduced. Pellets should not be stored until sufficient moisture has been removed or they will mold.

There are five general categories of feeds that require different conditioning for optimum production and pellet quality. They include high grain, heat sensitive, high natural protein, high urea-molasses, and complete dairy. High grain, for example, should be pelleted at high heat/high moisture to achieve maximum benefits. Heat sensitive feeds generally contain 5 to 25% sugars. These ingredients will caramelize at approximately 140°F, a temperature easily obtained in a thick die without any steam. When this caramelization occurs, lysine will be bound and become unavailable. This is especially a problem when pelleting diets for young animals, diets such as creep feeds.

Pellets can be burned and it is very evident. The pellets often have a very dark color and an unmistakable burnt odor. This can occur when the entire feed is pelleted, but is more often seen in compounded or textured feed. When pelleted alfalfa is used it is sometimes overheated during drying or pelleting. Often times the protein source, vitamins, minerals and other low level inclusion ingredients are pelleted and these pellets are then mixed with cracked or rolled grain. Because of the low grain level and the high temperatures needed to pellet protein feeds, pellets can be burned.

Pelleting has been shown to improve nutrient digestibility, feed efficiency and improved intake in several species. Some of the non-nutritive benefits of pelleting are: less dust, ease of handling and storage, elimination of sorting of ingredients and particles by the animal, reduced segregation during handling, reduced feed wastage, and in some cases improve palatability.

Although there are several advantages to pelleted feed, there are also some cautions that must be taken when considering pelleted feed for horses. Pelleted feeds may be consumed very rapidly and, if the grain used in the pellets has been finely ground and is particularly fermentable, this may lead to situations of colic. I feel that this is more of a management concern and can be controlled or avoided with proper formulation and pellet characteristics.

EXTRUSION

Extrusion cooking has become an important part of the feed industry. Basic to extrusion cooking of cereals is starch gelatinization. Gelatinization in feed is brought about by a combination of moisture, heat, mechanical energy, and pressure differential. Gelatinization enhances the ability of starch to absorb large amounts of water leading to improved digestibility in most cases and improved feed efficiency in some. Gelatinization also increases the speed at which enzymes can break down the starch into simpler, more soluble carbohydrates.

There are basically three types of extruders in use today: short time, high temperature (ST/HT) cookers, pressure cooking extruders and dry extrusion cookers. The most common are the ST/HT extruders. The process involves the following steps:

1. Steam preconditioning at atmospheric pressure at 150°F to 210°F.

2. A method of uniform moisture application.

3. The first portion of the extruder assembly works the moistened cereal or cereal mixture into a doughy consistency at temperatures of 180°F to 210°F.

4. The next section of the extruder raises the temperature of the dough to 230°F to 400°F during a very short time, 10 to 20 seconds. This is done both with the addition of heat to the extruder barrel and friction created by the screw configuration inside the barrel.

5. The last section of the extruder serves to form the gelatinized dough into the final shape by forcing the dough through specially designed dies.

6. A cutter slices the extruded material into the desired size material.

7. The extruded product must then be dried and cooled.

This ST/HT treatment minimizes the loss of available nutrients. Vitamins, in particular, were found to be most affected by this treatment. The increased popularity of this processing method has resulted in the development of many more stable vitamins and other additives.

References

AAFCO Official Publication. 1994. Association of American Feed Control Officials.

Coffman, F. 1961. Oats and Oat Development, in Feed Management, 1986, vol. 37, no. 11, p. 23.

Corn: Culture , Processing, Products. 1970. Ed. by G.E. Inglett, Avi Publishing Co., Inc., Westport, CT.

Feed Management, 1985, vol. 36, no. 7.

Feed Management, 1993, vol. 44, no. 9.

Feed Manufacturing Technology III. 1985. Ed. by R.R. McEllhiney, American Feed Industry Assn., Arlington, VA.

Soybeans: Improvement, Production, Uses. 1987. Ed. by J.R. Wilcox, ASA Publications, Madison. WI.

Wheat Chemistry and Technology. 1978. Ed. by Y. Pomeranz, American Association of Cereal Chemists, Inc., St. Paul, MN.

This paper was first published in "Feeding the Performance Horse," Proceedings for the 1994 Short Course for Feed Manufacturers

MEASURING THE DIGESTIBLE ENERGY CONTENT OF HORSE FEEDS

JOE D. PAGAN

Kentucky Equine Research, Inc., Versailles, Kentucky, USA

One of the most important measures of a horse feed's value is its energy content. Energy density determines how much feed must be fed to meet an animal's energy requirement. Level of intake in turn dictates the concentration of all other nutrients in the feed. Therefore, horse feeds cannot be properly formulated without knowledge of their energy contents. Unfortunately, it is not possible to directly measure the amount of useful energy contained in feed as you can with other nutrients such as protein and minerals. Instead, energy content must be estimated from other measurements.

In the United States, the energy content of horse feed is expressed as Digestible Energy (DE). There are several different ways that DE content can be estimated and this has led to a great deal of confusion about how much DE is actually in horse feed. This paper will review the various methods that are used to measure digestible energy and provide guidelines about how to accurately estimate DE from easily measurable constituents in feed.

Heat of combustion (gross energy)

When a substance is completely burned to its ultimate oxidation products (carbon dioxide, water and other gases), the heat given off is considered its gross energy or heat of combustion. This measure is the starting point in determining the energy value of feed. The determination is usually carried out in a bomb calorimeter. The bomb calorimeter consists of a bomb in which the feed is burned, enclosed in an insulated jacket containing water which surrounds the bomb and which thus provides the means of measuring heat production. The basic unit of heat energy is the calorie (cal), defined as the amount of heat required to raise 1 g of water 1°C, measured from 14.5 to 15.5°C. This unit is too small for use in horses, so the energy content of horse feed is usually expressed as kilocalories (kcal) or megacalories (Mcal). There are 1000 calories in a kcal and 1,000,000 calories in a Mcal. Measured in terms of the joule, the international unit of work and energy, 1 Mcal = 4.185 megajoules (MJ).

Table 1 contains the gross energy content of a number of pure substances and horse feeds. As you can see, fats contain over twice as much gross energy as carbohydrates. These differences are due to the relative amount of oxygen contained in each molecule, since heat is produced only from the oxidation which results from the union with oxygen from outside the molecule. In the case of carbohydrates, there is enough oxygen present in the molecule to take care of all the hydrogen present, and thus heat arises only from the oxidation of the carbon. In the case of fat, however, there is much less oxygen present and the combustion involves the oxidation of hydrogen as well as carbon.

The difference in gross energy between glucose and starch is because there is relatively more carbon in 1 g of starch than in 1 g of glucose and thus starch has a higher energy value.

The energy producing component of horse feed can be divided into three classes of nutrients: protein, fat, and carbohydrates. These three classes of nutrients typically have the following gross energy contents:

Carbohydrates	4.15 kcal/g
Fats	9.40 kcal/g
Proteins	5.65 kcal/g

These gross energy values for the three classes of nutrients explain the gross energy (GE) differences in the feeds listed in table 1. Oats have more GE than corn because they contain more protein and fat. Whole soybeans are high in protein and fat, so their GE is even higher.

Table 1. GROSS ENERGY VALUES OF PURE SUBSTANCES AND FEEDS (DRY MATTER BASIS)

Pure substance	Gross energy (kcl/g)	Feed	Gross energy (kcal/g)
Glucose	3.76	Corn	4.43
Starch	4.23	Oats	4.68
Seed fat	9.23	Soybeans	5.52
Lard	9.48	Timothy hay	4.51
Casein	5.86	Oat straw	4.43

Digestible energy (DE)

It should be obvious from table 1 that GE is a poor indicator of overall feed value since the GE of corn is identical to the GE of oat straw. Gross energy does not differentiate between various carbohydrate sources and starch and cellulose contain the same GE content. Therefore, to be useful as an indicator of productive energy, losses of energy must be accounted for. The first and largest loss of gross energy occurs in digestion. By determining the heat of combustion of the feces and subtracting this value from the GE, one obtains digestible energy (DE). Table 2 shows the results of a digestion trial in which the DE of three different feeds were determined (Pagan, 1982).

The GE of these diets was related to their composition. Diet 1 which contained the most starch and least protein had the lowest GE. Its digestibility, however, was highest and it consequently contained the most DE. This type of digestion trial is an accurate method to determine DE in the total diet, but it has two serious drawbacks. First, it is simply not practical to measure the DE content of every horse ration, since conducting a digestion trial is laborious and expensive. Secondly, measuring the GE of feces does not determine the DE of each individual feed, but rather the overall digestibility of the entire ration.

Table 2. DIGESTION TRIAL WITH 3 DIFFERENT FEEDS

Diet number	Alfalfa %	Corn %	Soybean meal %	GE feed (kcal/g)	GE feces (kcal/g)	DM digestibility	Digestible energy (kcal/g)
1	34	63	3	4.45	4.96	80.8	3.54
2	40	53	7	4.52	4.92	78.6	3.47
3	47	37	16	4.56	5.01	76.2	3.37

Total digestible nutrients (TDN)

Digestible energy can be estimated by first measuring the total digestible nutrient (TDN) content of the feed. TDN is calculated as: digestible crude protein (CP) + (digestible crude fat (EE) x 2.25) + digestible cell wall (NDF) + digestible non structural carbohydrate (NSC). Non structural carbohydrate = 100-CP-EE-NDF-ash. Fonnesbeck (1981) conducted 108 digestion trials with horses and measured both TDN and DE. The relationship between TDN and DE was best described as DE (kcal/kg) = 255 + 3660 x TDN.

Estimating DE from chemical composition

There are a number of ways that DE can be estimated for a feed using its chemical composition. One method is to determine the DE content of a large number of different rations and statistically relate the DE content to other components of the feed. At our laboratory we have conducted dozens of digestibility studies with a wide range of feedstuffs. From data with 30 different diets (120 observations) , we have developed a regression equation to predict DE from chemical composition. The rations studied ranged from pure alfalfa hay to a combination of sweet feed and fescue hay to pelleted concentrates fed with timothy hay.

The energy content of the various rations was calculated as percent total digestible nutrients (TDN %) and converted to DE using Fonnesbeck's equation.

The most complete equation to estimate DE from these data was:

DE (kcal/kg DM) = 2,118 + 12.18 (CP%) - 9.37 (ADF %) -3.83 (hemicellulose%) + 47.18 (fat %) + 20.35 (NSC) - 26.3 (ash %) (R^2=0.88).

Notice that as protein, fat and NSC increase, DE increases. As fiber and ash increase, DE decreases. This is because the digestibility of protein, fat and NSC tends to be quite high (>85%) while the digestibility of fiber tends to be lower (~40-45%) in most feeds. Ash doesn't contain any energy, so it would naturally lower the overall energy density of a feed.

KER also uses another method of determining the digestibility of individual feed ingredients. In this design, a basal ration of forage cubes is fed to horses and its digestibility content is measured. Individual feeds are then fed along with the forage and the overall digestibility is measured. By difference, the digestibility of the individual ingredient is determined. The digestibility of each organic component (protein, fat, NSC, and NDF) is multiplied by its heat of combustion to calculate DE content. It could be argued that feeding another ingredient along with the forage may change the digestibility of the forage. Even if this is true and the change in digestibility is credited to (or debited from) the ingredient, the overall estimate of digestibility is correct since these ingredients are always fed with some type of forage.

Table 3. DE CONTENT OF SEVERAL DIFFERENT COMMON HORSE FEED INGREDIENTS CALCULATED BY A NUMBER OF DIFFERENT METHODS (AS FED BASIS).

Feed	NRC (Mcal/lb)	KER Regression (Mcal/lb)	KER regression %NRC	Direct measurement (Mcal/lb)	Direct measurement %KER equation	Direct measurement % NRC
Oats	1.30	1.33	102.3	1.33	100	102.3
Corn	1.54	1.53	99.3	1.58	103.3	102.3
Wheat Midds	1.38	1.20	87.0	1.26	105.0	91.3
Molasses	1.18	1.17	99.2	1.20	102.5	101.7
Alfalfa Hay	0.94	0.96	102.1	1.0	104.2	106.4
Timothy Hay	0.80	0.86	107.5	0.85	98.8	110.0
Rice Bran	1.19	1.23	103.4	1.44	117.0	121.0
Beet Pulp	1.06	1.08	101.9	1.28	118.5 ·	120.7
Soy Hulls	0.77	0.82	106.5	1.17	142.7	151.9
Oat Hulls	0.65	0.79	121.5	0.51	64.6	78.5

KER's regression equation using data from the 30 different rations produces DE values which were very close to the NRC estimates for most of the feeds measured. Only wheat midds and oat hulls differed substantially from the NRC estimates (table 3).

The direct measurements of digestibility confirm that both the NRC and the KER equation accurately describe the DE content of cereal grains and hays. Both, however, grossly underestimate the DE content of high fat feeds (rice bran) and non-forage, high fiber feeds such as beet pulp and soy hulls. Both also overestimate the digestibility of poor quality fiber sources like oat hulls.

The fat from feed ingredients that contain high levels of fat is more digestible than fat found in forages and cereal grains. An equation based on diets that are fairly low in fat will tend to underestimate the energy contribution from high fat feeds. The KER equation was developed with rations ranging in fat content from 2.1% to 5.5%, so an allowance should be made for high fat feeds. If a feed contains more than 5% fat, add an extra 0.02 Mcal/lb (0.044 Mcal/kg or 0.18 MJ/kg) for each 1% fat over 5%. For example, the rice bran in the above example contains 15% fat, so 0.2 Mcal/lb (10% x 0.02 Mcal/lb) should be added to the DE calculated from the KER equation. This would yield 1.43 Mcal/lb (1.23 + 0.2) which is very close to the DE measured directly (1.44 Mcal/lb).

Both the NRC and KER equation underestimate the DE content of beet pulp and soy hulls. This is because the cell wall of these two ingredients is much more digestible than the cell wall found in most horse feeds. Likewise, the cell wall in oat hulls is less digestible than most forages and allowances should be made for this in calculating DE. The same is true for other poorly digestible fiber sources such as peanut hulls and rice hulls.

DE in grain mixes

There is a great deal of variation in the reported DE contents of various horse feeds. Some manufacturers routinely overestimate the DE content of their feeds and use these exaggerations to promote their product. In reality, the DE content of a grain mix can only be altered to a relatively small degree unless large amounts of fat or fiber are added. Let's examine an example of how composition affects DE. A simple grain mix of 40% oats, 40% corn, 10% molasses and 10% soybean meal would contain about 14% protein, 3.4% fat and 14% NDF. This mix would contain around 1,440 kcal/lb of DE. Adding 1% vegetable oil to the mix would only elevate the DE by 30 kcal/lb, so this mix would contain 4.4% fat and 1,470 kcal/lb. To reach a DE of 1,600 kcal/lb, 6% oil would need to be added to the diet and the total fat content of the feed would approach 10%. Manufacturers who claim that their 4-5 % fat feeds contain 1,600 kcal/lb need to recheck their figures (table 4).

Table 4. DE AND TOTAL FAT WITH DIFFERENT LEVELS OF ADDED FAT[1]

| | *% added fat* | | | | | | | |
	0%	1%	2%	3%	4%	5%	6%	7%
Total fat (%)	3.4	4.4	5.4	6.3	7.3	8.3	9.2	10.2
DE (kcal/lb)	1,440	1,470	1,490	1,520	1,550	1,570	1,600	1,620

[1] 14% protein grain mix containing 40% corn, 40% oats, 10% molasses, and 10% soybean meal.

Conclusions

The Digestible Energy (DE) content of most horse feeds can be estimated from a regression equation developed by KER that uses the crude protein, crude fat, ADF, hemicellulose (NDF-ADF), non-structural carbohydrate (NSC) and ash content of feed. This equation works well for most horse feeds except those that contain high levels of fat or that contain fiber which is either much more or less digestible than forage. A correction of 0.02 Mcal DE/lb should be applied for every 1% fat over 5% in a feed. Beet pulp and soy hulls contain highly digestible fiber and their DE contents are 20-50% higher than suggested by the NRC. Oat hulls have very poorly digestible fiber and DE values that are only 80% of NRC estimates.

Many manufacturers overestimate the DE content of their feeds. A typical grain mix without added fat will contain around 1,400-1,450 kcal/lb. A feed with 6% added fat and a total fat content of around 10% will contain around 1,600 kcal/lb. Feed manufacturers should review the DE values that they currently use in formulating horse feeds to insure that reasonable DE values are assigned to their feed ingredients.

References

Fonnesbeck, P.V. (1981). Estimating digestible energy and TDN for horses with chemical analysis of feeds. Journal of Animal Science Abstract No. 290, p. 241-242.

NRC, 1989. Nutrient Requirements of Horses, 5th Revised Edition. National Academy Press, Washington, D.C.

This paper was first published in Proceedings, Kentucky Equine Research 1997 Equine Nutrition Conference

NUTRIENT DIGESTIBILITY IN HORSES

JOE D. PAGAN

Kentucky Equine Research, Inc., Versailles, Kentucky, USA

Introduction

Many equine nutrient requirements are based on certain assumptions about how well horses digest and absorb nutrients. Unfortunately, a great many questions remain unanswered about nutrient digestibility in horses. How well do horses utilize different sources of nutrients? What nutrients interact with one another to affect digestibility?

Over the past five years, Kentucky Equine Research has conducted dozens of digestibility trials to evaluate different types of feeds and feed ingredients for horses. This paper will present a summary of the data collected in these various experiments. Together, these data represent one of the most comprehensive digestibility studies ever conducted in horses. Hopefully, the results of these studies will help refine the various nutrient requirements currently being used for horses and improve the precision with which horse feeds are formulated.

Materials and methods

Kentucky Equine Research uses a standardized experimental design to measure digestibility in horses. In this design, four mature horses are fed different experimental diets in a Latin square design (either 2x2 replicated or 4x4) over four collection periods. Each period consists of a 3 week adjustment period followed by a 5 day total fecal collection. The week before and during the 5 day collection period, the horses are housed in specially designed stalls that allow the complete and separate collection of urine and feces. While housed in these stalls, the horses are hand walked twice daily.

During the collection period, daily feed intake and total fecal output are measured. Subsamples of daily feed and feces are taken and frozen. These subsamples are dried and composited for chemical analysis. Both feed and feces are analyzed for dry matter, crude protein, ADF, NDF, crude fiber, fat, calcium, phosphorus, magnesium, potassium, zinc, copper, manganese, and ash. Digestibilities are calculated for each nutrient measured.

Table 1. AVERAGE NUTRIENT CONCENTRATIONS OF DIETS STUDIED (100% DRY MATTER BASIS)

Nutrient	Average concentration	Standard deviation	Maximum	Minimum
Crude protein	13.1 %	2.6 %	20.4 %	9.6 %
ADF	28.8 %	4.6 %	40.6 %	20.6 %
NDF	46.9 %	5.4 %	57.4 %	38.3 %
Hemicellulose	18.1 %	4.7 %	24.1 %	6.0 %
Crude fiber	22.8 %	3.9 %	31.8 %	15.4 %
Soluble CHO	28.9 %	5.0 %	36.9 %	18.3 %
Fat	3.6 %	0.8 %	5.5 %	2.1 %
Calcium	0.89 %	0.24 %	1.50 %	0.55 %
Phosphorus	0.39 %	0.09 %	0.58 %	0.20 %
Magnesium	0.22 %	0.03 %	0.29 %	0.17 %
Potassium	1.63 %	0.54 %	3.29 %	0.98 %
Iron	287 ppm	119 ppm	753 ppm	127 ppm
Zinc	84 ppm	38 ppm	147 ppm	20 ppm
Copper	22 ppm	8 ppm	38 ppm	7 ppm
Manganese	83 ppm	29 ppm	127 ppm	29 ppm
Ash	7.45 %	1.53 %	11.62 %	5.99 %

Thirty different diets (120 observations) have been evaluated using this design. These diets have ranged from pure alfalfa hay to a combination of sweet feed and fescue hay to pelleted concentrates fed with timothy hay. Table 1 lists the average concentration of each nutrient measured along with the standard deviation, maximum and minimum ranges. The majority of horses used in these studies have been Thoroughbreds, although Quarter horses, Appaloosas, and Warmbloods have also been included. Most of these horses have averaged between 1,100 and 1,320 lbs of body weight (500-600 kg). Because of the tight range of body weights of the experimental horses, all data are presented as total daily intakes rather than as a function of body weight.

Each experiment was conducted for a specific purpose, such as to evaluate the effect of adding distillers dried grains to horse feeds or to determine the effect that pelleting has on alfalfa hay, but for the purpose of the present study, all data have been combined into one data base.

As table 2 illustrates, these combined experiments represent a wide range of nutrient intakes for mature horses. While a variety of different feed ingredients were used in these studies, these data are only representative of forages and concentrates from a temperate environment. Tropical forages may behave differently because they contain inhibitory substances not found in temperate forages. (For a more detailed discussion of these factors, see the paper *Forages for Horses: More Than Just Filler*).

Table 2. AVERAGE NUTRIENT INTAKES OF DIETS STUDIED

Nutrient	Average concentration		Standard deviation		Maximum		Minimum	
Dry matter	7,119	grams	1,464	grams	10,541	grams	4,777	grams
Crude protein	946	grams	326	grams	1,808	grams	572	grams
ADF	2,097	grams	709	grams	4,266	grams	984	grams
NDF	3,371	grams	927	grams	5,427	grams	1,968	grams
Hemicellulose	1,275	grams	411	grams	2,191	grams	393	grams
Soluble CHO	2,007	grams	285	grams	2,627	grams	1,195	grams
Fat	254	grams	66	grams	469	grams	144	grams
Calcium	64	grams	27	grams	158	grams	33	grams
Phosphorus	28	grams	9	grams	57	grams	13	grams
Magnesium	16	grams	5	grams	27	grams	9	grams
Potassium	119	grams	53	grams	269	grams	47	grams
Iron	2,059	mg	1,250	mg	7,912	mg	773	mg
Zinc	567	mg	216	mg	885	mg	131	mg
Copper	149	mg	57	mg	282	mg	46	mg
Manganese	572	mg	201	mg	1,179	mg	210	mg
Ash	540	grams	199	grams	1,136	grams	299	grams

Nutrient digestibility

Nutrient digestibility can be expressed in two different ways. One way is as apparent digestibility. Using this calculation, the amount of a specific nutrient that is recovered in the feces is subtracted from the total daily intake of that nutrient. The amount that disappeared (intake - feces) is divided by the total daily intake to produce a percentage of intake. Table 3 shows the apparent digestibilities of the various nutrients measured. Apparent digestibility is a fairly crude way to evaluate digestibility since it only measures the total amount of a particular nutrient in the feces. There are two possible sources of these fecal nutrients. Some of the nutrient could be the undigested residue left from the feed, but some may have actually been excreted into the digestive tract from the horse's system or it might have sloughed off the intestinal wall. The fecal substances that originate from inside the horse are considered *endogenous* in nature and they result in an underestimation of *true* nutrient digestibility.

To overcome the interference of endogenous losses in the determination of digestibility, a statistical procedure called a Lucas test can be utilized. In this test, a range of nutrient intakes are studied. The amount of nutrient that is digested is regressed against its corresponding level of intake. This procedure is illustrated in figure 1. If there are real endogenous losses associated with a particular nutrient, then the calculated level of nutrient digested at a nutrient intake of zero will be a negative number. The slope of the regression line represents the *estimated true digestibility* for the nutrient. If the regression line intersects the vertical axis at or above zero, then there are no endogenous losses for that particular substance. For example, a horse would not be expected to have an endogenous loss of plant fiber (ADF or NDF). With these types of nutrients, apparent and true digestibilities should be fairly similar.

Table 3. AVERAGE APPARENT DIGESTIBILITIES OF DIETS STUDIED

Nutrient	Apparent digestibility	Standard deviation
Dry matter	62.0%	4.6%
Crude protein	71.0%	5.2%
ADF	39.9%	7.9%
NDF	45.4%	5.7%
Hemicellulose	51.9%	10.6%
Crude fiber	43.4%	14.5%
Soluble CHO	88.6%	5.2%
Fat	58.4%	19.2%
Calcium	44.0%	14.3%
Phosphorus	8.9%	9.8%
Magnesium	37.4%	9.1%
Potassium	75.4%	9.2%
Zinc	9.4%	11.0%
Copper	30.1%	11.6%
Manganese	8.9%	13.9%
Ash	43.3%	12.7%

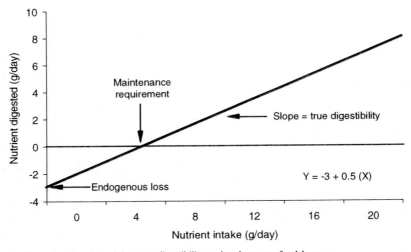

Figure 1. Lucas test for determining true digestibility and endogenous fecal losses

Table 4 contains the results of the Lucas tests for each nutrient measured. Most of the minerals measured had negative intercepts that were significantly different from zero, indicating that there are endogenous fecal losses for these nutrients. The slopes of the regression lines for the various minerals indicate that there is a great deal of difference in their true digestibilities. Calcium and potassium are readily digested from most equine diets, with estimated true digestibilities of about 75%. Magnesium true digestibility equals about 52%, while the estimated true digestibility of phosphorus is considerably lower (25%). The true digestibilities of the trace elements zinc, manganese and copper average 20.8%, 28.5% and 40.0%, respectively. The sources of trace minerals used in these diets were either from the naturally occurring mineral in the feed ingredients or added inorganic sources. The true digestibility of organic sources of these minerals is currently being investigated.

Table 4. ESTIMATED TRUE DIGESTIBILITIES AND ENDOGENOUS LOSSES FOR EACH NUTRIENT MEASURED.

Nutrient	True digestibility	Endogenous loss	Endogenous loss real[a]	R^2
Crude protein	86.1%	143.3g/d	yes	0.96
ADF	40.2%	12.4 g/d	no	0.85
NDF	45.0%	-112.3 g/d	no	0.85
Hemicellulose	54.2%	26.8 g/d	no	0.87
Soluble CHO	97.4%	179.3 g/d	yes	0.85
Fat	55.7%	-7.4 g/d	no	0.30
Calcium	74.7%	17.4 g/d	yes	0.94
Phosphorus	25.2%	4.7 g/d	yes	0.33
Magnesium	51.8%	2.2 g/d	yes	0.76
Potassium	75.3%	1 g/d	no	0.94
Zinc	20.8%	54 mg/d	yes	0.57
Copper	40.0%	38 mg/d	yes	0.71
Manganese	28.5%	110 mg/d	yes	0.40
Ash	67.8%	121 g/d	yes	0.81

[a] intercept of regression equation significantly different from zero ($p < 0.05$)

The true digestibility of protein in these various diets averaged 71%. Most of the diets studied had protein digestibilities close to this level with the exception of a high quality alfalfa hay from Arizona that averaged a protein digestibility of around 80%.

Regression analysis of fiber digestibility showed that these components did not produce endogenous losses. Estimated true digestibilities of ADF, NDF and hemicellulose were 40.2%, 45.0%, and 54.2%, respectively. Interestingly, low fiber intakes resulted in lower fiber digestibility than when high levels of fiber were being fed. Perhaps the fiber from grains (which represented a greater proportion of total at the low fiber intakes) was less digestible than the fiber from forages.

Energy content

The energy content of the various rations was calculated as percent total digestible nutrients (TDN %). TDN was calculated as: digestible crude protein + (digestible crude fat x 2.25) + digestible neutral detergent fiber + digestible soluble carbohydrate. Soluble carbohydrate (CHO) = 100-crude protein (CP)-ether extract (EE)-neutral detergent fiber (NDF)-ash. TDN averaged 61.4% for all of the diets measured with a range from 46.9% to 61.0%. TDN or digestible energy (DE) are useful values to calculate for a horse ration. Since these values are by nature biological assays, it would be impossible to directly determine these values for every feed. From the present study, regression equations have been developed that allow the calculation of TDN (or DE) from analyses routinely performed on horse feed and forage. TDN and DE are really interchangeable units of digestible energy since the heat of combustion of protein and carbohydrate are similar and the heat of combustion of fat is already accounted for in the equation used to calculate TDN. Therefore, to calculate DE as kcal/kg, simply multiply TDN% X 4400 or DE as kcal/lb, multiply TDN X 2000.

The most complete equation to estimate DE is: DE (kcal/kg DM) = 2,118 + 12.18 (CP%) -9.37 (ADF%) - 3.83 (hemicellulose %) + 47.18 (fat %) + 20.35 (NSC) - 26.3 (Ash %) (R^2=0.88). Notice that as protein, fat and soluble CHO increase, DE increases. As fiber and ash increase, DE decreases. This agrees well with what we know about the energy density and digestibility of these various components in horse feeds. It should also be remembered that these equations were developed with either all forage diets or mixtures of forage and concentrate. These equations tend to overestimate the energy density of straight grains, possibly because of the differences in fiber digestibility mentioned above.

Nutrient interactions

Table 4 contains the R^2 for each regression equation that was used to calculate true nutrient digestibility. R^2 describes how well the equation reflects the relationship between nutrient intake and disappearance. An R^2 of 1.0 means that the regression line perfectly describes the relationship between the two parameters measured. The closer R^2 gets to 0, the less related are the two values in the regression. R^2 for protein, calcium and potassium were quite high (0.94). This indicates that these nutrients were digested with only minor interference from other substances in the feed. Other nutrients like phosphorus, manganese and zinc had low R^2 (<0.60), indicating that there were other factors besides nutrient intake that significantly affected their digestibility.

Nutrient requirements

The maintenance requirements of calcium, phosphorus, magnesium, zinc, copper, and manganese can be calculated by dividing the mineral's daily endogenous loss by its estimated true digestibility. For example, the endogenous calcium loss averaged 17.4 grams/day and the estimated true digestibility of calcium equaled 74.7%. Therefore, to replace all of the fecal calcium losses and maintain the horse in zero calcium balance, a daily intake of 23.3 grams (17.4/0.747) would be required. Table 5 contains these maintenance estimates along with the 1989 NRC recommendations for the same minerals. The estimates of maintenance requirements from this study for calcium and phosphorus are very similar to NRC requirements. In this study, however, endogenous calcium losses were higher than estimated by the NRC, but so was true digestibility. These two factors combined resulted in the same daily requirement. Conversely, endogenous phosphorus losses were slightly lower than estimated in the NRC, but so was true phosphorus digestibility. Again, the two factors combined netted the same daily requirement.

Table 5. MINERAL REQUIREMENTS FOR MATURE HORSES

Mineral	Requirement estimated from present study		1989 NRC requirement (500-600 kg)	
Calcium	23.3	grams/day	20-24	grams/day
Phosphorus	18.5	grams/day	14-17	grams/day
Magnesium	4.2	grams/day	7.5-9.0	grams/day
Zinc	257	mg/day	328-388	mg/day
Manganese	385	mg/day	328-388	mg/day
Copper	95	mg/day	82-97	mg/day

Daily requirements for zinc were slightly lower than estimated by the NRC, but manganese and copper requirements were remarkably similar. The NRC did not use this method of calculation to arrive at its requirements for the trace minerals. Instead, it either used data from studies with cattle (manganese) or studies that determined the amounts of copper and zinc necessary to prevent deficiency symptoms.

These mineral requirements are only appropriate for mature horses at rest. Requirements for growth, pregnancy and lactation will certainly be higher. It remains to be determined how exercise affects the requirements for many of these nutrients.

This paper was first published in "Feeding the Performance Horse," Proceedings for the 1994 Short Course for Feed Manufacturers

EFFECT OF FEEDING FREQUENCY ON DIGESTION IN PONIES

AMY M. GILL AND LAURIE M. LAWRENCE
University of Kentucky, Lexington, Kentucky, USA

The horse is a grazing animal by nature. Free ranging horses spend an estimated 65-75% of their time grazing (Mayes and Duncan, 1986). However, many horses live in confinement. Many of these horses have increased nutrient requirements due to growth, work, gestation or lactation. These horses are often fed a high concentrate diet containing large amounts of starch. Several studies concerning physiological response to a single, large grain meal have been conducted. Source of starch and processing affect digestibility (Meyer *et al.*, 1993) and intake levels above 0.4% of body weight decrease starch digestion in the foregut and increase digestion in the hindgut (Potter *et al.*, 1992). Increased rate of passage decreases digestion prececally and decreases absorption of nutrients (Argenzio *et al.*, 1974; Hintz, 1989). Other physiological responses to a large meal include decreased plasma volume and increased plasma protein (Houpt, 1990).

Table 1. FEEDING SCHEDULE (schedule repeats every 12 hours)

Time of feeding	2 meals/d	4 meals/d	8 meals/d	16 meals/d
09.00 AM	X	X	X	X
10.30 AM				X
12.00 PM			X	X
13.30 PM				X
15.00 PM		X	X	X
16.30 PM				X
18.00 PM			X	X
19.30 PM				X

This experiment was designed to test the hypothesis that increased frequency of feeding will improve nutrient digestion. Four mature Shetland ponies were randomly assigned to one of four dietary treatments. Each horse was fed a complete feed containing forage and grain at 2 % of body weight as either treatment 1, 2 meals/d; treatment 2, 4 meals/d; treatment 3, 8 meals/d; or treatment 4, 16 meals/d (Table 1). The experimental design was a 4 x 4 Latin square design utilizing a 10-d period and a

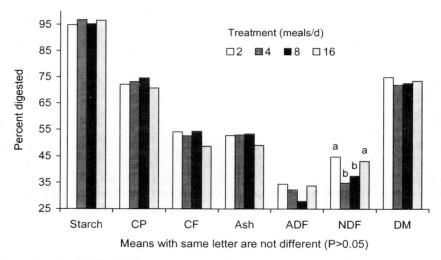

Figure 1. Effects of feeding frequency on digestion of nutrients in a complete feed

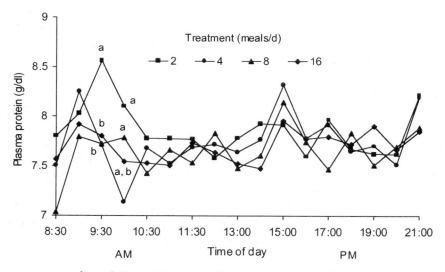

Figure 2. Effect of feeding frequency on plasma protein concentrations

3-d total fecal collection. Starch, crude protein (CP), dry matter (DM), crude fat (CF), acid detergent fiber (ADF), neutral detergent fiber (NDF) and ash digestibilities were determined. Plasma protein and hematocrit were also measured over a 12-h period to evaluate changes in plasma volume.

Feeding frequency did not affect digestion of starch, CP, DM, CF, ADF or ash. Feeding 2 or 16 meals/d increased digestion of NDF ($P<0.05$) (Figure 1). Plasma protein levels increased ($P< 0.05$) 30 minutes after the 9 AM feeding when ponies consumed 2 meals/d. At 10 AM, plasma protein decreased ($P<0.05$) when ponies fed 4 meals/d were compared to ponies eating 2 or 8 meals/d (16 meals/d treatment was not different from 4 meals/d treatment because of consistently lower concentrations) (Figure 2).

The present results do not support the hypothesis that increased frequency of feeding is associated with an increase in digestibility. The results may be due to the diet, as it was very low in fiber (26% NDF, 16% ADF). However, the large fluctuation in plasma protein concentration in this study is an indication that water balance is affected by large, infrequent meal feeding. Therefore, the present results suggest that increasing feeding frequency may regulate plasma volume which could be beneficial to stabled horses.

References

Argenzio, R.A., J.E. Lowe and D.W. Pickard. 1974. Digesta Passage and Water Exchange in the Equine Large Intestine. Am. J. Physiology, 226:1035-1042

Hintz, H.F. 1989. A Report on the Third Equine Colic Research Symposium. Equine Practice. Vol. 11, No. 6

Houpt, K.A. 1990. Ingestive Behavior. Veterinary Clinics of America: Equine Practice. Vol.6, No. 2

Mayes, E. and P. Duncan. 1986. Temporal Patterns of Feeding in Free Ranging Horses. Behavior. 96:105-129

Meyer, H., S. Radike, E. Kienzle, S. Wilke, and D. Kleffken. 1993. Investigations on Preileal Digestion of Oats, Corn, and Barley Starch in Relation to Grain Processing. Proceedings Equine Nutrition and Physiology Society.

NRC. 1989. Nutrient Requirements of Horses. Fifth Revised Edition

Potter, G.D., F.F. Arnold, D.D. Householder, D.H. Hansen and K.M. Brown. 1992. Digestion of Starch in the Small or Large Intestine of the Equine. European Conference on the Nutrition of the Horse. Hanover, Germany.

This paper was first published in Proceedings, Kentucky Equine Research 1997 Equine Nutrition Conference

EFFECTS OF MEAL FEEDING FREQUENCY AND ROUGHAGE ON BEHAVIORS OF STABLED HORSES

A.M. GILL, A. PARKER, S. LEAK, AND L.M. LAWRENCE
University of Kentucky, Lexington, Kentucky, USA

Aberrant behaviors such as wood chewing and cribbing are exhibited by horses in confinement but usually not by horses in free roaming conditions. Boredom and hunger are possible reasons for poor behavior in stabled horses. The purpose of this study was to determine the effects of grain feeding frequency and roughage availability on behavior of stabled horses. Four horses were adapted to box stalls for one week and then assigned to one of four treatments in a 4x4 Latin square design, with each period lasting one week. The treatments were four different diets: 1) eight meals per day with ad lib roughage; 2) eight meals per day with limited roughage; 3) two meals per day with ad lib roughage, and 4) two meals per day with limited roughage. Grain was provided every three hours for treatments 1 and 2 beginning at 7:00 AM, and at 7:00 AM and 4:00 PM for treatments 3 and 4. Feed was delivered to the horses via automatic feeders (Triple Crown® Freedom Feeder, Milford, Indiana). Total grain provided each day was the same for all treatments. Feed (hay and grain) and water consumption were measured throughout each period. The horses were videotaped on the final day of each period for two, ten hour periods, starting at 10:00 AM (daylight) and 10:00 PM (evening) to record all activity. The videotapes were read at three random, 5 minute segments per hour. Each videotape was evaluated for duration and frequency of each of the following states and behaviors: drinking, eating hay, chewing , walking, sleeping, standing alertly, cribbing, pawing, picking at bedding and scratching. The effects of the treatments were analyzed by ANOVA using SAS General Linear Models. No differences ($P>0.05$) between treatments were seen for duration or frequency of behaviors during the daylight period (figure 1 and 2). During the evening there was a significant difference ($P<0.05$) between treatments for duration of time spent eating hay (figure 3). Horses fed 8 times per day with ad libitum access to hay spent more time eating hay than horses fed 2 times per day with ad libitum access to hay. This difference was not seen for frequency of the behavior (figure 4). The feed consumption data will be analyzed to determine whether feeding grain 8 times per day increased the amount of hay consumed. Based on the diurnal patterns noted when behaviors were plotted by hour, cribbing appeared to be worse at midday and pawing was centered around feeding times but appeared to wane as the novelty of the feeders wore off. Most hay was eaten during daylight hours. The horses spent more than 25% of their time during daylight eating hay as compared to spending less than 15% of their time eating hay during the evening. The horses slept for less than 25% of the time observed during daylight as opposed to more than 50% during the evening. The horses slept periodically through the day, but slept for long periods starting at about midnight until approximately 7:00 AM. From these observations, it is recommended that automated feeders be set between the hours of 7:00 AM and 12:00 AM during a 24 hour period to help reduce aberrant behavior and prevent disruption of the natural behavioral patterns of the stabled horse.

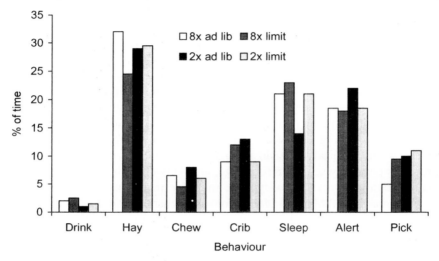

Figure 1. Duration of behaviours for stabled horses during daylight (10am - 8pm)

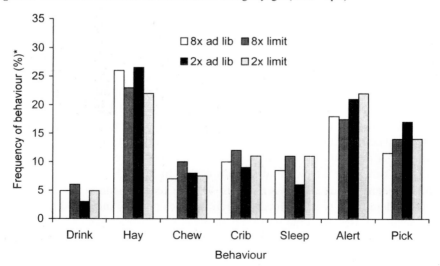

* % is of total frequency for all behaviours

Figure 2. Frequency of behaviours for stabled horses during daylight (10am-8pm)

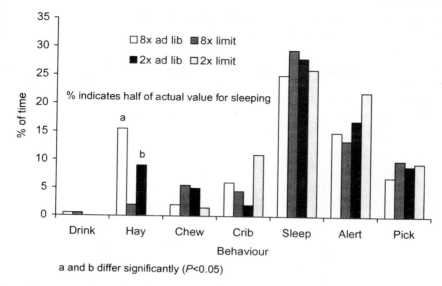

Figure 3. Duration of behaviours for stabled horses during nightime (10pm - 8am)

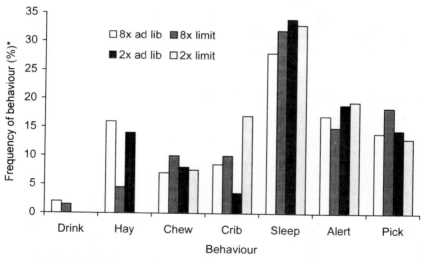

Figure 4. Frequency of behaviours for stabled horses during nightime (10pm - 8am)

This paper was first published in Proceedings, Kentucky Equine Research 1997 Equine Nutrition Conference

RESPONSES OF BLOOD GLUCOSE, LACTATE AND INSULIN IN HORSES FED EQUAL AMOUNTS OF GRAIN WITH OR WITHOUT ADDED SOYBEAN OIL

JOE D. PAGAN, T. ROTMENSEN AND STEPHEN G. JACKSON
Kentucky Equine Research, Inc., Versailles, Kentucky, USA

When fat is substituted for carbohydrate isocalorically in a horse's ration, blood glucose and insulin response to feeding is reduced (Stull *et al.*, 1987, Pagan *et al.*,1994). These studies, however, haven't shown if this response is simply due to reduced glucose in the diet or if fat affects glycemic response in some other manner. Therefore, this experiment was designed to evaluate whether adding fat to a grain meal would affect glucose and insulin response to feeding when the level of grain intake remained the same.

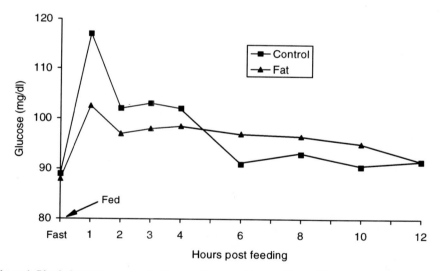

Figure 1. Blood glucose response to feeding a grain meal with and without added soyabean oil

Nine Thoroughbred horses were used in this two period switch-back design experiment. Five of the horses were in training and were physically fit and four were untrained. During period one, each horse was fed 2.27 kg of a grain mix (table 1) which consisted of 72% oats, 20% corn and 8% molasses at 7 AM. Five of the horses were also fed 200 ml (170 g) of soybean oil mixed into the grain. At 8 AM each horse was given 2.72 kg of mature bluegrass hay (table 1). Blood samples were taken from each horse by jugular catheter before feeding and at 1, 2, 3, 4, 6, 8, 10, and 12 hours post feeding. Water was available to the horses at all times. The same procedure was followed two weeks later with the soybean oil added to the grain of the four horses that served as controls during period 1.

The blood samples were collected in sterile glass tubes containing EDTA and centrifuged immediately. The plasma was pipetted into glass tubes and frozen. The samples were analyzed for lactate, glucose and insulin at the conclusion of the study. Lactate was measured using an automated L-lactate analyzer (YSI, 1500 Sport). Glucose was measured using an automated glucose analyzer (YSI, 2300 STAT). Insulin was measured using a commercially available radioimmunoassay (RIA) kit which had been validated for specificity and accuracy in equine plasma (BET Labs, Lexington, Kentucky).

Table 1. NUTRIENT COMPOSITION OF EXPERIMENTAL FEEDS (DRY MATTER BASIS)

Nutrient	Grain Mix	Bluegrass Hay	Soybean Oil
Dry matter (%)	84.7	93.0	100.0
Crude protein (%)	11.1	6.5	-
Acid detergent fiber (%)	11.0	44.3	-
Neutral detergent fiber (%)	22.1	73.0	-
Lignin (%)	2.8	5.8	-
Ether extract (%)	5.8	1.8	100.0
Soluble CHO (%)[1]	57.7	12.7	-

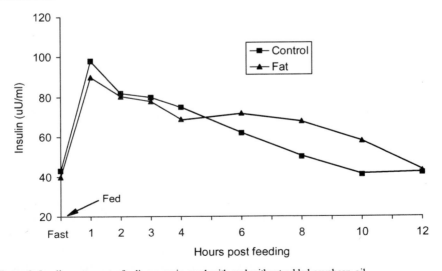

Figure 2. Insulin response to feeding a grain meal with and without added soyabean oil

Blood glucose was significantly lower (p<0.05) one hour after feeding (102.4 vs 117.2 mg/dl) when soybean oil was added to the diet (figure 1). Glucose remained lower (p<0.10) for 3 hours post feeding. After 6 and 10 hours, blood glucose was higher (p<0.10) in the fat supplemented group. Insulin was lower (p<0.10) in the fat supplemented group 1 hour after feeding (figure 2). After 8 and 10 hours, insulin was higher (p<0.05) in the fat supplemented group. Plasma L-lactate tended to be higher (p=0.14) in the control group 4 hours after feeding and higher in the fat supplemented group (p=0.20) 6 hours after feeding.

These data suggest that the addition of fat (soybean oil) to a grain meal will affect glucose and insulin response to feeding. These affects are independent of the amount of carbohydrate in the diet and may be due to differences in the rate of gastric emptying when fat is included in the diet.

This paper was first published in "Recent Advances in Equine Nutrition," Proceedings for the 1995 Short Course for Feed Manufacturers

SELENIUM SUPPLEMENTATION FOR HORSE FEED

HOWARD D. STOWE
Professor Emeritus, Department of Large Animal Clinical Sciences
Michigan State University, East Lansing, Michigan, USA

History and current selenium regulations

Selenium (Se) was established as a dietary essential after it was demonstrated that a liver necrosis in rats fed torula yeast could be prevented by supplementing the yeast with Se (Schwarz and Foltz, 1957). Soon thereafter, practical problems relating to Se deficiency, e.g. white muscle disease of calves, lambs and foals, and exudative diathesis of poultry, were recognized. Burns Biotech Corp. was quick to develop injectable products (L-Se, Bo-Se, E-Se and Mu-Se) which gave veterinarians sources of supplemental Se (and vitamin E) for prophylaxis and therapy of these problems. The problem areas of the US became associated with regions of Se-deficient soils (Kubota *et al.*, 1967). Ultimately, even human manifestations of Se deficiency (Keshan disease of children) in China became recognized (Keshan Disease Research Group, 1979).

The efforts to permit oral Se supplementation of livestock have been reviewed by Ullrey (1980, 1992a).The increasing prevalence of Se-responsive disease among US livestock through the 1960's prompted the American Feed Manufacturers Association (AFMA) to petition the Food and Drug Administration (FDA) for a GRAS (Generally Recognized as Safe) status for Se in March of 1970. The request was denied because the Director of the Board of Veterinary Medicine felt the AFMA petition did not show that food-producing animals would not be adversely affected by supplemental Se or that the Se residue in the products used for human food did not pose a carcinogenic risk. After AFMA supplied additional information on Se levels in typical livestock feeds, on background tissue Se concentrations, and on human Se intakes from Se-supplemented livestock, an official proposal to establish a food additive regulation governing the safe use of selenium in the feed of chickens, turkeys and swine was published in the Federal Register in June 1971. Almost 2.5 more years were required for sufficient data to be accumulated and/or generated to satisfy the FDA and United States Department of Agriculture (USDA) about the safety of Se supplementation of feeds for swine and poultry. On February 7, 1974, 17 years after the discovery that Se was an essential nutrient, it became legal to supplement swine and poultry (except laying hen) diets at 0.1 ppm (mg/kg).

It then took a special Selenium for Ruminant Animals Task Force, established in 1975, two years to assemble published information and develop new data to prepare a petition to permit addition of Se to the diets of sheep and cattle at 0.1 ppm. These efforts culminated in FDA actions and Federal Register notices between March 1978 and January 1979, permitting Se supplementation at 0.1 ppm in the diets of sheep and cattle of all ages and sexes. In 1981, approval was granted for Se supplements of 0.1 ppm in diets of laying hens. In 1982, Se supplementation of swine prestarter and starter diets was approved at 0.3 ppm.

In 1983, the National Research Council (NRC) subcommittee on Se in Nutrition concluded that the dietary requirement of most animals was in the range of 0.05 to 0.3 ppm. This conclusion, in part, was the basis for the 1987 FDA approval for Se supplementation at 0.3 ppm in complete feeds of the major food producing animals, poultry (including ducks), cattle (dairy and beef), sheep and swine.

While the animal nutrition community generally agrees that 0.3 ppm is an appropriate and safe rate of Se supplementation, FDA is currently under pressure, particularly from environmentalist groups, to roll this rate back toward the 0.1 ppm. These groups claim, among other things, that the 0.3 ppm rate is contributing to Se contamination of recovered irrigation waters (as in the Kesterson Reservoir in California) sufficient to kill the water fowl and other aquatic life inhabiting these ponds. In actuality, when the variety of sources of environmental Se are calculated, it has been demonstrated that the 47.5 tons of Se which would be required annually to supplement the feed for all US livestock at 0.3 ppm, represent less than 0.5% of the Se in the environment originating from other anthropogenic and natural sources such as fuel combustion, industrial uses, rainfall and leaching of seleniferous rocks by ground water (Ullrey, 1992b).

It is important to note that horses, zoo animals, llamas and other pets were never included in any of the FDA regulations on Se supplementation. FDA probably elected not to include these species, in part, because they did not contribute to the human food chain (at least in the USA) and because the petitions for approval of Se supplementation did not include data on the benefits of dietary Se supplementation of these species. Unfortunately, this situation has created a dilemma for those trying to conduct sound feeding practices for these species. The burning question is: "Why should FDA restrict nutritionally sound Se supplementation practices for animals which will not affect the Se content of the human food chain?"

One interpretation of the FDA stand on this matter came in the form of a 1990 Notice of Adverse Findings from the Center of Veterinary Medicine to the President of Peninsular Products, a Lansing, MI manufacturer of MEGA-SEL. This product is a punch-like liquid labeled to contain 0.003% Se and 50 IU vitamin E/oz and promoted as a more satisfactory source of Se for horses than the standard Se-premixes designed to be mixed into concentrates. Even though the recommended dose of MEGA-SEL (1 oz/d/500 lb) would provide a 1000 lb horse with only 1.8 mg supplemental Se per day (equivalent to ~0.18 ppm if the horse consumed 10 Kg dry matter per day), the company was requested to cease marketing the product because there was no approved food additive petition in effect (for horses) and no regulation permitting Se supplementation of equine diets. In contrast, a number of Veterinary Supply houses such as Butler Co., Vetpro Distribution Inc. and IDE Interstate, market a Se-containing oral supplement for horses (EQU SeE by Vet A Mix) and to my knowledge have not been requested to cease vending these products.

A petition for GRAS status for Se supplementation of equine diets was filed in May, 1991 by Real Selenium Inc. of Virginia. In July 1991, Real Selenium Inc. was notified that its petition could not be acted upon because it lacked the data and format required under section 21 CFR 5700.35 and the National Environmental Policy Act. At the time of writing, there is no new petition for GRAS status of Se as an equine dietary supplement.

Functions of selenium

It took about 15 years after the essentiality of Se was established, for investigators (Rotruck *et al.*, 1973) to determine one biochemical role of Se was as part of the enzyme, glutathione peroxidase (GSHpx). This is one of several cytosolic antioxidants which help protect cell membranes and organelles from oxidative damage. It is this antioxidant function which helps maintain muscle and vascular integrity and the competence of cells participating in the immune system. More recently, Se has been found to be a component of type I iodothyronine deiodinase (Beckett *et al.*, 1987; Behne *et al.*, 1992), a selenoenzyme which catalyzes the hepatic conversion of thyroxine (T4) to tri-iodothyronine (T3). This function would optimize utilization of thyroxine and/or formation of its tissue- active form (T3) if thyroid activity were limited by iodine deficiency. It is therefore possible that some clinical manifestations of hypothyroidism may be secondary to Se deficiency.

Clinical assessment of the selenium status of horses

Some of the first efforts to quantify the serum Se status of horses were conducted at the University of Kentucky (Stowe, 1967) using tedious Schoniger combustion flask technology for digestion, followed by fluorometric detection of the Se ion complex. Over time, several laboratories across the US have developed Se assay capabilities. Since 1982, the Clinical Nutrition Section of the Animal Health Diagnostic Laboratory (AHDL) at Michigan State University has provided serum and tissue Se analyses for diagnostic purposes on a fee for service basis and has generated a rather large Se data base on horses, food animals and exotic species. The expected or reference values developed from that data base for horses are as presented in

Table 1. A summary of the 1990 - 1991 serum Se data (Stowe and Herdt, 1992) from 599 adult horses (Thoroughbred, Standardbred, Quarter Horse) indicated their mean serum Se was 141 ± 35 ng/mL which is within the expected range for this age group and remarkably consistent with early estimates (Stowe, 1967).

Table 1. REFERENCE VALUES FOR SELENIUM IN SERUM, WHOLE BLOOD AND LIVER IN HORSES OF DIFFERENT AGES.[a]

Age (days)	Serum Se ng/mL	Whole blood Se[b] g/mL	Liver Se ug/g DM
1 - 9	70 - 90	98 - 135	1.2 - 2.0
10 - 30	80 - 100	112 - 150	1.2 - 2.0
31 - 300	90 - 110	126 - 165	1.2 - 2.0
301 - 700	100 - 130	140 - 195	1.2 - 2.0
<700	130 - 160	182 - 240	1.2 - 2.0

a Adapted from Stowe and Herdt, 1992.
b Whole blood Se values for equine species are 1.4 to 1.5 x serum Se.

While GSHpx values, expressed usually as enzyme units/gram of hemoglobin (EU/g Hb), are expected to correlate well with Se intake and serum Se under well controlled conditions, GSHpx is not a preferred indicator of Se status for clinical diagnostic purposes. This is because the detected enzyme concentrations are subject to storage times and temperatures and to the kind of hemolyzing agent used in the assays. Additionally, a complete GSHpx response to Se supplementation requires some 80 - 90 days, equal to the life span of equine red blood cells. This is because the Se-containing GSHpx is incorporated in the red blood cells only during erythropoiesis, the time when the red cells are formed. Whole blood GSHpx values for the equine species assayed by MSU AHDL range from 40 to 160 EU/g Hb without a detectable age effect.

What is the feed industry doing about Se supplementation of equine feeds?

It is my understanding that at least some formulators and manufacturers of equine concentrate (grain) mixes are incorporating a Se source sufficient to create ~0.3 ppm Se in the total dry matter consumed by horses, particularly for growth, performance and brood mares. Thus, if the grain mix comprises 50% of the dry matter intake, a reasonable Se concentration in the grain mix would be 0.6 ppm because diluting it 50% with Se-deficient roughage would result in a Se concentration of the total dry matter of ~0.3 ppm. This is the concentration FDA permits for food animal species and equine nutritionists have reason to believe that it is sound feeding management for horses as well, particularly when the Se status of the animals is monitored via serum or whole blood Se assays.

If the horse owner is unable to obtain Se-supplemented concentrates, appropriate quantities of Se could be provided by top-dressing Se premixes on the concentrate portion of each horse's daily ration and/or by providing access to a loose trace mineral salt mix with appropriate Se content.

So how much Se per day is reasonable? Assume a growing 200 kg (440 lb) horse consumed 3% of its body weight in dry matter daily, the total dietary dry matter would be 6 kg. (0.03 x 200 kg). It would take 1.8 mg (6 kg x 0.3 mg/kg) of Se to supplement that diet at 0.3 ppm Se. If Se 90/200 is the Se source, each ounce of that supplement contains 5.5 mg Se. So approximately 1/3 ounce (1.8 mg/5.5) of Se 90/200 would be an appropriate amount of Se supplement to top dress daily for a growing horse of that size.

Selenium toxicity and toxic reactions to injectable Se/vitamin E products

The maximum tolerable level (MTL) of dietary Se for horses is believed to approximate 2 ppm (NRC, 1980); therefore, there is a considerable margin of safety between the practiced 0.3 ppm rate of supplementation and the MTL. When Se was established as the element causing blind staggers and/or alkali disease in horses in the plains states in the 1930's (Franke, 1934), the affected horses had consumed products of seleniferous soils and/or plants capable of concentrating Se in their aerial parts to levels of several hundred ppm. Chronically affected horses developed cracked and very sore hooves, as well as impaired hair development, particularly of the mane and tail.

In 1991, the AHDL diagnosed Se toxicity among a group of 20 horses used in a feedlot operation in Nebraska. An initial serum sample taken from one affected horse had the highest serum Se concentration ever assayed in horse serum by the AHDL (928 ng/mL). The horses' hay, grown in western Nebraska and the primary nutrient source for these horses, was found to contain 20 ppm Se. As in the early cases of Se toxicity of horses, these horses experienced impaired hoof and hair development. Serum Se concentrations in these horses declined to the 250 - 325 ng/mL range within 8 weeks after the toxic hay was replaced by normal hay, and all but one of the horses recovered over time.

Untoward responses to injectable Se/vitamin E products have been observed in several species, and animal owners should be advised of the potential fatal effects of these products, even when used at recommended doses. The response is an immediate, usually fatal, anaphylactoid reaction. The reaction is not to the Se or vitamin E in the product but apparently to an emulsifying agent or preservative present in the product. An immediate injection of epinephrine or antihistamine into the horse experiencing the anaphylactoid reaction may save the animal but often is of no help. If the reaction is not fatal, the horse may develop a generalized edema and/or apparent blindness for a period of time. None of these untoward reactions is observed from oral administration of Se at appropriate rates.

Summary

"Determination of nutrient essentiality or of the quantitative requirements is not a political act" (Ullrey, 1980). The FDA, however, has assumed the authority to regulate essential Se additions to animal diets and now permits 0.3 ppm supplemental Se in the diets of poultry, sheep, swine and cattle. While horses are not included in this list, it is gratifying to know that feed manufacturers are providing appropriate options to people to meet the Se requirements of their horses on a scale comparable to that permitted in the food animal species. I would like to think that FDA will remain tolerant of these options because they are conducive to equine health and do not pose a threat to the human food chain. In the interim, it would be prudent for the equine industry to assemble a task force, as did the ruminant industry, to prepare a new petition or assist Real Selenium Inc. in resubmitting its petition for GRAS status of Se in equine feeds. The Equine Nutrition and Physiology Society might wish to play a role in this task.

References

Beckett, G.J., Beddows, S.E., Morrice, B.C., Nicol, F. and Arthur, J.R. 1987. Inhibition of hepatic deiodination of thryoxine is caused by selenium deficiency in rats. Biochem. J. 248:443-447
Behne, D., Kyriakopoulos, A., Gessner, H., Walzog, B. and Meinhold, H. 1992. Type I iodothyronine deiodinase activity after high selenium intake, and relations between selenium and iodine metabolism in rats. J. Nutr. 122:1542-1546.
Franke, K.W. 1934. A new toxicant occurring naturally in certain samples of plant food stuffs. I. Results obtained in preliminary feeding trials, J. Nutr. 8:597.
Keshan Disease Research Group. 1979. Observations on effect of sodium selenite in revention of Keshan disease. Chinese ME. J. 92:471.
Kubota, J., Allaway, W.H., Carter, D.L., Cary, E.E., and Lazar, V.A. 1967. Selenium in crops in the United States in relation to the selenium-responsive diseases of livestock. J. Agr. Food Chem. 15:448.
NRC. 1980. Mineral Tolerance of Domestic Animals. National Academy Press, National Academy of Sciences Washington, DC

Rotruck, J.T., Pope, A.L. Ganther, H.E. *et al.* 1973. Selenium: Biochemical role as a component of glutathione peroxidase. Science 179:588-590

Schwarz, K and Foltz, C.M. 1957. Selenium as an integral part of factor 3 against dietary necrotic liver degeneration. J. Amer. Chem. Soc. 79:3292-3293.

Stowe, H. D. 1967 Serum selenium and related parameters of naturally and experimentally fed horses. J. Nutr. 93:60-64.

Stowe, H.D. and Herdt, T.H. 1992. Clinical assessment of selenium status of livestock. J. Anim. Sci. 70:3928-3933.

Ullrey, D.E. 1980. Regulation of essential nutrient additions to animals diets (Selenium - a model case). J. Anim. Sci. 51:645-651.

Ullrey, D.E. 1992a. Basis for regulation of selenium supplements in animal diets. J. Anim. Sci. 70:3922-3927.

Ullrey, D. E. 1992b. Environmental impact of selenium supplementation of animal feeds. Dockets Management Branch (HFA-305), FDA Public Hearing, Bethesda, MD Aug. 25.

This paper was first published in "Feeding the Performance Horse," Proceedings for the 1993 Short Course for Feed Manufacturers

WHAT DOES YOUR HORSE WEIGH?

JOE D. PAGAN, STEPHEN G. JACKSON, AND STEPHEN E. DUREN
Kentucky Equine Research Inc., Versailles, Kentucky, USA

Determining what a horse weighs is the foundation of a logical feeding and management program. In addition to helping calculate daily intake requirements for hay and grain, accurate assessment of each horse's weight is necessary for the proper dosage of dewormers and other medications.

In mature horses, keeping track of weight gains or losses can help identify health problems related to teeth (which become worn and need periodic floating) or decreased digestive capability, either due to increasing age or disease. But older horses are more likely to be obese rather than too thin. Since an owner in most instances observes a horse daily, it is often easy to overlook the fact that the mare or stallion has become too fat. Obese horses are more prone to colic and founder, and fat mares have more difficulty foaling as well as getting back in foal. Recent studies also indicate that performance horses have ideal bodyweights at which the compete at their best, and minor fluctuations of as little as 30 pounds can mean the difference between victory and defeat.

Grow slow

In growing horses, there is a difference between maximum growth and optimum growth. Many breeds have been selected for early maturation, but if too much weight is gained daily (as opposed to skeletal growth), a variety of developmental ills can result, including osteochondritis dissecans (OCD) lesions, wobbler syndrome, rotational deformities and epiphysitis. Some of these problems are mechanical, and are the result of growth plates failing under the added strain of the overweight weanling or yearling. Some of these problems have a variety of origins, but are complicated by too rapid growth. Again, bimonthly or even weekly monitoring of the growing horses' weight can help identify which horses are at risk of these and other problems, and need to have their feed intake reduced to slow their weight gain. Since it has been found that skeletal growth is difficult to slow, there should be little concern that the horse's eventual size can be compromised. It is only the control of too rapid weight gain (i.e. fat) that is the intent of monitoring each individual's growth curve.

Guess your weight?

Yet while the old adage, " the eye of the master fattens the ox," has been repeated since antiquity, recent surveys have found that even experienced horseman routinely underestimate bodyweight. Two groups, one made up of 77 horsemen (average experience was 15 years) and the other of 62 equine practitioners were asked to participate in the University of Florida study.

In response to a questionnaire, both groups were asked why and how they determined bodyweight. Both groups (100% of veterinarians, and 94% of the horsemen) responded that determining appropriate dosages of medicines was their most important use of how much a horse weighed. Determining feed levels was second in importance to both groups (69% of the veterinarians, 72% of the horsemen), with about half of both groups being interested in weight assessment to help monitor growth rate.

Only 10% of the veterinarians and 12% of the horseman used a scale to weigh their horses. Although some in each group said that they did use a weight tape (21% of the veterinarians, 53% of the horsemen), the majority of the veterinarians (96%) and horsemen (68%) said they primarily made a guesstimate of the horse's weight.

Each group was then asked to estimate the weight of 5 mature horses, which had been weighed just before the test. Over 85% of both groups underestimated all the horses weights, by an average of 150 to 185 pounds. When the data were analyzed, it was found that there was no correlation between the accuracy of the estimations and years of experience. This led the researchers to conclude that underestimation of bodyweight was a common error among both lay horsemen and equine veterinarians.

Scales don't lie

Fortunately, even the most inexperienced horsemen can use several methods to determine how much their horses weigh. The most accurate method is to use a large portable scale. Such scales are now available which are relatively light (150 pounds), and can be easily loaded by two people into the bed of a light pick up, for transit. They are low to the ground (less than 4 inches), and horses of all ages soon learn to walk on, while a digital readout gives their weight in either pounds or kilograms. The process takes only minutes per horse, and yields a great deal of information, particularly if the data are then compared to the preceding weighings. Several computer programs can then take these data and graph the growth curve of that individual, as well as calculate daily gain (or loss) since the last weighing.

Unfortunately scales are pricey (around $3500) and so beyond the average farm's budget. However, some feed companies have purchased scales and provide regular weighing of their customers' horses for a nominal fee per head, at the same time recording the weights and keeping track of growth rates for the herd. They then can identify potential problem horses, and in consultation with the manager or owner, develop a strategy to manage the problem.

Tale of the tape

But there are alternatives to the purchase of a scale. The simplest is the weight tape. It has been long known that there is a correlation between girth measurement and weight. Many horses have had their girth measured and then had that figure compared to their weight as calculated on a scale. The averages of all these measurements were compared with the actual weights, and formulas were developed that translated a girth measurement into an actual weight. Weight tapes are not marked in inches, but in pounds, thus eliminating the calculation step and in many instances these weight tapes can provide a reasonable assessment of weight change.

However, because they only measure one parameter, girth, weigh tapes alone are not the most accurate alternative to weighing. Weight tapes can be as much as 5% or more off (50 pounds per 1000 pounds), and thus are not accurate enough for small, but potentially important, weight changes. There is also a certain amount of error possible depending on who is actually making the measurements, and whether they are taken in a consistent manner. Also, horses can be long backed or short coupled, and while they might share the same heart girth, the horse that stood over more ground could be assumed to weigh more. Similarly, the amount of flesh a horse is carrying can significantly affect any weight estimation.

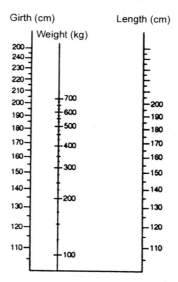

Figure 1. A simple way to estimate bodyweight, using girth and length measurements (as taken at the points in Figure 2). A ruler is used to connect the appropriate values, and the weight is read where the ruler crosses the weight scale.

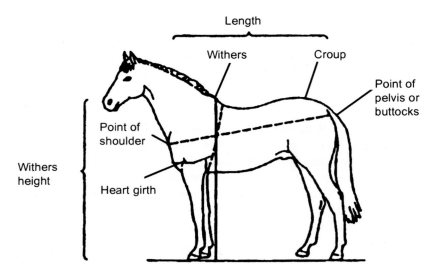

Figure 2. Where to measure girth and length.

A Better weigh

To help eliminate some of these inaccuracies, researchers at Texas A&M and elsewhere have developed descriptions to contrast the differences in horse's relative fatness or thinness graded in a scale of 1 to 10 (or in some instances 1-5). Such condition scoring gives the observer a framework by which horses can be con.)ared which, although not entirely objective, is an improvement over the pure guessti · .ate.

A combination of girth measurement, overall length and condition score is the most accurate alternative to actual weighing. Although it may take some time to be able to develop a system where the points are measured each time, this will come if care is taken. Similarly, familiarity with the condition score will increase the accuracy of the weight estimates, and will improve the horseman's eye, which will reap benefits in other areas of husbandry as well.

The condition score

Absolute weight is not the only important criterion by which to evaluate the horse. Appearance and condition have always been used as indicators of fitness and health. This condition score system was developed in an attempt to standardize these descriptions, to allow for easier comparison and communication.

0-Very poor
- ✓ Very sunken rump
- ✓ Deep cavity under tail
- ✓ Skin tight over bones
- ✓ Very prominent backbone and pelvis
- ✓ Marked ewe neck

1-Poor
- ✓ Sunken rump
- ✓ Cavity under tail
- ✓ Ribs easily visible
- ✓ Prominent backbone and croup
- ✓ Ewe neck-narrow and slack

2-Moderate
- ✓ Flat rump either side backbone
- ✓ Ribs just visible
- ✓ Narrow but firm neck
- ✓ Backbone well covered

3-Good
- ✓ Rounded rump
- ✓ Ribs just covered but easily felt
- ✓ No crest, firm back

4-Fat
- ✓ Rump well rounded
- ✓ Gutter along back
- ✓ Ribs and pelvis hard to feel
- ✓ Slight crest

5-Obese
- ✓ Very bulging rump
- ✓ Deep gutter along back
- ✓ Ribs buried
- ✓ Marked crest
- ✓ Fold and lumps of fat

This paper was first published in "Feeding the Performance Horse," Proceedings for the 1995 Short Course for Feed Manufacturers

COMPUTING HORSE NUTRITION: HOW TO PROPERLY CONDUCT AN EQUINE NUTRITION EVALUATION

JOE D. PAGAN

Kentucky Equine Research, Inc., Versailles, Kentucky, USA

Introduction

Feed manufacturers and horse owners place a great deal of emphasis on the nutrient content of the feeds and supplements that they produce or feed to their horses. Often, extremely rigid values are used for certain nutrients. For instance, horse owners will insist that they feed a 14% protein concentrate to their yearlings; 13% protein would be considered completely inadequate and 15% protein would be excessive. These preconceived ideas about the correct nutrient concentration for different classes of horses are more a product of tradition and misinformation than science. In fact, the concentration of a specific nutrient in a grain mix or supplement is only relevant when it is viewed in the context of a total ration. Therefore, it is important that we have a system to accurately evaluate the complete ration of the horse. Unfortunately, this is not as simple as it may first appear. Nutrition evaluations are based on a number of assumptions and estimates that may or may not be correct. This paper will outline the steps that should be followed when conducting a nutrition evaluation for horses. It will attempt to point out the weaknesses that are an unavoidable part of conducting such an evaluation and it will introduce a new computer software program that will make the evaluation process less tedious and more accurate.

The protocol

Every nutrition evaluation should follow the same series of steps. Omitting any of these steps can lead to serious errors in an evaluation. The obvious place to start with any nutrition evaluation is by classifying the type of horse that we are feeding. Different classes of horses have different nutrient requirements and they will eat different amounts of forage and grain.

Horses can be classed into the following broad categories:

Table 1. CLASSES OF HORSES

Growing horses	Broodmares	Adult horses
Suckling foals	barren	idle
Weanlings	early pregnant	light work
Yearlings	late pregnant	moderate work
Long yearlings	early lactation	heavy work
Two year olds	late lactation	geriatric

Within each class of horse, it is also important to know the horse's current body weight, its age and mature body weight if it is growing, and its rate of body weight gain or loss. Obviously, for a growing horse weight change will be as growth, but for adult horses weight changes will also have a large influence on nutrient requirements. For example, an adult horse that is too thin may need to gain weight to reach a desirable body condition. This extra weight gain will require additional dietary calories which will increase the horse's total daily energy requirement.

Nutrient requirements

Ration evaluations are intended to compare a horse's daily nutrient intake to a set of requirements to see how well the feeding program meets the horse's nutrient needs. This seems a pretty straight-forward accounting exercise, but what nutrient requirements should we use? The National Research Council (NRC) publishes a set of requirements for horses as it does for other species of livestock, so many nutritionists chose to use these numbers to evaluate a ration. Unfortunately, the NRC figures fall short in a number of respects. For the most part, NRC values represent *minimum* requirements for most nutrients. These are the levels of intake that are required to prevent frank deficiency symptoms. There is no allowance included as a safety margin to take into account factors which may increase the requirement for a nutrient. Different sources of nutrients may have different bioavailabilities and there may be other substances within a ration that interfere with the digestibility or utilization of the nutrient.

Digestible energy and protein are two NRC requirements that fairly accurately describe the needs of horses maintained under practical management conditions. These two requirements were for the most part developed from direct measurements of growth response and energy balance in a number of different experiments. Other requirements such as calcium and phosphorus were developed using more theoretical calculations involving estimates of endogenous losses and digestibility. Still others were based on values developed for other species or from single experiments that were far from conclusive. For most of the vitamins and minerals, we use values ranging from 1.25 times NRC to values as high as 3.0 times NRC. These more liberal requirements are based on KER's own research and experience in the field. All of these nutrient requirements are far from absolute and they will continue to evolve as more data become available. For now, though, we feel that our requirements adequately reflect what is needed by the horse under a wide range of conditions.

Types of evaluations

There are two ways that you can approach a ration evaluation. One way is to evaluate a current ration for nutrient adequacy by tallying up what is currently being fed and comparing that to the horse's requirements. This is actually more difficult that it may first appear since most horsemen don't actually know exactly what their horses are eating. There are a number of checks that can be used to more accurately estimate feed intakes and we will review those later. A second type of evaluation is one in which a ration is being developed for a horse. These types of evaluations are also tricky since the various feeds and levels of intakes selected must be practical and safe for the horse in question.

Both types of evaluations depend on the concept of *energy balance* to match feeds intake to requirements. Calculating energy balance allows a primary overall evaluation of how well a ration meets the horse's needs. Only after we are satisfied that the horse is in a reasonable state of energy balance will we proceed with the rest of the evaluation.

Energy is the key

The first step for every evaluation is to calculate the energy requirement of the horse. We currently use units of Digestible energy (DE) to describe dietary energy requirements. DE requirements can be expressed as kilocalories (kcal) or megacalories (Mcal), where 1 Mcal equals 1000 kcal. Joules are another unit of measure used to describe DE. To convert calories to Joules, simply multiply by 4.18. Therefore, 1 kcal = 4.18 kJ and 1 Mcal = 4.18 MJ. Digestible energy is actually a fairly crude method of describing the energy content of feed, since it is calculated by subtracting the energy lost in the manure from the gross energy (GE) content of the feed. There are large differences in how efficiently the digested energy is utilized from different feedstuffs, so DE requirements can only be viewed as ball park estimates that must be refined depending on the type of diet being fed. For example, a horse will require more DE to meet its energy requirement if it is eating an all forage diet than if it is eating a ration high in grain or added fat. More accurate systems of energy evaluation utilizing net energy (NE) have been developed, but have not been placed into widespread use because of a lack of information about NE requirements for various classes of horses and NE contents of different feedstuffs.

Table 2. ENERGY REQUIREMENTS FOR DIFFERENT CLASSES OF HORSE

Class of horse	Equation	Body weight (ADG)	DE (Mcal/day)
Weanling	$1.4 + (0.0136 \times BW^1) + (4.54 \times ADG^2)$	500 (1.75)	16.1
Yearling	$1.4 + (0.0136 \times BW) + (7.27 \times ADG)$	725 (1.25)	20.4
Two year olds	$1.4 + (0.136 \times BW) + (9.1 \times ADG)$	1000 (0.50)	19.6
Maintenance	$1.4 + (0.0136 \times BW)$	1100	16.4
Early pregnant[3]	(maintenance DE)	1100	16.4
Late pregnant[4]	(maintenance DE) x 1.2	1100	19.7
Early lactation[5]	(maintenance DE) + (0.04 BW x 0.36)	1100	32.2
Late lactation[6]	(maintenance DE) + (0.03 BW x 0.36)	1100	28.3
Light work	(maintenance DE) x 1.25	1100	20.5
Moderate work	(maintenance DE) x 1.50	1100	24.6
Heavy work	(maintenance DE) x 2.00	1100	32.8

[1] BW = body weight (lb)
[2] ADG = average daily gain (lb/day)
[3] early pregnant = 1st 8 months of pregnancy
[4] late pregnant = last 3 months of pregnancy
[5] early lactation = 1st 3 months of lactation
[6] late lactation = 2nd 3 months of lactation

Table 2 lists the DE requirements for various classes of horses. The maintenance DE requirement for horses is DE (Mcal/day) = 1.4 + 0.03 x body weight (Kg). Requirements for other classes of horses will depend on age, growth rate, reproductive status or work intensity. We will evaluate each of these classes later. For now, let's evaluate the mature, idle horse. An average 500 kg (1100 lb horse) horse requires 16.4 Mcal DE/day. Remember, this is an average figure and there will be great variation among individuals, but it gives us a place to start.

Once the energy requirement is established, a ration must be designed. A horse's ration must contain an adequate quantity of forage to maintain proper gut function. This amount, both in absolute terms and as a percentage of the total diet, will change depending on the age and physiological status of the horse. Table 3 provides guidelines for forage and grain intake in various classes of horse.

From this table we can see that a mature horse at maintenance needs to consume at least 1% of its body weight and 50% of its total ration as forage. How much digestible energy does this amount of forage provide? The answer depends on the type of forage selected. The next step in performing a ration evaluation is estimating the energy content of different feedstuffs. For grains and feeds, values from the literature are generally used. Table 4 lists some common equine feedstuffs and their estimated DE contents. It should be emphasized that these energy values are only estimates since very few actual DE determinations have been made on individual feed ingredients, and those that have been made have used mathematical formulas to calculate the energy content of individual grains. Only the DE content of forages can be determined directly.

If our 1100 kg horse were eating a midbloom timothy hay with a DE content of 0.80 Mcal/lb, then an intake of 1% BW (11 lbs) would provide only 8.8 Mcal of DE. This is far short of the horse's DE requirement (16.4 Mcal/day) and at this level of forage intake, supplemental grain would be required. With this minimal forage intake, the horse would require about 5.5 lbs of a concentrate containing 1.35 Mcal/lb. It is much more likely that a horse of this type would eat 2% of BW/day as hay. This level of hay intake (22 lbs) would provide 17.6 Mcal DE, a level that is fairly close to the horse's requirement, considering the relatively low efficiency with which DE is used from forage. But what about the mature horse that is maintaining its weight and condition (i.e. zero energy balance) just fine on 5 lbs of timothy hay per day and bluegrass pasture? The horse must be consuming around 16-17 Mcal of DE/day to maintain a constant body condition and only 4 Mcal are coming from the hay. Therefore, it must be eating enough pasture per day to provide an additional 12-13 Mcal DE. If bluegrass pasture contains about 1.0 Mcal DE/lb of DM, then the horse must be consuming 12 or 13 lbs of pasture dry matter per day. As you can see from this example, a horse can meet its DE requirements from a number of different sources. The ration most appropriate for an individual will depend on a number of factors related to management and forage availability. How well any of these rations meets the rest of the horse's nutrient requirements will be determined later in the evaluation, but for now we must quantify levels of intake for each feedstuff.

Table 3. EXPECTED FEED CONSUMPTION BY HORSES

| Horse | % of body weight | | % of diet | |
	forage	concentrate	forage	concentrate
Maintenance	1.0-2.0	0-1.0	50-100	0-50
Pregnant mare	1.0-2.0	0.3-1.0	50-85	15-50
Lactating mare (early)	1.0-2.5	0.5-2.0	33-85	15-66
Lactating mare (late)	1.0-2.0	0.5-1.5	40-80	20-60
Weanling	0.5-1.8	1.0-3.0	30-65	35-70
Yearling	1.0-2.5	0.5-2.0	33-80	20-66
Performance horse	1.0-2.0	0.5-2.0	33-80	20-66

The above example also assumed that the horse was in energy equilibrium or zero energy balance. In other words, energy intake exactly equalled energy expended so the horse neither gained nor lost weight. This is the goal when feeding a mature, idle horse, but often a horse will get fat while eating nothing but pasture. To calculate how much extra DE the horse is consuming over its maintenance requirement, follow these steps:

1)　weigh the horse repeated over several weeks at the same time per day

2)　calculate average daily weight gain

3)　1 lb of fat deposition requires about 7.5 extra Mcal of DE

A horse that is on pasture gaining 1.5 lbs per day (make sure it's fat deposition and not gut fill) must be consuming about 11 lbs of pasture dry matter more than is required to maintain constant body weight since most pasture contains about 1.0 Mcal DE/lb of dry matter. Adult horses can easily eat 2.5% (27.5 lbs) of their body weight per day as pasture dry matter, so it's easy to see how an 1100 lb horse can get fat on pasture alone! This level of pasture intake provides 27.5 Mcal DE/day, which is 11 Mcal over the maintenance requirement. This extra DE would produce 1.5 lbs of fat deposition per day, and in three months on this type pasture, your horse has gained 135 lbs of weight.

Table 4. DE CONTENT (MCAL/LB) OF COMMON EQUINE FEEDSTUFFS

Hays		*Pasture*		*Grains and supplements*	
As fed	*DE (Mcal/lb)*	*Dry basis*	*DE (Mcal/lb)*	*As fed*	*DE (Mcal/lb)*
Timothy (early bloom)	0.83	Alfalfa	1.34	Barley	1.49
Timothy (midbloom)	0.80	Bahiagrass	0.92	Beet pulp	1.06
Timothy (late bloom)	0.78	Bermudagrass	1.08	Corn	1.54
Alfalfa (early bloom)	1.02	Bluegrass	0.95	Molasses	1.20
Alfalfa (mid bloom)	0.94	Clover	1.14	Oats	1.30
Alfalfa (late bloom)	0.89	Fescue	1.01	Soybean meal	1.43
Bermuda grass	0.85	Orchard grass	1.04	Sweet feed	1.35-1.40
Bluegrass	0.72	Pangola grass	0.89	Vegetable oil	4.08

This same weight gain would result from 8 lbs grain per day fed along with 20 lbs of midbloom timothy hay. Many mature horses are fed this way and the horse will often gain 100 lbs before the owner notices that it is getting fat. In this situation, a ration evaluation would signal that this excess weight gain may be taking place. If so, the energy balance of the horse needs to be assessed. For more information about monitoring energy balance, see the paper *"What does your horse weigh?"* elsewhere in this book.

Calculating pasture intake

The amount of pasture eaten by any class of horse can be calculated by subtracting the DE intake from all other feedstuffs from the horse's daily energy requirement. Dividing this number by the pasture's calculated energy density yields daily dry matter intake. For example, a yearling that weighs 725 lbs with an average daily gain of 1.25 lbs/day should require 20.4 Mcal DE/day. If that yearling is eating 8 lbs of sweet feed (10.8 Mcal DE) and 4 lbs of mature alfalfa hay (3.6 Mcal DE), then it must be consuming around 6 Mcal of DE from pasture. Most grass pastures contain about 1 Mcal DE/lb, so this yearling must consume about 6 lbs of pasture dry matter per day. These intakes can then be used to evaluate the adequacy of the ration for other nutrients in addition to energy.

This method of calculating pasture energy intake works well provided that two assumptions are correct:

1)   The horse is really consuming the intakes of the other feedstuffs

2)   You have chosen the correct energy requirement

Often times, using the method described above for estimating pasture intake yields a negative number. If this occurs, then either the DE intake of the other feeds was too high or the calculated energy consumption was too low. Sometimes, horse owners report higher intakes for feeds than are actually eaten. This is particularly true for forage were hay is rarely weighed and large quantities are often wasted. Grain intake can also be overestimated since that coffee can that is used to measure grain doesn't hold nearly as much grain as coffee! Other times, the hay and grain intake may be correct, but the horse may be consuming more energy than calculated. This can happen if the horse is expending extra energy because of activity or to keep warm in cold weather or it may be that a young horse is growing faster than assumed. For example, a yearling needs about 5 lbs of additional grain (7.3 Mcal DE) per lb of gain. If average daily gain is higher than assumed, then the horse may eating significantly more DE than calculated.

Evaluating nutrient adequacy

After nutrient requirements are established and intakes estimated, the various feedstuffs should be sampled and analyzed for other nutrients. The accuracy of the entire nutrition evaluation depends on the use of proper methodology for sampling feedstuffs. The feeds should be thoroughly mixed and a representative sample taken. This is not difficult for pelleted feeds since each pellet is fairly uniform in composition. For textured feeds and home mixes, however, sampling is more critical. If an odd nutrient value is encountered, look to sampling error as a likely cause.

Sampling forages presents a challenge, especially when sampling pasture. A hay core can be used to get a representative hay sample for analysis. Pasture analysis is more difficult. The first question that must be addressed is whether the entire pasture should be systematically sampled or if only those areas heavily grazed should be sampled. Since horses tend to be "spot" grazers, it is probably best to sample the areas heavily grazed rather than the entire pasture.

When expressing feed intakes and nutrient composition, we use "air dry" values for hay and grain and "100 % dry matter" values for pasture. This is because hay and grain intakes are actually measured "as fed" and pasture intakes tend to be estimated. The moisture content of the pasture is not relevant to our evaluation and only confuses how to calculate intake.

WEANLINGS

Let's evaluate the ration of a 6 month old weanling. This is a March foal born in Kentucky, so the current evaluation would be in September. This particular foal is eating 8 lbs of a commercial concentrate containing 16% protein and 1.45 Mcal DE/lb. It weighs 550 lbs and is gaining an average of 1.87 lbs/day. Therefore, it would have a daily DE requirement of 17.4 Mcal (see table 2). The 8 lbs of grain provides 11.6 Mcal DE, leaving about 6 Mcal of DE needed from forage.

If this weanling were maintained on pasture without hay supplementation, then it would probably consume around 6 lbs of pasture dry matter. Table 5 contains a tabular evaluation of this feeding program. The top portion of this table contains the nutrient composition of the ration. Notice that the concentrate intake is expressed on an "as fed" basis while the lower portion provides the daily nutrient intake for DE, protein, lysine and a number of macro and micro minerals. In addition to the concentrate and pasture, it is assumed that this weanling will voluntarily consume about 30 grams (~ 1 ounce) of free choice salt per day.

This evaluation can also be presented graphically as in figure 1. This type of presentation expresses intakes of each nutrient as a percent of required supplied, thus eliminating the various units of measure that are confusing to the horse owner. In addition, a graphic presentation of this type shows the relative contribution that each ingredient makes to the overall nutrient intake of a ration.

Table 5. NUTRITION EVALUATION OF A 6 MONTH OLD WEANLING* EATING PASTURE PLUS A 16% PROTEIN GRAIN MIX. NOTICE THAT THIS TYPE OF RATION PROVIDES MORE PROTEIN THAN NECESSARY

Nutrient composition	Fall pasture	Grain ESF 1	Salt	Total nutrient	Supplied by ration	Required nutrients
Intake (lbs/day)	6.01	8.00	0.11	14.11		
Intake (kgs/day)	2.73	3.64	0.05	6.42		
Dry matter %	100.00	89.00	100.00	93.77		
Protein %	16.00	16.00		15.88		
Lysine %	0.56	0.72		0.65		
DE (mcal/kg)	2.20	3.10		2.69		
Calcium %	0.55	0.95		0.77		
Phosphorus %	0.30	0.75		0.55		
Magnesium %	0.20	0.38		0.30		
Sodium %	0.01	0.25	40.00	0.46		
Potassium %	1.70	0.68		1.11		
Zinc (ppm)	35.00	125.00		85.72		
Manganese (ppm)	70.00	125.00		100.62		
Copper (ppm)	12.00	45.00		30.61		
Selenium (ppm)	0.10	0.50		0.33		
Iodine (ppm)	0.05	0.40		0.25		
Cobalt (ppm)	0.10	0.20		0.16		
Daily intakes						
Dry matter (kgs/day)	2.73	3.24	0.05		6.02	6.25
Protein (kg/day)	436.80	581.60	0.00		1018.40	783.00
Lysine (g/day)	15.29	26.17			41.46	36.54
DE (Mcal DE/day)	6.01	11.27	0.00		17.27	17.40
Calcium (g/day)	15.02	34.53	0.00		49.55	44.25
Phosphorus (g/day)	8.19	27.26	0.00		35.45	29.50
Magnesium (g/day)	5.46	13.81	0.00		19.27	11.06
Sodium (g/day)	0.27	9.09	20.00		29.36	18.75
Potassium (g/day)	46.41	24.72	0.00		71.13	62.50
Zinc (mg/day)	95.55	454.38	0.00		549.93	500.00
Manganese (mg/day)	191.10	454.38	0.00		645.48	500.00
Cooper (mg/day)	32.76	163.58	0.00		196.34	150.00
Selenium (mg/day)	0.27	1.82	0.00		2.09	1.88
Iodine (mg/day)	0.14	1.45	0.00		1.59	1.25
Cobalt (mg/day)	0.27	0.73	0.00		1.00	0.94

* Class weanling 550.00 Body wt. (lbs); 250.00 Body wt (kgs); 500.00 Mature wt. (kgs); 0.85 ADG (kg/day); 1.87 ADG (lbs/day); 6.00 Age (months)

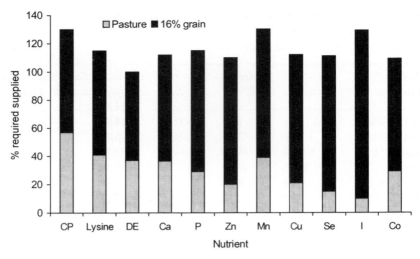

Figure 1. Weanling eating pasture plus a 16% protein grain concentrate

From this evaluation, it is apparent that a 16% protein concentrate is unnecessary to meet the weanling's protein requirement since the forage portion of the ration (pasture) is high in protein.

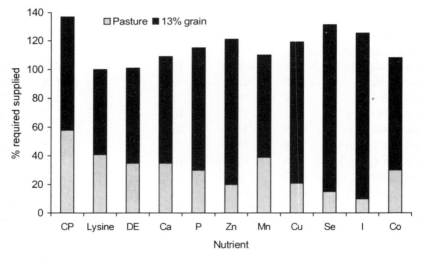

Figure 2. Weanling eating pasture plus a 13% concentrate

In this instance, a 13% protein grain mix will meet the weanling's protein requirements. If this type of mix is adequately fortified with other nutrients, then it is perfectly fine for weanlings grazing high quality pasture such as the type found in Central Kentucky.

Table 6 and figure 2 illustrate this type of ration.

Table 6. NUTRITION EVALUATION OF A 6 MONTH OLD WEANLING* EATING PASTURE PLUS A 13% CONCENTRATE.

Nutrient composition	Fall pasture	Grain ESF 1	Salt	Total nutrient	Supplied by ration	Required nutrients
Intake (lbs/day)	6.01	8.01	0.11	14.12		
Intake (kgs/day)	2.73	3.64	0.05	6.42		
Dry matter %	100.00	89.20	100.00	93.88		
Protein %	16.00	13.00		14.17		
Lysine %	0.56	0.59		0.57		
DE (mcal/kg)	2.20	3.17		2.73		
Calcium %	0.55	0.90		0.74		
Phosphorus %	0.30	0.70		0.52		
Magnesium %	0.20	0.30		0.26		
Sodium %	0.01	0.20	40.00	0.43		
Potassium %	1.70	0.40		0.95		
Zinc (ppm)	35.00	140.00		94.26		
Manganese (ppm)	70.00	100.00		86.46		
Copper (ppm)	12.00	40.00		27.78		
Selenium (ppm)	0.10	0.60		0.38		
Iodine (ppm)	0.05	0.40		0.25		
Cobalt (ppm)	0.10	0.20		0.16		
Daily intakes						
Dry matter (kgs/day)	2.73	3.25	0.05		6.03	6.25
Protein (kg/day)	436.80	473.20	0.00		910.00	783.00
Lysine (g/day)	15.29	21.29			36.58	36.54
DE (Mcal DE/day)	6.01	11.54	0.00		17.54	17.40
Calcium (g/day)	15.02	32.76	0.00		47.78	44.25
Phosphorus (g/day)	8.19	25.48	0.00		33.67	29.50
Magnesium (g/day)	5.46	10.92	0.00		16.38	11.06
Sodium (g/day)	0.27	7.28	20.00		27.55	18.75
Potassium (g/day)	46.41	14.56	0.00		60.97	62.50
Zinc (mg/day)	95.55	509.60	0.00		605.15	500.00
Manganese (mg/day)	191.10	364.00	0.00		555.10	500.00
Copper (mg/day)	32.76	145.60	0.00		178.36	150.00
Selenium (mg/day)	0.27	2.18	0.00		2.46	1.88
Iodine (mg/day)	0.14	1.46	0.00		1.59	1.25
Cobalt (mg/day)	0.27	0.73	0.00		1.00	0.94

* Class weanling 550.00 Body wt. (lbs); 250.00 Body wt (kgs); 500.00 Mature wt. (kgs); 0.85 ADG (kg/day); 1.87 ADG (lbs/day); 6.00 Age (months)

If this weanling had been raised on poorer quality pasture or fed only grass hay, then the 16% protein grain mix with higher levels of supplemental mineral would have been required. Table 7 and figure 3 show this type of ration where the foal is consuming the same quantity of concentrate along with orchardgrass hay. With this type of ration, protein may be marginal and lysine may actually be deficient. Also, calcium intake may be lower than optimal. In this instance, the text book "16%" for weanlings is probably justified.

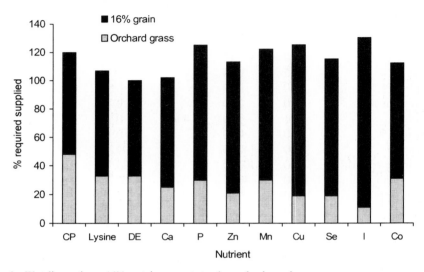

Figure 3. Weanling eating a 16% protein concentrate plus orchardgrass hay.

Evaluation software

Conducting an equine nutrition evaluation by hand calculation can be a tedious process. Therefore, Kentucky Equine Research has developed a software program to simplify the process. This program, called MicroSteed™, will automatically calculate nutrient requirements for each class of horse using either KER equations or those developed by the NRC. It also contains a large database of feed ingredients from various geographic region around the world including many commercial concentrates and supplements. This program is written for use in a Windows environment in a very user friendly format. It will automatically create stacked bar graphs such as the ones illustrated in figures 1-3. In addition, help screens contain useful information about typical horse weights and growth rates.

MicroSteed™ makes equine nutrition evaluation much simpler and more descriptive. However, it will produce accurate results only if the rules outlined in this paper are followed. Feed intakes that match energy status must be used and feedstuffs must be properly sampled and accurately analyzed. With these safeguards, a great deal can be learned from conducting thorough equine nutrition evaluations.

Table 7. NUTRITION EVALUATION OF A 6 MONTH OLD WEANLING* EATING ORCHARDGRASS HAY PLUS A 16% PROTEIN CONCENTRATE.

Nutrient composition	Fall pasture	Grain ESF 1	Salt	Total nutrient	Supplied by ration	Required nutrients
Intake (lbs/day)	7.04	8.01	0.11	15.16		
Intake (kgs/day)	3.20	3.64	0.05	6.89		
Dry matter %	89.10	89.00	100.00	89.13		
Protein %	11.40	16.00		13.75		
Lysine %	0.40	0.72		0.57		
DE (mcal/kg)	1.94	3.10		2.54		
Calcium %	0.34	0.95		0.66		
Phosphorus %	0.30	0.75		0.54		
Magnesium %	0.10	0.38		0.25		
Sodium %	0.01	0.25	40.00	0.43		
Potassium %	2.59	0.68		1.56		
Zinc (ppm)	36.00	125.00		82.76		
Manganese (ppm)	50.00	125.00		89.26		
Copper (ppm)	8.00	45.00		27.49		
Selenium (ppm)	0.11	0.50		0.31		
Iodine (ppm)	0.05	0.40		0.23		
Cobalt (ppm)	0.10	0.20		0.15		
Daily intakes						
Dry matter (kgs/day)	2.85	3.24	0.05		6.14	6.25
Protein (kg/day)	364.80	582.40	0.00		947.20	783.00
Lysine (g/day)	12.77	26.21			38.98	36.54
DE (Mcal DE/day)	6.21	11.28	0.00		17.49	17.40
Calcium (g/day)	10.88	34.58	0.00		45.46	44.25
Phosphorus (g/day)	9.60	27.30	0.00		36.90	29.50
Magnesium (g/day)	3.20	13.83	0.00		17.03	11.06
Sodium (g/day)	0.32	9.10	20.00		29.42	18.75
Potasium (g/day)	82.88	24.75	0.00		107.63	62.50
Zinc (mg/day)	115.20	455.00	0.00		570.20	500.00
Manganese (mg/day)	160.00	455.00	0.00		615.00	500.00
Copper (mg/day)	25.60	163.80	0.00		189.40	150.00
Selenium (mg/day)	0.34	1.82	0.00		2.16	1.88
Iodine (mg/day)	0.16	1.46	0.00		1.62	1.25
Copper (mg/day)	0.32	0.73	0.00		1.05	0.94

* Class weanling 550.00 Body wt. (lbs); 250.00 Body wt (kgs); 500.00 Mature wt. (kgs); 0.85 ADG (kg/day); 1.87 ADG (lbs/day); 6.00 Age (months)

This paper was first published in "Recent Advances in Equine Nutrition," Proceedings for the 1995 Short Course for Feed Manufacturers

THE PERFORMANCE HORSE

CHOKE POINTS:WHAT FACTORS LIMIT PERFORMANCE IN THE EQUINE ATHLETE?

JOE D. PAGAN

Kentucky Equine Research, Inc., Versailles, Kentucky, USA

Introduction

Horses are unique among large domestic animals in that they are not raised specially to produce meat, milk or wool. Instead, horses are raised to be athletes, with work as their main productive function. There are large numbers of different types of work that horses perform, ranging from high speed racing at speeds of over 45 miles per hour to long distance endurance racing for 50 miles or more to draft work where horses pull or carry heavy loads. The basic driving force behind all of these various types of work is the conversion of stored chemical energy into mechanical energy for muscular movement.

A number of physiological systems in the horse work in unison to provide fuels and oxygen to the working muscle and to remove waste products that are produced from its metabolism. All of these systems function together to produce efficient movement of the horse's limbs and body. The study of exercise physiology can be divided into several broad categories including:

- the cardiovascular system
- the respiratory system
- the muscular system
- biomechanics and conformation
- hematology and
- nutrition.

Each of these systems can be viewed as a link in a chain. If any particular link is weak, then the performance of the whole animal suffers. The study of equine exercise physiology therefore entails methodically evaluating each physiological system to assess its role in limiting performance.

Choke points

Any one of the various physiological systems involved during exercise may limit oxygen consumption. If one particular system limits oxygen uptake and utilization, then the horse will only be able to perform at that level regardless of how well all of its other physiological systems operate.

Respiratory system

The oxygen which is consumed by the working muscle originates from the air. Air contains about 21% oxygen and the horse must inspire air at a rate that is high enough to supply the body with as much as 90 liters of oxygen per minute. The amount of air which the horse can inspire is a product of its respiratory rate x tidal volume. Respiratory rate during the gallop is linked mechanically to stride frequency so the horse takes a breath with every step. Respiratory rate can reach in excess of 150 breaths per minute and tidal volume can be as high as 12 liters per breath. Thus, the horse inspires and expires at a rate of over 2.5 times per second and during this extremely short period, the lung must be able to transport oxygen from the air in the lung into the blood.

There are several potential problems with the horse's respiratory system. First, many horses have a partial paralysis of the muscles in the larynx which reduces the size of the wind pipe. This problem in its advanced stages is called roaring because of the noise the horse makes during exercise. Even a small reduction in the size of the wind pipe can greatly reduce the amount of air that can reach the lungs. Fortunately, surgical procedures can often greatly improve the performance of a horse afflicted with this disease.

Another potential problem is damage to the lung itself. One of the problems that can occur with the lung is called chronic obstructive pulmonary disease (COPD) or "heaves." COPD is a hyperallergenic response of the respiratory system similar to that seen in human asthma. Affected horses may cough, develop a nasal discharge and have excessive tearing of the eyes. Respiratory rate is increased, and lung elasticity is diminished.

The most important aspect of treatment for "heavey" horses is recognition of its cause: exposure to dust, mold spores and respiratory irritants such as ammonia. Horses affected with COPD are best kept outside and managed in pastures rather than in stalls. When this is not possible, horses should be bedded on dust free bedding such as shredded paper or peat moss.

Another common problem in performance horses is exercise induced pulmonary hemorrhage (EIPH) or "bleeding." Horses with EIPH bleed from the lungs during intense exercise which greatly reduces the efficiency of transfer to oxygen into the blood stream. The cause of bleeding is still unclear, but the most common treatment currently is the use of the diuretic furosemide (Lasix).

Conformation and biomechanics

Another system that can limit a horse's performance is conformation and biomechanics. A horse with faulty conformation may perform poorly for two reasons. First, conformationally incorrect horses are likely to be unsound. Lameness is the number one factor limiting performance in all types of horses. Often the conformation faults which lead to unsoundness do nothing to reduce the biomechanical efficiency of the horse if the horse does not become lame. In fact, many of the best racehorses have very crooked legs that do not reduce their racing ability. Instead, these faults ultimately shorten the horse's racing career.

A second type of conformation defect never adversely affects the horse's soundness. Rather, these horses are simply poor movers and they expend extra energy when they work. This type of biomechanical inefficiency is especially harmful for racehorses since they must work much harder to do the same amount of work and therefore fatigue earlier than more biomechanically correct individuals. Also, since respiratory rate is linked to stride frequency, poor movers with short strides have higher respiratory rates with reduced oxygen transfer in the lungs. This greatly reduces their aerobic capacity.

Cardiovascular system

Once oxygen has entered the bloodstream, it must be transported to the working muscle and waste products removed. The horse has a very advanced cardiovascular system for transporting blood. Cardiac output (CO) is a measure of how much blood the heart can pump per minute. CO is the product of heart rate (HR) x stroke volume (SV). HR in resting horses varies from 25-45 beats per minute and averages around 32-35. Horses have maximal HRs of 220-250 beats per minute. SV is around 0.8 - 1.2 liters per beat. Therefore, at maximal exercise, CO can reach over 250 liters per minute. This is comparable to pumping a 55 gallon drum of blood through the heart each minute! This massive CO is one reason that horses are such good natural athletes.

As a horse becomes more fit, SV tends to increase and HR at a particular speed decreases. Measuring the speed at which a horse can exercise at a specific HR (i.e., 180 or 200) gives a good indication of its relative fitness. Low cost HR monitors are available which enable horsemen to monitor their horse's training progress in the field.

Since oxygen is carried through the blood stream in red blood cells, the number of these cells can affect performance. Horses have the ability to store as many as half of their red blood cells in their spleen when they are not exercising. When strenuous exercise begins, these cells are mobilized into the blood stream where they double the blood's oxygen carrying capacity. A deficiency of red blood cells (anemia) could possibly limit performance, but this usually only happens when the horse has suffered some type of infection or illness. Nutritional anemia is fairly rare in performance horses.

Nutrition

Supplying nutrients to the working muscle to produce energy is certainly an important factor affecting performance. How feeding affects the supply and utilization of energy by the muscle is still not completely resolved. There is no doubt that feeding does affect performance, but it remains to be determined what are the best sources of energy for the horse and when they should be fed relative to exercise. Also, the role that electrolytes play in maintaining optimal muscle function and in the prevention of exercise related diseases remains largely unresolved. A number of research groups are currently evaluating these questions and hopefully more will be known about this important area in the not too distant future.

Conclusion

The exercising horse depends on a number of different physiological systems to supply fuel to the muscles and remove waste products during exercise. Any one of these systems may limit the horse's ability to perform. To properly evaluate a horse's performance potential, each system must be methodically examined. Once the weak link in the performance chain is identified, specific training and management steps can be implemented to improve that individual horse's athletic ability.

This paper was first published in "Feeding the Performance Horse," Proceedings for the 1993 Short Course for Feed Manufacturers

FORM FOLLOWS FUNCTION? HOW DOES CONFORMATION AFFECT THE PERFORMANCE HORSE?

STEPHEN G. JACKSON

Kentucky Equine Research, Inc., Versailles, Kentucky, USA

In learning to evaluate conformation, you need a good understanding of all the factors that should be considered when you thoroughly evaluate each individual. The factors can be categorized under a series of major selection criteria: BALANCE, MUSCLING, STRUCTURAL CORRECTNESS and QUALITY. Travel is considered under structural correctness since the horse's structure will directly determine how it will travel. This system was developed to logically organize all selection factors, making them not only easier to learn, but easier to recall when evaluating a horse.

Balance

Balance is one of the most important selection criteria, but sometimes the most difficult to comprehend or visualize. It is defined as the way a unit's component parts fit together to form the functioning whole, or the blending of parts to form the entire horse. Balance is evaluated from the side, from 25 to 30 ft away.

A well balanced horse (Figure 1) should have a long neck, a long sloping shoulder, a long hip, a deep heartgirth and hindrib and should be relatively short in the back compared to the underline. A poorly balanced horse, on the other hand, may have some areas which are relatively shorter or longer than others. For example, a poorly balanced horse may have a short neck, a short steep shoulder, a long back, a short hip and/or be hollow in either its heartgirth or hindrib.

Length of neck is important, because the horse uses its neck and weight of its head as a counterbalance to maintain equilibrium during movement. The longer the neck (lever), the more leverage the horse will have while executing maneuvers. For example, the hunter will raise its head and neck just before taking a jump; a cutting horse will bend its neck and orient its head just before changing direction and the reining horse will raise its head and neck during a sliding stop.

Not only is length important, but also trimness and how the neck ties into the forequarter. Horses with long, clean, trim necks that tie smoothly into the withers and high into the forequarter will have more suppleness and flexibility in their movements compared to horses with short, thick, cresty, low tying necks.

Shoulder length and slope are extremely important. Horses with long, well-sloped, well-laid-in shoulders will have a wider range of movement, will give a smoother ride and will develop less unsoundness in the forelegs. Both length and slope of the shoulder are evaluated by visualizing the scapula's spine (Figure 2). A longer shoulder will permit a greater range of movement by allowing for greater muscular contraction. The result will be a greater efficiency of movement. Since the shoulder bone (scapula) and the arm bone (humerus) work together as part of the "shock absorbing mechanism," it is clear that a well-sloped shoulder will permit more cushion or absorption of the concussive forces during movement than a short, steep shoulder. In addition to length and slope, the shoulder should blend well or be well laid into both the neck and barrel.

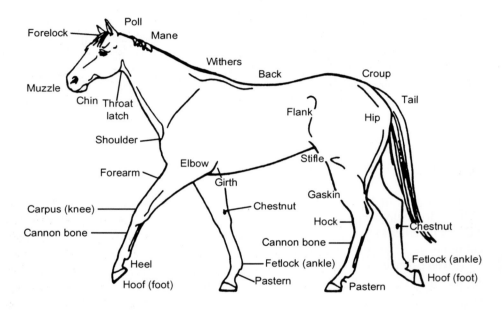

Figure 1. Parts of the body

The back lies from the withers to the loin (coupling) and should be strong and relatively short compared to the underline (Figure 1). Horses with long, well-sloped shoulders will often give the impression of being short in their backs. A short back will be more capable of withstanding the weight of the rider and equipment and will provide more strength and support for mares while they are carrying their foals. A long underline will permit a longer stride resulting in greater efficiency of movement. Long backs may appear strong in young horses, but will weaken with age and use, leaving the horse weak and sway backed.

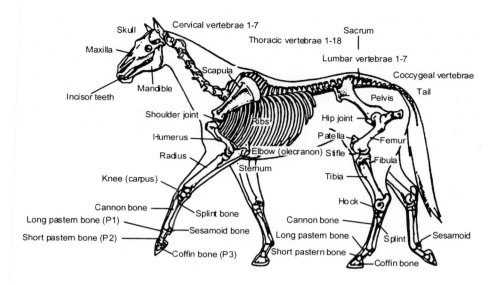

Figure 2. The horse's skeleton

Muscling

All movement originates from the contraction and relaxation of muscle. The horse depends on muscle for a variety of functions: to move its body from one place to another (locomotion), to move food through its digestive system, to run its heart and even to vibrate certain parts of its body that it cannot reach to chase away pests. However, since the horse is an athlete, it is evaluated for the muscling responsible for locomotion and control. Muscling is located over the entire body from the knees and hocks up. However, certain areas of the body should possess additional volume and definition of muscling. These areas are the chest or pectoral region, the forearm, shoulder, loin, croup, stifle and gaskin (Figure 1). The most desirable kind of muscling is long, smooth and deep tying muscle rather than short, bunchy muscling. All 7 of the major muscle mass areas contribute significantly to the horse's ability to perform as an athlete.

The chest or pectoral region should have ample muscling that carries down the insides of both forelegs and ties smoothly into the knees giving a "V" like appearance. Horses that are wide through the floor of the chest cavity and possess ample muscling will have more extension and lateral movement power than narrow-fronted, light muscled horses.

Evidence of muscling in the forearm will ensure that the horse will have more power and strength during extension. This muscling should be bulging, but long and should tie down well into the knee.

Ample shoulder muscling is important to bind the foreleg to the trunk. Also, shoulder muscling is useful during jumping and for forward and lateral movement.

A well-muscled loin is important for strength and support to withstand the weight of rider and equipment. Muscles in this region play an important role in coordinating the fore and rear quarters during movement as well as aiding vertical extension and jumping.

A well-muscled loin should not be confused with the undesirable condition known as being "roach backed," when the spine is abnormally elevated in the lumbar area. Light muscling in the loin will permit the back to become weak with age and use. Adequate muscling in the croup will ensure that the horse has sufficient power for impulsion and drive off of the rear quarters as well as for stopping, jumping and backing. Since the obese horse will tend to deposit fat in the area of the croup, the croup should be closely examined to distinguish between fat or muscling.

The horse gets much of its locomotive power from the stifle or thigh area. Therefore, muscling in the stifle is necessary for jumping and stopping and for manipulation of the rear quarters. Horses should be as thick, or thicker through the center of the stifle as they are through the point of the hip. Besides thickness, depth of muscling in the stifle is important. The stifle should tie in deep toward the gaskin from the side view and the quarter should be deep and wide. Horses that lack ample muscling in the stifle will not be as thick through the center of the stifle as they are through the point of the hip.

Gaskin muscling is important for power in the flexion and extension of the rear legs. Muscling in the gaskin should be prominent in both the inside and outside areas and should be tied smoothly into the hock.

Structure, correctness and soundness

Horses should be serviceably sound. Young animals should show no defects in conformation that may lead to unsoundness. You must first know and recognize normal structure and function before you can identify unsoundness. An unsoundness is defined as any deviation in form or function that interferes with an individual's usefulness. A blemish is an abnormality which may detract from an animal's appearance but does not affect his serviceability. Some definitions and locations of unsoundnesses and blemishes are given on the following pages. Examples of blemishes can be wire cuts, rope burns, shoe boils and capped hocks.

For the horse to perform properly he must have sound feet and legs. The feet should be tough, well rounded and roomy with deep open heels. They should be set directly under the knees and hocks and should be straight as viewed from the front and rear.

The legs should be straight and the knees and hocks should be deep, wide and free from coarseness.

The bone should appear flat, be clean, hard and free from puffiness. It should be of adequate strength and substance to properly support the horse during strenuous activity. The tendons should be well defined.

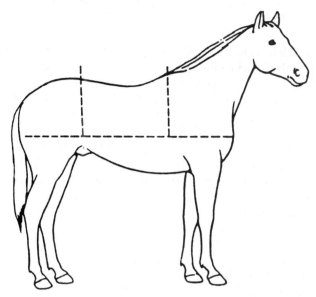

Figure 3. Balance is evaluated by dividing the body into three equal parts.

Unsoundnesses and blemishes

As noted before, some conformational variations are unsightly without affecting performance, while others do need to be avoided. Here we will look at the horse from the front, side and rear and look at some of the more common conformational idiosyncrasies.

The knees

Few horses when viewed from the front have flawless conformation. Because the front legs carry over 60% of the horse's weight, horsemen have long understood the need to avoid some of the conformational defects as being unsuitable for the performance animal. These include:

Bench knees. When the cannons (as viewed from the front) fail to come out of the center of the knees. This fault very often causes large splints to develop.

Bow-knees. Bow-kneed horses often stand over the outside of their front feet. This faulty position brings undue weight upon the outside position of the front feet, especially the outside lateral cartilages, often causing early formation of "side bones."

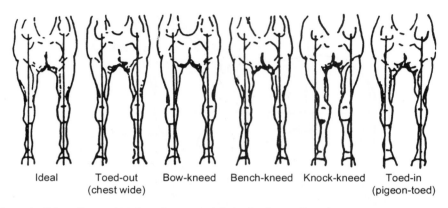

| Ideal | Toed-out (chest wide) | Bow-kneed | Bench-kneed | Knock-kneed | Toed-in (pigeon-toed) |

Figure 4. Schematic representation of correct and faulty frontleg conformation.

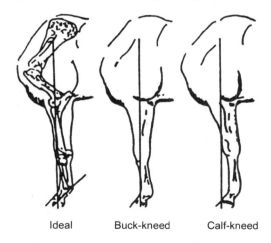

| Ideal | Buck-kneed | Calf-kneed |

Figure 5. Conformation of the forelimb viewed from the side.

Knock-knees. Horses that stand in at the knees or are too close at the knees. Knock-kneed conditions are caused by the bones of the upper and lower leg not entering and leaving the knee squarely.

Pigeon-toed. A pigeon-toed horse appears to be standing with the aim of the hoof turned toward the center of the body. Such a horse commonly exhibits paddling as a result of this imperfection.

Buck-knees. Buck-kneed horses are ones over-at the knees or whose knees protrude too far forward when viewed from the side. Buck-knees are not considered as severe a fault as calf knees.

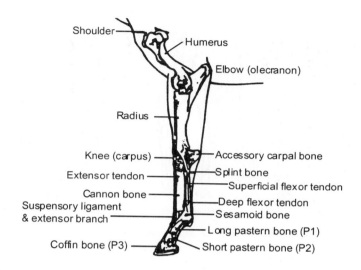

Figure 6. Basic anatomy of the equine forelimb.

Calf-knees. Knees (when viewed from the side) that break backward. They are objectionable because bowed tendons and knee ailments often develop.

The hind legs

Although they do not bear as much weight as the front legs, the hind legs provide the propulsion for the body and conformation is important here also.

Bow-legged. When a horse stands pigeon-toed on its hind feet, with the points of its hocks turned outward, it is said to stand bow-legged behind. Such horses go wide at the hocks, making collected performance impossible. A horse should work with its hocks fairly close together, not wide apart

Cow-hocked. A cow-hocked horse stands with the point of the hocks turned inward, while being base wide and splay-footed.

Camped out. The rear legs are set out behind the back of the hip. Usually starts at the hocks and continues down the lower leg.

Sickle hocked. The rear legs have too much set to the hocks and when viewed from the side, resemble a sickle.

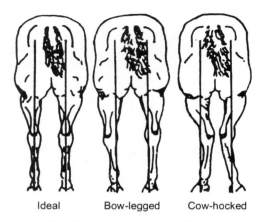

| Ideal | Bow-legged | Cow-hocked |

Figure 7. Correct and faulty conformation of the hindlegs (rear view).

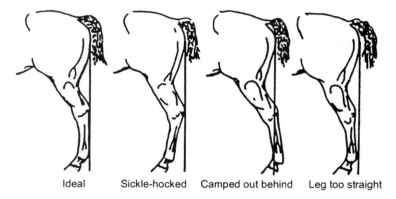

| Ideal | Sickle-hocked | Camped out behind | Leg too straight |

Figure 8. Correct and faulty conformation of the hindlegs (side views).

Other common defects

Blood spavin. An enlarged or varicose vein on the inside of the hock; does not cause
lameness.

Bog spavin. A soft filling of the natural depression on the inside and front of the hock.

Bone spavin. A bony enlargement on the inside and front of the hock where the base of the hock tapers into the cannon bone of the lower leg. Bone spavin is an inheritable weakness and one of the most destructive conditions affecting a horse's usefulness. The lameness is most evident when the animal is used following rest.

Bowed tendons. A thickened enlargement of any one or all of a group of tendons and ligaments (usually the superficial flexor tendon, deep flexor tendon and suspensory ligament) which occupy the posterior space in the cannon region between knee and fetlock joint or between hock and fetlock joint. Bowed tendon is the name horsemen apply to ruptured tendon tissue and is more commonly seen on front legs than on rear legs.

Capped hocks, knees and elbows. Swellings located respectively, on the point of the hock, front of the knee and tip of the elbow. They are caused by injuries which result in excess secretion of the synovial fluid.

Curb. Enlargement of the hock tendon or ligament on the upper part of the cannon just below the point of the hock; caused by injury or strain.

Fistula. An inflamed condition in the withers region, commonly thought caused by bruising. Fistula and "poll evil" are very similar except for location.

Forging. A defect in the way-of-going, characterized by the striking of the supporting forefoot by the striding hindfoot on the same side.

Founder (laminitis). A serious ailment of the fleshy laminae. It can be caused by overeating, overwork, giving hot animals too much cold water or inflammation of the uterus following foaling. All feet may be affected, but the front ones are more susceptible.

Hernia or rupture. The protrusion of any internal organ through the wall of its containing cavity. It usually means passing part of the intestine through an opening in the abdominal muscle. A hernia is a genetic imperfection.

Hip down. Fracture of the hip bone with a falling away; may cause lameness with a crooked hitching gait; due to injury.

Interfering. A defect in the way-of-going, characterized by the striking of the fetlock or cannon of the supporting leg by the opposite foot that is in motion.

Navicular disease. Inflammation of the navicular bone area due to faulty conformation caused by excessive concussion to the foot (nerved horses are considered unsound).

Osselet. Abnormal bony growth at the fetlock joint.

Parrot mouth. A hereditary imperfection in how the teeth come together It is caused by the lower jaw beng shorter than the upper jaw (also known as "overbite"). The reverse of this condition, "monkey mouth" or "underbite," is caused by the lower jaw being longer than the upper jaw.

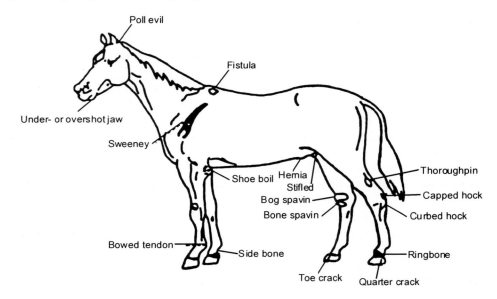

Figure 9. Some common blemishes and unsoundnesses of the horse.

Ring bone. Bony enlargement near the coronary band which may involve the pastern joint or coffin joint; usually associated with stress and faulty conformation.

Side bone. Loss of flexibility of the lateral cartilages usually in the forefeet caused by ossification; excessive concussion and poor conformation contribute to the condition.

Splint. Calcification between the splint and cannon bones due to injury, stress or faulty conformation.

Stifled. Dislocation of the patella causing a fixation of the leg in an extended position due to injury; faulty conformation may be a contributing factor.

Sweeney. Atrophy or degeneration of the shoulder muscle(s) due to loss of nerve supply.

Thoroughpin. A puffy condition in the hollow of the hock. The puff can be seen mostly on the outside, but is movable when palpated. Thoroughpin rarely causes lameness.

Windpuff. A puffy enlargement of the pastern joint, also referred to as "windgall." The enlargement is a fluid filled distension of the bursa (joint sac or capsule).

Travel or way of going

Although the degree of action of the horse will vary somewhat with the type and breed, the usefulness of all horses depends on their action and their ability to move in various types of racing, driving, hunting and riding. In all types and breeds, the motion should be straight and true with a long swift and elastic stride.

Length. Distance from the point of breaking over to the point of contact of the same foot.

Directness or trueness. The line in which the foot is carried forward during the stride.

Spring. Manner in which the weight is settled upon the supporting structure at the completion of the stride.

Step. The distance between imprints of the two forelegs or two hindlegs.

Stride. The distance between successive imprints of the same foot.

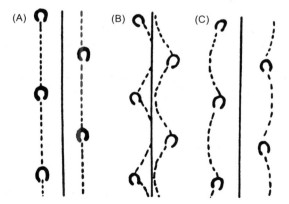

Figure 10. A. Normal foot moves in a straight line.
B. "Base-wide," or "Toed-out" feet move forward in inward arcs, "winging."
C. "Base Narrow," or "Pigeon Toed" feet move forward in wide outward arcs, "paddling."

Evaluating travel is a challenge similar to evaluating structural correctness in that deviations in the flight of the feet may range from slight to severe with some deviations being more serious than others. For example, both dishing (winging in) and paddling out are common deviations. However, dishing is a much more serious fault. If the condition is severe enough, interference between the supporting and striding legs and feet may occur.

In addition to evaluating trueness of stride, you should also observe length of stride. A short, choppy stride will result in poor ground coverage and a rough gait. Conversely, an extremely long, over reaching stride may lead to interference between the fore and rear feet and legs.

The following are some of the most common traveling faults typically associated with or caused by structural deviations. It is not uncommon for a structurally correct horse to be faulty in its movement or for a structurally incorrect horse to move in a fairly true manner.

Paddling out is commonly associated with horses that stand pigeon-toed or toed-in. The flight path of the feet tend to follow an outward arc.

Dishing (winging in) is commonly associated with horses that stand splay-footed or toed-out. The flight path of the feet tend to follow an inward arc.

Winding (rope walking) is a twisting of the striding leg and foot around the supporting leg and foot. The tracks appear very close or nearly in a straight line

Forging is the contact between the sole or shoe of the fore foot with the toe of the rear foot due to over reach.

Scalping is another form of over-reaching in which there is contact between the coronary band of the hind foot and the toe of the fore foot.

This paper was first published in "Focus on Equine Nutrition," Proceedings for the 1996 Short Course for Feed Manufacturers

ENERGY AND THE PERFORMANCE HORSE

JOE D. PAGAN

Kentucky Equine Research, Inc., Versailles, Kentucky, USA

Introduction

Among the nutrients that are important to the performance horse, energy is the dietary factor most affected by exercise. Energy is not a nutrient *per se* but is, rather, a measure of a feed's potential to fuel body functions and exercise.

This discussion of equine energetics will encompass two separate, yet closely related, topics. The first deals with the particular pathways and substrates used by the horse to produce a chemical intermediate that fuels muscle contraction during exercise and depends on the intensity and duration of the exercise. The second topic is related to how various sources of energy in the horse's diet can be used to provide or replace the energy used during exercise.

Energy generation during exercise

The main productive function in horses is work. This may vary from high speed racing at speeds up to 45 miles/hour for short distances to endurance racing at slower speeds for 50 miles or more, to draft work where horses pull or carry heavy loads for variable amounts of time. The basic driving force behind all of these different types of equine performance is the conversion of chemically bound energy from feed into mechanical energy for muscular movement.

Since horses do not eat continuously while they exercise, feed energy must be stored in the horse's body for later release. There are a number of different storage forms that the horse can utilize, including intramuscular glycogen and triglycerides and extra muscular stores such as adipose tissue and liver glycogen. Many factors determine the proportion of energy derived from each storage form including speed and duration of work, feed, fitness, muscle fiber composition and age of the horse.

Work capacity depends on the rate at which energy is supplied to and used by muscles for contraction. A molecule called adenosine triphosphate (ATP) is used to produce muscular activity (figure 1). The most direct way to form ATP is by the cleavage of another compound, called creatine phosphate (CP). However, since muscle contains only small amounts of CP and ATP, the supplies are exhausted after a short duration of exercise. Prolonged exercise would not be possible unless there were ways for ATP to be resynthesized at the same rate at which it were used. Two fundamental reactions resynthesize ATP:

1)   *Oxidative phosphorylation* breaks down carbohydrates, fats and protein into energy (ATP) with the involvement of oxygen. The use of oxygen qualifies this as an aerobic reaction.

2)   *Glycolysis* breaks down glucose or glycogen into lactic acid. This reaction doesn't use oxygen and is considered anaerobic.

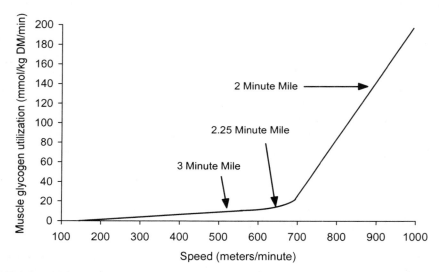

Figure 1. Muscle glycogen utilization as a function of speed

Large quantities of energy can be derived from the utilization of intramuscular (triglyceride and glycogen) and extracellular (free fatty acids from adipose and glucose from the liver) fuels. The total amount of fuel stored in a 1,000 lb (450 kg) horse is shown in Table 1.

Table 1. AMOUNTS OF FUEL STORED IN HORSE MUSCLE.

Fuel	Tissue	Grams
triglyceride	muscle	1,400-2,800
triglyceride	adipose	40,000
glycogen	muscle	3,150-4,095
glycogen	liver	90-220

Muscle fiber types

The horse has three basic types of muscle fiber: Type I, IIA, and IIB. These fiber types have different contractile and metabolic characteristics (table 2). Type I fibers are slow contracting fibers while types IIA and IIB are fast contracting. The type I and IIA fibers have a high oxidative capacity and can thus utilize fuels aerobically while type IIB fibers have a low aerobic capacity and tend to depend on anaerobic glycolysis for energy generation. All three fiber types are very high in glycogen while only type I and IIA have triglyceride storage.

Table 2. METABOLIC CHARACTERISTICS OF DIFFERENT MUSCLE FIBER TYPES.

Classification	Type I ST	Type II FTH (II A)	FT (II B)
Speed of contraction	slow	fast	fast
Max. tension developed	low	high	high
Oxidative capacity	high	intermediate to high	low
Capillary density	high	intermediate	low
Lipid content	high	intermediate	low
Glycogen content	intermediate	high	high
Fatiguability	low	intermediate	high

Substrate utilization during exercise

The amount of ATP used by a muscle depends directly on how fast it is contracting. While walking, the muscles contract very slowly and expend relatively small amounts of ATP. During this type of exercise, type I fibers are primarily recruited and energy generation is entirely aerobic. At this speed, the muscle burns predominantly fat. Fat stores are plentiful and they can be mobilized and metabolized fast enough to regenerate what ATP is used at a walk. As speed increases from a walk to a trot to a canter, type I fibers alone are no longer capable of contracting rapidly enough to propel the horse. At this point, type IIA fibers are also recruited. These fibers are also aerobic, but they use a combination of glycogen and fat for energy generation. Glycogen (or glucose) can be metabolized aerobically twice as fast as fat for ATP generation and as speed increases, fat becomes simply too slow a fuel for energy generation. As the horse increases speed to a fast gallop, type IIB fibers are recruited and energy generation no longer remains purely aerobic. Anaerobic glycolysis is the fastest metabolic pathway available to generate ATP and the horse must depend heavily on this to maintain high rates of speed. Anaerobic glycolysis results, however, in lactic acid accumulation and fatigue soon develops as the pH in the muscle begins to fall.

The endurance horse typically travels at speeds which can be maintained almost entirely through aerobic energy generation. Only during hill climbing and for short intervals is the horse's ATP demand too great for aerobic regeneration. Fatigue in endurance horses is much more likely to result from glycogen depletion than from lactic acid accumulation.

Racehorses, eventers and many of the western performance horses perform at much higher intensities of exercise. These horses depend heavily on anaerobic glycolysis for energy generation and fatigue is most likely to result from lactic acid accumulation rather than glycogen depletion.

Substrate utilization in the horse can be investigated by using biopsy techniques of both the muscle and the liver. These biopsies are safe and can be taken repeatedly to determine how much muscle glycogen is used at different intensities of work. In addition, substances in the blood and respiratory gases can be used to paint a metabolic picture of substrate utilization during various intensities of exercise. The middle gluteal muscle is the most convenient muscle to biopsy when studying intramuscular substrate utilization. This muscle typically contains between 500 and 700 millimole (mmol) of glycogen per kilogram (kg) of dry weight. During endurance exercise (7.5 to 11.5 mph), horses will typically use muscle glycogen at a rate from 0.5 to 1.5 mmol/kg/min. The remainder of the energy generated at this rate of speed comes from fat oxidation. As speed increases, muscle glycogen utilization increases. At a speed of around 650 meters/min. (a 2:25 mile), ATP production can no longer be completely satisfied by aerobic pathways. At this point, anaerobic pathways become an important source of energy. In shifting to this type of energy production, the use of glycogen and the accumulation of lactic acid increase exponentially.

Figure 1 shows the amount of muscle glycogen used per minute in relation to speed. These data are compiled from a number of different breeds. Notice that when the horse runs at speeds of less than 650 meters/minute, very little glycogen is used. However, when speed is increased, the horse crosses what is known as its *"anaerobic threshold"* and the use of muscle glycogen increases dramatically.

The basic reason for this increase is that anaerobic glycogen utilization is 12 times less efficient than aerobic glycogen utilization. When glycogen is metabolized aerobically, 36 ATPs are produced, but when glycogen is metabolized anaerobically, only 3 ATPs are produced (2 molecules of lactate are also produced).

Dietary energy considerations

Dietary energy is usually expressed in terms of kilocalories (kcal) or megacalories (Mcal) of digestible energy. Digestible energy (DE) refers to the amount of energy in the diet that is absorbed by the horse. Digestible energy requirements are calculated based on the horse's maintenance DE requirement plus the additional energy expended during exercise. Basically, DE can be provided by four different dietary energy sources: starch, fat, protein and fiber (table 3).

Table 3. DIETARY ENERGY SOURCES AVAILABLE TO THE PERFORMANCE HORSE.

Energy source	Starch	Fat	Protein	Fiber
Common feed source	Corn (70%) Barley (66%) Oats (50%)	Vegetable oil Animal fat	Soybean meal Alfalfa	Hay Beet Pulp
Site of absorption	small intestine	small intestine	small intestine	large intestine
Form(s) absorbed	glucose	lactic acid	glycerol FFA	amino acids, acetate, propionate, butyrate
Aerobic Energy	yes	yes	yes	yes
Anaerobic Energy	yes	no*	no	no*

*Form absorbed cannot be used anaerobically, but these energy sources can be used to make glucose, an anaerobic substrate.

Starch

Starch, a carbohydrate composed of a large number of glucose molecules, is the primary component of cereal grains, making up 50 to 70% of the grain's dry matter. Of the grains commonly fed to horses, corn has the highest starch content. Starch is a versatile energy source for the performance horse. Horses break down starch into glucose units in the small intestine, where it is absorbed into the blood. Once in the blood, these glucose units can be used for a number of different purposes:

1) They can be oxidized directly to produce ATP.
2) Blood glucose can be used to make muscle glycogen, liver glycogen or body fat.

Muscle glycogen is an important fuel for energy generation during exercise. In addition, glycogen is stored in the liver where it is available for the production and release of glucose into the blood during exercise. Maintaining blood glucose levels during exercise is of prime importance since glucose is the only fuel that is available to the central nervous system. Hypoglycemia is another potential cause of fatigue in exercised horses.

Starch is the dietary energy source of choice for glycogen synthesis since starch digestion results in a direct rise in blood glucose and insulin, two of the most important factors involved in glycogen synthesis.

There is a limit, however, to the amount of starch which a performance horse's ration should contain. If large amounts of starch are fed in a single meal, the small intestine's ability to digest and absorb the starch may be overwhelmed, and a substantial amount of the starch may pass into the large intestine where it will be rapidly fermented to lactic acid by bacteria. An increase in acid will lower the pH of the hind gut. This may kill other bacteria and lead to the release of endotoxins into the blood. The combination of these two factors may lead to colic or laminitis.

Fat

Fat is a less versatile energy source than starch since it can only be oxidized aerobically to produce energy or stored as body fat. Fatty acids cannot be converted to glucose or used to synthesize glycogen.

There is reason to believe, however, that feeding fat may have a sparing effect on muscle glycogen in endurance horses. Research which I conducted in Sweden with Standardbred horses indicated that feeding fat to horses resulted in a greater mobilization and utilization of fat during long distance exercise. In this experiment, horses fed high levels of soybean oil (15% of the concentrate) had higher concentrations of free fatty acids in their blood than horses fed high carbohydrate or high protein diets. Respiratory quotients (RQ) were also lower in the fat fed horses during these exercise tests, indicating that a greater proportion of their energy was being generated from fat than in the control group of horses. Unfortunately, the horses fed the high fat diets had lower muscle and liver glycogen storage than the control group. Therefore, it is important to supply adequate starch in the horse's diet as well.

Protein

If the protein requirement of a performance horse exceeds its requirement, then the extra protein can be used as a source of energy. The amino acids from this extra protein are broken down by the liver, and the nitrogen from the protein is excreted as ammonia. The carbon "skeletons" that are left can be oxidized to produce ATP or used to make glucose or fat.

Excessive protein intake should be avoided in the exercised horse for a number of reasons:

1)   Water requirements increase with increased protein intake.

2)   Urea levels increase in the blood leading to greater urea excretion into the gut, which may increase the risk of intestinal disturbances such as enterotoxemia.

3)   Blood ammonia increases causing a number of problems such as nerve irritability and disturbances in carbohydrate metabolism.

Increased ammonia excretion in the urine may also lead to respiratory problems because of ammonia buildup in the stall.

Fiber

Fiber is an energy source that is often overlooked in horse nutrition. Horses have a highly developed hind gut which houses billions of bacteria and protozoa capable of fermenting large quantities of fiber. The endproducts of fiber fermentation can be used as energy sources throughout the day since fermentation continues long after a meal has been eaten.

Since proper gut function is essential to the health and well-being of the horse, fiber should be considered an essential nutrient. Hay should be fed at a rate of intake equal to at least 1% of body weight per day. Grasses that are less mature at harvest make the best horse hay. An interesting alternative energy source for performance horses is beet pulp, a by-product of the sugar beet industry, made by drying the residual pulp after the sugar has been extracted. It contains a high percent of fermentable fiber and its DE content is similar to oats.

Conclusion

The rations of performance horses should include a mixture of energy sources. In this regard, moderation is the key. Excessive amounts of starch should be avoided as this may lead to colic, founder, or "tying up" in horses. Too much fat may compromise glycogen storage and excessive protein may lead to problems associated with ammonia production. Fiber must be included in the diet to maintain proper hind gut function. Including the correct mixture of these energy sources in the performance horse's ration should reduce problems associated with feeding and allow the horse to utilize energy generating substrates most efficiently during exercise.

This paper was first published in "Feeding the Performance Horse," Proceedings for the 1992 Short Course for Feed Manufacturers

THE GUT DURING EXERCISE

STEPHEN E. DUREN

Kentucky Equine Research, Inc.,Versailles, Kentucky, USA

Introduction

Popularity of the horse for athletic competition, coupled with the tremendous economic importance of the horse, has stimulated increased study of equine exercise physiology. Studies in equine exercise physiology have taken many different avenues, two of the most popular being cardiopulmonary and muscular adaptations to exercise and nutrition of the "equine athlete." Although progress has been made in each area, only recently have studies been conducted which bridge the two fields of study.

In an effort to link diet with exercise performance, many studies have evaluated differences in performance associated with manipulation of various dietary ingredients. Several studies have shown a positive performance response to manipulation of assorted dietary ingredients, fat (vegetable oil) being one of the ingredients receiving a great deal of study. Other researchers have begun to look at not only what we feed athletic horses, but also when we feed these horses prior to exercise. The response of the digestive system is a key factor in determining which ingredients to manipulate and ultimately when to manipulate them. To understand fully how the digestive system can influence exercise performance, one must first appreciate the size and weight of the equine digestive system. Next, one should understand the impact that feeding has on the digestive system, and what impact exercise has on gut function and nutrient digestibility. Finally, this information must be summarized into a series of recommendations relative to what and when to feed horses that are involved in different types of exercise.

The equine digestive system

Anatomically, horses have developed a specialized digestive system which allows them to not only survive, but thrive on high fiber diets (Figure 1). The cecum (C) and colon (D) collectively account for approximately 64% of the empty weight of the horse's digestive system (Meyer *et al.*, 1993). These two structures, known as the hindgut, are estimated to hold between 24 - 36 gallons of liquid (Householder *et al.*, 1993), and house billions of bacteria and protozoa that ferment plant fiber. The horse's small, one compartment stomach (A) makes up less than 7% of the empty weight of the digestive system (Meyer *et al.*, 1993), and stresses the need for a continual intake of feedstuffs. The small intestine (B) is the single longest and heaviest (empty tissue weight) structure in the horse's digestive system, making up 27.5% of the total gastrointestinal tract weight.

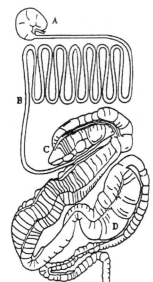

A   Stomach
B   Small intestine
C   Cecum
D   Colon

Figure 1. The horse's digestive tract

Taken together, the empty tissue weight of the stomach, small intestine and large fiber fermenting hindgut account for approximately 5% of the body weight of the mature horse. A fed (non-fasted) horse, however, has a fluid capacity within the digestive system of nearly 50 gallons (Householder *et al.*, 1993). After accounting for the weight of the digesta and associated fluid, a much larger percentage of the horse's body weight is associated with the digestive system. This can be appreciated when one considers that a partial fast (24 hours) can result in a 3.5% decrease in body weight for mature physically conditioned ponies (Duren, 1990).

The impact of feeding

One does not have to feed many horses before realizing that horses have a profound cardiovascular response to feeding. The noise associated with rattling buckets in a feed room can send a stable of horses into a pre-feeding frenzy. This phase of feeding is known in the scientific literature as the anticipation/ingestion phase. The anticipation/ingestion phase refers to the period when the animal is aware of an upcoming feeding and continues during ingestion of food. Horses, like many other animal models, respond to the anticipation/ingestion phase of feeding with increased cardiovascular activity. This cardiovascular response generally decreases after the ingestion of food (postprandial phase). In ponies, the cardiovascular response to feeding remains elevated for more than one hour following consumption of a grain meal (Duren, 1990).

Along with cardiovascular changes in response to feeding, changes can also occur in the distribution of blood flow within the body. The distribution of blood flow within the body is controlled by two mechanisms. It is controlled centrally through the nervous system, and locally by the environmental conditions in the immediate vicinity of the blood vessels (Berne and Levy, 1988). Central control of blood flow is mediated by the autonomic nervous system and primarily by the sympathetic nerve fibers (Goodman and Gilman, 1985). Increased sympathetic nerve activity (excitement/panic) causes vasoconstriction in the arterioles of the abdominal viscera, while causing vasodilation of arterioles in skeletal muscle. This scheme shunts blood away from the digestive system to working muscles in an adrenaline driven "flight" response.

Local control of peripheral blood flow appears to be adjusted to the existing metabolic activity of the tissue (Berne and Levy, 1988). According to the metabolic model of tissue blood flow, any intervention that results in an oxygen supply that is inadequate for the requirements of the tissues gives rise to the formation of vasodilator metabolites. These metabolites are released from the tissue and act locally to dilate the arterioles, increasing the flow of blood and the supply of oxygen.

Blood is distributed and redistributed to the various tissues of the body by a combination of central and local control of arteriolar smooth muscle. Duren (1990) reported that in fasted ponies (24 hour fast), 20.4% of cardiac output (blood flow) is distributed to the various tissues of the digestive system, while 79.6% of the blood flow is found in other tissues including skeletal muscle (Figure 2). Once a horse is fed, the amount of blood distributed to the gastrointestinal tract increases (Duren, 1990). This mesenteric hyperemia is confined to the digestive organs actively engaged in digestive functions. Muscle blood flow does not change as a function of feeding in ponies. The net result of feeding in horses is a redistribution of cardiac output (Figure 3) such that 27.4% of blood flow is distributed to the various tissues of the digestive system, while 72.6% of the blood flow is found in non-digestive tissue (Duren, 1990).

Besides changing the distribution of blood flow within the body, feeding has the obvious result of increasing the amount of material in the digestive system. This has a profound impact on the body weight of the animal. Meyer (1987) summarized that for every one kilogram of dry hay intake, approximately 10 kg of water is ingested. Eating hay stimulates saliva production (Meyer, 1987) and an increase in the secretion of digestive juices into the gastrointestinal tract. Much of the fluid in these secretions comes from blood plasma, resulting in a drop in plasma volume (Pagan, 1997). Decreased plasma volume then stimulates a thirst response and horses drink water. Fiber also has the capacity to bind water in the digestive system.

This facilitates the holding of water in the hindgut as the amount of fiber in the diet increases. Van Soest (1984) reported that fiber binds water at a rate of 1 - 5 ml/g of fiber. The amount of water ingested with mixed diets (forage + concentrate) is roughly half that of all forage diets.

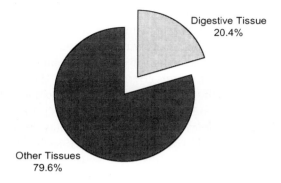

Figure 2. Estimated distribution of cardiac output in fasted ponies at rest.

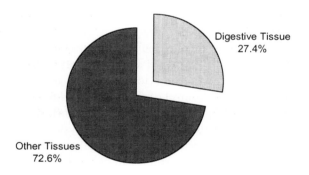

Figure 3. Estimated distribution of cardiac output in fed ponies at rest.

With changes in fluid content of the gut a characteristic of different feeds, the type of diet fed to performance horses can have an impact on body weight during exercise. This can be illustrated by calculating the energy requirement for a given performance horse, then calculating the amount of feed necessary to satisfy this requirement. The amount of feed necessary to maintain energy balance in a performance horse being fed either a 100% forage diet, a 50% forage plus 50% oat diet, or a 45% forage, 45% oat, 10% vegetable oil diet would be different due to the increased energy content of the mixed diets. Kronfeld (1997) calculated that a performance horse would consume 22.2 kg of forage compared to 16.6 kg of mixed feed and 12.9 kg of mixed feed plus vegetable oil to maintain body weight. The fat supplemented diet reduced feed intake by 22%, fecal output (gut fill) by 31% and water requirement by 12 %. Similarly, Pagan*et al.*, (1997) reported that performance horses working at moderate intensity consumed 10% more feed when fed an all forage diet compared with a mixed forage and grain diet. Further, the horses on the all forage diet consumed 33% more water than horses eating the mixed diet. To summarize these research reports, it appears the higher the fiber content of the diet, the greater the fluid content of the digestive system and the more weight carried by the horse.

Exercise and gut function

Limited information exists regarding changes in blood flow distribution during exercise in fed compared with fasted horses. Duren (1990) measured blood flow distribution during exercise in eight fed ponies and eight fasted ponies. The fasted group did not receive feed during the 24 hours preceding data collection. During this 24-hour period, these ponies were housed in a stall containing water and salt, but devoid of bedding material. The fed treatment group was provided free-choice alfalfa hay, water and salt during the 24 hours preceding data collection. In addition, these ponies consumed a pelleted grain concentrate at a rate of 0.7% of body weight 1.4 hours preceding data collection. Each group of ponies was monitored at rest and during 30 minutes of treadmill exercise. The treadmill was positioned at a 7% incline and set at a speed of 28 km/hour such that the ponies reached a heartrate greater than 150 beats/minute. This intensity of exercise is approximately 75% of heart rate maximum.

   Blood flow to the digestive tract decreased during exercise in both fasted and fed ponies; however, blood flow was consistently higher throughout exercise in fed ponies (figures 4 and 5).

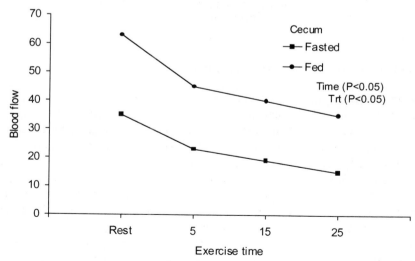

Figure 4. Blood flow (ml/100g tissue/min) to the cecum in fasted and fed ponies at rest and during exericse. SEM for cecum was 5.8

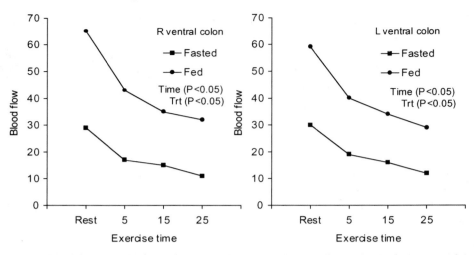

Figure 5. Blood flow (ml/100g tissue/min) to the right ventral colon and left ventral colon in fasted and fed ponies at rest and during exercise. SEM for right ventral colon and left ventral colon were 5.3 and 4.6 respectively.

It is speculated that fed ponies had an elevated blood flow at rest, associated with increased digestive tissue oxygen demand, and the increased sympathetic tone produced during exercise was not large enough to totally reverse this hyperemia. As would be expected, blood flow to the locomotor and respiratory muscles increased during exercise in both fed and fasted ponies (Duren, 1990). However, blood flow to both locomotor (figure 6) and respiratory muscles (figure 7) was higher in fed than in fasted ponies.

Duren (1990) speculated that fed ponies worked harder during exercise, as evidenced by increased muscle blood flow, due to increased gut fill associated with feeding. Since the fed ponies exercised at approximately 75% of heart rate maximum, they were able to increase heart rate, cardiac output and stroke volume (figure 8) to deliver an increased amount of blood to both the digestive tract and working muscle.

With the knowledge that blood flow is shunted away from the gastrointestinal tract during exercise, the next logical question may be: what is the effect of exercise on nutrient digestibility? Most digestibility studies in horses have been conducted with idle horses confined to metabolism stalls. The values obtained from these studies are used for all classes of horses including the performance horse. Pagan *et al.,* (1997) reported that exercise resulted in a small but statistically significant decrease in dry matter digestibility. In that study, exercise consisted of walking, trotting and cantering approximately 5 miles/day on an inclined (3°) treadmill. It is not known if the 1% decrease in dry matter digestibility reported by Pagan is actually biologically significant to the animal, but it does pose some interesting questions:

1)   At what level of exercise intensity and duration would one expect to negatively influence nutrient digestibility?

2)   Does the term "over training," a situation when the performance and body weight of a horse actually decline during heavy training, represent potential limits in digestive efficiency?

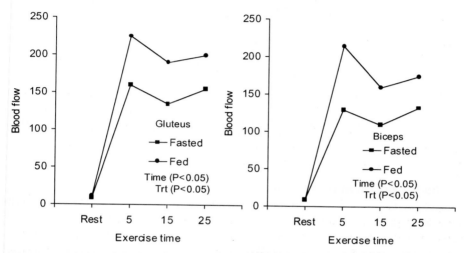

Figure 6. Blood flow (ml/100g tissue/min) to the crural diaphragm and costal diaphragm in fasted and fed ponies at rest and during exercise. SEM for crural diaphragm and costal diaphragm were 16.5 and 21.9 respectively.

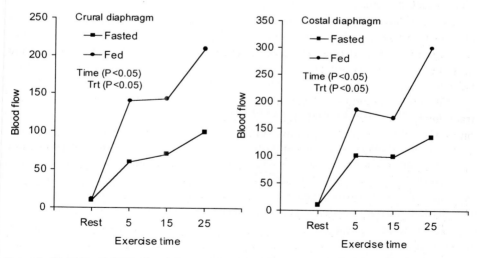

Figure 7. Blood flow (ml/100g tissue/min) to the gluteus medium and biceps femoris in fasted and fed ponies at rest and during exercise. SEM for fluteus medius and biceps femoris were 16.5 and 21.9 respectively.

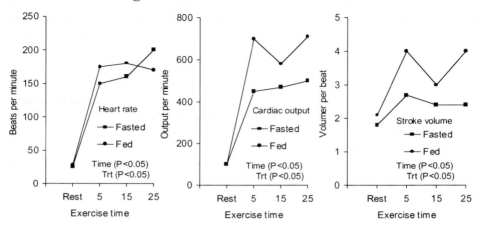

Figure 8. Heart rate (beats/min), cardiac output (9 ml/min/kg) and stroke volume (ml/beat/kg) in fasted and fed ponies at rest and during exercise. SEM for heart rate, cardiac output and stroke volume were 4.6, 40.3 and 0.2, respectively.

Feeding the performance horse

The preceding pages have detailed: the size and weight of the equine digestive system; changes in the distribution of blood flow associated with feeding; differences in gut fill and water intake associated with different diets and changes in blood flow and nutrient digestibility associated with exercise. From this information, one must attempt to determine the type of diet and the pre-exercise feeding schedule that will allow horses to perform at optimal levels. The following are some guidelines which may help in answering those questions. For the following examples, exercise performance has been classified into the following categories: 1) high intensity, short duration, 2) moderate intensity, medium duration, and 3) low intensity, long duration.

High intensity, short duration exercise

During high intensity, short duration exercise, the horse is working at near heart rate maximum. The horse can only maintain performance, at this level of exertion, for a short period of time (less than 10 minutes). One example of this type of exercise is flat track racing. Due to the short duration of this exercise, it is generally thought that nutrients needed to fuel muscle contraction must be stored in the muscle prior to exercise. Therefore, feeding horses with the intention of "loading" the blood with nutrients to be metabolized during short-term exercise does not appear beneficial. In fact, Stull and Rodiek (1995) and Pagan (1997) reported that grain feeding within four hours prior to submaximal exercise caused large declines in blood glucose during exercise. These declines in blood sugar may be detrimental to exercise performance since glucose is the only fuel metabolized by the central nervous system.

Feeding large fiber meals prior to exercise is not warranted either, since fiber would increase the "dead" weight carried by the horse. Since the speed at which an animal can travel is related to body weight, additional body weight would only serve to slow the animal. Racing officials routinely handicap horses by assigning additional weight to superior runners. If racing officials can potentially change the outcome of a race by assigning as little as 4 lb, what would be the impact of a short-term fast (12 hours) on body weight? Longer periods of fasting would further decrease body weight; potential problems including digestive upset, however, may occur with re-feeding these horses.

FEEDING RECOMMENDATIONS

High intensity, short duration exercise

Hay feeding - eliminate 12 hours prior to exercise
Grain feeding - do not feed within eight hours of exercise
Water - no restrictions

Moderate intensity, medium duration exercise

During moderate intensity, medium duration exercise, the horse is working at a heart rate between 50% and 75% of maximum. Exercise of this intensity may be tolerated for several hours. This type of exercise may include a variety of "show events" in which horses perform in a number of classes throughout the day. Since speed is not the primary concern, the weight (gut fill) of the animal does not appear to be critical. These horses would benefit from small frequent forage meals (partially to eliminate boredom). Grain meals should be avoided within eight hours of performance. This would eliminate large fluctuations in blood glucose associated with feeding and postprandial exercise.

FEEDING RECOMMENDATIONS

Moderate intensity, medium duration exercise

Hay feeding - small frequent meals, avoid large single meals
Grain feeding - eliminate grain within eight hours of exercise
Water - no restrictions

Low intensity, long duration exercise

During low intensity, long duration exercise the horse is typically working at less than 50% of heart rate maximum. At this intensity, exercise can be tolerated all day. Trail riding and some endurance rides are examples of this type of exercise. These horses have increased requirements for water and electrolytes due to the duration of exercise. They would benefit from the water and electrolyte holding characteristics of high fiber diets. The fiber should be of high quality (low degree of lignification) such that fermentation can occur thereby making these nutrients available for absorption. The use of "super" fibers including soybean hulls and beet pulp is warranted due to their high fermentation and water holding capacity. Meals provided during the ride should also maximize forage consumption since forage will stimulate water intake and help maintain hydration. Grain intake should be minimized during the ride in an effort to avoid fluctuations in blood sugar. Dietary fat is recommended to increase the energy density of the diet and to decrease the amount of grain needed in the diet.

FEEDING RECOMMENDATIONS

Low intensity, long duration exercise

Hay feeding - free access to high quality forage (high digestible fiber, low crude protein content)
Grain feeding - eliminate or minimize during day of the ride
Water - no restrictions
Electrolytes - provide pre-ride and early during ride (prior to significant dehydration).

References

Berne, R.M. and M.N. Levy. 1988. Physiology. 2nd Ed. C.V. Mosby Company. St. Louis, MO.

Duren, S.E. 1990. Blood flow distribution in fasted and fed ponies at rest and during endurance exercise. Dissertation. University of Kentucky, Lexington, Kentucky.

Duren, S.E., M. Manohar, B. Sikkes, S. Jackson and J. Baker. 1992. Influence of feeding and exercise on the distribution of intestinal and muscle blood flow in ponies. Pferdeheilkunde, 9/1992 pp. 24.

Goodman, L.S. and A.G. Gilman. 1985. The Pharmacological Basis of Therapeutics. 7th Ed. Macmillan Publishing Co. New York, NY.

Householder, D.D., P.G. Gibbs, G.D. Potter and K.E. Davison. 1993. Digestive system of the horse and feeding management guidelines. In: Horse Industry Handbook. American Youth Horse Council, Inc.

Kronfeld, D.S. 1997. Dietary fat affects heat production and other variables of equine performance especially under hot and humid conditions. Eq. Vet. J.

Meyer, H. 1987. Nutrition of the equine athlete. In: Equine Exercise Physiology 2. J.R. Gillespie and N.E. Robinson, Eds. ICEEP Publications, Edwards Brothers, Inc. Ann Arbor, MI.

Meyer, H., M. Goenen and B. Stadermann. 1993. The influence of size on the weight of the gastrointestinal tract and the liver of horses and ponies. Proc. 13th Equine Nutrition and Physiology Society.

Pagan, J.D. 1997. Carbohydrates in equine nutrition. Proc. 7th Equine Nutrition Conference, Kentucky Equine Research, Inc. (In Press)

Pagan, J.D., P. Harris, T. Brewster-Barnes, S.E. Duren and S.G. Jackson. 1997. The effect of exercise on the digestibility of an all forage or mixed diet in Thoroughbred horses. Proc. 15th Equine Nutrition & Physiology Society. (In Press).

Stull, C.L. and A.V. Rodiek. 1995. Effects of postprandial interval and feed components on stress parameters in exercising Thoroughbreds. Proc. 14th Equine Nutrition and Physiology Society.

Van Soest, P.J. 1984. Some physical characteristics of dietary fibers and their influence on the microbial ecology of the human colon. Proc. Nutr. Soc. 43:25.

This paper was first published in Proceedings, Kentucky Equine Research 1997 Equine Nutrition Conference

PROTEIN REQUIREMENTS OF EQUINE ATHLETES

LAURIE M. LAWRENCE
University of Kentucky, Lexington, Kentucky, USA

Protein catabolism as a fuel source during exercise

How much protein does an athlete require? This question has been pondered by athletes and trainers for decades, if not centuries. It has been suggested that the first support for eating high protein diets came from the work of von Liebig who stated that muscle protein provided the primary fuel for muscle contraction (Wilmore and Freund, 1986), but it appears that even early Greek athletes believed that adding meat to their diets would improve performance (Hickson and Wolinski, 1989). Subsequently, the use of protein as a fuel for exercise was discounted. For example, the 1978 NRC for horses states that exercise does not increase the protein requirement. There is little doubt that quantitatively, carbohydrate and fat are much more important fuels for exercise than protein. Nonetheless, recent studies suggest that some protein may be used during exercise, and that under certain situations, protein may contribute up to 15% of the energy utilized during exercise.

The evidence for the catabolism of protein during exercise comes from the observation of metabolic changes during exercise and from studies using radioisotope- labelled amino acids. When amino acids are used for energy, the carbon skeleton is combusted, but the amino group is not used for energy. Therefore, the amino group must be transported from muscle and then used for synthesis of non-essential amino acids or excreted as urea. Nitrogen is transported from muscle following a transamination reaction in which the amino group is removed from one amino acid and attached to pyruvate, forming alanine. The alanine is transported in the blood to the liver where the nitrogen can be used to form urea and the pyruvate is used for gluconeogenesis. Several studies have documented that plasma alanine concentrations increase with exercise in horses (Miller and Lawrence, 1988; Essen-Gustavsson *et al.*, 1991; Miller-Graber *et al.*, 1991) indicating that some amino acid catabolism is occurring in equine muscle during exercise. In addition, plasma urea concentrations increase following long term exercise (Snow *et al.*, 1982), which is another indication that protein catabolism is occurring during exercise. No studies have examined whether specific amino acids are preferentially catabolized during exercise in the horse; however, studies with humans and rats suggest that the branched chain amino acids, especially leucine, are most important (Young, 1986). Most amino acids in the body are contained in structural proteins, but there are some amino acids free in the plasma and there appear to be some liable proteins in the liver that could provide amino acids for energy production. In addition, exercise may make amino acids available by altering protein turnover, either by increasing protein degradation or decreasing protein synthesis (Booth and Watson, 1985).

Protein use for lean tissue accretion

Some athletes consume high protein diets in order to support changes in body composition, such as increased muscle or lean body mass. This practice is based on the assumption that individuals in training actually do increase lean body mass. In some cases, the absolute amount of lean body mass is not affected by training, although the percentage of the body that is lean mass may be increased. That is, training may result in a reduction in body fat, but not necessarily an increase in muscle mass. In humans, an increase in lean body mass will occur most commonly as a result of strength training. Wilmore and Freund (1986) indicate that weight lifters may experience periods of negative nitrogen balance during heavy training even when protein intakes are high. Effects of training on lean body mass are more likely to occur in the early phases of training and in young athletes that are growing and training simultaneously.

Table 1. DIETARY CRUDE PROTEIN REQUIREMENTS OF 500 KG WORKING HORSES FROM THE 1978 AND 1989 NRC.

Type of work	1978	1989
None (maintenance)	630 grams	656 grams
Light	630 grams	820 grams
Moderate	630 grams	984 grams

Protein requirements of athletic horses

In 1978, the National Research Committee Subcommittee on Horse Nutrition indicated that a 500 kg horse in heavy work had the same protein requirement as a similar horse at maintenance, about 630 g of crude protein. Unfortunately, this recommendation was somewhat impractical because it is difficult to formulate palatable diets that meet a hard-working horse's energy needs without exceeding the protein requirement. In 1989 the crude protein recommendations for working horses were increased (Table 1). The NRC cites several reasons for increasing the crude protein requirement. Horses may lose 1 to 1.5 g N/kg of sweat; thus heavy sweating horses might lose 5-7 g of nitrogen during exercise (Meyer 1987). Freeman *et al.* (1988) reported that nitrogen retention increased with physical training in horses. In that study, nitrogen losses in sweat were not accounted for and thus the amount of retained nitrogen may have been overestimated; however, in either case it could be concluded that exercise increased the nitrogen requirement. Meyer (1987) indicates that an additional reason for increasing endogenous fecal nitrogen losses associated with the higher dry matter intake.

There is probably little controversy concerning the recommendation that regular exercise can elevate the dietary protein requirement of horses. However, there is still considerable discussion as to the extent of the elevation. The 1989 NRC recommendation for horses in hard (intense) work (1320 g) is more than double the 1978 recommendation. The 1989 NRC recommendations for work were arrived at by maintaining the same protein:calorie ratio in the diets for working horses as in the diets for adult horses at maintenance (40 g CP/Mcal DE). Meyer (1987) also suggests using the nutrient:calorie ratio as a guide to determining an adequate protein intake. While these recommendations provide a practical way to adjust protein intake for working horses, they are not necessarily accurate estimates of need. Studies that accurately estimate protein or amino acid requirements of horses in work have not been performed. Some estimate of the appropriateness of the NRC (1989) recommendations may be gained by comparing these recommendation to those made for human athletes. Several sources suggest that 1.0-1.5 g of protein per kilogram of body weight is sufficient for most human athletes (Young, 1986; Dohm, 1984; Wilmore and Freund, 1986). Only weight lifters in rigorous strength training may require more than 2 g of protein per kilogram of body weight (Wilmore and Freund, 1986). If these recommendations are applied to 500 kg horses, the protein requirement would be estimated to be between 500 g (at 1 g/kg BW) and 1000 g (at 2 g/kg BW) per day. These values are well below the crude protein recommendations for working horses; however the types of protein consumed by humans and the types of protein consumed by horses are considerably different. While horses frequently consume low quality protein from forages and cereal grains, humans consume high quality protein from animal sources. Once the differences in digestibility and quality of protein are accounted for, the recommendations for human and equine athletes become more comparable. No studies have been conducted to determine whether protein quality is important for equine athletes. However, in humans, it has been reported that 2.0 g of protein per kg BW from lower quality protein sources (vegetable and fish protein) could be replaced by 1.3 g of protein per kg BW from higher quality sources (meat) (Wilmore and Freund, 1986). Hickson and Wolinski (1989) suggest that the preference of early Greek athletes for meat in their diets may have been related to an improvement in protein quality over the more typical vegetarian diet of the time.

Will protein or amino acid supplementation benefit the equine athlete?

Several authors have reviewed the effects of protein supplementation on human athletes with the general conclusion being that protein supplementation (above 1.5 g/kg BW) has little observable benefit (Horstman 1972; Dohm 1984; Wilmore and Freund 1986; Young 1986 Hickson and Wolinski 1989). In horses, studies have typically found no positive effects of high dietary protein. In fact Patterson *et al.* (1985) concluded that horses at medium or hard work had similar indices of protein status when they consumed isocaloric diets with protein intakes of 0.8 g CP/kg BW or 1.2 g CP/kg BW. However, the intensity of the actual training program in that study is somewhat difficult to interpret. The authors indicated that all horses lost weight while on the study, and the weight loss was greatest in the horses on the lowest protein diet. Furthermore, the horses on the higher protein diet recovered more easily when the horses performed a 1.6 km track test.

Several research experiments have examined the effects of dietary protein on metabolic responses to exercise (Miller *et al.,* 1988, Miller-Graber *et al.,* 1991[a,b]; Pagan *et al.,* 1987). In two of these studies, lactate accumulation during exercise was lower when horses received a diet containing a high level of protein (Miller *et al.,* 1988; Pagan *et al.,* 1987) but in a third study lactate accumulation was unaffected by dietary protein level (Miller-Graber, 1991[a]). Pagan *et al* reported that muscle glycogen was somewhat lower in horses receiving a high protein diet; Miller-Graber *et al* found no effect of protein level on muscle glycogen concentration. At this point, there are no solid research data to support the theory that protein supplementation may be beneficial to equine athletes. Even in the human area, benefits have only been sporadically reported, usually with weight lifters, for which the equine world has no real counterpart.

Because the branched-chain amino acids are the primary amino acids catabolized during exercise, researchers have also evaluated supplementation of these amino acids (especially leucine). Glade (1989) has reported that horses receiving a branched-chain amino acid supplement had lower lactate levels than unsupplemented horses; however, the lactate levels were so low (below the anaerobic threshold) and the work bout so mild (walking on an inclined treadmill) that the relevance of these results is questionable. Further research in this area is necessary before recommendations concerning positive benefits can be made.

Can a high protein diet negatively affect horses?

Although many trainers provide high dietary protein in an effort to improve performance there may be negative effects instead. Glade (1979) surveyed feeding practices in Thoroughbred race horses and found a positive correlation between race time and dietary protein intake; race time was increased by 1 to 3 seconds for every 1000 g of CP ingested above the 1978 recommendation. Meyer (1987) indicates that digestible protein intakes above 2 g/kg BW should be avoided in endurance horses because of effects on water intake, urea and ammonia metabolism. Although an elevation in plasma ammonia level was not observed, Miller-Graber *et al.* (1991[b]) found that exercising horses consuming 1741 g CP/d (> 3 g CP/kg BW) excreted more urea in sweat and had higher plasma urea levels than horses consuming 863 g of CP. In addition, these authors measured urinary orotic acid clearance. Orotic acid production increases when the urea cycle is impaired or when the capacity of the urea cycle to cope with excess nitrogen is overwhelmed. An increase in orotic acid production appeared to be present post-exercise in the horses consuming the high protein diet, suggesting that an intake of 1741 g of CP per day may have exceeded the capacity of the urea cycle. As noted previously, muscle glycogen levels may be affected by dietary protein level (Pagan *et al.*, 1987) which may be detrimental to some types of athletic endeavors. Another potentially deleterious effect of excessive protein intake is increased urinary nitrogen excretion. Meyer (1987) suggests that increased urinary nitrogen may contribute to increased aerial ammonia levels which could negatively impact on respiratory health.

Conclusion

The National Research Council (NRC) Subcommittee on Horse Nutrition increased the dietary crude protein allowance for working horses in 1989. The recommendations were based on some experimental information and practical considerations. Comparison of the recommendations for horses to those used for human athletes suggests that the NRC allowances are adequate. There is no evidence in either the human or equine research literature that protein supplementation above the recommended levels is beneficial to athletic performance. Some studies have suggested that high dietary protein intakes may have metabolic effects that would be deleterious to performance, but critical performance testing has not been conducted.

References

Booth F.W. and P.A. Watson. 1985. Control of adaptations in protein levels in response to exercise. Fed Proc. 44:2292.

Dohm, G.L. 1984. Protein nutrition for the athlete. Clin Sports Med. 3(3):595.

Essen-Gutavsson B., E. Blomstrand, K. Karlstrom *et al.* 1991. Influence of diet on substrate metabolism during exercise. Equine Ex Physiol. 3:288.

Freeman D.W., G.D. Potter, G.T. Schelling *et al.* 1988. Nitrogen metabolism in mature horses at varying levels of work. J Anim Sci. 66:407.

Glade M.J. Nutrition and performance of racing Thoroughbreds. Equine Vet J 1983;15:31.

Glade M.J. Effects of specific amino acid supplementation on lactic acid production by horses exercised on a treadmill. Proc Eleventh Equine Nutr Physiol Symp 1989:244.

Goodman M.N. and N.B. Ruderman. Influence of muscle use on amino acid metabolism. In, Terjung RL, (ed), Exercise and Sports Science Rev, Franklin Inst Press, Philadelphia 1982:1.

Hickson J.F. and I. Wolinski. Human protein intake and metabolism in exercise and sport. In, Hickson J.F., Wolinski I. (ed), Nutrition in Exercise and Sport, CRC Press, Boca Raton 1989:5.

Horstman D. Nutrtion. In, Morgan W.P. (ed) Ergogenic Aids and Muscular Performance, Academic Press NY 1972:343.

Meyer H. Nutrition and the equine athlete. Equine Exer Physiol 1987;2:644.

Miller P.A. and L.M. Lawrence. The effect of dietary protein level on exercising horses. J Anim Sci 1988;66:2185.

Miller-Graber P.A., L.M. Lawrence, J.H. Foreman *et al*. Dietary protein level and energy metabolism during treadmill exercise in horses. J Nutr 1991[a];121:1462.

Miller-Graber P.A., L.M. Lawrence, J.H. Foreman *et al*. Effect of dietary protein level on nitrogen metabolites in exercised Quarter Horses. Equine Exer Physiol 1991[b];3:305.

NRC. Nutrient Requirements of Horses. National Academy Press, Washington DC 1978.

NRC. Nutrient Requirements of Horses. National Academy Press, Washington DC 1989.

Pagan J.D., B. Essen-Gustavsson, A. Lindholm and J. Thornton. The effect of dietary energy source on exercise performance in Standardbred Horses. Equine Exer Physiol 1987;2:686.

Patterson P.H., C.N. Coon and I.M. Hughes. Protein requirements of mature working horses. J Anim Sci 1985;61:187.

Snow D.H., M.G. Kerr, M.A. Nimmo and E.M. Abbot. Alterations in blood, sweat, urine and muscle composition during prolonged exercise in the horse. Vet Rec 1982;110:377.

Wilmore J.H. and B.J. Freund. Nutritional enhancement of athletic performance. In, Winnick, M (ed). Nutrition and Exercise. John Wiley & Sons, NY 1986:67.

Young V. Protein and amino acid metabolism in relation to physical exercise. In, Winnick, M (ed). Nutrition and Exercise. John Wiley and Sons, NY 1986:9.

This paper was first published in "Feeding the Performance Horse," Proceedings for the 1992 Short Course for Feed Manufacturers

BLOOD ANALYSIS AND ITS RELATIONSHIP TO FEEDING THE PERFORMANCE HORSE

PER SPÅNGFORS
Euro-VETS AB, Simlångsdalen, Sweden

Introduction

The discussion in this paper concerns the performance horse, and cannot without proper adjustments be extrapolated to the young growing horse or the pregnant mare.

There is a great danger with blood analyses in that you get a figure on a piece of paper. Most people regard that figure as the absolute truth, and that this figure is static until you take the next blood sample. If the person in question also compares that figure with a reference value and finds his horse's value within the expected limits for health, then the clinical picture is of no concern to him, and no matter how the horse looks, he is sound according to the blood test. If the horse starts in a competition and fails, the person raises his eyebrows and wonders why the blood test failed to tell him that the horse was in no condition to compete.

This somewhat pessimistic scenario could be one reason why people are beginning to lose faith in the analyses. This person should have realized that the figure in his hand is a photograph of a dynamic situation, and was only valid for that particular situation. He should also know that the clinical picture of his horse is the truth, no matter what the blood test and normal values say, and he should have consulted a specialist about the interpretation of the analyses, but the absolute truth is never revealed.

Why use clinical chemistry in the feed industry?

The use of body fluids (blood, urine, milk) for the development of new feeds for the performance horse is possible because we now know more about the desirable reactions after feeding. As a complement to classical methods (digestibility trials, field studies) and in conjunction with exercise physiology trials, the benefits for the feed industry to add clinical chemistry to these research models should be:

1) Good estimate of the metabolic responses after feeding, including fuel utilization and hormonal responses.

2)   Possible to measure waste product production during rest and exercise.

3)   Gives valuable information of the mineral metabolism and turn-over.

4)   Can be used to fine tune the balance of nutrients in a complete feed.

5)   For cheap and easy follow-up studies after feed composition adjustments.

Basic facts

There is an enormous amount of information hidden in a blood sample and a lot of parameters to choose between. Therefore, it is essential to consider some basic facts before the sample is drawn.

1)   The purpose of the test:
     a) Health test
     b) Disease diagnostics
     c) Nutritional control
     d) Performance prognosis

2)   What type of blood to take
     e) Venous (blood to the heart)
     f) Arterial (blood from the heart)

3)   Parameters to analyze

4)   What kind of test-tubes
     g) Serum (no anticoagulant)
     h) Heparin (Sodium or Lithium)
     i) EDTA (Potassium)
     j) Fluoride (for glucose analyses)
     k) Other

5)   When to take the sample
     l) Before and/or after feeding
     m) Before and/or after training

6)   Method of controlling the results
     n) Lab's reference values
     o) The horse itself (previous tests)

7)   Treatment of the sample
     o) Immediate analysis
     p) Stored in ice water or room temperature
     q) Centrifuged or whole blood

Evaluation of feed with blood-tests

Evaluation of feeds by biochemical analyses of blood requires a strategy somewhat different from other sampling techniques. The horse must be its own control and the samples must be taken in narrow intervals. An overnight fast is essential and the first sample is taken before feeding. After feeding, blood is collected with 30 minutes to 1 hour intervals until 4 hours post feeding. The first sample, before feeding, reflects the absorption of nutrients from the hindgut and the metabolic response to hindgut fermentation. The other samples reflect the absorption of nutrients from the small intestines and the metabolic response to that absorptive phase. This is hence a good way to study the hormonal changes after feeding and can therefore be used to interpret how long after feeding the horse is work intolerant. It is also possible to get a rough idea how long the feed takes to pass the small intestines (when certain values return to "before feeding" figures).

Urine and mineral studies

Many studies of minerals including electrolytes use a technique called urine fractional excretion, FE (sometimes called creatinine clearance or fractional clearance). The renal clearance of a mineral is expressed as a percentage of the excretion of creatinine.

A urine sample and a blood sample are taken no more than one hour apart. Both the serum and the urine are analyzed for the studied minerals and creatinine. The fractional excretion ratio is calculated from the equation:

$$\frac{\text{Mineral } urine}{\text{Mineral } serum} \times \frac{\text{Creatinine } serum}{\text{Creatinine } urine} \times 100$$

This technique assumes that the urine excretion of creatinine is constant which is not always the case. There are some inborn errors as we shall comment.

Creatinine is a degradation product of creatine, an energy rich compound found in muscles as phosphocreatine. The formation of creatinine in non-meat eating animals is dependent on 1) the rate of synthesis of creatine (from amino acids arginine, glycine and methionine), 2) the formation of creatinine from creatine and 3) the muscle mass (Finco, 1989).

Creatinine is highly soluble in water and is therefore equally distributed in intra and extra cellular tissues. The urine excretion is consequently constant with these important exceptions. A) The formation of creatinine from creatine rises in exercising animals. B) The excretion of creatinine is lowered in kidney diseases (even in sub clinical cases) (Finco, 1989). C) Creatinine excretion can also be affected by diet even if no creatinine is present in the feed (Lindberg and Jacobsson, 1992), and creatinine was found to be significantly lower in urine when NDF (neutral detergent fibre) content in the feed was high due to added sugar beet pulp. The creatinine in plasma was not measured in this study. D) Dehydration probably also affects FE. E) Furthermore, the excretion of the mineral in question is not constant and is sometimes elevated after feeding, for example sodium after grain rich diets, and sometimes delayed, as for phosphorous because of the main absorption site in the hind gut.

When using fractional excretion technique to study mineral losses the horse must not be exercised prior to sampling (24 hours). The horse must be healthy and hydrated and the samples must be taken at a constant interval from feeding, in order to be comparable. The feed itself must be evaluated for the effect of creatinine. If these criteria cannot be filled, total urine collection must be done in a balanced trial.

Calcium sediments in horse urine due its alkaline nature. Repeated measurements are therefore difficult to attain. An inadequate intake of calcium stimulates the secretion of parathyroid hormone (PTH). PTH also decreases the renal reabsorption of phosphate. PTH is often successful in maintaining the serum calcium through mobilization of bone calcium, and increased intestinal uptake of calcium, whereas the serum phosphate tends to drop. Inadequate calcium intake gives us the picture of normal serum calcium, low serum phosphate and increased FE % of phosphate.

Direct methods of assessing calcium nutrition are also possible and several methods are described (Caple, *et al.*, 1982).

Minerals suitable for FE studies or total urine collection trials

Calcium	Magnesium	Silicon
Chloride	Phosphorous	Sodium
Chromium	Potassium	Sulfur
Fluorine	Selenium	Zinc
Lead		

NORMAL FE RANGES

	FE % Hay diet	Grain based diet
Magnesium	>20	>15
Phosphate	0-0.2[1]	0-0.5[2]
Sodium	0.04-0.54[1]	0.02-1[2]
Potassium	35-80[1]	15-65[2]
Chloride	0.7-2.1[1]	0.04-1.6[2]

[1]Harris *et al.*, 1991 [2]Traver *et al.*, 1976

Statistical revision of the results

The results from a trial, including blood tests, need special procedures when it comes to the statistical handling.

Many parameters from such trials show a non-normal distribution. This makes the figures unsuitable for common parametric techniques, such as ANOVA and regression, for raw data interpretation. A non-parametric method, for example rank sum tests or ANOVA on ranks, must be used. Another way to cope with this problem is to do some form of transformation of the raw data.

As we analyze many parameters from the same individual, the independent variables are all related to one another. This must not be the case in regression procedures. This situation is called multicollinearity. When the independent variables are correlated (as more or less all analyzed parameters are), they all hold some common information. In regression models all independent variables must contribute with unique information (Glantz *et al.*, 1990).

There are two kind of multicollinearity; structural multicollinearity, when the independent variables are a function of each other, and sample-based multicollinearity, which occurs when many parameters are measured on the same individual. There are several ways to measure multicollinearity and to solve the problem. One way to resolve structural multicollinearity is to collect more data under other circumstances to break up the relationship (Glantz *et al.*, 1990).

As we often use a rather small number of horses in nutritional research, it is extremely important to check the raw data for influential data points which are outliers. There are several ways to identify and quantify influential data points (Glantz *et al.*, 1990).

In nutritional research we deal with a multi-variate situation. To conduct classical trials with a small number of experiments and using t-test and ANOVA for interpretation, is not always the best way, but definitely the cheapest. A better, but far more expensive method, is to design the trial for multi-variate evaluation, such as principal component analysis (Mardia *et al.*, 1989).

Discriminant analysis is also a good way to see that your trial was correct, in that afterwards you can let the computer suggest which feed the horses probably have eaten, according to the blood results. If the computer does the right classification as in reality, your trial was successful. You can also see which blood-parameters have the strongest influence on the classification (Mardia *et al.*, 1989).

Pitfalls and errors

In all analytical work there are inherent errors. Sampling technique, storage after sampling and laboratory errors are the most prominent errors affecting the result of a blood test.

One type of laboratory error is suspected if we make ten analyses on the same sample, and we get ten different values. We measure the variation in the analytical results as coefficient of correlation (CV=Standard deviation/mean $*100$). As the horse itself has a very low variation in most parameters, an inferior analytical machine is responsible for most of the variation in the test results. From such a machine it is difficult to see the variation contributed by the feed. CV under 2% is a must for most parameters when dealing with horse-blood. Just as important as the precision, is the accuracy of the measured parameters. This means that the values from the machine must have a clinical significance. Not many machines and analytical methods can give these low variations and acceptable accuracy. The laboratory must spend a lot of effort to accomplish this, with methods validated for horses.

Robots for pipetting and highly automated routines are essential for a good result. For hematology, automated systems for measuring, cell counting and white cell differential counts are necessary. This equipment costs of course a lot of money, but unfortunately it is necessary when dealing with blood tests from horses.

Blood tests to evaluate nutritional status in individuals

Interpretation of blood tests is an art. It takes knowledge, intuition and fantasy to do a good job. You have to see patterns in the figures and understand the dynamics between the different parameters. To be an experienced interpreter, the feed-back from the veterinarians, trainers and horse owners is essential. First when you compare the real situation with the test results in discussion with the horse handler, you can develop your skill in reading test results.

From the discussion above it is clear that in order to use blood samples to evaluate nutritional status, it all depends on how you do it. If you have a reliable laboratory and know which parameters to analyze, and when to take the samples, it is possible to make a good guess on the nutritional status for some nutrients (see list above).

As a general rule, it is much easier to see when something is wrong, than to see when the situation is optimal. In other words, it is easy to see when you can expect poor performance, but almost impossible to see when the horse is in perfect shape. Or, it is easy to see a copper deficiency, but impossible to see when copper for this horse is optimal.

We use blood tests to scan all the individuals in a stable, and we can get a rough picture of the health status, performance status and nutritional status by doing this. We encourage the trainers/horse owners to take the samples at least once a month. One must use the test results as a complement to what you see and what you feel about the horse when in training. We find a good clinical relevance in the test results, but we also find imbalances among the parameters, and are often able to correct these imbalances before clinical symptoms occur.

What is normal?

Normal range is a statistical way to help understanding non-normal situations. But as it is just a statistical value, many exceptions exists. Furthermore, we can have many different normal ranges, one for the whole population (widest range), one for clinical situations (most used range), and one for performance evaluations (narrowest range). Every laboratory must have their own set of normal values, as analysis procedures, analytical temperatures, hardware and sample handling differ among laboratories. To simply use literature values is meaningless.

The best normal values come from the horse itself. Previous blood tests from the same horse can be used if the samples are sent to the same laboratory and have been taken on similar occasions as the previous ones. It is hence a good practice to standardize your sampling procedures and make notes of sampling conditions for future use.

Interpretations

Most of the parameters analyzed from blood give an unspecific picture of the biochemical processes. Consequently, we have to analyze many unspecific parameters in order to get a more specific illustration of the situation. By doing this we see patterns in the figures, and do not necessarily have to have values outside the normal ranges to spot pathologic situations. This in turn makes each blood test more difficult to explain.

Many nutritional imbalances affect the hormonal system. And as metabolic active hormones always have more than one target organ, and there are many correlations between parameters, you can be certain to find more than one parameter diverging from normal. This is why you can see a pathologic pattern if you analyze many parameters.

Many metabolic active hormones are possible to analyze even in mailed blood samples, such as insulin, cortisol, T4 and T3, while others, growth hormone (GH), insulin-like growth factor-1 (IGF-1), glucagon, parathyroid hormone (PTH) and calcitonin, are for research or hospitalized horses only. To measure hormone levels requires special attention and is best used to confirm a suspected disturbance discovered by the ordinary blood test.

It is of little use to analyze hormones without making a stimulation or inhibition test, because hormone levels show a natural variation during the day due to feeding, exercise or circadian rhythm. Thus, insulin, T4, T3, and cortisol can be stimulated by glucose tolerance tests and T4 and T3 alone by giving thyroid releasing hormone (TRH). Tolerance tests often give valuable information of an individual's response-status, and can give information on how this particular horse should be fed.

Summary

Blood analysis is a good complement to conventional methods for the development of new feeds or for characterizing existing feeds. It is necessary for the laboratory to use validated methods with high precision and accuracy. Several parameters must be analyzed to get a more specific picture of the dynamic processes. Sampling technique and sample handling is a crucial factor, as well as the statistical revision.

Table 1. SOME COMMONLY ANALYZED PARAMETERS IN HORSE BLOOD AND THE POSSIBLE USE OF THE DIFFERENT PARAMETERS FOR THE FEED INDUSTRY AND FOR EVALUATION OF NUTRITIONAL STATUS.

Group	Parameter	Used for feed evaluation	Comments
1) Hormones	insulin	Yes	Metabolic evaluations
	thyroxine (T4)	Yes	and to follow responses
	triiodothyronine (T3)	Yes	from feed and exercise
	cortisol		
2) Fuels	glucose	Yes	Responds on feeding
	triglycerides	Yes	and exercise
	fatty acids	Yes	
	cholesterol	Yes	
	glycerol		
	amino acids	Yes	
	pyruvate		
3) Waste products	urea	Yes	Responds on feeding
	lactate	Yes	and exercise
	ß-OH butyrate	Yes	
	bilirubin		
	ammonia	Yes[1]	
	creatinine	Yes[2]	
	urate		
4) Enzymes	AST[3]	Yes	High values can reflect cell
	CK[4]	Yes	damage or increased production.
	ALP[5]		In general, high starch diet, high
	GT[6]	Yes	enzymes.
5) Minerals	calcium	Yes[1]	Apart from copper the
	magnesium	Yes	interpretations of the
	phosphorus	Yes	test results are very
	copper	Yes	difficult except when low
	zinc	Yes[1]	values are found which has
	iron	Yes[1]	a high diagnostic value.
	selenium	Yes	
6) Electrolytes	sodium	Yes[1]	Along with some of the
	potassium	Yes[1]	minerals, urine is the best fluid
	chloride	Yes[1]	for analysis
7) Vitamins	B$_{12}$	Yes	Good indicators of feed quality.
	folate		Retinol requires special
	retinol	Yes	procedures for evaluation[7]
	tocopherol	Yes	

Table 1. (CONT'D)

8) Serum proteins	total protein albumin		Reflects indirectly nutritional status (but also excessive losses
	globulins fibrinogen		via intestine). Albumin is a big protein reservoir
9) Acid/base balance	O_2 CO_2 HCO_3^-	Yes Yes	Can reflect acid/base status after feeding. O_2, CO_2 is independent, HCO_3^-, pH pH dependent of CO_2 [8]
10) Haematology	red/white cells hematocrit haemoglobin MCV [9] differential count		Requires sophisticated equipment for nutritional studies. Haemoglobin concentration is more affected by horones and protein intake than dietary iron.

1) Requires special care and/or sampling techniques for evaluation
2) In mineral studies in conjunction with analysis of urine
3) Aspartate aminotransferase (GOT) [4)5)]
4) Creatine kinase
5) Alkaline phosphatase
6) Glutamyltransferase
7) Loerch et al., 1979
8) Stewart, 1981
9) Mean Corpuscular Volume (Mean red cell volume)

Blood analysis is also an excellent tool for determining nutritional status in an individual horse. But the exceptions are many. Knowledge of the dynamic processes involved and a critical eye is a must. Normal values should be used with great care and previous samples from the same horse to compare with is the preferable method.

Table 2. SOME BLOOD PARAMETERS AND THEIR RESPONSE TO FEEDING.

Parameter	Postprandial reaction	Optimal reaction for performance	Comments
Glucose and insulin	elevated[1]	higher peaks- longer work intolerance	The higher starch content of the feed higher peaks of both.
Cortisol	NA[1,2]	is a stress factor if mean level is high	Cortisol increases the breakdown of glycogen and body fat. Exercised induced release.
Thyroxine (T4)	sparse elevation	normal levels enhances performance	Is an antagonist to insulin but is sometimes lowered (hypothyroidism) in the post absorptive phase (adverse reaction to the feed).
Triiodothyronine (T3)	elevated	as T4, is an insulin antagonist	The conversion of T4 to T3 is stimulated by insulin-higher peaks than T4. T3 enhances performance.
Fatty acids	lowered	high levels - glycogen sparing effect	Elevated in the hindgut- absorptive state. Excellent fuel for all horses. Utilization of FA as a fuel is proportional to plasma concentration in man[3].
Cholesterol	NA[2]	important carrier of vitamins	The mean level is strongly to the fat content of the feed up to a certain limit[4].
Urea	sparse elevation	high levels - negative	High levels increase water consumption and urine formation. Uses bicarbonate when synthesized. Reflects the protein quantity and quality of feed. (Protein/energy balance).
Ammonia	lowered	high levels in fatigue	Strong inverse Correlation to ATP levels in muscles of exercised horses[5].
AST	NA[2]	low levels good for performance	Mean levels higher for starch rich diets than in fiber rich diets.

Table 2. (CONT'D)

CK (CPK)	variable	as for AST	Mean levels higher for starch rich diets than in <u>fat</u> rich diets.
GT	NA[2]	low levels good for performance	High grain diets increase synthesis due to higher stress hormone levels and gives high mean levels in serum (feed stress indicator). Fibre/fat rich diets give lower values. Sometimes very high levels when long term feeding of high fat diets.
Magnesium	elevated	low levels negative for performance	In magnesium deficient horses serum levels are normal due to decreased urinary output. Muscle and urine levels are better indicators of Mg-status.
Phosphate	often lowered	narrow range for optimum performance[7]	Low levels not only by low absorption but also by high urinary output. Inorganic phosphorous is the lowest level of energy, ATP the highest.
Copper	NA[2]	as for phosphorous	Mean plasma levels is a good indicator of feed levels on a long term basis. Liver storage normalizes low intake for several months. Strong inverse correlation to plasma iron (and zinc of healthy horses). Copper deficiency increases MCV in exercising horses and lowers white cell count in nonexercising horses.
Iron	NA[2]	as for phosphorous	Iron deficiency rarely seen. Often high levels in copper deficient horses.
Sodium	sometimes elevated	as for phosphorous	High grain diets give higher peaks. Glucose sodium coupled uptake as in pigs not demonstrated in horses but likely.

Table 2. (CONTD)

Potassium	Often lowered	as for phosphorous	High feed levels in conjunction with high sugar levels (molasses) can give a mild transient hyper-kalemia. Low dietary cation/anion balance give low concentration in plasma.
Chloride	varies	influencing acid/base status	Abundant negatively charged ion in serum. Increased urinary excretion in hay diets.
Vitamin B$_{12}$	NA[2]	high levels good for performance	Reflects cobalt status and hindgut microbe activity. Synthesized by hindgut microbes. High levels are seen in well balanced diets with high fibre quality and adequate cobalt intake.
Tocopherol	elevated	high levels good performance	Plasma values follow feed content. Levels must be correlated to plasma lipids[8].
pH	varies		Often postprandial acidosis in high grain diets. Fibre and/or fat rich diets usually don't affect pH levels.
Haemoglobin	NA[2]	low and high levels negative	Is a poor indicator of iron status. Affected by hormones (T3) and protein intake. Low plasma copper influence HGB.
MCV	NA[2]	as for phosphorous	MCV can, on a long term basis, be affected by nutrients, such as copper.

[1]Stull *et al.*, 1988
[2]NA-Not Affected, means that the concentration in blood is not markedly raised or lowered up to 4 hours after feeding but the mean levels are influenced by feeding.
[3]Jansson *et al.*, 1982.
[4]Hambleton *et al.*, 1980
[5]Harris *et al.*, 1991
[6]Snow *et al.*, 1987
[7]Denny *et al.*, 1987
[8]Horwitt *et al.*, 1972

References

Caple, I.W., Doake, P.A. and Ellis, P.G., 1982; Assessment of the Calcium and Phosphorous Nutrition in Horses by Analysis of Urine. Australian Veterinary Journal, vol. 58:125-135.

Denny, J.E.F.M., 1987; Thoroughbred Blood Serum Inorganic Phosphate Concentrations in Relation to Feeding Regime and Racing Performance. Journal of the South African Veterinary Association, June: 85-87.

Finco, D.R.; 1989, Kidney Function, In Clinical Biochemistry of Domestic Animals, Ed. Jiro J. Kaneko, 4th ed., s 527-537.

Glantz, S.A., Slinker, B.K., 1990. Primer of Applied Regression and Analysis of Variance. New York:McGraw-Hill.

Hambleton, P.L., Slade, L.M., Hamar, D.W., Kienholz, E.W. and Lewis, L.D., 1980; Dietary Fat and Exercise Conditioning Effect on Metabolic Parameters in the Horse., J. Anim. Sci. 51, 1330-1339.

Harris, P.A. and Snow, D.A.; 1991, Role of Electrolyte Imbalances in the Pathophysiology of the Equine Rhabdomyolysis Syndrome; In Equine Exercise Physiology 3:435-442.

Harris, R.C., Marlin, D.J., Snow, D.H. and Harkness, R.A., 1991; Muscle ATP Loss and Lactate Accumulation at Different Work Intensities in the Exercising Thoroughbred Horse. Eur. J. Appl. Physiol. 62:235-244.

Horwitt, M.K., Harvey, C.C., Dahm Jr. C.H., et al., 1972; Relationship Between Tocopherol and Serum Lipid Levels for Determination of Nutritional Adequacy. Ann. NY Acad. Sci., 203:223-236.

Jansson, E. and Kaijser, L. 1982; Effect of Diet on the Utilization of Blood-borne and Intramuscular Substrates during Exercise in Man. Acta Physiol. Scand. 115:19.

Lindberg, J.E. and Jacobsson, K.G., 1992; Effects of Barley and Sugarbeet Pulp on Digestibility, Purine Excretion and Blood Parameters in Horses. Proc. Europäische Konferenz ber die Ernährung des Pferde, 116-118.

Loerch, J.D., Underwood, B.A. and Lewis, K.C., 1979; Response of Plasma Levels of Vitamin A to a Dose of Vitamin A as an indicator of Hepatic Vitamin A Reserves in Rats., J. Nutr. 109:778.

Mardia, K.V., Kent, J.T. and Bibby, J.M., 1989. Multivariate Analysis. Academic Press, Inc. San Diego, CA 92101.

Snow, D.H., Gash, S.P. and Rice, D., 1987; Field Observations on Selenium Status, Whole Blood Glutathione Peroxidase and Plasma Gamma-Glutamyl Transferase Activities in Thoroughbred Racehorses. Equine Exercise Physiology 2, 494-505.

Stewart, P.A.; 1981. How to Understand Acid-Base. Elsevier, North Holland, Inc. New York, N.Y.

Stull, C.L. and Rodiek, A.V., 1988; Responses of Blood Glucose, Insulin and Cortisol Concentrations to Common Equine Diets. J. Nutr. 118:206-213.

Traver, D.S., Coffman, J.R., Moore, J.N., Salem, C.A., Gamerr, H.E., Johnsson, J.H., and Tritchler, L.G.; 1976, Urine Clearance Ratios as a Diagnostic Aid in Equine Metabolic Disease. Proc. Am. Ass. Equine Practors. 22, 177-183.

This paper was first published in "Feeding the Performance Horse," Proceedings for the 1993 Short Course for Feed Manufacturers

SKELETAL MUSCLE FUNCTION AND METABOLISM

S.J. VALBERG and J.M. MACLEAY

Department of Clinical and Population Sciences, College of Veterinary Medicine, University of Minnesota, St Paul, Minnesota, USA

Skeletal muscle provides the explosive power of the jumper and cutting horse, the stamina of the endurance horse and the fine motor control of the advanced dressage horse. In this paper the pertinent aspects of muscle function and metabolism that confer this remarkable athleticism will be discussed.

Structure

Skeletal muscle consists of bundles of long spindle shaped cells called muscle fibers that attach to bone by tendinous insertions. The blood vessels and nerves that nourish and control muscle function run in thin sheets of connective tissue that surround bundles of muscle fibers. Each nerve branch communicates with one muscle fiber at the motor end. The nerve and all the muscle fibers that it supplies are together termed a motor unit. Each time that a nerve is stimulated all of the muscle fibers under its control will contract.

A muscle's unique ability to contract is conferred by the highly organized parallel, overlapping arrangement of actin and myosin filaments. These repeating contractile units or sarcomeres extend from one end of the cell to another in the form of a myofibril. Each muscle fiber is packed with myofibrils that are arranged in register giving skeletal muscle a striated appearance under the microscope. Muscle contraction occurs when the overlapping actin and myosin filaments slide over each other, serving to shorten the length of the muscle cell from end to end and mechanically pulling the limb in the desired direction. The sliding of the filaments requires chemical energy in the form of ATP.

Muscle fiber types

Different forms of myosin (isoforms) can be found in different muscle fibers and these different isoforms affect the speed with which a muscle cell can contract. In addition, fibers with specific contractile speeds will also possess characteristic metabolic energy producing capacities (Table 1). Type 1 fibers contract slowly, are ideally suited for endurance and are able to hold a tetanic twitch for long durations without fatigue. Their resistance to fatigue is in part related to their high density of mitochondria which confer a high aerobic or oxidative capacity. In addition to having the highest oxidative capacity, type 1 fibers also have the highest lipid stores, the highest density of capillaries, the lowest glycogen stores and the lowest glycolytic enzyme capacity of the three fiber types. Fast-twitch muscle fibers or type 2 fibers are readily divided in the horse into type 2A and 2B fibers. Type 2B fibers have the fastest contractile speed, the largest cross-sectional area, the highest glycogen stores and glycolytic capacity and the lowest oxidative capacity. As such they are ideally suited to short fast bursts of power. Type 2A fibers are intermediate in contractile speed and metabolic properties between type 1 and type 2B fibers.

Table 1. THE PROPERTIES OF MUSCLE FIBER TYPES IN THE UNTRAINED HORSE

	Type 1	*Type 2A*	*Type 2B*
Speed of contraction	slow	fast	very fast
Fatigability	low	intermediate	high
Oxidative (aerobic) capacity	high	intermediate	low
Glycolytic (anaerobic) capacity	low	high	high
Glycogen content	low	high	high
Fat content	high	intermediate	low

Most large muscles in the horse contain a mixture of muscle fiber types. The muscle fiber composition, the percentage of type 1, 2A and 2B fibers, and muscle fiber cross-sectional areas vary greatly between muscle groups, among individual horses and between breeds. These proportions are not constant, as training can alter the fiber composition and fiber size in the same muscle over time. Propulsive locomotor muscles such as the gluteus contain a predominance of fast-twitch type 2 muscle fibers, with the highest density of type 1 fibers located deeper within the muscle. In general, Quarter horses and Thoroughbreds have the highest percentage of fast-twitch muscle fibers, 80-90%; Standardbreds an intermediate number, 75%; and donkeys have the lowest percentage of type 2 fibers in locomotor muscles. With growth and training, there is a change in the length and breadth of a fiber, and a change in the proportion of fiber types rather than an increase in the number of muscle fibers. In young horses intensively trained at speed, the proportion of type 2A fibers increases concomitant with a decrease in type 2B fibers.

Muscle fiber recruitment

When a muscle contracts during exercise, it does so in response to a predetermined recruitment of particular muscle fibers. This orderly recruitment of muscle fibers leads to smooth, coordinated movement. Each motor contains fibers of the same type. As exercise begins, a select number of motor units are recruited to provide the power to advance the limb. At slow exercise intensities, type 1 muscle fibers and a small number of type 2A muscle fibers are stimulated. The force produced by any muscle is proportional to the cross-sectional area that is active. As the speed or duration of exercise increases, more muscle fibers will be recruited and this occurs in the order of their contractile speed. Only at near-maximal exercise intensities or after several hours of submaximal exercise are type 2B fibers recruited.

Excitation - contraction - coupling

When a nerve is stimulated, a wave of electrical depolarization occurs that quickly reaches the neuromuscular junction. In response, the nerve terminal releases acetylcholine which binds to the motor-end plate of the muscle fiber and initiates electrical depolarization of the muscle cell membrane. Electrical depolarization of the muscle cell membrane triggers the release of calcium that is sequestered in intracellular membranous storage sites (sarcoplasmic reticulum) into the myoplasm via the calcium release channel. Increased concentrations of intracellular calcium allows the interaction of actin and myosin filaments which then slide over each other in a rachet like fashion to produce a contraction (cross-bridge cycling). Tension is generated as the shortening filaments tug both ends of the myofiber toward the middle. Muscle must relax after each contraction by actively pumping calcium back into the storage sites preventing actin-myosin interaction. In addition, ion pumps in the cell membrane actively repolarize the muscle cell membranes. All of the processes necessary for relaxation are active, meaning that they require energy in order for them to occur.

Metabolic responses to exercise

ENERGY PATHWAYS

The basic unit of energy in the cell is adenosine triphosphate or ATP. This molecule stores energy in the form of a high energy phosphate bond. When cleaved, the products include adenosine diphosphate (ADP), inorganic phosphate (Pi), and energy for use in cellular functions. During muscle contractions, ATP is utilized for actin-myosin cross-bridge cycling, and cell membrane and sarcoplasmic reticulum ion pumps. The processes of glycogenolysis, glycolysis, the Krebs cycle, oxidative phosphorylation by the electron transport chain, oxidation of free fatty acids (FFA), and purine nucleotide deamination all serve to supply the muscle cell with ATP (figure 1). A number of interdependent factors appear to influence the metabolic pathways used for energy production during exercise in the horse. These include the speed and duration of exercise; the muscle fiber composition; the properties of the muscle fibers recruited, including capillarization, oxidative and glycolytic capacities; and the availability of oxygen and different energy substrates.

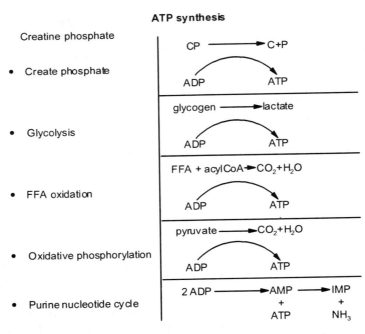

Figure 1. Skeletal muscle metabolic pathways used to supply ATP for muscle contractions.

Energy Sources

Creatine phosphate serves as a small store of immediate energy within the muscle fibers. Initially, cleavage of the phosphate from ATP or the creatine phosphate molecule supplies energy until ATP production from glucose or glycogen begins. Glucose is stored in the body in the form of glycogen, a long, branched polymer of glucose molecules. The largest deposits of glycogen are in the liver and muscle cells. Up to 8% of the liver's weight and up to 1-2% of the muscle's weight may be in the form of glycogen. Sympathetic stimulation of the nervous system, as occurs in exercise, causes an increase in the circulating levels of epinephrine and glucagon. These hormones activate phosphorylase enzymes that breakdown glycogen to phosphorylated glucose molecules. The muscle or liver cells shift from glycogen formation to glycogenolysis to supply free glucose. When this process occurs in the liver, free glucose is released into the blood stream. Muscle cells obtain glucose from the blood and from glycogen stored within the muscle cell. Fat serves as another energy-rich fuel source. Free fatty acids released from adipose tissue or from the liver can be taken up by the muscle cells and burned aerobically. Small intracellular triglyceride stores are also present within type 1 and 2A muscle fibers.

Metabolic pathways

Anaerobic pathways such as glycolysis, creatine phosphate and the purine nucleotide cycle are found within the cell cytoplasm. This pathway, which converts glucose to pyruvate and then lactate, provides 2 molecules of ATP for each molecule of glucose metabolized. Aerobic pathways such as the Krebs cycle, oxidation of FFA and the electron transport chain are located within the cell's mitochondria and provide the bulk of ATP for the cell so long as oxygen is plentiful. Specific transport mechanisms are present in the outer mitochondrial membrane to move FFA and pyruvate into the mitochondria for further metabolism. The efficiency of mitochondrial pathways is demonstrated by the ability to generate 38 molecules of ATP from oxidation of one molecule of glucose or the generation of up to 146 molecules of ATP from oxidation of a FFA.

AEROBIC EXERCISE

At submaximal exercise speeds, oxygen is readily available and slow-twitch fibers as well as fast-twitch fibers with a high oxidative capacity are recruited. Intramuscular supplies of ATP and creatine phosphate (CP) are quickly utilized and energy must be derived from glycolytic or oxidative pathways. A drop in the ATP: ADP + Pi ratio activates glycolysis, and ATP for contraction will then be provided by the metabolism of glycogen to pyruvate. Pyruvate is converted to acetyl-CoA in the mitochondria and is completely oxidized by the Krebs cycle and the electron transport chain. The amount of blood-borne substrates (glucose and FFA) available for oxidation increases within 15 minutes of submaximal exercise in conjunction with increasing concentration of cortisol and low insulin concentrations. High rates of oxidative phosphorylation result in inhibition of phosphofructokinase and a slowing of glucose oxidation in favor of beta-oxidation of FFAs. As such, the rate of intramuscular glycogen utilization steadily declines over time as the oxidation of FFA increases. Oxidative metabolism is highly efficient. It provides much more ATP per molecule of substrate (glucose or FFA) then glycolysis without altering intracellular pH. By using FFA, intramuscular glycogen stores are spared. Fatigue during prolonged submaximal exercise occurs when a combination of the following occurs: intramuscular glycogen concentrations become depleted, muscle temperatures become markedly elevated, electrolyte concentrations are altered or neuromuscular fatigue occurs (Table 2). Very little lactic acid accumulates at fatigue in horses performing submaximal exercise.

Table 2. FACTORS THAT CONTRIBUTE TO FATIGUE DURING AEROBIC AND ANAEROBIC EXERCISE INTENSITIES.

Aerobic exercise	Anaerobic exercise
• glycogen depletion	• lactic acidosis
• hyperthermia	-inhibition of PFK
• electrolyte depletion	-decreased muscle tension
• myalgia and motivation	• depletion of CP and ATP

PFK= phosphofructokinase
CP= creatine phosphate
ATP= adenosine triphosphate

ANAEROBIC EXERCISE

With any form of exercise a small amount of anaerobic metabolism occurs, but at submaximal speeds the majority of energy is produced by aerobic metabolism. As the speed of exercise increases so does the energy demand placed on the muscle. More muscle fibers are recruited including type 2B fibers and more oxygen is consumed by the horse until it reaches a speed where the delivery of oxygen or the ability to utilize oxidative processes becomes limiting. At the point of maximum oxygen consumption (VO2max) any further energy must be generated by anaerobic glycolysis or deamination of ATP (figure 2). By converting pyruvate to lactate, NADH is oxidized to NAD thereby further facilitating glycolysis. With their rich supply of glycolytic enzymes and limited capacity for oxidative phosphorylation, type 2B fibers are uniquely suited for anaerobic glycolysis. With type 2B fiber recruitment at speeds at and beyond the point of maximal oxygen uptake, an exponential rise in blood lactate accumulation occurs (figure 2). The advantages of anaerobic glycolysis are that oxygen is not required and that it provides a rapid supply of ATP. Depletion of glycogen stores does not limit maximal exercise because anaerobic glycolysis is inhibited by a lactic acidosis before total muscle glycogen is depleted. Low intramuscular pH caused by lactate and hydrogen ion accumulation inhibits phosphofructokinase enzyme, which is the rate limiting step in glycolysis (Table 2). Muscle pH can fall as low as 6.4 following maximal exercise at which point both glycolysis and excitation contraction coupling are inhibited. The ability to buffer or remove hydrogen ions becomes very important for muscle function during maximal exercise. Intracellular buffering of hydrogen ions occurs by proteins and dipeptides such as carnosine. Diffusion and active transport of lactate into the general circulation where bicarbonate acts as a major blood buffer are also important for intramuscular pH. The amount of lactic acid in the circulation following exercise is in part directly related to the percentage of low oxidative type 2B fibers in the muscle and the duration of high intensity exercise.

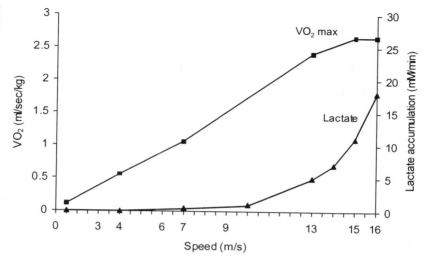

Figure 2. The oxygen consumption and rate of lactate accumulation in a Thoroughbred horse. (Data courtesy of Dr. JH Jones).

At top speeds, as the intramuscular stores of ATP and energy demands outstrip its innate ability to produce ATP, the cell turns to its last venue of energy production. Surplus ADP in the cell is converted to ATP and AMP in a process called the myokinase reaction (figure 3). At low intramuscular pH, AMP deaminase enzymes are activated and this deaminates AMP into IMP, NH^{3+} and Pi to catalyze the production of ATP from ADP. Short term, this produces ATP for muscle contraction from the excess of intramuscular ADP. However, ammonia diffuses from the cell and the total nucleotide pool is depleted. Plasma ammonia levels begin to increase at a threshold beyond the onset of lactic acid accumulation and correlates strongly with a depletion of ATP within the muscle cells. Before intracellular stores of ADP and ATP are replenished IMP must be reaminated. The reamination of IMP into ADP and ATP takes at least 30-60 minutes. Ultimately, fatigue appears to be related to depleted ATP stores within muscle fibers (Table 2). The levels of lactate and ATP in individual fibers during maximal exercise may be more important for the onset of fatigue than the measured concentrations in whole muscle samples. Depleted fibers might develop a sustained painful contracture similar to rigor, and impair the horse's ability to maintain maximal speed.

The effect of training

ENDURANCE TRAINING

Endurance training in horses changes the contractile and metabolic profile of skeletal muscles. After a short period of training, the volume density of mitochondria, and

Purine nucleotide cycle

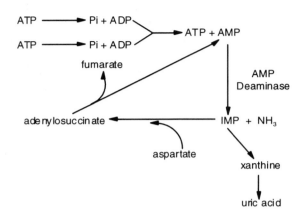

Figure 3. The purine nucleotide cycle.

thus the oxidative enzyme capacity, all increase. Over a 6 month period the ratio of type 2A:2B fibers increases, the cross-sectional area of type 2B muscle fibers decreases, and the capillarization of all fiber types increases. These adaptations favor the delivery of oxygen and blood-borne substrates, the early activation of oxidative metabolism and the utilization of FFA in muscle fibers. By sparing muscle glycogen, endurance is enhanced, and fatigue is delayed.

SPEED TRAINING

With training at high intensities, the speed at which a horse begins to accumulate lactate should gradually increase, delaying the onset of lactate accumulation and ATP depletion. This is accomplished by an increase in the oxidative capacity (by increased mitochondrial volume) and capillarization of all muscle fiber types, including type 2B fibers. Training of 2 and 3 year-old Standardbred and Thoroughbred racehorses in Scandinavia had been shown to reduce the percentage of type 2B fibers and increase the percentage of type 2A fibers as well as decrease the cross-sectional area of type 2B fibers. Although an increase in oxidative capacity may be metabolically advantageous, a decrease in the percentage of type 2B fibers and a decrease in their cross-sectional areas may also deleteriously affect their speed and force of contraction. Muscle must have the ability to generate energy via anaerobic glycolysis for race horses to be successful. Obviously a balance is required between skeletal muscle fiber metabolic and contractile properties for optimum speed and endurance. Since the muscle fiber composition and fiber properties vary so greatly between horses, achievement of this balance may be different for each horse.

References

Snow, D.H. and Valberg S.J.: Muscle anatomy, physiology and adaptations to exercise and training. In Rose, R.J. and Hodgson, D.H. (eds) The Athletic Horse: principles and practice of equine sports medicine. Philadelphia, PA, W.B. Saunders Co., 1994.

Hodgson D.H.: Energy considerations during exercise. In Rose, R.J. (ed)Vet Clinics of North America, Equine Practice, vol 3, Philadelphia, PA, W.B. Saunders Co., 1985.

This paper was first published in Proceedings, Kentucky Equine Research 1997 Equine Nutrition Conference

THE USE OF NUTRITIONAL ERGOGENIC AIDS IN HORSES

LAURIE M. LAWRENCE
University Of Kentucky, Lexington, Kentucky, USA

What is an ergogenic aid?

The word "ergogenic" is derived from the Greek work "ergon" (work) and "genic" (producing). Thus, ergogenic aids are factors that can increase or improve work production. Improved work effort may occur as a result of increased strength, increased speed, increased endurance, etc. Many things fall into the category of ergogenic aids for human athletes including equipment, pharmacological agents, nutritional supplements and even psychological aids such as hypnosis and mental imaging. The purpose of this review is to examine the usefulness of some nutritional supplements purported to have ergogenic effects in horses. Within the scope of this paper a nutritional supplement will include compounds or elements that can be administered orally and have a nutritionally oriented function.

How do ergogenic aids work?

In order for something to have an ergogenic effect, it must be able to affect some aspect of exercise physiology, preferably an aspect of exercise physiology that is limiting to the athlete in question. Therefore, it is imperative that the metabolic or physiologic function of the aid in question be known. Many substances are marketed without any factual evidence to elucidate their function, or descriptions of their functions are too vague to provide useful information. For example, describing a product's metabolic function as "oxygen building" is meaningless. The merit of substances without a known function should be viewed with some skepticism. Coyle (1984) suggests that ergogenic aids can function in the following general ways:

1)   They may act as a supplementary fuel source for energy production.

2)   They may affect the flux of fuels through the energy pathways.

3)   They may delay or minimize the affects of end product accumulation, such as heat or lactic acid.

4)   They can affect the nervous system by affecting coordination, recruitment of muscle fibers or psychological effects.

Table 1 lists a number of compounds that are used as ergogenic aids in human and equine athletics with a brief description of their proposed metabolic or physiologic role. In some cases the role of each compound in exercise is not known.

Table 1. PARTIAL LIST OF COMPOUNDS THAT ARE USED AS ERGOGENIC AIDS IN HORSES AND HUMANS.

Compound	Metabolic/physiological function
B12 (cyanocobalamin)	Coenzyme in reactions: methyl malonyl COA to succinyl COA cycling of 5-methyltetrahydrofolate to folate
Folic acid	Methyl donor; coenzyme in purine synthesis; RBC synthesis
Pyridoxine (B6)	Coenzyme in amino acid metabolism; heme synthesis pantothenate. Constituent of coenzyme A; essential for metabolism of fat and carbohydrate
Thiamin (B1)	Cofactor in pyruvate dehydrogenase complex (pyruvate to acetyl COA)
Vitamin E	Antioxidant
Coenzyme Q10	Antioxidant; electron transport
Vitamin C	Antioxidant; collagen synthesis
Iron	Heme synthesis (oxygen transport)
Phosphorus	ATP synthesis; 2,3 diphosphoglycerate synthesis (oxygen dissociation from hemoglobin)
Dimethyl glycine (DMG)	Methyl donor; other ??
Carnitine	Fatty acid transport into mitochondria
Bee Pollen	Source of various nutrients; other ??
Gingseng	?????
Sodium bicarbonate	Alkalinizing agent; delay metabolic acidosis

Once the function of a specific substance is determined, its usefulness as an ergogenic aid can be evaluated. In order to evaluate whether specific substances may be capable of reducing the limiting aspect of a certain exercise bout, it is necessary to understand the metabolic or physiological mechanisms that limit different types of exercise. For example the factors that cause fatigue in endurance horses are dramatically different from the factors that cause fatigue in Thoroughbreds racing a mile and a half. Therefore a substance that is effective in Thoroughbreds may be of no use to an endurance horse (and vice versa). An understanding of the function of each compound and an understanding of the metabolism and physiology of each type of athlete is also important because some compounds that may be helpful to some types of athletes could actually be detrimental to other types of athletes.

Do ergogenic aids work?

Maybe. Sometimes. The unfortunate truth regarding ergogenic aids is that the body of research is very small even when animal and human studies are considered together. Many of the studies that have been conducted have used inadequate designs to compare treated and untreated individuals. It is not uncommon to find studies where subjects were tested in an untreated (control) condition one week and then tested several weeks later after receiving the ergogenic supplement. In this type of design, it is not possible to determine whether any change in performance was a result of the supplement or a result of training progress during the supplementation period. Thus, studies should be designed to balance or randomize treatment order and ensure that controls and treated individuals are always tested under the same conditions. In addition, humans must be tested in a "blind" situation so that they are not aware of their treatment; otherwise, psychological rather than physiological changes will be measured. Even though animals may not be subject to a psychological boost from some supplement, animal studies must also be conducted in a situation where the handlers are blind to the treatment. This requirement is especially important in equine studies where riders or drivers can have a huge impact on the performance of the horse.

Conclusions relative to the efficacy of a particular treatment should be based on sound statistical methods. However, in many performance situations this practice is problematic. First, it is essential to be able to accurately measure "performance." Second, it is essential that differences detected as statistically significant are also biologically significant, and that biologically significant effects can be detected statistically. A one or two second change in race time would be considered biologically significant by most trainers but might be difficult to identify as statistically significant without a large number of animals or repetitions. When tested in a research environment some ergogenic aids or practices appear to have a positive effect on some subjects but the differences between the treated group and the controls are not statistically significant at the conventional 5% level of acceptance. This situation occurs because performance criteria are often subject to great variability resulting from individual differences. Because of limited resources, many studies are restricted to such a small number of subjects that it is often unrealistic to expect to find a performance difference that can be identified at the 5% level of significance. Although the "0.05" level of significance is a good discriminator for most experimental studies, in studies with small sample sizes it may be useful to select a different level of significance for testing hypotheses. At the very least, when treatments produce changes that are different at $0.1 > p > 0.05$, follow up research is warranted. Another problem associated with these types of studies is the lack of dose response information that leads to difficulty in selecting the appropriate treatment rate and adaptation period.

Because of the limited number of studies that have been performed and the difficulties involved in conducting those studies, contradictory evidence exists for almost every ergogenic aid. In addition, very few substances have been tested with adequate controls in real performance situations. Particularly with horses, it is difficult to translate laboratory results obtained on a treadmill to potential effects on the race track or in the show arena. In a perfect world, each ergogenic aid would be tested in a laboratory situation to identify metabolic and physiological functions, ideal dose rate and adaptation period; and then field tested to identify actual performance effects. Since it is not a perfect world, assessment of the value of ergogenic aids must be made on the information available and on new information. The following is a brief discussion of some of the more common nutritional supplements reputed to have an ergogenic benefit in horses.

B vitamins

The normal equine diet contains most B vitamins, with the exception of B12 which can be synthesized and absorbed in the gut. The microbial population in the large intestine is also capable of synthesizing other B vitamins including thiamin. It has generally been accepted that the levels of B vitamins provided by typical diets and microbial synthesis are not deficient for horses. However, the absence of classical vitamin deficiency signs does not necessarily imply optimal vitamin status. In human studies, deficient vitamin intakes (combined B1, B2, B6 and C) have been reported to negatively impact physical performance even though general health was not affected (van Dokkum *et al.*,1989; van der Beek *et al.*, 1985).

Because of its role in the conversion of pyruvate to acetyl COA, thiamin has received particular attention as an ergogenic aid. In 1989, the NRC increased the recommendation for thiamin from 3 mg/kg to 5 mg/kg, based on the study of Topliff *et al* (1981) in which three horses received three levels of dietary thiamin (2, 4, and 28 mg/kg) in a Latin square design. Blood lactate levels following 30 minutes of exercise were lower in horses receiving the highest level of thiamin, but the lactate levels were relatively low (below the proposed anaerobic threshold) for all treatments. Studies using a larger number of horses and more rigorous exercise test have not been conducted but are warranted since Knippel *et al* (1986) have reported that thiamin supplementation increased the anaerobic threshold in cyclists. The study by Topliff et al is useful because it delineates a range of thiamin levels that should be studied. Horses receiving the highest dose of thiamin excreted significantly more thiamin in the urine and were in positive thiamin balance compared to the 4 mg/kg dose rate.

Antioxidants

A number of compounds with antioxidant functions including vitamin E, vitamin C, beta-carotene and coenzyme Q10 are supplemented to athletes. Antioxidants protect the cells and tissues from oxidant damage caused by the free radicals produced during exercise. An excellent review of this area has been published (Witt *et al.*, 1992). Vitamin E deficient animals may have reduced physical performance, particularly in regard to fatigue time during endurance exercise (Witt *et al.*, 1992). However, vitamin E deficiency does not appear to occur commonly in the horse. In fact, Petersson *et al.* (1991) fed horses a low vitamin E diet (< 15 ppm) without producing any clinical signs of vitamin E deficiency. In that study, the horses responded similarly to an exercise test performed after 4 months of the low vitamin E diet and after 1 month on a repletion diet (vitamin E supplemented). In addition, horses in a mild training program responded similarly to depletion and repletion as nonexercised horses.

While vitamin E adequacy is undoubtedly important for optimal physical performance, supplementation of vitamin E or other antioxidants above recommended levels has not consistently improved performance. Witt *et al.* (1992) suggest that vitamin E supplementation will not improve maximal aerobic or performance capacity. Shelle *et al.* (1985) fed supplemental vitamin E to horses and did not find any effect on their indicator of oxidative damage/protection, glutathione peroxidase. Supplementation with Coenzyme Q10 has failed to improve measures of physical performance of fitness in horses and normal humans (Rathgeber-Lawrence *et al.*,1991; Braun *et al.*, 1991). Studies with vitamin C in humans have produced conflicting results (Bucci, 1989) and are difficult to extrapolate to horses because to differences in ascorbic acid metabolism.

Hematinics

Hematinics (blood builders) are used to a large extent in the horse industry, although there is very limited research support for this practice. The compounds in this category (used alone or in combination) include iron, copper, zinc, pyridoxine, B12, and folic acid. These nutrients are involved in hemoglobin synthesis and erythropoiesis.

The availability of adequate hemoglobin is essential for oxygen transport. In humans a hemoglobin concentration of 15 to 16 g/dL is considered a desirable level for optimal performance, and low levels will impair maximal oxygen transport (Weaver and Rajaram, 1992). The occurrence of "sports anemia," a decrease in hemoglobin levels in athletes, has been described in human athletes (Pate, 1983). In humans, this condition may occur as a result of increased plasma volume in response to training, or from depleted iron stores and increased hemoglobin losses due to exercise (Weaver and Rajaram, 1992). There is some indication that horses can suffer a decline in hematologic parameters during a training program, but the source of this decline has not been defined (Carlson, 1987). Human athletes, especially women, may have marginal iron intakes and appear to benefit from iron supplementation (Lyle *et al.*, 1991; Weinstein *et al.*, 1989). Colgan *et al* (1992) have suggested that endurance athletes can also benefit from supplementation with zinc, folate, pyridoxine, B12 and ascorbate in addition to iron.

Iron deficiency in horses appears to occur rarely under practical feeding conditions (NRC, 1989). Kirkham (1971) found little response of equine hematological parameters to various hematinics. Roberts (1983) reported that performance horses on typical diets in Queensland were probably B12 adequate, but might require additional folate.

Comparisons of hematological parameters and responses to exercise in horses and humans must be made carefully. Distinct differences exist between the two species. Horses store a large percentage of their red blood cells in the spleen. During exercise splenic release of stored cells can increase packed cell volume and hemoglobin values by 50% or more. The spleen does not function similarly in humans. Consequently, measures of hemoglobin taken at rest are relatively representative of the hemoglobin that will be available during exercise in humans, but not in horses. Any small increase in resting hemoglobin produced by a hematinic in horses would be overshadowed during exercise by the increase resulting from splenic release of red blood cells.

Are ergogenic aids ethical?

Sodium bicarbonate is an example of an ergogenic aid that has become the topic of considerable controversy in the racing industry. Sodium bicarbonate is administered pre-race to enhance the buffering capacity (bicarbonate reserve) of the blood and delay metabolic acidosis. Sodium bicarbonate has been studied extensively in human athletes, usually at doses of 200 to 300 mg/kg body weight. A review on the use of sodium bicarbonate in humans has been published (Linderman and Fahey, 1991). Sodium bicarbonate administration does not appear to increase maximum power output, but rather increases the time that intense exercise can be sustained. It is not useful for endurance activity and may have negative effects if administered to dehydrated, electrolyte depleted subjects.

Several studies have evaluated the use of sodium bicarbonate in exercising horses (Kelso *et al.*, 1987; Lawrence *et al.*, 1987; Lawrence *et al.*, 1990; Roberts *et al.*, 1991; Greenhaff *et al.*, 1991a; Greenhalff *et al.*, 1991b; Harkins *et al.*, 1992). Performance enhancement (race time) was suggested by two studies (Kelso *et al.*, 1987; Lawrence *et al.*, 1990) if a level of significance of $p < 0.1$ is accepted. In other studies, race times of treated and untreated horses were essentially the same (Greenhaff *et al.*, 1991; Harkins *et al.*, 1992). Only one of the studies that measured race time was conducted using a test that would be predicted to identify an effect of sodium bicarbonate. Greenhaff *et al*, Harkins *et al*, and Kelso *et al* used Thoroughbreds racing 1 mile or less. Since human studies have suggested that tests of 2 minutes are necessary to identify differences due to sodium bicarbonate treatment, the tests used in these studies may have been sub-optimal. In addition Gordon *et al* (1991) have suggested that sodium bicarbonate appears to have the greatest benefit for interval type tasks; therefore, the Standardbred race horse, which may have an intense warm-up, may have the greatest response. The metabolic responses to sodium bicarbonate in horses resemble those in humans suggesting that an ergogenic benefit is possible.

In practice, sodium bicarbonate has gained wide acceptance as an ergogenic aid in Standardbred racing. Sodium bicarbonate is frequently administered with a nasogastric tube along with glucose and other compounds. The dose rate used in practice may exceed those that have been tested by research studies. Numerous editorials have been written condemning the use of sodium bicarbonate, because of possible damage to the horse's health and a negative impact on the image of racing (Bergstein, 1989; 1991). The use of sodium bicarbonate on Standardbred tracks is currently prohibited in some racing jurisdictions including Illinois and Ontario. In Illinois, blood samples are obtained pre-race and screened for aberrant pH, sodium and bicarbonate levels. Gordon *et al* (1992) indicated that governing bodies of human athletics have not specifically banned the use of sodium bicarbonate because of its ergogenic effects, but there may be concern over its effect on urine pH and possible drug testing complications.

References

Bergstein S. Milkshakes: A bad idea the sport can do without. Harness Horse 1989;54(36):6.

Bergstein S. Chicago leads the way in ridding the sport of a scourge - milkshakes. Harness Horse 1991;45(28):7.

Braun B., Clarkson P.M., Freedson P.S., and Kohl R.L. Effects of coenzyme Q10 on exercise performance, maximal oxygen consumption and lipid peroxidation. Med Sci Sport Ex 1991;23(4):578 (abstract).

Bucci L. Nutritional ergogenic aids. In, Nutrition in Exercise and Sport. Hickson J.F. and Wolinski, I. (eds). 1989 CRC Press, Boca Raton.

Carlson G.P. Hematology and body fluids in the equine athlete: A review. Equine Exer Physiol 1987;2:393.

Colgan M., Fiedler S., and Colgan L.A. Micronutrient status of endurance athletes affects hematology and performance. Int J Appl Nutr 1991.

Coyle E.F. Ergogenic aids. Clin Sports Med 1984;3(3):731.

Gordon S.E., Kraemer W.J., and Pedro J.G. Increased acid base buffering capacity via dietary supplementation: anaerobic exercise implications. Int J Appl Nutr 1991.

Greenhaff P.L., Hanak J., Harris R.C. *et al.* Metabolic alkalosis and exercise performance in the Thoroughbred horse. Equine Exer Physiol 1991a;3:353.

Greenhaff P.L., Harris R.C., Snow D.H., *et al.* The influence of metabolic alkalosis upon exercise metabolism in the Thoroughbred horse. Eur J Appl Physiol 1991b;63:129.

Harkins J.D. and Kammerling S.G. Effects of induced alkalosis on performance in Thoroughbred during a 1600 m race. Equine Vet J 1992;24(2):94-8.

Kelso T.B., Hodgson D.R., Witt E.H., *et al.* Bicarbonate administration and muscle metabolism during high intensity exercise. Equine Exer Physiol 1987;2:438.

Kirkham W.W., Guttridge H., Bowden J., and Edds G.T. Hematopoietic responses to hematinics. JAVMA 1971;159:1316.

Knippel M., Mauri L., Belluschi R., *et al.* The action of thiamin on the production of lactic acid in cyclists. Med Sport 1986;39(1):11.

Lawrence L.M., Miller P.A., Bechtel P.J., *et al.* The effect of sodium bicarbonate ingestion on blood parameters in exercising horses. Equine Exer Physiol 1987;2:448.

Lawrence L.M., Kline K.H., Miller-Graber P.A., *et al.* Effect of sodium bicarbonate in racing Standardbreds. J Anim Sci 1990;68:673.

Linderman J. and Fahey T.D. Sodium bicarbonate and exercise performance. An update. Sports Med 1991;11:71.

Lyle R.M., Sedlock D.A., Weaver C.M., *et al.* Effect of oral iron therapy vs increased consumption of muscle foods on hemoglobin in exercising women. Med Sci Sport Exer 1991;23(4):577 (abstract).

National Research Council. Nutrient Requirements of Horses. Nat Acad Press, 1989, Washington DC.

Pate R.R. Sports anemia: A review of current literature. Phys Sport Med 1983;11:115.

Petersson K.H., Hintz H.F., Schryver H.F. and Combs G.F. The effect of vitamin E on membrane integrity during submaximal exercise. Equine Exer Physiol 1991;3:315.

Rathgeber-Lawrence R., Ratzlaff M., Grant B.D. and Grimes K.L. The effects of coenzyme Q10 as a nutritional supplement on musculoskeletal fitness in the exercising horse. Equine Athlete 1991;4(3):1.

Roberts A., Lawrence L., Schryver H.F., *et al.* Metabolic changes in exercised horses given sodium bicarbonate. Proc 12th Equine Nutr Physiol Symp 1991, Calgary Alberta.

Roberts M.C. Serum red cell folate and serum B12 levels in horses. Aust Vet J 1983;60:106.

Shelle J., Van Huss W., Rook J.S. and Ullrey D.E. Relationship between selenium and vitamin E nutrition and exercise in the horse. Proc 9th Equine Nutr Physiol Symp 1985, East Lansing, MI.

Topliff D.R., Potter G.D., Kreider J.L. and Creger C.R. Thiamin supplementation for exercising horses. Proc 7th Equine Nutr Physiol Symp 1981, Warrenton, VA.

van der Beek E.J., van Dokkum W., Schrijver J., *et al.* Impact of marginal vitamin intake on physical performance in healthy young men. Proc Nutr Soc 1985;44:27A (abstract).

van Dokkum W., van der Beek E.J., Schrijver J., *et al.* Vitamin restriction and functional performance in man. Amer J Clin Nutr 1989;49:1138 (abstract).

Weaver C. and Rajaram S. Exercise and iron status. J Nutr 1992;122:782.

Weinstein Y., Epstein S., Magazanik A., *et al.* Hematological profile of exercising young females: The effects of oral iron supplementation. Med Sci Sports Exer 1989;21(supp 2):543 (abstract).

Witt E.H., Reznick A.Z., Viguie C.A.,*et al.* Exercise oxidative damage and effects of antioxidant manipulation. J Nutr 1992;122:766.

This paper was first published in "Feeding the Performance Horse," Proceedings for the 1992 Short Course for Feed Manufacturers

ELECTROLYTES AND THE PERFORMANCE HORSE

JOE D. PAGAN

Kentucky Equine Research, Inc., Versailles, Kentucky, USA

Electrolytes are substances that dissociate in solution into electrically charged particles called ions. In the horse, electrolytes play an important role in maintaining osmotic pressure, fluid balance, and nerve and muscle activity. During exercise, sodium (Na^+), potassium (K^+), chloride (Cl^-), and magnesium (Mg^{++}) are lost in the sweat and urine. Loss of these electrolytes causes fatigue and muscle weakness, and decreases the thirst response to dehydration.

It is important to have some idea of the magnitude of loss of electrolytes from the horse during exercise before a feeding program can be developed to replace these losses. Since most of the electrolyte loss in the horse occurs through sweating, one method of calculating electrolyte requirements can be based on different amounts of sweat loss. Body weight loss during exercise is a good way to estimate the amount of fluid lost, where 1 kg (2.2 lbs) of body weight loss equals 1 liter of fluid.

Table 1 contains the levels of Na^+, Cl^-, K^+, and Mg^{++} required per day by a horse at rest, and after exercising hard enough to lose either 5, 10, 25, or 40 liters of sweat.

Table 1. TOTAL DAILY ELECTROLYTE REQUIREMENTS (GRAMS/DAY) AS A FUNCTION OF SWEAT LOSS.

| Electrolyte | Rest | Sweat loss (liters/day) | | | |
		5 liters	10 liters	25 liters	40 liters
Sodium (Na^+)	10	27	43	93	142
Chloride (Cl^-)	10	41	71	163	254
Potassium (K^+)	25	34	43	70	97
Magnesium (Mg^{++})	10	12	13	19	24

The amount of fluid loss will depend on a number of factors such as duration and intensity of exercise, temperature and humidity. Therefore, the best way to determine this loss is to weigh the horse before and after exercise. This after exercise weight should be taken before the horse is allowed to drink. A racehorse training in Florida will obviously lose more sweat than one training in England, but for the sake of comparison we will consider that during a routine workout, sweat loss in a racehorse will amount to between 5 and 10 liters. Losses of 25 liters might occur during a normal endurance ride, and 40 liters of fluid loss would probably only be seen in an exhausted, dehydrated endurance horse in serious danger of dying.

Researchers at the Universities of Tennessee and Georgia measured weight loss, water loss and electrolyte balance in horses competing in a 3-day event in New Jersey (Andrews, *et al.*, 1993). Even though the environmental conditions during this event were fairly mild, the horses lost a significant amount of body water and electrolytes during the competition. The 48 horses measured in this study lost an average of 18.4 liters of body water during the cross country phase of the three day event.

At the 1996 Olympic Games in Atlanta, several 3-day event teams weighed their horses daily throughout the competition. Figure 1 shows the average body weights of the three teams that won medals at the games (Australia-Gold, USA-Silver and New Zealand-Bronze). During the endurance day, the average weight loss of these three teams was 18.4 kg.

Many people don't have a good idea of their horse's daily sweat loss or don't have access to a scale to weigh their horse before and after exercise. Therefore, a more general set of recommendations based on work intensity can be used. Table 2 contains daily requirements of electrolytes for 500 kg horses at maintenance and at light, moderate and heavy work. These values were calculated by Dr. Helmet Meyer, a German researcher who has extensively studied electrolyte requirements in horses (Meyer, 1987).

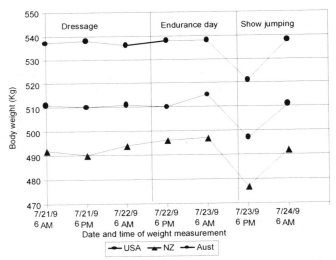

Electrolytes and rhabdomyolysis

Equine rhabdomyolysis, or tying up is a common problem in performance horses. There are a number of possible causes of tying up, but recent research from England suggests that many cases of tying up are related to electrolyte imbalances. Using urinary fractional electrolyte excretion tests, researchers at the Animal Health Trust in Newmarket evaluated the electrolyte status of 144 horses which had suffered repeated attacks of tying up (Harris and Snow, 1992). One hundred of these horses had electrolyte balances outside of normal ranges. Of these 100 animals, 72 suffered no more attacks of the condition after receiving proper electrolyte supplementation.

Table 2. DAILY REQUIREMENTS OF SODIUM, POTASSIUM, CHLORIDE, AND MAGNESIUM FOR HORSES EXERCISING AT DIFFERENT INTENSITIES. (GRAMS/DAY)

		Work intensity		
Electrolyte	*Rest*	*Light*	*Moderate*	*Heavy*
Sodium (Na$^+$)	10	20	50	125
Chloride (Cl$^-$)	10	25	70	175
Potassium (K$^+$)	25	30	44	75
Magnesium (Mg^{++})	10	11	14	15-19

It is the author's impression that many cases of tying up are caused by electrolyte deficiencies resulting from inadequate forage intake. A major source of potassium for horses is forage. Hays typically contain from 10 to 20 grams of potassium per kg. When fed in adequate amounts, hay provides a great deal of a performance horse's potassium requirement.

Besides providing large quantities of potassium, forage helps maintain water balance in exercised horses. German research has shown that horses fed adequate forage maintained water and potassium balance better during exercise than horses fed a high concentrate diet (Meyer *et al.*, 1987). Unfortunately, forage is very low in sodium and marginal in chloride. Therefore, supplemental sodium and chloride are required by the performance horse. A portion of the sodium and chloride required by the performance horse can be provided by a salt lick. Research at Cornell in the US has shown that horses at rest will voluntarily consume about 50 grams per day from a salt block (Schryver *et al.*, 1987).

Supplementing electrolytes

Although it is theoretically possible to fulfill an exercising horse's electrolyte needs with plenty of good quality forage and free choice salt licks, many equine practitioners have reported that supplemental electrolytes are important and beneficial for maximum performance. Besides aiding in the prevention of tying up, electrolytes help horses rebound from hard work sooner, return to feed quicker and begin the necessary rebuilding phase that occurs after exertion.

While electrolytes are essential to the performance horse, electrolyte preparations must be properly formulated to meet the horse's needs. Unlike human preparations, equine electrolyte replacements should not be largely sugar (although some sugar aids in rapid uptake from the gastrointestinal tract). Electrolytes should be formulated to replace the amounts of loss from the horse during exercise.

In summary, electrolytes are essential nutrients for the performance horse. Since horses lose large quantities of electrolytes in sweat, requirements increase with exercise intensity and sweat loss. Adequate intakes of good quality forage and a free choice salt lick will help meet much of the electrolyte requirements of the performance horse. In addition, a commercial electrolyte supplement can help prevent electrolyte depletion, but it should be evaluated to determine whether useful amounts of the critical electrolytes are being supplied.

References

Andrews, F.M., Ralston, S.L., Sommardahl, C.S., *et al.*, 1993. Weight loss, water loss, and cation balance in horses competing in a 3-day event. Proc. Thirteenth Equine Nutr Physiol Symp:203.

Harris, P.A. and Snow, D.H., 1991. Role of electrolyte imbalances in the pathophysiology of the equine rhabdomyolysis syndrome. In: Equine Exercise Physiology 3:435.

Meyer, H., 1987. Nutrition of the equine athlete. In: Equine Exercise Physiology 2:644.

Meyer, H., Perez, H., Gomda, Y. and Heilemann, M. 1987. Postprandial renal and faecal water and electrolyte excretion in horses in relation to kind of feedstuffs, amount of sodium ingested and exercise. Proc. Tenth Equine Nutr Physiol Symp:67.

Schryver, H.F., Parker, M.T., Daniluk, P.D. *et al.* 1987. Salt consumption and the effect of salt on mineral metabolism in horses. Cornell Vet., 77:122.

TRACE MINERALS FOR THE PERFORMANCE HORSE: KNOWN BIOCHEMICAL ROLES AND ESTIMATES OF REQUIREMENTS

STEPHEN G. JACKSON

Kentucky Equine Research Inc., Versailles, Kentucky, USA

In the absence of conclusive experimental data concerning the requirements for any nutrient, the nutritionist is faced with the dilemma of ignoring that nutrient or compiling information which enables an educated guess at the intake of a nutrient adequate to support a specific physiological function. The lack of conclusive experimentally derived data concerning the trace mineral requirements of all classes of horses is astonishing but the lack of data concerning the trace mineral requirements of the athletic horse is staggering. The literature concerning trace minerals and the horse is beginning to allow educated assessment of the requirements for growing horses and brood mares for selenium, zinc, copper, manganese, iron and more recently iodine and chromium. These minerals all play crucial roles in the physiological response to exercise, in energy metabolism and in tissue conservation during a period of insult brought about by exercise. Surely the performance horse has distinct needs for these as well as other nutrients in order to perform an athletic task effectively. The following is a discussion of the roles of certain trace minerals in exercise and where possible an estimation of the trace mineral needs of the athletic horse.

Iron

It is probably fitting that a discussion of trace mineral requirements of the athletic horse begin with a discussion of iron. Iron is, at least from the standpoint of the layman, the first trace mineral that is considered in terms of supplementation. A recent survey conducted at a California race track indicated that a large majority of trainers had their horses on some type of iron supplement (Carlson, 1994). This concern with iron stems from the well known function of iron as part of the heme molecule. This is but one of the important functions of iron but is the basis of the interest in iron and the performance horse. The ancient Greeks recognized iron deficiency anemia and were said to have consumed water in which an iron sword had been placed in order to correct the symptoms of iron deficiency. As early as 1886 it was shown that pure crystals of horse hemoglobin contained 0.33 % iron. Cytochromes, catalases and peroxidases are other iron containing compounds and were discovered as early as the late 1800's. The cytochromes, like hemoglobin, are involved in oxygen utilization via electron transport.

Hemoglobin requires iron for its synthesis and is the component of the red blood cell which allows oxygen to be carried to the tissues. It appears that the cytochromes and enzymes associated with tissue metabolism as well as myoglobin take precedence in the supply of iron in the body and as such the first deficiency symptom associated with iron is anemia. The anemia associated with iron deficiency is hypochromic, microcytic anemia. There are few instances when practical diets would result in iron deficiency anemia. In the previously mentioned study of Carlson, horses which received supplemental iron had iron levels which fell into the normal range for iron in adult horses. Very few of the horses examined had any evidence of anemia and those with resting hematocrits below 34% (defined as anemia) showed no evidence of impaired iron status. This scenario is frequently the case and furthermore it is rare that a horse with lowered hematocrit responds to supplemental iron with a concomitant increase in hematocrit. Clinically significant anemia in the athletic horse is indeed a rare entity. One of the significant aspects of iron metabolism which buffers the horse and other animals from iron deficiency anemia is the ability of the body to conserve iron. Approximately 67% of the iron in the body is contained in the red blood cells in the form of hemoglobin. Red blood cells are formed in a process known as erythropoiesis and remain in the circulation for about 150 days. When these red cells "die," iron contained in the heme molecule is recycled and utilized to synthesize new heme molecules and red blood cells. As such, there is rarely net loss of iron from the body. It is interesting to note that exceptions to this are severely parasitized horses, horses with gastric ulceration that leads to blood loss and perhaps in horses which suffer from severe EIPH (exercise induced pulmonary hemorrhage). A recent study indicated that in excess of 80% of the horses on the race track had some degree of gastric ulceration or at least some erosion of the gastric mucosa. Whether this problem has resulted in net blood and therefore iron loss is still subject to some speculation. The fact that iron recycling is effective and iron deficiencies are rare is apparent from the lack of effectiveness of some of the iron tonics in increasing packed cell volume and hemoglobin concentrations in the blood of horses in training. More times than not, low hematocrits are an indicator of infection, low grade systemic disease or even perhaps marginal B-Vitamin status brought about by stressed large colon or cecal microbial populations and not a deficient dietary intake of iron.

Iron appears to be efficiently absorbed at low levels of intake. Iron absorption is decreased as iron intake increases and with the presence of high concentrations of copper, zinc, manganese, cadmium and cobalt. Additionally, due to the effective iron conservation mechanism, net iron excretion is low and that iron appearing in the feces appears to result primarily from unabsorbed dietary iron rather than from net endogenous fecal losses. Work conducted by Lawrence (1987) in Florida has failed to show an increase in hemoglobin, packed call volume or serum iron when ponies were supplemented with high levels of iron.

There appears to be some iron lost in the sweat. Meyer (1986) estimates that the concentration of iron in horse sweat is about 21 mg/l. Horses in intense exercise may lose as much as 25 - 30 liters of sweat per day and this sweat loss would represent a net iron loss in the sweat of 500 mg/day (25 1 X 21 mg/l). With these sweat losses and the possibility of greater synthesis of hemoglobin and myoglobin (muscle iron containing compound) in the athletic horse there may be reason to believe that the athletic horse has greater requirements for iron than does the mature sedentary horse. Practical dietary constituents contain from 40-50 ppm iron for the cereals, 100-150 ppm iron for the oilseed meals and from 200-1000 ppm iron for many of the forages. Care must be taken in sampling of pastures to avoid soil contamination. Soil in forage samples results in abnormally high iron values and may lead to errors in assessing the iron status of the diet. Another factor to consider in assessing the iron concentration in a manufactured feed is the amount and source of any dicalcium phosphate in the diet. Rations containing much dical, especially supplements or mixing pellets, may contain as much as 1000 ppm iron. It is probable that most of this is iron oxide which is poorly absorbed. Questions still remain, however, as to the impact of this iron on the efficiency of absorption of other minerals.

The National Research Council, Nutrient Requirements of Horses (NRC, 1989) lists the iron requirement of the performance horse as 40 mg/kg of dry matter (ppm). Assuming a dry matter intake of roughly 12 kg for the horse at high work intensities this would result in an iron requirement of roughly 500 mg/day. For horses in intense work that are losing a great deal of sweat this may only be enough iron to replace that iron lost in sweat and therefore may be a bit low in terms of meeting the horses' iron requirement. There is no reason to believe that the requirement is any higher than 40 ppm for the horse at light to moderate work intensity. Meyer (1986) suggest that the iron requirement of the 500 kg horse is 500, 600 and 1200 mg/day for light, moderate and heavy exercise. Unfortunately, it will be a long time before the people doing the feeding are convinced that some of the expensive hematinics don't really make their horses run faster and jump higher. Hopefully at the levels at which iron is fed it is fairly innocuous. It is just possible that in attempts to stimulate the "blood picture" some horsemen are unwittingly causing interactive deficiencies of other minerals.

Manganese

The best known function of manganese is its role in bone formation. Manganese is needed in several of the steps necessary in the formation of chondroitin sulfate and in the synthesis of the organic matrix of bone which is predominantly a mucopolysaccharide ground substance. Manganese is required in the synthesis of chondroitin sulfate (ring any bells?, this is one of the new wave of supplements for the performance horse) and appears to be required in the enzymes galactotransferase and polymerase required in the synthesis of chondroitin sulfate from beta-D-glucuronide and 1,3-N-acetyl-D-galactosamine. Manganese deficiency is expressed as a disorganization of the cells making up the epiphyseal plate, a narrowing of the epiphyseal plate and a reduction of blood vessel migration into the growth plate. Additionally the cartilage of the growth plate in manganese deficient animals contains lower levels of chondroitin sulfate than do the growth plates of normal animals. With respect to this function of manganese it stands to reason that two and three year old horses in which skeletal maturation is not complete may have a slightly higher requirement for manganese than do older animals.

Manganese is also known to be an activator of several enzymes such as arginase, thiaminase, carnosinase and deoxyribonuclease. Manganese is required for oxidative phosphorylation in the mitochondria and as such is very involved in regeneration of ATP from ADP, a reaction critical for the maintenance of adequate concentrations of the high energy phosphagens in the athletic horse. It is unlikely that a Mn deficiency would be rate limiting in the production of ATP but this demonstrates the crucial role that trace minerals play as co-factors and components of various of the enzymes. Manganese is also known to be involved in fatty acid synthesis and in amino acid metabolism either as a co-enzyme or as an activator of enzymes . Manganese also is an effective chelating agent allowing for more efficient and rapid transfer of amino acids.   Because of the role that Mn plays in energy metabolism through various roles in lipid metabolism and carbohydrate metabolism it is of interest in the formulation of performance horse diets. In most areas of the world manganese deficiency does not appear to be of concern in horses grazing fresh forage. Mn concentrations in forage range from 50 - 300 ppm and these levels should meet the requirements of most horses. However, cereal grains contain less Mn and may range in Mn concentration from 5 ppm (corn) to 15 ppm (barley). In the athletic horse on high grain diets and consuming grass hay of variable quality it is probable that some supplemental manganese may be required. It is our practice to supplement performance horse diets with 80-100 ppm manganese with about 1/3 of the supplemental Mn coming from chelated manganese and 2/3 from manganous oxide. High concentrations of calcium and phosphorus in feeds or forages may inhibit manganese absorption and this should be taken into account in the formulation of feeds for all classes of horses. It is interesting to note that some of the forages I have sampled from around the world that are the highest in manganese are also the highest in calcium. Some forages in Ireland for instance may have from 200-300 ppm Mn and 1% calcium. Unlike in the US when these calcium concentrations are found in mixed grass/legume swards, these calcium concentrations are common in pure swards of ryegrass. Whether there is a significance to this is still under investigation.

There is little, <0.2 mg/l , manganese in horse sweat and as such one would expect manganese losses in sweat to be minimal. We currently would think that 350 mg/day of Mn should be adequate for horses at low work intensities and think that horses' requirement for this mineral should be met with 500 mg/day for horses at moderate to high work intensities.

Selenium

Selenium is recognized as an essential nutrient as well as an environmental toxicant. The selenium requirements listed for domestic livestock may be as much a political compromise as an accurate assessment of the physiological needs for the mineral. Selenium is best known as an essential component of the selenium dependent enzyme glutathione peroxidase and functions as part of the cellular antioxidant defense system. Selenium functions much as does vitamin-E in a role of biological antioxidant and indeed there are a number of deficiency symptoms of selenium that may be partially corrected by vitamin-E and vice-versa. The antioxidant defense system allows for the trapping of free radicals and superoxides which cause oxidative damage to lipid membranes. Simply put, glutathione peroxidase converts reduced glutathione to oxidized glutathione and destroys peroxides by converting them to harmless alcohols. This conversion of the peroxides prevents them from reacting with lipid membranes and causing loss of membrane integrity.

It follows that since exercise results in increased oxygen delivery to the tissues and oxidation of energy substrate resulting in the generation of reactive oxygen by-products, peroxides, the selenium requirement for the athletic horse should be increased. Shellow (1985) did a trial with sedentary geldings fed a basal diet and three levels of supplemental selenium, 0.05, 0.1, and 0.2 ppm supplemental selenium to assess the impact of feeding supplemental selenium on plasma and whole blood selenium and on glutathione peroxidase which has been thought to be an accurate indicator of selenium status. They reported that there was a linear increase in plasma selenium over time until a level of 0.14 ppm was reached in the plasma and then selenium plateaued regardless of the amount of selenium that was fed. There was no difference in peak plasma selenium values between 0.1 and 0.2 ppm supplemental selenium. When the basal selenium level of the diet, 0.06 ppm was added to the supplemented selenium, this experiment suggested that a requirement of 0.16 ppm in the total diet was appropriate. Shellow (1985) was unable to find a relationship between dietary selenium level and glutathione peroxidase activity and suggested that plasma selenium may be a better indicator of selenium status than is glutathione peroxidase. It is interesting to note that in this experiment there was a significant difference in plasma and whole blood selenium due to the relatively high concentration of selenium associated with the red blood cells. Whole blood selenium is higher than is plasma selenium and it is important that the distinction be made in the interpretation of blood test results.

Stowe (1993) has suggested that the appropriate concentration of selenium in the total diets of horses is 0.3 ppm. This would mean that if a concentrate mix was

50% of the diet and the forage component of the diet was 0.06 ppm se, the grain mix would need to be roughly 0.6 ppm. There have been few studies dealing directly with the relationship of selenium requirements to exercise. Shelle (1983) investigated the effect of supplemental selenium on plasma selenium and on glutathione peroxidase in Arabian and crossbred horses subjected to a conditioning program. He reported that conditioning increased erythrocyte glutathione peroxidase activity and suggested that horses at high work intensities may have higher requirements for selenium than the 0.1 ppm requirement suggested by the NRC. Supplementing horses with 1-2 mg of selenium and 1000 mg of vitamin E has long been thought to prevent exertional rhabdomyolysis in some horses. It is probably done in response to the "leakage " of muscle enzymes into the plasma from the muscle. Appearance of high levels of LDH, SGOT and CPK in the plasma has been indicative of muscle damage and the thought was that the muscle membrane was subjected to reactive peroxides resulting in damage to the membranes and leakage of the enzymes into the circulation. Unfortunately not all horses have responded to supplementation with selenium and vitamin E and ceased to tie-up. It is still a good idea to evaluate the diets of horses that tie-up and rectify selenium and vitamin E deficiencies should there be any. More recently, another interesting role of selenium has been revealed. Selenium appears to be part of the enzyme Type I iodothyronine deiodinase. This is a selenoenzyme which catalyzes the conversion of thyroxine (T4) to triiodothyronine (T3) which is the tissue active form of the thyroid hormone. It is interesting to speculate whether some of the clinical manifestations of hypothyroidism may in fact be secondary to selenium deficiency.

Our current recommendations for selenium in the performance horse range from 2.5 to 3.5 mg/day depending on work intensity, weight, and other environmental factors. We do not recommend selenium and Vitamin-E injections as there have been numerous reports of anaphylactic reactions to the injection of some of the commercial preparations of these nutrients. In most cases the horses affected by the anaphylaxis died and since dietary selenium and vitamin E are well absorbed and result in increased plasma levels of these two nutrients it is not worth the risk to use the injection.

Iodine

Much like selenium, iodine has suffered in relative obscurity since the margin between adequate and toxic has been over-stressed. The only known function of iodine is as part of the thyroid hormones thyroxin and triiodothyronine. The classical deficiency symptom for iodine is a hypoiodine goiter and the classic toxicity is a hyperiodine goiter. As such the only real way to assess the adequacy of the diet is to evaluate the ration. Thyroxin and the tissue active form of the hormone, triiodothyronine (T3), serve a multitude of metabolic and regulatory roles. The thyroid hormones affect all of the organ systems, muscle metabolism, the nervous system, respiration and the cardiovascular system. Thyroxin also controls growth rate and cell division, metabolic rate and oxidative metabolism.

In the athletic horse, perhaps the most important role of thyroxin is control of basal metabolic rate and cellular energy metabolism. Thyroid hormone stimulates respiration in the mitochondria resulting in increased oxygen consumption and energy production. There has been a great deal of interest in the use of supplemental, synthetic thyroxin in the performance horse. This use of Thyrol-L is predicated on what appears to be a fairly common hypothyroxemia among performance horses. Unfortunately, no one has done the research to ascertain whether this apparent lack of thyroactive hormones is due to a lack of iodine in the diet, a lack of selenium for the conversion of T4 to T3 or to dysfunction of the thyroid gland. Additionally there are some known goiterigenic compounds such as kale, cabbage, Brassica, and perhaps Kentucky 31 tall fescue which interfere with iodine uptake and thyroid function.

Current NRC recommendations for iodine are for 0.1 ppm (mg/kg of dry matter). At this level of intake a dry matter intake of 10 kg per day would result in only 1 mg of iodine intake. This is a little less than half of our current recommendations for iodine. We would propose that the 500 kg horse at light work requires 1.75 mg of iodine, at moderate work 2.5 mg and in intense training 2.75-3.0 mg/day of iodine. There is still a great deal of work to be done in understanding the relationship between dietary iodine and thyroid function but I suspect it will be the next trace mineral topic that is in vogue.

Chromium

The recognized function of chromium is as a component of glucose tolerance factor (GTF). GTF is thought to potentiate the action of insulin in Cr-deficient tissue. Insulin has anabolic characteristics as it promotes glucose uptake by the cell, stimulates amino acid synthesis and inhibits tissue lipase. Because of its role in carbohydrate, lipid and protein metabolism and in the clearance of blood glucose it is interesting to consider the requirements of the athletic horse for chromium. Chromium excretion is greater in athletic than in sedentary humans and the chromium requirement is increased by physical activity. Chromium supplementation has increased lean body mass in humans and pigs and has resulted in a partitioning effect on nutrients which favors tissue anabolism and muscle protein accretion. In calves chromium excretion is greater during stress and chromium supplementation has resulted in a stimulation of the immune system and less mortality and morbidity in shipped feedlot cattle. Certainly this aspect of chromium is interesting when we consider the performance horse and the kind of stresses that they may see. There has been a great deal of research on chromium in humans, rats and pigs owing to the crucial role insulin status plays in diabetes. There is very little research work that has been done in other species of animals and only a few reports in horses.

Pagan *et al.* (1995) reported that supplementing performance horses with 5 mg/day of chromium in the form of chromium yeast had a beneficial effect on the response of horses to exercise stress. Horses were subjected to a standard exercise test on a high speed treadmill and blood and heart rate were monitored. Horses in that experiment receiving chromium cleared blood glucose following a meal more quickly than control horses, showed lower peak insulin values and lower cortisol levels. Chromium supplemented horses also had higher triglyceride values during exercise indicating perhaps more efficient fat mobilization. There was no difference in the heart rate in response to exercise between the two groups but peak lactic acid concentrations in the chromium supplemented group of horses were significantly lower than for the controls.

Work on chromium continues in our laboratories at Kentucky Equine Research. There is gathering evidence from the field that chromium supplementation may have a positive impact on horses known to have chronic problems with exertional rhabdomyolysis. One of the features of horses that routinely tie-up is a problem with normal glucose and glycogen metabolism. It may be that the role of chromium in GTF assists in clearing glucose and may make glycogen utilization and storage more efficient. Trainers that have had horses on Metaboleeze (the KER chromium supplement) have commented that horses appear less nervous and more work tolerant than non-supplemented horses. Current work with chromium is progressing in the areas of the laminitic horse and in other conditions thought to be related to insulin insensitivity.

The good news is that everyone pretty well realizes that chromium is an essential nutrient for man and animals; the bad news is that chromium is not GRAS listed (generally recognized as safe) by the FDA. As such, it is currently not legal to add chromium yeast to commercial feeds as a source of organic chromium in the US. If a horseman wants to supplement with chromium he may do so in one of two ways: 1) he may buy chromium at a human health food store or 2) he may get a prescription from a veterinarian for Metaboleeze from KER. We have set the chromium requirement for the performance horse at 5 mg/day but know that a great deal more research needs to be done to titrate this requirement and elucidate further the beneficial effects of chromium in the diets of horses in training.

Zinc and copper

There has been a great deal of attention given to the requirements of the young horse and the broodmare for copper and zinc. The role of copper in the copper dependent enzyme lysyl oxidase and that enzyme's role in the formation and maturation of cartilage has obviously stimulated interest in copper as it relates to developmental orthopedic disease in young horses. Additionally, zinc has long been known to play a role in the maintenance of epithelial integrity and in keratogenesis. The use of copper and zinc supplementation in modern horse feeds for all classes of horses stems from the possible role of these two nutrients in reducing physitis, osteochondrosis, wobbler syndrome and other manifestations of developmental orthopedic disease.

It is interesting to note that in addition to its role in cartilage and bone metabolism, copper is also involved in hemoglobin formation and in nerve conductivity and coordination. Copper is also involved in other enzymes such as tyrosinase and cytochrome oxidase to name but a few of the more well known of the enzymes containing a copper moiety or which need copper as a co-factor. There does not really seem to be a down side to the inclusion of copper at the levels we now use. Currently we would recommend the performance horse receive 131, 170 and 187 mg/day of copper for light, moderate and heavy work respectively. We also would typically use bioplexes (chelates) to provide 30% of the supplemental copper in most of our rations. These allowances are not a great deal more than those of the NRC for the performance horse. Current NRC recommendations are for 10 ppm copper or 10 mg/kg of dry matter intake. We would think that with calcium intakes being higher due to the use of legume hays and with typical feeds ranging from 0.6 - 1.0 % calcium, there is justification for higher copper inclusion rates. There is a small loss of copper in the sweat of horses and probably is no greater than 4 mg/l of sweat. Still this may result in sweat losses of 80-100 mg of copper per day.

Zinc is involved as a co-factor in a multitude of enzyme systems. Alcohol dehydrogenase, carbonic anhydrase and carboxypeptidase are but a few of the Zn requiring enzymes. In addition to the role as enzyme activator/co-factor, there are in excess of 200 zinc containing proteins. 50 to 60 % of the zinc in the body is stored in the muscle. Zinc deficiency has resulted in reduced insulin levels and reduced glucose tolerance along with increased insulin resistance especially in the peripheral tissues. There has been a noted decrease in glucose utilization in zinc deficient animals with a concomitant increase in fat catabolism. There is a lowering of resting R.Q. in zinc deficiency which would be characteristic of increased fat catabolism. In terms of bone metabolism zinc deficiency directly inhibits the effectiveness of somatomedin in stimulating cartilage growth and the classical symptom of zinc deficiency is disrupted keratogenesis.

There is a significant amount of zinc that is lost in the sweat. Meyer (1986) has determined the loss of zinc in the sweat to be 20-21 mg/l of sweat. Obviously in the hard working horse this zinc loss can be substantial. High levels of calcium and copper can reduce zinc absorption so the kind of hay being fed may have an impact on the amount of zinc required by the horse. Increased levels of protein or increased protein intake has been shown to reduce zinc absorption and increase zinc excretion. These classic and well documented physiological and biochemical functions of zinc along with the relatively high zinc losses in the sweat have resulted in the development of more liberal allowances for zinc than the NRC proposes. We would currently recommend the zinc intake of the performance horse in moderate and heavy work needs to be 500 mg/day and think that 400 mg/day is probably adequate for the horse at light work intensities. Regarding copper, it is our general practice to use bioplexes as 30% of the supplemental zinc in the ration. Another note of interest: when the efficacy of hoof supplements is considered, the inclusion of zinc-methionine along with biotin and 3 grams of methionine appears to result in greater growth of the stratum germinativum and the tubular horn of the hoof wall than does the feeding of biotin alone.

The trace mineral nutrition of the performance horse remains an educated guess. It is encouraging to see more emphasis on trace mineral nutrition in the horse and particularly in the athletic horse. Hopefully over the next several years we will be able to more thoroughly elucidate the trace mineral requirements of the horse and accurately describe their metabolic functions. Until then hopefully the requirements that NRC and KER have derived will be of some use in preventing deficiency and enhancing the horses' ability to cope with the stress of exercise.

References

Carlson, G.P. 1994. Forty years later - can we diagnose and treat anemia yet? Proceedings 16th Bain-Fallon Memorial Lectures. Aus. Eq. Vet. Assn. Queensland, Australia.

Lawrence, L.M ., E.A. Ott, R.L. Asquith and G.J. Miller. 1987. Influence of dietary iron on growth, tissue mineral composition, apparent phosphorus absorption and chemical properties of bone. Proc. 10th Equine Nutr. and Physiol Soc Symp , Ft.Collins, Colorado.

National Research Council. 1989. Nutrient requirements of horses. National Academy Press, Washington D.C.

Meyer, H. 1987. Nutrition of the equine athlete. In: Proceedings 2nd International Conference on Equine Exercise Physiology. J.R. Gillespie and N.E. Robinson eds. San Diego, California.

Pagan, J.D., S.G. Jackson and S.E. Duren. 1995. The effect of chromium supplementation on the metabolic response to exercise in Thoroughbred horses. Proc. 14th Equine Nutr. And Physiol. Soc. Symp., Ontario, California.

Shelle, J.E., W.D. Vanhuss, J.S. Rook and D.E. Ullrey. 1985. Relationship between selenium and vitamin E nutrition and exercise in horses. Proc. 9th Equine Nutr. and Physiol. Soc. Symp., Lansing Mich.

Shellow, J.S., S.G. Jackson, J.P. Baker and A.H. Cantor.1985. The influence of dietary selenium levels on blood levels of selenium and glutathione peroxidase activity in the horse. J. Anim. Sci., 61:590.

Stowe, H.D. 1993. The horse feed manufacturer's dilemma regarding selenium supplementation. Proc. Feeding the Performance Horse. Kentucky Equine Research, Versailles, Kentucky.

This paper was first published in Proceedings, Kentucky Equine Research 1997 Equine Nutrition Conference

FAT SOLUBLE VITAMINS AND THE PERFORMANCE HORSE

KATHLEEN CRANDELL

Kentucky Equine Research, Inc., Middleburg, Virginia, USA

Introduction

Feeding vitamin supplements to horses has become commonplace. There are questions about the necessity of this practice, and the dangers involved. Fat soluble vitamins (A, D, E, and K) in particular can be a problem because of their ability to build up toxic levels in the body. In the horse, the amounts of these vitamins needed to prevent deficiency or produce toxicity have been established, but very little work has been done on the effect of exercise on these requirements. This paper addresses functions, forms and requirements of fat-soluble vitamins in the horse.

Fat-soluble vitamins

Vitamins are complex organic compounds, present in minute amounts in natural foodstuffs, that are essential to normal metabolism. Lack of said vitamins in the diet results in deficiency disease. Vitamins are a mixed group of compounds that are not similar to each other but are grouped by function, and are differentiated from trace elements by their organic nature. Although there are two general categories of vitamins, fat-soluble and water-soluble, this article focuses on those that are fat soluble.

Fat soluble vitamins are those that occur in nature in association with lipids and are absorbed along with dietary fats; conditions favorable to fat absorption would also be favorable to absorption of fat-soluble vitamins. Because of their lipid nature, fat-soluble vitamins can be stored in appreciable amounts in the body and are excreted in the feces via the bile. However, the relative ease of accumulating fat-soluble vitamins makes them more likely to cause problems in excessive amounts (particularly A and D).

Level of fat in the diet may affect absorption of the fat-soluble vitamin A, D, E, and K, as well as the requirement for vitamin E. Fat-soluble vitamins may fail to be absorbed if digestion of fat is impaired.

Many vitamins are delicate substances that can suffer loss of activity due to unfavorable circumstances encountered during processing or storage of premixes and feeds. Stress factors for vitamins include humidity, pressure (pelleting), heat, light, oxidation-reduction, rancidity, trace minerals, pH, and interactions with other vitamins, carriers, enzymes, and feed additives (NRC, 1973). Rancid fats destroy vitamins A, D and E. Dicumerol, found in certain plants, interferes with blood clotting by blocking the action of vitamin K. Certain sulfonamides may reduce intestinal absorption of vitamin K.

Vitamins represent only a minute fraction of animal feeds, amounting to less than 0.1% by weight and about 1-2% of the cost (depending on the diet used and the level of supplementation required). What many consumers do not understand is that a balanced vitamin fortification for meeting requirements of the animal will more than offset the cost of adding vitamins in the health and vitality of the animal.

Vitamin A

FUNCTIONS

Vitamin A is perhaps the most important of the vitamins and is indispensable for support of growth and health of a horse. Deficiency causes loss of vision, defects in bone growth, defects in reproduction, defects in growth and differentiation of epithelial tissues, and lowered resistance to disease and infection.

FORMS OF THE VITAMIN

Active

Vitamin A is a generic term describing several forms of retinoids. The most abundant forms which are found in use in the body are retinol, retinal, and retinoic acid. These forms of vitamin A will bind easily to other compounds. Transported forms commonly found in the corporal circulation are retinol bound to a binding protein and esters such as retinyl palmitate and retinyl acetate. Esterification makes vitamin A more stable. For that reason, synthetic or animal sources of vitamin A typically are in the form of esters.

Inactive

Although vitamin A does not occur in plant products, its precursor, carotene, does in several forms. However, only about 20 of the over 600 carotenes have provitamin A activity. These compounds are commonly referred to as provitamin A because the body can transform them into the active vitamin. Conversion usually occurs in the intestinal mucosa, but can occur to a lesser extent in the liver and adipose tissue as well. The most biologically active of the carotenes is ß-carotene, which theoretically could be split by the enzyme 'ß-carotene 15, 15'-dioxygenase' enzyme to form 2 vitamin A. Unfortunately, the actual conversion rate is much lower. From one mg of ß-carotene the horse can only get approximately 0.01-0.05 mg of vitamin A. Rate of conversion is affected by many factors: age, activity, level of intake, environmental temperature, and the individual's vitamin A intake and status.

DIETARY SOURCES

Natural

Naturally occurring vitamin A can be found in fish oils, milk fat, egg yolk and liver. Typically these are not feeds eaten by a horse. Carotenes are the natural source of vitamin A for the horse, since they are found in abundance in green forages. Unfortunately, much of the carotene content is destroyed by oxidation in the process of field curing. Horses are not able to absorb sufficient quantities of ß-carotene from hay to meet their requirement, except possibly well made early bloom alfalfa hay (Fonnesbeck and Symons, 1967).

Synthetic

Sources of supplemental vitamin A are derived primarily from fish liver oil and from industrial chemical synthesis. Forms of vitamin A typically used as feed additives are all-trans retinyl palmitate and acetate. Since vitamin A is easily destroyed by oxidation they are stabilized by coating the vitamin in fat or gelatin and adding antioxidants.

REQUIREMENT

National Research Council (NRC) recommendations for vitamins are usually close to the minimal amount necessary to prevent deficiency signs, but not necessarily the optimal amount needed by the animal. Feeding at the NRC recommended level may lead to suboptimum performance even though the animal appears normal. In a 40 week study, growing ponies fed the NRC recommended level appeared normal, but upon postmortem examination exhibited lesions suggestive of vitamin A deficiency (Donoghue and Kronfeld, 1980). Optimal supplementation of vitamin A for the horse has been hypothesized to be more than twice (Greiwe-Crandell *et al.*, 1997) and possibly as much as 5 times (Donoghue *et al.*, 1981) the NRC recommendation.

Maintenance

Horse grazing high quality pastures during the growing season are easily receiving their full vitamin A requirement (in the form of carotene). Likewise, if the horse is consuming large quantities of very green alfalfa hay, vitamin A might not be a problem. If the horse subsists on hay and grains, then it will need supplementation. The NRC recommends that diets for all horses should provide 30 to 60 IU of vitamin A activity and retinol or equivalent per kg of body weight per day (NRC, 1989). Even if the horse is grazing, additional vitamin A is not harmful as long as the amount given is not excessive. Vitamin A supplementation has been found to decrease the amount of carotenes converted in the animal.

Performance

Very little research on vitamin A supplementation of the performance horse has been done. Abrams (1979) supplemented four Thoroughbred race horses in training over a two year period with 50,000 IU/d of Vitamin A to a diet of hay, oats and bran. The supplemented horses were sound for 64% more races than the other four horses on the study not receiving the Vitamin A. In addition, by the second year of training, all horses not receiving the vitamin A were plagued with lameness, particularly with tendon problems. The horses receiving the vitamin A were all sound and fit for racing. Butler and Blackmore (1982) sampled 71 two and three year old Thoroughbreds in race training in England monthly for 6 months. Mean plasma level were 16.5 ug/dl, which were low/normal values. Since these are horses in intense training, the low plasma levels may be indicative of an increased utilization of vitamin A with exercise. Further work is needed to define vitamin A requirements for exercise in the horse.

TOXICITY

Vitamin A

Oversupplementation of vitamin A appears to be more of a problem than under-supplementation because vitamin A can be very toxic in excessive amounts (Donoghue *et al.*, 1981). Symptoms of mild toxicity (100 times the NRC recommended levels) are difficult to define in the attitude of the horse, but the obvious signs are the same as mildly deficient horses: slowed growth, dull hair coat and poor muscle tone. Severe toxicity (up to 1000 times the NRC recommended level) results in depression, alopecia, ataxia, severe bone deformation and eventually death. Blood values of intoxicated horses may increase to up to 6 times the normal range (normal = 17-50 g/dl). In addition, low red blood cell count and low levels of cholesterol and albumin may be indicative of vitamin A intoxication (Donoghue *et al.*, 1981). The NRC has proposed an upper safe limit of 16,000 IU of vitamin A per kg of dry diet per day for chronic administration (NRC, 1989).

Carotenes

Carotenes have not been found to be toxic at any level of intake because the body appears to down-regulate the activity of the enzyme responsible for converting the carotene into vitamin A (McDowell, 1989). The only symptom of excessive carotene intake may be a yellowing of the skin due to an increase in storage of carotenes in adipose tissue, but this does not appear to have any effect on the overall health of the animal.

Vitamin D

FUNCTIONS

Vitamin D can be considered a vitamin only in the sense that, under modern farming conditions, many animals are raised in total confinement with little or no exposure to natural sunlight. Vitamin D is actually a hormone and adequate sunlight results in the production of sufficient vitamin D from 7-dehydrocholesterol in the skin. Hence vitamin D is not required in the diet if sufficient amounts of sunlight are received. Sufficient vitamin D must be present for calcium and phosphorus to be absorbed; a vitamin D deficiency markedly reduces absorption of both minerals. Lack of adequate photoproduction of vitamin D_3 or inadequate dietary supplementation of vitamin D leads to the failure of bones to calcify normally. This metabolic disease is known as rickets in the young and osteomalacia in adults.

FORMS OF THE VITAMIN

Plant and animal

The two major natural sources of vitamin D are cholecalciferol (vitamin D_3, which occurs in animals) or ergocalciferol (D_2, which occurs predominantly in plants). Vitamin D_2 and D_3 are not equally utilized by the horse; it appears that D_3 may be many times more potent a source than D_2 (Harrington and Page, 1983).

Activation

Vitamin D_3 produced in the skin goes to the liver. Dietary vitamins D_2 and D_3 are absorbed in the distal small intestine. The absorbed vitamin D is transported via the lymph-blood system to the liver where it is hydroxylated to 25-hydroxycholecalciferol. This form is then secreted back into the blood stream where it is further hydroxylated in the kidney to either 1,25-dihydroxycholecalciferol or 24,25-dihydroxycholecalciferol. The conversions of these vitamin D metabolites are under hormonal control. Low blood calcium stimulates the secretion of parathyroid hormone (PTH), which in turn stimulates the of release of these metabolites. Vitamin D metabolites have a three-fold effect: an increase in the absorption of calcium, phosphorus, and magnesium in the intestines, an increase in the release of calcium and phosphorus from the bone, and an increase in the resorption of calcium in the kidney.

DIETARY SOURCES

Intracorporal

Vitamin D_3 (cholecalciferol) results primarily from ultraviolet irradiation of 7-dehydrocholesterol synthesized by the tissues of the horse and present in the skin. The vitamin is then transported to the liver for utilization.

Sun cured feeds

Vitamin D_2 (ergocalciferol) results from ultraviolet irradiation of ergosterol, which is synthesized by plants. This process does not occur until the plant has been cut and is exposed to sunlight. Leaves have a higher concentration of D_2 than stems.

Other sources

Foods naturally rich in vitamin D_3 include fish oils and egg yolks; in vitamin D_2, sun cured forages. Many commercial horse feeds include vitamin D in the formulation in case the animals are not receiving enough vitamin D from other sources.

REQUIREMENT

Modern horsemanship practices may predispose the horse to suboptimal intakes of vitamin D. Restricting the amount of turnout for horses to less than 2 hours a day prevents their bodies from having time to convert sufficient vitamin D in the skin. In addition, during winter, conversion is less efficient because of the lower intensity of light and is further compounded by the use of blankets covering much of their bodies. During summer, horses tend to be turned out at night when it is cool and kept inside when the sun is shining. Furthermore, hays that have been dried artificially with little exposure to sunlight will not contain much vitamin D.

Maintenance

No absolute requirement has yet been established for the horse. However, supplementation with 800 to 1000 IU of Vitamin D per kg of dry diet has been found to be adequate to prevent deficiency symptoms in growing horses. For the adult, 500 IU of vitamin D per kg of dry diet may be sufficient (NRC, 1989). Supplementation at this level with no exposure to sunlight does not produce bones as strong as those in a horse that is maintained outside (Shorafa *et al.*, 1979). Optimal supplementation for horses with limited access to sunlight is not yet known.

Performance

Extensive bone remodeling was found in young horses undergoing race training resulting in changes in calcium, phosphorus and vitamin D levels in serum and bone (Nielsen *et al.*, 1995). Logically, anything that stresses the bone structure of the animal (such as carrying the weight of the rider, jumping or intensive training) will increase the amount of bone remodeling, and therefore, may increase the need for vitamin D. An increase in vitamin D intake has been found to increase efficiency of calcium and phosphorus absorption in the intestinal tract (Cromwell, 1996) which would increase the supply of these nutrients as needed in times of stress due to exercise. Much more work needs to be done on vitamin D supplementation in the exercising horse.

TOXICITY

Outward signs of vitamin D toxicosis are depression , decreased appetite with weight loss, and limb stiffness. When young ponies were fed 14,000 IU vitamin D per kg body weight daily, acute toxicity and severe calcification of the lungs, heart, kidney and other organs occurred within 10 days. Chronic toxicity (calcification of kidneys, rarefication of bone, severe weight loss and death after 3 to 4 months) occurred when 3500 IU vitamin D per kg of body weight per day was fed (Hintz*et al.*, 1973).

The tolerable dose varies with the intake of calcium and possibly other nutrients which influence calcium metabolism, such as phosphorus, magnesium, protein and vitamin A. The NRC suggests that a level of 50 times the requirements may be harmful to horses.

Vitamin E

FUNCTIONS

Vitamin E has numerous functions in the body, many of which are still not completely understood. Vitamin E is essential for the integrity and optimum function of reproductive, muscular, circulatory, nervous and immune systems. Its action as a natural antioxidant is seen as the underlying factor of most vitamin E functions. Vitamin E is considered to be the most effective natural lipid-soluble chain-breaking antioxidant. The action of vitamin E is very important in cell membranes, protecting them from peroxidative damage. This is especially important in the mitochondrial membrane, where enzymes involved in respiratory chain energy production are located. Selenium , like vitamin E, also acts to prevent lipid peroxidation, however with differing mechanisms. The two complement each other, one appearing to be able to compensate for the absence of the other. Signs of deficiency, such as nutritional muscular dystrophy, are often the same as those seen with selenium deficiency. Other diseases associated with low serum vitamin E include degenerative myelopathy and degenerative myeloencephalopathy.

FORMS OF THE VITAMIN

Natural

There are at least eight forms of vitamin E found widely distributed in nature: four tocopherols (α, β, δ, and γ) and four tocotrienols (α, β, δ, and γ). The majority of vitamin E activity in animal tissues is generally assumed to be α-tocopherol and when it is present it is used preferentially (Ullrey, 1981). Tocopherols are extremely resistant to heat but readily oxidized. Natural vitamin E is subject to destruction by oxidation, accelerated by heat, moisture, rancid fat, and certain trace minerals (McDowell, 1989). Horses have the capability to store much less vitamin E than vitamin A; nevertheless, stores are thought to be able to compensate for about 4 months of inadequate vitamin E intake. An increase in the requirement for vitamin E that usually occurs with increasing intakes of oils high in polyunsaturated fatty acids has not been observed in the horse (Siciliano and Wood, 1993).

Synthetic

Since esterification stabilizes vitamin E, commercial supplements usually contain tocopheryl acetates.

DIETARY SOURCES

Found in plants

Vitamin E is abundant in green growing pastures (45 to >400 IU/kg), particularly in alfalfa (McDowell, 1989). The content diminishes with maturation, especially after going to seed. Harvesting the forage diminishes the quantity of vitamin E present (10-200 IU/kg). Storage of the hay further decreases the amount of vitamin A as much as 50% in the first month of storage. Vitamin E is abundant in the germ of grains and oils pressed from the germ (wheat germ oil, 1330 IU/kg). Vegetable oils such as corn and soybean oil are relatively high in vitamin E (50-300 IU/kg). In practice, the vitamin E content of other feedstuffs is variable and not readily predictable because of handling and storage time. Therefore, it is common practice to supplement animal feeds with vitamin E.

Added to feeds

No differences were found in the utilization of natural versus synthetic forms of vitamin E added into the feeds of exercising horses (Gansen *et al.*, 1995). However, the natural vitamin E was fed at one-third the amount of the synthetic vitamin E. This would suggest that the natural form is more available than the synthetic form.

REQUIREMENT

Maintenance

Significant confusion of actual vitamin E requirement exists because of the difficulty in determining the amount needed to prevent deficiency symptoms and the amount needed to produce optimal immune function. The NRC (1989) recommends 50 IU of vitamin E per kg of dietary dry matter in the total diet for the maintenance horse, and 80 to 100 IU in foals, pregnant and lactating mares, and working horses.

Performance

Vitamin E appears to be the most researched vitamin at this time in production animals, and in particular, its effects on improving performance. Since the main function of vitamin E is to protect the cell against peroxidative damage, lipid peroxidation as a result of exercise may be influenced by the concentration of vitamin E present in the diet. Several studies have reported evidence of oxidative stress occurring with exercise in both humans and rodents (Siciliano and Lawrence, 1996). Serum vitamin E decreased in horses undergoing exercise conditioning and fed a diet low in vitamin E (< 18 IU/kg dry matter) over a period of four months. However, no improvement in performance of a standardized exercise test following vitamin E supplementation for one month was reported (Petersson *et al.*, 1991). Total diet concentrations of 44 IU per kg dry matter increased blood levels of vitamin E but did not increase performance (McNeniman and Hintz, 1992). Because of the nature of vitamin E, benefits of supplementation during exercise would more likely be seen in long duration exercise, such as endurance riding. Unfortunately, little if any work has been done with horses in this field.

TOXICITY

Signs of vitamin E toxicity in the horse have not been produced. However, in other animals, very high intakes have been found to interfere with utilization of other fat-soluble vitamins. The NRC (1989), therefore, takes a conservative upper limit for vitamin E supplementation of 100 IU/kg of dry diet or 20 IU/kg of body weight per day.

Vitamin K

FUNCTIONS

The major function of vitamin K is in blood coagulation. In fact, the Danish discoverer of the vitamin named it after its function "koagulation" (Danish spelling). The vitamin is required for the activation of the four plasma clotting factors. Recently, vitamin K has also been found to have a role in the activation of a number of other proteins throughout the body, some specifically identified in the skin and bone.

FORMS OF THE VITAMIN

Microbial form

Vitamin K_2 (menaquinone) is the compound synthesized by intestinal microbes, being absorbed from the small intestine by a passive, noncarrier-mediated process.

Plant form

Vitamin K_1 (phylloquinone) is the compound found in green plants. It is absorbed in the proximal small intestine by an energy-requiring process. Phylloquinone also appears to be the form that is stored for a limited amount of time (< 24 hours) in the liver.

Synthetic

Vitamin K_3 (menadione) is a synthetic product and appears to be absorbed from both the colon and small intestine by passive processes.

DIETARY SOURCES

Natural

It is generally assumed that vitamin K is synthesized by microorganisms of the cecum and colon in sufficient quantities to meet requirements. Coprophagy (eating feces) will reintroduce highly available synthesized vitamin K to the intestines. This practice has made defining absolute requirements difficult to quantify.

Green leaves are the richest natural source of vitamin K, and the vitamin remains present even after the green has diminished. The nature of the diet of the horse, pasture and/or hay, should provide more than adequate quantities of vitamin K.

Added to feeds

Phylloquinone is the safest form for supplementation of vitamin K in the animal but also the most expensive. The water soluble forms of menadione are less expensive and are used commonly in animal feeds.

REQUIREMENT

Maintenance

Dietary requirements of vitamin K have not been determined for the horse (NRC, 1989). Phylloquinone in pasture or in good quality hay and menaquinones synthesized by intestinal bacteria presumably meet those requirements in all but the most unusual of circumstances. High calcium diets fed to pigs have been found to greatly increase the vitamin K requirement (Hall *et al.*, 1991). In horses, high calcium diets are usually a result of high alfalfa intakes, and alfalfa is an excellent source of vitamin K. Conditions which interfere with vitamin K function are impaired fat absorption, gastric ulcers, mycotoxins in the feed, long term antibiotic treatment, dicumarol in the feed (found in spoiled sweet clover hay) and warfarin (rat poison).

Performance

No research has been done on the requirement for vitamin K during exercise. Clinical responses of some "bleeders" to vitamin K therapy suggest that some performance horses may require additional supplies of vitamin K (Wakeman *et al.*, 1975).

TOXICITY

No problems have been found with excessive intakes of phylloquinone. However, menaquinones administered orally have been found to be toxic at 1000 times the dietary requirement. Phylloquinone injectables appear safer than menadione injectables, as parenteral administration of menadione bisulfite has been found to cause acute renal failure in horses (Rebhun *et al.*, 1984).

Summary

While research has shown the importance of the fat-soluble vitamins for normal body function, absolute requirements in the horse are less well defined. Factors which complicate quantifying requirements of fat-soluble vitamins are body stores and intracorporal production of the vitamins. More extensive research is needed on the vitamin requirements of the performance horse. Modern equine management practices may not always allow the horse to obtain sufficient quantities of the vitamins from the sources that nature intended. Addition of vitamins to the diet of the horse supplies a sense of security that the animal is receiving at least the minimum that is necessary.

References

Abrams, J.T. 1979. The effect of dietary vitamin A supplements on the clinical condition and track performance of racehorses. Biblthca Nutr. Dieta. 27:113.

Cromwell, G.L. 1996. Metabolism and role of phosphorus, calcium and vitamin D3 in swine nutrition. In: M.B. Coelho and E.T. Kornegay (Ed.) Phytase in animal Nutrition and Waste Management. BASF Reference Manual p.101.

Donoghue, S., and D.S. Kronfeld. 1980. Vitamin-mineral supplements for horses with emphasis on vitamin A. Compendium Cont. Edu. 8:S121.

Donoghue, S., D.S. Kronfeld, S.J. Berkowitz, and R.L. Copp. 1981. Vitamin A nutrition of the equine: growth, serum biochemistry and hematology. J. Nutr. 111:365.

Fonnesbeck, P.V. and L.D. Symons. Utilization of the carotene of hay by horses. J. Anim. Sci. 26:1030.

Gansen, S., A. Lindner, and A. Wagener. 1995. Influence of a supplementation with natural and synthetic vitamin E on serum alpha tocopherol content and V_4 of Thoroughbred horses. In: Proc. 14th Equine Nutr. And Physiol. Soc. Symp. p. 68. Ontario, CA.

Hall, D.D., G.L. Cromwell, and T.S. Stahly. 1991. Effects of dietary calcium, phosphorus, calcium: Phosphorus ration and vitamin K on performance, bone strength and blood clotting status of pigs. J. Anim. Sci. 69:646.

Harrington, D.D. and E.H. Page. 1983. Acute vitamin D_3 toxicosis in horses: case reports and experimental studies of the comparative toxicity of vitamins D_2 and D_3. JAVMA 182:1358.

Hintz, H.F., H.F. Schryver, and J.D. Lowe. 1973. Effect of vitamin D on calcium and phosphorus metabolism in ponies. J. Anim. Sci. 37:282.

McDowell, L.R. 1989. Vitamins in Animal Nutrition: Comparative Aspects to Human Nutrition. Academic Press, Inc. San Diego, CA.

McNeniman, N.P., and H.F. Hintz. 1992. Effect of vitamin E status on lipid peroxidation in exercised horses. Equine Vet. J. 24(6):482.

Neilsen, B.D., G.D. Potter, L.W. Greene, E.L. Morris, M. Murray-Gerzik, W.B. Smith, and M.T. Martin. 1995. Does the onset of training alter mineral requirements in the young racing Quarter Horses? In: Proc. 14th Equine Nutr. And Physiol. Soc. Symp. p. 70. Ontario, CA.

NRC. 1973. Effect of Processing on the Nutritional Value of Feeds. National Academy of Sciences, Washington, D.C.

NRC. 1987. Vitamin Tolerance of Animals. National Academy Press, Washington D.C.

NRC. 1989. Nutrient requirements of horses. (5th Ed.) National Academy Press, Washington D.C.

Petersson, K.H., H.F. Hintz, H.F. Schryver, and G.F. Combs, Jr. 1991. The effect of vitamin E on membrane integrity during submaximal exercise. In: G.B. Persson, A. Linkholm, and L.B. Jeffcott (Ed.) Equine Exercise Physiology 3. ICEEP Publications, Davis, California, p. 315.

Rebhun, W.C., B.C. Tennant, S.G. Dill, and J.M. King. 1984. Vitamin K_3-induced renal toxicosis in the horse. J. Am. Vet. Med. Assoc. 184:1237.

Shorafa, W.M., J.P. Feaster, E.A. Ott and R.L Asquith. 1979. Effect of vitamin D and sunlight on growth and bone development of young ponies. J. Anim. Sci. 48:882.

Siciliano, P.D., and C.H. Wood. 1993. The effect of added dietary soybean oil on vitamin E status of the horse. J. Anim. Sci. 71:3399.

Siciliano, P.D. and L.M. Lawrence. 1996. The role of vitamin E nutrition in the exercised horse. In: . M.B. Coelho (Ed.) Vitamin E in Animal Nutrition and Management. BASF Reference Manual p. 461.

Ullrey, D.E. 1981. Vitamin E for swine. J. Anim. Sci. 53:1039.

Wakeman, D.L., E.A. Ott, B.H. Crawford, and T.J. Cunha. 1975. Horse Production in Florida. Bulletin No. 188, Florida Dept. of Agriculture and Consumer Services, p.75, Gainesville, FL.

This paper was first published in Proceedings, Kentucky Equine Research 1997 Equine Nutrition Conference

TESTING FOR DRUGS, MEDICATIONS AND OTHER SUBSTANCES IN RACING HORSES

THOMAS TOBIN,[1] J.D. HARKINS,[1] W.E. WOODS,[1] N. C. HALL,[1] ANTONIO QUEIROZ-NETO,[2] SCOTT D. STANLEY, [3] AND GEORGE D. MUNDY[4]

[1]*The Maxwell H. Gluck Equine Research Center, Department of Veterinary Science, University of Kentucky, Lexington, Kentucky, USA,* [2]*Departamento de Morfologia e Fisiologia, Animal Faculdade de Ciencias Agrariais e Veterinarias de Jaboticabal, Unesp. Sao Paulo, Brazil,* [3]*Truesdail Laboratories, Inc., Tustin, California,* [4]*The Kentucky Racing Commission, Lexington, Kentucky, USA*

Summary

Testing for drugs in horses starts with the taking of samples. Samples, usually blood and urine, should be split immediately after they are drawn and the referee portion of the sample stored independently of the sample to be analyzed. The sample to be analyzed is then shipped in a secure fashion to the laboratory for analysis.

In the analytical process, drugs are subjected to liquid/liquid extraction and screened for the presence of illegal medications. The most commonly used screening method is thin layer chromatography. Other screening methods include gas chromatography and high pressure liquid chromatography and, more recently, immunoassay, including enzyme linked immunosorbent assay (ELISA). ELISA screening is particularly sensitive and rapid. Due to the sensitivity of immunoassay-based screening, most high-potency medications are first detected on ELISA screening.

If an agent is detected in the screening process, its presence in the sample is confirmed by other methods, but most especially by gas chromatography-mass spectrometry. The qualitative detection of drugs in forensic samples is a well developed art, and most drugs can be identified in blood or urine samples with a high degree of accuracy. Drugs can be quantitated in blood or urine with an accuracy of plus or minus 25% or better. These scientific determinations on a sample can be independently verified in the referee samples and form the scientific basis for the regulatory process of medication control.

These techniques detect much more than medications administered to horses, and one of the challenges of equine drug testing is to fairly and equitably distinguish between natural substances in horse urine and medicinal substances. In this review we examine the techniques used or that may be used to make this distinction for a number of dietary, environmental and endogenous substances found in horse urine.

229

Introduction

Racing has the longest established, most elaborate, broadly based and technically accurate systems for drug testing of any human endeavor (Tobin 1981). The medication of racing horses was formally declared illegal by the English Jockey Club about 1903. The first reported medication violation, using frogs as the test animal, and "determining" from their croaks whether the drug was present, was reported in Russia in about 1905. The first medication violation reported by analytical chemistry was reported in 1912. Since then, analytical chemistry and drug testing have made major strides, and analytical chemistry is now an established discipline. However, interpretation of the forensic significance of the analytical findings regarding the types of rules that can be enforced and how these rules should be defined, drafted and interpreted, is currently the subject of much debate within the industry.

Sample collection

Since the expense of collecting a blood sample is small and blood is the only sample from which drug concentration data can be interpreted with any confidence, both blood and urine should be collected. Additionally, a decision must be made regarding the nature of the blood sample drawn. While plasma was once the sample of choice for forensic work, the advent of enzyme linked immunosorbent assay (ELISA) has rendered serum the more satisfactory sample. This is because the presence of proteins in plasma samples can inhibit the ELISA reaction and our experience with these assays suggests that serum is more satisfactory, with less likelihood of non-specific inhibition of the ELISA system. Alternatively, plasma samples can be extracted to avoid the interfering problems with plasma proteins and to maintain the efficacy of ELISA testing.

Urine samples should be drawn into a chemically clean container. If the urine sample is stored cold and shipped to the laboratory promptly, there should be no significant problems with changes in the urine sample. Beyond this, drugs such as furosemide or other diuretics should generally not be used to obtain a urine sample since they act to dilute certain drugs and drug metabolites in equine urine, and are therefore likely to interfere with the testing process.

Blood versus urine

The backbone of drug testing in North America today is post-race urine testing. Urine testing is generally superior to blood testing since urine is available in relatively large amounts (200 ml plus), tends to contain higher concentrations of the parent drug than does the corresponding blood sample, and almost invariably contains much greater (50 fold greater) concentrations of drug metabolites than a corresponding blood sample. On the other hand, urine is slow and difficult to collect, and because of the lack of correlation between blood and urinary concentrations of drugs and drug metabolites, it is difficult to determine the forensic significance of a given urinary concentration of a drug.

In contrast, blood samples are easy to collect, and once a drug is identified and quantitated in blood, one can usually estimate its pharmacological effect with a reasonable degree of accuracy. The principal problem with blood testing is that the sample volume is small and the concentration of drug available in the sample, especially the concentration of drug metabolites, tends to be small. This is a major problem with blood testing, and it means that, given the current state of the art, blood testing is always used in conjunction with post-race urine testing for effective medication control.

Currently, the state of Kentucky takes post-race urine samples only, and testing of Kentucky samples is carried out by one of us (SDS) at Truesdail Laboratories Inc. in Tustin, California. Following collection at Kentucky tracks, the samples are shipped in a secure container to Truesdail, where they arrive the next day. The box is opened in the presence of a witness, the volume and pH (acidity) of each sample is noted, and the analytical process begins.

Pre-race testing and post-race testing

PRE-RACE TESTING

Pre-race testing, which is no longer performed on a significant basis in North America, was based entirely on blood sampling, although at one time pre-race testing in Hong Kong was based on urine sampling. In classical American pre-race testing, the blood sample was drawn two to four hours before the race and subjected to screening and, if possible, gas chromatography-mass spectrometry (GC/MS) analysis. In theory, pre-race testing allowed the chemist to detect a medicated horse before it ran, and then to scratch the horse, and in this way prevent the running of an illegally medicated horse. Pre-race testing was thus seen as the ultimate drug testing strategy, the one that could actually prevent the use of medication to manipulate the betting payoff, which post-race testing cannot do (Tobin *et al.,* 1979).

The problem with pre-race testing is that the testing technology has never been sensitive enough to detect the use of high-potency, illegal medications pre-race. Using thin layer chromatographic (TLC) screening systems, acidic drugs such as phenylbutazone and furosemide can be detected but, as a general rule, TLC-based testing does not have sufficient sensitivity to detect the abuse of high-potency, basic, illicit drugs pre-race. This is all the more so because horses are post-race tested for illegal medications and no medication that can be readily detected in urine is likely to be used. This restricts the illegal use of medications to relatively potent drugs that are unlikely to be detected in urine, and if a medication is undetectable in urine it is, in general, highly unlikely to be detectable in blood. For this reason pre-race testing based on TLC had an extremely poor record of detecting high potency illegal medications pre-race, and the concept of pre-race testing required a much more sensitive drug detection technology than TLC-based testing. It was largely to answer this need for more sensitive pre-race testing that ELISA tests were initially introduced into chemical analysis.

Chemical analysis of the sample

Classical chemical analysis of a blood or urine sample is a three step procedure. The first step is extraction of the drug from the blood or urine, the second step is screening of the sample for suspected drugs, and the third step is confirmation of the presence of the drug. The first step in this analysis is the extraction process, which is performed by a procedure called liquid-liquid extraction.

LIQUID-LIQUID EXTRACTION

Liquid-liquid extraction is based on the transfer of the drug from blood or urine (aqueous phase) into a solvent that does not mix with water. Liquid-liquid extraction of drugs follows the extraction rule (Blake and Tobin 1986). By this rule, acidic drugs extract under acidic conditions, and basic drugs extract under basic conditions. To implement this rule, the analyst takes small portions of the sample (usually about 2 to 3 ml) and makes them either acidic or basic. To make the urine acidic, about 5 ml of an acidic buffer is added which changes its pH value to about 4.0. To make the urine basic, a few drops of ammonium hydroxide are added, which will change the pH of the urine to about 9.0.

To extract the drug, an organic solvent such as dichloromethane is added, and the sample is placed on a mechanical shaker for about 5 minutes or more. For the acidic sample, acidic drugs move into the dichloromethane, while for the basic sample, basic drugs move into the dichloromethane. The sample is centrifuged to allow the dichloromethane to separate from the aqueous layer, which is pipetted off. The drugs are now contained in the dichloromethane layer, which is evaporated down to a small volume in order to concentrate the drugs. This small volume will contain all the drugs, therapeutic medications, environmental substances and natural products extracted from the urine, and at this point the chemist is ready to submit the extract to screening procedures.

DRUG SCREENING

The screening tests that the chemist uses have been, until recently, almost invariably chromatographic tests. In chromatography, the drug is placed in a mobile phase, which moves past a stationary phase. Depending on the affinity of the drug toward the stationary phases, and thus the amount of time that the drug spends on the stationary phase, the drug may move right along with the mobile phase, may stay immobile on the stationary phase, or may be anywhere in between. Based on this principle, the chromatography may be performed on thin layer plates, or in a gas or liquid chromatographic system. However, by far the most commonly used screening system is TLC or HPTLC (High Performance Thin Layer Chromatography).

Thin layer chromatography

In thin layer chromatography, the urine extract is spotted onto a thin layer of silica (generally less than 1 mm thick) on a glass plate, along with appropriate standards. The plate is then placed in a glass tank and "developed" by allowing a solvent mixture to run up the plate by capillary action. As the solvent (mobile phase) runs up the plate, the different drugs in the sample move along the plate at different rates, characteristic of the drug and dependent on TLC conditions. However, in the last analysis, the test yields only one single piece of information about the drug, which is that it chromatographs in the same way as the standard.

IMMUNOASSAY BASED TESTING

While TLC based testing is relatively inexpensive, broad in scope, and sufficiently sensitive to allow the detection of many medications, particularly in urine, there are many medications that are difficult to detect by TLC in blood or urine. For these drugs the only testing modality with the requisite sensitivity and flexibility has generally been immunoassay, and immunoassay has been suggested to be the most practical approach to the problems of equine medication control (Tobin *et al.*, 1988). This is especially true in the case of pre-race testing, where the volume of sample available is small and the concentration of drug present in the sample is low. For these reasons, the sensitivity of immunoassay techniques renders this a very attractive technology, and, about nine years ago, we began a broad scale approach to developing immunoassays for use in equine drug testing. Since it is conceptually and practically the simplest testing format, we will restrict this discussion to ELISA tests, although other non-isotopic test formats are also available.

Performing an ELISA test is relatively simple. As shown in Figure 1, the antibody to the drug is bound to the bottom of the test well. The assay is started by adding

20 μl of the standard, test or control samples to each well, along with 100 μl of the drug-horseradish peroxidase (drug-HRP) solution. During this step, the presence in the sample of free drug or cross-reacting drugs or metabolites competitively prevents the antibody from binding the drug-HRP conjugate. The degree of antibody:drug-HRP binding is therefore inversely related to the amount of drug in the sample. After ten minutes of incubation the fluid is removed from the microtiter wells, and the wells are washed three times. During this process the antibody and bound drug remain fixed to the bottom of the wells. Substrate (tetramethylbenzidine) is then added to all wells, a color-producing reaction occurs between the substrate and antibody-bound drug-HRP enzyme in the wells, and their absorbance read at 560 nm in a microwell reader. Higher optical absorbance corresponds to lower drug concentration in the sample.

These ELISA tests can be particularly potent and effective in drug detection. They can be as sensitive as radioimmunoassays (RIA), the test can be completed within about one hour and a good ELISA is comparable to a RIA in terms of accuracy.

For example, a simple morphine ELISA was particularly effective in terms of detection of opiates. Figures 2 and 3 show, respectively, the time course and sensitivity of the morphine ELISA, a typical "run" on a series of track samples, and in Table 1, the results of the introduction of this test into routine post-race testing. As shown in Table 1, of 166 samples screened in the Western United States, 18 were "flagged" by ELISA and of these, 13 confirmed to contain a narcotic substance by GC/MS (McDonald *et al.*, 1988).

Table 1. ELISA SCREENING OF POST-RACE URINE SAMPLES FOLLOWED BY GC/MS ANALYSIS

Sample date	No. urine samples	No. flagged by ELISA	No. positive by GC/MS analysis	Drug identified
10-3,4-87	34	5	3	Oxymorphone
10-4-87	16	1	1	Oxymorphone
10-11-87	8	1	1	Oxymorphone
10-17-87	36	3	2	Oxymorphone
10-17,18-87	27	3	1	Oxymorphone
10-20-87	21	4	4	Oxymorphone
10-27-87	24	1	1	Oxymorphone
TOTALS*	166	18	13	Hydromorphone

*9 Days Racing

Post-race urine samples from two racing jurisdictions were screened for morphine and its analogues by the ELISA test and then subjected to gas chromatography/mass spectrometry (GC/MS). The dates on which the samples were collected, the number of samples in each analysis batch, and the number of samples flagged "suspicious" by ELISA are presented in the first three columns. The results of GC/MS analysis of the flagged samples are shown in columns four and five. About 72% of the ELISA identifications were determined by GC/MS to contain either oxymorphone or hydromorphone. For some of the unconfirmed ELISA identifications, insufficient sample was available for complete GC/MS evaluation of their opiate status. Reproduced with permission from *Res. Comm. Chem. Pathol. Pharmacol.*

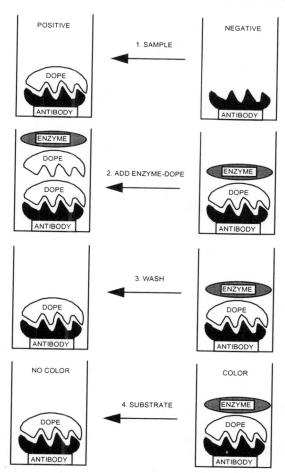

Figure 1. Reaction sequence of the one-step ELISA test. Antibody to the drug is bound to the well, and test and control samples are added directly to the well. In control samples those sites remain free and bind the drug-enzyme conjugate when this is added. In "positive" sample wells, the drug-enzyme conjugate cannot bind, because the antibody sites are already occupied. Unbound drug-enzyme is removed by the wash step, and the substrate is added to develop the test. An absence of color, indicating that no drug-enzyme complex bound to the antibody, represents a positive test. Reproduced with permission from *Res. Comm. Chem. Pathol. Pharmacol.*

Similar patterns of medication violations positives were seen across the western United States whenever these immunoassay tests were introduced. In general about 1% to 5% of the early samples tested were found to contain a narcotic analgesic. Similarly, when the mazindol test was introduced in early 1988, about 2 to 5 % of the early samples were confirmed by GC/MS (Prange *et al.,* 1988). The efficacy of these ELISA tests in racing chemistry was clear, and their ability to control the use of high potency medications was established.

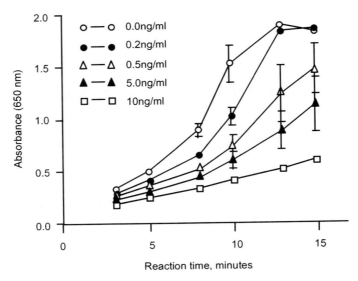

Figure 2. Time course of ELISA reaction in the presence of increasing concentrations of morphine. The symbols show the time course of the ELISA reaction in the presence of the indicated concentration of morphine. Reproduced with permission from *Res. Comm. Chem. Pathol. Pharmacol.*

Establishing the ELISA based immunoassays (Table 2) exposed deficiencies in TLC as a screening methodology. No TLC method for buprenorphine existed, so use of this drug was completely uncontrolled. Similarly, sufentanil abuse was uncontrolled and even "bragged on" by horsemen until the advent of this technology. While TLC methods for cocaine, oxymorphone and mazindol existed, these methods were unable to detect the small doses of these drugs being used in horses. This was especially so for mazindol, where the TLC-detectable dose was about 400 mg/horse, while the dose used on the track was about 4 mg/horse (Prange *et al.,* 1988). Overall, the great sensitivity and speed of the ELISA tests rendered them highly effective screening tests and far superior to TLC as a screening method for high potency drugs.

It is, however, worth noting that once an effective test became available abuse of these medications stopped at once, and did not resume. This was clearly demonstrated when business disputes and marketing strategies among competing ELISA companies left the western United States without access to ELISA tests for a period of at least one year through 1989. Then, beginning in 1990, ELISA tests again became commercially available to western testing laboratories. When these tests were re-introduced into the western United States there was no evidence of a return to the frequent pattern of abuse of narcotic analgesics characteristic of this region prior to 1987.

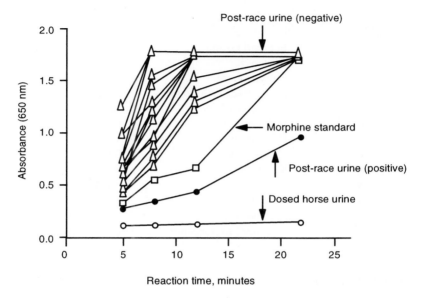

Figure 3. One-step ELISA reaction in a series of post-race urine samples. The open triangles (△) show the activity in this one step ELISA test of post-race urine samples. The open squares (□) show the effect of 0.5 mg/ml of morphine added to this system. The open circles (O) show ELISA activity in a dosed horse urine, and the solid circles (●) show ELISA activity in a sample subsequently determined to contain oxymorphone.

Table 2. EFFICACY OF PCFIA AND ELISA TESTS

Drug	State	TLC status	Immunoassay positives
Buprenorphine	New Mexico	No test	Multiple (>50)
Oxymorphone	New Mexico	Low sensitivity	Multiple (>30)
Sufentanil	Oklahoma	No test	10/300*
Mazindol	Western States	Low sensitivity	Multiple (>20)
Cocaine	California	Low sensitivity	2/83*
Acepromazine	Illinois	Fair sensitivity	Multiple**(>25)

*The table compares the TLC and immunoassay status of 6 drugs for which immunoassay tests have been introduced since August 1987. Figures marked by an asterisk represent the ratio of positives called to total number of samples tested.
**Acepromazine initially detected in pre-race samples.
Reproduced with permission from *Res. Comm. Chem. Pathol. Pharmacol.*

Table 3. PARTIAL LIST OF COMMERCIALLY AVAILABLE ELISA TESTS

Alfentanil	Dexamethasone	Meperidine
Amphetamine	Diprenorphine	Mepivacaine
Anileridine	Doxapram	Methylprednisolone
Azaperone	Droperidol	Nalbuphine
Barbiturate Group	Ethacrynic Acid	Nandrolone
Benzodiazepine Group	Etorphine	Opiate Group
Boldenone	Fentanil Group	Oxymorphone/Oxycodone
Bronchodilator Group	Fentanyl	Pentazocine
Bumetanide	Fluphenazine	Phenylbutazone (Blood Only)
Buprenorphine	Furosemide (Blood Only)	Procaine
Butorphanol	Glycopyrrolate	Promazine Group
Caffeine/Pentoxifylline	Haloperidol	Pyrilamine
Carfentanil	Haloperidol Metabolites	Reserpine
Clenbuterol	Isoxsuprine	Sufentanil
Cocaine/Benzoylecgonine	Ketorolac	Sulfamethazine
Corticosteroid Group	Levallorphan	THC Metabolites
Cromoglycate	Lofentanil	Theophylline
Dantrolene	Mazindol	Triamcinolone Acetonide
Detomonine	Mazindol Metabolites	Tricyclics Group

Drug confirmation

GAS CHROMATOGRAPHY-MASS SPECTROMETRY

Mass spectrometry (MS) has become the standard instrumental method for confirmation of the presence and identity of a drug in a sample. Samples containing as little as picogram quantities of analyte can be measured as long as the material can exist in the gaseous state at the temperature and pressure of the ion source. The mass of the analyte can typically range from 10-800 Atomic Mass Units. The major advantages of MS are its initial sensitivity over most other analytical techniques and its specificity in confirming the presence of suspected compounds.

Mass spectrometry provides both qualitative and quantitative information about the atomic and molecular composition of organic as well as inorganic materials. After solvent extraction to partially isolate the drug from the sample, the material to be analyzed is further separated by gas chromatography (GC) or, occasionally, by liquid chromatography (LC) and the separated components from the GC or LC are successively introduced into the vacuum chamber of the mass spectrometer. In the "ion source" of the MS, the sample components are bombarded by a beam of electrons or by a reagent gas such as methane. The collision of the electron beam and sample molecules produces molecular ions of the parent compound and its fragments. The resulting positive ions are accelerated through an electromagnetic field, which separates them based on their mass/charge ratio. Once separated, the ions strike a detector, which analyses the number of ions at each mass. The resulting mass spectrum is a plot of counted ions versus mass of the ions.

The mass spectrum is characteristic of the individual particular drug. The pattern produced by the drug and its fragment ions may be visualized as a molecular "fingerprint" and thus the spectrum is routinely accepted as evidence of the drug's identity. The chromatographic characteristics of the drug also add to its confirmation. The mass spectrometer is sensitive down to sub-nanograms (trillionths of a gram) levels and is very rapid; it can develop a full mass spectrum in a fraction of a second.

A state-of-the-art GC/MS system consists of a GC for sample separation, a mass spectrometer, and a computerized data system to precisely control the instrument and to collect and analyze the chromatographic and mass spectral data. It may also contain a computerized library of reference spectra to aid in the identification of unknown samples.

UNEQUIVOCAL IDENTIFICATION OF SUBSTANCE

By the time the chemist has completed his TLC, immunoassay, and GC/MS analyses, sufficient evidence will have been accumulated for the analyst to be persuaded as to the presence of the drug or drug metabolite in the sample. If the medication is a prohibited drug, the analyst is in a position to issue a chemical finding. This act of formally reporting to the authority the presence of a chemical substance initiates a sequence of administrative events that may end in significant disciplinary action against certain individuals, and is only undertaken when the analyst is absolutely certain that he is able to unequivocally identify the material present in the sample.

Since issuing an analytical report may eventually result in substantial penalty to the trainer, the analyst's findings may be challenged in a formal proceeding. Under these circumstances, the analyst will want to make as good a case as possible for the presence of the material in question, and the quality of the analytical chemistry should be sufficient to allow unequivocal chemical identification of the drug.

THE SPLIT (REFEREE) SAMPLE

As a general rule, the field of analytical chemistry is a rigorous and accurate discipline. If a well-trained chemist with a well-equipped laboratory performs the analysis and reports an analytical finding, then the results reported are virtually always repeatable in a similarly equipped and staffed laboratory. However, if the analyst is inexperienced, or not well-trained, or under pressure, then errors can be made, as in any other field of human endeavor.

The most important independent check on the ability and integrity of the chemist is to have available a split or referee sample, which is an independently sealed and stored sample. If the trainer so desires, this sample can be sent to an analyst of his (or her) choice, and the analytical work repeated. In this author's experience, analytical reports from high caliber laboratories on which administrative actions are based are virtually always repeatable. On the other hand, there have been instances where identifications have not turned out to be repeatable in the hands of an independent chemist, so the precaution of holding a split or referee sample is important. When the analyst is confident of the quality of the analytical work being done in the laboratory, the analyst should welcome requests for split or referee samples; these should be seen primarily as an opportunity to have the quality of the analytical work independently verified.

VETERINARY REVIEW/THRESHOLDS

With the increase in scope and sensitivity of medication testing, the bulk of the chemical findings reported by analysts are not illegal medications improperly used, but rather are trace residues of legal and appropriate therapeutic medications. The frequency of these findings in recent years has created somewhat of a dilemma for the industry. Under the old rules, any finding of a foreign substance led to confiscation of the purse and suspension of the trainer. Under the new and highly sophisticated techniques available to analytical chemists, however, routine and rigorous application of this approach would close down racing.

The solution to this problem is two-fold. In the first place, all analytical reports should be formally reviewed in writing by a veterinarian experienced in the field of racing administration and pharmacology to determine the regulatory significance of the finding. California, which has just appointed an Equine Medical Director, is the first major racing state to take this approach to the problem. One of us (GDM) serves in a similar capacity in the state of Kentucky.

No veterinarian, no matter how well trained or experienced, can have at his fingertips answers to all of the problems that can arise from the application of sophisticated analytical chemistry to 10-40,000 post-race urines/year. For this reason both the California and Kentucky Boards / Commissions function in close conjunction with university based research programs to enable them to respond appropriately when questions concerning findings of drugs, therapeutic medications, and environmental and dietary substances in racing horses arise.

The second portion of the solution is formal thresholds or cutoffs for therapeutic medications in racing horses. Again, California has been the first state to implement this solution, with the recent establishment of thresholds for eight therapeutic medications as set forth in table 3, and one of us (TT) has an active research program in the area of thresholds for therapeutic medications in racing horses.

Table 4. APPROVED AND PROPOSED "THRESHOLDS" FOR MEDICATIONS
IN RACING HORSES MARCH 30, 1995

Phenylbutazone	5 µg/ml	Plasma	North America (ARCI)
Oxyphenbutazone	5 µg/ml	Plasma	North America (ARCI)
Furosemide	50 ppb	Plasma	Oklahoma
Flunixin	1 µg/ml	Plasma	California
Flunixin	0.1 µg/ml	Plasma	Pennsylvania
Naproxen	1 µg/ml	Plasma	California
Procaine	25 ppb	Plasma	Canada
Procaine	10 ppb	Urine	California
Acepromazine	25 ng/ml	Urine	California
Mepivacaine	10 ng/ml	Urine	California
Promazine	25 ng/ml	Urine	California
Albuterol	1 ng/ml	Urine	California
Atropine	10 ng/ml	Urine	California
Benzocaine	50 ng/ml	Urine	California
Theobromine	2 µg/ml	Urine	International
Arsenic	0.3 µg/ml	Urine	International
Salicylate	6 µg/ml	Blood	International
Salicylate	750 µg/ml	Urine	International, California
DMSO	15 µg/ml	Urine	International
DMSO	1 µg/ml	Plasma	International
Hydrocortisone	1 µg/ml	Urine	International

Bicarbonate

In recent years, there has been considerable interest in the use of $NaHCO_3$ in athletes to counteract the acidosis associated with intense exercise. The accumulation of hydrogen ions (H^+) during intense, short-duration exercise suppresses glycolysis through the inhibition of the enzyme phosphofructokinase (Hood *et al.*, 1988; Wilkie, 1986). During intense exercise the H^+ associated with lactate formation are buffered by HCO_3^- in the reaction:

$$H^+ + HCO_3^- \rightarrow H_2CO_3 \rightarrow H_2O + CO_2$$

Carbon dioxide is eliminated through respiration, and HCO_3^- is depleted. As blood $[HCO_3^-]$ decreases, H^+ accumulate causing blood pH to decrease. The goal of $NaHCO_3$ administration is to augment the blood bicarbonate buffering system thereby delaying the accumulation of H^+.

Studies using human athletes have delayed the onset of fatigue with $NaHCO_3$ during moderately heavy but not supramaximal exercise. For $NaHCO_3$ to be beneficial to performance, work bouts must last at least 2 minutes in duration (Costill *et al., 1984*). Sodium bicarbonate provides no beneficial effect during long term aerobic exercise since lactic acid buildup is not a problem in that type of work. In fact, endurance exercise produces alkalosis.

In studies using equine athletes, the fatigue-delaying effects of $NaHCO_3$ are equivocal; however, anecdotal evidence and the perception that $NaHCO_3$ can improve performance, particularly in Standardbreds, is substantial. Since a majority of Standardbred races last longer than 2 minutes and Standardbred trainers use multiple pre-race warm-up heats, pre-race treatment with $NaHCO_3$ may supply an ergogenic benefit to Standardbred racing horses. Mixtures of $NaHCO_3$, water and confectionery sugar, known as "milkshakes," administered by nasogastric tube have been used to a considerable extent at Standardbred race tracks. It is estimated that as many as 90% of trainers at some Standardbred tracks have used these concoctions (Bergstein, 1989).

Following $NaHCO_3$ administration, renal and respiratory compensatory mechanisms will seek to return systemic acid-base balance to normal. Renal mechanisms respond to acid-base changes by altering the excretion of electrolytes, H^+, and HCO_3^-. Horses fed a grain mixture containing 2.0% $NaHCO_3$ (about 0.4 g/ kg) had a urine pH of 8.20 compared to 7.46 for horses not consuming $NaHCO_3$ (Robb and Kronfeld, 1986). The urine pH of human athletes following an 800 meter run was 6.17 during recovery following a placebo but was increased to 7.61 when athletes were given $NaHCO_3$ (0.3 g/kg BW) before the run (McKenzie, 1988).

Several racing organizations have ruled that concoctions containing $NaHCO_3$ are not permitted. The Illinois Racing Board regards the tubing of a horse on race day as a violation of its rules. Furthermore, an excess of $NaHCO_3$ is a rules violation because it is a foreign substance that changes the normal physiological state of the horse (Milbert, 1991). In Illinois, any horse not being treated with furosemide for exercise-induced pulmonary hemorrhage that has a pre-race plasma $[HCO_3^-]$ of 38 units or higher, blood pH above 7.43, and a [Na] over 147 mEq/L, is promptly retested. If the second test shows similarly high levels, the stewards are requested to scratch the horse (Bergstein, 1989).

Dietary, environmental and endogenous substances in racing horses

With the increasing sensitivity of equine drug testing, the incidence of detection of dietary, environmental and endogenous substances in post-race blood and urine samples has increased. We have categorized these substances under three headings: dietary substances, environmental substances and endogenous substances.

DIETARY SUBSTANCES

Definition

A dietary substance is any substance that is part of the normal and ordinary feeding of horses. In this section we are concerned with substances that yield materials in post-race samples that trigger administrative actions. With dietary substances there are generally clear-cut geographic, seasonal and food source influences on the appearance of these materials in post-race samples.

Salicylate

Salicylic acid (Salicylate), the prototype Non Steroidal Anti-Inflammatory Drug (NSAID), is found in the post-race urine of all horses and has long been recognized as "normal" in horse urine. Based on a number of studies, thresholds of 6.0 g/ml and 750 g/ml of salicylate in plasma and urine respectively were established. These thresholds are internationally recognized, and the 750 g/ml threshold is being reviewed for adoption as the urinary threshold for this agent in California. Salicylate is an ARCI Class 4 agent (Moss *et al.,* 1985).

Hordenine

Hordenine is a plant alkaloid closely related structurally and pharmacologically to epinephrine. It gets its name from *Hordeum vulgare* or barley, a common source of hordenine. Other common sources include Reed Canary grass, brewers grains and sprouting barley. Like salicylate, hordenine is likely to be found in a large number of post-race urine samples if they are examined at high enough sensitivity. There are, however, regional reports of unusually high concentrations of hordenine being found in the post-race urines of horses racing in Minnesota and also in Queensland. It seems likely that these geographically related high concentrations of hordenine are also seasonally related (Frank *et al.,* 1990). There is no formal threshold for hordenine. Hordenine is not classified by ARCI. Some European laboratories report hordenine to their authorities.

Dimethyl sulfoxide (DMSO)

DMSO is found in all horse urines and is thought to be entirely of dietary origin. DMSO and its metabolite, dimethylsulfone (MSM) therefore occur normally in horse urine. In horses on a diet of Lucerne hay, urinary concentrations as high as 5 μg/ml of DMSO in urine have been reported. DMSO is a Class 5 substance in the ARCI classification system. DMSO is often readily identifiable in post-race urine samples and some US labs report DMSO to their authorities. The international thresholds for DMSO are 1 µg/ml in plasma and 15 µg/ml in urine (Crone, 1995).

Morphine

Morphine is found in significant quantities in hay grown in certain parts of Australia and worldwide in poppy seed used in baked products such as bagels and muffins. Occasional low concentrations of morphine or its metabolites in post-race horse urine in eastern Australia have been traced to horses eating feed contaminated with poppy capsules. Another possible source of morphine is codeine, which is metabolized to morphine in man and presumably also in the horse; the pharmacological activity of codeine in man may be due to its metabolism to morphine. Findings of morphine in post-race urine samples may therefore be associated with contaminated hay in certain geographic areas, inadvertent feeding of poppy seed bagels, accidental contamination from prescription codeine or with morphine from other sources. Because poppies grow wild in Australia, there are clear seasonal and geographic influences on the incidence of morphine identifications in this country. No published or unpublished thresholds for morphine have been reported; however, Australian researchers use chemical-ionization GC/MS procedures to identify equine urine samples where morphine is derived from *P. setigerum* contamination of cereal crops (Batty, 1995). Morphine is an ARCI Class 1 agent.

Scopolamine

Scopolamine is an alkaloid closely related to atropine that is available as a pharmaceutical agent and also from various plant sources. The most common plant source of scopolamine in the US is "jamestown" or jimson weed, which grows wild across much of the southern United States. Scopolamine identifications are rarely reported in racing horses, and unequivocally distinguishing between pharmaceutical scopolamine and scopolamine from plant sources is far from trivial. However, a seasonal finding of jimson weed in close association with horses and an associated finding of scopolamine in post-race urines clearly raises the possibility of environmental contamination (Feenaghty, 1982). Within the last two years, a number of scopolamine identifications have been made in the US and elsewhere. Scopolamine is an ARCI Class 3 agent. No published or unpublished thresholds for scopolamine have been reported.

Bufotenine

Bufotenine or NN-dimethylserotonin is an indole alkaloid found in the leaves and seeds of *Piptadenia* and also from *Amanita*. Bufotenine is also hallucinogenic, and materials from frog and toad skin are sometimes ingested for their hallucinogenic effects. At least one identification of bufotenine in a post-race urine sample has been reported in the US, and a number of identifications have been made outside the US. Although no penalty was assessed, no formal threshold for this agent in post-race urine exists. Bufotenine is not classified by ARCI. No seasonal or geographic associations for bufotenine identifications have so far been reported.

Arsenic

Arsenic is ubiquitous in nature and is found in all horse urines. However, it can be used as a tonic in small amounts and as a "stopper" in large amounts. A threshold was therefore needed to distinguish between normal arsenic and unusually high concentrations of arsenic in post-race urines. Crone and his co-workers analyzed 4,000 post-race samples in Hong Kong between 1983 and 1988. The international threshold for arsenic is now 0.3 µg/ml of arsenic in urine (Crone, 1995). While it is highly likely that there are geographic influences on arsenic concentrations in post-race urine, these are not described. Arsenic is not classified by ARCI.

ENVIRONMENTAL CONTAMINANTS

Definition

Environmental contaminants are substances brought into the environment of the horse by man and are unlikely to be found in horses not closely associated with man. Horses may be exposed to these materials pre-race, in which case metabolites of the materials will be found in the post-race samples. Identification of parent contaminant alone in the absence of metabolites is presumptive evidence of post-collection contamination.

Caffeine

Caffeine is the most widely used psychoactive agent in the world. It is consumed daily by humans in considerable (125 mg) amounts. Caffeine is extensively metabolized in the horse, with only about 2-3% of a dose being excreted in the urine as unchanged caffeine. A finding of caffeine in a urine sample with associated metabolites generally means that the caffeine went through a horse. Finding of caffeine without associated metabolites generally means that the caffeine did not go through a horse, with the implication that the caffeine resulted from post-collection contamination. Because of the widespread environmental presence of caffeine, Hong Kong has an unpublished threshold of 0.01 µg/ml in plasma and 0.03 µg/ml in urine. Malaysia also has an in-house threshold of 0.01 µg/ml in plasma (Cheng, 1988). Caffeine is an ARCI Class 2 agent.

Theobromine

Theobromine is 3,7-dimethylxanthine, and for two decades theobromine from cocoa husk was the most commonly identified material in horse urine in England. It proved very difficult to remove cocoa husk from the feed, so the approach was taken of developing a threshold. Studies were carried out at the Horse Racing Forensic Laboratory in England, and 2 µg/ml in urine was established as the regulatory threshold (Greene, 1983). Theobromine is an ARCI Class 4 agent.

Nicotine

Nicotine is ubiquitous in the human environment, and is occasionally identified in post-race urine samples from horses. The metabolism of nicotine in the horse has not been described; however in man cotinine and trans-3-hydroxycotinine are its major urinary metabolites. Based on what is known of the metabolism of nicotine in humans, the likelihood of free nicotine entering horse urine by any route other than contamination is small. In the absence of cotinine or other nicotine metabolites, a nicotine identification is presumptive evidence of post-collection contamination (Stanley, 1993). Nicotine is not currently classified by ARCI.

Cotinine/trans-3-hydroxycotinine

These agents are the major urinary metabolites of nicotine in man. Their identification in horse urine in significant concentrations is presumptive evidence that the horse was exposed to nicotine, such as bedding on tobacco stalks. They are not classified by ARCI (Stanley, 1993).

Cocaine

Cocaine is ubiquitous in certain human environments, and cocaine and/or its metabolites have been found in tongue ties, in saliva samples from horses entering races and in post-race urine samples from horses. Most of these identifications have been at relatively low concentrations, and their pharmacological and forensic significance is often unclear. In Illinois, control of the use of cocaine on tongue ties has been implemented by use of a pre-race cocaine ELISA. Application of this test allows pre-race detection of cocaine contamination; the trainer is then invited to withdraw his horse, and most elect to do so. This approach avoids the problem of determining the source, pharmacological effect and forensic significance of trace detections of cocaine or its metabolites in post-race urine. Determining the significance of traces of cocaine or its metabolites in post-race samples is made more difficult by the fact that cocaine spontaneously hydrolyses to breakdown products difficult to distinguish from authentic metabolites (Jensen, 1995). Cocaine is classified as an ARCI Class 1 agent.

ENDOGENOUS SUBSTANCES

Definition

Endogenous substances are substances that are specifically synthesized within the horse and are independent of dietary or other sources.

Hydrocortisone

Hydrocortisone is an endogenous corticosteroid hormone produced by the adrenal gland and essential to normal life. It is also available as an injectable pharmaceutical, and its release in the horse can be specifically stimulated by administration of ACTH. To control its use in racing horses, a urinary threshold of 1 g/ml has been established. Hydrocortisone is an ARCI Class 4 agent.

Testosterone

Testosterone is normal in the plasma and urine of geldings and fillies but at very low concentrations. Testosterone can also be used for its anabolic actions in fillies and geldings. To control this use of testosterone, a threshold for this agent is required. The Australian authorities use a threshold of 100 ng/ml of testosterone, although by what method this threshold was devised is not quite clear (Batty, 1995). Testosterone is an ARCI Class 4 agent.

Acknowledgments

The investigation reported in this paper is in connection with a project of the Kentucky Agricultural Experiment Station and is published as a Kentucky Agricultural Experiment Station Article with approval of the Dean and Director, College of Agriculture and Kentucky Agricultural Experiment Station.

Publication #201 from the Kentucky Equine Drug Testing and Research Programs, Department of Veterinary Science and the Graduate Center for Toxicology, University of Kentucky.

Supported by grants entitled "Development of a Test for Procaine in Horses" and "Thresholds and Clearance Times for Therapeutic Medications in Horses" funded by the Equine Drug Council and the Kentucky Racing Commission, Lexington, Kentucky, and the National Horsemen's Benevolent and Protective Association, New Orleans, Los Angeles and the Conselho Nacional de Pesquisa (CNPq), Brazil.

References

Batty D. Morphine and the Australian analytical experience, in Proceedings. Workshop on "Testing for Therapeutic Medications, Environmental and Dietary Substances in Racing Horses," Maxwell H. Gluck Equine Research Center, Department of Veterinary Science, University of Kentucky 1995;93-97.

Bergstein S. "Milkshakes": A bad idea the sport can do without. Harness Horse 1989; 54:6.

Blake J.W. and Tobin T. Testing for drugs in horses. J Equine Vet Sci 1986; 6:93-97.

Cheng A.S. Threshold levels of prohibited substances in horse body fluids and their relevance to the rules of racing — with particular reference to caffeine, in Proceedings. 7th International Conference of Racing Analysis and Veterinarians 1988;97-99.

Costill D.L., Verstappen F., Kuipers H., *et al.* Acid-base balance during repeated bouts of exercise: Influence of HCO_3. Int J Sports Med 1984; 5:228-231.

Crone D.L. Arsenic and DMSO thresholds, in Proceedings. Workshop on "Testing for Therapeutic Medications, Environmental and Dietary Substances in Racing Horses," Maxwell H. Gluck Equine Research Center, Department of Veterinary Science, University of Kentucky 1995;63-69.

Feenaghty D.A. Atropine poisoning: Jimsonweed. J Emergency Nursing 1982; 8:139-141.

Frank M., Weckman T.J., Wood T., *et al.* Hordenine: pharmacology, pharmacokinetics and behavioral effects in the horse. Equine Vet J 1990; 22:437-441.

Greene E.W., Woods W.E. and Tobin T. Pharmacology, pharmacokinetics, and behavioral effects of caffeine in horses. Am J Vet Res 1983; 44:57-63.

Hood V.L., Schubert C., Keller U., *et al.* Effect of systemic pH on pHi and lactic acid generation in exhaustive forearm exercise. Am J Physiol 1988; 255:F479-F485.

Jensen R. Personal communication. 1995.

McDonald J., Gall R., Wiedenbach P., *et al.* Immunoassay detection of drugs in racing horses. III. Detection of morphine in equine blood and urine by a one step ELISA assay. Res Comm Chem Pathol Pharmacol 1988; 59:259-278.

McKenzie D.C. Changes in urinary pH following bicarbonate loading. Can J Sport Sci 1988; 13:254-256.

Milbert N. Illinois horsemen say "No thanks" to milkshakes. Hoofbeats 1991; 59:27-32.

Moss M.C., Blay P., Houghton E., *et al.* Normal and post-administration concentrations of salicylic acid in thoroughbred horses, in Proceedings. 6th International Conference of Racing Analysts & Veterinarians, Hong Kong 1985;97.

Prange C.A., Brockus C., Stobert D., *et al.* Immunoassay detection of drugs in racing horses. V. Detection of mazindol in equine blood and urine by a one step ELISA assay. Res Comm Subst Abuse 1988; 9, 13-30.

Robb E. and Kronfeld D. Dietary sodium bicarbonate as a treatment of exertional rhabdomyolysis in a horse. *J Amer Vet Med Assoc* 1986; 188:602-605.

Stanley S.D., Gairola C.G., Diana J., *et al.* Development and characterization of an ELISA for cotinine in biological fluids. Inhalation Toxicology 1993; 5:403-413.

Tobin, T. Drugs and the Performance Horse. CC Thomas, Springfield, IL, 1981;85-110.

Tobin T., Maylin G.A., Henion J., *et al.* An evaluation of pre- and post-race testing and blood and urine testing in horses. J Equine Med Surg 1979; 3:85-90.

Tobin T., Watt D.S., Kwiatkowski S.,*et al.* Non-isotopic immunoassay drug tests in racing horses: a review of their application to pre- and post-race testing, drug quantitation, and human drug testing. Res Comm Chem Pathol Pharmacol 1988; 62, 371-396.

Wilkie D.R. Muscular fatigue: effects of hydrogen ions and inorganic phosphate. Fed Proc 1986; 45:2921-2923.

This paper was first published in "Recent Advances in Equine Nutrition," Proceedings for the 1995 Short Course for Feed Manufacturers

RECENT DEVELOPMENTS IN EQUINE NUTRITION RESEARCH

JOE D. PAGAN

Kentucky Equine Research, Inc., Versailles, Kentucky, USA

Introduction

Several important equine nutrition meetings were held during 1992 and 1993. The first European Horse Nutrition Conference was held in Hannover, Germany and the Equine Nutrition and Physiology Society (ENPS) held its scientific meeting in Gainesville, Florida. At each of these meetings, new information of relevance to feed manufacturers was presented. This paper will review papers from each of these meetings as well as present results of research that until now has not been published.

Blood flow

At the Hannover meeting, Dr. Steve Duren presented interesting results from his Ph.D. dissertation from the University of Kentucky (Duren *et al.*, 1992). This experiment was conducted to compare hemodynamics and blood flow distribution in fasted and fed ponies at rest and during treadmill exercise. In the first portion of the experiment, hemodynamics and blood flow distribution were measured in fasted ponies at rest. The 24 hour fast imposed prior to data collection resulted in a 3.5% decrease in body weight.

From this experiment, Dr. Duren concluded that digestive tissue blood flow is the lowest in the esophagus and rectum, two tissues devoid of absorption capabilities. Digestive tissue blood flow was the highest in the glandular region of the stomach followed by the duodenum of the small intestine, two tissues with large secretory capacity. Blood flow to the pancreas was twofold greater than any digestive tissue, again attributed to secretory potential. Finally, it was concluded that fasted ponies divert 20.4% of their cardiac output to the digestive system.

In the second portion of this experiment, postprandial hemodynamics and blood flow distribution were determined in resting ponies. The ponies consumed 0.71% of body weight of a pelleted grain concentrate plus free-choice alfalfa hay, 1.2 hours preceding data collection. Feeding resulted in an elevated stroke volume, which led to a trend for elevated cardiac output. It was concluded that feeding resulted in mesenteric hyperemia, evident by increased blood flow to the small intestine, cecum, ventral colon, dorsal colon and small colon in fed ponies. This is the first known report of mesenteric hyperemia in the pony. This hyperemic effect was not present in the stomach, indicating that, contrary to popular belief, the continued presence of food in the stomach does not stimulate an increase in gastric blood flow. Feeding resulted in pancreatic hyperemia, which was attributed to increased pancreatic secretion during digestion. Kidney blood flow also increased following feeding. It was speculated that increased intravascular volume associated with water absorption, or increased kidney function associated with nitrogen excretion, caused renal hyperemia. Despite the increased blood flow to the digestive system, muscle blood flow was not different between fasted and fed ponies. Thus, it is hypothesized that increased blood flow to the digestive system was accomplished by slight increases in cardiovascular performance, coupled with small, hard to detect, changes in blood flow distribution in other vascular beds. Finally, it was concluded that fed ponies divert 27.4% of their cardiac output to the digestive tract, compared to 20.4% in fasted ponies.

The final phase of this experiment compared hemodynamics and blood flow distribution in fasted and fed ponies during exercise. Hemodynamic and blood flow determinations were made at rest and during 30 minutes of treadmill exercise. Exercise began 24 hours postprandial in fasted ponies and 1.4 hours postprandial in fed ponies. Heart rate, cardiac output, stroke volume and arterial blood pressure all increased during exercise, and each displayed a treatment x time interaction. This interaction indicated the magnitude of difference in response between fasted and fed ponies was dependent on exercise time. However, heart rate, cardiac output, stroke volume and arterial pressure were consistently higher in fed than in fasted ponies. Blood flow to the digestive tract decreased during exercise in both fasted and fed ponies; however, blood flow was higher throughout exercise in the fed ponies. It is speculated that fed ponies had an elevated blood flow at rest, associated with increased digestive tissue oxygen demand, and the increased sympathetic tone produced during exercise was not large enough to totally reverse this hyperemia. Blood flow to the locomotor and respiratory muscles increased during exercise and each displayed a treatment x time interaction. Again, this interaction indicated the magnitude of difference in response between fasted and fed ponies was dependent on exercise time. However, blood flow in each locomotor and respiratory muscle was higher in fed than in fasted ponies. It is surmised that fed ponies work harder during exercise, as evidenced by increased muscle blood flow, due to increased gut fill associated with feeding. Blood flow to the non-exercising masseter muscle did not differ during exercise and was not different between treatment groups.

BOTTOM LINE

The results of this experiment indicate that during exercise, both hemodynamics and blood flow distribution are affected by feeding. Since the fed ponies exercised at approximately 75% of heart rate maximum, they were able to increase heart rate, cardiac output and stroke volume to deliver an increased amount of blood to both the digestive tract and working muscles. This invites the next question: What would happen during maximal exercise? Would blood be completely shunted away from the digestive tract regardless of digestive status, or would exercise tolerance be hindered by digestive hyperemia? More research is needed to answer this question.

Biotin and hoof condition

At the ENPS meeting, Swiss researchers reported the results of an experiment conducted at the Spanish Riding School in Vienna (Linden, *et al.*, 1993). Forty-two Lipizzaner stallions were used in a double-blind trial over two and a half years to study the efficacy of dietary biotin on hoof condition. The horses were divided into two groups: 26 animals (group B) received 20 mg d-biotin daily and 16 horses (group C) were fed a placebo. Assessments were made of overall hoof condition, horn histology and the white line using a scoring system which ranged from 0 (= no irregularities) to 3 (= severe defects).

Initial overall hoof scores were 1.73 and 1.66 for groups B and C, respectively. After 9 months, the score for group B was 1.27, compared to 1.47 for group C (P<0.01). The improvement in group B continued subsequently. Average horn histological scores at the start were 1.81 and 1.75 for groups B and C, respectively. After 19 months, the score for group B was 1.52, significantly better (P<0.05) than group C which was unchanged. White line condition improved (P<0.05) from 2.01 initially to 1.67 after 19 months for group B. The white line score of group C was unchanged. Horn tensile strength averaged 4.0 kp/mm^2 at the start. After 30 months, the tensile strength of group B increased to 4.5 kp/mm^2, compared to 3.7 kp/mm^2 for group C (P<0.05). Biotin had no significant effect on horn growth rate.

BOTTOM LINE

The results demonstrate the beneficial effects of d-biotin supplementation on hoof condition of Lipizzaner horses, by reducing the incidence and severity of horn defects, increasing tensile strength and improving the condition of the white line. However, contrary to popular belief, biotin did not improve hoof growth rate. Also, it takes a long time before all of the beneficial effects of feeding biotin become apparent.

Feeding fat for performance

Kentucky Equine Research, in conjunction with the Waltham Centre for Equine Nutrition and Care, presented results of a study evaluating the effects of feeding fat to racehorses at the ENPS meeting (Pagan *et al.*, 1993). Nine thoroughbred racehorses were used in a six month long exercise study to evaluate the effect that different types of energy sources have upon metabolic response during a series of standardized exercise tests. The horses were fed diets containing either high carbohydrate, soybean oil (10%), coconut oil (10%) or a mixture of soybean oil (5%) and coconut oil (5%). Each horse was fed the high carbohydrate (control) diet for a four week period at the beginning of the experiment. The horses then performed a five day standardized exercise test (SET-5) to determine baseline fitness and ability. Using data from the SET-5, the horses were divided into four groups and fed one of the four diets for a three week period followed by two weeks of standardized exercise tests. The first test (SET-5) consisted of 1600 m gallops on five consecutive days at speeds from 7 to 11 m/s on an inclined (6°) high speed treadmill. Blood samples were taken five minutes post exercise for determination of lactate, glucose, ammonia, FFA and triglycerides. Heart rate was measured throughout exercise. A second test (SET-1) consisted of two minutes walking, four minutes trotting, and eight minutes galloping at speeds between 8 and 9 m/s on the inclined treadmill. These speeds produced heart rates of between 180 and 220 beats/minute (ave. 200). Blood samples were taken at rest, after the trotting warm up, at four minutes and eight minutes of the gallop as well as at five and ten minutes after the gallop. After the first period, the horses were switched to another diet according to a Latin square arrangement and the trial was repeated. V_{LA4} measured during the Set-5 was significantly lower (10.15 m/s) in the control diet than when either the soy (10.52 m/s), coconut (10.46 m/s) or mixed (10.69 m/s) oils were fed (P<0.05). V_{200} measured during the SET-5 averaged 9.58, 9.71, 9.49, and 9.51 m/s in the control, soy, coconut, and mixed diets, respectively. V_{200} was significantly higher in the soy diet than in either the coconut or mixed diets. During the SET-1 there was no difference in average HR, while lactate was lower in the coconut diet than in the control throughout the test. Blood glucose was not significantly different during or after exercise during SET-1.

BOTTOM LINE

Addition of fat to the diets of Thoroughbred racehorses affected metabolic response to exercise by reducing lactic acid production. This is certainly an important effect since high lactic acid production is associated with fatigue in racehorses. The long term effects of feeding high fat diets to performance horses remains to be determined.

Fat digestibility

Our laboratory just completed a series of digestion trials to compare the digestibility of three different fat sources in mature horses. Four horses were used in a 4 X 4 Latin square design trial to evaluate the effect of feeding a sweet feed along with either soybean oil, a 4-80 spray dried animal fat (4% protein, 80% fat, Milk Specialties Company, Dundee, Illinois) or a new 100% dry fat product (Start to Finish Energy Pak, Milk Specialties Company, Dundee, Illinois).

During each one month period, each horse was fed one of the four rations which consisted of 20% grass hay, 47% high fiber pellets, and 33% sweet feed with or without added fat. The various fats were supplemented at a rate equal to 5% of the grain intake as added fat. The nutrient compositions of the hay, pellets and grain are shown in table 1.

Table 1. NUTRIENT COMPOSITION OF FEEDS (DRY BASIS)

	Grass hay	Sweet feed	Fiber pellet
Dry matter	91.25%	86.5%	86.4%
Protein	14.2%	16.0%	14.1%
ADF	33.8%	11.2%	38.2%
NDF	56.9%	21.8%	57.2%
Crude fiber	27.5%	8.6%	30.6%
Fat	3.4%	5.0%	2.7%
Calcium	0.72%	0.91%	1.16%
Phosphorus	0.31%	0.76%	0.24%
Magnesium	0.19%	0.24%	0.25%
Potassium	2.22%	1.02%	1.57%
Zinc	23 ppm	134 ppm	46 ppm
Copper	9 ppm	39 ppm	10 ppm
Manganese	45 ppm	94 ppm	43 ppm
Ash	7.34%	6.99%	7.27%

During each 4 week period, the horses were fed their experimental rations for a three week acclimation period followed by a five day complete collection digestion trial. During the collection period, daily feed intake and total fecal output was measured. Subsamples of daily feed and feces were taken and frozen. These subsamples were dried and composited for chemical analysis. Both feed and feces were analyzed for dry matter, crude protein, ADF, NDF, fat, calcium, phosphorus, magnesium, potassium, zinc, copper, manganese, and ash. Digestibilities were calculated for each nutrient measured.

The apparent digestibility of the various nutrients are shown in table 2.

The addition of these various fats did not adversely affect the digestibility of any of the other nutrients measured. In fact, it appears that the 4-80 fat actually improved the digestibility of several of the minerals. The 4-80 fat was also highly digestible, equaling the digestibility of the soybean oil. The ration containing Energy Pak had an apparent fat digestibility equal to 80% of the soybean oil or 4-80 diets.

Of the three fats tested, the Energy Pak dry fat seemed most palatable followed by the soybean oil. The 4-80 was least palatable and it took the horses several days to become accustomed to the taste. Every horse accepted the Energy Pak at first offering.

Table 2. APPARENT NUTRIENT DIGESTIBILITIES (%)

	Control	*Soy oil*	*4-80*	*Energy Pak*
DM	64.34	63.87	64.66	62.43
CP	71.98	69.27	72.05	70.06
ADF	49.78	48.15	48.33	46.23
NDF	53.59	50.53	51.19	52.61
CF	54.12	52.46	51.49	52.56
fat	53.72	68.26	69.62	54.61
Ca	42.74	42.51	46.74	41.01
P	11.28	14.49	18.22	11.63
Mg	30.49	30.69	36.49	30.36
K	80.03	78.11	79.31	77.57
Zn	6.77	8.78	15.94	5.87
Cu	25.53	24.17	31.09	18.63
Mn	0.75	3.43	7.09	1.06
ASH	46.81	44.57	47.87	45.19

BOTTOM LINE

Adding fat to a sweet feed, hay, fiber pellet ration at a level equal to 5% of the grain intake did not adversely affect digestibility of any nutrients. Diets containing soybean oil and 4-80 dry fat had similar fat digestibilities while the fat digestibility of the diet containing Energy Pak was about 80% of these values. The Energy Pak, however, was the most palatable of the three fats and it was also easy to feed since it was in a dry form.

Do fat babies become good athletes?

The detrimental effects of rapid growth on skeletal soundness have been well established in horses, but what effect does excessive fatting have on subsequent performance in the equine athlete? Cecil Seamen of Thoroughbred Analyst in Lexington may just have the answer. Thoroughbred Analyst is a consulting company that advises Thoroughbred racehorse buyers of a horse's athletic potential based on its biomechanical conformation. A series of 15 measurements of body dimensions are taken of yearlings and these measurements are used to rate the horse's mechanical probability of success on a scale of A+ down to C.

From 1980 until 1988, 10,190 Thoroughbred yearlings have been measured at major sales in Kentucky, New York and England. In addition to the rating described above, the yearling's body condition was also evaluated. Each yearling's height, length and girth measurements were extrapolated to 40 months of age using computer generated growth curves. These measurements were compared to measurements taken from winners of Classic and Graded Stakes which were taken at the time of their stakes victories. This group included such elite racehorses as Riva Ridge, Spectacular Bid and A.P. Indy. Body weights were estimated for each group based on the relationship between heart girth, length and height.

The yearlings were divided into 3 categories based on estimated weight:

    1) Ideal (less than 60 lbs overweight)

    2) Overweight (>60 lbs and <120 lbs overweight)

    3) Obese (>120 lbs overweight)

The race records of these 10,190 yearlings were purchased from Bloodstock research and the horses' racetrack performances were compared to both their mechanical probability scores and their body condition at sale time. As expected, the high probability horses (A+,A, A-,B+) performed much better than the low probability horses (B, B-, C). High probability horses earned an average of $48,775 per starter compared to only $26,206 for the low probability horses. Over 10% of the high probability horses won stakes races compared with only 5% of the low probability horses.

Among the low probability horses, body condition as a yearling didn't have much of an affect on racing performance. Apparently, other factors such as conformation limited these horses' ability to compete in quality races. The high probability horses, however, were greatly affected by body condition as yearlings. Yearlings with ideal body weights went on to earn an average of $62,732 per starter while yearlings which were obese earned an average of only $36,198 per starter! 12.41 % of the yearlings with ideal body weights won stakes (7.41% graded) while oniy 7.85 % of those yearlings that were obese managed to win in stakes company (3.44 % graded). Yearlings which were in between in body condition were also intermediate in both earnings and stakes victories.

It should be emphasized that body weight was estimated when the horses were yearlings. Therefore, body weight may have changed greatly by the time the horses began racing depending on their diet and training regime.

Why the obese yearlings performed poorly is open to debate. Perhaps the fat yearlings never lost the extra pounds and therefore were forced to carry excess weight into their races. Or maybe obesity in young animals changes their metabolism so that they are less efficient at generating energy during a race. Research in rats suggests that this may be the case. Regardless of the reason, the bottom line is that excessive fatness in young horses not only increases the risk of skeletal damage, but it also diminishes their subsequent racing ability, at least in good individuals.

References

Duren, S.E., M. Manohar, B. Sikkes, S. Jackson, and J. Baker. 1992. Influence of Feeding and Exercise on the Distribution of Intestinal and Muscle Blood Flow in Ponies. Europäische Konferenz über die Ernährung des Pferdes. Tierärztliche Hochschule Hannover.

Linden, J., H. Josseck, W. Zenker, H. Geyer and J. Schulze. 1993. The Effect of D-biotin Supplementation on Hoof Condition in Lipizzaner Horses. In: Proc. 13th ENPS, Gainesville, FL.

Pagan, J.D., W. Tiegs, S.G. Jackson and H.Q. Murphy. 1993. The Effect of Different Fat Sources on Exercise Performance in Thoroughbred Racehorses. In: Proc. 13th ENPS, Gainesville, FL.

This paper was first published in "Feeding the Performance Horse," Proceedings for the 1993 Short Course for Feed Manufacturers

THE EFFECT OF PRE-EXERCISE B-VITAMIN SUPPLEMENTATION ON METABOLIC RESPONSE TO EXERCISE IN THOROUGHBRED HORSES

T. ROTMENSEN, JOE D. PAGAN AND STEPHEN G. JACKSON
Kentucky Equine Research, Inc., Versailles, Kentucky, USA

Performance horses are often administered large quantities of B-vitamins before exercise in an attempt to improve performance. B-vitamins play an important role in the conversion of pyruvate into acetyl Co-A for use in aerobic energy generation. A reduction in the conversion of pyruvate to acetyl Co-A will result in lactate production which may contribute to fatigue during exercise. To evaluate whether B-vitamin supplementation before exercise can affect performance, a 2 X 2 Latin square experiment was conducted. During the first of two periods, four trained 3 year old Thoroughbreds (3 geldings and 1 filly) were divided into 2 groups and fed either a sweet feed and hay diet (CONTROL) or the control diet plus extra B-vitamins the evening before and morning of a standardized exercise test (SET) on a high speed treadmill. The B-vitamins were provided in an oral form from a commercial product (Lactanase, Vita-Flex Nutrition Co., Inc.) which contained 500 mg thiamine, 35 mg riboflavin, 35 mg niacinamide, and 450 mg of d-pantothenic acid per dose. This was added to the evening feed the night before the SET and in the morning feed which was fed 3 hours before the SET. The sweet feed used in this experiment was also fortified with B-vitamins so that both groups received daily B-vitamin supplementation throughout the experimental period (table 1). The SET consisted of a 2 minute warm-up

Table 1. VITAMIN CONCENTRATIONS.

Vitamin	One packet(mg)	Vitamins provided by sweet feed	NRC[1] recommendation
Thiamin	500	31 mg/day	46.5 mg/day
Riboflavin	35	31.9 mg/day	18.6 mg/day
Niacinamide	35	142.4 mg/day	NR[2]
d-Pantothenic acid	450	65.1 mg/day	NR[2]
Vitamin A	-	33936.4 IU/day	22500 IU/day
Vitamin D	-	4331.3 IU/day	2785 IU/day
Vitamin E	-	188.2 IU/day	743 IU/day

[1] NRC 1989 for working horse; moderate intensity; 500 kg
[2] No recommendation given

Table 2. V_{LA4} AND V_{200} DURING SET

	CONTROL	B-vitamin supplementation	Standard error	Level of significance
V_{LA4} (m/s)	10.80	10.47	0.17	NS
V_{200} (m/s)	9.63	9.55	0.03	NS

walk followed by an 800 m trot (~4 m/s), then 800 m gallops of 8 m/s, 9 m/s, 10 m/s and 11 m/s. These gallops were followed by an 800 meter warm-down trot and 2 minute walk. At the end of each speed, heart rate was measured and a blood sample was taken from an indwelling jugular catheter. Blood was also taken at 15 and 30 minutes after exercise. After period 1, the diets were switched and the protocol repeated. The lactate-velocity relationship was determined by regressing the logarithm of lactate against speed and was expressed as V_{LA4}. The heart rate-velocity relationship was determined by linear regression and was expressed as V_{200}. There was no statistical difference (p>0.10) for either V_{LA4} or V_{200} between control and B-vitamin treatment (table 2). There was also no difference in plasma glucose either during or after the SET.

Additional B-vitamin supplementation before exercise did not appear to affect metabolic response in horses already receiving daily B-vitamin supplementation. It remains to be determined whether this type of B-vitamin supplementation will affect exercise response in horses receiving no supplemental vitamins.

This paper was first published in "Recent Advances in Equine Nutrition," Proceedings for the 1995 Short Course for Feed Manufacturers

EFFECT OF DIETARY VITAMIN E SUPPLEMENTATION ON THE EXERCISING HORSE

P.D. SICILIANO, A.L. PARKER, AND L.M. LAWRENCE

University of Kentucky, Lexington, Kentucky, USA

Vitamin E plays an important role in cellular antioxidant mechanisms, and vitamin E deficiency has been associated with decreased muscle integrity in some species. Because exercise may challenge some of the antioxidant defenses found in muscle cells, the effect of vitamin E supplementation on exercising horses was studied. Nineteen horses were randomly assigned to one of three diets for 90 days. The three diets were 1) a basal diet containing less than 44 ppm vitamin E; 2) the basal diet supplemented with 80 ppm vitamin E (d,l α-tocopheryl acetate); and 3) the basal diet supplemented with 300 ppm vitamin E (d,l α-tocopheryl acetate). The basal diet was adequate in all nutrients (NRC, 1989) except vitamin E for horses in moderate work. During the 90-day period horses were exercised 5 d/wk. Blood and muscle samples were obtained on days 0, 30 and 90 for determination of serum and muscle vitamin E levels. At the end of the 90-day period, all horses completed a repeated submaximal exercise test. Blood samples were taken before and 0, 1, 3, 6, 24, 48 and 72 hours after exercise for determination of creatine kinase (CK) and aspartate amino transferase (AST) activities which were used as indicators of muscle damage. The exercise test used in this study had previously been shown to cause an elevation in serum CK and AST activities post-exercise. Muscle samples were obtained before and after exercise for determination of thiobarbituric acid reactive substances and conjugated diene concentrations.

Mean serum and muscle vitamin E concentrations were not different (P>0.05) among groups on day 0 of the 90-day sampling period. Serum vitamin E concentrations declined in horses receiving either the basal diet or the diet supplemented with 80 ppm vitamin E (P<.05 and P<.06, respectively) during the 90-day sampling period. A similar trend was observed for muscle vitamin E concentrations in horses receiving those diets. Muscle and serum vitamin E levels did not decline in horses receiving the diet supplemented with 300 ppm vitamin E and on days 30 and 90 horses receiving this diet had higher vitamin E concentrations than horses receiving either the basal diet or the diet supplemented with 80 ppm vitamin E (Figure 1). These data may indicate that the current NRC recommended level of vitamin E supplementation (80 mg/kg diet) is not adequate to maintain vitamin E concentrations in regularly exercising horses.

Seventeen horses completed the exercise test at the end of the 90-day sampling period. Mean serum CK and AST activities were increased in all groups after the exercise tests. However, the increases in CK and AST activities observed in the horses consuming the vitamin E supplemented diets (80 or 300 ppm) were not different from the increases in the horses receiving the basal diet. Similarly, muscle thiobarbituric acid reactive substances and conjugated diene concentrations were not different among groups. Thus, an effect of vitamin E supplementation on muscle integrity in exercising horses was not observed.

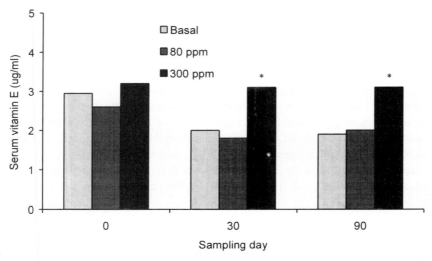

Figure 1. Serum vitamin E concentrations in exercised horses receiving diets containing varying levels of vitamin E. *Horses receiving the basal diet supplemented with 300ppm vitamin E had higher serum vitamin E concentrations than horses receiving the basal diet or the diet supplemented with 80ppm vitamin E. (Source: Siciliano, P.D. *et al*, (1997). Effect of dietary vitamin E supplementation on the integrity of skeletal muscle in the exercising horse. Journal of Animal Science.)

This paper was first published in Proceedings, Kentucky Equine Research 1997 Equine Nutrition Conference

THE EFFECT OF CHROMIUM SUPPLEMENTATION ON METABOLIC RESPONSE TO EXERCISE IN THOROUGHBRED HORSES

JOE D. PAGAN, STEPHEN G. JACKSON, AND STEPHEN E. DUREN
Kentucky Equine Research, Inc., Versailles, Kentucky, USA

Introduction

Chromium has been recognized as an essential nutrient in humans for many years (Mertz, 1992). Though chromium may well be involved in other physiological processes, at present its only known role is as a component of glucose tolerance factor (GTF) which potentiates the action of insulin. Therefore, it is involved in carbohydrate metabolism and other insulin dependent processes such as protein and lipid metabolism. A number of recent experiments have evaluated the effect of supplemental chromium in a wide range of species including humans, cattle, pigs, and turkeys. In these studies, chromium supplementation has increased lean muscle deposition (humans and swine), improved immune response (cattle), and reduced cortisol production caused by heat and transport stress (cattle and swine). No research, however, has been conducted with chromium in horses. Therefore, the following study was conducted to determine the effect that chromium supplementation has on metabolic response to exercise in trained Thoroughbred horses.

Material and methods

Six trained Thoroughbred horses (4 gelded males, 2 females) were used in this 2 period switch-back design experiment. The horses were divided into two groups which received identical diets with one group (CHROM) also receiving 5 mg of chromium from a chromium yeast product (Co-Factor III, Alltech, Inc.). The diet consisted of a textured grain mix, forage cubes and orchard grass hay. Amounts and compositions are listed in Tables 1 and 2. At the conclusion of the first period, the diets were switched and the horses repeated the same exercise and testing regime.

During each 14 day period, the horses were exercised on a high speed treadmill (Beltalong, Eurora, Australia) inclined to 3° according to the schedule outlined in table 3. Heart rate was monitored on a daily basis (Hippocard PEH 200). At the end of each period, the horses performed a standardized exercise test (SET) on the treadmill. On the test day, each horse received 1.36 Kg of hay cubes 5 hours before the SET and 1.81 kg grain 3 hours before the test. Blood samples were collected from an indwelling jugular catheter after an 8 hour overnight fast, before grain was fed and hourly after feeding for 3 hours. The SET began at 3 hours post feeding and consisted of a 2 minute warm-up walk followed by an 800 m trot (~4 m/s), then 800 m gallops of 8 m/s, 9 m/s, 10 m/s and 11 m/s. These gallops were followed by an 800 m warm-down trot and 2 minute walk. During the SET, a blood sample was taken after the warm-up trot, during the last 15 seconds of each gallop and after the warm-down walk. Blood samples were also collected at 15 and 30 minutes post exercise. Heart rate was recorded at each speed.

Table 1. NUTRIENT CONCENTRATIONS OF EXPERIMENTAL FEEDS

Nutrient	Sweet feed	Orchard grass hay	Forage cubes	Chromium yeast
Dry matter (%)	85.5	91.0	91.6	92.3
Crude protein (%)[1]	14.2	15.8	16.7	48.6
Acid detergent fiber (%)[1]	9.8	34.9	37.3	3.7
Neutral detergent fiber (%)[1]	19.3	54.5	49.9	17.9
Lignin %[1]	2.4	5.9	8.0	-
Ether extract (%)[1]	4.7	3.2	2.2	0.9
Soluble CHO (%)[1,2]	55.85	17.08	21.47	26.33
Calcium (%)[1]	0.71	0.76	1.40	0.15
Phosphorus (%)[1]	0.62	0.40	0.27	1.22
Magnesium (%)[1]	0.22	0.16	0.24	0.21
Potassium (%)[1]	0.86	3.20	1.96	1.84
Sodium (%)[1]	0.241	0.012	0.03	0.084
Iron (ppm)[1]	363	135	460	157
Copper (ppm)[1]	30	7	7.9	51
Zinc (ppm)[1]	98	19	22	192
Chromium (ppm)[1]	2.6	0.30	0.74	1008

[1] dry matter basis
[2] soluble CHO = 100-CP-EE-NDF-Ash

Table 2. DAILY FEEDING SCHEDULE

	Sweet feed	Orchard grass hay	Forage cubes[1]	Chromium yeast
07.00 am	1.81 kg		1.36 kg	
12.00 pm		1.13 kg		
17.00 pm	1.81 kg		1.36 kg	5 grams
22.00 pm		1.13 kg		

[1] AlfaOats, Canadian Agra Bio-cube, Kincardine, Ontario

Table 3. EXERCISE SCHEDULE

	Period 1	*Period 2*
3 times per week	1600 m @ 7 - 8 m/s	1600 m @ 8 - 9 m/s
4 days before SET	1600 m @ 10 m/s	1600 m @ 10 m/s
3 days before SET	no exercise	no exercise
2 days before SET	1600 m @ 8 m/s	1600 m @ 8 m/s
1 day before SET	no exercise	no exercise

Each blood sample was placed in a sterile tube containing EDTA and centrifuged immediately. The plasma was pipetted into glass tubes, measured for lactate and glucose and then frozen. Plasma glucose was measured using an automated glucose analyzer (YSI, 2300 STAT). Lactate levels were measured using an automated L-lactate analyzer (YSI,1500 Sport). The following day, the frozen plasma was analyzed for triglycerides and cholesterol (Eppendorf 5060 Automated Analyzer, Gibbstown, New Jersey). At the conclusion of the study, all of the frozen plasma samples were analyzed for insulin and cortisol using commercially available radioimmunoassay (RIA) kits which had been validated for specificity and accuracy in equine plasma (BET Labs, Lexington, Kentucky). Variables were analyzed by analysis of variance using animal, period and treatment as main effects (NCSS, Kaysville, Utah).

Results

Plasma glucose (figure 1) in both groups peaked 1 hour after the grain meal the morning of the SET. Glucose tended to be higher in the control (CON) horses at this time (121.8 vs. 116.8 mg/dl, p=0.18). At the onset of exercise, glucose was still elevated above fasting levels in both groups. During exercise, glucose decreased with each step. Glucose was significantly lower than the CON (p<0.05) in the CHROM group after the 8 m/s and 9 m/s steps. During the warm-down phase of the SET, glucose rebounded to fasting levels in both groups and glucose was not different (p>0.10) 15 or 30 minutes post exercise.

Plasma insulin (figure 2) increased following feeding in both groups. Insulin peaked in the CON group 1 hour after grain, while the peak in the CHROM group didn't occur until 2 hours after grain was fed. Blood insulin was lower in the CHROM group than the CON (163 vs 129 uU/ml, p<0.10) 1 hr after grain feeding.

Plasma lactate (figure 3) increased in both groups throughout the SET, peaking in both groups following the final gallop step. Lactate was lower in the CHROM group (8.65 vs. 7.55 mmol/l, p=0.08) after the 11 m/s step.

Cortisol (figure 4) was significantly lower in the CHROM group 3 hours after feeding (p<0.01), after the warm-up trot (p<0.05) and after the 8 and 11 m/s steps (p<0.10).

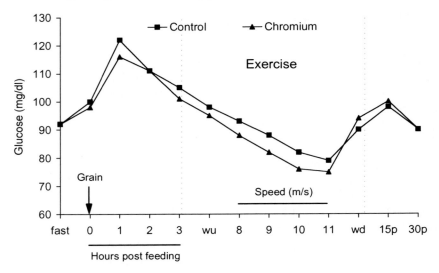

Figure 1. Plasma glucose (mg/dl)

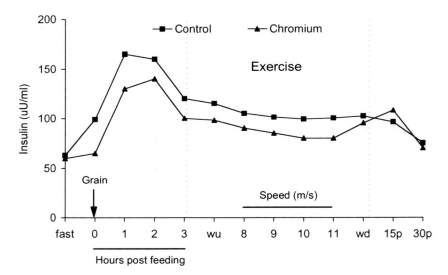

Figure 2. Plasma insulin (uU/ml)

Triglycerides (figure 5) tended to be higher in the CHROM group than the CON following the 10 and 11 m/s steps and were significantly higher in the CHROM group 15 and 30 minutes post exercise ($p<0.05$). Heart rate (figure 6) and cholesterol were unaffected by diet.

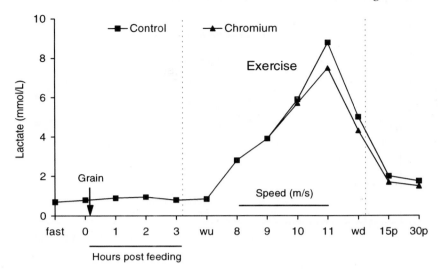

Figure 3. Plasma lactate (mmol/l)

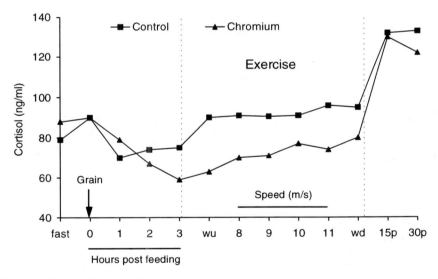

Figure 4. Plasma cortisol (ng/ml)

Discussion

Supplementation with an organic form of chromium affected insulin response to a grain meal in these exercised horses. This response is consistent with findings in humans (Anderson *et al.*, 1991a) and pigs (Evock-Clover *et al.*, 1993) where

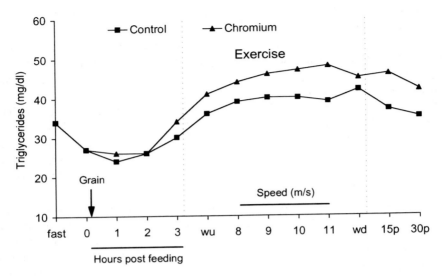

Figure 5. Plasma triglycerides (mg/dl)

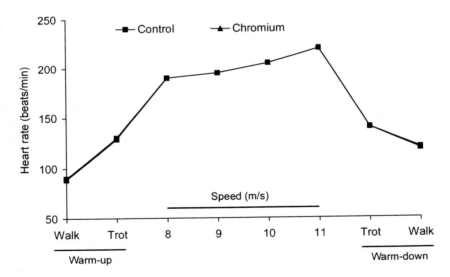

Figure 6. Heart rate (beats per minute)

chromium supplementation increased glucose tolerance and insulin sensitivity. Trivalent chromium, as a constituent of glucose tolerance factor (GTF), is thought to facilitate interactions between insulin and insulin receptors on target tissues such as muscle and fat.

Plasma cortisol was also affected by chromium supplementation. Cortisol concentrations were lower in the CHROM group 3 hours after feeding and during exercise and this effect may have also been related to differences in insulin status. Cortisol acts antagonistically to insulin and this may be the underlying metabolic role of cortisol in stress (Munck *et al.*, 1984). The function of cortisol may be to prevent insulin from causing dangerous hypoglycemia. In a previous study with trained Thoroughbreds (Pagan *et al.*, 1994), high insulin levels post feeding were associated with high cortisol production.

Elevated triglycerides in the CHROM group during and after exercise may have also been related to insulin production. Insulin inhibits lipid mobilization from adipose. The increase in triglycerides in the CHROM group may have been the result of high lipid mobilization during exercise. Free fatty acids mobilized during exercise that were not taken up and oxidized by the working muscle may have been used to resynthesize triglycerides in the liver.

Plasma lactate was lower after the fastest step of the SET in the chromium supplemented horses. The reason for this decrease is unknown, but may be related to a change in carbohydrate and lipid metabolism brought about by a reduction in insulin production or increase in tissue insulin sensitivity. Since lactate accumulation has been implicated as a contributing factor to fatigue during strenuous exercise, this reduction in lactate accumulation can be interpreted as being beneficial for the performance horse. The horses used in this experiment had been in training for several months before the start of this experiment and they continued to exercise throughout the study. Research in humans has shown that chromium excretion is related to exercise intensity (Anderson *et al.*, 1991b). This may explain why these horses responded to chromium supplementation while untrained, sedentary horses in a subsequent study (Pagan, unpublished data) did not. Chromium is a nutrient, not a drug. Therefore, it is reasonable to only expect a metabolic response in horses that are deficient in chromium. More research is needed to determine which factors affect chromium status in horses and what levels of supplementation are effective.

References

Anderson, R.A., Polansky, M.M., Bryden, N.A. and J.J. Canary. 1991a. Supplemental-chromium effects on glucose, insulin, glucagon, and urinary chromium losses in subjects consuming controlled low-chromium diets. Am. J. Clin. Nutr. 54: 909-916.

Anderson, R.A., Bryden, N.A., Polansky, M.M. and J.W. Thorp. 1991b. Effect of carbohydrate loading and underwater exercise on circulating cortisol, insulin and urinary losses of chromium and zinc. Eur. J. Appl. Physiol. 63:146.

Evock-Clover, C.M., Polansky, M.M., Anderson, R.A., and N.C. Steele. 1993. Dietary chromium supplementation with or without somatotropin treatment alters serum hormones and metabolites in growing pigs without affecting growth performance. J. Nutr. 123: 1504-1512.

Mertz, W. 1992. Chromium, history and nutritional importance. Biol Trace Elem. Res. 32:3.

Munck, A., Guyre, P.M., and N.J. Holbrook. 1984. Physiological functions of glucocorticoids in stress and their relation to pharmacological actions. Endocrine Reviews 5: 25-44.

Pagan, J.D., Burger, I. and S.G. Jackson. 1994. The long-term effects of feeding fat to 2 year old Thoroughbreds in training. 4th ICEEP, Queensland, Australia (abstr.).

This paper was first published in "Recent Advances in Equine Nutrition," Proceedings for the 1995 Short Course for Feed Manufacturers

THE EFFECTS OF NIACIN SUPPLEMENTATION ON NIACIN STATUS AND EXERCISE METABOLISM IN HORSES

A.L. PARKER, L.M. LAWRENCE, S. ROKURODA AND L.K. WARREN
University of Kentucky, Lexington, Kentucky, USA

The National Research Council (1989) currently does not list a dietary niacin requirement for horses because hindgut synthesis and niacin naturally occurring in feeds are believed to be adequate to meet the needs for most horses. However, because niacin plays a key role in energy metabolism, many exercising horses receive dietary niacin supplementation. Two studies were conducted to examine the effects of niacin supplementation on the exercising horses.

In the first trial, 4 mature Thoroughbred geldings were used in a two period cross-over design exercise trial to examine the effects of acute nicotinic acid (NA) dosing on exercise metabolism. The basal diet consisted of 60% timothy hay and 40% heavy racehorse oats and a commercial vitamin mineral supplement and contained approximately 27 mg NA/kg DM. Horses were housed in box stalls and exercised 4 d/wk on a high-speed treadmill. Horses performed two exercise tests on the treadmill 7 days apart. Prior to the first exercise test, horses were randomly assigned to a control group or NA dosed group. NA dosed horses received 4.5 g NA mixed with 25 g applesauce orally 2 hours before performing the exercise test. Applesauce was used as a carrier for the NA. Horses were fasted 12 hours prior to the beginning of the test. The exercise test consisted of an 18 minute warm-up phase (12 minutes at 3% grade and 4.0 m/s, and 6 minutes walk at 0% grade and 1.9 m/s), followed by a 7 minute step test at 10% grade. The step test began at 2.0 m/s and the speed was increased 1 m/s every minute until a final speed of 8 m/s was reached. At the conclusion of the final step, the speed was decreased to 1.9 m/s and the treadmill was lowered to 0% grade. Heart rate (HR) and blood samples were obtained before the beginning of the exercise test, every 3 min throughout the warm-up, at the end of each step of the step test and every 5 minutes during a 30 minute recovery phase. No differences were found for plasma FFA or plasma lactate concentrations between the two treatments. Mean plasma lactate concentrations were 7.0 ± 3.1 and 6.7 ± 2.1 mmol/L when horses received the control diet or were dosed with 4.5 g NA, respectively. A time by treatment interaction was detected ($P < 0.05$) for plasma glucose concentrations during the warm-up phase. However, this effect was absent during the step test and recovery phases. Furthermore, point-by-point analysis failed to demonstrate differences ($P > 0.05$) between the two treatments. Heart rates were similar between the two groups throughout the exercise test. The mean maximum HR achieved was 190.3 ± 4.6 and 191.0 ± 8.5 beats/min when horses received the control diet or the 4.5 g NA, respectively.

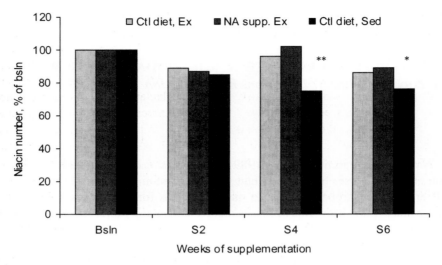

Figure 1. Niacin status as a percentage of week 0 (baseline) (**$P<0.05$; *$P<0.1$). Time effect ($P<0.01$). Time * trt interaction ($P<0.1$).

In humans, the determination of the NAD:NADP ratio in red blood cells has been used to assess niacin status, which can be increased with niacin supplementation. Using this method, a preliminary study showed horses to be niacin "deficient" by human standards. To determine the effect of 6 weeks of niacin supplementation on niacin status and exercise metabolism in the horse, a second experiment was conducted using 11 mature Thoroughbred geldings in a randomized repeated measures design experiment. Horses were assigned to one of 3 groups: 1) sedentary, no nicotinic acid supplementation, 2) exercise, no NA supplementation and 3) exercise, 3 g/d NA supplementation. The basal diet consisted of 58% timothy hay and 42% concentrate and contained approximately 29 mg of NA/kg DM. Sedentary horses were kept in 3x12 m sheltered pens and received no forced exercise. Exercised horses were housed in box stalls and were exercised 5 times/wk on a high-speed treadmill. Blood samples were obtained prior to supplementation (week 0) and at 3, 5, and 7 weeks of supplementation for determination of NAD and NADP levels. On weeks 0 and 7, the exercised horses performed a 30 minute exercise test on the treadmill. Horses were fasted 12 hours prior to the beginning of the exercise test, which consisted of a 15 minute warm-up (12 minutes at 3% grade and 4.0 m/s, and 3 minutes at 0% grade and 1.9 m/s), followed by a 14 minute step test at 10% grade beginning at 2 m/s and increasing 1 m/s every 2 minutes until a final speed of 8 m/ s was reached. Blood samples were obtained before the start of the exercise test, every 3 minutes throughout the warm-up phase, at the end of each step of the step test and every 5 minutes during a 30 minute recovery phase. Plasma FFA concentrations were higher at week 7 than at week 0 for both exercised groups. However, the differences were significant only for the exercised control group during the step test (time by week; P<0.01) and recovery phase (time by week; P<0.1). In the recovery phase, FFA concentrations in the control group tended to be higher (P<0.1) 15 minutes post-exercise and were higher at 20 (P<0.05), 25 (P<0.01) and 30 minutes (P<0.01) post-exercise in the week 7 versus week 0 exercise test. Plasma FFA concentrations in exercised NA supplemented horses were not increased (P>0.05) at week 7 compared to week 0. Plasma lactate concentrations did not differ (P>0.05) from week 0 to week 7 for either exercised group. Mean plasma lactate concentrations at the end of the step test were 12.15 ± 2.08 mmol/L at week 0 and 11.19 ± 1.92 mol/L at week 7 for control horses. For horses receiving the NA supplemented diet, mean plasma lactate concentrations at the end of the step test were 18.50 ± 10.36 mmol/L at wk 0 and 17.81 ± 8.88 mmol/L at week 7. Differences in niacin status existed between treatment groups at week 0. Thus, all niacin status values were expressed as a percentage of week 0 (baseline), allowing each group to serve as its own control (Figure 1). No differences were observed between exercised groups over the 6 week period. However, sedentary control horses had lower (P<0.05) niacin status than either exercised group at week 4 and week 6. At week 6, horses in the sedentary control group tended to have a lower (P<0.1) niacin status than the exercised control group, but not the exercised NA supplemented group. A time effect (P<0.01) was observed, and a tendency (P<0.1) for a time by treatment effect occurred, reflecting the lower niacin status values in the sedentary control group at week 4 and week 6.

In summary, neither acute nor chronic NA supplementation appears to affect exercise metabolism in the horse. Furthermore, niacin status in the horse was not affected by 6 wk of NA supplementation.

This paper was first published in Proceedings, Kentucky Equine Research 1997 Equine Nutrition Conference

THE INFLUENCE OF TRIMETHYLGLYCINE ON THE UNTRAINED AND TRAINED HORSE EXERCISING TO FATIGUE

L.K. WARREN, K.N. THOMPSON, L.M. LAWRENCE AND
T. BREWSTER-BARNES
University of Kentucky, Lexington, Kentucky, USA

Because fatigue has been associated with the accumulation of lactate, there is considerable interest in methods which reduce lactate accumulation during intense exercise. The compound N,N-dimethylglycine (DMG) has been theorized to prevent lactic acid build-up during exercise; however, inconsistent findings have been reported. Despite the controversial effectiveness of DMG, it continues to be marketed as an ergogenic aid for horses. The purpose of this study was to evaluate the effect of trimethylglycine (TMG) (Finnsugar Bioproducts, Helsinki, Finland), a relative compound to DMG, in untrained and trained horses before, during and after a high-intensity exercise test. Eight mature untrained Thoroughbred horses (5 geldings, 3 mares) were randomly assigned to the control or the TMG treatment group. TMG was top-dressed on the morning grain ration at a rate of 80 mg/kg body weight for 14 days prior to, but not including the day of, the exercise trial. Horses performed an incremental exercise test on a high-speed treadmill beginning at 6 m/s on a 10% grade and increasing 1 m/s every minute thereafter until the horse fatigued. Following the exercise test, treatment groups were switched and the horses were tested a second time. After a 60 day conditioning program, horses were tested again with the same treatment protocol, this time as trained individuals. The addition of TMG did not alter the effect of exercise on plasma lactate, glucose, free fatty acids or triglyceride concentrations during exercise in the untrained horse. However, plasma lactate concentrations were lower at 10 minutes (P<0.10) and 60 minutes (P<0.05) post-exercise when untrained horses received TMG (Figure 1). In addition, plasma free fatty acids were lower (P<0.05) before exercise and at 12 hours post-exercise when untrained horses recieved TMG (Figure 2). After training, no differences (P>0.05) due to TMG supplementation were observed in any of the blood or exercise variables measured before, during or after exercise. However, training affected (P<0.05) all variables measured, including prolonging (P<0.05) time to fatigue and reducing (P<0.05) lactate accumulation. The results of this experiment suggest that supplemental TMG may have a beneficial effect on post-exercise lactate oxidation in the untrained horse. However, this finding was not supported by a similar affect on lactate metabolism in the trained horse. Although the horses exhibited a training effect, TMG supplementation produced no additive effects in the trained horse. Therefore, based on the results of this study, TMG appears to offer no benefit to the horse as an ergogenic aid.

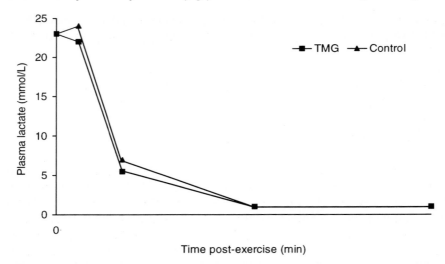

Figure 1. The effect of TMG on the post-exercise plasma lactate concentration in the untrained horse (*P<0.10; **P<0.05) (from Warren *et al.*, 14th ENPS, Ontario, CA, January 1995)

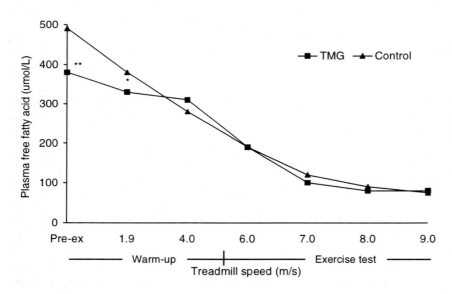

Figure 2. The effect of TMG on the plasma free fatty acid concentration before and during exercise in the untrained horse (*P<0.10; **P<0.05) (from Warren *et al.*, 14th ENPS, Ontario, CA, January 1995)

This paper was first published in "Recent Advances in Equine Nutrition," Proceedings for the 1995 Short Course for Feed Manufacturers

THE EFFECT OF FEEDING RESTRICTED DIETS ON THYROID HORMONE CONCENTRATIONS AND METABOLIC RESPONSES IN THE EXERCISING HORSE

D. POWELL, L. LAWRENCE, B. FITZGERALD, K. DANIELSEN[1,]
A. PARKER, S. ROKURODA AND A. CRUM
University of Kentucky, Lexington, Kentucky, USA
[1]Halsetreina 17, 7027 Trondheim, NORWAY

Caloric restriction and exercise can produce changes in peripheral thyroid hormone concentrations in humans and animals which may have the potential to affect metabolism or performance during physical activity. This study investigated the effects of short-term feed restriction and the percentage of concentrate versus roughage contained in the diet on T_4 and T_3 concentrations and metabolic responses to feeding a small meal and to exercise. Four treatments were assigned to four healthy mature Thoroughbred geldings in a 4x4 Latin square design. The four treatments consisted of 1) a nutritionally adequate high roughage ration (70:30% roughage:concentrate) [AHR]; 2) a nutritionally adequate high concentrate ration (40:60% roughage:concentrate) [AHC]; 3) a diet restricted to 70% of 1 [RHR]; 4) a diet restricted to 70% of 2 [RHC]. Diets AHR and AHC met or slightly exceeded the NRC (1989) nutrient recommendations for horses undergoing moderate work. Body weights were measured at the beginning and end of each treatment period. At the end of each period, a diet was fed which allowed for any weight loss that occurred during the feeding period to be regained. Following the 7-day weight-gaining period, the treatments were switched and the same procedure followed until all horses completed all treatments.

On day 9 of each feeding period, each horse was fed 1.0 kg of oats between 0900 and 0930 hours. Blood samples were taken pre-feeding, immediately after and 30 minutes after completion and then every hour for 7 hours for determination of thyroid hormone (T_4 and T_3), glucose, insulin and free fatty acid (FFA) concentrations. On day 11 or 12 of each treatment period, horses performed a 25 min exercise test on a high speed treadmill. Horses were not fed the morning prior to the test and all tests were conducted between 0800 and 0900 hours. The test consisted of a 17 minute warm-up phase, immediately followed by an 8 minute step test at a 10% grade, where the speed was increased every min beginning at 2 m/s and ending at 9 m/s. Blood samples obtained pre-exercise, during exercise and during recovery were analyzed for T_4, T_3, lactate, glucose, insulin and FFA concentrations.

Meal feeding produced an increase (P<0.01) in the T_4 and T_3 concentrations when horses received the AHR and AHC diets but not when they received diets RHR or RHC (Figure 1). T_4 concentrations were lowest when horses received the AHC diet. When horses received diet RHR, they had a greater increase (P<0.05) in glucose post feeding (1 kg oats) than when fed the other diets. During the exercise test, horses had higher T_4 concentrations and a higher T_4/T_3 ratio throughout the step test and recovery periods (P<.05) when they received the RHR diet (Figure 2). T_3 concentrations tended to decline when horses received the RHR diet during the step test (Figure 2). Similarly, there was a time x diet effect (P<0.05) during the recovery phase when T_3 declined in horses receiving the RHR diet. Insulin concentrations were highest (P<0.05) during the step test when horses received the AHC diet. A time x diet interaction tended (P=0.20) to occur with glucose during the step test when horses received diets RHR and RHC, while FFA concentrations in the horses consuming diet RHR tended (P=0.15) to have a greater response during exercise.

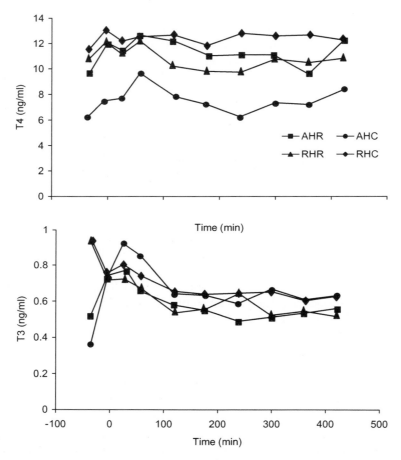

Figure 1. Mean serum concentrations of thyroxine (T_4) and triiodo-thyronine (T_3) in horses fed adequate high roughage (AHR), adequate high concentrate (AHC), 70% of intake of AHR (RHR) or 70% of intake of AHC (RHC) during a meal feeding.

These data suggest that T_3 and T_4 increase in response to meal feeding in horses receiving nutrient adequate diets, but this response may not occur when horses have been subjected to short-term feed restriction. Short-term diet restriction and diet composition may affect peripheral conversion of T_4 to T_3 in exercising horses.

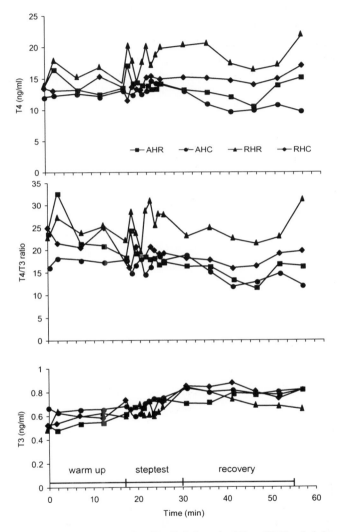

Figure 2. Mean serum concentrations of thyroxine (T_4), triiodothyronine (T_3), and T_4/T_3 ratio in horses fed adequate high roughage (AHR), adequate high concentrate (AHC), 70% of AHR (RHR) or 70% of AHC (RHC) diets during an exercise test.

This paper was first published in Proceedings, Kentucky Equine Research 1997 Equine Nutrition Conference

THE LONG-TERM EFFECTS OF FEEDING FAT TO TWO YEAR OLD THOROUGHBREDS IN TRAINING

JOE D. PAGAN, IVAN BURGER[1] AND STEPHEN G. JACKSON
Kentucky Equine Research, Inc., Versailles, Kentucky, USA
[1]Waltham Centre for Nutrition and Care, Melton Mowbray, UK

A number of short-term studies (2-4 weeks) have demonstrated improved metabolic response to exercise with fat supplemented diets. No longer term studies have been conducted to evaluate how fat supplementation affects the health and metabolic response of horses to exercise over an extended training period. Therefore, the following seven month study was conducted using 12 two year old Thoroughbreds to evaluate the long-term effects of feeding a fat supplemented diet during medium intensity, aerobic training. The control group (n=6) was fed grass hay and a fortified sweet feed (CON) and the other group (FAT)(n=6) received hay, sweet feed, a supplement pellet and 400 ml of soybean oil. This amount of oil supplementation supplied about 12% of the DE intake of the FAT group. After 2, 4, and 7 months, the horses performed 2 standardized exercise tests (SETs) on a high speed treadmill. The first test (STEP) consisted of sequential steps of 800 m at speeds of about 4, 8,9,10, and 11 m/s. The second test (SET30) consisted of 30 minutes of trotting at about 4 m/s.

Hematological parameters

Hematological parameters measured in samples taken 4 hours after feeding before each STEP for both treatment groups were within ranges reported previously for two year old Thoroughbreds in training (Allen and Powell, 1982). Neither dietary treatment nor training affected any of these hematological parameters.

Serum chemistry

Values for AST, GT, SDH, total bilirubin, total protein, cholesterol and bile acids from resting samples taken before each STEP were within ranges normally reported for healthy horses (Blackmore and Brobst, 1981) and none was affected by diet. Cholesterol and bile acids were elevated in both treatment groups after 2 months of training compared with samples taken later in the study. At this point in the study, the horses were turned out at night in grass paddocks which were fairly lush with spring forage.

Resting plasma hormone levels

Concentrations of insulin, cortisol and thyroxine measured in blood samples taken 4 hours after feeding before each STEP are shown in table 1. Diet did not statistically affect any of these measurements. There was, however, a difference ($P<0.01$) between 2 month and 7 month cortisol and thyroxine concentrations for both treatment groups. Cortisol was higher and thyroxine was lower at 2 months of training than at 7 months.

Table 1. RESTING PLASMA HORMONE LEVELS[1]

Hormone	Initial	2 months	4 months	7 months
CONTROL Insulin (uU/ml)	39.46 ±5.4	55.98 ±17.2	46.16 ±11.3	86.54 ±24.1
FAT Insulin (uU/ml)	43.29 ±12.4	48.03 ±15.4	51.30 ±10.9	45.47 ±3.84
CONTROL Cortisol (ng/ml)	59.94 ±21.97	101.80 ±28.05	43.09 ±5.4	37.13 ±4.7
FAT Cortisol (ng/ml)	45.41 ±19.7	78.27 ±17.6	42.90 ±13.3	35.80 ±3.3
CONTROL Thyroxine (ng/ml)	20.94 ±4.4	15.47 ±2.7	28.88 ±5.9	25.65 ±3.26
FAT Thyroxine (ng/ml)	16.93 ±2.1	15.69 ±3.9	26.11 ±3.7	27.32 ±2.0

[1] mean ± standard deviation

Table 2. V_{LA4} AND V_{200} DURING STEP[1]

	Initial	2 months	4 months	7 months
CONTROL V_{LA4} (m/s)	8.65 ±0.72	10.16 ±0.99	9.67 ±0.59	10.08 ±0.49
FAT V_{LA4} (m/s)	8.62 ±0.60	9.62 ±0.80	9.59 ±0.49	10.03 ±0.65
CONTROL V_{200} (m/s)	9.15 ±0.65	9.54 ±0.80	9.88 ±0.46	10.33 ±0.51
FAT V_{200} (m/s)	10.05 ±1.00	10.07 ±1.08	10.34 ±0.52	10.78 ±0.78

[1] mean ± standard deviation

Standardized step-wise exercise test (STEP)

V_{200} and V_{LA4} measured at the beginning of the experiment and after 2, 4, and 7 months of training are shown in table 2. Training significantly increased V_{LA4} and V_{200} in both treatment groups ($P<0.05$). Diet, however, had no effect on these measurements. Figures 1-3 show plasma glucose, insulin, and cortisol response during the 7 month STEP. Four hours before the 7 month STEP, CONTROL horses were fed 2.27 kg of sweet feed and FAT horses received 1.59 kg of sweet feed, 113 g supplement pellet and 200 ml of soybean oil. The horses received no hay the morning of the STEP.

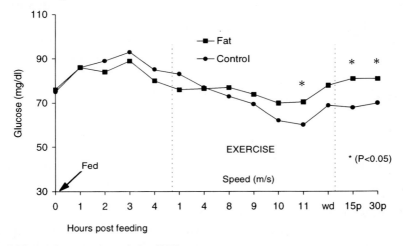

Figure 1. Plasma glucose response during STEP

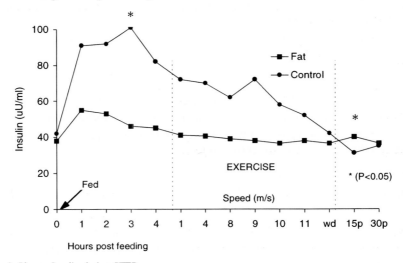

Figure 2. Plasma Insulin during STEP

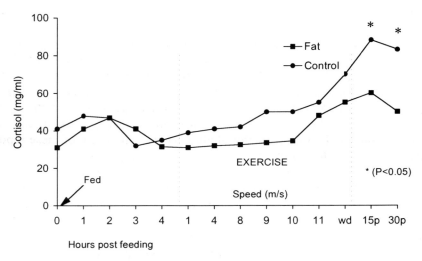

Figure 3. Plasma cortisol during STEP

GLUCOSE

Plasma glucose concentration was similar in the two treatment groups after an overnight fast. Glucose peaked in both groups 3 hours after feeding. After the onset
of exercise, blood glucose decreased continually in the CONTROL horses from a pre-exercise level of 85.2 mg/dl to 61.2 mg/dl after the fastest exercise step (11 m/s). After the last exercise step, blood glucose was higher in the FAT horses (71.0 mg/dl) than in the CONTROL horses (61.2 mg/dl) ($P<0.05$). Fifteen minutes after exercise, glucose in the FAT group had returned to preexercise levels (81.8 mg/dl) and was higher ($P<0.05$) than in the CONTROL group (66.7 mg/dl).

INSULIN

Insulin was higher ($P<0.05$) 3 hours after feeding in the CONTROL group than in the FAT horses (102.9 vs 46.5 uU/ml).   Insulin dropped throughout exercise and during recovery in the CONTROL horses. At 15 minutes after exercise, insulin was lower ($P<0.05$) in CONTROL horses (29.8 uU/ml) than in the FAT group (38.7 uU/ml).

CORTISOL

Cortisol was similar for both treatment groups before exercise. Cortisol increased in both groups throughout exercise and during recovery. At 15 and 30 minutes after exercise, cortisol was higher ($P<0.001$) in CONTROL horses than in the FAT group.

Discussion

A primary objective of this study was to determine whether feeding a fat supplemented diet to horses in training for an extended period of time (7 months) affected their health or athletic performance. Anecdotal reports have suggested that feeding fat supplemented diets to horses during intense training may lead to a number of problems including reduced packed cell volume (PCV), liver dysfunction, hypothyroidism and a generalized reduction in performance described as "running out of gas" near the end of a race. The results of this study do not support any of these reports. Hematological values taken throughout the 7 month training period were not affected by diet. Horses in the fat supplemented group had PCV, hemoglobin and RBC levels that averaged slightly lower than the CONTROL horses, but these differences existed at the beginning of the study before the horses were assigned to either diet. The horses were assigned to each diet based on V_{LA4} values determined during the initial SET and these differences in hematological values were simply a coincidence. None of these values changed significantly throughout the 7 month training period.

There was no evidence of liver dysfunction in either treatment group. GT is an enzyme which is found in highest concentrations in the liver, pancreas and kidney. Increases in plasma concentrations are associated with increased synthesis in the hepatobiliary system and GT has been used as a sensitive measurement of chronic hepatic damage (Snow *et al.*, 1987a). There was no difference in serum GT levels between diets. Both groups had normal levels throughout training. In addition, other serum chemistry that might indicate a problem with liver function (AST, SDH, total bilirubin, bile acids, cholesterol) was unaffected by diet.

Plasma total thyroxine (T4) was also unaffected by diet. Thyroxine concentrations were higher in both groups at 7 months than after 2 months of training ($P<0.01$). It has been reported that training increases thyroxine secretion in horses and humans, but changes in the ratio of bound to free thyroxine tend to cause total thyroxine levels to remain unaffected by exercise (Thornton, 1985). However, thyroxine levels tend to be highest during times of rapidly declining temperatures and tend to return towards the annual mean when temperatures reach a stable level of cold (Irvine, 1983). In warm weather, thyroxine concentrations tend to be low. The initial samples were obtained in early March when temperatures were consistently cold. The 2 month samples were collected in late April when temperatures were warmer and the 7 month samples were taken in early October when temperatures had begun to fall. Therefore, the variation that was seen in resting thyroxine concentrations may have been due to fluctuations in the environmental temperature.

V_{200} and V_{LA4} have been used to measure the state of fitness and endurance capacity of horses (Persson, 1983). Training significantly improved V_{200} and V_{LA4} in each treatment group. Diet, however, did not significantly affect heart rate or lactate response to exercise. These results do not agree with a previous study conducted in our laboratory (Pagan *et al.*, 1993), in which a diet containing 10%

soybean oil resulted in a significant increase in both V_{200} and V_{LA4} compared to a control diet. The differences in results between these two studies may be due to the composition of the control diet used in each study. In the present study, the control diet contained 42% oats and 31% corn as whole and coarse cracked grains, while in the previous study the control diet was pelleted and contained 36% ground oats and 43% ground corn. Since corn is higher in starch than oats, perhaps the total starch content of the diet affected the results. In addition, grinding corn increases its prececal digestibility in horses (Meyer *et al.*, 1993). The effect of starch intake and grain processing on metabolic response to exercise warrants further investigation.

Although diet had no effect on V_{200} or V_{LA4}, there were differences in hormonal and glycemic response to exercise. During the STEP there was a significantly greater drop in plasma glucose in the CONTROL fed horses. This drop was probably the result of increased uptake of glucose by the working muscle under the influence of insulin since plasma insulin was elevated in the CONTROL group before exercise began. An increase in insulin results in enhanced glucose uptake and glycogen synthesis, enhanced lipogenesis and decreased lipolysis (Lawrence, 1990). As a result, during exercise there will be increased use of blood glucose and a decreased use of fat as a result of lower FFA availability. An exercise induced hypoglycemia has been shown to cause fatigue during severe exercise lasting an hour or longer in humans (Costill *et al.*, 1977).

Replacing carbohydrate with fat reduced post feeding peaks in both insulin and glucose and thus reduced the fall in blood glucose during strenuous exercise. This response could be beneficial to horses performing prolonged strenuous exercise. These exercise tests were conducted 4 hours after feeding. It should be noted, however, that if exercise is performed after either an overnight fast or an 8 hour delay after feeding, these large drops in blood glucose concentration during strenuous exercise no longer occur even with high carbohydrate-low fat diets (Lawrence *et al.*, 1993, Pagan *et al.,* 1995).

Feeding a fat supplemented diet to reduce postprandial blood glucose and insulin response may be beneficial if feeding occurred 3-4 hours before exercise. In the present study, there were also no detrimental effects on performance during the SETs. While these tests were intense (HRs >210), they were still not maximal and tests of similar intensity have resulted in only small decreases in muscle glycogen (Pagan *et al.*, 1987). Thoroughbred racehorse training has been shown to reduce muscle glycogen by 19-25% (Snow and Harris, 1991) and racing can result in drops of 25-33% (Harris *et al*, 1987). Since muscle glycogen repletion depends on increases in both blood glucose and blood insulin (Snow *et al.*, 1987b) it is possible that feeding fat supplemented diets for an extended period of time to racehorses in race training may result in a progressive decline in muscle glycogen which may ultimately compromise the horse's racing performance. A combination of a low carbohydrate-high fat diet has been used in horses undergoing intense exercise to reduce muscle glycogen storage and decrease performance (Topliff *et al.*, 1983, Topliff *et al.*, 1985). The effect of feeding fat supplemented diets to racehorses for extended periods of time still needs to be resolved. The present study used training regimes and exercise tests that were more comparable in intensity to those used in sport horses than in Thoroughbred racing. Under these conditions, feeding a level of fat equal to about 9-10% of the daily grain ration caused no detrimental effects on either health or exercise response. All of the horse studied tolerated this level of fat in their diets and were able to maintain similar weight gains as CONTROL horses, but with reduced grain intakes. Adding fat reduced the fall in blood glucose experienced in the CONTROL horses during the STEP and this may help delay fatigue in horses exercising intensely for extended periods of time.

References

Allen, B.V. and Powell, D.G. (1983). Effects of training and time of day of blood sampling on the variation of some common haematological parameters in normal Thoroughbred racehorses. In Snow DH, Persson SO, Rose R. (eds): Equine Exercise Physiology. Cambridge, England, Granta Editions.

Blackmore, D.J. and Brobst, D. (1981). Biochemcial Values in Equine Medicine, The Animal Health Trust, Newmarket, England.

Costill, D.L., Coyle, E., Dalsky G., Evans, W., Fink, W. and Hoopes, W. (1977). Effects of elevated plasma FFA and insulin on muscle glycogen usage during exercise. J.Appl. Physiol.:Respirat. Environ. Exercise Physiology. 43(4) 695-699.

Dickson, W.M. (1993). Endocrine glands. In Swensen, M.J. and Reece, W.O. (eds.): Duke's Physiology of Domestic Animals, eleventh edition, Cornell Unviersity Press, Ithaca,NY. pp. 657-660.

Harris, R.C., Marlin, D.J. and Snow, D.H. (1987). Metabolic response to maximal exercise of 800 and 2000 m in the Thoroughbred horse. J. Appl. Physiol. 63, 12-19.

Irvine,C.H.G. (1983). The role of hormones in exercise physiology. In Snow DH, Persson SO, Rose R. teds): Equine Exercise Physiology. Cambridge, England, GrantaEditions.

Lawrence, L.M. (1990). Nutrition and fuel utilization in the athletic horse. The Veterinary Clinics of North America, vol.6, no. 2, pp. 393-418.

Lawrence, L., Soderholm, L.V., Roberts, A., Williams, J. and Hintz, H. (1993). Feeding status affects glucoe metabolism in exercising horses. J. Nutr. 123:2152-2157.

Meyer, H., Radicke, S., Kienzle, E., Wilke, S. and Kleffken, D. (1993). Investigations on preileal digestion of oats, corn, and barley starch in relation to grain processing. Proc.13th ENPS, Gainesville, FL. pp. 92-97.

Pagan, J.D., Essen-Gustavsson, Lindholm, A., and Thornton, J. (1987). The effect of dietary energy source on exercise performance in standardbred horses .

In Gillespie, J.R. and Robinson, N.E. (eds.) Equine Exercise Physiology 2, ICEEP Publications, CA, pp. 686-700.

Pagan, J.D., Tiegs, W., Jackson, S.G., and Murphy, H.Q. (1993). The effect of different fat sources on exercise performance in throughbred racehorses. Proc. 13th ENPS, Gainesville, FL. pp. 125- 129.

Persson, S.G.B. (1983). Evaluation of exercise tolerance and fitness in the performance horse. In Snow DH, Persson SO, Rose R. (eds): Equine Exercise Physiology. Cambridge, England, Granta Editions.

Rodiek, A., Bonvicin, S., Stull, C. and Arana, M. (1991). Glycemic and Endocrine responses to corn or alfalfa fed prior to exercise. In Persson, S.G.B., Lindolm, A., and Jeffcott, L.B. (eds.) Equine Exercise Physiology 3, ICEEP Publications, CA. 323-330.

Snow, D.H., Gash, S.P., and Rice, D. (1987a). Field observations on selenium status, whole blood glutathione peroxidase and plasma gamma-glutamyl transferase activities in Thoroughbred racehorses. In Gillespie, J.R. and Robinson, N.E. (eds.) Equine Exercise Physiology 2, ICEEP Publications, CA, pp. 494-505.

Snow, D.H., Harris, R.C., Harman, J.C. and Marlin, D.J. (1987b). Glycogen repletion following differnet diets. In Gillespie, J.R. and Robinson, N.E. (eds.) Equine Exercise Physiology 2, ICEEP Publications, CA, pp. 701-710.

Snow, D.H. and Harris, R.C. (1991). Effects of daily exercise on muscle glycogen in the Thoroughbred racehorse. In Persson, S.G.B., Lindolm, A., and Jeffcott, L.B. (eds.) Equine Exercise Physiology 3, ICEEP Publications, CA pp.299-304.

Tabata, I, Ogita, F., Miyachi, M., and Shibayama, H. (1991). Effect of low blood glucose on plasma CRF, ACTH, and cortisol during prolonged physical exercise. J. Appl.Phys. 71(5): 1807-1812.

Thomton, J.R. (1985). Hormonal responses to exercise and training. The Veterinary Clinics of North America, vol. 1, no. 3, pp.477-496.

Topliff, D.R., Potter, G.D., Dutson, T.R., Kreider, J.L., and Jessup, G.T. (1983). Diet manipulation and muscle glycogen in the equine. Proc. 8th ENPS, Lexington, KY. pp.119-124.

Topliff, D.R., Potter, G.D., Dutson, T.R., Kreider, J.L., and Jessup, G.T. (1985). Diet manipulation, muscle glycogen metabolism and anaerobic work performance in the equine. Proc. 9th ENPS, East Lansing, MI. pp. 224-229.

This paper was first published in "Recent Advances in Equine Nutrition," Proceedings for the 1995 Short Course for Feed Manufacturers

THE INFLUENCE OF TIME OF FEEDING ON EXERCISE RESPONSE IN THOROUGHBREDS FED A FAT SUPPLEMENTED OR HIGH CARBOHYDRATE DIET

JOE D. PAGAN, IVAN BURGER[1] AND STEPHEN G. JACKSON
Kentucky Equine Research, Inc., Versailles, Kentucky, USA
[1]Waltham Centre for Equine Nutrition and Care, Melton Mowbray, UK

Recent research (Pagan *et al.*, 1994) demonstrated that feeding supplemental fat to Thoroughbred horses altered blood glucose and insulin levels compared to a grain based diet and these changes influenced substrate selection during a standardized exercise test. All of the exercise tests in this experiment were conducted 4 hours after feeding. It is not known if this is the best time to feed horses before exercise or if the high fat diets would yield a different response if the feeding interval were altered. Therefore, the following experiment was conducted to evaluate the influence of time of feeding on exercise response in horses receiving either a traditional sweet feed or a fat supplemented diet.

Six Thoroughbreds were used in a two period switch-back design study. During period one, 3 horses were fed a fat supplemented diet (FAT) (sweet feed + 340 g soybean oil/day) while 3 horses received a control ration of sweet feed (CON). These horses had been eating these diets for 8 months. Weekly during period one, the horses performed a standardized exercise test (SET) on a high speed treadmill inclined to 3°. This exercise test was performed at 3 different times after eating: 1) after an overnight fast 2) 3 hours after eating 3) 8 hours after feeding. The time of feeding was assigned within each dietary treatment in a 3X3 Latin square design so that each horse was tested weekly at a different time of feeding. At the end of period one, the horses' diets were switched and they continued in training for a 1 month adjustment period. At the end of the adjustment period, the horses repeated the three week SET schedule as in period 1. The SET consisted of a 2 minute walk at 1.4 m/s, 800 meter trot at 4.3 m/s, 800 meter gallop at 7.7 m/s, 1600 meter gallop at 11.0 m/s, 800 meter trot at 4.2 m/s and 2 minute walk at 1.4 m/s. Blood samples were taken before feeding, hourly until the beginning of the SET and then after the trot, at the end of the 800 meter gallop at 7.7 m/s, after 800 meters and at the end of the 11.0 m/s gallop, after the warm-down trot and walk and 15 and 30 minutes post exercise. During the SET, heart rate was measured and blood was analyzed for glucose, lactate and insulin.

Heart rate was significantly higher when the horses were fed 3 hours before exercise at 7.7 m/s ($p<0.10$) and during the warm-down trot ($p<0.05$). During the warm-up walk, fat supplemented horses had lower heart rates (75 b/min vs 81 b/min, $p<0.10$). Insulin (figure 1) was significantly higher in the 3 hour fed horses at the beginning and throughout exercise ($p<0.01$). Insulin was lower in the fat supplemented horses following the warm-up (p<0.05) and during exercise (p<0.10). Blood glucose (figure 2) was higher after the 3 hour feeding at rest and following the warm-up (p<0.01). During exercise, blood glucose dropped in the 3 hour fed horses and was significantly lower during and after the 11 m/s gallop. Lactate (figure 3) was unaffected by time of feeding or diet during exercise. Fifteen minutes post exercise, however, the 3 hour fed horses had significantly lower (p<0.05) plasma lactate levels.

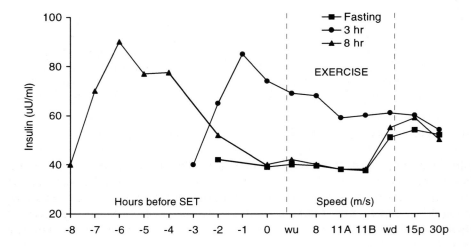

Figure 1. Effect of time of feeding on plasma (control and fat treatments combined)

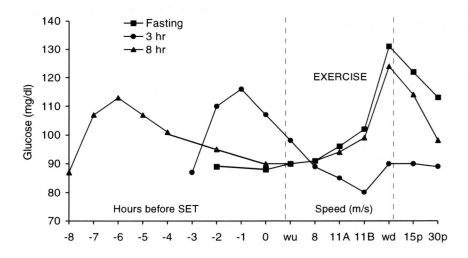

Figure 2. Effect of time of feeding on plasma glucose (control and fat treatments combined)

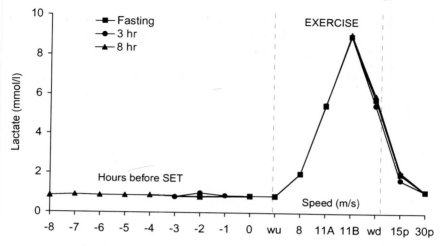

Figure 3. Effect of time of feeding on plasma lactate (control and fat treatments combined)

Time of feeding affected plasma glucose and insulin before, during and after exercise. Horses fed 3 hours before exercise experienced large drops in blood glucose during exercise. These drops were probably due to elevated insulin levels at the beginning of the SET. Fat supplementation did not affect blood glucose during exercise. However, glucose was higher in the FAT groups (p<0.05) 15 and 30 minutes post exercise.

This paper was first published in "Recent Advances in Equine Nutrition," Proceedings for the 1995 Short Course for Feed Manufacturers

THE EFFECT OF FEEDING AFTER EXERCISE ON GLUCOSE AND GLYCOGEN RESPONSES IN THE HORSE

T. BREWSTER-BARNES, L.M. LAWRENCE, L.K. WARREN,
P.D. SICILIANO, A. CRUM AND K. THOMPSON
University of Kentucky, Lexington, Kentucky, USA

Carbohydrates, especially muscle glycogen, are key sources of energy for working muscle and when muscle glycogen is depleted during exercise, fatigue occurs rapidly. Because glycogen is a valuable substrate during exercise, replenishment of its stores is extremely important. Diets high in soluble carbohydrate should have a positive effect on muscle glycogen repletion but some studies have noted that glycogen resynthesis in horses is slow even when high grain diets are fed. If repletion to pre-exercise levels does not occur, subsequent performances may be negatively affected. In humans, feeding carbohydrates soon after exercise affects the uptake of glucose by muscle and increases the synthesis of muscle glycogen as compared to feeding a carbohydrate source several hours after exercise. Typically, horses are not fed the grain portion (soluble carbohydrate source) in the diet during the early (< 1.5 hours) post-exercise (PE) period. However, feeding the grain meal closer to the end of exercise may be more beneficial for the horse, if muscle glycogen resynthesis can be affected. Enhanced glycogen resynthesis after exercise could be important for horses that compete on consecutive days, such as 3-day eventers. In this experiment, four conditioned Thoroughbred geldings were used in a 4X4 Latin square experiment to determine the effect of feeding a carbohydrate source during the early or late post-exercise (PE) period on blood glucose and muscle glycogen responses. In each collection period, three horses were exercised for 1 hour and one horse served as an unexercised control. Each exercised horse received a meal of oats at a different times PE; either 1.5 hours PE, 4 hours PE or divided into two smaller meals at 1.5 and 4 hours PE. The unexercised control horse received a meal of oats at a similar time of day as the exercised horses. Venous blood samples were taken every 30 minutes for 6 hours after consumption of the test meal. Blood samples were analyzed for plasma glucose and serum insulin. Muscle biopsies were taken at rest, after exercise, prior to feeding, 6 hours after feeding and 26 hours after the initial biopsy. After feeding, exercised horses had a lower glucose peak and insulin concentrations post-feeding (P<0.05) than the controls. These results suggest that exercise has a residual effect on the horse that produces altered glucose and insulin responses to a meal. In humans, exercise is known to have an effect on glucose transport into muscle and the same effect may occur in the horse. Feeding at different times after exercise also affected glucose and insulin responses. When the horses were fed 4 hours PE they had lower insulin concentrations, plasma glucose peak and slower glucose clearance rate than when they were fed 1.5 hours PE (P<0.05). The exercise test resulted in limited glycogen depletion (< 20%). Muscle glycogen concentrations were lower at 4 hours PE as compared to immediately after exercise or 1.5 hours PE (P<0.05). At 6 hours post-feeding, glycogen concentrations continued to be lower in horses fed 4 hours PE than in horses fed 1.5 hours PE (P<0.05). The results from this experiment suggest that feeding 1.5 hours PE, as opposed 4 hours PE, prevents the further depletion of muscle glycogen stores. Although there were some differences in glucose metabolism, time of feeding after exercise did not affect the muscle glycogen concentrations in biopsies obtained 26 hours PE. The absence of an effect was possibly related to the low level of glycogen depletion produced by the exercise test. Even though the horses worked over a distance of 18 km, the work intensity was minimal. A more strenuous test that produces more severe glycogen depletion should be used in subsequent studies to evaluate the effect of the feeding program on muscle glycogen resynthesis in the horse.

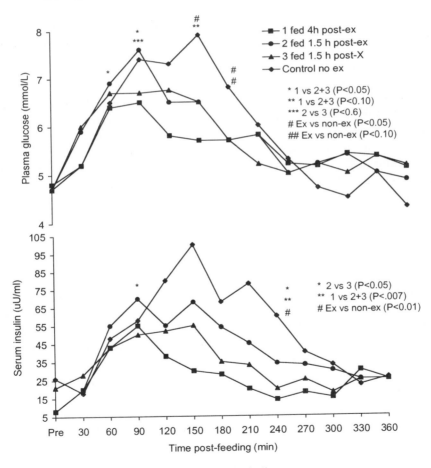

Figure 1. Plasma glucose and serum insulin concentrations after feeding

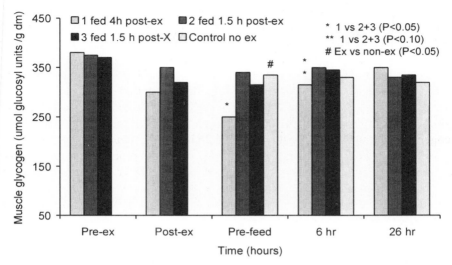

Figure 2. Muscle glycogen concentrations before and after exercise, prior to feeding, 6h post feeding and 26h post feeding

This paper was first published in "Recent Advances in Equine Nutrition," Proceedings for the 1995 Short Course for Feed Manufacturers

THE EFFECT OF DIET ON WEIGHT LOSS AND PLASMA VARIABLES IN ENDURANCE EXERCISED HORSES

K. DANIELSEN, L. LAWRENCE, P. SICILIANO, AND K. THOMPSON
University of Kentucky, Lexington, Kentucky, USA

Endurance rides impose great physiological stress on horses, particularly in hot environments. One of the physiological consequences of endurance exercise is the dehydration that can result from large sweat losses. Sweat losses as high as 8 to 9 % of body weight (about 80 to 90 lb for a 1000 lb horse) have been measured during long term exercise (Snow *et al.*, 1982). Because large sweat losses may affect the performance and/or health of the horse, strategies that assist the horse in maintaining fluid and electrolyte balance during endurance exercise may be beneficial. Absorption of fluid from the gastrointestinal (GI) tract into the extracellular fluid may be important in exercising horses (Carlson *et al.*, 1987), and Meyer (1987) has suggested that the composition of the diet consumed prior to competition may affect the amount of water available in the GI tract during competition.

This study was conducted to determine whether diet composition could affect electrolyte and water balance in horses during endurance-type exercise. Two crossover design experiments, each using four horses, were performed to compare the effect of consuming a high hay/low concentrate diet to a limited hay/moderate concentrate diet. Changes in body weight and plasma total protein concentrations were used to monitor dehydration. In experiment 1, the diets were controlled only the night before the exercise test. Water intake was lower when horses received the limited hay diet ($P<0.001$). Average weight loss during the exercise test was 2.8% of body weight and was not affected by treatment. Plasma protein concentration increased during exercise, but there were no diet differences ($P>0.05$). In experiment 2, horses were adapted to the diets for 7 days prior to the exercise test and a more strenuous exercise test was used. Again, water intake was lower ($P<0.01$) when the horses received the limited hay diet. During exercise, both groups lost about 4% of body weight, but the increase in total protein concentration was lower ($P<0.05$) in the horses receiving the high hay diet (figure 1). Horses receiving the high hay diet also maintained a higher plasma potassium concentration during exercise ($P<0.05$).

The increased water intake and the lower plasma protein concentration associated with the hay diet may indicate that high hay diets are beneficial to horses involved in endurance type exercise. Currently, studies are underway to evaluate whether the source and/or type of fiber in the diet can affect water balance during exercise.

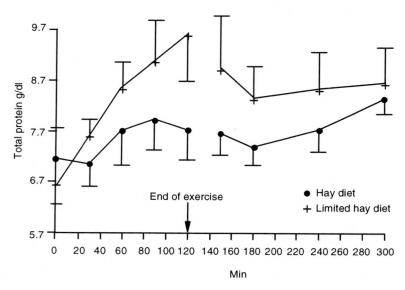

Figure 1. Changes in plasma concentrations of total protein during exercise (0–120 minutes) and recovery (150–300 minutes) for horses on a high hay diet and a limited hay diet in Experiment 2. Bars represent standard error of means (n=4)

References

Carlson, G.P. (1987) Hematology and Body Fluids in the Equine Athlete: A Review. In: Equine Exercise Physiology 2. Gillespie, J.R. and N.E. Robinson. ICEEP Publications. Davis CA p393-425

Meyer, H. (1987) Nutrition of the Equine Athlete. In: Equine Exercise Physiology 2. Gillespie, J.R. and N.E. Robinson. ICEEP Publications. Davis CA p644-673

Snow, D.H., M.G. Kerr, M.A. Nimmo and E.M. Abbott (1982) Alterations in blood, sweat, urine, and muscle composition during prolonged exercise in the horse. Vet Rec. 110:377-384.

This paper was first published in "Recent Advances in Equine Nutrition," Proceedings for the 1995 Short Course for Feed Manufacturers

THE EFFECT OF EXERCISE CONDITIONING AND TYPE ON SERUM CREATINE KINASE AND ASPARTATE AMINO-TRANSFERASE ACTIVITY

PAUL D. SICILIANO[1], LAURIE M. LAWRENCE[1], KRISTIN DANIELSEN[1], DEBRA M. POWELL[1] AND KENT N. THOMPSON[2]
[1]Department of Animal Science, [2]Department of Veterinary Science, University of Kentucky, Lexington, USA

Exertional myopathies result in a several fold increase in serum muscle enzymes (SME) (e.g. creatine kinase and aspartate amino-transferase). However, smaller, yet significant, increases are noted following exercise in clinically normal horses. The physiological significance of these increases are uncertain; but in humans, increases in SME are associated with muscle soreness. Periodic evaluation of post-exercise elevations in SME has been suggested to be useful in monitoring the status of the muscular system during training in horses.

The following experiment was conducted to investigate the effect of type of exercise and state of physical condition on post-exercise elevation in SME in order to develop an exercise test for use in future studies on dietary effects which may influence the equine muscular system during training.

In experiment 1 five mature, unconditioned, Thoroughbred geldings performed an initial submaximal exercise test (UC) prior to any conditioning, and a final test (C) following 8 weeks of conditioning. Serum creatine kinase (CK) and aspartate amino-transferase (AST) activity was measured before and for 72 hours post-exercise. Plasma lactate was used as an indicator of exercise conditioning. Serum CK and AST activity remained increased ($P<0.05$) above pre-exercise from 0-24 hours, and 0-8 hours post-exercise, respectively. There was a time by exercise conditioning interaction ($P<0.05$) for AST, CK, and plasma lactate resulting in an attenuated response of each variable following exercise test C as compared to following exercise test UC. These results indicate that submaximal exercise can elevate serum AST and CK, and conditioning can attenuate these changes. A second study using eight mature Thoroughbred horses was conducted to evaluate the effect of two different types of exercise, short term high intensity (STHI); and repeated submaximal (RS) on serum AST and CK activities. Serum AST and CK activities during the post-exercise period were higher ($P<0.05$) in response to the RS test as compared to the STHI test.

The results of this study indicate greater leakage of intracellular muscle enzymes from the skeletal muscle occur in unconditioned horses during repeated submaximal exercise. An exercise model employing repeated submaximal exercise in unconditioned horses may be a useful model for studying the physiological significance of post-exercise elevations in SME. In addition, this test may be useful in evaluating the effect of various nutrients which are thought to be important in maintaining the integrity of skeletal muscle (e.g. vitamin E).

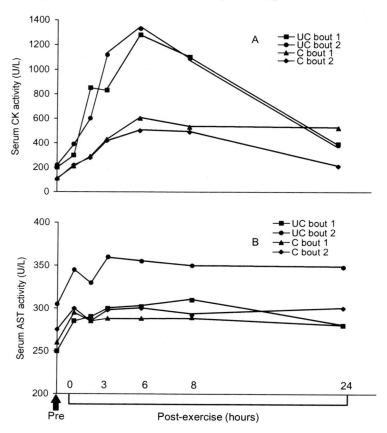

Figure 1. Serum CK response (panel A) to two bouts (1 & 2) of repeated submaximal exercise conducted 48 hours apart before (UC) and after (C) exercise conditioning in experiment 1. Exercise conditioning (UC vs C) $P<0.05$; time by exercise conditioning $P<0.05$. pooled S.E. = 316.
Serum AST response (panel B) to two bouts (1 & 2) of repeated submaximal exercise conducted 48 hours apart before (UC) and after (C) exercise conditioning in experiment 1. Exercise conditioning (UC vs C) $P<0.05$; time by exercise conditioning $P<0.05$; bout (1 vs 2) $P<0.05$; bout by exercise condition $P<0.05$. Pooled S.E. = ±20. (From: Siciliano *et al.*; 4th ICEEP, Brisbane Australia)

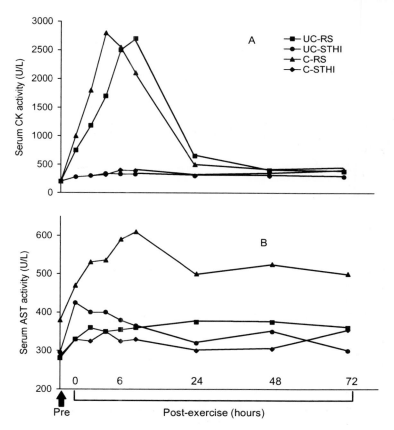

Figure 2. Serum CK response (panel A) to repeated submaximal (RS) and short term high intensity exercise (STHI) before (UC) and after (C) in experiment 2. Exercise test (RS vs STHI)*P*<0.05. Pooled S.E. = ±933. Serum AST response (panel A) to repeated submaximal (RS) and short term high intensity exercise (STHI) before (UC) and after (C) exercise conditioning in experiment 2. Exercise test (RS vs STHI)*P*<0.05; time by exercise test *P*<0.05; exercise test by exercise conditioning *P*<0.05. Pooled S.E. = ±93. (From: Siciliano *et al.*; 4th ICEEP, Brisbane Australia)

This paper was first published in "Recent Advances in Equine Nutrition," Proceedings for the 1995 Short Course for Feed Manufacturers

THE EFFECT OF WARMING-UP ON RESPONSE TO EXERCISE

S. ROKURODA, L. LAWRENCE, A. PARKER, L. WARREN, D. POWELL AND A. CRUM

University of Kentucky, Lexington, Kentucky, USA

Warm up before exercise/competition is believed to prevent injury and improve performance. Few studies have examined the benefit of warm-up on horses, although various warm-up methods are used for competitive horses. This experiment examined physiological and metabolic effects of warm-up on Thoroughbred horses.

Four mature Thoroughbred geldings were used as the experimental units. During the two months prior to the initiation of the study, horses were exercised 4-5 times a week, with the combination of trot and canter on a high speed treadmill. Horses were individually housed in 3x4m box stalls and were fed twice a day at 8:00 am and 4:00 pm except on testing days when the morning meal was withheld. At the end of the conditioning phase horses were assigned to treatments in a two period cross-over design experiment. In the first period, two horses performed an 18 minute low intensity warm-up (LW) prior to completing a step-wise exercise test and two horses performed an 18 minute moderate intensity warm-up (MW) prior to the exercise test. In the second period the treatments were switched. LW consisted of 18 minutes of walk at 2m/s on a 0% grade treadmill, and MW consisted of 5 minutes at 2m/s on 0% grade, 4 minutes at 4m/s (0% grade), 3 min at 4m/s (10% grade), 3 minutes at 4m/s (0% grade), and 3 minutes at 2m/s (0% grade). Upon completion of the warm-up exercise, all horses performed a step-wise exercise test (2-7m/s) on a 10% grade with 2 minute intervals between each step. The exercise tests were separated by 7 days, and treatment order was balanced. The response variables were heart rate, skin and rectal temperatures, packed cell volume (PCV), plasma lactate, plasma free fatty acids (FFA), and plasma glucose.

During the 18 minute warm-up, there were time x treatment effects on heart rate, PCV, skin temperatures, rectal temperatures, and plasma lactate concentration ($p<0.05$), with MW producing higher values for all variables. Heart rate during the 12th minute of the warm-up averaged 141.5 bpm when the horses performed the MW compared to 53.8 bpm when they performed LW. Plasma FFA concentrations declined during the first 12 minutes of MW, but remained constant during the same period when horses performed the LW. MW produced higher heart rate, PCV and skin temperatures at the initiation of the step test, but there were no differences between the treatments for these variables at the end of the step test. Plasma lactate levels at the beginning of step-wise exercise test were not significantly different between the treatments. Plasma

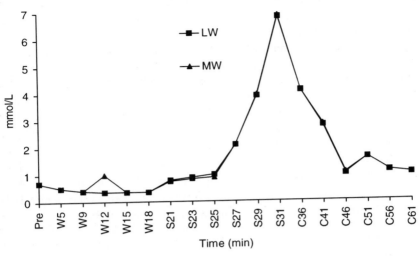

Figure 1. Effect of warm up intensity (low=LW; moderate=MW) on plasma lactate response during the warm-up (W5 - W18), step test (S21 - S31) and recovery (C36 - C61).

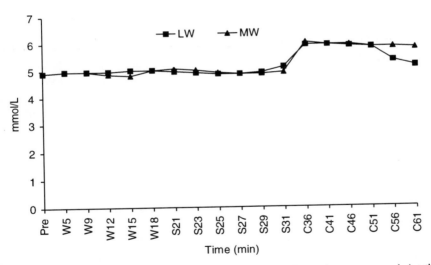

Figure 2. Effect of warm up intensity (low=LW; moderate=MW) on plasma glucose response during the warm-up (W5 - W18), step test (S21 - S31) and (C36 - C61). There was a time x treatment effect (p<0.0002) during the step test.

lactate increased (p<0.05) during the step test, but there were no treatment effects (Figure 1). During the step-wise exercise test, there was a time x treatment effect for plasma glucose (Figure 2). When horses completed the MW, they had lower plasma glucose concentrations at the end of the step-wise test (p<0.05). There was no effect of warm-up intensity on changes in FFA nor TG during the step-wise exercise test. There were no effects of the warm-up intensity found on any variables during the recovery period.

Warm-up increases tissue temperature which is believed to facilitate metabolism and muscle contraction, increase cardiac output, and dilate capillary beds in muscle; thus increasing blood flow and oxygen availability. In this study the MW seemed to be the more ideal type of warm-up because it produced a higher temperature increase than in LW, without significant lactate build-up. In addition, higher heart rate and PCV occurred during MW as expected. Despite the differences in physiological and metabolic responses during warm-up, there were no differences in heart rate or lactate responses during the step-wise exercise test. Horses in this study were not maximally exercised, so it is possible that treatment differences would have become apparent with a more difficult test. Warm-up intensity did appear to influence blood glucose responses to the step test. At the end of the exercise test glucose level in MW became lower than in LW, while the response of plasma FFA to the step test was not affected by warm-up intensity. This was an unexpected result: the warm-up was expected to facilitate fat utilization, and thus conserve glucose. These results may indicate that the MW for this particular exercise test was not beneficial over LW.

This paper was first published in Proceedings, Kentucky Equine Research 1997 Equine Nutrition Conference

FEEDING MANAGEMENT

MYTHS AND WIVES' TALES OF FEEDING HORSES "SOME TRUTH, SOME FICTION"

STEPHEN G. JACKSON
Kentucky Equine Research, Inc., Versailles, Kentucky, USA

"Oh, but if you don't soak beet pulp before you feed it, it will swell up in the stomach and cause it to rupture." This is but one of the countless wives' tales concerning the feeding of horses. Almost every one has been exposed to these tidbits of wisdom that "everyone that has fed a horse surely knows." There are more of these anecdotal, pseudo-true myths surrounding horse feeding than seen associated with any other class of livestock including man. Where do these truisms come from, are they founded in any fact, why do they persist and does it really matter? In this paper I would like to discuss a number of the more prevalent myths and wives' tales and at least from my perspective "set the record straight." We might as well start with the oldest and most common of them all!

"Bran mashes"

Since I can remember I have been told that there is nothing better for a horse than an occasional bran mash. To tell you the truth, I was 30 years old before I even knew how to make one, have had horses all of my life and have yet to make one! Bran mashes are made in a number of ways and one could write a pretty lengthy book entitled "recipes from around the world for bran mashes." Most of these mashes at least have one thing in common, they contain wheat bran. Most are made with hot water, wheat bran, perhaps some oats or even some sweet feed and corn, soy or safflower oil, maybe even some boiled flax seed.

Wheat bran has been thought to have a laxative or mild cathartic effect. Research has failed to indicate that this is the case. A study conducted at Cornell University in which 50% wheat bran was added to a diet of hay and grain found that fecal moisture was not different between horses receiving wheat bran and those on the control diet that received no wheat bran. Furthermore, the digestibility of wheat bran was not affected by soaking in warm water. Another reason some cite as a reason for feeding bran is that it is high in fiber. Indeed bran is higher in fiber than, say, corn. But oats are actually higher in fiber and certainly all hays are higher in fiber than is bran. So if bran is not a laxative, does not contribute significantly to fiber intake and does not impact positively on fecal moisture when water is available to the horse, is there any positive side to the practice of feeding bran mash? Perhaps the only thing one might see as a possibility, is the water a horse consumes via the bran mash. In cold environments, when water intake may be sub-optimal, this could provide some insurance in terms of maintaining hydration. But, if heated waterers are available this advantage disappears. Bran may also provide some nutrients to the horse, though there are usually more effective ways to get this job done!

In the final analysis, bran mashes are innocuous but do not provide the "magic" oftentimes attributed to them. If a horseman gets a warm fuzzy feeling by doing a bran mash or, more importantly, gets the whole of good stable management done more effectively, then by all means feed the bran.

"Beet pulp must be soaked prior to feeding"

This is an often expressed opinion of "horse nutrition experts." The rationale behind the thought that one should always soak beet pulp is based on the water holding capacity of shredded beet pulp and the fact that the volume occupied by beet pulp after soaking is especially greater than that occupied by the dry stuff. Further, it is surmised that if one feeds dry beet pulp it will absorb water in the form of saliva in the esophagus and gastric juices in the stomach, swell up and then cause either choke or gastric rupture. Helmut Meyer, a noted German researcher, would subscribe to the latter theory and maintains that feeding beet pulp is a risky practice.

There have been literally thousands of tons of high beet pulp feed fed to horses (i.e. Replete, Respond, Complete Advantage, Sweet Rely), the majority of it fed straight out of the bag without being soaked. I have never (I know, never say never) heard of a horse choking or busting a gut due to these feeds swelling up in the stomach. So is there some explanation for the difference of opinion between myself and Dr. Meyer? The answer is, possibly! The high beet pulp feeds that we characteristically would see on the market range in molasses content from 20-30 %. It is probable that this amount of molasses does two things in the feed. First, the beet pulp soaks up a great deal of the molasses and swells to some extent and second, the molasses coats the beet pulp which prevents it from absorbing saliva and swelling in the esophagus.

Although I have mixed shredded beet pulp with sweet feed on my own farm with no problem, when I mix it with oats on the farm I generally would add some water just to be on the "safe side." This is one of those situations that calls for a bit of a "better safe than sorry" attitude even though my experience suggests that the soaking is not necessary.

"When I feed my horse high protein feed it goes *DITZO*"

All over the world this is one of the most frequent questions/comments I get. My general reply would go something like this: "There are no data, either scientific or otherwise, which would suggest that protein concentration or intake has anything to do with mental attitude." But there is actually a twist to this query. Many times the second retort is, "But when I feed my horse more feed it make him really spooky." This defines the problem many horsemen have in differentiating between energy and protein. Still, even after volumes have been written about a high protein (relative term) feed not necessarily being a high energy feed, people labor under the misconception that high protein means high energy means ditzo horses. NOT TRUE.

"Corn/oats are a heating feed"

This myth actually has two interpretations according to how one defines heating. When some people say this they mean temperature hot while others mean mental hot! First and easiest things first, let's address body temperature. If we think back about basic digestive physiology and the energy diagram, we remember the terms heat production and heat increment. Heat production is the sum of net energy for maintenance and heat increment. Heat increment is also referred to as specific dynamic action or heat of nutrient metabolism and is the heat associated with the digestion and metabolism of various feed stuffs. Feeds that are higher in fiber have a greater heat increment because it takes more work to digest these feeds, hence the heat involved in digesting fibrous feeds in the winter time is a valuable source of heat to regulate body temperature. If one were to rank nutrients from highest to lowest heat increment the rank would be as follows; fibrous feeds such as hay (higher the fiber, the higher the heat increment), concentrates and the lowest, fat. This is why in hot environments fat may be added to livestock diets and does not appreciably add to heat load. When temperature increases feed intake decreases and as such energy density must increase to maintain growth and productivity. Increasing fat level in the diet is the easiest way to both increase energy density and decrease heat increment of the diet. One would therefore conclude that both oats and corn would be less "heating" than hay. The flip side to this coin is related to the effect of body insulation, especially fat, on body temperature regulation. Unfortunately, I have first hand experience with how increasing fat cover can increase heat load during exercise. If a horse is being fed more energy than required and is storing fat, increasing insulation, then certainly they get hot. This is not due to the dietary constituents, but rather to the amount of feed being fed and level of fitness of the horse. So are corn and oats heating feeds (temperature)? NO.

With respect to the other definition of hot, mental 'hot'. Most people that feel that their horse's mental attitude is bad because of feed are drawing a corollary between the sugar and hyper child syndrome and the behavior problems they see in their horses. Again a part of this is the observation that "when I feed more grain, my horses get high." My typical response is, "You have basically two choices, you can train a horse into submission or you can starve him into submission." One would expect a horse to feel better, if they are in a positive energy balance. The key is to direct this "energy" in a positive fashion resulting in superior, more brilliant performance. Especially in the western pleasure horse industry five years ago, some horses were fed too little to make them go slow. They were lethargic, sluggish and really felt bad and as consequence did not want to go anywhere. As a judge, I was instructed to not place any horse that looked "intimidated or emaciated." Finally this trend in training western pleasure horses is beginning to lose its popularity.

Even though I do not subscribe to the opinion that feeds make horses high, I do think that more work needs to be done in this area. What impact, for instance, does a high carbohydrate meal have on requirements for B-vitamins (thiamine) and if the requirements for these vitamins are not met is there a concomitant deterioration in disposition/nervousness? Certainly one could construct a pretty convincing story to this effect. Until more definitive research is done, I am inclined to not believe that starch/sugar intake per se have anything to do with a horse becoming hyper beyond the effect that the increased calories have. Interestingly, there was a recent paper in the Journal of the American Medical Association that compared hyper children fed sugar to those not receiving sugar and found no difference in the degree of hyperactivity! There goes another truism of behavior and diet.

"I want a feed that gives my horse energy but does not make him fat"

I want one of these feeds for myself, too! Would it not be great to be able to eat all of the energy giving food (especially if it tasted good) you wanted and not get fat! Again, we are dealing here with a lack of knowledge about energy balance. Dietary energy not required for maintenance is available for productive functions including growth, lactation, work and fattening to name a few. Put simply, if caloric intake is greater than caloric expenditure the result is fattening. More frequently than not the people that ask for these products are owners of easy keepers that many times do not get adequate exercise. "My pony is fat and does not want to go. How can I give him more energy?" When I'm fat I don't want to go either! Sadly, this lack of *go* is a result of inadequate physical conditioning rather than lack of energy intake. The best solution for most of these cases, whether human or animal, is more push-aways and more push-ups (push away from the table and push up the hill).

"Molasses causes colic"

This is a commonly heard wives' tale that is not based on fact but needs to be qualified. Molasses used in the manufacture of horse feeds is predominantly sugarcane (blackstrap) or sugar beet molasses or may be blends of these and various fats or oils. Molasses is classified historically as an energy feed and has a digestible energy (DE) value similar to oats (3.4 mcal/kg) on a dry matter basis. Molasses ranges from 70-80 % dry matter and depending on source of the molasses may contain from 0.5 to 7% protein. By far the largest component of the dry matter in molasses is sugar, which explains the high DE value of molasses. Molasses is used most frequently in feeds for its effect on palatability, and on improving the homogeneity of the feed. It reduces sifting out of ingredients, dustiness and fines.

So why is it frequently said that molasses may cause colic? There are two obvious relationships that molasses may have to digestive upset. Especially in hot environments, (and depending on the brix of the molasses), there is a greater tendency of "sweet feeds" to mold than in the case of pelleted feeds or dry mixes. Part of this problem can be eliminated by using some mold inhibitors in the feed and/or molasses. Many molasses contain some propionic acid to deal with this problem. The other and more obvious question one must deal with is the possibility that the amount of sugar in the molasses will overwhelm the ability of the small intestine to absorb glucose, resulting in some of the glucose (sugar) reaching the cecum where it would be fermented, much like starch that escaped digestion in the small intestine. I really do not think that this is a valid argument considering the amounts of molasses that are frequently fed in many sweet feeds. Most sweet feeds contain only from 5-10% molasses. Again we can go back to the example of the feeds containing large amounts of beet pulp. These feeds contain on average three times the molasses that a typical sweet feed would contain and are actually used in many cases in horses that chronically colic. So, even though one might jump through some hoops and come up with a reason that molasses might cause colic, the reality is that it is very doubtful if it does.

"Pellets cause horses to choke"

This wives' tale is a holdover from the days when people were trying to find ammunition to justify not feeding pellets. There is no reason at all to think that horses are any more likely to choke on pellets than on any other physical form of feed if they are fed and eat in a normal manner. If, on the other hand, horses bolt their feed there is as great a chance that they may choke on pelleted feed as on other forms of feed. The solution to the problem of choke is to feed in shallow, rather than deep, feed troughs. For the aggressive eater, several large smooth stones should be placed in the feed trough. This requires the horse to sort around the rocks to eat and therefore rate of intake is slowed. There is every reason to believe that if there is not some kind of esophageal pathology which prevents normal peristalsis, there is no difference in choke rate between types of feed.

If there is something wrong with the esophagus, the best way to feed the affected horse is to make a gruel or very liquid mash out of the feed to be offered. I have been involved in several cases of this sort and have found that dissolving pelleted feeds, adding some corn oil and even using some dissolved alfalfa pellets to provide some fiber, is an effective way of meeting nutrient requirements. I have used this strategy in the short term while esophageal lesions heal and in the long term where there are permanent esophageal strictures.

"Crimped oats are better than whole oats"

There is a pervading opinion among horsemen that crimped oats are significantly more digestible than whole oats. Most of the digestibility studies that have been conducted comparing crimped and whole oats indicate that there is at most a 6% increase in the digestibility of crimped oats when compared to whole oats. In addition to the total tract digestibility experiments that have been done, Meyer in Germany has recently reported that the difference in the preileal digestibility of oat starch from whole and rolled oats is minimal. This indicates that there is in most cases no real justification for using crimped oats over whole oats. The only time when this may not hold true is for older horses with bad teeth and perhaps for very young horses. For the older horse a pelleted or extruded ration is more appropriate anyway, so this may well be a moot point.

"If horses are getting *pot bellies* deduce their grain intake"

This is a common one. Many times people mistake large bellies for fat and have a tendency to reduce the grain part of the ration. When one reduces concentrate intake, the horse is forced to rely more heavily on forage to meet nutrient requirements and may show an increase in the size of the barrel. However the real cause of hay bellies in many horses is a loss of condition down the top line that makes the barrel or belly appear to be bigger than it really is.

In many instances, one may help this situation by increasing the amount of concentrate that a horse receives along with an increase in exercise. If one really thinks about it, the main times when a horseman complains about hay bellies are in young horses just post-weaning, or in mature horses that are on pasture and receiving little exercise. Rarely do we hear complaints from a racehorse trainer (most race horses are receiving about 15 pounds of hay and from 12 - 15 pounds of concentrate) or from trainers of other high performance horses. Also, people fitting halter horses rarely have queries about big bellies.

Horses tend to deposit fat over the crest of the neck, behind the shoulder, over the ribs and over the croup and tail head, not on the underline as a human might do. I have seen far more hay or pot bellies on thin horses, ones that have little fat cover over the ribs, than on truly fat horses.

"I feed corn oil to prevent impaction"
("sort of like my vet giving my horse mineral oil")

Mineral oil is used when horses colic or founder for two reasons. First, mineral oil coats the gut which prevents the absorption of toxins by a damaged intestinal lining and second, because it does have a lubricating effect on the intestinal tract and allows the horse to pass a fecal mass. Additionally, mineral oil has a laxative effect as well.

What one must remember is that mineral oil is totally inert in the GI tract. There is absolutely zero absorption of mineral oil and all of the "oil" gets back to the hind-gut to exert its effect. Corn oil or other vegetable oils (soy, safflower, canola etc.) on the other hand are very highly digestible. Vegetable oils are about 85-90% digestible. Furthermore, fat digestion takes place predominantly in the small intestine. These feed ingredient fats are emulsified in the small intestine by bile acids, micelles are formed and absorbed in the small intestine. Very little if any of these dietary fats make it into the cecum and large colon to act in a manner similar to that of mineral oil.

So, in essence mineral oil may indeed grease the chute whereas vegetable oils do not have this effect. An interesting footnote here is actually feeding mineral oil. It is probable that when significant amounts of mineral oil are fed, there may be some decrease in the absorption of the fat soluble vitamins but if anything feeding vegetable oils may enhance the absorption of these vitamins.

"I feed trace mineral salt - *that's enough, isn't it?*"

The typical trace mineral salt has a composition similar to that listed below:

Salt	- not less than 94%
Salt	- not more than 97.5%
Zinc	- not less than .350%
Iron	- not less than .340%
Manganese	- not less than .200%
Copper	- not less than .033%
Iodine	- not less than .007%
Cobalt	- not less than .005%

It is obvious that far and away the largest component of TM salt is salt or sodium chloride. This is not all bad as this is for many horses the only salt source that is available, but it does not do the job as far as trace minerals are concerned. Dr. Harold Hintz at Cornell University did a study in which the voluntary intake of a salt block was measured by repeatedly weighing a salt block after horses had access to it each day. Based on those data one would expect voluntary consumption to be from 1.8-2 oz. per day. Using the above composition of TM salt, intake of the various minerals would be as follows:

Salt	- 54.6 grams
Zinc	- 196 mg
Iron	- 196 mg
Manganese	- 112 mg
Copper	- 18 mg
Iodine	- 3.92 mg
Cobalt	- 2.8 mg

The intake of salt would come close to meeting the sodium and chloride requirements of the sedentary horse and if taken with forage, zinc, manganese and iron would be provided in an amount close to that required but intake of other nutrients would be negligible. For performance and young horses, a TM salt block alone falls short of really addressing trace mineral needs and their feed must be fortified to satisfy these requirements.

"High protein causes developmental orthopedic disease (DOD)"

One of the most common of the wives' tales revolves around the various and sundry syndromes that people attribute to protein. Maladies ranging from "too much energy" to growth disorders are all attributed to too much protein. In order to address these questions and comments, one must first understand why people are inclined to blame protein to begin with. Most people identify feed according to its protein level with little regard to the concentration of other nutrients in the ration. The question, "what do you feed your horse?" is often answered, "I feed a 14% sweet feed." The horseman has immediately said the only nutrient that they really know anything about is protein. Therefore, when perceived problems arise this nutrient is the first thing that they think about. There is far too much emphasis on protein in the marketing and purchase of feeds and far too little emphasis on other important nutrients. There are no data to suggest that the protein concentration in concentrates has anything to do with the occurrence of DOD in young horses. Furthermore, there are times when the protein intake from concentrates may be only a small percentage of total protein intake. A classic example is the young horse in central Kentucky. These horses may receive (yearlings) eight to ten pounds of a 14 to 16 percent protein concentrate in the springtime, yet have ad-libitum access to pasture that might be from 22-26% protein. People pass judgement that it is the protein in the concentrate that is the problem, without even considering the nutrient concentrations in the pasture. Even more surprising is that many times a person that might be feeding a

14% protein feed may also be feeding a really good quality alfalfa hay and not realize that the protein concentration in that hay may be as much as 22%.

The fact of the matter is, there is far more justification for thinking that inadequate protein or an inappropriate protein:calorie ratio could cause these sorts of problems than for thinking that excess protein is causing problems.

"Free choice minerals allow the horse to *eat what he needs*"

There are some horsemen that still subscribe to the philosophy that says if "cafeteria style minerals" are put out, the horse will eat only those minerals that they need. There is no evidence that the horse has the ability to selectively consume those minerals for which they specifically have requirements above what is provided by the basal diet. This would be slightly akin to saying that you and I are able to determine that our diets are deficient in a specific mineral and seek sources of that mineral. I can see myself deciding, based on some metabolic or physiological indicator, thinking "I believe I am deficient in copper, let me chew on a penny for a while" or "Oh no! my potassium status is marginal. I better eat a banana!"

There are, of course, perceived exceptions to this line of thinking. There is some evidence that animals may be able to regulate sodium and chloride intake if free choice salt is available. Additionally, a phosphorus deficiency is classically identified by pica, or an insatiable appetite. One must wonder if this deficiency symptom occurs after body phosphorus stores are already far below optimum levels.

It is far more appropriate to design livestock (horse) diets such that required intakes of minerals are achieved than to take the chance that animals are able to determine what they need and select sources of those nutrients to meet requirements.

"Horses that practice coprophagy are *missing something*"

I do not think that anyone knows why some horses eat their feces. There are probably several viable explanations. One could really assume that from an evolutionary standpoint this is normal rather than abnormal behavior. It kind of makes sense that the horse would view feces as another way of obtaining nutrients (i.e. extraction of nutrients from the feces or recycling nutrients such as microbial protein).

There are several instances when horses are commonly observed to practice coprophagy. The very young foal may be seen eating the feces of its dam, probably a method of inoculating the gut with bacteria. The horse on limited fiber or caloric intake may eat feces to fulfill a need for fiber and/or calories. In either instance, supplying adequate feed and/or fiber may or may not cause a cessation of the behavior. Most frequently adding fiber to the diet yields the best results as far as eliminating the habit of eating feces. Many times we find the show horse, especially the easy keeper on limited feed intake and on a sporadic and inadequate exercise program, to be more prone to coprophagy. One must think that this habit may be behavioral, and primarily a result of boredom and in some instances have may absolutely nothing to do with nutrition.

"New hay must go through a sweat before being fed"

A great many people think that hay must cure in the barn for a certain amount of time prior to being fed to horses. This feeling is probably due to the observation that hay sometime heats after baling. Hay heats due to continued respiration of the plant material after it has been cut. The extent to which this process continues is to a large extent a function of the moisture content of the hay at the time of baling. One would expect a little continued respiration as soluble sugars in the plant tissues are broken down, but if too much heat is produced internal combustion of the hay may result in the hay barn burning down.

My general response to people is: If hay is heating enough that there is some hesitancy about feeding it to a horse, I sure do not want it in my barn! I have on numerous occasions gone and picked up hay out of the field in an afternoon and fed it to horses in the barn that evening and have never had any detrimental reactions. The other thing to consider is the fact that if there is adequate moisture to promote "heating" of the hay, then there is every chance that the hay also will mold to some extent. If the hay is going to heat and mold, I do not want to buy and feed it anyway.

"First cutting hay is not good for horses"

This may or may not be true! The accuracy of this statement depends almost entirely on the species or type of hay being fed/purchased and the maturity of the hay when it is cut. Many times hay producers get only one cutting of some types of grass hay so if you cull that cutting, then you are culling that type of hay. More frequently than not when this statement is made it refers to alfalfa hay. There is every chance that first cutting hay will contain more weeds and grasses than subsequent cuttings of hay and because weather conditions may vary, many times the first cutting of hay is taken when the plants are more mature than for later cuttings. If a hay producer does a good job of weed control and cuts each hay crop at the ideal stage of maturity, these differences disappear.

If a first cutting of hay is of similar or like nutritive value to that of later cuttings of hay, then there is absolutely no justification for rejecting it in favor of later cuttings of hay.

"Alfalfa causes kidney damage in horses"

This old belief requires no other discussion further than a loud and definitive NO! There are no data, scientific or otherwise that would indicate that the renal system of the horse is compromised in any way by the feeding of alfalfa hay. Again, people know that alfalfa is higher in protein than some other types of hay and as a justification for falsely indicting protein for a multitude of ailments, have added renal damage.

"Timothy hay is superior for horses"

Untrue! The hay that is best for horses is that hay that provides the best mix of nutritive value, economy and effective fiber. Timothy in fact is many times the most expensive hay one can get. This is particularly true when the cost of nutrients is considered. There are many times that timothy hay may cost as much as $300.00/ ton on the racetrack and provide little nutritional value. Again, tradition and misunderstanding of the nutritive value of hay and forage rears its ugly head.

"Coastal bermuda hay causes colic"

There is no evidence to support this belief! Personally, I have fed coastal hay all of my life with no increase in the amount of GI upset over that experienced by horsemen that do not choose to feed coastal. My family raises coastal in Texas and are able to harvest more nutrients per acre using this hay than for any other appropriate forage crop that they could raise. Coastal Bermuda grass is very responsive to the application of nitrogen fertilizer and this is reflected in the variability one sees in looking at the chemical composition of coastal hay grown in different parts of the country or indeed within a given state. The rules for assessing the quality of coastal hay are the same as for any other type of hay.

Obviously, the list of misconceptions and myths surrounding feeding horses goes on and on. These are but a few of the more common ones. Hopefully by examining these truisms from an accurate and nutritionally sound perspective some of the misinformation can be corrected and these wives' tales dispensed with.

This paper was first published in "Feeding the Performance Horse," Proceedings for the 1994 Short Course for Feed Manufacturers

FEEDING THE THREE-DAY EVENT AND DRESSAGE HORSE

TERESA HOLLANDS
Dodson & Horrell, Ltd, Northamptonshire, UK

Eventing and dressage in Great Britain

Great Britain is one of the most successful nations in the world when it comes to horse trials (eventing), and our riders have been consistently successful in World, European and Olympic Games. No other country boasts the number and variety of events, so much so that many of the world's leading riders choose to base themselves in England to take advantage of the opportunities.

Top class event horses come in all shapes and sizes and because Horse Trials demand such a wide range of equine abilities it is almost impossible to design a blueprint.

The size of the industry

In Great Britain, there are an estimated 500,000 horses - 17,000 of these are in training for racing, 7127 are registered event horses and 4171 are registered dressage horses. The actual numbers of horses competing at advanced dressage level and advanced eventing levels are very small indeed, 157 and 718 respectively. Having said that, both sports attract a large spectator and support following and are an inspiration to the far greater numbers competing at the lower levels.

The largest number of events are one-day horse trials. Two-day horse trials add steeplechase and roads and tracks to the cross-country giving competitors a chance to practice the technical and practical skills they will need for a 3-day event.

The ultimate test is the 3-day event. Each test takes place on a separate day starting with dressage. Day 2 is the roads and tracks, separated by the steeplechase - followed by cross-country. The final day is show-jumping day.

Badminton Horse Trials in Avon attracts a crowd of over 400,000 people on Saturday, the cross-country day. It is actually as famous for its shopping aisles as the horses!!

The event horse needs to have soundness and toughness to withstand the rigors of cross-country - the requirements for speed and stamina mean that Thoroughbred blood is preferable. They need good paces for dressage and an athletic jump. The event horse therefore represents quite a challenge to the nutritionist.

The NRC Requirements (1989) make no allowance for breed, temperament or management of horses; the only two criteria that are taken into account are the weight of the horse and its workload.

If one assumes that a pure dressage horse and an event horse are the same weights and are doing the same work, then there is no scientific justification to assume different dietary requirements - as our current knowledge stands. However, there is a definite perception in most riders' minds that the requirements are different.

The NRC does acknowledge that the requirements are minimum amounts needed to sustain normal health and performance and that the following should be borne in mind:

- digestive and metabolic differences among horses that result in some horses being "hard keepers" and others "easy keepers," and appropriate adjustments in feed intake to compensate for this variation;

- variation in production and performance capabilities of the animal and expectations of the owner;

- health status of the animal;

- variations in the nutrient availability in feed ingredients;

- interrelationships among nutrients;

- previous nutritional status of the horse;

- climatic and environmental conditions;

This is why it is so valuable for a nutritionist to be a practical horseman.

Cuddeford (1995) summarizes some of the metabolic diferences between horses and ponies; these differences can be applied to different "types" of horses.

Obviously, the types of feed available will influence the feeding strategies applied. There are several different feeds available that are uncommon in other countries.

Micronized feeds

Undigested starch in the large intestine can cause multiple metabolic problems, from poor performance through to laminitis and colic. The main energy sources fed to performance horses are the cereals which contain high levels of starch.

The activity of the horse's amylase is only 8-9% that of a pig's, so that any manufacturing process which aids the breakdown of starch is of benefit. Micronizing is the cooking of cereals under an infra-red cooker. When infra-red rays penetrate grain or seeds, they cause the molecules of the material to vibrate at a frequency of

80-170 million megacycles/sec. This causes rapid internal heating and a rise in water vapour pressure. The material becomes soft and plastic, causing it to swell and fracture. Immediate flaking gelatanises the starches.

Table 1. AMOUNT OF STARCH DIGESTED BY ENZYMES IN ROLLED CEREAL COMPARED TO MICRONIZED CEREAL.

Cereal	Barley	Wheat	Maize
% starch digested in rolled cereal	32	28	43
% starch that could end up in large intestine	68	72	57
% starch digestion in micronized cereal	98	90	74
% in large intestine	2	10	26

(University of Newcastle; Shetty, Lineback and Seib 1974)

Obviously, the more starch that is 'pre-digested' the less risk there is in undigested material reaching the large intestine.

Extrusion, which is more common in the USA, has a similar affect but the UK market is resistant to the appearance of extruded products. The majority of compound mixes (sweet feed) or muesli contain flakes, but only a few companies use totally micronized flakes. There is a perceived practical increase in digestibility of mixes over straights, leading to reduced intakes and more cost-effective feeding.

A three year study using *in vitro* techniques and fistulated ponies is being sponsored by Dodson and Horrell (the largest producers of micronised feeds) into the "Degradability of starch and non-starch polysaccharides in processed and unprocessed feeds."

Haylages

Great Britain's hay production is declining and the production of haylages is on the increase. The hay available is generally poorly dried due to our climatic conditions and therefore dusty. This is obviously a potentially damaging situation for the performance horse, who needs to be able to utilize lung capacity to maximum potential.

Although the case histories described in this paper are all feeding hay, a large proportion of event and dressage horses are fed haylage as an alternative to hay.

Haylage is made from mature grass which is cut and wilted for 24 hours, baled and compressed. This results in mild lactic acid, anaerobic fermentation - in effect pickling the grass.

Typical analysis of Haylage

DM	55%	DE 9-11 MJ/KG
Protein	9-12%	Ca 2.5-4.0 g/kg
MAD Fibre	32-36%	P 1.7-2.5 g/kg

There are typical problems associated with feeding haylages mainly due to their high water content and cost. People will only feed the same weight of haylages they do hay - in effect halving the fibre intake. In addition, horses appeared to be receiving extra energy from haylage compared to hay. This resulted in a reduced usage of compounds and therefore a reduction in vitamin, mineral and dry matter intakes. A recent 4X4 Latin Square digestibility trial at the Royal (Dick) Vet School, Edinburgh, Scotland gave the following results.

Table 2. DIGESTIBILITY COEFFICIENTS IN PONIES

	Haylage	*Timothy hay*	*% Increase*
Organic matter	0.52	0.45	15
ADF	0.42	0.38	10.5
Crude protein	0.62	0.36	72
Energy DE	0.55	0.43	28

Because of the reduction in dry matter intakes in horses being fed haylages, many horses developed behavioral abnormalities such as wood chewing, dung eating and similar. Consequently, there is a trend in Great Britain to soak hay. Until recently this was avoided in large yards as it was recommended to soak for 24 hours. However, recent work (Warr and Petch, 1992) indicates that a half hour soak is sufficient to reduce the respiratory challenge and to minimize nutrient loss.

Chaffs

In order to further extend fibre intake, chaff is commonly added to concentrate feeds. Generally speaking, 'a scoop' per feed is added (1 lb, 0.5 kg) to bulk out the feed. There are 4 main types of chaff available in Great Britain: molassed straw chaffs, containing between 40%-60% molasses; limestone and straw; high temperature dried alfalfa with 10%-20% molasses; a straw and alfalfa 50:50 mix and unmolassed pure hay and straw chaffs. The increased rate of chewing for fibre (Meyer, Ahleswede and Reinhardt, 1975) in comparison to cereals is the main reason these chaffs are added to the feeds.

What management and nutrition tricks maximize performance? What is performance?

Performance is defined in the dictionary as 'realism of potential.' In simple terms performance can be defined as getting the best from one's horse at whatever level it is being used. Management tricks are as important as nutrition and certainly daily turnout is beneficial to all performance horses. The racing industry has much to learn from other performance industries. 99% of top event and dressage horses are turned out daily for two hours even when they are at peak fitness; their welfare is improved by this. Limits on performance will include genetics, ability of horse and rider, training, commitment and expectation.

Obviously when one looks at diet, it is necessary to consider long term nutritive factors such as energy sources, roughage types and intakes as well as short term nutritive factors such as glycogen and glucose. Although according to the NRC (1989), the energy requirements for a horse doing a similar workload and similar bodyweight are identical, the diet can be manipulated to utilize different energy sources depending on the type of work involved. The following tables indicate how work type can be linked to energy type.

Table 3. TO ILLUSTRATE ENERGY SOURCES AVAILABLE TO A HORSE.

		Energy substrate obtained from		
Energy source	*Dietary source*	*Small intestine*	*Large intestine*	*Cells*
Starch	cereals	glucose	VFA's lactic acid	glycogen fatty acids
Fibre	roughage	-	VFA's	glycogen fatty acids
Fatty acids	oil/fat	fatty acids	VFA's	fatty acids
Proteins	roughage cereals	amino acids	VFA's microbial protein	fatty acids glucose (glycogen)
Sugars	molasses sugar beet	glucose	VFA's lactic acid	glycogen

Many top eventers and dressage riders come from a long history of association with horses, and many of their feeding practices are based on years of practical experience. As with many large yards, cost is very important and nutrition is often compromised.

Table 4. HOW THE HORSE USES ENERGY SOURCES.

Energy source	Relative energy content	Relative speed of metabolism	Relative efficiency of use of energy
Starch	high	fast	high
Fibre	low	slow	high
Fatty acids	very high	slow	very high
Proteins	high	moderate	moderate
Sugars	high	very fast	moderate

Table 5. WHY NUTRITION IS LINKED TO EXERCISE PHYSIOLOGY. EXERCISE EFFECTS MUSCLE TYPE WHICH INFLUENCES DIETARY ENERGY SOURCE.

Exercise level	Muscle fibre types (dominant)	Dietary energy sources
Low walking	I	roughage
Endurance	IIA	roughage, cereals
Trotters driving	IIA, IIB	roughage, cereals, oil
3-day eventing	IIA, IIB	roughage, cereals, oil
Show jumping	IIA, IIB	roughage, cereals, oil
Racing	IIB	cereals, roughage

The following graphs summarize typical feeding practices from some of the top event and dressage yards in Great Britain.

There is a distinct difference between the energy and appetite intakes of dressage and event horses (Figure 1). Typically the horses surveyed were Thoroughbred eventers and Warmblood dressage horses; this suggests the NRC perhaps overestimates energy requirements for the Thoroughbred type horse (being fed about 20% less energy than recommended) and possibly underestimates that of the heavier horse type. Interestingly the rider's perception is that the stuffy warmblood needs more energy to do its work; however this could be contra-indicative and simply result in increased weight gain. The difference in energy intakes could also be a reflection of the different body conditions.

There is no clear pattern to the feeding of protein and obviously lysine intake reflects the protein intakes (Figure 2). It should be noted that if these horses were being fed straights as opposed to compounds, their lysine intake would most definitely be compromised. It should be remembered that high protein intakes can be detrimental to performance, due to the energy required to remove the excess nitrogen and of course the build up of ammonia in the stable.

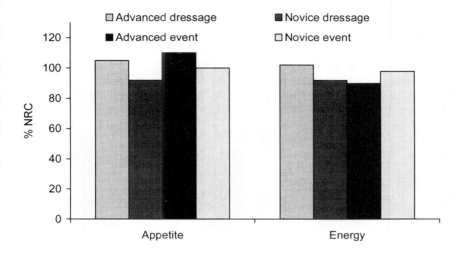

Figure 1. Nutrient intakes as a percentage of NRC (1989)

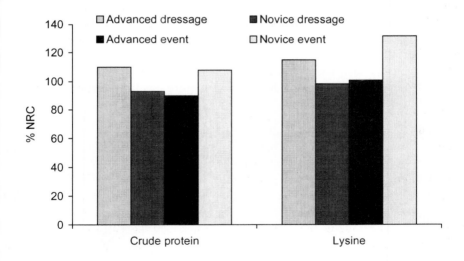

Figure 2. Nutrient intakes as a percentage of NRC (1989)

When calcium to phosphorus ratios are 1:1 or lower, the diets should be altered. Because all these horses are being fed compound feeds (Dodson and Horrell) the Ca:P ratio is not reversed, which is often seen on unsupplemented straight diets. Although in all cases phosphorus is being fed excess to requirement, it should be remembered that some of this will be in the form of phytates, whose availability is still unresearched (Figure 3).

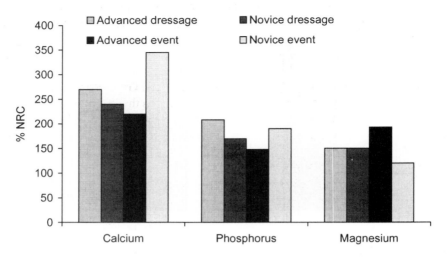

Figure 3. Mineral intakes as a percentage of NRC (1989)

The high potassium intakes are as a direct effect of reasonable forage intakes. This excess could be further exacerbated by high molassed feeds (molasses being high in K 4.2%). This could be considered contra-indicative due to potassium's diuretic effect, especially for horses that are working hard in hot climates...sweat. Sodium intake is typically low, hardly surprising when most compound feeds contain on average 1% salt. Most working horses will require electrolyte supplementation (Figure 4).

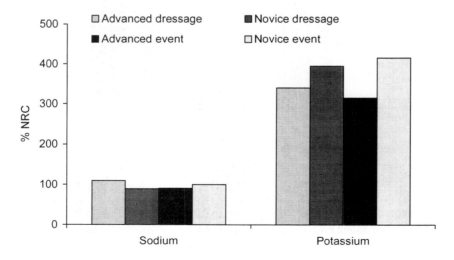

Figure 4. Mineral intakes as a percentage of NRC (1989)

Nearly all groups of horses were on additional vitamin and mineral supplementation which is surprising as nearly all minerals are already fed excess to requirement. These were not used in the calculations. Will there be any competing for copper and zinc uptake? This is one argument for the inclusion of bioplexes in feeds; however a lot more work needs doing on the role of bioplexes in equine nutrition before we can substantiate their benefits. Interestingly, in Great Britain there is still a belief in the veterinary profession and some nutritionists that iron supplementation is important. Iodine is universally over-supplemented, it is not at the 5 mg/kg toxic levels, but it does throw into question the NRC recommendations (Figures 5 and 6).

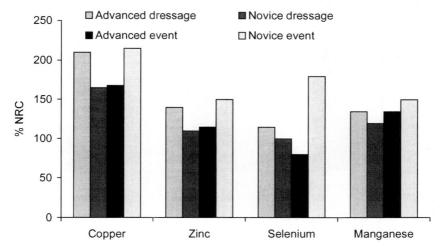

Figure 5. Trace mineral intakes as a percentage of NRC (1989)

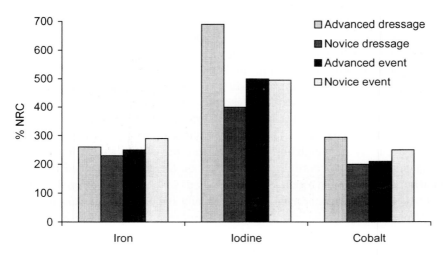

Figure 6. Trace mineral intakes as a percentage of NRC (1989)

Why do feed compounders put such high levels of vitamin A into their rations? Commercial pressure and the numbers game is perhaps the only reason. Are the horses absorbing the vitamin efficiently or perhaps there is a poor uptake? These percentages represent an intake of up to 172,000 IU of vitamin A a day for an individual horse who is eating 9.5 kg of food a day ... i.e. 18,105 IU/kg, which is over the maximum tolerance level (Figure 7).

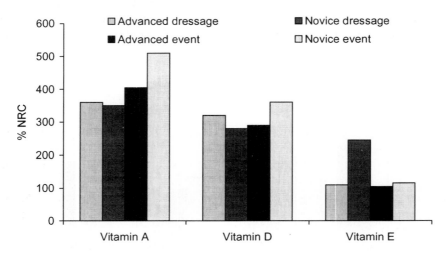

Figure 7. Vitamin intakes as a percentage of NRC (1989)

Although vitamin E intakes are higher than NRC, many nutritionists recommend higher levels (J. Pagan, personal communication). Although it is suggested that horses turned out for part of the day can manufacture vitamin D, the natural production of D in England is not sufficient (Dr. Frape, personal communication).

There is obviously a large discrepancy between nutrient intakes in the 'real' world and those obtained under controlled experimental conditions. All these case histories discussed are competing at world level without any apparent compromises. Some of the horses are also used for breeding and the different nutrient intakes do not hinder the continued success of their offspring. There may be several reasons for the apparent discrepancies: a) incorrect weight of horses, many yards use weight tapes, the accuracy of weigh formulas available have been called into question; b)daily intake varying according to personnel on the yard; c) a need to see well rounded horses resulting in a general overfeeding d) a lack of research on the apparent different needs for different breeds of horses. Finally and probably the most influential, a misinterpretation of work load. There is no simple physiological way of measuring work. People's perception of hard work is very contradicting. A horse working at Grand Prix Level will be working very hard for the duration of his test and during the last half hour of warm up. How does this compare with a fast sprint around a steeplechase or a slog around a cross country course? Would a TB breed exert less energy doing the same task as a warmblood? How high have the heart beats been raised and perhaps more importantly, for what duration? The old wives tales on feeding and some of the suspicion of scientists by practical, professional horsemen and women would be dissipated if exercise physiologists and nutritionists (both equine and human) could work more closely together to answer some of the questions. The more you delve into the nutrition of equines, the more questions evolve. That is why the whole field of equine nutrition is so exciting and why we are all here today!!

References

Cuddeford, D., 1995. Are ponies really small horses? Proceedings, International Conference on Feeding Horses.

Derksen, F.J., 1993. Chronic obstructive pulmonary disease (heaves) as an inflammatory condition. In: Equine Vet Journal, 25:257-258.

McGorum, B.C., Dixon, P.M. and Halliwell, R.E.W., 1993. Responses of horses affected with chronic obsructive pulmonary disease to inhalation challenges with mould antigens. In: Equine Vet Journal, 25:261-267.

Meyer, Ahleswede and Reinhardt, 1975. Duration of feeding, frequency of chewing and physical form of the feed for horses. DT Tierärztl Wschr 82:34-38.

Meyer, H. 1987. Nutrition of the Equine Athlete. In: Equine Exercise Physiology 2, 644-673.

Tremblay, G.M., Ferland, C., Lapointe, J.M., Vrins,A., Lavoie, J.P. and Cormier, Yvon, 1993. Effect of stabling on bronchoalveolar cells obtained from normal and COPD horses. In: Equine Vet Journal, 25:194-197.

Warr, E.M. and Petch, J.L., 1992. Effects of soaking hay on its nutritional value. In: EVE 5(3) 169-171.

Woods, Pamela S.A., Robinson, N.E., Swanson, M.C., Reed C.E., Broadstone, R.V. and Derksen, F.J., 1993. Airborne dust and aeroallergen concentration in a horse stable under two different management systems. In: Equine Vet Journal, 25:208-213.

This paper was first published in "Recent Advances in Equine Nutrition," Proceedings for the 1995 Short Course for Feed Manufacturers

FEEDING PRACTICES IN AUSTRALIA AND NEW ZEALAND

P.J. HUNTINGTON AND G.J. JENKINSON
Rhône-Poulenc Animal Nutrition, West Footscray, Australia

Introduction

As well as producing top golfers, beer and sailors, Australia and New Zealand are great horse producing countries. Australia has the second largest horse population in the western world and New Zealand horses have long plundered Australia's richest races. There are about 36,000 active racehorses in Australia who complete at 410 racetracks for US $140 million prize money. Horses are bred and trained in a variety of climatic regions and can be kept outdoors all year round.

New Zealand as a comparison has a total population of 3.5 million, about the same as the Australian city of Melbourne. It is made up of two main islands, the North and the South. In New Zealand pastures remain green and of high quality nearly all year. The double attraction of the Australian racing scene is the higher stakes and 25% higher value of the Australian dollar, as this helps offset the expense of air flights to the successful raiders.

This paper describes some of the common feeding practices in Australia and New Zealand, particularly where they differ from those used in North America or Europe.

Pastures

Snow falls only very rarely in areas where horses are kept, so horses can graze all year round. Horses on studs are not stabled at night and have access to pasture all day. Many pastures are poorly managed and suffer from overgrazing by horses, and inadequate pasture renovation. Although the country is large, many horse farms are overstocked and pastures suffer accordingly. In temperate areas of Australia, pastures dry off over summer and autumn which creates a need for supplementary feeding of horses at this time of year. Pastures are usually based on ryegrass and clover.

In Queensland, introduced tropical grasses such as kikuyu, buffel and seteria are common. These have high oxalate levels which interfere with calcium and phosphorus digestibility and can lead to the development of nutritional secondary hyperparathyroidism. In areas of North Queensland, pasture species such as *Morinda*

Spp or *Neptunia amplexicaulis* can accumulate selenium and cause selenium toxicity. Australia has an abundance of poisonous plants with regional distributions, although most of the intensively stocked areas with horses are relatively free of poisonous plants.

Climatically the North Island of New Zealand is a warmer, higher rainfall area and is host to the main Thoroughbred breeding studs. The South Island of New Zealand has traditionally been the main breeding area for Standardbreds. Pastures are mainly rye grass and clover in both islands. South Island pastures experience snowfalls from May through to September. Poisonous plants are not a concern in New Zealand horse pastures. Pastures rarely dry off over summer in the North Island; however they do dry off in the South Island.

Roughage

Australian horses are fed roughage in the form of hay, chaff, pellets and cubes. Lucerne (alfalfa) is the most common hay fed to horses, followed by grass (meadow) hay and oaten hay. Lucerne and grass hay are packed in small bales and the unit of feeding is a biscuit (flake). Unfortunately, wide variation in the density of hay and the width of a biscuit means that the weight of a particular biscuit can vary from one kg to three kg. Under those circumstances, nutritional evaluation can be inaccurate unless the weight is actually measured.

The value of grass hay can vary widely according to the composition of the grasses, time of hay making and other factors. A high clover content will increase the nutrient content of the hay and good quality clover hay can approach lucerne hay in value. The climatic conditions at the time of hay making are usually favorable and Australian hay is generally free of dust, molds and other contaminants. Prices for hay vary substantially according to its type, quality, balance between supply and demand and transport costs. Oaten hay is fed less commonly because production is lower and storage is more difficult. It is fed in sheaves or bales.

In times of drought, demand for hay by other livestock can create severe shortages and this has led to the development of several novel fiber sources. Lupin hulls contain 46% fiber and 8.5% crude protein and are used as a cheap fiber source in pellets and textured feeds. Rice hulls have also been used successfully in high fiber pellets and for mixing in with other feedstuffs. They are also used as bedding and unfortunately horses that eat the bedding can develop impaction colic.

Australian horses are fed large quantities of chopped hay or chaff. Chaff is made in commercial chaff mills that produce 40 kg bags or it can be produced on the farm using a small scale chaff cutter. Racehorses are often fed a mix of oaten or wheaten chaff and lucerne chaff. Immature oats or wheat crops are cut for chaff several weeks before harvest. The timing varies each season but is described as the 'early heading stage' or no more than 7 days after flowering. At this stage you can squeeze "milk" out of the head of the grain and the nutrient content of the stalk is higher than at harvest. It is made into sheaves which are stocked for drying in the paddock over several weeks, then cut into 5mm segments as chaff. Most commercial chaff is "steam cleaned" to remove dust and allow easier cutting. Some chaff is rough cut and contains portions of longer fiber. Good quality chaff should not contain any formed grain, but chaff often does contain grain.

The principal advantage of chaff is that it can be mixed in with the concentrate portion of the feed and the horse consumes roughage with the concentrate. This can slow down the intake of concentrate and prevent starch overload in the large intestine. Horse owners commonly overestimate the weight of chaff fed because it is very light and may weight only 300g/2 liters for oaten or wheaten chaff and 250g/2 liters for lucerne chaff. Although chaff is principally fed as a source of roughage it is desirable that it contains high energy levels for horses in hard work. This is usually subject to considerable variation. The nutrient content of lucerne chaff is usually superior to cereal chaff (table 1). There is considerable debate as to the merits of oaten chaff over wheaten chaff and vice versa.

As in Australia, New Zealand lucerne and oaten chaff are main forms of roughage added to hard feed. Meadow and lucerne hay are fed in similar quantities to stabled performance horses.

The hay making season is shorter and more difficult in New Zealand, and therefore a great deal of care is needed to ensure hay is cured correctly. There are very limited additional sources of roughage available, unlike Australia with bran and pollard (2nd grade flour) being available in fluctuating quantities depending on the demand of the dairy season.

Table 1. NUTRIENT CONTENT OF SELECTED AUSTRALIAN FEEDSTUFFS (AS FED)

Feed	DE** MJ/kg	CP %	Fat %	Fiber %	Ca g/kg	P g/kg	Zn mg/kg	Cu mg/kg
Lupins	14.5	30	5.5	13	2	3	27	3.5
Sunflower Seeds	17	1020	1.5	23	4	9.2	97	3.7
Lupin Hulls	6.6	8.5	1.7	46	3	1.8	--	--
Rice Hulls	--	2	0.4	4.0	0.8	0.7	--	--
Coprice M*	13.2	12	5.4	7.5	10.5	6.7	60	14
Sustaina	13.4	11	8.5	6	4.5	3.5	30	65
Cereal Chaff	4-7	5-8	1.5	30-35	2-3	2-3	41	4.5
Rice Pollard	16	13	19	9	0.5	12	30	8

*Composition of pellets and sweet feed varies and some contain higher mineral and vitamin inclusion levels than others.
**4.18MJ = 1Mcal

Average intakes for performance horses would be 2.5 kgs of meadow or lucerne hays with approximately 300 to 400 grams of oaten or lucerne chaff. Access to pasture varies from nil to about 2.5 hours if available. Most racing stables have access to pasture and would often cut about 6kg of pasture for stabled horses.

Concentrates

Australians have traditionally fed more "straights" than premixed textured or pelleted feeds, although this pattern is changing with the development of better quality feed mill products. Oats are by far the most common grain fed to horses based on safety, price and the fact that there is no need for further processing. Corn or maize is higher priced than oats and cannot compete on a cost/MJ basis but it is often necessary to increase the energy density of the ration. It is usually fed in amounts of less than 1 kg. Barley is perceived by many to be a "non-heating" feed and is fed either steam rolled or boiled, but again it is usually fed in small amounts. Sorghum is an economical grain but is not widely used.

Bran has been a popular ingredient, particularly for combination in a wet feed (bran mash) with various supplements, but its use is now declining. Pollard is popular with people wanting to put condition on horses without feeding extra grain. Rice pollard is also used by some owners for conditioning, due to its high fat content.

Feed mills produce both pelleted and textured feeds but there is still a substantial prejudice against pellets by horsemen. Up until recently, many processed feeds have been inappropriately formulated. In addition the mineral and vitamin premixes added to the feeds have usually been inadequate for use in high performance horses or fast growing horses without extra supplementation. Many of these feeds are not used according to instructions, but are diluted with other grains which further diminishes the value of the vitamin and mineral premixes in the feeds. Rice based pellets (Coprice M) have been popular for a number of years. Those are high energy pellets (Table 1) purported to offer "cool conditioning." Some lower energy textured feeds contain lucerne or oaten chaff as a source of fiber. These are popular with riders of horses in light work. Recently some feeds for performance and growing horses have been produced containing high levels of fat. An example is Mitavite Sustaina, a feed for racehorses (Table 1).

In New Zealand, a limited amount of commercially prepared feed is fed to both Thoroughbred and Standardbred racehorses with tradition and skepticism being the main reasons for this. Sixty percent of trainers might feed about 2 kgs of a balanced concentrate, the rest being basic oats and chaff feeders with some additional additives.

The price of grain in New Zealand is significantly higher than in Australia and this may go some way to explaining why 90% of the oats in New Zealand are crushed and crimped as opposed to the reverse in Australia.

Costs of bagged oats in Australia	$A28 cents per kg
Costs of bagged oats in New Zealand	$A48 cents per kg
	(A $1.00 = US $0.70)

Protein supplements

In racing horses, protein supplementation is usually provided by the feeding of lupins, sunflower seeds, tick beans, soybean meal and peas. These also contain a higher energy content than traditional grains (Table 1). Linseed meal and cottonseed meal were common "meal" supplements but these have declined in popularity recently. Lupins are becoming increasingly popular as they represent good value, and they are a palatable energy and protein source with high digestible fiber content. However lupins have low levels of methionine and tryptophan. The contention that linseed meal or sunflower seeds makes horses "look better" is likely to be due to the high oil content, as both provide relatively poor quality protein. On the breeding farms the value of soybean meal is increasingly being recognized and it is fed as a soybean meal or full fat soybean meal. However some breeders still use protein supplements with lower quality protein e.g. sunflower seeds, cottonseed meal.

Where horses have access to 12 hours or more of good pasture in New Zealand, protein supplementation is not the major limiting factor. For example the foal ration of a major feed company supplying the total hard feed in a fully prepared ration was 14.5% protein.

Good pastures fluctuate between 16% and 28% protein. Protein supplements to racehorses are mainly full fat soya and sunflower even though sunflower seeds are very expensive.

Supplements

Australian horse trainers are major users of supplements as most people do not use prepared feeds, or use them as only part of the concentrate intake. There are many brands and types of feed supplements marketed for horses and these promise a variety of benefits for the horses. There is a strict registration process but despite this, many products provide spurious claims or contain inadequate supplementary minerals or vitamins. Some formulations are quite dated and they do not provide sufficient supplementary minerals and vitamins. It is common for a product to contain a particular ingredient, but not contain enough to make a meaningful contribution to balancing the horse's diet.

Overuse of supplements is common and many horses are fed five or six supplement products including several sources of the same nutrient. Iron supplements are still common despite the fact that all diets contain adequate iron intakes from natural sources. Most owners have little concept of the mineral and vitamin needs of their horses and labels are often difficult to understand, hence the choice of supplements becomes difficult. Most supplements are powders although liquid electrolytes, vitamins, buffers and iron supplements are available. Some products are presented in a pelleted form to enhance intake of the supplement. Many of these products contain protein supplements in addition to minerals and vitamins.

Feeding practices with racehorses

A survey on the feeding of racehorses in Sydney has recently been published (Southwood *et al.*, 1993). The survey work of Southwood *et al* (1993) revealed a number of interesting findings about feeding practices near Sydney. The results emphasize the dependence on straight grains as only 1 TB stable fed a sweet feed as the only concentrate feed. The average amount of sweet feed used was 1.6 kg and 0.75 kg by Thoroughbred (TB) and Standardbred (SB) trainers whilst 15% of trainers fed some rice based pellets.

The average daily roughage intake of 3.3 kg (TB) and 4.1 kg (SB) is less than recommended minimum intakes, particularly for Thoroughbred horses. The average chaff intake was 1 kg (TB) and 2.2 kg (SB) with 88% trainers feeding lucerne chaff at an average of 33-45% of chaff intake. SB trainers used chaff as the principal roughage source whilst TB trainers used hay.

In this survey TB trainers fed an average of 129 MJ/day and SB trainers 132 MJ/day based on average body weights of 490 kg and 440 kg respectively. There was significant variation in daily intake that presumably relates to workload, as would the increased energy intake in SB horses. It appears that TB trainers work horses for a shorter duration than trainers in the USA or Europe. Trainers fed more crude protein than NRC recommendations with an average of 1450 g or 12% dietary protein. The mean calcium and phosphorus intakes were slightly higher than NRC recommendations and only 20% of trainers used a calcium supplement, yet approximately 30% of diets required additional calcium. Iron intakes were over 200% of requirements, yet iron supplements and injections were popular. Some trainers fed potassium deficient diets, presumably due to low roughage intakes.

Salt was fed by 25% of trainers with higher intakes (70g) by SB horses than TB horses (30g). Electrolyte supplements were fed by only 44% of trainers so many horses in this study would have been electrolyte deficient. Twenty five percent fed commercial naturalizing agents and a considerable number fed sodium bicarbonate. About 20% of trainers fed glucose whilst only 14% added fat and the average amount of oil fed was less than 125 ml. Injectable vitamins were used more commonly than oral vitamins, although 25% trainers fed extra vitamins.

Most trainers thought the major problems with feeding is getting horses to eat enough as they reach racing condition or after gallops and races. This is the reason for the low roughage intake by most trainers; however the low roughage intake may also lead to inappetence as could the feeding of large meals twice daily, amino acid imbalances or B vitamin deficiencies. Ninety percent of trainers changed feeding prior to racing with a decreased roughage intake, increased grain intake and increased supplement intake being common practice. Seasonal variations were also evident with increased salt and electrolyte intake in summer and greater maize and barley intakes in winter.

Tying up and excitability are other feed related problems that are addressed by feed substitution, reduced feed intake and supplementation. Veterinary or nutritional advice on feeding practices was considered to be important by relatively few trainers.

The daily feeding program of six leading Thoroughbred trainers is listed in Table 2 along with the nutrient content of those diets (Table 3). These are average feeds for a horse in full work. Some trainers feed twice a day but most feed three times a day. Most trainers feed insufficient roughage and this may be related to the high incidence of tying up in Australia. It is rare to find trainers who feed ad lib hay. Inadequate electrolyte supplementation may also contribute to the incidence of tying up. Some trainers do not feed lucerne as they consider it may lead horses to tie up and makes them "thick in the wind." A lot of feeding is done on the basis of following traditional practices, but there is an increasing use of premixed textured feeds which contain sufficient mineral and vitamins so that supplements are unnecessary. Whilst some use these feeds as designed, others use them as only a part of the concentrate ration which reduces the impact of the vitamin and mineral additives in the prepared feed.

Table 2. EXAMPLES OF RACING DIETS FED TO THOROUGHBREDS IN FULL WORK

Ingredient (kg)	Trainer A	B	C	D	E	F
Oats	5.4	1.3	6	5.2	5.9	4.2
R Oats	--	1.8	--	--	--	--
R Barley	--	0.6	--	--	--	--
Cr Maize	1.55	0.6	2.1	--	0.8	0.9
Lupins	0.3	--	0.33	1.8	--	--
Peas	--	--	0.33	--	0.4	--
Tick Beans	--	0.4	--	--	0.4	0.875
Bran	0.3	0.53	0.2	0.3	--	0.3
Sunflowers	0.25	0.2	0.1	0.1	0.4	0.075
Pellets	--	0.7	--	--	--	--
Oil	--	--	0.2	--	--	0.12
Cereal Chaff	0.4	1.8	0.45	0.8	0.65	1.8
Lucerne Chaff	0.3	0.75	0.7	0.8	0.9	1.2
Lucerne Hay	1.7	--	1.5	2	0.75	1.0
Oaten Hay	1.35	--	1.4	--	--	--
Supplements	5	2	3	1	5	4
Pasture		+			+	+

Surprisingly few horses are put out in a paddock to graze during the day although some trainers do give horses a few days on grass after a race. Trainers fear that horses won't eat the hard feed if they spend too much time grazing. Some stables have absolutely no access to grazing apart from a short "pick" whilst horses are being walked in the afternoon. Where a trainer has stables outside a city and has day yards it is more common to put the horse out to graze during the day.

Table 3. NUTRIENT CONTENT OF THOROUGHBRED RACING DIETS

Nutrient		A	B	C	D	E	F
Protein	g	1300	1071	1500	1690	1285	1727
Digestible energy	MJ	130	101	152	130	125	132
Vitamin A	IU	88258	45990	108350	150000	69400	144812
Vitamin D	IU	715	2664	13500	5800	6890	7887
Vitamin E	IU	2171	162	445	1425	255	387
Vitamin K	mg	6	2	7	31	7	12
Thiamin (B1)	mg	45	32	164	74	175	87
Riboflavin (B2)	mg	176	46	148	99	137	100
Niacin	mg	1079	246	594	395	360	337
Pyridoxine (B6)	mg	138	23	47	43	80	50
Pantothenic Acid	mg	331	77	137	185	200	162
Vitamin B12	ug	393	72	441	140	50	0
Folic Acid	mg	36	4	60	21	6	12
Biotin	mg	2	1	2.5	17	2	2
Calcium	g	41	24	38	77	36	59
Phosphorus	g	35	31	40	51	34	42
Magnesium	g	38	13	22	32	7	25
Potassium	g	89	55	78	100	75	118
Sodium	g	33	15	34	36	32	10
Iron	g	1371	1458	1863	2470	2010	2475
Zinc	mg	680	306	513	700	650	575
Copper	mg	71	51	133	200	96	87
Manganese	mg	398	414	430	788	440	562
Iodine	mg	0.8	0.5	1.5	1.3	1.0	1
Cobalt	mg	0.9	0.7	1.5	1.2	0.8	1.25
Selenium	mg	4	1	3	3.9	3.5	5

Most New Zealand trainers feed 3 times a day, with some feeding 4 times a day. Owners and trainers tend to feed through conscience and have difficulty understanding that more feed does not necessarily mean horses will run faster. Some dramatic improvements have been experienced by identifying energy requirements and lowering grain intakes to be more in line with the horses' weight and workload.

Most commercial trainers do not have this problem, as their experience has identified maximum intakes.

Feeding on stud farms

Feeding practices on studs vary widely throughout Australia. The size of the stud and the number of horses, climate, pasture development, irrigation, breed, location and commercial status all influence the feeding practices. Board rates vary from A $8 to A $12 for mares and young horses on Thoroughbred studs and A $2 to A $3 on Standardbred studs. This means that Standardbred horses are usually fed hay or oats only, apart from very commercial farms or unusual circumstances.

Examples of feeding programs for 12 month yearlings are listed in Table 4. Relatively few studs weigh young horses, so assessment of growth rate is subjective. Breeders are now realizing the problems created by pushing large amounts of grain into young horses. However demands by yearling purchasers for large, fat yearlings at sales force many breeders to overfeed yearlings.

Table 4. FEED INTAKE OF 12 MONTH OLD THOROUGHBRED YEARLINGS ON AUSTRALIAN STUDS (kg)

Feed	A	B	C	D	E	F
Oats	5	4	3.2		1	
Pellets				3	3	4
Sweet Feed						
Lupins	1					
Tick Beans		0.5				
Sunflowers		0.5				
Soybean Meal				0.5	0.4	
Lucerne Chaff	0.5	0.5	1.3	3		
Lucerne Hay	2	2			3	2.5
Cereal Chaff			0.7			
Grass Hay				1.25		
DCP g				50		
Limestone g	0.5	25				
Supplements	1	1	1			

*All yearlings have access to pasture

Creep feeding is relatively uncommon, but foals usually have the opportunity to eat from the mare's feed bin. Whilst it is usual to feed supplementary minerals to young horses, many breeders are not aware of how much copper and zinc are needed by young horses for rapid growth and minimal developmental orthopedic diseases.

Laboratory testing of the nutrient content of feeds is rare apart from protein testing of oats and some hay. This is due to a combination of ignorance of the benefits of testing and the high costs involved.

Feeding on studs in New Zealand has changed dramatically over the last five years mainly through the bad experiences of overfeeding, when it was common to sell to the Australian market by the pound. The downturn in returns for the New Zealand yearling led to studs wanting to identify what was needed and what was not required.

Pasture analysis on a seasonal basis is now common and structured feeding programs justified by nutritional benefits and cost.

Most of the Thoroughbred studs in New Zealand are feeding commercially prepared steam flaked or extruded textured feeds to their sale yearlings. The convenience and labor savings to the commercial studs together with the definable nutritional contributions are the main reasons for this switch in feeding practices.

References

Southwood L.L., D.L. Evans, W.L. Bryden and R.J. Rose (1993) Nutrient Intake of horses in Thoroughbred and Standardbred stables, Aust Vet J 70:164-168.
Southwood L.L., D.L. Evans, W.L. Bryden and R.J. Rose (1993) Feeding practices in Thoroughbred and Standardbred stables, Aust Vet J 70:184-185.

This paper was first published in "Feeding the Performance Horse," Proceedings for the 1994 Short Course for Feed Manufacturers

SOME ASPECTS OF FEEDING THE ENDURANCE HORSE

PER SPÅNGFORS
SLR, Forskning, Sweden

Feed the hindgut

The low enzyme activity in the saliva and in the small intestine for the digestion of starch and sugars tells us that the horse's main energy source is not supposed to be sugars. Instead, the primary energy source should be volatile fatty acids (VFAs) from microbial fermentation in the large intestine. These VFAs are either used directly as fuel in the cells or they are transformed to other energy molecules, such as glucose. Longer chain fatty acids can also be derived from dietary fat, which is absorbed mainly from the small intestine.

The horse which is best prepared for demanding tasks, such as endurance races, is the horse with a high microbial activity from beneficial microbes in the hindgut. Ideally, 60-75% of the horse's energy requirement should come from hindgut fermentation. The lower value is sufficient for a racehorse, and the higher value for the endurance horse. You can regulate the proportion of energy from the hindgut by the fibre content in the feed. If you have less than 15% crude fibre in the diet, the horse's digestive tract functions like a pig or a human. With a high fibre content, the horse becomes more dependent on microbial fermentation and VFAs from the hindgut.

Water and electrolyte reservoir

High fibre content in the feed can also have a microbe-sparing effect in the hindgut. When the ingesta passes from the large colon to the small colon, fluid with a high microbe content is squeezed from the solids and re-enters the large colon. This effect is more pronounced when the fibre content in the feed is high. When the fluid is separated from the solids, peptidase, water soluble molecules and small undigested particles are also recycled into the large intestine for further digestion. In that way the fecal losses of valuable nutrients is much less in horses fed fibre-rich feeds. Indigestible solids will leave the horse quickly and in this way stimulate the appetite.

This fluid-barrier also prevents water and electrolyte losses via the faeces. If properly fed, the large intestine serves as a big reservoir for water and electrolytes. If the diet is rich in starch that escapes enzymatic digestion in the small intestine, starch particles will hold the water in the large intestine due to osmosis. Thus it will be difficult to use the water in the large intestine to compensate for the dehydration that always occurs during an endurance race. In an experiment at my laboratory, 4 horses received equal amounts of energy, by either grass hay (1.5 kg/100 kg BW) or grass hay (0.7 kg/100 kg BW) and oats (0.5 kg/100 kg BW). We collected blood, faeces and urine for analysis. As seen in figure 1, the retained sodium (in percent of the intake) is significantly higher for horses getting the high fibre feed. The retention of potassium, as shown in figure 2, is the same between the two diets. Where sodium goes, water goes. Therefore, we can conclude that a high fibre diet also increases the water reservoir in the large intestine.

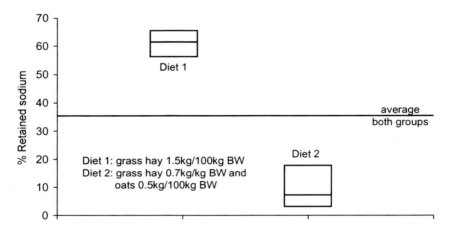

Figure 1. Retained Sodium as a percent of intake

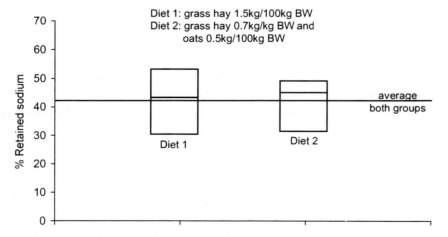

Figure 2. Retained Potassium as a percent of intake

The blood samples showed a postfeeding increase in serum-sodium when the horses were fed oats as shown in figure 3. As the sodium peak occurred 1 hour after feeding, we can assume that the sodium was absorbed in the small intestine. This did not happen when the horses were fed hay. The oats have a higher concentration of starch, that is digested to glucose by enzymes in the small intestine. From research conducted with pigs, we know of a glucose-sodium coupled uptake. This means that when glucose is absorbed through the intestinal wall, sodium is carried along with the glucose molecule. Because of this coupling, which is positive in a piglet with diarrhoea, sodium is absorbed and enters the blood. Unfortunately this sodium, if it is not needed in the metabolism, is immediately excreted in the urine. Orally given electrolytes between meals probably suffer the same fate. At least we can assume this if the electrolyte mixture also contains glucose.

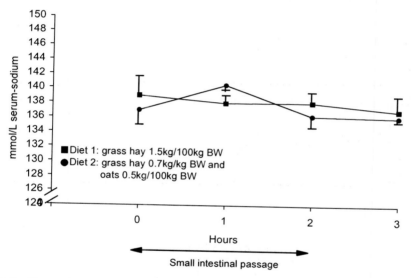

Figure 3. Changes in serum sodium after feeding

If the sodium escapes uptake in the small intestine, as with the hay diet, we create a buffer of electrolytes in the large intestine, which can be used in times of electrolyte depression. This is why the retained sodium is higher when horses get a high fibre diet.

Ideal endurance feeds

From the discussion above it is easy to understand the importance of a good quality hay. In Sweden we use grass hay with a high percentage of timothy and other meadow grasses. We harvest the hay shortly after blooming, in order to increase the fibre content. We don't want more than 80-90 g crude protein per kg in the hay when fed to competition horses. This will be discussed below. We use metabolizable energy in Sweden when we calculate energy needs and the best hay for horses is a hay with no more that 8.5 MJ metabolizable energy per kg as fed (1.0 Mcal DE/lb).

Fat is a popular source of energy for endurance horses. We use a fluid vegetable fat with 30% linoleic acid and 5-6% in the ration is common. We have found that horses suffering from muscle problems like tying up improve on a high fat/fibre diet. The serum enzymes used for diagnosing the muscle breakdown decrease rapidly and remain low if the horses are kept on this type of diet. This feed holds 11% of the fluid fat mentioned above, and 22% crude fibre with high digestibility. We also add 2000 mg vitamin E per kg. We are now evaluating this feed on a scientific basis.

Fat is not only a source of energy, but should also be regarded as a carrier for fat soluble vitamins and as a source of essential fatty acids such as linoleic acid.

Avoid protein excess

The protein need in an adult horse is very low. The excess nitrogen is a poison and must be made harmless. This energy consuming process takes place in the liver via the formation of urea which is excreted in the urine. When the urea is excreted, water goes with it. Horses on a high protein diet usually have a higher water demand. When urea hits the floor in the box, bacteria convert the nitrogen to ammonia. If horses are kept indoors over night, as is common in Sweden, you can smell the difference between a stable with a high protein diet and one with a low protein diet, when you open the stable door in the morning. This is detrimental for an endurance horse who has to have his lungs in good shape.

During an endurance race, the filtration rate in the kidney is lowered in order to save valuable water. For this reason we always see a linear increase in urea in the blood during endurance competitions. If you start the race with a high urea concentration, soon the level in the blood will become dangerously high which may lead to a number of negative metabolic events.

It is not only the protein level in the feed that affects the urea concentration in the blood. The small intestinal digestibility of the protein source is also important. Protein which escapes enzymatic digestion in the small intestine is transformed by bacteria into ammonia when it enters the large intestine. The ammonia produced in the hind gut eventually reaches the liver where it is converted to urea.

The balance between energy and protein in the feed is also important in order to lower the urea in the blood. We see the lowest urea concentration when we have 5-6 g digestible protein per MJ metabolizable energy.

Fatty acids and glycerol

In a properly fed hindgut, there are nutrients to keep a horse going for days without feed, if you take it easy. But the more speed you demand from your horse, the more important will the glucose metabolism from glycogen be. Glucose is stored in muscles and liver in the form of glycogen. When you push on and the horse moves more rapidly it gets more dependent on glucose coming from glycogen. The glycogen stores are constantly being refilled, even during work, but it is a slow process, so if the speed is very high, the breakdown and formation of glycogen doesn't keep pace.

If the duration of the work is long, as in endurance riding, you can't feed the horse properly during the race. So the horse must use other sources for the formation of glucose in order to save the glycogen stores. Propionic acid from the hindgut fermentation of fibre is probably the most important precursor for glucose but glycerol from the breakdown of body fat is also important. It seems that the horse has an enormous capacity to form glucose from propionic acid and glycerol.

When we measure volatile fatty acids in plasma after feeding, we never detect propionic acid in venous blood in the resting horse, because it is immediately transformed to glucose in the liver. Postprandial increases of acetic and butyric acid are always detected. As we also measure the hormonal changes in the blood after feeding, we can assume that the postprandial peaks of acetic acid are derived from the feed, and not from endogenous formation in the liver, as seen in the pig. Acetic acid from the hindgut fermentation of fibre and from body fat is also an excellent fuel for muscle cells.

The conditioned horse is also capable of using long chain fatty acids as energy in muscle cells after degradation to shorter carbon units. Sources of long chain fatty acid are dietary fat and body fat.

Feeding strategy is a question of hormones

The most important hormone that regulates energy coming from the small intestine is insulin. Insulin has three important functions. It promotes glycogen formation in the liver, fat storage and protein synthesis in muscles. The net result from these three tasks is that insulin promotes storage and not usage of energy and this makes the horse work intolerant as long as the insulin level is high. Insulin is always elevated after a meal as long as the feed passes the small intestines. The more starch and sugars in the feed, the higher is the insulin peak.

The other important hormone involved in energy metabolism is thyroxine. Thyroxine has many functions in the body, but three of them are very important for the endurance horse. Thyroxine promotes breakdown of glycogen in the liver, the formation of glucose from volatile fatty acids and glycerol, and it increases oxygen consumption in the muscle cells. There are also indications that thyroxine actually promotes the uptake of volatile fatty acids from the large intestine. All of these effects are beneficial for the endurance horse because they promote usage of stored energy.

Thyroxine is therefore an insulin antagonist. We always see a postprandial decline in thyroxine. If the horse is constantly on a high starch diet, the basal insulin level is high and consequently the thyroxine concentration is low. It is not difficult to realize the detrimental effect if an endurance horse constantly would have low thyroxine levels. To avoid this, the endurance horse must be kept on a high fibre/low starch diet.

The hormonal and energy substrate shift that occurs after feeding, when the feed passes the small intestine, also tells us that you should not feed the endurance horse too close to the start of the race. This is because the feed must enter the large intestine so that the hormonal levels shift back to large intestinal uptake levels, with normal insulin and thyroxine levels.

If we give horses feeds where the main energy extraction occurs in the large intestine, we want the passage time in the small intestine to be as short as possible. Pellets or cubes are the structure of choice because these are consumed faster, and have a faster stomach and intestine passage time. In this way we reduce the postfeeding work intolerance phase. The horse can be fed more often and soon after feeding be ready for training. If you use these feeds it is even possible to feed a tired horse during a long race, rest him for 1-2 hours, and then finish with a fresh horse.

Macro- and micro-minerals

The mineral most discussed in the endurance field is calcium. Nature regards calcium as a very important ion. We can presume this since all mammals have been equipped with two hormones and one vitamin with the mission to regulate the calcium level in the tissues. No other mineral is so thoroughly regulated.

This reminds us of a time in the Precambrian ocean where life began, and calcium was a rare ion. When life came up from the sea it enclosed the ocean inside a cell membrane, and started to look for a way to move that cell. When the vertebrate animals were formed, the calcium ion became the most important extracellular ion. The Precambrian ocean is still, in a sense, in every living cell today and the ions in the cells are called intracellular ions. One of the most important intracellular ions is magnesium.

For a long time the mineral levels have been more or less constant in the soil and hence in the plants growing in that soil. Local variations have been known for generations by the farmers cultivating the fields. But we live in a variable time with heavy industrial influence on the environment. In Sweden the rain-clouds from northern Europe pour acid rain over our meadows. This has changed the mineral concentrations in the fields. Magnesium and many micro-minerals such as copper, zinc, cobalt and molybdenum seem to be the most influenced ions, and their concentrations in the soil are rapidly decreasing while aluminum and cadmium are increasing.

Today we can see deficiency diseases never seen before. As an example, we have just diagnosed a horse with both molybdenum and copper deficiency, which is very contradictory, since in ruminants a deficiency in one of these ions always is associated with excess in the other. This gives us new problems to cope with when formulating new feeds. In this paper, though, we will focus on magnesium.

Magnesium deficiency - a common problem?

Magnesium deficiency is perhaps the oldest known deficiency in animals. Chinese researchers have found eggshells from dinosaurs, 70 million years old. These eggshells contain 30 times less magnesium than normal. These scientists have perhaps found the reason why these animals suddenly disappeared off the face of the earth. An environmental change is postulated as a probable cause.

Magnesium deficiency has been known to appear in horses for a long time, but always together with calcium deficiency. Five years ago we diagnosed the first horse with magnesium deficiency as a solitary finding. Since then a lot of horses have been diagnosed with this deficiency. Unlike earlier finds, the calcium levels in these horses are high.

Magnesium is an intracellular ion. 60% of the magnesium in the body is bound to the apatite crystal in the skeleton while 20% is in the muscles. The muscle store seems to be the primary tissue affected in times of low magnesium intake. Because most of the magnesium in the body is tightly bound to apatite, this pool of magnesium can't be used in times of low intake. Therefore, the horse must meet its daily need of magnesium from the feed. But because calcium and magnesium are chemically alike, both ions use the same uptake and transport mechanisms in the body. We call it a competitive action. But as said before, calcium is regulated by hormones and vitamin D, so magnesium always comes off as a loser. From this we can postulate two theses. Magnesium deficiency can appear when magnesium intake is low or when calcium intake is high and magnesium intake is marginal.

The clinical picture is very variable but one symptom is always present. The horse is work intolerant because of muscle tiredness. Other symptoms that usually appear include hypersensitivity in the skin, muscle tremor, hot temperament when trained, intermittent severe hind leg lameness and paresis with the horse standing up but not able to move, or lying down unable to get up.

The diagnosis of magnesium deficiency is difficult, because serum magnesium only reflects recent magnesium intake, and does not tell us anything about the magnesium content in the muscles. When low magnesium intake has been present for a while, the body tries to compensate for the low intake and shuts off the urinary excretion of magnesium. If that has happened, the serum magnesium is normal to high despite low muscle content and low daily intake. Urine magnesium is a slightly better indicator of magnesium defeciency because low magnesium in the urine tells us that the low intake has been going on for a while. The best way for an accurate diagnosis is via muscle biopsy and analyses of magnesium concentration in the muscle tissue.

There are two ways to improve magnesium content in the muscles. First, of course, you have to increase the daily intake of magnesium. We do this by adding a few grams of magnesium oxide to the diet. At the same time, if possible, we lower the calcium intake if it is excessive. We have found that a calcium/magnesium ratio of 1.5-2.0:1 is ideal for the daily intake, with the higher value for maintenance and the lower for intense work. The quotient recommended by the NRC is 2.6-2.7:1. Comparisons between recommended daily intake levels of calcium and magnesium in Sweden and the US are shown in figures 4 and 5.

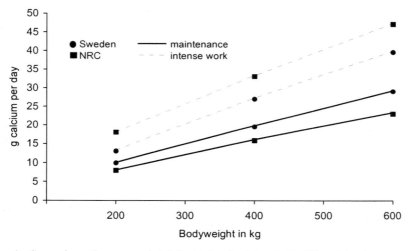

Figure 4. Comparison of recommended daily intake of calcium in the US and Sweden

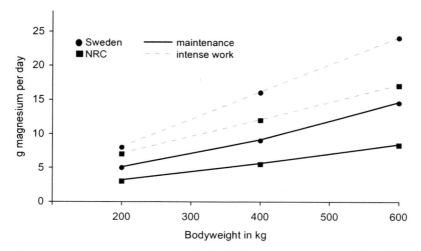

Figure 5. Comparison between recommended daily intake of magnesium in the US and Sweden

Excessive magnesium intake is not recommended. It alters the pH in the intestines and can cause serious problems with metabolic disorders and intestinal formation of concretions. For this reason also, magnesium phosphate should not be used as a feed additive.

Conclusions

Endurance horses are extreme athletes. As in all athletic activity with a long duration in either humans or animals, the feed is the difference between failure and success.

The duration of the energy sources is the vital point. Long time work also means large losses of sweat, and the water balance disturbance that goes with it. Waste products are created in large amounts and must be disposed of. Despite all this, there is a natural way to cope with all these postulations.

Try to provide the hindgut with fuel to keep the microbe activity at an optimum. Avoid large amounts of small intestinal energy, and use moderate protein levels. The protein must have a high small intestinal digestibility. Electrolytes are best provided as a natural part of the feed, in order to build a reservoir in the hindgut. Water must be provided unlimited. Use a structure and composition of the feed to make it pass the small intestines quickly, and feed the horse small amounts as often as possible to avoid large hormone and energy peaks.

This paper was first published in "Feeding the Performance Horse," Proceedings for the 1992 Short Course for Feed Manufacturers

FEEDING THE ENDURANCE HORSE

STEPHEN E. DUREN

Kentucky Equine Research, Inc., Versailles, Kentucky, USA

Introduction

To understand how to feed an endurance horse and ultimately how to manufacture a feed for endurance horses, it is necessary to understand the sport of endurance riding and the nutritional needs of the endurance horse. The following paper will provide a brief description of endurance riding while outlining the nutrition opportunities and critical nutrients for endurance horses. Finally, information will be presented on feeding management strategies and tips for manufacturing an endurance horse feed.

Endurance riding - the sport

The sport of endurance riding began many years ago as a pursuit by military groups to establish the "best" horse for cavalry purposes. The first modern endurance ride, held in 1955, was a one-day, 100-mile race from Lake Tahoe, California to Auburn, California. From this beginning, thousands of endurance rides are held annually throughout the world. Most endurance rides range in distance from 25 to 100-plus miles per day, over a multitude of different terrains. The ride with the reputation for being one of the most demanding is the "Tevis Cup." This one-day ride covers 100 miles through the Sierra Nevada Mountains with total changes in elevation amounting to nearly 40,000 feet (Figure 2).

The basic rules for endurance riding are simple: the first horse to finish, in acceptable condition, is the winner. There is no minimum amount of time allowed for the race, giving horse and rider the opportunity to set a quick pace. The rides are supervised by veterinarians and open to any breed of horse. Most breeds have been tried as endurance horses. Many competitive endurance horses are Arabian or Arabian crosses. Other breeds, including Thoroughbreds, Quarter Horses, Mustangs, Appaloosas, Morgans, Standardbreds and Mules, have been used successfully. Endurance horses have a physical look which could be described as small and wiry, without excessive muscling. Typical body weight measurements would be in the range of 850 to 1050 pounds. From a body condition standpoint, most endurance horses are moderately thin, resembling human endurance runners. The small, lightly muscled physique of endurance horses is advantageous both for reducing thermal load and for traveling up and down mountains.

The people involved in endurance riding also are unique. Any person who would ride a horse for 40 to 50 miles/week, and then ride for 100 miles on Saturday, could be classified as "determined." Endurance riders are very serious about both their horses and their sport. They have a genuine desire to do the best for their horses, and most feel that they have a personal bond with the animal. They have formed many of their nutrition opinions based on what others in the sport have told them, and on personal experience.

Nutritional opportunity

An endurance horse ridden at a medium trot (250 meters/min) could potentially complete a 25-mile endurance course in about 3 hours, a 50-mile endurance course in just over 5 hours and a 100-mile course in approximately 11 hours. Given these estimates for "competition time," a tremendous opportunity exists for nutrition to influence the performance of an endurance horse. In addition, endurance horses are routinely rested and fed during the ride further increasing the impact that proper nutrition would have on performance. Contrast this with the racing Quarter Horse which completes a 440 yard sprint in less than twenty seconds, or the competitive Thoroughbred racehorse which can complete a 1 1/4 mile race in just under two minutes. There have been volumes of information published regarding manipulating exercise performance in horses doing relatively short bouts of exercise. However, the real opportunity for a diet and dietary manipulation to influence performance lies in events which last longer than a few minutes.

The speed at which the exercise bout is performed also will influence the ability of diet to modify performance. In the case of short, intense (anaerobic) bouts of exercise, the animal is forced to generate energy for muscle contraction as fast as possible. This limits the type of fuel a muscle can utilize and the method by which the fuel is burned. The endurance horse, on the other hand, performs an extended exercise bout at a much slower (aerobic) speed. This provides an opportunity for the muscles to select a fuel and obtain the maximum energy production from that fuel. In endurance situations, fuel (feed) can actually be ingested, absorbed and circulated to the muscle for conversion to energy while the exercise is still being performed.

Critical nutrients

There are several key nutrients which will directly influence the performance capability of the endurance horse. These nutrients include: energy, electrolytes and water.

ENERGY

The main productive function in endurance horses is work. This work may vary from relatively slow speed exercise over long distances, common in 100-mile rides, to exercise conducted at faster speeds over the shorter (25- to 50-mile) endurance courses. Energy is the dietary nutrient which will directly influence whether an endurance horse can go the distance. Energy is not a nutrient per se, but rather a measure of a feed's potential to fuel body functions and muscle contraction during exercise. Muscle contraction, in turn, will move the legs and ultimately the horse across the ground during the ride. The endurance horse takes in, via the gastrointestinal tract (GI tract), a variety of feed types (fiber, starch, fat, protein) which can be used to fuel muscle contraction (Figure 1). Since horses are not able to eat continuously during a ride, feed must be digested and stored within the body to be used later as fuel during exercise. These different fuels are transferred between blood, liver, adipose tissue and the muscle cell. Stored energy in the form of muscle and liver glycogen (sugar), intramuscular and adipose triglycerides (fat) along with feed taken in during the ride will provide energy for muscle contraction.

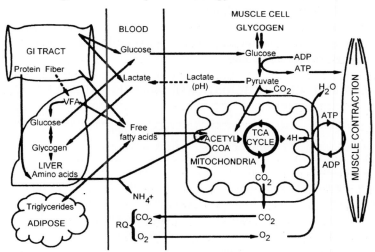

Figure 1. Feed types used to fuel muscle contraction (fiber, starch and protein).

For muscle contraction to occur, the chemically bound energy from feed must be converted into mechanical energy. This conversion process occurs in the muscle cell, and utilizes adenosine triphosphate (ATP) as the "currency" for muscle contraction (Figure 1.) The most direct method to form ATP is by the breakdown of another compound, creatine phosphate (CP). However, since muscle contains only a small amount each of CP and ATP, the supply of ATP is quickly depleted with the onset of exercise. For an endurance horse to exercise for a prolonged period of time, ATP must be resynthesized at the same rate at which it is being used. Two fundamental reactions resynthesize ATP: 1) Oxidative phosphorylation, breaking down carbohydrates, fats and protein, in the presence of oxygen, producing energy (ATP). The involvement of oxygen qualifies this as an aerobic reaction. 2) Glycolysis, breaking down glucose or glycogen into lactic acid. This reaction does not use oxygen and is considered anaerobic. There are several factors which will determine both the choice of fuel and the pathway used to generate ATP. These factors include: muscle fiber type, the speed and duration of exercise, type of feed provided, and animal fitness.

The horse has three basic types of muscle fiber (Table 1): Type I, IIA and IIB. These fiber types have different contractile and metabolic characteristics. Type I fibers are slow-contracting fibers while Types IIA and IIB are fast-contracting. Type I and IIA fibers have a high oxidative capacity and thus can utilize fuels aerobically while Type IIB fibers have a low aerobic capacity and depend on anaerobic glycolysis for energy generation. All three fiber types store glycogen, while only Types I and IIA have significant triglyceride storage. It is not surprising that different breeds of horses will have different percentages of the muscle fiber types. For example, racing Quarter Horses typically have more Type IIA and IIB fibers and fewer Type I fibers than Arabian horses. This would help explain why one breed, the Arabian, is known for endurance. Unfortunately, within a breed, the differences in muscle fiber type distribution are so small that muscle fiber typing as a predictor of performance is of limited value.

Table 1. METABOLIC CHARACTERISTICS OF DIFFERENT MUSCLE TYPES.

	Type I	*Type IIA*	*Type IIB*
Classification	*Slow twitch*	*Fast twitch high oxidative*	*Fast twitch*
Speed of contraction	slow	fast	fast
Maximum tension developed	low	high	high
Oxidative capacity	high	intermediate to high	low
Capillary density	high	intermediate	low
Lipid (fat) content	high	intermediate	low
Glycogen content	intermediate	high	high
Fatiguability	low	medium	high

The speed of muscle contraction determines how fast the animal is able to move. Since the amount of ATP used by a muscle depends directly on how fast it is contracting, the faster an animal moves the greater the ATP requirement. While walking, the muscles contract very slowly and expend relatively small amounts of ATP. During this type of exercise, Type I fibers are primarily recruited and energy generation is entirely aerobic. At this speed, the muscle burns predominantly fat. Fat stores are plentiful, and they can be mobilized fast enough to regenerate what ATP is used for muscle contraction. As speed increases from a walk to a trot to a canter, Type I fibers alone are no longer capable of contracting rapidly enough to propel the horse. At this point, Type IIA fibers are also recruited. These fibers are also aerobic, but they use a combination of glycogen and fat for energy generation.

Glycogen (glucose) can be metabolized twice as fast as fat for ATP generation, and as speed increases, fat becomes simply too slow a fuel for energy generation. As the horse increases speed to a fast gallop, Type IIB fibers are recruited and energy generation no longer remains purely aerobic. At these speeds, the requirement for ATP has exceeded the ability of the horse to deliver enough oxygen to the muscle to produce the energy by aerobic means. Anaerobic glycolysis takes over as a rapid metabolic pathway to generate ATP. Anaerobic glycolysis results, however, in lactic acid accumulation, and fatigue soon develops as the pH in the muscle begins to fall.

The speed at which endurance horses typically travel is within the range which can be maintained almost entirely through aerobic energy production. Only during the "controlled runaway" some riders use at the beginning of a ride, the "end of race" sprints and during hill climbing would the energy production shift toward anaerobic means and then, only for a short time. Therefore, fatigue in an endurance horse is much more likely to result from depletion of glycogen and/or triglyceride stores than lactic acid accumulation.

Dietary energy is usually expressed in terms of kilocalories (Kcal) or megacalories (Mcal) of digestible energy. Digestible energy (DE) refers to the amount of total energy in the diet that is actually absorbed by the horse. The DE requirements for different types of horses are calculated based on the horse's maintenance DE requirements plus the additional energy expended during exercise. Table 2 lists the amount of DE required above maintenance at various speeds. For example, a 450 kg (990 lb) endurance horse would have a maintenance DE requirement of 14.9 Mcal/day (DE = 1.4 + 0.03BW, NRC, 1989). Using the values in table 2, this same endurance horse ridden at a medium trot (250 meters/min) by a 75 kg (165 lb) rider for 3 hours, would have an additional energy requirement of 14.9 Mcal/day (Pagan and Hintz, 1986). The total energy requirement would be nearly 30 Mcal of DE/ day, a value the NRC, 1989, would classify as intense work. The total DE requirement (maintenance + exercise) can be provided by four different dietary energy sources: starch, fat, fiber and protein.

Table 2. DIGESTIBLE ENERGY (DE) REQUIREMENTS ABOVE MAINTENANCE AT VARIOUS SPEEDS

Gait	Speed (meters/min.)	DE (Mcal/Kg BW*/hr)
Slow walk	59	0.0017
Fast walk	95	0.0025
Slow trot	200	0.0065
Medium trot	250	0.0095
Fast trot/slow canter	300	0.0137
Medium Canter	350	0.0195

*Weight of horse plus rider and tack

STARCH

Starch, a carbohydrate composed of a large number of glucose (sugar) molecules, is the primary component of cereal grains, making up 50 to 70% of the grain's dry matter. Of the grains commonly fed to endurance horses, corn has the highest starch content, followed by barley and then oats. Horses break down starch into glucose units in the small intestine, where it is absorbed into the blood. Once in the blood, these glucose units can be used for a number of different purposes including: 1) being oxidized to produce ATP or 2) being used to make muscle glycogen, liver glycogen or body fat.

Starch is the dietary energy source of choice for glycogen synthesis. Starch digestion results in a direct rise in blood glucose and insulin, two of the most important factors involved in glycogen synthesis. Muscle glycogen is a versatile fuel for energy generation during endurance exercise, since glycogen can be metabolized either aerobically (with oxygen) or anaerobically (in the absence of oxygen). In addition, glycogen stored in the liver is available for the production and release of glucose into the blood during exercise. Maintaining blood glucose levels during exercise is of prime importance since glucose is the only fuel that is available to the central nervous system. In endurance horses, hypoglycemia (low blood sugar), as a result of prolonged exercise, can be a cause of fatigue.

FAT

Corn oil and soybean oil along with animal fat are the most common sources of fat in the horse's diet. These fat products contain roughly 2.25 times as much DE as an equal weight of corn, oats or barley. Numerous digestion studies have confirmed that fat is both very palatable and extremely well digested. Fat is a less versatile energy source than starch since it can only be oxidized aerobically to produce energy or be stored as body fat. Fatty acids, derived from fat metabolism, can not be converted to glucose or be used to synthesize glycogen.

Fat is, however, an extremely useful dietary energy source. Research studies have concluded that feeding fat to horses resulted in a greater mobilization and utilization of fat during long distance exercise (Pagan *et al.*, 1987). In essence, it appears horses trained their enzyme systems to utilize fat, thereby sparing the use of muscle and liver glycogen. Further, endurance horses in heavy training have a very high daily DE requirement. Often these endurance horses can not or will not eat enough feed to meet their energy requirements. The result is a steady decrease in body condition. In these instances, adding fat will increase the energy density of the diet so that less feed is required to maintain body weight. Hintz *et al.* (1978) did in fact report that endurance horse consuming fat-supplemented diets required less feed to maintain body weight.

FIBER

Fiber (hay/pasture) is an energy source that is often overlooked in horse nutrition. Horses have a highly developed hindgut which houses billions of bacteria capable of fermenting large quantities of plant fiber. Volatile fatty acids (VFA's), the endproduct of fiber fermentation, are absorbed from the hindgut and transported to the liver. Once in the liver, VFA's can be converted to glucose and be stored as liver glycogen or be converted to fat, and be used to fortify the body's fat stores. Fiber, therefore, can be used as an energy source throughout the endurance ride since fermentation of fiber and absorption of VFA's continues long after a meal has been eaten.

An endurance horse's intestinal health is critical to success. Normally, the digestive system of the horse is active, moving feed ingredients through the length of the tract. Inactivity of the digestive system, due to dehydration and/or electrolyte imbalances, can cause severe colic and even death. Research conducted in Germany (Meyer *et al.*, 1987) has underscored the importance of fiber in maintaining gut health. Their experiments have shown that a diet high in fiber resulted in an increased water intake. Further, animals supplemented with a simple hay and salt diet had 73% more water in their digestive tracts after exercise and approximately 33% more available electrolytes than animals on a low fiber diet. The additional water and electrolytes in the digestive tract of the high fiber animals is probably due to the high water holding capacity of plant fiber. More importantly, the water and electrolyte pool created by a high fiber diet can be used to combat dehydration and electrolyte imbalances which derail so many endurance horses. Another important attribute of a digestive system full of fiber is maintenance of blood flow to the digestive system during exercise. The physical presence of fiber in the digestive system will help insure that blood is not totally diverted away from the digestive system with the onset of exercise. Duren (1990) reported the percentage of cardiac output (blood flow) distributed to the digestive system was higher in fed ponies compared to fasted ponies during exercise. For an endurance horse, maintenance of blood flow to the digestive system will aid in the ability of gut tissue to remain active and could prevent colic.

Fiber in the form of hay/pasture has been discussed as an excellent energy source for endurance horses. In addition to forage fiber sources, there are so-called "super fibers." These super fibers have the same beneficial aspects of forage fibers for maintaining gut health and fluid and electrolyte balance, but contain more energy. The additional energy is the result of both a high fiber content and a low lignin (non-digestible fiber) component. Therefore, these ingredients have more fiber which is available for microbial digestion. These super fibers (e.g. beet pulp, soybean hulls, almond hulls, oat hulls) contain energy equivalent to oats and barley, but they would be safer to feed because they do not produce the symptoms of grain overload.

PROTEIN

If the protein intake of an endurance horse exceeds its requirement, then the extra protein can be used as a source of energy. The amino acids associated with the extra protein are broken down by the liver, and the nitrogen is excreted as ammonia. The carbon skeletons that are left can be oxidized to produce ATP or used to make glucose or fat. Excessive protein intake should be avoided in endurance horses for a number of reasons. First, water requirements increase with increased protein intake. This can be devastating for endurance horses which typically struggle to maintain proper hydration. Second, accumulation of nitrogen end-products (ammonia and urea) in the blood can lead to nerve irritability and disturbances in intestinal function and carbohydrate metabolism. Further, increased ammonia excretion in the urine may lead to respiratory problems associated with ammonia buildup in the stall.

ELECTROLYTES AND WATER

Energy metabolism within the body is not 100% efficient. A certain amount of energy is lost from each chemical reaction in the form of heat. In order for the horse to remain healthy and continue to exercise, excess heat must be dissipated from the body. If the horse is unable to rid itself of this heat, body temperature can rise to the point where it becomes life-threatening. For horses, the main route of heat dissipation is through a form of evaporative cooling known as sweating. In evaporative cooling, the sweat gland takes fluid from the circulatory system and secretes it out to the surface of the skin. Once the hot fluid (sweat) is on the skin, it spreads out and evaporates. This takes heat away from the body. Unfortunately, sweating also takes water and electrolytes away from the body.

As water is lost from the blood, the remaining blood becomes thicker. This increased blood viscosity, decreases perfusion potential, and negatively influences tissue oxygenation. With intense exercise, water loss can become so extreme that blood volume is decreased and further sweating is not possible. If the horse is not re-hydrated, death from heat stroke will occur. The National Research Council (NRC, 1989) has cited research that indicates non-working horses require 2-3 liters of water/kg of dry matter intake. This would equate to 20-30 liters (6 to 8 gallons) of water for a 1000 lb. horse. It is thought that exercise conducted in a hot, humid environment may increase the water requirement by 300 percent (Lucke and Hall, 1978 as cited by the NRC, 1989), giving a total water requirement of 90 liters (24 gallons).

Electrolytes are substances that dissociate in solution into electrically charged particles called ions. In horses, electrolytes play an important role in maintaining osmotic pressure, fluid balance and nerve and muscle activity. During exercise, sodium (Na^+), potassium (K^+), chloride (Cl^-), calcium (Ca^{++}) and magnesium

(Mg++) are lost in the feces, urine and sweat. Loss of these electrolytes causes fatigue and muscle weakness, and decreases the thirst response to dehydration. Therefore, it is vital to replenish electrolyte losses in competitive endurance horses. For a detailed discussion of electrolytes, exhaustion, and the performance horse, see *Tied Up With Electrolytes - Or Not?* by Pat Harris contained herein.

Feeding management strategies

FORAGE

Of the feeds offered to endurance horses, forage is by far the most important. Horses have evolved as grazing animals and have a unique ability to take in large amounts of forage (up to 3.5% of body weight). The horse, in concert with the bacteria in the hindgut, utilize this forage primarily for energy production. The ability of the horse to effectively utilizes forages is evident if one considers that many horses are maintained on all-forage (hay/pasture) diets. Occasionally, a competitive endurance horse can be maintained solely on good quality pasture, but this is certainly the exception and not the rule. In addition to being a steady source of energy for the endurance horse, forage is essential to maintain intestinal health. A diet containing large amounts of good quality fiber can increase the water consumption, and provide a reservoir for both water and electrolytes. This water and electrolyte reservoir can be utilized throughout the ride to minimize dehydration and electrolyte imbalances. Finally, the presence of fiber in the digestive system can help insure that blood is being distributed to the digestive system during the ride. This maintenance of blood flow to the digestive system will aid in the ability of gut tissue to remain active and could help prevent colic.

A logical question often asked is "What type of forage do I feed my endurance horse?" To actually determine which hay to buy, one should consider the fiber, digestible energy (DE), protein and calcium content of the hay. First, to prevent digestive upset, it is absolutely essential to provide the horse's hindgut with an adequate source of digestible fiber. This would mean maximizing the use of good quality hay/pasture with a high NDF value and a low ADF value. Second, the digestibility and thus the DE content of any given plant decreases with maturity. Therefore, horse owners should avoid feeding extremely mature forages. Since endurance horses 1) do not have high protein requirements, and 2) have to expend energy and use extra water to get rid of excess protein, select a hay with a lower protein content (8% to 14% as-fed). Finally, since chronic over-supplementation with calcium can cause problems with endurance horses, avoid high calcium hays. With these selection criteria, the endurance horse would be well suited with free-choice access to a good quality grass hay. A mixed alfalfa/grass hay is also acceptable provided it is predominantly grass.

GRAIN CONCENTRATES

Most competitive endurance horses are unable to maintain body weight on all forage diets. These horses need additional sources of energy that come in the form of starch, fat, fiber and protein. These energy sources are found in most commercial grain concentrates. With the information presented in this paper outlining the benefits of starch for energy production, it may sound like "the more starch the better." This is not the case. There is a limit to the amount of starch which an endurance horse's diet should contain. If a large amount of starch is fed in a single meal (ie. greater than 5 lbs of grain/meal), the small intestine's ability to digest and absorb the starch may be overwhelmed, and a substantial amount of the starch may pass into the large intestine. Once in the large intestine (cecum, colon), a cascade of reactions occur which can result in laminitis (founder) or colic.

There also is a limit to the amount of fat which can be added to the diet. First, from a palatability standpoint, horses will indicate when they have reached their peak level of fat intake by refusing to eat the feed. The threshold level of fat necessary to reach this stage varies with the horse and the type of fat; however, grain concentrates with over 20% added fat (top-dressed) are prone to feed refusal. The other limitation on the amount of fat that can be added to the diet occurs in situations where calories from fat are replacing calories from starch. These high fat, low starch diets can limit the amount of starch available for glycogen synthesis and actually decrease liver and muscle glycogen stores (Pagan et al., 1987). Grain concentrates which have between 7 and 10% added fat appear optimum for endurance horses. To obtain the best results with the addition of fat to the diet, begin adding the fat during the conditioning phase of training and continue throughout the season. This will expose the muscles to high levels of fat and condition the body to use fat as an energy source. The combination of dietary fat and fitness will allow endurance horses a greater mobilization and utilization of fat during long distance exercise. The addition of fat only on "race days" will be of limited value.

Just as there were limitations in the amount of starch and fat appropriate for endurance horses, so are there limits on the amount of protein. The actual protein requirement for the endurance horse is only about 8 to 10% of the total diet. This is much lower than is actually fed to endurance horses because there are few ingredients that are this low in protein. For example, corn is around 9% protein, oats 11.5%, timothy hay 10% and alfalfa hay 15 - 20% protein. Therefore, it is not practical to restrict protein intake to the horse's actual requirement. Instead, protein content of the ration should be monitored and not allowed to become extremely high.

TIME OF FEEDING

Specific information relating time of feeding prior to exercise with endurance horse performance is not available. Research efforts have mainly concentrated on time of feeding prior to a relatively short bout of exercise. In these studies, a diet is typically fed at a given time prior to exercise and blood indicators of metabolism and stress are monitored throughout the exercise protocol. Pagan *et al.* (1995) have demonstrated changes in plasma glucose and plasma insulin prior to and during exercise as a result of feeding time. These differences in plasma metabolites did not result in any marked differences in exercise performance. Further, Stull and Rodiek (1995) reported the composition of the diet and the timing of the meal prior to exercise can be manipulated to influence glucose availability in the blood before and during exercise. However, stress measurements (lactate and cortisol) did not respond to feeding time. Both of these studies are interesting since they were able to change plasma glucose levels as a result of pre-exercise feeding. However, it is possible the duration of the exercise protocol was not long enough to see a difference in stress. With endurance horses, the exercise protocol would definitely be long enough to determine the affect of feeding. In addition, endurance horses are fed at rest points during the ride so time of feeding and the composition of the meal may have a dramatic influence on exercise performance. Kentucky Equine Research is currently working on the design of an experiment which could evaluate feeding time prior to exercise in endurance horses.

Manufacturing an endurance feed

To manufacture a grain concentrate for endurance horses, several points need to be addressed. First, the energy content of the feed is probably the most important factor. Energy should be available from a combination of sources. Fortification with processed starch in the form of cracked corn, rolled barley or crimped oats will be the basis of the feed. Addition of energy in the form of vegetable oil or a quality animal fat product is the next step. Finished grain concentrates for endurance horses should contain between 7 and 10% fat. With the many benefits that fiber has both for energy production and for maintenance of proper digestive function, inclusion of additional fiber is justified. Adding any one, or a combination of, the "Super Fibers" (beet pulp, soybean hulls, almond hulls or oat hulls) at a rate of 10 to 40% would be beneficial. The next criterion the finished grain concentrate will be judged on is protein content. For endurance horses, high protein and high performance do not go together. Finished grain concentrates, therefore, should contain 12% protein or less. Electrolytes would seem like an obvious group of minerals to add to an endurance horse feed. Unfortunately, most endurance riders have worked out their own schemes for dosing horses with electrolytes. This eliminates the need to put a lot of time into figuring out proper electrolyte inclusion in grain concentrates. The addition of plain salt at a rate of 0.5% is adequate. Other nutrients which warrant consideration include: vitamin E, selenium, and B-vitamins. Vitamin E and selenium are both involved in antioxidant reactions within the body. Vitamin E should be added at a rate of 100 IU/lb of finished feed, with selenium adjusted to provide 0.3 ppm of total diet. A B-vitamin package should be added to the grain concentrate to account for any potential deficiencies which may occur due to stress. These products are water soluble and safe to add. Finally, the total grain concentrate must be balanced for other essential nutrients including vitamins and minerals.

If manufacturing a complete (forage + grain) pellet for endurance horses is your intention, the energy and protein content of the product is critical. It is essential that enough grain (starch) be included in these products to raise the energy content. A product with approximately 30% grain with added fat should be appropriate. The protein content of this product should not exceed 14%, so use alfalfa sparingly. Finally, most endurance riders do not like to feed pelleted products. The conception that only "trash" goes into pellets is alive and well in endurance riding circles. Therefore, pelleted products will take a bit more marketing skill. The United States Forest Service is doing their part to help you market these products by requiring that feed used in the "back country" be certified as weed seed free. The pelleting process is recognized by the Forest Service as a method to control weed seeds. Therefore, any pelleted horse feed is currently acceptable in the National Forest.

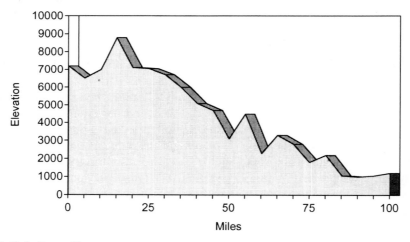

Figure 2. Tevis Cup profile map

References

Duren, S.E., 1990. Blood flow distribution in fasted and fed ponies at rest and during endurance exercise. Ph.D. Dissertation, University of Kentucky.

Hintz, H.F., M.W. Rose, F.R. Lesser, P.F. Leids. K.K. White, J.E. Lowe, C.E. Short and H.F. Schryver, 1978. The value of dietary fat for working horses I. Biochemical and Hematological evaluations. J. Equine Med. Surg. 2:483.

Meyer, H., H. Perez, Y. Gomda and M. Heilmann, 1987. Postprandial renal and recal water and electrolyte excretion in horses in relation to kind of feedstuffs, amount of sodium ingested and exercise. In: Proceedings of the 10th Equine Nutrition and Physiology Symposium. p. 67.

N.R.C., 1989. Nutrient requirements of horses. 5th revised edition. National Academy Press, Washington, DC.

Pagan, J.D., B. Essen-Gustavson, A. Lindholm and J. Thornton, 1987. The efect of dietary energy source on exercise performance in Standardbred horses. In: Equine Exercise Physiology 2. J.R. Gillespie and N.E. Robinson (Editors) p. 686.

Pagan, J.D., I. Burger and S.G. Jackson, 1995. The influence of time of feeding on exercise response in Thoroughbreds fed a fat supplemented or high carbohydrate diet. In: Proceedings of the 14th Equine Nutrition and Physiology Symposium. p. 92.

Pagan, J.D. and H.F. Hintz, 1986. Equine energetics II. Energy expenditure in horses during submaximal exercise. J. Animal Science 63:822.

Stull, C.L. and A.V. Rodiek, 1995. Effects of postprandial interval and feed components on stress parameters in exercising Thoroughbreds. In: Proceedings of the 14th Equine Nutrition and Physiology Symposium. p. 17.

This paper was first published in "Recent Advances in Equine Nutrition," Proceedings for the 1995 Short Course for Feed Manufacturers

FEEDING AND FITTING: THE HALTER AND SALES HORSE

STEPHEN G. JACKSON
Kentucky Equine Research, Versailles, Kentucky, USA

There are two groups of horses that are assessed and therefore valued to a large extent on their looks, conformation and the way they are "turned out"; the halter or "in hand" horse and the sales horse. There are vast sums of money riding in the balance that literally can be made or lost depending on the job that the feeder and fitter does. We have all heard the adage "fat is a pretty color" and that sales and halter horses are simply fed all they want to eat and gotten too fat. In the modern sales and show arena simply fat is far from being enough. To be really successful in fitting sales horses and halter horses the "fitter" must be able to differentiate between fit and fat.

It may come as a surprise that one would consider the western halter horse and the Thoroughbred sales weanling and yearling in the same context. But let's face it, the horse sale is a horse show and many times horses are worth more on sale day than they will be the rest of their lives. Fitting these horses is a combination of superior nutrition, superior health management, superior and specific exercise and superior genetics, tempered with more hard work and attention to detail than most people are willing to do (that is why sales agents and halter horse trainers have a job). In the following paper I will outline what has worked for me in the preparation of halter babies for futurities, halter horses for the major Quarter Horse shows, and in the preparation of sales weanlings, yearlings and broodmares for the major Thoroughbred sales. In consideration of this topic I specifically cast anabolic steroids in a very negative light as I see them as unnecessary, unethical and detrimental to the long term utility of the horse.

The weanling

Fitting a weanling is perhaps the biggest challenge of all. When one prepares a weanling for a show or sale it is critical to understand the nutrient requirements of the horse and the critical balance between feed intake and exercise as they impact on condition and soundness. Fitting the weanling for halter futurities may, in fact, be more difficult than fitting the sales weanling since most of the major weanling futurities are earlier in the year than are the weanling sales and there is more emphasis on overall fitness at futurities than there is at the sales. The weanling feeding program should be based on a balanced ration using palatable, easily assimilated nutrient sources that meet the weanling's requirements for protein, energy, minerals and vitamins. All too often people fall into the trap of feeding all-grain feeds to weanlings that may encourage fattening but do little to insure optimum growth and bone development. It is crucial that people understand that "high" protein does not cause bone problems! and in fact more cases of acquired flexural deformities and metabolic bone disease are caused by improper mineral balance and over feeding energy than from any other nutritional cause. The amount of feed that an individual foal/weanling will tolerate is extremely dependent upon the individual and it is crucial to adjust individual feeding levels based on individual performance (growth rate and degree of fatness). I would usually expect to be feeding a light horse (Quarter horse, Thoroughbred, Paint, Appaloosa) weanling intended for the futurity or weanling sales a minimum of 1 lb of feed per month of age right up until the time of the futurity. In general one would be best served to feed a 16 - 18 % protein concentrate to these horses in addition to really good quality hay that was harvested in early stages of maturity. I prefer a heavy mixed alfalfa hay for these horses as this maximizes the utilization of fibrous feeds in meeting the energy requirements of these horses and as such decreases the amount of starch the weanling has to deal with. Also, in using a high quality, early cut hay one tends to minimize the appearance of gut-fill that is often associated with a hay of high lignin content. In selecting the appropriate concentrate feed for the weanling it is important that the total nutrient profile of the feed be considered, not just the protein concentration. All too often, due to formulation errors on the part of the feed manufacturer or misuse of a feed (primarily cutting sweet feed with oats) by the consumer, the nutrient calorie ratio of grain mixes fed to weanlings is all wrong. Consumers should be educated to the fact that the nutrient profile of a feed designed for a specific class of horses is critical and that by "tinkering" with a feed this critical balance of nutrients is destroyed. Similarly, feeds formulated for older horses do not get the job done with respect to macro and micro-mineral intake when fed at appropriate levels to meet the young horse's energy requirements.

Beyond the feed trough the real art involved in fitting weanlings is the exercise and "rubbing" they receive. Although I am not an advocate of longeing for the sales or show weanling under 5 months of age, I think that judicious use of longeing, free longeing ("round-penning"), ponying and hand walking can be very useful tools depending on the individual. Foals run, romp and play nearly from birth, and to think that a careful program of forced exercise is detrimental and risky is folly. Daily grooming, rinsing with warm water, braiding or banding of manes and conditioning of tails are all necessary for weanlings if optimum fitness is to be achieved. With respect to turn-out there are several factors to be considered and somewhat of a difference between what works for the sales weanling and what works for the show weanling. In general, turn-out for the futurity baby works to a limited extent. If feed intake is limited and weanlings are turned out on good pasture, they tend to get a little belly on them; on the other hand, if weanlings are turned out in the evening after the strong sun for a little time on good pasture or in barren paddocks, this time out can be very effective in encouraging exercise. One must let the individual serve as a guide in this respect. Some halter futurity babies will tolerate pasture turnout and some will not. For sales weanlings this appears to be a little less critical as it is more acceptable for sales weanlings to carry both a little hair and a little belly.

Sales and show weanlings should be blanketed as soon as night temperatures drop to below 50 degrees. In many cases the blanket and hood serve to make the hair lay, as much as to make the hair remain short. It seems that hair growth and shedding for the weanling are somewhat heritable as is hair quality in general. The use of artificial lights may be of value in some programs. Day length should remain a constant 15 hours through the use of lights if they are to be used. One negative aspect of the use of lights for weanlings is that they appear to become refractory to the lights over time (in other words, you can only fool mother nature for so long). In the past I have had weanlings under lights that as yearlings were a real challenge to get fit the next spring. I guess if someone else buys the weanling this is their problem but if for one reason or another the weanling does not sell, the problem then becomes mine. For the above reason, I would suspect that more people are not using lights on weanlings than are using them.

Weanlings should be on a rigorous deworming program. Weanlings should be dewormed every 30 - 60 days alternating between anthelmintics. Although I would most frequently use purge de-wormers, there are instances when I have used Strongid C for horses that I can't get to slip hair or that appear to be dull and that do not want to put on any condition.

Show and sale weanlings should receive at least 2 oz of added fat per feeding and I have used as much as 9 oz. of fat per day in some instances when it was critical that more energy intake be achieved without increasing starch (grain) intake. If horses are gradually adjusted to fat intake, a great deal of energy may be fed to the weanling in the form of fat. Other useful nutritional tools include using beet pulp in the ration and selecting for very immature hays that have maximum digestibility .

The last thought for the weanling deals with weaning time. In general I have found 5 months of age to be the most ideal time to wean, all things considered. However, I really like to let the individual weanling tell me when to wean. If a weanling is top-heavy and too fat or starts to get erect in the pasterns or show severe physitis, I have no qualms about weaning as early as 3 months of age so that I can carefully control nutrient intake. Additionally, late August or early September futurities present a unique problem especially for April and later foals. My general rule of thumb is that I will wean a foal at least 45 days before a futurity or if that is too early for late foals I will wean 5 days before a futurity. Forty-five days gives me adequate time to get the weanling over the post-weaning slump and into good shape, and five days pre-futurity weaning does not give the weanling time to fall apart. Although some people take mares and foals to the horse show together, I will not do so!

Identify your horse **and feed accordingly**

Big, scopy, precocious individuals
The type that almost preps himself. Keep him out of the sun and avoid injuries. On 8- to 10-pounds of grain, good hay, and moderate exercise, he will be an attractive addition to any consignment.

Weedy individuals
The type of individual that requires as much energy as possible in order to gain condition for sale. This type of horse will need additional daily feedings, and alternate forms of energy, like oil and beet pulp, should be considered.

Fat individuals
The type of horse that stays fat no matter how much you limit their intake. They need to maintain their intake of roughage, and a pelleted supplement may be used to satisfy protein requirements. Controlled exercise is needed.

Feeding and fitting the yearling

Yearlings in some ways are easier to fit than weanlings. Since we are in most cases talking about horses that are at least 12 months of age there are fewer skeletal wrecks that we can precipitate when we start our fitting or "prep" program. In discussion of the fitting process it is appropriate that we start with the feeding program. Yearlings do best on a 13-14% protein ration balanced for macro and micro-minerals and fat and water soluble vitamins. Feeding rates for yearlings are extremely variable depending on growth history, skeletal size, individual metabolism, actual age in months and availability and quality of forage. In the preparation of sales yearlings I have seen feed intakes range from 2#/day of a supplement pellet (i.e., KER ALLPHASE) to 16#/day of a fortified sweet or pelleted feed. Most generally it seems to take more feed to get a colt fit than it does for a filly. The real key here is realization that "the eye of the master fattens the ox." What works in the feeding program for one yearling may totally miss the mark for another! Comments made concerning hay type and quality for the weanling apply to the yearling as well.

Besides the base feed, there are some tools of the trade that fall into the nutrition category. First, I always use some supplemental fat. I have used vegetable oil alone or a mixture of vegetable oil and animal fat (i.e., Fat Pak 100 from Milk Specialties).

I think that using at least 4 oz. per day of an unsaturated fat high in essential fatty acids (linoleic, linoleic and arachidonic acids) is preferable to using only saturated fats. The manner in which the fat is provided in the diet is a choice for the horseman but in many instances it makes more sense to top-dress the fat rather than use a fat added feed. As for the "grain" portion of the ration, the amount of fat that is appropriate to use is going to be highly individual. This is due to the fact that there are two main reasons that we are using fat to begin with. First there is the hair effect and second there is the energy effect. The hair effect is easy, 2 oz per day of vegetable fat. The energy source rationale is the interesting application of fat and also beet pulp (to be discussed below). My use of high levels of fat intake in the yearling is to reduce the amount of starch that must be fed to achieve a specified energy intake. When I reach 10 lbs of feed intake in the yearling I start to really consider the advantages of supplemental fat. I have had big, rugged, raw boned yearlings on as much as 12 oz. of vegetable oil per day with absolutely no detrimental effect.

In addition to fat, many of my prep and show rations will contain beet pulp. Unlike the weanling, there is a real possibility of laminitis and starch over-load colic in the yearling. By using beet pulp as a feed ingredient, one can reduce the amount of starch that a horse has to consume while keeping at relatively high levels of energy intake. It is probable that beet pulp, a source of readily digestible fiber, is digested predominantly in the hind-gut and absorbed as volatile fatty acids therefore reducing the starch/glucose load, the amount of starch that may enter the cecum un-digested, and contributing to the maintenance of cecal homeostasis. All of these results are positive! Most rations that I use would contain 10% beet pulp (shreds, not pellets) and I have gone as high as 25% beet pulp in the concentrate ration. NOTE: At least for a time one will notice loose feces in many horses that are put on beet pulp. This increase in fecal moisture is totally innocuous and usually does not persist more than a week. Certainly I would rather have a horse a "little loose" than a "little tight."

For other ages and classes of sales and halter horses the feeding and fitting techniques are the same as for the weanling and yearling. Emphasis should always be placed on the individual in terms of feed intake levels and exercise programs. The goal should be individual fitness. That takes an individually tailored feeding and fitting program. It is critical to understand that fit and fat are not the same and that lots of feed without a concomitant increase in the exercise program results in a horse that is patchy in its fat cover and more prone to disorders of the gut such as colic, laminitis and enterotoxemia.

Fitting tools

The essentials of fitting halter and sale horses really only start with the feed bucket. Hair quality and athletic appearance are crucial if a professional appearance is to be achieved. The exercise program that one uses to get horses fit may be very different from farm to farm and indeed even from horse to horse. I feel like the most useful tool on a sales prep or training operation is a covered round pen. I prefer a pen that is round and a minimum of 50 feet in diameter. The ground surface needs to be very forgiving and absorb concussion effectively. For this application I would opt for sand, tanbark or shredded rubber over a gravel base (class I sand works well for a base). The surface should be a minimum of 6 inches deep. If this kind of forgiving surface is used the occurrence of splints and other exercise stress related blemishes can be minimized. Even though my preference is for a covered round pen, open topped pens can be very effective in some parts of the country especially with a little thought about drainage prior to construction of the pen. It should be pointed out that there are many uses for a covered round pen. Mares and foals can spend their first day "outside" in these structures especially in inclement weather, they can be used for post-surgical turnouts, turnouts for horses off the track before they go to larger pastures or paddocks, stallions can be exercised in them, if tanbark is used as a surface they make excellent breeding sheds and so on and so on.

Once the exercise area is built, design of the exercise program is the next order of business. I personally favor a free longeing or loose-line exercise program. It is *critical* that the person doing the longeing understand the importance of controlling the session. If a longe line is used it should remain loose and one should avoid putting pressure on the horse's head. When the head is pulled to the center of the circle, undue pressure is put on the inside leg and there is a much greater chance of "popping" splints. Horses should always have splint boots on while being longed. I generally start horses on the longeing program at the walk but do not go ballistic if they want to jog or trot some. The initial session will be five minutes duration in both directions. It is crucial that horses be worked the same amount of time in both directions every time that they work. Over a period of a week I will work weanlings up to seven minutes both directions and yearlings up to 10 minutes both directions. I always start in each direction with a minute of walking and then move to a long trot. I have found that a square, two-beat trot is safer and easier on the legs than is the canter. Older horses may be worked longer as fitness levels increase and body condition dictates.

Other possibilities for exercise techniques include hand walking, ponying, swimming, use of a mechanical horse walker and treadmilling. The traditional method of choice for fitting Thoroughbred yearlings is hand walking. I have always been of the opinion that the main fitness achieved using this methodology occurs in the person doing the walking rather than in the horse. However, there are some horses that for one reason or another cannot take a more rigorous exercise program. Horses are walked from twenty minutes to an hour each at a brisk walk and where possible, up and down hills. I have one friend that walks his yearlings 5 miles each at a brisk walk. Last year all of his help quit him and he prepared 7 yearlings for the sales by himself. You better believe that he was a fit son of a gun when he got finished. One positive aspect of hand-walking is that the horses are really taught to lead! Lead ponies are really effective for fitting sales horses and halter horses if one has an appropriate place to pony the horses. Horses may be ponied at the walk and the trot and if the pasture or paddock is big enough the yearling can be ponied in a straight line avoiding the lateral torque on the legs which may occur when some other methods are used. Swimming is beyond the reach of most people but is effective for sales or show horses that may have borderline soundness. Mechanical horse walkers are used in many parts of the country very effectively in a manner much the same as the covered round pen. The main difference is that horses are usually only walked and not trotted on the walker. One disadvantage of the walker is the tendency for horses that have been fit on a walker to drag along when being led. Treadmills are great tools if used judiciously. I think that horses can be fit very effectively on the treadmill at the walk and trot and the newer, high speed treadmills are fairly easy on a horse's legs. When we use a treadmill for fitting yearlings or show horses, we use sessions of five minutes to begin with and if the treadmill is adjustable, a 6% incline. One personal observation concerning the use of the treadmill is the tendency for horses to roll their shoulders rather than really breaking cleanly over and bending their knees. As with any exercise method, one should be alert to changes in the feet and legs which may indicate an impending soundness problem or blemish. Common problems which necessitate reducing work load or backing completely off the exercise program include: splints, windpuffs, thoroughpins, joint effusion (swelling) in any joint but particularly the ankles, hocks and stifles, active physitis, foot soreness, tendinitis or any signs of lameness. It is essential that horses that are receiving a great deal of feed be exercised every day. People seem to be inclined to think that exertional rhabdomyolysis (tying up) is strictly a problem affecting performance horses but there are a significant number of halter horses that tie up due to the large starch intakes that are characteristic for these horses and due to the tendency for people to skip exercise days therefore setting a horse up for a management induced episode of tying up. Another caution for horses being prepared for halter competition and sales is heat stress. Because most of these horses are fit in the summer months, heat stress and even heat stroke are real possibilities. Careful observation of the horse can prevent this problem. Horses that are not sweating when worked hard should be stopped immediately. This is particularly true in areas where anhidrosis is common.

During and after an exercise bout is an ideal time to work on conformational deficits. Horses with thick cresty necks should be exercised in a neck sweat and then be tied in the stall after exercise for a cooling out period. The shape of a horse's neck and therefore the balance of a horse can be improved significantly using a sweat. Likewise, there are individuals that may benefit from a throatlatch sweat or even a full shoulder sweat. Horses that are particularly coarse in the throat benefit from wearing a throat collar all of the time (care should be taken that the mane is protected from the collar when these are used). Another quite useful tool for fitting horses is a set of side-reins and a bitting rig. Horses with thin weedy necks, ewe necked horses and horses that appear to have their necks put on upside down (thin on top and a belly to the neck below) should be exercised in side-reins. This makes the horse arch the neck and can significantly change the appearance of the shoulder and neck. When reins are first used they should be adjusted loosely and only after the horse has worn them a couple of times should they be tightened and the horse be made to really go to work.

Now the most important and most neglected part of fitting the horse, RUB TIME. If a really good hair coat is to be achieved, horses must be groomed vigorously on a daily basis. I find that immediately following exercise is a good time for an initial grooming. If you don't sweat grooming a horse then you are probably not doing a good job! The best tool for the job is a small (about the size of the hand) flexible rubber curry. The horse should be thoroughly and vigorously curried all over the body and then a medium soft brush should be used followed by a rub rag. Most horses should have one good grooming per day followed by a light "knock-off" later. I usually will give a horse a bath with plain water daily and use a mild soap one time per week. Manes should be washed and unruly manes should be braided or banded to get them to lay smooth. Tails should *not* be brushed unless plenty of Show-Sheen is used first and the tail is completely dry. Then, prior to brushing they should be picked out by hand and then put in a loose braid and bagged. Usually once a horse is fit the only time the tail is really picked and brushed thoroughly is on the morning of a show. Yearlings and weanlings that are turned out in groups should have their tails treated with something that is unpalatable to other yearlings (one of the best is a paste made from fish oil and cayenne pepper). There is nothing that detracts more from the balance and symmetry of a yearling than a chewed off tail. Regular foot care is also a must for horses to be shown at halter and for sale horses. I would generally show weanlings and yearlings unshod and other horses shod all the way around. By convention, Thoroughbred sales horses are shod in front and barefoot behind with the exception of weanlings which are sold barefoot and two-year-old in training horses which are sold shod all the way around. Even though biotin, zinc and methionine supplementation may help some horses with bad feet, nothing can take the place of regular trimming in terms of producing a good foot on a sales or show horse.

Obviously there are as many tricks of the trade as there are trainers and what techniques work for some may not work for others. The important thing is to design a program and stick to it. Modifications may be necessary along the way but the critical aspect of getting this job done is daily attention to detail. One should not get caught in the trap of thinking that there is some magical feed ingredient that is going to turn a sow's ear into a silk purse. Great genetics, good feed and hard work beat steroids, poor genetics and lack of preparation every time.

This paper was first published in "Recent Advances in Equine Nutrition," Proceedings for the 1995 Short Course for Feed Manufacturers

FEEDING THE WESTERN PERFORMANCE HORSE

STEPHEN G. JACKSON

Kentucky Equine Research Inc., Versailles, Kentucky, USA

Summary

Feeding the western performance horse in a manner consistent with nutrient requirements is predominantly a function of properly identifying energy needs. This class of performance horses may have energy requirements ranging from maintenance to energy requirements similar to those of the race horse in intense training. Although energy is not the only nutrient for which there is an increase in requirement as work intensity increases, for many of the other nutrients increased requirements associated with work are met simply by increasing feed intake to meet the increased requirement for energy. In reality the main nutrients other than energy that must be dealt with specifically are electrolytes, trace minerals, and vitamin E.

Introduction

Western performance horses in the US probably are the most numerous of the performance horses being ridden and trained. Activities and level of work intensity within an event or activity vary widely from the recreational western pleasure horse to the professional reining horse or NCHA caliber cutting horse. As such, accurate identification of nutrient needs is sometimes difficult. For example, the amount of feed necessary for the very solid non-pro reining horse may be totally inadequate for a horse in intense reining training headed for the Derby or Futurity. It is necessary to try to group these horses by event and work intensity to establish a base-line set of feeding recommendations and make adjustments depending on individuality, actual response to work and training and on the role that forage plays in the overall feeding program. To do this I have taken the liberty of dividing the typical western event into light, medium and intense categories of work and have then given a best estimate of the requirements for these levels of work. Due to the critical role that forage plays in any horse's diet, I have separately discussed forage and have tried to reinforce that when talking about specific classes of horses. Finally, I would be remiss if I did not mention body style when discussing the feeding programs for some of these performance horses since nutrition plays such a large role in the perceived frame that these horses go in.

The forage component

The loss of horses in the western performance horse industry to colic and laminitis is large. These losses are due in large part to the failure of the horseman and trainer to realize the critical aspect of adequate fiber in the horse's diet. Not only can fibrous feeds meet a large portion of the horse's nutrient needs for all classes of nutrients but also the "balanced cecum" can serve as a tremendous buffer against gut pathology and dehydration. The best estimate of voluntary forage intake by horses is somewhere between 3 to 4% of body weight per day in forage dry matter. Using these numbers, it is likely that many of the western performance horses could meet most of their nutrient requirements using a diet of good quality fiber alone. This kind of feeding program in the industry is certainly the exception rather than the rule. I know of trainers in Arizona using alfalfa pellet alone, in California using alfalfa cubes alone and personally have fed only hay and a "guilt cup" of feed to western pleasure horses in training.

Table 1 shows the predicted energy value of some commonly fed hays for horses.

Table 1. AVERAGE DIGESTIBLE ENERGY AND PROTEIN CONCENTRATIONS IN HAYS COMMONLY FED TO HORSES (DRY MATTER BASIS).

Forage	DE	Protein	Forage	DE	Protein
Alfalfa	1.1	20	Timothy	0.7	7
Coastal	0.9	11	Clover	1.0	15
Oat	0.8	9	Bahiagrass	0.8	8
Lespedeza	1.0	18	Fescue	0.9	12
Mixed	1.0	15	Pangola	0.8	9

Assuming that energy requirements for these horses range from 18 Mcal to 34 Mcal of digestible energy (DE) per day, it is easy to see that many of the horses in question can meet their energy requirements from hay alone. For example, if a horse requires 20 Mcal of DE per day it would have to eat 28, 20 and 16.5 lbs. of hay per day that contained 0.7, 1.0 and 1.2 Mcal of DE per lb. respectively. Assuming the horse weighed 1100 lbs these intakes would represent 2.5, 1.8 and 1.5 percent of body weight per day in hay intake. These numbers are well within the capacity of the horse to eat hay. Even though these numbers work in theory, in practice this feeding management routine is the exception rather than the rule due to tradition, ease of feeding and lack of availability and storage for these amounts of hay in many parts of the country. Therefore, a practical thumb rule is to always meet at least 50% of the western performance horse's energy requirements with fibrous feeds with an absolute minimum forage intake of 1% of body weight per day. Adhering to theses "rules" will result in greater economy, fewer gut problems, fewer stable vices and probably most importantly, in a happier horse.

The horse doing light work

Western performance horses that fit into the light work category include:

Western pleasure horses
Trail horses
Recreational roping horses (less than 6 head per day)
Equitation horses
Western riding horses

There may be instances when horses used in other events fit into this category and times when horse listed above may fit better into the moderate work category but for purposes of a basic discussion of nutrient needs and feeding management, these horses group quite nicely. Table 2 shows a basic list of nutrient requirements for horses that have been grouped in this category and for comparative purposes maintenance requirements have been listed as well.

Table 2. DAILY REQUIREMENTS FOR SELECTED NUTRIENTS FOR WESTERN PERFORMANCE HORSES DOING LIGHT WORK (1100 LBS MATURE WEIGHT)

Nutrient	Mature	Two Year Old	Maintenance
Digestible energy (Mcal)	20.5	22	16.4
Crude protein (g)	820	900	656
Calcium (g)	25	29	29
Phosphorus (g)	18	16	14
Magnesium (g)	9.4	8.2	7.5
Potassium (g)	31.2	28	25
Selenium (mg)	1.5	1.5	1.0
Vitamin A (IU x 1000)	22	20	15
Vitamin E (IU)	600	600	500

It should be obvious that the difference in nutrient requirements between maintenance and horses doing light work is actually quite small. The maintenance requirement for DE for the size of horse listed is 16.4 Mcal of DE while light work is 20.5 Mcal, a difference of 4 Mcal or roughly 6 lbs of grass hay, 4 lbs of legume hay or 2.5 lbs of a typical sweet feed. Protein requirements are a mere 164 grams over maintenance and the other nutrients follow this trend. For all practical purposes, a two year old in training doing these types of work can be treated as a mature horse in terms of the types and amounts of feed required to meet nutrient needs.

Now that the nutrient requirements are stated the real challenge is to convert these numbers into a practical feeding program. Recall that we are going to meet at least 50% of the DE requirement with hay and or other fibrous feed. This would mean that for horses doing light work at least 10 Mcal of DE per day is going to be provided by hay. Going back to Table 1 this would mean that we would start with a basal ration of 14 lbs of timothy or coastal hay, 12 lbs of a mixed alfalfa/grass hay and 10 lbs of a straight alfalfa, lespedeza or clover hay. The remaining energy required over and above that provided by the hay would be 10 mcal of DE. Therefore, assuming that most concentrate rations provide 1.4 Mcal per lb. this would mean that the horse would be fed 7 lbs of grain per day. This is pretty close to the average grain intake that one might see fed to these horses on a practical basis.

At this point we have really only considered energy in the feed intake equation, and obviously there are other important nutrients. It is very difficult to make protein a real factor if practical diets are being fed in amounts adequate to meet energy needs. My general suggestion to horsemen is to feed a 12 - 14% protein grain mix to all performance horses and that when energy requirements are being met then nearly by definition, protein requirements are met as well. For example, assume a 7% protein timothy hay was being fed (14 lbs from above example = 6.3 kg) and a 12% grain mix at 7 lbs per day, 3.18 kg. Protein intake would be as follows:

hay 6300 g x .07 = 441 g/d
grain 3180 g x .12 = 381 g/d
total protein intake = 822 grams/day (required = 820 g)

It is apparent that even when horses are being fed a relatively poor quality timothy hay, protein requirements are being met using a 12% protein grain mix. The important thing here is for people to understand that at least when grass or grass/legume mixed hays are being fed, it does not really matter if a 12, 13 or 14% protein grain mix is fed. Feeding a 13 or 14 % grain mix in the above example would mean an increase in 32 and 64 grams per day respectively. This difference is of academic significance only but it seems that people really get hung up on this protein thing.

The other nutrients in the diet fall in line if one is feeding a well formulated, fully fortified feed. A typical nutrient profile one might encounter for one of these feeds is 0.65 % calcium, 0.5 % phosphorus, 0.25 % magnesium, 0.3 ppm selenium and 4,000 IU/lb vitamin A. If the concentrations of the above nutrients, plus or minus, are in the feed then one can be assured that the requirements for all nutrients are being met. There really should be no need for supplements for these horses other than for the ones discussed at the end of this paper that have application for all classes of performance horses. The obvious exception is salt. Even though most manufacturers would include salt as 0.5% of the grain concentrate, it is a good idea to provide a free-choice trace-mineral salt source, either loose or block to all horses, even those not in work.

Besides using a fortified textured or pelleted feed, many people like to use bulk grains as the concentrate part of the ration. Even though this is perfectly fine in terms of meeting energy requirements, the macro and micro mineral requirements are not generally met using this method of feeding. If on the other hand, grain plus

1-2 lbs per day of a supplement pellet (ie KER ALLPHASE or VI-PRO-MIN) is used all nutrient requirements are generally met. These mixing or supplement pellets are generally available from most manufacturers and are very highly fortified and formulated to address the deficiencies in cereal grains. This method of feeding allows a trainer, producer or horse owner a great deal of flexibility in the feeding program as energy and other nutrients are unlinked. One can then start with a "daily unit" of pellet and add that amount of grain necessary to achieve the appropriate body condition for the individual.

Some last thoughts on feeding this group of performance horses: Even though these horses are not doing a great deal of work in terms of caloric expenditure, they are still athletes. Flexibility, muscular fitness, cardiovascular fitness and soundness are still of extreme importance. It is rare that we see a flexible, fit, cardiovascularly fit, fat athlete. As such for these horses to carry excessive finish or fat can only be described as potentially detrimental to their performance. The modern "look" for a pleasure horse is sleek, streamlined and hard. The definition of the really good performance horse is elegance, symmetry and balance. This definition is difficult to achieve in the fat horse. Just as fit and fat are different for the halter horse, fit and thin are different for the performance horse. Judges have been instructed by breed associations to discriminate against horses that look emaciated, dull and worn out and that appear to be intimidated. The way to get a horse that is supposed to go slow to do so is through appropriate training and NOT through starvation. It takes energy to be balanced, round, cadenced and pure in movement. These attributes of the western performance horse are not achieved by restricting feed and/or water intake. In conclusion for the horse being trained, shown and worked in the events that I have indicated are light work, it is energy balance in the individual that ultimately is going to be the critical aspect of getting the job done right. "The eye of the master fattens the ox." Thumb rules concerning the feed intakes predicted to be required for these horses are meaningless without the horsemanship of the feeder.

Feeding for moderate work

All but a very select few of the remaining western performance horses can be put in this category. Events covered in the moderate work category would be:

Reining	Steer roping (> 6 head per day)
Working cow horse	Calf roping
Cutting	Team penning
Ranch work	Barrel racing
Pole bending	Steer wrestling

This category contains the largest portion of the real using horses, horses that have speed and anaerobic metabolism as any significant component of their work. The training program for these horses when compared to the typical pleasure horse or trail horse would generally consist of longer and more intense daily training sessions and more intensity of work during the event at the horse show. A greater amount of aerobic as well as anaerobic fitness is required for these horses when compared to those horses doing light work. Even with individual variation in the actual amount of feed these horses take to maintain energy balance, requirements presented in Table 3 are a good place to start when trying to establish feeding programs that meet nutrient requirements for horses engaged in these activities.

The 1989 NRC suggests that 50% of the diet of horses doing moderate work may be comprised of forage and 50% of grain. As for horses doing light work there are certainly instances when horses are consuming high quality forages (good pasture or legume hay) when all of the protein and energy requirements may be met by the forage component of the diet. Most of the time when this is possible, it is when horses are maintained outside on pasture except when they are being ridden and trained. This is just simply not how the majority of western performance horses are managed. More frequently than not horses in training for or being shown in western performance events are housed in stalls with limited if any turn-out and this fairly well necessitates the feeding of grain. Assuming that 50% of the DE requirements can be met by hay and that these horses require 24 Mcal of DE per day then 12 Mcal must be provided by hay and the remaining 12 by grain or concentrate. Going back to our previous assumptions the 12 Mcal required from the hay or forage portion of the diet could be provided by 17 lbs, 12 lbs and 10 lbs of grass, mixed grass/legume and legume hays respectively, these figures would represent 1.7, 1.1 and 0.9 % of body weight per day respectively for the 1100 lb horse. These kinds of hay intakes are certainly well within the capability of the horse to consume fibrous feeds. Using our 1.4 Mcal/lb figure for grain mixes, grain intake for horses doing moderate work would need to be in the neighborhood of 9 - 10 lbs/day.

Table 3. DAILY REQUIREMENTS FOR SELECTED NUTRIENTS FOR WESTERN PERFORMANCE HORSES DOING MODERATE WORK (1100 LBS. MATURE WEIGHT).

Nutrient	Mature	Two year old
Digestible energy (Mcal)	24	24
Crude protein (g)	984	800
Calcium (g)	30	34
Phosphorus (g)	21	19
Magnesium (g)	11.3	9.8
Potassium (g)	31.2	32.2
Selenium (mg)	2.0	2.0
Vitamin A (IUx1000)	22	20
Vitamin E (IU)	800	800

The above intakes are going to be a function of training intensity, stage of training (maintenance of training level takes less work than getting to the peak), individual response to training and feed efficiency differences between horses. Additionally, if more than 50% of the DE requirements are met by forage then grain intake can be reduced. As for light work, a fully fortified pelleted or textured feed (12 -14% protein) or a supplement pellet plus straight grain fed at levels which meet energy requirements will insure that other nutrient needs are met.

Unlike horses doing light work, there is a considerable risk for horses at moderate work intensities to develop muscle problems. It is critical for horses to be ridden every day, to be worked within their metabolic means, and to have feed intakes reduced on light work days if tying up and other types of muscle pathology are to be prevented. For horses at risk, I have found that maximizing the role of forage in the diet, adding fat and beet pulp to the diet to replace some of the starch calories and insuring adequate electrolyte intake all help to prevent muscle problems from occurring or help in the maintenance of horses that have tied up. Oil or fat intakes of 12 oz/day can easily be tolerated by these horses and concentrate rations with as high as 25% beet pulp are excellent for horses at higher intensities of work. It is also well to remember that a strictly aerobic, stress-free warm-up period is effective in helping to promote normal metabolism (besides being good for the horse's brain). If more people spent more time with these horses at the walk and long trot a great many physical and mental disasters could be averted. Even though people would like there to be a real difference in the way one feeds reiners, cutters, snaffle bit horses and roping horses, they really, from a nutritional point of view, are pretty much the same horses.

Horses at high work intensity

The western performance horse doing intense work is the exception rather than the rule. When we think about horses doing heavy work, we generally think about the high goal polo pony, the race horse or the upper level 3-Day Event horse rather than western horses. On the other hand some really professional western performance horses may fit into this category! Some of the horses that may want to be fed like a race horse include barrel racing horses headed for a futurity, upper level cutting horses and reining futurity prospects in the final stages of preparation for shows. Some might even argue that some really top team roping horses get enough riding to warrant being in this nutritional classification. Table 4 lists the nutrient requirements of the horse at high work intensities.

In most instances it is fairly impractical to think that 50% of a hard working horse's energy requirements can be met by forages. For example, if one met 50% of the 34 Mcal DE requirement of the hard working horse with timothy hay, this would necessitate a hay intake of roughly 27 lbs of this hay per day or 2.7% of a 1000 lb horse's body weight per day. This is obviously reaching the horse's capacity

Table 4. DAILY REQUIREMENTS FOR SELECTED NUTRIENTS FOR WESTERN HORSES DOING INTENSE WORK (1100 LBS MATURE WEIGHT).

Nutrient	Required	Nutrient	Required
Digestible energy (Mcal)	33	Potassium (g)	49.9
Crude Protein (g)	1200	Selenium (mg)	2.5
Calcium (g)	40	Vit A (IU x 1000)	22
Phosphorus (g)	29	Vit E (IU)	1000
Magnesium (g)	15.1	Salt (g)	90

to consume dry matter. For higher quality hays the problem is not quite so severe and indeed some high goal polo ponies play the Argentine Open off of really good quality pasture. However the reality works better than the theory and it is commonplace for horses at intense or heavy work loads to be fed free choice hay and limit feed grain. Research has indicated that when this is done the horse will voluntarily consume about 15 lbs of hay. Making the assumption that this hay is worth about .9 Mcal per lb the DE consumed from hay would be 13.5 Mcal per day leaving a deficit of roughly 20 Mcal per day that must be derived from the grain mix. Using our figure of 1.4 Mcal per lb for a typical grain mix this would necessitate that the horse consume from 14 - 15 lbs of grain per day. Interestingly, these numbers are nearly identical to the numbers found to be fed to race horses in hard training at the race track. We must forever be cognizant of the fact that these are average numbers and there is an extreme degree of variation in actual intake of feed between individuals. It is also important to identify methods of decreasing the starch load of horses consuming a great deal of feed. Probably the most effective way of accomplishing this is by using a fat-added feed or by top-dressing with fat at the time of feeding. Modern performance rations may contain fat at 5 - 10 % of the grain mix. All of the answers are not in terms of the net effect of feeding fat to the horse but it is apparent that the horse readily utilizes fairly large amounts of animal fat or vegetable oil. Another effective and fairly popular method of replacing starch calories is the use of sugarbeet pulp. Beet pulp is a readily fermentable fiber source that has roughly the same DE value as oats but unlike oats the energy derived from beet pulp is derived from fermenting the fiber to produce VFAs which when absorbed in the cecum contribute to the energy economy of the horse. Another viable source of readily fermentable fiber that can effectively be used in the diets of performance horses is soy hulls. Practical diets containing as much as 30% soy hulls can be made and are readily consumed by the horse. This source of fiber necessitates a pelleted feed and may therefore reduce the number of consumers willing to feed it. The real key to meeting these horses' energy requirements in a safe and efficacious manner is feeding management: small meals, frequently fed, with reliance upon a variety of energy precursors.

Supplements for the working horse

If the basal ration is properly formulated and fortified with adequate macro and micro minerals as well as with fat and water soluble vitamins there are few supplements that really should be necessary. In most instances the only plausible arguments that can be made for supplements are for a good electrolyte, a biotin supplement and an extra vitamin E and selenium supplement. In extraordinary cases when horses have been stressed one may also consider a probiotic and perhaps a B-complex vitamin supplement. Electrolytes are discussed in other papers in this proceedings but it is worth mention here as well. More times than not, simply providing free-choice salt is all of the electrolyte supplementation that is necessary. In those instances when another electrolyte supplement is considered, an electrolyte should be chosen that effectively replaces electrolytes actually lost in sweat. Biotin supplements, if used, should provide at least 15 mg/day of biotin, 3 grams per day of methionine and 200 mg of zinc. There is some indication that chelated zinc sources may be most effective in this application. When using a supplemental source of vitamin E and selenium one should try to find a supplement that provides 1000 mg of vitamin E and 2 mg of selenium. Extra B-complex vitamins may be warranted due to the unusually high levels of starch intake associated with feeding the high performance horse and the role that these vitamins play in starch metabolism. There appears to be some validity to feeding supplemental thiamine to horses that appear to have particularly nervous dispositions. When this is done I generally recommend thiamine intakes of 1000 mg/day. Additionally, even with the most meticulous feeding management routine, cecal function may be somewhat compromised due to large pH shifts associated with undigested starch entering the cecum. Maintenance of cecal homeostasis is critical and cecal acidosis may be the second largest cause of anorexia in the performance horse, second only to gastric ulcers. Due to the positive effects of yeast-culture on cecal metabolism it has been our tendency to include yeast culture in the diets of performance horses.

In summary, meeting the energy needs of performance horses tends to be the most important aspect of feeding for performance. When a well formulated and PROPERLY fortified feed is fed in adequate quantities to meet energy demands, nearly by definition, other nutrient requirements are met as well. There is no magical formula that legally makes horses run faster and jump higher. The real key to feeding to maximize performance is attention to detail, reliance on high quality forage in the feeding program and adjustment of feed intake to meet individual needs.

This paper was first published in "Recent Advances in Equine Nutrition," Proceedings for the 1995 Short Course for Feed Manufacturers

GROWTH AND BROODMARE NUTRITION

THE EQUINE SKELETON

HOW DOES BONE GROW AND HOW DO ABNORMALITIES IN THE DEVELOPMENTAL PROCESS AFFECT SOUNDNESS?

C. WAYNE MCILWRAITH
Colorado State University, Ft. Collins, Colorado, USA

Normal long bone development

Long bones develop from cartilage by a process of endochondral (within cartilage) ossification (Fig 1). In the fetus, the bone anlages (early bone templates) are composed entirely of cartilage. Centers of ossification (bone formation) develop in the center of the future long bone (diaphysis) and also at the ends of these long bones (epiphysis). As ossification proceeds, a bony epiphysis develops at each end and a bony diaphysis develops in the center. Between these two centers of ossification is a metaphyseal growth plate (also called physis) and this is what enables the limb to continue to lengthen after birth as the foal grows. Eventually, the epiphyseal center of ossification and the diaphyseal center of ossification will unite and this results in bony closure of the physis.

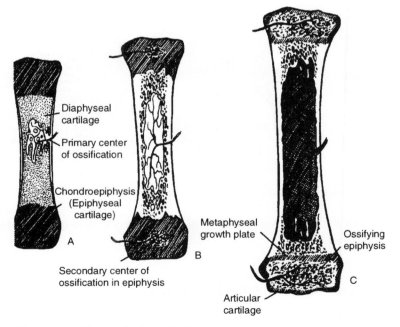

Figure 1. Diagram of ossification of a developing bone

The physes close at various stages. As a generalization, the ones nearest the foot (distal) close before the ones further up the leg (proximal). There is variation within each growth plate as well and knowledge of this growth pattern and closure pattern is critical to manipulation of deformities in the limb.

Ossification of the epiphyses at the ends of the long bones is also critical for an understanding of both joint development as well as defects in this ossification, such as osteochondrosis, the most important condition of which is osteochondritis dissecans (OCD). A diagrammatic representation of the development of the joint is in Figure 2. As can be seen in the diagram, epiphyseal ossification gradually proceeds out and stops at a certain stage. When it ceases, there is a layer of cartilage left at the joint surface called articular cartilage. This should never ossify. Obviously there is physeal cartilage retained as well, up to a certain stage, but this eventually ossifies. Ossification of the epiphysis requires blood vessels and these are provided through cartilage canals. Prior to ossification, the cartilage that contains cartilage canals and blood vessels is called epiphyseal cartilage. Cartilage that remains at the end of ossification and lines the joint is called articular cartilage and is devoid of blood vessels. It also has a very specific structure to provide motion at the joint surface. These aspects will be discussed in more detail when considering OCD.

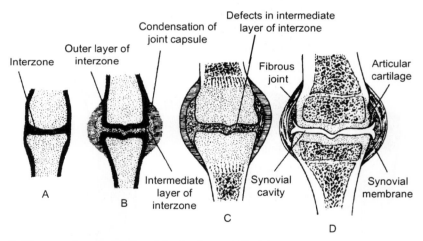

Figure 2. Diagrammatic representation of the development of a joint.

The anatomy of the metaphyseal growth plate or physis is also quite complicated and is illustrated in Figure 3.

Abnormalities of bone and joint development

There are various abnormalities involved in the developmental process. They are generally classified under the term developmental orthopedic disease (see below).

These abnormalities may involve defects in endochondral ossification by which the bone is formed, abnormalities in bone lengthening or metabolic changes within the bone after it is formed, and as the horse goes into training many of these have yet to be identified.

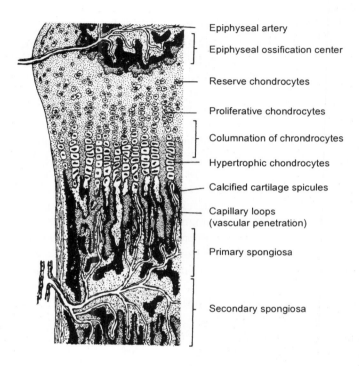

Epiphyseal artery

Epiphyseal ossification center

Reserve chondrocytes

Proliferative chondrocytes

Columnation of chrondrocytes

Hypertrophic chondrocytes

Calcified cartilage spicules

Capillary loops
(vascular penetration)

Primary spongiosa

Secondary spongiosa

Figure 3. The anatomy of the metaphyseal growth plate or physis

In general, we look at two sets of major orthopedic problems in the horse:

1) developmental problems, discussed under the umbrella of developmental orthopedic disease, and

2) traumatically induced or degenerative problems.

Many of these conditions are only seen at an end stage. For instance, we now recognize that chip fractures in the carpus of the racehorse are secondary to long term degenerative conditions in the subchondral bone. Similarly, stress fractures when they occur in the racing athlete are probably not an acute event but rather a final breakdown in bone structure due to localized osteoporosis associated with bone remodeling.

Developmental orthopedic disease

DEFINITION

The term developmental orthopedic disease (DOD) was coined in 1986 to encompass all orthopedic problems seen in the growing foal. It came out of a blue ribbon panel sponsored by the American Quarter Horse Association. It is a term that encompasses all general growth disturbances of horses and is therefore nonspecific. It is felt that one has to be nonspecific when talking about the various limb anomalies of young horses because previous terms such as metabolic bone disease and osteochondrosis implied that they all had a common cause and pathogenesis (mechanism of disease development). It is still to be determined how closely related the various forms of DOD may be but it is important that the term not be used synonymously with osteochondrosis. It is considered inappropriate for all subchondral cystic lesions, physitis, angular limb deformities and cervical vertebral malformations to be presumed to be manifestations of osteochondrosis (a condition defined below). The spectrum of conditions currently classified as DOD were previously designated as metabolic bone disease. However, it is felt that this term is misleading because it refers specifically to bone, whereas many of these problems are seen essentially as joint and growth plate problems. Severe forms of DOD are seen sometimes when there is little or no aberration in bone histomorphometry, implying questionable change in bone metabolism. Developmental orthopedic disease has become the generally accepted term.

When the term developmental orthopedic disease was first coined, it was categorized to include the following.

1.   ***Osteochondrosis*** - Osteochondrosis is a defect in endochondral ossification (definition above) that can result in a number of different manifestations, depending on the site of the endochondral ossification defect. These manifestations include osteochondritis dissecans, which is a disease process of the articular surface of joints. As mentioned previously, the epiphyseal ossification center advances out until ossification ceases, leaving a layer of cartilage. This layer of cartilage becomes the articular cartilage. If there is a disturbance in endochondral ossification, an area of retained cartilage can be formed with a consequent defect in the bone. Cracking can then proceed in this retained cartilage to give a flap or fragment of cartilage that may contain bone. These flaps and fragments on the surface of the joint result in osteochondritis dissecans (detailed in another paper).

Another manifestation of osteochondrosis may include some subchondral cystic lesions (Figure 4). These are radiolucent cyst-like structures that occur in epiphyseal bone. Not all subchondral cystic lesions or bone cysts are necessarily the result of osteochondrosis. Recently in a project funded by the American Quarter Horse Association, we demonstrated that subchondral cystic lesions can develop from defects in the joint surface and in mature animals. However, there is no question that some subchondral bone cysts occur as a result of endochondral ossification. These cysts are also discussed in another paper. Osteochondrosis can also result in lesions in the physis or metaphyseal growth plate. Cervical vertebral malformations (wobblers) are also included. The exact role of osteochondrosis and the pathogenesis of cervical vertebral malformation are still uncertain. In some instances, angular limb deformities will be associated with retained cartilage associated with the physis and this would be evident on radiographs. Such cases are a small minority of angular limb deformities.

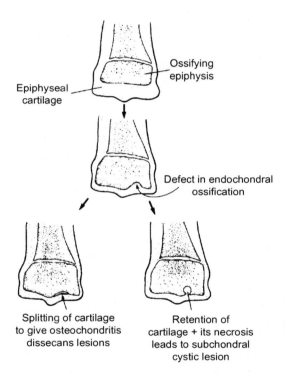

Figure 4. Diagram of pathogenesis of osteochondritis dissecans and subchondral cystic lesions in relation to the generalized condition of osteochondrosis.

2. *Acquired angular limb deformities*

3. *Physitis*

4. *Subchondral cystic lesions*

5. *Flexural deformities* (may be secondary to osteochondrosis or physitis)

6.   *Cuboidal bone abnormalities*

7.   *Juvenile osteoarthritis*

The above problems are considered DODs. Individual instances may or may not be associated with osteochondrosis.

CLINICAL DIAGNOSIS OF DOD VERSUS RADIOGRAPHIC SURVEYS

There has been a problem or a point of confusion between reports of clinical instances of DOD and radiographic surveys of horses not necessarily showing clinical signs. This has led to some questionable conclusions, not only regarding the causative factors of DOD but also the effect of treatment or the significance of various problems. There are many instances where radiographs on a prepurchase examination will show OCD, for instance, but that OCD may not be causing clinical problems because the fragment has not separated. That is why it is important to distinguish between the two. Most of the major radiographic studies have involved Standardbred horses. In one study in Quebec, each horse's racing performance at two years of age was related to the radiographic lesions diagnosed at approximately 17 months of age and before training (there were two generations of 41 and 32 yearlings, respectively; five stallions and 46 mares were also radiographed). No complete clinical examinations or lameness diagnoses were made. Radiographic lesions were found in 31 (25%) of the horses (8 adults and 23 yearlings), of which 60% had a single problem, and 40% had between two and four radiographic problems. Subchondral bone cysts were detected in 14 (11.3%) horses (6 carpus, 5 fetlock, 4 pastern, 2 hock, and 2 stifle). Juvenile osteoarthritis lesions were diagnosed 78 times in 35 (47.9%) of the yearlings (40 pastern, 13 fetlock, 11 carpus, 8 coffin, 6 hock) based primarily on the basis of osteophytes. Sesamoiditis was also diagnosed in yearlings. The average winnings and number of starts were compared between radiographically normal horses, the OCD or subchondral bone cyst horses, and the juvenile OA horses; no significant differences were found. Although the radiographic lesions did not seem to be associated with poor racing performance, the authors of the study noted the lack of clinical data and the relatively small numbers. What we need are improved studies in which clinical signs are correlated with radiographs and possibly more important, all horses are radiographed and then followed so we know how many of those horses with x-ray changes develop clinical problems. This would solve many of the current issues at the yearling sales.

The high incidence of clinically apparent physitis and flexural deformities was emphasized in another study in Canada. Mild to moderate physitis and flexural deformities (concurrent with physitis in most cases) occurred in 88% of 42 weanlings between weeks 6 and 8 of a study looking at the effect of dietary energy and phosphorus on blood chemistry and development of growing horses. In these instances, the clinical signs largely resolved on their own by five weeks. Dietary treatment did not influence the incidence, nor was it related to daily weight gain. There has been another study defining incidence of DOD in Thoroughbred horses in Ireland over a period of 18 months. It was found that angular limb deformities and physitis together constituted 72.9% of the cases treated. The peak incidence of DOD problems occurred between weaning and the end of December. In a retrospective study, 193 of 1,711 (11.3%) were treated for DOD (21 had more than one type) and are detailed as follows: angular limb deformities - 92, physitis - 64, flexural deformities - 18, wobblers - 7, and osteochondritis dissecans, juvenile arthritis or other joint problems - 28. More than half the animals treated (53.9%) recovered completely, that is they achieved expected sale value as yearlings; 27.5% showed incomplete recovery and mild to moderate loss of sale value; and 18.7% were either killed or lost much of their sale value. It was also noted that 67.7% of the animals showed some evidence of DOD, but only 11.3% were deemed to need treatment. This study was a good start and points out the need to have definition of what disease process we have. I think it can be seen from these studies that when "developmental orthopedic disease" occurs, it commonly involves angular limb deformities and physitis problems that spontaneously self-correct. It is the ones that often do not self-correct, such as OCD subchondral bone cysts, that we need to investigate further.

OSTEOCHONDROSIS

Osteochondrosis was initially defined as a disturbance of cellular differentiation in the growing cartilage. It is considered to be a result of the failure of endochondral ossification and may affect either the articular epiphyseal cartilage complex (previously diagramed and illustrated in Figure 4) or the metaphyseal growth plate (also in Figure 4). It was considered that the loss of normal differentiation of the cartilage cells means the transitional calcification of the matrix, which is important for bone formation, did not take place. Therefore, ossification ceases and cartilage is retained. This retained cartilage then undergoes cellular death (necrosis) in the basal layers and it is proposed that subsequent stresses give rise to fissures in the damaged cartilage and that progressive breakdown of the cartilage can then lead to the syndrome designated as osteochondritis dissecans or subchondral bone cysts.

That these entities are part of the generalized condition of osteochondrosis has resulted from studies in other species and extrapolation to the condition in the horse. There is still considerable argument about the exact association and with more experience, one comes up with more cases that don't quite fit the pattern. For example, we see cases of osteochondritis dissecans in the stifle that do not have thickened cartilage or a defect in the bone and that do not quite fit with the retained cartilage phenomenon. However, they could still fit with some developmental abnormality. At this stage, we therefore like to say that osteochondrosis may lead to osteochondritis dissecans or subchondral cystic lesions. It also may occur in the physis and lead to retained cartilage in that area. It is currently presumed that many instances of subchondral bone cysts result from osteochondrosis. On the other hand, we have demonstrated the development of bone cysts secondary to a defect. In early work, osteochondrosis was suggested to be a generalized condition and therefore occurred in multiple sites. However, based on our clinical material, it was found that osteochondritis dissecans will be found in a particular joint and a lesion will commonly occur in the same joint but will not occur elsewhere. We feel that certain biomechanical factors and perhaps insults at certain stages of development may also be important factors. Causative factors associated with osteochondrosis are discussed further below.

Osteochondritis dissecans

There is general agreement that this condition involves a dissecting lesion with the formation of a chondral or osteochondral flap. Flaps may become detached and form joint mice. Blood vessels from the periphery of the joint frequently remain in communication with cartilage flaps or detached flakes, leading to calcification or ossification of the avulsed cartilage. It is commonly considered that release of debris from under the flap causes synovitis and pain, but we don't think it is that simple now because we find instances where the cartilage is intact but the horses still have lameness and synovial effusion.

Subchondral cystic lesions

Subchondral cystic lesions have also been proposed as a manifestation of osteochondrosis by a number of authors and there is pathologic evidence to support this. When we have a yearling horse with a large subchondral cystic lesion in one stifle and a defect in the other, we feel comfortable assuming the cause to be osteochondrosis. However, we also get subchondral cystic lesions that develop in all the horses and in some instances, we have noted them developing after a cartilage surface defect. We have also experimentally produced them by creating a defect into the subchondral bone.

Physitis

Physitis has also been described as epiphysitis and physeal dysplasia. It has even been suggested earlier that epiphysitis was the same as osteochondrosis but this is incorrect. In many instances, we have pain and swelling at the growth plate without any evidence of retained cartilage. Most cases of physitis do not have any radiographic lesions that are particularly significant and they resolve with time.

Angular limb deformities

As with these other syndromes, they will be discussed in more detail. Angular limb deformities involve deviations in the limbs as looked at from the front or back, such that the deviation is excessive from side to side from the horse's point of view. Many angular limb deformities cause no problems and resolve themselves.

Cuboidal bone malformation

Cuboidal bone malformation certainly represents a delay in endochondral ossification. Usually it is a result of either prematurity or a delay of ossification caused by hyperthyroidism. Usually the condition manifests as a carpal deformity or a hock deformity because of a collapse of the cuboidal bones in this area. They have collapsed because of insufficient ossification of the bones by the time they are bearing weight on them. They are treated by casting in a position that takes weight off the bones and the cuboidal nature of the bone can return if treatment is initiated sufficiently early.

CAUSATIVE FACTORS OF OSTEOCHONDROSIS

Certain etiologic factors have been recognized that contribute to the development of these lesions. These factors have been varied, but the idea that there is a multifactorial etiology (a number of causes contributing to it) has generally been accepted. Much of the information is from clinical and pathologic reports, as well as experimental studies in the horse. The experimental studies in the horse have given some answers but have also created confusion. The primary problem has been that the lesions are often somewhat different than what we most commonly encounter as veterinarians looking at clinical cases. However, we have identified major factors that seem to predispose the growing animal to osteochondrosis type problems, including rapid growth, genetic predisposition, nutritional excesses or imbalances and superimposed trauma on the cartilage. In pigs it has been demonstrated that a high growth rate is the main reason for high incidence of osteochondrosis and that the high growth rate is the result of both genetic selection and caloric intake. Some genetic predispositions have been demonstrated in the horse and increased energy will increase the incidence of osteochondrosis. However, it is not a simple cause/effect relationship. We will now discuss the various factors that have been implicated in contributing to this complex disease.

Genetic predisposition

Radiographic studies in Swedish Trotters and Warmbloods have shown progeny of one stallion from each breed having a significantly high frequency of OCD amongst his progeny, compared with the progeny of the other stallions. In another study in Denmark, radiographic evidence of a significantly high proportion of osteochondrosis in the progeny of one of eight stallions, even though the stallion itself did not show radiographic signs of osteochondrosis, was seen. Since that time, there have been two more studies on the heritability of osteochondrosis in the hock of Standardbred Trotters.

There has been little work done in the United States with regard to heredity and we certainly haven't been able to develop any type of screening program for osteochondrosis in stallions and mares that will ensure freedom from that condition. However, it would appear very likely that there are genetic components to this disease. Individual instances of certain stallions and mares producing these individuals have been seen.

Growth and body size

Fast growth was implicated with a high incidence of osteochondrosis in dogs and pigs. There have been anecdotal reports of this in the horse. However, the controlled studies that have been done in the horse question whether growth rate is indeed a factor. It has been pointed out that the most intense phase of growth occurs in the first three months of life and if growth was a big factor, we expect this would be the time that most lesions would occur but this is not when we see them clinically. At this stage, the evidence implicating growth rate and body size in the pathogenesis is largely unsubstantiated, at least with any definitive studies. Growth rate is obviously associated with a number of factors. In one study done at Ohio, foals with a higher number of lesions had similar growth rates to those with fewer or no lesions, suggesting that rapid growth may not be a necessary predisposing factor in the development of cartilage lesions. Growth was based on measurements of body weight, height, and cannon bone circumference and it was part of a study on the effect of dietary copper.

Mechanical stress and trauma

It has certainly been recognized that mechanical stresses often precipitate clinical signs with OCD and it is presumed that this is by separating the OCD flap or fragment from the parent bone. Whether trauma or physical stress is involved in the primary induction of an OCD lesion is controversial. However, some people do tend to feel this is the case and we do recognize there are certain predisposing sites for the occurrence of OCD, suggesting possible mechanical factors. A notable veterinary bone and joint pathologist, Dr. Roy Pool, feels that shear forces may disrupt capillaries in the subchondral bone (bone under the cartilage) and give rise to chondrocyte or cartilage cell damage. This is based on histologic observations of various lesions.

Nutrition

As discussed previously, the idea of overnutrition as a cause of OCD has been extrapolated from work in dogs and pigs. There has been an increased incidence of OCD lesions noted in horses fed 130% of what the National Research Council (NRC) recommends for carbohydrate and protein. A second study in Australia by Dr. Kate Savage, which was very well controlled, showed that high energy diets (120% NRC requirements) consistently produced lesions of osteochondrosis in weanling foals compared to a control diet based on 100% NRC requirements. Some people have focused on "high protein" being a problem but this has not been demonstrated.

Many generalizations have been made about excessive growth causing OCD and this is based on the early work done in Sweden in 1978 which was primarily extrapolated from pigs. However, even when the pig work is carefully looked at, a direct association is not demonstrated in some studies. Unfortunately, the correlation of growth and OCD has led to the practice of virtually starving horses (onto grass hay and water) in an attempt to reduce the incidence (which it has not). This creates a whole new malnutrition situation. It may be that lowering energy and protein is a good part of the protocol in some instances to prevent OCD but the possibility of inducing other nutritional imbalances needs to be carefully considered and compensated for.

It has also been pointed out that overfeeding can induce endocrine imbalances (see *Endocrine factors* below).

Mineral imbalances

Various mineral imbalances have been implicated as causative factors with OCD, including high calcium, high phosphorus, low copper and high zinc. Although high calcium levels have been implicated, experimental research in the horse with three times the NRC level of calcium in the diet failed to produce lesions of osteochondrosis. High phosphorus diets (five times NRC) did produce lesions of OCD in young foals.

Low copper has been implicated as a cause. An epidemiologic study on clinical cases of DOD implicated low copper levels as the most consistent factor. In experimental studies, it has been noted that a marked copper deficiency (1.7 ppm - a very artificially low level) produced OCD-like lesions and flexural deformities. In another study in Thoroughbred foals in which osteochondrosis developed before weaning, seven had serum copper and ceruloplasmin concentrations below normal. In a third controlled experiment in Canada with high (30 ppm) and low (7 ppm) copper diets, there was a much higher incidence of lesions seen in the foals fed the low copper diet. However, it is to be noted that most of the changes were present in the cervical vertebrae rather than the limbs where we commonly see clinical problems.

Excessive zinc intake has been related to equine osteochondrosis. Generalized osteochondrosis has been seen in foals raised near a zinc smelter. The relationship between zinc and copper (it has been suggested that high zinc suppresses copper levels) is still being elucidated.

Endocrine factors

It has been postulated by one investigator that the production of osteochondrosis lesions in association with overfeeding is mediated by the endocrine system. Certainly the long-term administration of dexamethasone has produced osteochondrosis-type lesions and it is considered that glucocorticoids induced a parathyroid hormone resistance at the level of the osteocyte causing an inhibition of normal remodeling. Glucocorticoids also induced decreased GAG levels and this decrease in turn inhibits capillary penetration of the cartilage which is a very important step in forming bone from cartilage. The failure of ossification could also be mediated through induced defects in vitamin D metabolism. Corticosteroids are also a potent inhibitor of lysyl oxidase which is involved in cross-linking of collagen in cartilage and bone. It is felt this could be a way of inducing lesions.

Site vulnerability

Because the lesions of equine osteochondrosis occur at specific anatomic sites, this obviously suggests site vulnerability. This predilection could be related to an ossification defect or trauma caused by excessive stress in that region. In nearly all instances, the sites of occurrence of OCD are very close to the limits of articulation and we know from basic research that the makeup of the cartilage between articulating and nonarticulating surfaces is different.

OCD lesions are frequently bilateral in the stifle and hock and quadrilateral in the fetlock joint, although they frequently involve different joints in the same animal. It is felt this may suggest a "window of vulnerability" in the endochondral ossification of that specific joint when an environmental insult may have occurred. If the causative factor was present intermittently or for a transient period during the foal's growth period, this would explain the development of the disease in only one pair of joints. It is not possible from these data to ascertain different periods of onset of the disease process in different joints.

Exercise

As has been discussed under traumatic arthritis, adequate exercise in foals would logically be important for the maintenance of cartilage and bone quality. There are some data suggesting a "protective" effect of exercise. This particular study was done on early weaned Warmblood foals and there was a dramatic reduction in the incidence of OCD in foals subjected to forced exercise and a high energy diet compared with foals fed the same diet but with limited exercise.

The various developmental orthopedic diseases will now be considered in more detail.

OSTEOCHONDRITIS DISSECANS

Osteochondritis dissecans (OCD) is a disease subset of osteochondrosis. This condition affects the articular (joint) cartilage and also often involves the subchondral bone just beneath the cartilage surface. The cause of OCD has generally been considered a defect in endochondral ossification at the joint surface (this process was previously mentioned with regard to ossification of this secondary epiphysis). The paradigm has been that for some reason endochondral ossification does not occur correctly at a site, leaving an area of thickened retained cartilage which then is secondarily displaced as a flap or fragment. This end result is certainly attained, but more recent data from studies we have done suggest that it is not as simple as this. For instance, we have had OCD lesions that have no thickening of the cartilage and no defects in the bone. We have also had lesions develop after endochondral ossification is complete and when we had a normally appearing surface. There is still a lot to learn about this complicated disease.

The important situation is, however, that these lesions do occur in the joint and if they result in flaps or fragments, lead to an arthritis situation. We will now go through the clinical features of this disease in each of these joints.

OSTEOCHONDRITIS DISSECANS OF THE FEMOROPATELLAR (STIFLE) JOINT

The stifle joint is one of the principal joints affected with OCD. Stifle OCD can be diagnosed in almost any breed but it is more common in Thoroughbreds. Approximately 60% of affected horses will be one year of age or less at the time the condition becomes symptomatic. However we also see the disease show up clinically even after horses have won stakes races. The difference is when the retained cartilage fragment or flap becomes displaced. As a generalization, when animals show up at a younger age with OCD, they tend to have more severe lesions.

Clinically the animals present with joint swelling due to synovial effusion and varying degrees of lameness. Severe cases can be very lame and be confused with wobblers because of the difficulty they have flexing the stifles in getting up and down. In older animals, an increase in the level of exercise may be part of the history. Horses will often have a bunny-hop gait behind and also could be confused with a neurologic problem. Some horses will be very subtle in their lameness. A joint distention (when the disease is clinically significant) is a regular feature. Careful palpation of the joint may identify free bodies or the surface irregularity associated with the damage within the joint. Bilateral involvement is common in the stifle so careful examination of both stifles should be completed. In one major study of cases we operated, 57% of animals had bilateral involvement.

Table 1. BREED DISTRIBUTION OF 161 HORSES PRESENTED FOR FEMOROPATELLAR OCD

Breed	Number	Percentage
Thoroughbred	82	50.9
Quarter Horse	39	24.2
Arabian	16	9.9
Warmblood	9	5.6
Crossbred	5	3.1
Paint Horse	3	1.9
Appaloosa	3	1.9
Other	4	2.5

Table 2. AGE DISTRIBUTION OF 161 HORSES PRESENTED FOR FEMOROPATELLAR OCD

Age (yr)	Number	Percentage
<1	22	13.7
1	68	42.2
2	36	22.4
3	21	13.0
≥4	14	8.7

(From Foland, McIlwraith and Trotter. Equine Vet J, 1994.)

Lateral to medial radiographs provide the best means of diagnosis regarding specific location of the lesion and its size. The most common location is on the lateral trochlear ridge of the femur and shows up as an area of flattening, irregularity or concavity. The area of the trochlear ridge adjacent to the bottom portion of the patella is most commonly involved. Various degrees of mineralization may be present within the flap tissue, affecting the radiographic signs, and free bodies may also be identified. OCD can also primarily affect the patella or the medial trochlear ridge of the femur. Generally the extent of damage to the joint identified at surgery is more extensive than would be predicted from radiographs. Although other joints can be involved concurrently, this is uncommon. In one study of 161 horses with stifle OCD, 5 also had OCD affecting the rear fetlocks, 4 had hock OCD and 1 had OCD of a shoulder joint.

Treatment

In general, arthroscopic surgery is recommended for the treatment of most of these cases. However, it has been recently identified that in low grade lesions detected very early, stall confinement could allow healing with presumably reattachment of any separated cartilage. When there is a significant concave defect or flaps or fragments identified, arthroscopic surgery is recommended. The joint is thoroughly explored and this usually gives a better assessment of all damage. Suspicious lesions are probed and loose or detached tissue is elevated and removed. Loose bodies are also removed. The defect site is then debrided down to healthy tissue. Animals are usually stall rested for two weeks after surgery at which time hand walking is started. Restricted exercise is continued for two to three months after surgery, when training is started or the horse is turned out (the total period of convalescence depends on the amount of damage).

In a recent study of 252 stifle joints in 161 horses, followup information was available for 134 horses. Of these 134 horses, 64% returned to their previous use or anticipated use (racing), 7% were in training, 16% were unsuccessful, and 13% were unsuccessful due to reasons unrelated to the stifle. The success rate was higher in horses having smaller lesions.

OSTEOCHONDRITIS DISSECANS OF THE TARSOCRURAL (HOCK) JOINT

OCD occurs in a number of locations in the hock, including the intermediate ridge of the tibia (most common), the lateral trochlear ridge of the talus, the medial malleolus of the tibia and the medial trochlear ridge of the talus (descending incidence). It is a very common disease in Standardbreds but is also very common in Quarter Horses and Arabians.

The most common clinical sign of hock OCD is joint distention of the tarsocrural joint. This manifests clinically as a "bog spavin," which simply refers to the prominent swelling seen along the medial or inside aspect of the joint. Lameness can also be seen but it is not common and it is rarely prominent. All ages of horse can be affected. Often in racehorses the disease does not show up until the horses are in training. In nonracehorses, the cases that are going to be clinical commonly show up as yearlings prior to going into training. The disease is confirmed with radiographs.

The location of OCD lesions in 318 tarsocrural joints is shown in Table 3 (taken from a study by McIlwraith, Foerner and Davis, 1988).

Table 3. LOCATION OF OCD LESIONS IN 318 TARSOCRURAL JOINTS

No. Joints	Location
244	Intermediate ridge (dorsal aspect) of distal tibia
37	Lateral trochlear ridge of talus
12	Medial malleolus (dorsal aspect) of tibia
11	Intermediate ridge of tibia plus lateral trochlear ridge of talus
4	Intermediate ridge plus medial malleolus of tibia
3	Intermediate ridge plus medial trochlear ridge of talus
3	Medial trochlear ridge of talus
3	Lateral trochlear ridge of talus plus medial malleolus of tibia
1	Lateral and medial trochlear ridge of talus
318	Total

Treatment

When clinical signs are present in association with OCD lesions in the hock, surgery is the recommended treatment. It is to be noted that the disease is often diagnosed as an incidental finding on radiographs of horses prior to sale. If there is no joint effusion or lameness, we do not normally recommend surgery. In some instances in racehorses, lameness may be the only problem seen and it is only seen at racing speed or upper levels of performance. Certainly resolution of the joint effusion can only be expected with removal of abnormal tissue. The horses are treated arthroscopically with removal of fragments and debridement of any damage. The postoperative management is similar to OCD of the stifle but the convalescence time may be faster as many of the lesions are localized and not involving a major articulating surface.

In a study involving 183 horses mentioned previously, 76% raced successfully or performed at their intended use after surgery. If secondary osteoarthritic change is identified at surgery in the cartilage, the prognosis is less favorable. Resolution of the joint distention so there is a normal hock with no fluid is a critical criterion of success for nonracehorse owners. It was found in this study that the resolution of effusion was inferior for lesions involving the lateral trochlear ridge of the talus compared to the intermediate ridge of the tibia, so we take this into account when giving a realistic prognosis to owners.

OSTEOCHONDRITIS DISSECANS OF THE FEMOROPATELLAR JOINT

The most common manifestation of OCD in the fetlock joint is fragmentation and irregularity on the distodorsal (front) aspect of the sagittal ridge and condyles at the bottom of the cannon bones, which is an intra-articular part of the fetlock. This condition affects all breeds but we have seen many cases in Thoroughbreds and Arabians. A second condition that some people have described as OCD is fragmentation at the back of the fetlock off the proximal palmar or plantar aspect of the first phalanx or long pastern bone. Debate continues as to whether these fragments are truly OCD or whether they represent small avulsion fragments. A third disease that has been classified as OCD of the fetlock occurs on the distal back part of the end of the cannon bone condyles and this appears to be a trauma-related condition of racehorses and should not be considered as OCD. The first two entities will be considered separately below.

OCD OF THE DORSAL ASPECT OF THE DISTAL METACARPUS OR METATARSUS IN THE FETLOCK JOINT

Joint filling is the most common clinical sign with lameness being variable in both appearance and severity. Fetlock flexion tests are usually positive. It is not unusual for all four fetlocks to be involved and it is quite common for bilateral forelimb or hindlimb involvement. The condition is diagnosed on radiographs. It is another one of the problems that cause controversy at yearling sales.

We divided the lesions into three types because it does affect the prognosis as well as treatment.

Type I OCD

This involves flattening or a defect in the sagittal ridge or condyles without any fragment. This is obviously diagnosed by x-ray. Most of these cases get better with conservative treatment and do not need surgery. Not only will they get better clinically with loss of the joint filling but also remodel radiographically.

Type II OCD

This involves a defect as in Type I but also there is a fragment present within it. Based on followup with conservative treatment, these cases don't generally get better with conservative treatment and require arthroscopic surgery. The prognosis for surgery in turn is related to a number of factors. The most favorable cases are hind fetlocks versus front fetlocks and ones with no spurs on radiographs and no secondary osteoarthritic damage.

Type III OCD

These have a defect in the primary area but also free all loose bodies within the joint. They have the same need for surgery as well as the same result as Type II lesions.

With regard to the overall prognosis, it is not as good as with stifle or hock OCD because commonly secondary articular cartilage erosion or wear lines develop in the joint by the time they are operated.

Proximal Palmar/Plantar fragments of the first phalanx

Two types of fragments have been identified in this location. Type I fragments usually involve the hind fetlocks and are located between the middle of the bone and its caudomedial (most common) or caudolateral (less common) borders. Type II fragments are also called ununited proximoplantar tuberosities of the proximal phalanx and these lesions occur almost exclusively in the hind limb. These are much less frequent. Both of these entities have been identified frequently in radiographic surveys completed in yearling Standardbreds, supporting a developmental concept. However, more recently it has been advocated (based on dissections and examination of the fragments) they are traumatic avulsions due to a pull on the short distal sesamoid ligament. However, it is agreed by all parties that they are present before a year of age.

With the common Type I fragment, joint filling is uncommon and a vague lameness is usually the main presenting sign. Most times cases are not diagnosed clinically until they are in training. Flexion tests are often positive and block of the fetlock area confirms the site of the problem. These cases are treated by arthroscopic surgery and have a high success rate.

With Type II fragments, they are often unassociated with any clinical signs and are incidental findings at radiography. If they are associated with clinical signs, most will still ossify on their own and surgery is not usually necessary.

Osteochondritis dissecans of the shoulder joint

This a severe problem and represents the worst type of OCD affecting horses. Generally large areas of the joint surface are involved and secondary osteoarthritis is common. It is fortunately less common than other sites and seems to affect Quarter Horses and Thoroughbreds with a similar incidence.

Most cases with shoulder OCD present at one year of age or younger with a history of forelimb lameness of variable severity. Many of these horses will have prominent lameness and if lameness has been present for many weeks, muscle atrophy will also be seen. Because of the altered gait and use of the limb, many cases also develop an upright or clubfooted appearance to the foot and the foot may appear smaller on the affected limb. Deep pressure over the shoulder joint will often cause discomfort. The diagnosis is confirmed with x-rays.

We have never seen conservative treatment solve the problem of OCD in the shoulder. Arthroscopic surgery has been used as a treatment with 50% of the cases becoming sound and the horses going on to do what they are supposed to do. If extensive degenerative arthritic changes are present on radiographs at the time of initial examination, the prognosis for an athletic career is unfavorable. With more localized lesions, the prognosis is much more favorable. The shoulder is a difficult area for surgery due to the depth of the joint below the muscles in the area. Surgery is easier on younger animals due to smaller muscle mass and the only fortunate aspect of OCD in the shoulder is that the clinical signs of lameness show before they are a year of age.

Subchondral cystic lesions
(also called bone cysts or osseous cyst-like lesions)

These are commonly recognized abnormalities of bones and joints that may or may not cause lameness. The ones that concern us the most in terms of soundness are articular cystic lesions that occur in the subchondral bone or epiphyseal bone and communicate with the joint.

Subchondral cystic lesions can occur in multiple sites in horses (see Table 4).

Controversy exists as to whether these lesions are a manifestation of osteochondrosis secondary to joint trauma, or a combination of both. Currently we feel that they have a multifactorial etiology and some are associated with retention of cartilage (a defect in endochondral ossification) but others occur secondary to a defect in the subchondral bone. This defect is probably most commonly a traumatically induced fracture or erosion. Because many of them occur in young growing animals, they are certainly considered to be one of the developmental orthopedic diseases. When seen in yearlings (and they are quite common in this situation in Quarter Horses and Arabians and to a lesser extent, Thoroughbreds), and particularly when they occur bilaterally, they are certainly considered to be a manifestation of osteochondrosis (discussed at the beginning of these notes as well). When they are due to osteochondrosis, it is felt that cartilage gets retained deeply, undergoes necrosis and leads to the problem. In other instances when seen in older horses, it is felt that they probably result from a defect. It has also been recently proven experimentally that a defect can produce such lesions.

The most common location of subchondral cystic lesions in horses is the medial femoral condyle within the stifle. Less common sites include the proximal tibia, distal aspect of the metacarpus and metatarsus (cannon bones), distal aspects of the radius and in the carpal bones, the proximal radius within the elbow, in the phalangeal bones associated with the pastern and coffin joints, in the shoulder and in the acetabulum of the hip.

Table 4. SITES OF OCCURRENCE OF SUBCHONDRAL CYSTIC LESIONS IN HORSES

Joint	*Specific location*
Stifle	Medial femoral condyle Lateral femoral condyle Proximal tibia
Carpus	Distal medial radius Cuboidal carpal bones
Elbow	Proximal medial radius Distal medial or lateral humerus
Fetlock	Distal metacarpus/metatarsus Proximal first phalanx Sesamoids
Pastern	Distal first phalanx Proximal second phalanx
Coffin	Third phalanx Navicular bone
Shoulder	Glenoid
Hock	Trochlear ridge of talus Tarsal bones
Hip	Acetabulum Proximal femur

SUBCHONDRAL CYSTIC LESIONS OF THE STIFLE

In the stifle, most horses present with a clinical problem between one and three years of age and they usually present to a veterinarian because of a unilateral lameness. A small percentage of horses may be lame in both hind limbs. The severity of the lameness is variable and usually ranges grade 1-3/5. Periods of work usually worsen the lameness and improvement occurs with rest.

Obvious signs of swelling (joint effusion) within affected joints are usually absent or minimal. Mild effusion of the stifle joint was reported in 15/41 cases we recently published. The diagnosis is confirmed with x-rays and the clinical significance of the x-ray lesion confirmed with intra-articular analgesia. In general, if clinical signs have become apparent in association with a cyst in the stifle, the recommendation is for surgical enucleation of the lesion. That is because with conservative management our success rate has been 20% or less, whereas our success with surgery is approximately 70%. The cases are operated arthroscopically.

SUBCHONDRAL CYSTIC LESIONS OF THE FETLOCK

These cases present with obvious lameness and usually have some filling in the fetlock joint. The lameness can be made worse by flexing the fetlock. These horses will respond to intra-articular blocks of the fetlock. Radiographs confirm the diagnosis. The cystic lesion either occurs in the bone under the articular surface of the condyle or the central sagittal ridge of the distal metacarpus or metatarsus (cannon bone). Cystic lesions are occasionally seen on the opposing surface of proximal P1 but are commonly insignificant clinically. We have also seen a very poor response to conservative management of these cases and arthroscopic surgery is recommended. A recent paper by Hogan, McIlwraith, Honnas, Watkins and Bramlage reported very good results with surgical treatment.

SUBCHONDRAL CYSTIC LESIONS OF THE CARPUS

Subchondral cystic lesions occur within the carpus (knee) but quite a few of these were incidental findings. If they persist and cause clinical signs, then we recommend surgery.

SUBCHONDRAL CYSTIC LESIONS OF THE PASTERN JOINT

When these occur singly, they are often incidental or cause only temporary lameness. More commonly they are multiple, involving the distal surface of the first phalanx. When they are multiple, they generally have severe secondary osteoarthritis (the only subchondral entity that shows this) and the only treatment available is fusion of the pastern.

SUBCHONDRAL CYSTIC LESIONS OF THE ELBOW

It is a relatively uncommon but a significant cause of lameness in the elbow. The diagnosis is based on upper limb lameness (usually after eliminating lower limb lameness), intra-articular anesthesia to prove the condition is the problem, and radiographic confirmation. We have had equal results in treating these cases with conservative versus surgical treatment. Conservative management is tried initially.

Angular limb deformities

Angular limb deformities in the young horse can take the form of a lateral or medial deviation of the limb. The angulation can arise in association with uneven elongation from the growth plate (physis) or alternatively can be involved in abnormalities of the cuboidal bones of the carpus and tarsus. Most commonly the problems are associated with uneven physeal growth and involve the physes of the distal radius, metacarpus and metatarsus or tibia (in that order). When a deviation results in the lower part of the limb going out (lateral), it is termed *valgus* while a deviation to the inside (medial) is termed *varus*. The total nomenclature for angular deformities is derived by combining the name of the involved joint or the joint immediately distal to the affected growth plate and the type of deviation. For example, a lateral deviation of the distal limb due to an affected distal radial growth plate or abnormal cuboidal bones of the carpus would be termed carpal valgus.

The etiology of angular limb deformities is complex and thought to be multifactorial. In Figure 5 it can be seen that the two main categories of factors include perinatal and developmental. Perinatal factors are usually involved when a foal is born with an angular limb deformity, whereas foals that are normal at birth but develop an angular limb deformity are more likely to suffer from one or more of the developmental factors.

It is to be noted that carpal valgus is a normal deformity in the young foal and that most of these correct naturally. There have been no nutritional factors consistently associated with this disease.

In managing these cases, one must first realize that depending on the location there is a typical growth curve for each of the physes. In the carpus, the growth plate stays open for two years and there is diminishing rate of lengthening that continues for over a year. On the other hand, when the deformity involves the fetlock, the time available for manipulation of the growth curve is much lower. All effective elongation in the physis at the distal metacarpus or metatarsus ceases around three months of age.

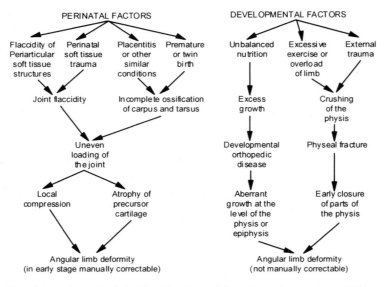

Figure 5. The etiology of angular limb deformities (adapted from *Equine Surgery*, Auer, 1992)

When an angular limb deformity involves the joint's bones itself, such as the carpus or tarsus, this needs to be recognized radiographically and is treated with braces or casts to maintain the limb in alignment while the cuboidal bones reconstitute. This problem occurs relatively infrequently. When it does, it is often associated with a premature foal or a hypothyroid foal.

When the more common situation of growth imbalance associated with the physis occurs, the management depends on the location. In the fetlock, it is generally considered an emergency and periosteal stripping is done at one to two months. The ideal time is one month and it should be done by two months. At three months, the amount of correction that can be attained is much lower and the blemish following periosteal elevation is more obvious. With carpal valgus, there is much more time for manipulation and periosteal strippings between two and six months are quite common. The principle of periosteal stripping is to transect periosteum (which acts as a normal restraining device to physeal lengthening on that side) and allow a speed-up of cartilage growth in the physis (hence, lengthening) on that side. It is a simple complication-free procedure. If the problem is not diagnosed until it is too late to obtain sufficient benefit from periosteal stripping, a second more drastic option is stapling or screw and wire fixation of the physis. The principle here is to halt growth on the fastest growing side to allow continued growth on the opposite side of the physis and straightening of the limb.

Physitis (Epiphysitis)

Physitis is also known as epiphysitis but because the problem is associated with the growth plate, the first term is more correct. The term has also been called physeal dysplasia, although not all the factors involved in what goes wrong are understood. In some instances, obvious osteochondrosis is present and radiographically retained cartilage and lipping at the edges of the physis are seen. In other instances, there is lameness and swelling associated with the physis but no abnormalities on radiographs. Microfractures may be involved. The cause of physitis is still uncertain. People have associated it with hard ground and there is no question that there are "bad seasons" for it.

In most instances, the prognosis for natural resolution of the problem is good. The foals are confined to some extent and the amount of confinement versus exercise titrated with careful observation. Horses usually present clinically between four and eight months of age. However, occasionally horses up to two years of age can be affected. The signs are usually seen in the distal radius and distal metacarpus or metatarsus. Less commonly they are seen in the first phalanx and distal tibia. The lameness varies from slight to overt.

TREATMENT

The treatment of physitis is aimed at correcting any possible nutritional deficiencies, excesses, or imbalances but in many instances none of these are recognized. Restriction of exercise is indicated when moderate to severe lameness is present and nonsteroidal anti-inflammatory drugs may relieve some of the pain associated with this condition. As mentioned previously, physitis is normally a self-limiting disease with resolution occurring when skeletal maturity is reached and growth at the affected physis ceases.

Physeal fractures

More drastic injuries to the growth plate may occur. As depicted in Figure 4, there is vulnerable tissue when cartilage cells die and undergo calcification. Fractures can occur along this plane and sometimes propagate through bone as well. These are traumatic events unrelated to any known factors in management or nutrition.

Bone disease in the athletic horse

Obviously, athletic horses sustain many forms of bone injury including chip fractures in the joint, slab fractures in the joint, stress fractures in the cannon bone, and stress fractures in the upper bone, such as the humerus, tibia and pelvis. The questions are always asked as to whether these lesions are associated with poor bone development (low calcium), or various other trace mineral imbalances.

Very little definitive data associating these problems with "bad bone" exist. There has been considerable work recently on the development of microtrauma in subchondral bone leading to more drastic injuries. It is also known that stress fractures are associated with vulnerability in the bone remodeling process.

This paper was first published in "Focus on Equine Nutrition," Proceedings for the 1996 Short Course for Feed Manufacturers

PROTEIN AND ENERGY REQUIREMENTS OF GROWING HORSES

LES BREUER

L.H. Breuer & Associates, East Alton, Illinois, USA

Introduction

There are several good sources of information on feeding young horses including the NRC Nutrient Requirement of Horses (NRC, 1989), textbooks (Cunha, 1991; Evans, Borton, Hintz and Van Vleck, 1977; Lewis, 1995) and various university extension publications. Since most feeding recommendations are based directly or indirectly on NRC nutrient recommendations, the NRC recommendations will be evaluated for accuracy and adequacy for feeding horses in the real world of the commercial horse industry. This paper will attempt to approach the subject with practical concerns of the horse producer in mind.

Some questions of practical concern are:

1. How important is mare feeding to milk production and foal growth?

2. Is it necessary to supplemental feed (creep feed) suckling foals?

3. How much protein should creep feeds and weanling feeds contain?

4. How much hay and how much concentrate should be fed to weanlings and yearlings?

5. Do colts and fillies need to be fed differently?

6. Can young horses be harmed by overfeeding? By underfeeding?

The values used in the discussion to follow are intended to apply to typical Thoroughbred, Standardbred, Quarter Horse and other light breeds with mature body weights of 1150 to 1200 lbs. The values can be lowered or raised for smaller and larger horses.

Rates of gain are used which have been observed in horse operations which are competitive in their segment of the horse industry. Discussions about whether moderate growth would be better than rapid growth are useful and this area deserves much more study. However, horse operations which are producing animals for weanling and yearling sales, halter shows, two and three year old racing, or just

407

want horses which "look" competitive really have little choice. Their goal has to be rapid growth, if not maximum growth, with as few developmental and health problems as possible. Rapid growth rates obviously require liberal amounts of energy and protein. The questions are: When? How much? In what form? To answer these questions, it is helpful to break the entire growth period into the management phases of suckling, weanling, yearling and 2 year old.

Suckling foals

The most growth in the shortest period of time occurs in the foal from birth to weaning. It is normal on successful commercial horse farms for foals to grow from about 10% of mature body weight at birth to nearly 50% of mature body weight at weaning (Hintz, Hintz and Van Vleck, 1979; Thompson, 1995). Daily gains are 2.3 to 2.4 lb. per day during the suckling phase for foals weaned at 6 months of age and even greater for earlier weaned foals. The weights shown in the NRC tables for weanlings appear to be 10% to 15% below the industry norm.

Mare milk is the only significant food the suckling foal receives during the first few weeks of its life and normally continues to be its major source of nutrients until the foal is 4 to 5 months of age. NRC concluded from their data review that mares produce an amount of milk equivalent to about 3% of their body weight for the first 12 weeks of lactation and an average of about 2% of their body weight during the next 12 weeks. Lactation studies (Zimmerman, 1981) in which mare caloric intakes required to maintain body weight are determined while producing milk to support rapid growth rates in their foals indicate that NRC DE recommendations for lactating mares are 10% to 12% low. Calculations based on weight gains of foals receiving mare milk and known amounts of supplemental feed indicate that mares are producing milk in the 4%-3% of body weight range rather than the 3%-2% range assumed by NRC. The additional milk would account for the higher DE requirements observed in the lactating mare studies.

Rapid growth rates in foals result in rapid increases in body weight, and consequently rapid increases in DE requirements for maintenance, while at the same time milk production by the mare begins to decline. Clearly, the foal must have other sources of nutrients if it is to continue to grow at rapid rates. Pasture studies with mares and foals (Breuer, 1974) indicate that older foals get significant amounts of nutrients from high quality pasture. The same would be expected when high quality hay is available to the foal. Under such conditions, foals consume supplemental concentrate at a rate of about 1% of body weight. Calculations indicate that under pasture conditions, older foals probably consume about 3% of body weight as feed dry matter, approximately equally divided between mare milk, pasture or hay, and concentrate. When pasture or hay is limited or poor quality, or mare milk production is low, voluntary concentrate intake will increase (Zimmerman, 1981).

Weanlings

To feed weanlings properly requires good management and the application of more nutritional knowledge than that required for any other class of horse. It is not unusual to see weanlings which are thin and pot-bellied with rough hair. Foals are seen which have been weaned two or three months and have gained little or no weight since weaning. Some owners accept such poor performance in weanlings as normal and unavoidable. It may be normal for some and it is arguable as to whether this is harmful to the horse but it can be avoided by paying attention to the following:

1. Psychology of weaning.
2. Health care.
3. Rations with proper nutrient density and balance.

The first two factors are outside the scope of this paper but are important in order to reduce psychological and physiological stressors to a minimum during the weaning period. Conversely, a balanced diet and a full belly will probably increase immunity to and/or help with recovery from some of the disease problems and possibly help with the psychological problems as well.

Daily weight gains for weanlings of 1.4 to 1.9 lbs. per day suggested by NRC appear to be reasonable based on experimental (Breuer, Kasten and Word, 1970; Breuer, 1974) and farm observations (Hintz, *et al.*, 1979; Thompson, 1995). However, NRC suggested dry matter intakes for weanlings of up to 3.5% of body weight appear to be too high. Practical and experimental observations indicate that 450 lb. to 500 lb. weanlings will consume a maximum of 2.8% to 2.9% of body weight of air dry matter. Thus, the total air dry matter intake for a 500 lb. foal can be expected to be about 14.5 lb. per day after a 2 to 3 week adjustment period. NRC estimates that the DE requirements of a 500 lb. weanling are 15.2 Mcal and 17.7 Mcal DE per day for weight gains of 1.4 and 1.9 lbs. per day, respectively. Therefore, the caloric densities required in 14.5 lbs. of feed theoretically should be about 1.05 and 1.22 Mcal DE per lb. for weight gains of 1.4 and 1.9 pounds per day. Using good hay and grain, a caloric density of 1.05 Mcal per lb. can be achieved with a ration composed of about 70% hay and 30% grain. Anyone with experience feeding weanlings knows they won't gain 1.4 lbs. per day on this ration. It will definitely take a lower hay:grain ratio to realize this moderate rate of gain. So where does theory go wrong? A couple of possibilities are: (a) hay DE is used less efficiently for gain than grain DE, i.e., net energy for gain in young horses is a lower percentage of digestible energy in hay than in grain, as is well recognized in ruminants and/or, (b) weanlings need more DE for gain than estimated by NRC.

Experimental data indicate that weanlings require about 5% more DE for gain than NRC recommends and that the percentage hay in the ration can be no more than 20% to 25% for rapid gains of 1.8 lbs. to 1.9 lbs. per day and 35% to 40% hay for more moderate gains of 1.3 lbs. to 1.4 lbs. per day. NRC recommends a constant 30% hay in the ration regardless of whether moderate or rapid gains are expected.

Yearlings / two year olds

Normal weight gains in yearlings range from 0.75 to 1.25 lbs. per day depending on prior feeding and development history. Yearlings which have been fed for rapid gains during the suckling and weanling phases and fed for rapid gains as yearlings will become obese, especially in the case of fillies. Yearlings which have been underfed previously may need to be fed for rapid growth similar to weanlings according to body weight rather than age. This should be done carefully to avoid DOD problems.

Experiments with yearlings which have been fed for rapid gains as suckling foals and for moderate or rapid gains as weanlings similar to common industry practice indicate that NRC recommendations for DE for gain in yearlings are as much as 15% below requirements. It may be that the NRC equation for DE requirements for growth which has a correction factor based on age doesn't adequately account for differences in previous feeding and growth histories. Possibly the equation could be improved by using body weight as a correction factor. Higher maintenance requirements due to the high level of activity in yearlings may also contribute to the apparent higher DE requirement for growth in yearlings.

Data from breeding farms (Hintz, *et al.*, 1979; Thompson, 1995) and experimental results show that colts and fillies grow at similar rates up to about a year of age but colts appear to continue to grow into their yearling year at slightly higher rates than fillies. Colts need to be fed enough additional feed to account for higher gains of 0.2 lbs. to 0.3 lbs. per day as well as any higher maintenance requirement due to the large amount of voluntary activity in yearling colts which are kept in groups or are allowed to exercise in groups.

Similar to yearlings, amounts to feed 2 year olds depend on how close they are to reaching mature weights which in turn depends on previous feeding and development history. A gain of 0.25 lbs. per day will add 100 lbs. of weight a year which should be adequate under most practical conditions. This will need to be modified if horses are put in training.

Protein requirements of growing horses

Protein requirements for growth in horses are primarily determined by requirements for the amino acids contained in the protein. This author and coworkers (Breuer and Word, 1967; Breuer and Word, 1968; Breuer, *et al.*, 1970; Breuer and Golden,

1971) demonstrated a lysine requirement in young horses thirty years ago which has been confirmed by numerous researchers (Borton, Anderson and Lyford, 1973; Hintz, Schryver and Lowe, 1971; Hintz, Schryver and Lowe, 1971;Ott, Asquith, Feaster and Martin, 1979, Ott, Asquith and Feaster, 1981; Potter and Huchton, 1975). The NRC lysine recommendations are based on a ratio of lysine to digestible energy which is decreased slightly as horses progress from weanlings to yearlings and 2 year olds. Actually these ratios only apply to a rather narrow range of weight gains and will underestimate lysine requirements in young, rapidly growing horses and overestimate requirements in older, slow growing horses. An analysis of studies on lysine requirements in horses shows that the lysine to digestible energy ratio varies widely with differences in growth rates as shown in the following table:

Daily gain (lb./day)	Lys:DE ration (gm/Mcal)	Ration protein %
1.00	1.27	11.0
1.25	1.59	12.5
1.50	1.91	14.0
1.75	2.22	15.5
2.00	2.54	17.0
2.25	2.86	18.5
2.50	3.18	20.0

The NRC values for lysine to DE ratios of around 2 gm lysine per Mcal DE would be expected to support weight gains of 1.5 lbs. to 1.75 lbs. per day which are usually satisfactory gains for 6 month old foals. However, higher lysine levels are needed in rations for orphan foals or early weaned foals and in creep feeds, especially if mare milk is severely restricted.

The ration protein levels required to meet the amino acid requirements are determined by the amino acid content and availability in the ingredients used in the ration. The values shown in the table are based on a corn-oats-soybean meal feed. Values can be lowered if higher quality protein sources or synthetic amino acid supplements are used. It should be noted that the protein levels apply to the complete ration. If a significant amount of hay is fed, the protein level in the grain feed may need to be adjusted depending on the protein content of the hay.

Studies of other amino acids in horses are limited. The other amino acids do not appear to be of much practical significance in feeding young horses. Lysine is the first-limiting amino acid in typical horse ration ingredients and if the lysine requirement is met using these ingredients, the requirements for the other amino acids will likely be met. If large amounts of unusual ingredients or synthetic amino acid supplements are used, then levels of other essential amino acids may be a concern. A recent study (Graham, Ott, Brendemuhl and TenBroeck, 1994) in yearling horses showed that threonine at 80% of the lysine level was adequate. Adequacy of other essential amino acid levels have to be evaluated in animal studies and/or by comparing to known requirements in simple stomached species such as swine, rats, and humans.

Lowering protein levels to reduce growth rates to help with DOD problems in young horses is a common recommendation in the horse industry. This practice will reduce weight gains as well as bone growth as measured by wither height. There is no question that gross over-feeding or over-consumption of high protein grain feeds will help precipitate DOD problems in susceptible horses. However, there are no definitive data showing that the feeding levels and growth rates recommended by NRC or in this paper are likely to raise the incidence of DOD problems. Practical experience with numerous feeding trials, controlled and uncontrolled, indicate that selection of the proper ration for the class of animal with respect to its amino acid and mineral content, and feeding the ration at the recommended level, will result in minimal DOD problems. There should be a concern of how nutrient restrictions will affect the expression of the genetic potential of the horse for size and structure. Reducing protein intake without a concurrent reduction in caloric intake should change the composition of gain to more fat and less muscle. If possible, it would be preferable to reduce both caloric and protein intake and try to maintain a normal muscle and fat content at the lower rate of gain.

Summary

Protein and energy nutrition can be used in horse farm management to regulate the growth and development of young horses. It does not have to be a largely uncontrolled process as is often the case. At a time when horse farm economics are a great concern, the proper application of nutritional knowledge in developing horses can result in the production of the desired animal with the highest possible feed efficiency.

References

Breuer, L.H., and J.D. Word. 1967. Studies on complete pelleted rations for horses. Proc. 22nd Texas Nutr. Conf., p.188.

Breuer, L.H., and J.D.Word. 1968. Studies on the dietary amino acid requirement of the equine. Fed. Proc. 27:730.

Breuer, L.H., L.H. Kasten and J.D. Word. 1970. Protein and amino acid utilization in the young horse. Proc. 2nd Equine Nutr. Physiol. Symp., p.16.

Breuer, L.H., and D.L. Golden. 1971. Lysine requirements of the immature equine. J. Anim. Sci.33:227.

Breuer, L.H. 1974. Feeding the breeding and the growing- developing horse. Proc. Maryland Nutr. Conf., p.102.

Borton, A., D.L. Anderson and S. Lyford. 1973. Studies of protein quality and quantity in the early weaned foal. Proc. 3rd Equine Nutr. Physiol. Symp., p.19.

Cunha, T.J. 1991. Horse Feeding and Nutrition, 2nd ed., Academic Press, NY.

Evans, J.W., A. Borton, H.F. Hintz and L.D. Van Vleck. 1977. The Horse. W.H. Freeman, San Francisco.

Graham, P.M., E.A. Ott, J.H. Brendemuhl and S.H. TenBroeck. 1994. The effect of supplemental lysine and threonine on growth and development of yearling horses. J. Anim. Sci. 72:380

Hintz, H.F., J.E. Lowe and H.F. Schryver. 1969. Protein sources for horses. Proc. Cornell Nutr. Conf., p.65.

Hintz, H.F., H.F. Schryver and J.E. Lowe. 1971. Comparison of a blend of milk products and linseed meal as protein supplements for young growing horses. J. Anim. Sci.33:1274.

Hintz, H.F., R.L Hintz, L.D. Van Vleck. 1979. Growth rate of Thoroughbreds:Effect of age of dam, year and month of birth. J. Anim. Sci. 48:480.

Lewis, L.D. 1995. Horse Feeding and Nutrition, 2nd ed., Academic Press, NY.

NRC. 1989. Nutrient Requirements of Horses, 5th ed., Nutrient Requirements of Domestic Animals. National Research Council. National Academy Press. Washington, DC.

Ott, E.A., R.L. Asquith, J.P. Feaster and F.G. Martin. 1979. Influence of protein level and quality on the growth and development of yearling foals. J. Anim. Sci. 49:620.

Ott, E.A., R.L. Asquith and J.P. Feaster. 1981. Lysine supplementation of diets for yearling horses. J. Anim. Sci. 53:1496.

Potter, G.D., and J.D. Huchton. 1975. Growth of yearling horses fed different sources of protein supplemented with lysine. Proc. 4th Equine Nutr. Physiol. Symp., p.19.

Thompson, K.N. 1995. Skeletal growth rates of weanling and yearling Thoroughbred horses. J. Anim. Sci. 73:2513.

Zimmerman, R.A. 1981 Energy needs of lactating mares. Proc. 7th Equine Nutr. Physiol. Symp., p.127.

This paper was first published in "Focus on Equine Nutrition," Proceedings for the 1996 Short Course for Feed Manufacturers

ENERGY REQUIREMENTS OF LACTATING MARES AND SUCKLING FOALS

JOE D. PAGAN

Kentucky Equine Research, Inc., Versailles, Kentucky, USA

Lactation places higher nutrient demands on the mare than any other stage of her life. Mares in early lactation produce large quantities of milk rich in protein, energy, vitamins and minerals. One of the most common mistakes made by horsemen is to underfeed mares during this period. Therefore, an understanding of the energy requirements of mares for milk production is essential to correct this problem and reduce associated reproductive disorders.

Satisfying the mare's requirements for milk production may only be part of the solution to feeding lactating mares and their foals. Does mare's milk provide enough energy and nutrients to support the type of foal growth expected by today's horse breeder? Recent research suggests that it may not. This paper will evaluate energy requirements for lactation in mares and present data showing that supplemental feed for the foal is necessary to support optimal foal growth.

Energy requirements for lactation

The energy requirements of lactating mares are usually calculated using a factorial method which estimates:

1. The mare's maintenance energy requirement.
2. The added energy required to produce milk.

The amount of energy needed to produce milk is in turn calculated based on estimates of:

1. Milk yield.
2. Milk energy content.
3. Efficiency of utilization of dietary energy for milk production.

The current NRC Nutrient Requirements for Horses (5th edition, 1989) makes the following estimates of these parameters:

1.   Maintenance DE (Mcal/day) = 1.4 + 0.03 BW (kg)

2.   Mares of light breeds produce milk equal to 3.0% BW/day during early lactation (1-12 weeks)

3.   Mare's milk contains 475 kcal GE/kg of milk

4.   Mares convert DE into milk energy (GE) with 60% efficiency.

Using these assumptions, a 500 kg mare would require 16.4 Mcal DE for maintenance + 11.9 Mcal DE to produce milk, or a total daily DE requirement of 28.3 Mcal DE/day.

In addition to the NRC, there are a number of other systems that have been used to estimate energy requirements for lactation in mares. In an excellent recent review, Doureau *et al* (1988) in France summarized these various systems (Table 1). The assumptions used in the calculation of each set of requirements vary somewhat from country to country , but overall estimates of energy required for lactation are remarkably similar. Only Abrams' (1984) estimate from the United Kingdom varied significantly from the others. This estimate, however, was based on a fairly low milk yield.

The French group has done extensive research on energy requirements in the horse. Their estimate of 30.4 Mcal DE/day is higher than any the other groups, but it agrees with DE intakes commonly seen in lactating mares under field conditions (Pagan, unpublished data) and with a large body of research data collected at Purina's research facility in Grey Summit, Missouri.

At Purina's research farm, research has been conducted for many years on the energy requirements of mares and their suckling foals. The results from 7 years of study including 164 lactation records are summarized in Table 2. Many of the same mares were included in the study over a number of lactations. None the less, these data represent the most information accumulated to date on energy requirements in lactating mares.

The mares in the Purina study consumed an average of 33.44 Mcal DE/d and gained an average of 0.25 lbs/d during the 35th through 91st day of lactation. Assuming that this weight gain was all fat deposition and that horses utilize DE for fattening with an efficiency of 55% (Pagan and Hintz, 1986), then 1.92 Mcal DE/d was used for weight gain by these mares. Therefore, these Quarter horse mares needed 31.5 Mcal DE/d to maintain zero energy balance during the second and third months of lactation. Adjusted to a 1100 lb (500 kg) mare weight, this DE requirement would equal 30.6 Mcal DE-d, 16.4 Mcal for maintenance and 14.2 Mcal for milk production. If these mares produced 3.0% for their body weight per day as milk (15 kg), and this milk had a GE content of 525 kcal/kg (a reasonable GE content for this stage of lactation), then these mares would convert DE to GE in milk with an efficiency of about 55%. This GE content is higher than used by the NRC and the efficiency of absorption is slightly lower. These assumptions, however, are in agreement with

Table 1. ENERGY REQUIREMENTS ACCORDING TO DIFFERENT SYSTEMS FOR A 500 kg (1100 LB) LACTATING MARE[1]

	Total requirements (Mcal DE/day)	Maintenance Basis for calculation	Requirements (Mcal DE/day)	Lactation Basis for calculation	Requirements (Mcal DE/day)
Norway (Nedkvitne, 1976)	28.9	DE (Mcal/d) = 138.3 BW (kg)$^{0.75}$	14.6	Milk yield = 18 kg Milk GE - 476 kcal/kg NE/DE = 0.60	14.3
U.S.A. (N.R.C., 1989)	28.3	DE (Mcal/d) = 1.4 + 0.03 BW (kg)	16.4	Milk yield = 15 kg Milk GE = 475 kcal/kg NE for milk/DE = 0.60	11.9
F.R.G. (Meyer, 1979)	27.5	DE (Mcal/d) = 140 BW (kg)$^{0.75}$	15.0	Milk yield = 13.5 kg Milk GE = 550 kcal/kg NE for milk/DE = 0.66	12.5
United Kingdom (Abrams, 1984)	23.0	12.1 Mcal DE for 450 kg horse, linear relationship with weight	13.5	Milk yield = 10 kg Milk GE = 524 kcal/kg NE for milk/DE = 0.65 ME/DE = 0.85	9.5
France (I.N.R.A., 984)	30.4	DE (Mcal/d) = 147 BW (kg)$^{0.75}$	15.5	Milk yield = 15 kg Milk GE = 550 kcal/kg NE for milk/DE = 0.65 ME/DE = 0.85	14.9

[1]Adapted from Doreau *et al* (1988)

the French system. It appears from these data that the DE requirements for lactating mares is about 8% higher than estimated by the NRC.

Table 2. SUMMARY OF 164 MARE LACTATION RECORDS[1,2]

Variable	Mean	Standard deviation	Minimum	Maximum
Mare weight (lbs)[3]	1132.50	96.90	884.00	1382.00
Mare DE intake (Mcal/d)	33.44	3.34	24.79	39.97
Mare ADG (lbs/d)	0.25	0.55	-1.16	1.61
Foal DE intake[4] (Mcal/d)	3.05	1.77	0.02	8.63
Foal ADG (lbs/d)	2.41	0.40	1.23	3.21

[1] Data from Purina Mills, Inc. research farm
[2] Records for 35-91 days of lactation
[3] 7 day postpartum mare weight
[4] Foal DE intake as supplemental feed

Supplemental energy required by the suckling foal

The 1989 NRC does not give specific feeding recommendations for the suckling foal other than to say that supplemental feed prior to weaning may be desirable in foals nursing mares that are poor milkers. This differs from the previous NRC edition (1978) which recommended that suckling foals three months of age receive 6.89 Mcal DE/d as supplemental feed.

What is the expected growth rate of a foal of this age and does the mare produce enough milk to support this growth rate?

The 1978 NRC suggested that a 3 month old foal weighing 341 lbs should gain 2.64 lbs./day. Hintz *et al* (1979) reported on growth rates in 1,992 Thoroughbred foals. These foals averaged about 2.65 lbs gain/day during the second and third months of lactation. Quarter horse foals in the Purina study averaged about 2.41 lbs ADG over this same time period. These foals consumed an average of 3.05 Mcal DE per day as supplemental feed over this two month period. Regression analysis of these data (weighted for mare weight) yields the equation:

Foal ADG (lbs./day) = 2.08 + 0.109 (foal DE (Mcal DE/d))

Using this equation, foals would need to consume 5.23 Mcal of supplemental DE/ day to gain 2.65 lb/day during the second and third months of lactation. No supplemental feeding would result in a growth rate of 2.08 lbs/day. These figures agree with Doureau *et al* (1982) who stated that foals require 15 kg of milk per kg liveweight gain at 8 weeks of lactation. Fifteen kilograms per day is the expected lactation. Thus, milk alone during this period of lactation could only be expected to support a growth rate of 2.1-2.2 lbs./day, a growth rate which is below that desired by today's horseman.

Figure 1 describes the relationship between suckling foal growth and supplemental DE intake during the second and third months of lactation. Typical foal concentrates contain around 1.5 Mcal DE/lb. Therefore, a foal of this age would need to eat about 3.5 lbs.of this type feed per day to support the type of growth rate typically seen under commercial conditions. It is not known how much hay and pasture a suckling foal will consume, but these energy sources should be kept in mind when deciding how much supplemental grain to feed. Ideally, weighing the foal regularly can aid in adjusting its grain intake.

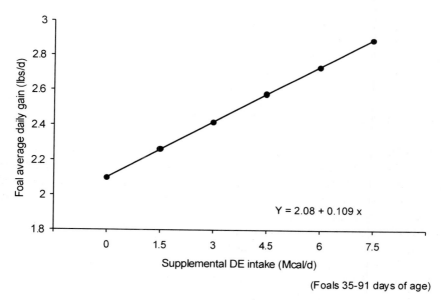

$Y = 2.08 + 0.109 x$

(Foals 35-91 days of age)

Figure 1. The relationship between foal growth and supplemental DE intake

It should also be noted that higher supplemental DE intakes may result in elevated growth rates which are undesirable since accelerated growth at this early age may contribute to developmental orthopedic disease in foals. It would therefore seem unwise to allow suckling foals free access to supplemental feed in a "creep" feeding arrangement. Instead, the foal should be fed a weighed amount of supplemental feed when the mare is fed. This can easily be accomplished by simply tying up the mare at meal time. It is a good management practice to feed both the mare and the foal at least twice daily, and three or four times per day if possible.

In conclusion, 1100 lb mares require about 30.5 Mcal DE/day during the first three months of lactation. 16.4 Mcal DE would be required by the mare for maintenance and 14.2 Mcal DE would be required to produce 15 kg of milk. This level of milk production is inadequate to support optimal foal growth during the second and third months of lactation. Around 5 Mcal supplemental DE would be required by a three month old foal. In using the rule of thumb of 1 lb. of feed per month of age would seem to satisfy the suckling foal's supplemental DE requirement.

References

Abrams, J.T., 1984. Foods and feeding. In: Horse Management. Academic Press, London. J. Hickman (ed.). pp. 93-151.

Doureau, M., W. Martin-Rosset and S. Boulot, 1988. Energy Requirements and the Feeding of Mares during Lactation: A review. Livestock Production Science, 20 (1988), pp. 53-68.

Doureau, M., W., Martin-Rosset and H. Dubroeucq, 1982. Production laitiere de la jument. Liaison avec la croissance du poulain. C.R. 8eme Journee d' etude du CEREOPA, CEREOPA, Paris, pp. 88-100.

Hintz, H. F., R. L. Hintz, and L. D. Van Vleck, 1979. Growth Rate of Thoroughbreds. Effect of Age of Dam, Year and Month of Birth and Sex of Foal. Journal of Animal Science. 48, 480-487.

I.N.R.A., 1984. Le Cheval. Reproduction, Selection, Alimentation, Exploitation. I.N.R.A., Paris, R. Jarrige and W. Martin-Rosset (eds.).

Meyer, H., 1979. Ernahrung des Pferds. In: Pferdezucht und Pferdefutterung. Eugen Ulmer, Stuttgart, H. Lowe and H. Meyer (eds.), pp. 262-397.

NRC. 1989. Nutrient Requirements of Horses, Fifth Revised Edition. National Academy Press, Washington, D.C.

NRC. 1978. Nutrient Requirements of Horses, Fourth Revised Edition. National Academy Press, Washington, D.C.

Nedkvitne, J.J., 1976. Forelesningar om foring av hestar. Agric. Univ. Norway, pp. 24-26.

Pagan and Hintz, 1986. Equine Energetics. I. Relationship Between Body Weight and Energy Requirements in Horses. Journal of Animal Science, 63, pp. 815 - 821.

DELIVERING ESSENTIAL NUTRIENTS TO YOUNG, GROWING HORSES

STEPHEN E. DUREN

Kentucky Equine Research, Inc., Versailles, Kentucky, USA

Introduction

The goal of raising performance horses is to produce sound athletes. One potential pitfall in raising this type of horse is unsoundness resulting from Developmental Orthopedic Disease. The term Developmental Orthopedic Disease (DOD) includes all general growth disturbances resulting from any alteration in normal bone formation (Lewis, 1995). DOD has many manifestations in growing horses including: 1) physitis, 2) wobblers syndrome, 3) angular limb deformities, 4) flexural leg deformities and 5) osteochondritis dissecans. The causes of DOD have been debated over the past ten years. Currently, the most common causes of DOD are thought to be: trauma to the metaphyseal growth plate or articular cartilage, genetics, rapid growth, nutritional imbalances and environment. With nutrition being one potential factor in DOD, adequately fortifying and properly balancing the diets for young growing horses is very important.

To properly fortify and balance a diet for a young growing horse, it is essential to have an understanding of which nutrients are most critical for proper skeletal growth. Further, one must have an understanding of the requirements for these critical nutrients. Understanding the critical nutrients and their requirements is only the first step in properly feeding growing horses. With so many different feedstuffs available, all with very different nutrient profiles, a working knowledge of feeding practices including the amount and type of feed provided and the expected growth rate of the horse is important. The following paper will discuss the essential nutrients for proper skeletal growth along with their requirements. In addition, some of the many different methods available to deliver essential nutrients to growing horses will be explored.

Critical nutrients for growth

The critical nutrients required for growth among different animals are basically similar. All animals require energy, protein (amino acids), minerals and vitamins. However, the actual nutrients which are considered in balancing diets for various farm animals are very different. For example the nutrients which are actively balanced in poultry diets are listed below.

Energy

Protein   *Amino acids*
                 Methionine
                 Cystine
                 Lysine
                 Threonine
                 Tryptophan
                 Arginine

Minerals   *Macro*   *Micro*
                 Calcium   Copper
                 Phosphorus   Iodine
                 Sodium   Iron
                 Potassium   Manganese
                 Chloride   Selenium
                                      Zinc

Vitamins   *Fat-soluble*   *Water soluble*
                 A   Choline
                 D   Pantothenic acid
                 E   Pyridoxine
                 K

As one can see, the list of nutrients is considerable. There are several reasons for this intense accountability of nutrients. First, the digestive system of the chicken does not provide extensive microbial synthesis of nutrients. Second, chickens are typically confined and gather their entire nutrient requirement from a complete diet provided to them.

In horses, the list of critical nutrients for growth is smaller. Although many nutrients are required, the most critical nutrients for growth of young horses are listed below.

Energy

Protein   *Amino acid*
                 Lysine

Minerals   *Macro*   *Micro*
                 Calcium   Copper
                 Phosphorus   Zinc

A complete discussion of energy and protein requirements of young, growing horses is provided elsewhere in these proceedings. Therefore, this paper will focus on the critical minerals necessary for proper skeletal growth.

Calcium

Calcium is the first mineral often considered in the diets of young horses. Calcium makes up about 35% of bone structure (El Shorafa *et al.*, 1979), with approximately 99% of the calcium in the body found in the bones and teeth (Lewis, 1995). Calcium is also involved in other body functions including muscle contraction and blood clotting mechanisms. Inadequate calcium intake by the developing foal can lead to rickets, which is characterized by poor mineralization of the osteoid tissue and the probability of enlarged joints and crooked long bones (NRC, 1989). The scientific data pointing to the ill-effects of a calcium-deficient diet have also been reported in the field. Knight and co-workers (1985) reported a negative linear relationship between dietary calcium intake and perceived severity of DOD in young horses. Excess calcium has also been fed to young horses. In a study reported by Jordan and co-workers (1975) feeding five times the calcium requirement was not detrimental provided the level of phosphorus in the diet was adequate.

Phosphorus

Phosphorus is also a critical mineral for proper skeletal development. Phosphorus is often considered with calcium since it also is a major component of bone, making up 14 - 17% of the skeleton (El Shorafa *et al.*, 1979). Two major problems can exist with growing horses relative to phosphorus supplementation. The first is inadequate phosphorus in the diet. A simple phosphorus deficiency can result in DOD and bone demineralization. The second condition is excessive phosphorus content in the diet, a situation in which phosphorus concentration is actually greater than calcium concentration, and phosphorus interferes with calcium absorption.

Copper and zinc

Copper is required by growing horses as a component of several copper-dependent enzymes involved with elastin and collagen formation (NRC, 1980). Young growing horses with inadequate copper intake do not suffer from slow growth rate; instead, normal or rapid growth continues but without adequate copper for normal bone and cartilage development. The end result is foals with decreased bone density and DOD (Lewis, 1995). Cymbaluk and co-workers (1981) reported that copper absorption by the horse decreases with increasing copper intake giving horses a high tolerance to excess copper ingestion. The NRC (1989) reported the maximum tolerance level of copper to be 800 mg/kg diet.

Zinc is required as a component of many metalloenzymes involved in protein and carbohydrate metabolism. Low zinc concentration has been correlated with an increased incidence of DOD in growing horses (Knight *et al.*, 1985). The NRC (1989) reported the maximum tolerance level of zinc to be 500 mg/kg diet.

Nutrient requirements

The National Research Council has published a booklet listing the Nutrient Requirements of Horses. The most recent edition of this booklet is the fifth revised edition published in 1989 (NRC, 1989). In this publication, a subcommittee of six equine nutrition research scientists reviewed the equine nutrition literature and updated the nutrient requirements of horses. The requirements stated in the booklet represent the *minimum* amounts needed to sustain normal health, production and performance of horses. In the introduction of this publication, the subcommittee suggested that consideration be given when applying these recommendations to, among other things, the individual variation in horses, expected performance and different environmental conditions. Therefore, the NRC should be viewed as a good starting place for the formulation of horse rations, and not as the only or best source of information.

Due to the frequency of publication of updated NRC guidelines, the last revision already seven years old, the NRC cannot contain the most up-to-date information. In an effort to remain current with advances in equine nutrition, Kentucky Equine Research continuously reviews new research, and also conducts and publishes research done in our laboratory. As a result of these efforts, Kentucky Equine Research has modified certain NRC requirements to be more practical in the production of sound, athletic horses. Modifications of NRC requirements which appear in this text along with modifications appearing in the MicroSteed™ computer program are safe additions to horse diets and are currently being used by the staff of Kentucky Equine Research.

The requirements for those nutrients critical to growth of young horses appear in the following tables. In each table, the minimum requirement established by the NRC, 1989, appears followed by the requirements established by Kentucky Equine Research.

Table 1. NUTRIENT REQUIREMENTS FOR 4-MONTH-OLD WEANLING (385 LBS) GAINING 1.87 LBS PER DAY, 1100 LB MATURE WEIGHT.

Requirement	Ca (g/d)	Phos (g/d)	Cu (mg/d)	Zn (mg/d)
NRC '89	34	19	50	198
KER	39	26	150	450

Table 2. NUTRIENT REQUIREMENTS FOR 6-MONTH-OLD WEANLING (473 LBS) GAINING 1.43 LBS PER DAY, 1100 LB MATURE WEIGHT .

Requirement	Ca (g/d)	Phos (g/d)	Cu (mg/d)	Zn (mg/d)
NRC '89	29	16	52	207
KER	36	24	150	450

Table 3. NUTRIENT REQUIREMENTS FOR 6-MONTH-OLD WEANLING (473 LBS) GAINING 1.87 LBS PER DAY, 1100 LB MATURE WEIGHT.

Requirement	Ca (g/d)	Phos (g/d)	Cu (mg/d)	Zn (mg/d)
NRC '89	36	20	59	237
KER	42	28	150	450

Table 4. NUTRIENT REQUIREMENTS FOR 12-MONTH-OLD YEARLING (715 LBS) GAINING 1.10 LBS PER DAY, 1100 LB MATURE WEIGHT.

Requirement	Ca (g/d)	Phos (g/d)	Cu (mg/d)	Zn (mg/d)
NRC '89	29	16	67	270
KER	45	30	150	450

Table 5. NUTRIENT REQUIREMENTS FOR 12-MONTH-OLD YEARLING (715 LBS) GAINING 1.43 LBS PER DAY, 1100 LB MATURE WEIGHT.

Requirement	Ca (g/d)	Phos (g/d)	Cu (mg/d)	Zn (mg/d)
NRC '89	34	19	76	303
KER	50	33	150	450

Table 6. NUTRIENT REQUIREMENTS FOR 18-MONTH-OLD YEARLING (880 LBS) GAINING 0.77 LBS PER DAY, 1100 LB MATURE WEIGHT.

Requirement	Ca (g/d)	Phos (g/d)	Cu (mg/d)	Zn (mg/d)
NRC '89	27	15	79	317
KER	46	31	150	450

Now that we have established the critical nutrients for growth and their requirements, it is time to apply this information to feeding growing horses.

Understanding the variables

To begin the process of providing essential nutrients to growing horses, one must realize that methods of feeding vary greatly throughout the United States and the world. Many feeding variables exist, each providing a series of challenges for delivering the proper amount of diet fortification. The following are several examples of common feeding variables.

Availability and quality of natural and/or stored forage

The types of forages (pasture and/or hay) which are available to young growing horses have a significant impact on diet fortification. Young, growing horses are capable of eating 1.5 - 2% of body weight in high quality pasture or hay per horse per day. Depending on the nutritive value of the hay or pasture, this can have a profound influence on the nutrient intake of the growing horses, and thus the remaining nutrients which need to be supplied by grain supplementation. For example, the difference in nutritive value between alfalfa and timothy hay is immense, with alfalfa typically having more energy, protein and calcium than timothy hay. Further, the difference between hay or pasture utilized in a young, vegetative state vs. a mature state is important, since the nutritive value and the intake of forage decreases with increased maturity.

Amount of supplemental feed (grain) typically fed

The amount of grain fed to young, growing horses varies widely throughout the world. For example, the normal amount of grain fed to a yearling Thoroughbred in central Kentucky is much greater than typically fed to a yearling Thoroughbred in Washington. The amount of grain accepted as a "normal" intake for a Quarter Horse weanling halter prospect is much greater than fed to a Quarter Horse weanling not intended for show. These basic differences in the amount of grain considered to be "acceptable" will have large implications on the amount of fortification which should be contained in these grain mixtures. Unfortunately, many manufacturers pay little attention to the amount of grain which is actually being fed by the horse-owner.

Desired growth rate

The rate at which growing horses gain weight is a function of the amount of feed provided and their genetic capacity for growth. The body weight of a growing horse can be controlled by adjusting the intake of calories. Horse-owners who desire rapid weight gain in young horses will typically provide a larger proportion of calories from grain concentrates. Since these horses are eating more pounds of grain per day, the concentration of nutrients in that grain can be less. On the other hand, horse breeders who do not stress rapid weight gain in young horses typically feed fewer pounds of grain. Grain concentrates for these horse breeders must be more concentrated since fewer pounds are provided to the horse. Both the fast-growing and slower-growing horses need proper dietary fortification; however, the amount of energy (calories) provided with this fortification must be different.

Ability to feed horses individually

In many areas of the world growing horses are fed individually a measured amount of feed on a daily basis. This is the best case scenario for feeding young horses. Unfortunately, many breeders of horses are unable to feed their young stock individually. In these situations young horses are fed in groups where one horse potentially can monopolize the feed. A feed product destined for use in this type of situation would need to have a low energy content, or a low intake, to prevent excessive growth, but still have a safe level of fortification to provide each horse with critical nutrients for growth.

Each of these variables provides a series of challenges for delivering the proper amount of diet fortification. The following are actual diets which can be formulated to address these common feeding variables.

The diets

In the following examples, several feeding programs will be developed for a 12-month-old yearling weighing 715 lbs, gaining 1.1 lbs per day with an expected mature weight of 1100 lbs. The nutrient requirements for this horse are listed in Table 4.

EXAMPLE 1

The first feeding situation is an example for supplying critical nutrients using three different levels of grain intake (moderate, low, and minimal). In this example, the yearling diet consists of free-choice access to good quality pasture, with supplemental grain feeding twice daily. In Figure 1, the yearling is on a moderate grain intake (8 lbs/horse/day) with an estimated intake of pasture dry matter of 12 lbs/horse/day. The level of fortification found in the pasture (DM) and the level of fortification necessary in the grain concentrate (as-fed) to balance the remainder of critical nutrients are shown below.

Ingredient	Ca (%)	P (%)	Cu (ppm)	Zn (ppm)
Pasture	0.37	0.27	15	28
14% Textured feed	0.80	0.60	35	95

The same yearling on a low grain intake is shown in Figure 2. In this example, the yearling is receiving 4.5 lbs of grain/horse/day with pasture dry matter intake estimated at 15.5 lbs/horse/day. Since the yearling is eating fewer pounds of grain/ day, the concentration of nutrients in that grain must be higher to satisfy the nutrient requirements. The level of fortification necessary in the low intake grain concentrate is shown below, compared with the nutrient profile of the grain used in the previous example.

Ingredient	Ca (%)	P (%)	Cu (ppm)	Zn (ppm)
14% Textured	0.80	0.60	35	95
Low intake sweet feed	0.95	0.80	70	200

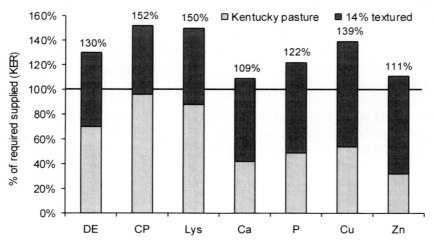

Figure 1. Yearling - high grain intake

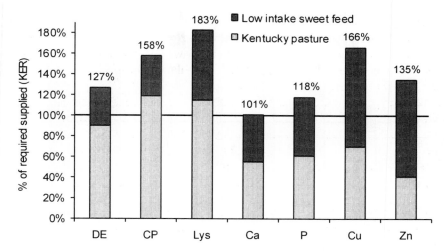

Figure 2. Yearling - moderate grain intake

Finally, there are horse feed clients who want to feed the absolute minimum amount of grain necessary to their horses. On good quality pastures, it is possible for the yearling in this example to consume enough pasture to satisfy requirements for digestible energy and protein to maintain a moderate level of growth (1.1 lbs/horse/day). However, the concentration of critical nutrients (calcium, phosphorus, copper and zinc) will not be adequate in a pasture-only diet. To properly balance a diet in this situation, it is estimated the yearling will consume nearly 16 lbs of pasture dry matter/day along with 1.25 lbs of supplement/horse/day. The nutrient profile of this diet is depicted in Figure 3. The nutrient profile of the supplement pellet is shown below.

Ingredient	Ca (%)	P (%)	Cu (ppm)	Zn (ppm)
14% Textured feed	0.80	0.60	35	95
Low intake sweet feed	0.95	0.80	70	200
Supplement pellet	5.00	2.00	300	800

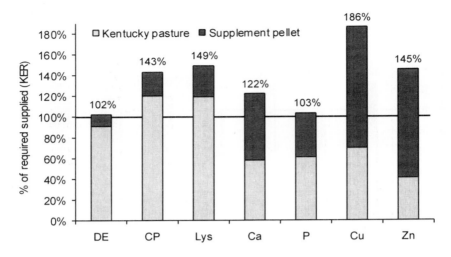

Figure 3. Yearling - supplement pellet

EXAMPLE 2

In this scenario, the horse owner is free-choice feeding good quality alfalfa hay to our example yearling. The alfalfa diet is supplying adequate energy, protein and calcium to support the desired moderate growth rate, but is marginal in phosphorus, copper and zinc. This is a situation very common to young growing horses in the west, where high quality alfalfa hay is common. To properly balance this diet, one would want to feed a low intake supplement pellet which provided essential phosphorus, copper and zinc, but did not add a significant amount of energy, protein or calcium since these nutrients are already in excess. In Figure 4, a final diet consisting of alfalfa (15.5 lbs/horse/day) and 1.5 lbs of a specially designed mixing pellet to be fed with alfalfa hay is shown. The nutrient profile of this mixing pellet is unique since it contains low protein (9%), an inverted ratio of calcium to phosphorus and high trace mineral concentrations. In formulating such a product, it is essential this supplement pellet be used only in diets for horses eating predominantly alfalfa hay (greater than 50% of the forage consisting of alfalfa).

Ingredient	Ca (%)	P (%)	Cu (ppm)	Zn (ppm)
Supplement pellet - alfalfa	0.50	2.60	200	800

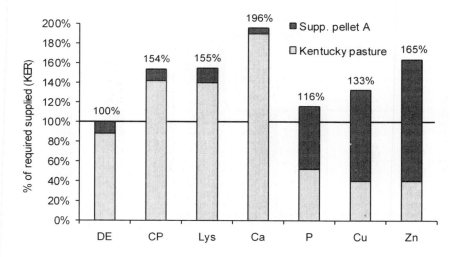

Figure 4. Yearling - maximum forage

EXAMPLE 3

Despite the best efforts of the owners, our example yearling has developed DOD. The veterinary surgeon involved has suggested an energy restricted diet to avoid any further rapid weight gain. It is important to realize that an energy restricted diet will decrease the rate of gain; however, the skeleton of the yearling will continue to grow. The end result is a yearling which has grown taller, but has become progressively thinner. Since the skeleton of the yearling continues to grow even on an energy restricted diet, it is important that the horse receive adequate levels of essential nutrients required for growth. In figure 5, the yearling can be fed at approximately 70% of energy requirements with adequate nutrients to support continued skeletal growth. The diet consists of 11 lbs of mixed hay (alfalfa/grass) plus 2.5 lbs of a protein, vitamin and mineral supplement pellet (All-Phase).

Ingredient	Ca (%)	P (%)	Cu (ppm)	Zn (ppm)
Mixed hay	0.85	0.26	6	25
All-Phase pellet	3.00	2.00	140	340

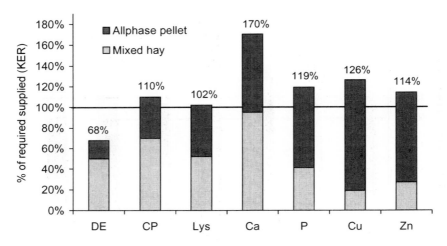

Figure 5. Yearling - DOD diet

EXAMPLE 4

The directions on the feed bag suggest that our example yearling receive the grain concentrate at a minimum rate of 8 lbs/horse/day. These directions were placed on the bag in order for the horse to get adequate diet fortification. Unfortunately, the owners of the horse do not want to feed any more than 5 lbs of grain/horse/day. If they only feed 5 lbs of this grain/horse/day along with a mixed hay (14 lbs/horse/ day) the yearling will be marginal in phosphorus, copper and zinc intake (Figure 6). A method which can be used to provide the requirement of essential nutrients while still adhering to the owners' maximum of 5 lbs of grain/horse/day rule is shown in Figure 7. In this situation, the intake of mixed hay remains constant while the level of grain concentrate is dropped from 5 lbs/day to 3.5 lbs/day. The remaining 1.5 lbs, which has been set aside for grain intake, is provided as a supplement pellet rather than the normal grain. The finished diet will then consist of 14 lbs of mixed hay/horse/day, 3.5 lbs of grain concentrate and 1.5 lbs of supplement pellet (All-Phase).

EXAMPLE 5

Finally, there are horse owners who raise young horses in situations which do not allow them to feed grain and/or supplement pellets on a daily basis. Hay and/or pasture are available free-choice, but supplemental grain feeding is not possible. The young horses still require diet fortification, but this fortification must be provided with a free-choice supplement. This free-choice supplement must be palatable and self limit intake. Fortified molasses blocks can be used to accomplish this goal.

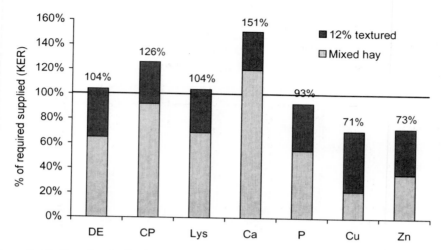

Figure 6. Yearling - low fortification

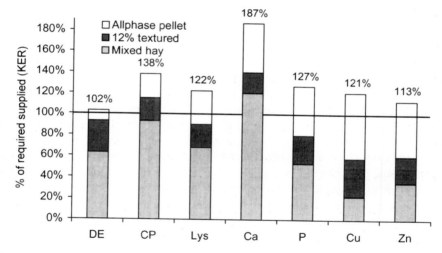

Figure 7. Yearling - balanced diet

Figure 8 depicts a diet for our example yearling. In this diet, the yearling is eating approximately 17 lbs of mixed hay/day along with 3 lbs/day of a well-fortified molasses block. It is important that the concentrations of nutrients which are contained in the block are appropriate for the actual intake. In other words, the intake of these blocks by young horses needs to be monitored to insure proper fortification. If intake of these blocks is grossly over or under the recommended intake, the blocks will do a poor job of balancing the diet. The appropriate level of nutrient fortification in a free-choice molasses block with a targeted intake of 3 lbs/horse/day is shown below.

Ingredient	Ca (%)	P (%)	Cu (ppm)	Zn (ppm)
Mixed hay	0.85	0.26	6	25
Forti-Sweet Block	1.75	1.00	135	245

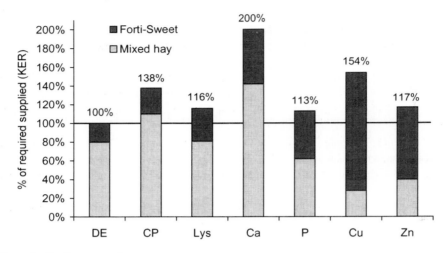

Figure 8. Yearling - no grain

Conclusion

Nutrition imbalances have been recognized as one potential cause of DOD in young, growing horses. Therefore, it is important that the diets of young horses be properly balanced with nutrients known to be critical to proper development. In young, growing horses the major nutrients of concern are protein, energy, calcium, phosphorus, copper and zinc. Each of these nutrients has minimum requirements put forth by the National Research Council (NRC, 1989). Kentucky Equine Research has elevated the requirements for these essential nutrients to allow an increased margin of safety, and to make them more practical in the production of sound, athletic horses. Understanding the essential nutrients and their requirements is the first step in properly feeding young horses. Next, one must understand the many variables associated with feeding including: 1) the availability and quality of natural and/or stored forage, 2) the amount of supplemental feed (grain) typically fed, 3) the desired growth rate and 4) the ability to feed horses individually. Once this information is put together, a properly balanced grain or supplement can be designed to balance the diet.

References

Cymbaluk, N.F., H.F. Schryver, and H.F. Hintz. 1981. Copper metabolism and requirements in mature ponies. J. Nutr. 111:87.

El Shorafa, W.M., J.P. Feaster, and E.A. Ott. 1979. Horse metacarpal bone: Age, ash content, cortical area, and failure-stress interrelationships. J. Anim. Sci. 49:979.

Jordan, R.M., V.S. Meyers, B. Yoho, and F.A. Spurrell. 1975. Effect of calcium and phosphorus levels on growth, reproduction and bone development of ponies. J. Anim. Sci. 40:78.

Knight, D.A., A.A. Gabel, S.M. Reed, L.R. Bramlage, W.J. Tyznik, and R.M. Embertson. 1985. Correlation of dietary mineral to incidence and severity of metabolic bone disease in Ohio and Kentucky. P. 445 in Proc. 31st Am. Assoc. Eq. Pract., F.J. Milne ed. Lexington, KY.

Lewis, L.D. 1995. Equine Clinical Nutrition: Feeding and Care. Williams and Wilkins, Baltimore, MD, USA.

N.R.C., 1980. Mineral Tolerance of Domestic Animals. National Academy Press. Washington, DC, USA.

N.R.C., 1989. Nutrient Requirements of Horses. 5th revised edition. National Academy Press. Washington, DC, USA.

This paper was first published in "Focus on Equine Nutrition," Proceedings for the 1996 Short Course for Feed Manufacturers

GROWTH MANAGEMENT OF YOUNG HORSES TO ACHIEVE DIFFERENT COMMERCIAL ENDPOINTS

STEPHEN G. JACKSON

Kentucky Equine Research, Inc., Versailles, Kentucky, USA

Unlike other livestock, horses are bred, kept and raised solely for the enjoyment of man. The number of breed associations in existence is testament to the fact that uses of the horse are varied. The purpose for which one breed of horse is raised may have no relationship to the primary purpose of another breed. There are differences between breeds in use or function and within breeds there is variation in type and use. Probably nowhere is this more true than in the "stock horse" breeds where horses may be used for halter, rail classes, racing, cattle classes and so on. The reality that we as nutritionists deal with is widely divergent nutritional management required to achieve different commercial endpoints. It is really of no significance to tell a man raising futurity horses that he is feeding a young horse too much feed. If he does not maximize growth and condition early on, he will not win a prize come futurity time. When making feeding and feed recommendations one must be acutely aware of the goal the horseman is trying to achieve with his or her horses.

The horses

As I perceive the industry of raising young horses, the horses fit into a few pretty widely divergent categories based on how they will be used and marketed. Each of these classes of horses have unique nutrient requirements needed to support the level of growth and differences in body composition which will allow them to be successful. These horses can't be divided solely by age at which they are going to be marketed as there are differences in what is expected even for horses of the same age. The types of horses that we deal with in designing nutrition programs are as follows:

Futurity weanlings
Weanlings to be sold as weanlings
Weanlings to be kept
Halter yearlings
Summer sale yearlings
Fall sale yearlings
Yearlings to be retained

It is prudent for us to discuss the physiology of growth that must be considered in dealing with young horses which are to be "used" prior to maturity. In all of the classes of horses above except for yearlings to be retained, the common denominator is that the growth curve must be moved to the left. Speeding physiological maturity is not simply a matter of adding weight but if done correctly, means increasing skeletal growth, muscle protein accretion and fat deposition. Many people think the futurity weanling or halter yearling is simply a fat weanling or yearling. If the feeding management, fitting and exercise programs are done correctly these "fat" young horses not only carry more condition but are also taller for their age and have greater muscle mass as well. The goal, then, is to encourage greater physiological maturity at an earlier chronological age. To get this done and not sacrifice quality of growth and skeletal integrity is the real challenge.

Nutrient requirements for growth "and fattening"

The basis for proper growth requires that the requirements for all nutrients be met in a manner that allows growth to proceed in a balanced and synchronized manner.

Nutrient requirements for growth listed in the NRC publication, "Nutrient Requirements of Horses" or those requirements that Kentucky Equine Research (KER) has derived from the research concerning growing horses should be considered a commercial starting point. The requirements listed by the NRC are described as being minimum values for normal growth and those of KER are optimum rather than minimum values.

For a producer in the business of raising two-year-olds to race or to show the KER requirements are quite adequate. When a producer needs to alter normal growth, precision and care need to be practiced in meeting nutrient requirements.

When a commercial feed is formulated, the concentration of nutrients in the feed is based on an estimate of the dry matter intake for the specific class of horse to which the feed is to be fed. Additionally some kind of thought should have gone into the type of forage that might be fed and the average nutritive value of the forage. This approach is usually close to correct if the assumptions are correct. The horse is generally pretty forgiving and tolerates a wide range of nutrient intakes without too many problems. When programs like the ones shown in tables 1 and 2 are used, there is the potential for problems. On one end of the spectrum, large amounts of unfortified cereal grains are fed. These programs many times result in the horse being fed far more phosphorus than calcium and in frank deficiencies of many of the trace minerals. The other extreme, while intended to be nutritionally more correct, results in excessive intakes of many nutrients. If a legume or heavy mixed hay is fed this is particularly true for calcium and protein. Although there are no definitive data which show that calcium intakes like those seen in table 2 are detrimental, there is no justification for exceeding the requirement for any nutrient to the extent seen here. This is one of the major problems with feeding a grain mix to horses based simply on the concentrations

Table 1. TYPICAL HAY AND OATS FEEDING PROGRAM FOR WEANLINGS. (SIX MONTH OLD WEANLINGS WEIGHT OF 550 LBS. DRY MATTER BASIS)

Daily nutrient intake	Mixed hay	Oats-grain	Requirements (KER)	Total nutrients	% of required supplied
Intake (lb/day)	7.02	9.00		16.02	
DM (lb/day)	6.18	8.03	16.5	14.21	
Protein (lb/day)	1.09	1.06	1.92	2.15	112
Lysine (oz/day)	0.39	0.56	1.29	0.96	74
DE (Mcal/day)	5.74	11.66	17.40	17.40	100
Ca (g/day)	27.12	3.27	44.25	30.40	69
P (g/day)	8.93	13.91	29.50	22.84	77
Mg (g/day)	7.98	5.73	14.75	13.70	93
Na (g/day)	3.19	2.05	22.50	5.24	23
Cl (g/day)	12.76	3.68	33.75	16.45	49
K (g/day)	76.26	16.36	52.50	92.63	176
Cu (mg/day)	31.91	24.55	150.00	56.45	38
Se (mg/day)	0.29	0.86	1.88	1.15	61
Zn (mg/day)	63.82	143.18	450.00	207.00	46
Iodine (mg/day)	0.26	0.45	1.50	0.71	47
Mn (mg/day)	143.59	147.27	500.00	290.86	58

Table 2. WEANLING FEEDING PROGRAM FEATURING A 16% PROTEIN COMMERICAL CONCENTRATE AND ALFALFA HAY.

Daily nutrient intake	16% pellet	Alfalfa hay	Requirements (KER)	Total nutrients	% of required supplied
Intake (lb/day)	9.00	8.00		17.01	
DM (lb/day)	8.10	7.24	15.00	15.33	
Protein (lb/day)	1.44	1.44	1.61	2.89	180
Lysine (oz/day)	0.94	1.04	1.08	1.98	183
DE (Mcal/day)	12.27	8.15	14.58	20.42	140
Ca (g/day)	36.82	46.55	36.14	83.36	231
P (g/day)	28.64	6.91	24.09	35.55	148
Mg (g/day)	12.27	11.27	12.05	23.55	195
Na (g/day)	17.18	5.09	20.45	22.27	109
Cl (g/day)	22.09	13.82	30.68	35.91	117
K (g/day)	28.64	84.36	47.73	113.00	237
Cu (mg/day)	163.64	41.45	150.00	205.09	137
Se (mg/day)	1.76	1.82	1.70	3.58	210
Zn (mg/day)	450.00	98.18	450.00	548.18	122
Iodine (mg/day)	1.23	0.55	1.36	1.77	130
Mn (mg/day)	409.09	120.00	500.00	529.09	106

that by convention have been recognized as appropriate. In reality, the appropriate feed for any class of horse should be based on intake, type of forage fed and the nutrient concentrations in all of the dietary constituents. While a "16 percent" may be appropriate for a young horse on grass hay, a "12 percent" may be the most appropriate feed for a young horse on a high intake of legume hays. This is why a thorough evaluation of the entire program is necessary if the nutrient requirements of the horse are to be accurately met.

Many times when feeding programs are put together, little or no emphasis is put on the forage feeding program. Nutrient requirements are met using a concentrate feed and nutrients derived from the forage are considered bonus nutrients. When confinement systems are used and when horses are raised in "pipe corrals" this is not as much of a concern as when good pasture is available. Weanlings that are raised on good quality pasture should be fed in a manner very different from that used when horses are on poor quality pasture or when pasture does not really fit into the nutrition equation.

Futurity weanlings

By definition weanlings that are going to be prepared for futurities are kept in the barn from the time they are weaned until the time they are shown. This makes meeting their nutrient requirements easier in some respects than is the case for sale weanlings or weanlings that are going to be kept for later marketing goals. One important consideration is weaning time. Weaning time is affected by the month of birth of the foal, the milk production of the mare and the date of the futurity. January, February and March foals can be weaned later than can April and May foals. It is possible to wean January and February foals at 5 months and still get them ready for the futurities, March foals generally should be weaned at 4 months and later foals need to be weaned at 3 months or alternatively, just prior to the futurity. If weaning time is too close to the futurity, it is likely that the weanling will appear pot-bellied due to a nearly unavoidable post-weaning slump.

Once weaned, the foal should be fed a very palatable feed. The feed should be offered in three or more small feeds rather than in two large ones. It is common for some producers to offer feed free-choice to horses destined for futurities and seven lbs of feed per day is a working minimum needed to get adequate condition by show date. Table 3 shows the nutrient intake that weanlings may see in the time leading up to the futurity. In addition to lots of feed, most show weanlings are being confined to stalls much of the day and are put on some kind of a forced exercise program. Getting nutrient intake right is important for these horses. I would generally recommend a legume hay for futurity weanlings or at least a very high quality grass hay that is cut in early stages of maturity. I use some added fat in the diet and have used as much as 4 ounces of vegetable oil per feeding. Exercise is critical for these horses to achieve some definition of muscle and to prevent them from becoming heavy middled. If a producer insists on feeding their weanlings free-choice, I use a higher fiber oat-based feed, appropriately fortified for the type of forage being fed. Using a higher fiber feed increases safety and using oats as the starch results in less soluble carbohydrate reaching the cecum. The following feeding program might be typical of the program I would use in fitting weanlings for a fall futurity.

Concentrate - 9 lbs
Hay   - 8 lbs
Vegetable oil - 6 oz

Concentrate intakes need to be adjusted depending on the age and condition of the horse. Obviously, the foal in the period immediately post-weaning will not eat as much feed as the weanling just prior to futurity time.

Table 3. TYPICAL RATION USED TO PREPARE FUTURITY WEANLINGS FOR SHOW. (DRY MATTER BASIS, 6 MONTH OLD WEANLINGS WEIGHING 500 LBS.)

Daily nutrient intake	13% Protein concentrate	Mixed hay	Requirements (KER)	Total nutrients	% of required supplied
Intake (lb/day)	9.00	9.00		18.00	
DM (lb/day)	7.83	7.92	15.00	15.75	
Protein (lb/day)	1.2	1.4	1.61	2.60	162
Lysine (oz/day)	0.76	0.51	1.08	1.27	118
DE (Mcal/day)	11.45	7.36	14.58	18.82	129
Ca (g/day)	27.00	34.77	36.14	61.77	171
P (g/day)	27.95	11.45	24.09	36.41	151
Mg (g/day)	9.41	10.23	12.05	19.64	163
Na (g/day)	7.36	4.09	20.45	11.45	56
Cl (g/day)	9.00	16.36	30.68	25.36	83
K (g/day)	28.64	97.77	47.73	126.41	265
Cu (mg/day)	151.36	40.91	150.00	192.27	128
Se (mg/day)	1.64	0.37	1.7	2.00	118
Zn (mg/day)	388.64	81.82	450.00	470.45	105
Iodine (mg/day)	1.47	0.33	1.36	1.80	132
Mn (mg/day)	261.82	184.09	500.00	445.91	89

All of this nutritional management is of little benefit if the other components of the fitting program are not optimized. Horses should be exercised daily, groomed intensively and be on a good deworming program. Doing the little thing well is the difference in having a fit horse and simply having a weanling that is fat.

Sales weanlings

Designing a feeding program for the sales weanling entails attention to the individual. In the Thoroughbred business, most of the weanling sales are in the fall of the year. In order for the weanlings to bring the greatest return to the producer they need to carry a bit more condition than weanlings which are going to be retained for sale as yearlings. Hair quality is important. Some producers are body clipping their weanlings about three weeks prior to the sale while others use blankets to make the hair lay. Another alternative is to put the weanlings under artificial lights. Increasing or maintaining light at 15 hours per day retards hair growth and this technique is fairly effective. I hate to buy a weanling that has been "under lights" since it seems that getting the hair right on a yearling that has been under lights as a weanling is more difficult than for non-lighted weanlings.

Feeding the sales weanling is a little different from the futurity weanling in that pasture generally plays a greater role in nutrient intake and as such not as much concentrate feed is required. Assuming that good quality forage is available, it is rare that I would have a sales weanling eating as much as eight lbs of feed per day. This of course will vary with the foaling date of the weanling, pasture availability and the shape or conformation of the weanling. Heavier muscled, rounder, earlier maturing weanlings require less feed than do weanlings that are more angular and taller.

I generally use some vegetable oil for sales weanlings to get some bloom and to add some non-carbohydrate energy. If a sales weanling is showing a little too much middle I might use some beet-pulp shreds at 10% of the concentrate intake or some really high quality alfalfa hay.

For any weanling one should remember that in order for fattening to occur, the nutrient requirements for skeletal growth and muscle protein accretion must be exceeded or some nutrient in the diet must limit true growth so that excess calories may be used for fattening. If, for instance, total protein in the diet is limiting, calories over and above those used for muscle protein accretion will be converted to body fat rather than being used to promote protein synthesis. When one is trying to fatten a horse the nutrient:calorie ratio should be increased (i.e. more calories/gram of growth substrate). This is one reason why increasing the caloric density of the diet results in greater fattening.

Weanlings to be retained

Weanlings that are not going to sales or shows should be fed in a more conservative manner than the weanlings previously discussed. Generally the best way to assess the impact of the feeding program of these weanlings is through assessment of body condition. Weanlings should maintain a thrifty appearance. One should not be able to easily see the ribs but should be able to easily palpate the ribs. Monitoring weight along with a good condition scoring system should allow for the accurate assessment of quality and quantity of growth. It is easy for us to say that a weanling should be fed a specific grain mix but care should be taken that the grain mix complements the type of forage being fed. When good quality pasture is available I recommend that feed intake be limited to around one pound of feed per month of age up to a maximum of 7 lbs of feed per day. Once this maximum is achieved the condition of the individual should be monitored and adjustments made in feed intake that are appropriate for the weanling in question.

Yearlings

If yearlings are to be shown or sold, basic requirements must be exceeded to the extent that increased fattening is desired. Normal growth rates of yearlings in central Kentucky show a characteristic increase in the spring of the year that corresponds to an increase in pasture availability. It is this increase that causes the yearlings to begin to get fat in late March and early April. The quality of the pasture is such that caloric requirements for growth are exceeded and calories are converted to fat rather than being used for growth. Concomitantly, growth rate has begun to decline in the 12 -15 month old horse and fewer nutrients are needed to support skeletal growth and muscle protein synthesis. All of these things in concert allow the yearling to begin "putting on condition."

Unlike weanlings, skeletal maturity of the yearlings allows them to be fed at an accelerated rate without having such a negative impact on bone growth. It is interesting to see how few yearlings are lost to osteochondritis dissecans (OCD), wobbler syndrome, flexural deformity and other metabolic bone problems after March of their yearling year. It is fairly safe to push a yearling on after this time.

Before discussion of the feeding program for yearlings it is prudent for us to realize that the feeding program is but one of the variables in making the yearling sales or halter horse get fit! So much of the ultimate appearance of the horse at the show or sale depends on the exercise program, how much grooming the horse gets and on genetics. Sometimes the success or failure of a yearling program is based more on these factors than on the feeding management program per se. I have seen numerous instances when the feeding programs were identical for two farms but where the final product at the sales or at the show was entirely different. Fitting yearlings is a paper in and of itself but suffice it to say that lots of dollars have been left on the table by people that fed them right but fit them wrong.

Halter yearlings

Halter yearlings are produced by a continuation of the feeding program begun for the weanlings. Fat or condition is cumulative and in order to achieve the halter fit look, it takes some time. It generally takes 90 - 120 days from the pasture to the show ring depending on the condition of the yearling when it arrives to start the fitting process.

There are as many feeding programs to fit the yearling for show as there are trainers and fitters. I know people that do a good job fitting yearlings on alfalfa pellets or alfalfa cubes and a supplement, while others use straights (cereal grains) and a supplement pellet or complete pelleted or textured feeds. The critical aspect of the program is meeting nutrient needs, not so much how they are met. Also critical is to recognize differences between individuals and to design programs that cater to those individual needs.

Similar to weanlings, yearlings being fit for show are rarely turned out to pasture. Most of the halter yearlings in the world spend about 22 hours a day in the stall. Their time out of the stall consists of 30 minutes in the round pen, an hour tied to the wall with a neck sweat on and thirty minutes in the wash rack getting rubbed on. Hay intake of halter yearlings is limited to not more than 1.5 percent of body weight per day and concentrate intakes range from 10 - 15 lbs of feed per day. Lower end concentrate intakes are seen when good quality alfalfa hay is being fed while the upper end of the range is characteristic of programs that utilize coastal hay or other grass hays. The important thing to realize when feeding yearlings for halter is to minimize meal size as much as possible. There are a great many really good yearlings that colic or founder due to grain overload. Much of this is preventable if smaller meals are fed more frequently. In fitting yearlings it is imperative that individuals be fed according to their own set of requirements. If a yearling is too thin he needs more groceries and if he is too fat, feed should be cut back! If these horses get shaky on their knees, caloric intake should be decreased until they are stable and then feed should be gradually increased. Nutritional tools that are useful in fitting the yearling for show include vegetable oil or other fat sources and beet pulp. When it is difficult to "finish" a yearling, the addition of these two components to the diet will get the bloom that is necessary.

Sales yearlings

Sales yearlings are really the same as show horses but not as extreme. Buyers now are looking for the athletic yearling rather than simply the fat yearling. Even so, ribby, ill prepared yearlings are not going to bring top dollar in the sales ring. Most of the yearling sales are held in the summer or early fall. The horses are from 14 - 18 months of age. Obviously younger horses, April, May and June foals have to be pushed harder than is the case for earlier foals in order for them to carry the same condition as their older contemporaries.

I would start the prep program in earnest about 90 days before the anticipated marketing target. This generally includes alteration of the turn-out program so that yearlings are in during the day and out at night. This turn-out schedule keeps the yearling from getting sunburned and also makes individualizing the program easier. For sales yearlings it is an absolute travesty to present a group of yearlings for sale that have had their tails chewed off. I recommend that yearlings have something kept in their tails from weaning time onward. Any number of formulas work for this purpose. The more popular ones include axle grease and cayenne pepper, fish oil and pepper, Cribox, No Chew, etc. Don't wait until you have horses coming in with their tails chewed off to start using something. Use something in the tails as a matter of habit!

Table 4. EXAMPLE "PREP RATION" WHICH MIGHT BE FED TO YEARLINGS LEADING UP TO THE KEENELAND SEPTEMBER YEARLING SALE.

Daily nutrient intake	Protein concentrate	Mixed hay	Mixed pasture	Vegetable oil	Requirements (KER)	Total nutrients	% of Required supplied
Intake (lb/day)	10.00	10.00	3.81	0.5		24.31	
DM (lb/day)	8.70	8.80	3.81	0.5	20.00	21.80	
Protein (lb/day)	1.33	1.55	0.71		2.42	3.59	149
Lysine (oz/day)	0.85	0.56	0.27		1.63	1.69	103
DE (Mcal/day)	12.73	8.18	3.46	2.04	24.37	26.41	108
Ca (g/day)	30.00	38.64	9.52		48.31	78.16	162
P (g/day)	27.73	12.73	5.20		32.21	45.65	142
Mg (g/day)	10.45	11.36	4.16		16.10	25.97	161
Na (g/day)	8.18	4.55	0.69		27.27	13.42	49
Cl (g/day)	10.00	18.18	2.60		40.91	30.78	75
K (g/day)	31.82	108.64	31.69		63.64	172.15	271
Cu (mg/day)	168.18	45.45	19.05		163.64	232.69	142
Se (mg/day)	1.82	0.41	0.16		2.27	2.38	105
Zn (mg/day)	431.82	90.91	69.27		545.45	592.00	109
Iodine (mg/day)	1.64	0.36	0.14		1.82	2.14	118
Mn (mg/day)	290.91	204.55	173.18		545.45	668.64	123

Designing a sales yearling feeding program that works is a matter of looking at the requirements of the individual within the group and feeding the yearling as an individual. How much one needs to feed depends on the amount and quality of forage available. Even in central Kentucky, concentrate intakes necessary to achieve optimum condition vary widely between farms. On those farms with really good pasture it takes less feed than on farms that are overstocked. On farms where a significant amount of good quality legume hay is fed it generally takes less feed than when only grass hay is fed. There are some thumb rule minimums for grain intake that serve as a good starting point. It is rare that I would have a yearling on less than seven pounds of feed per day in addition to liberal intakes of good forage and rare also to see a yearling eating more than 14 pounds of feed in the days leading up to the sales. In addition to the basal concentrate, I use added fat. Oil intakes may range from 2 - 6 oz. per feeding on a two times a day feeding routine. When yearlings are fed three times per day, 4 oz. of vegetable oil per feeding is generally my upper end. A representative example prep ration is shown in table 4. This ration covers most of the nutritional bases when fed with free-choice salt. Preparing sales yearlings is a function of controlling energy balance and body composition. Getting horses to peak at the sales requires that the feeding program be closely monitored and started early. Allowances should be made for foaling date and sex of the yearling as fillies get fatter faster than do colts. If the sale is a long distance from where the yearlings are prepped a little insurance condition needs to be added to account for shrink in transit. If a yearling has a little too much middle coming up to the sale I generally do not worry as the stress of the sale will cause the yearling to "tuck-up" some and not look bad.

When a yearling is getting potbellied I do not reduce grain intake. I either increase hay quality, bed on shavings, limit pasture turnout, increase exercise or do all of these things depending on the severity of the problem. On more than a few occasions we have decreased feed intake to near zero on a set of horses in order to make them lose weight only to weigh them 30 days later and find they have gained as much as anything in the barn. If good quality pasture is available horses will increase intake and gain the same as some horses that are getting a lot of grain. The only way I know of to get some of these horses to tighten is to limit turnout and increase exercise.

Remember that you must know your marketing target and understand how horses are expected to look at that time in order to be successful. Time spent at the sales looking at horses is an investment in your business. If you do not understand the customer's goals then you can't make valid recommendations.

This paper was first published in "Focus on Equine Nutrition," Proceedings for the 1996 Short Course for Feed Manufacturers

THE EFFECTS OF YEAST CULTURE SUPPLEMENTATION ON GROWTH OF THOROUGHBRED FOALS AT WEANING

A.S. GRIFFIN[1] , L.M. LAWRENCE[1], J.P. LEW[2], C.H. WOOD[1], AND T. BREWSTER-BARNES[1]

[1]University of Kentucky, Lexington, Kentucky, USA   [2]McCauley Bros Inc., Versailles, Kentucky, USA

For many years the horse industry has been interested in promoting rapid foal growth in an effort to enhance profitability. In the sale ring, premiums are paid for larger foals when all other factors are equal. Of the factors under the horseman's control, nutrition is a primary target for increased growth. The amount and type of nutrients available to growing horses change dramatically when foals are weaned from their dams, particularly when weaning occurs at an early age. One objective of this study was to evaluate the effect of weaning on growth rate in foals. Another objective was to evaluate the effects of yeast culture supplementation on foal growth during the weaning period. Forty mare/foal units from three central Kentucky Thoroughbred farms were blocked on each farm by age and sex and assigned to a commercial yeast culture (Diamond V "XP", Diamond V Mills, Cedar Rapids, Iowa) or a placebo look-alike supplement. The yeast culture and placebo treatment groups were on average 3.8 and 3.7 months of age, respectively, at the onset of the study. Treatments were assigned at least 2 weeks prior to weaning, and in most cases at least 1 month prior to weaning. Each mare/foal unit was individually fed at least once a day and the respective supplement was top-dressed on the grain ration at a rate of 56.8 g/d for mares and 28.4 g/d for foals. Foals were evaluated prior to the treatment (pretrt), less than one week prior to weaning (prewean), and at 1, 2, 3, 4, 6 and 8 weeks after weaning. Factors which include body weight, skeletal measurements, bone density, and subjective behavior characteristics such as coat condition and general attitude were evaluated. During the course of this study, three foals were eliminated due to illness or injury. Average age at weaning was about 4.9 months, but the range was 2.2 to 6.5 months. There were no gender differences in initial pretreatment weights or age at weaning ($P>0.01$). Across treatments, preweaning average daily gain (ADG) was 0.9 kg ($\pm$ 0.3). ADG decreased in the first week post-weaning to 0.3 kg ($\pm$ 0.7), but then increased after the first week post-weaning (Figure 1). Growth depression was calculated as a percentage by subtracting post-weaning ADG from preweaning ADG and dividing by preweaning ADG. A positive correlation ($r=0.63$, $P<0.01$) existed between ADG in the 2-3 week period prior to weaning and growth depression in the first week post-weaning. Thus, the more rapidly growing foals encountered more weaning depression. However, growth depression during the first week was not related to age at weaning ($P>0.01$). Yeast culture supplementation did not affect body weight at any time during the study. Yeast culture supplemented foals were numerically heavier than the controls; however, these weights were not significantly different during any time period (Figure 2).　　Differences among farms existed for age at weaning and ADG prior to and immediately following weaning (P<0.01). Variations in management and weaning practices at farms may have contributed to a lack of treatment effect. Skeletal measurements, bone density and subjective characteristics are currently being analyzed and will be reported at a later date.

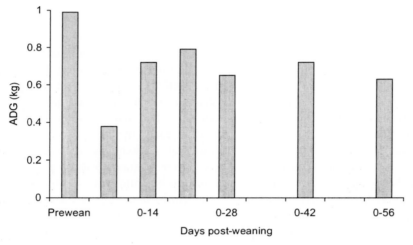

Figure 1.　Average daily gain

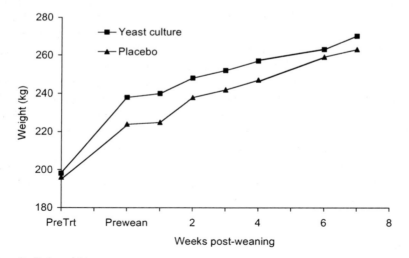

Figure 2.　Body weights

This paper was first published in "Recent Advances in Equine Nutrition," Proceedings for the 1995 Short Course for Feed Manufacturers

A SUMMARY OF GROWTH RATES OF THOROUGHBREDS IN KENTUCKY

JOE D. PAGAN

Kentucky Equine Research, Inc., Versailles, Kentucky, USA

Summary

Over a three year period (1993, 1994, and 1995), a total of 350 Thoroughbred colts and 350 Thoroughbred fillies in Central Kentucky were weighed monthly on a portable electronic scale through 18 months of age. Wither height and condition score were also measured in about half of the foals. In order to estimate mature body size in these horses, 472 brood mares were weighed 60 to 90 days after foaling. In addition, 25 Thoroughbred breeding stallions were also weighed. The average body weight of the brood mares equaled 570 kg and the average weight of the stallions equaled 580 kg. At 14 days of age, colts and fillies weighed an average of 77.7 and 76.1 kg and had average heights of 107.3 and 106.3 cm, respectively. Colts were heavier and taller than fillies throughout the study and at 490 days averaged 9.9 kg heavier (427.8 kg vs 418.0 kg) and 1.6 cm taller (153.4 cm vs 151.8 cm). The greatest difference in condition score between sexes occurred at four months of age when the fillies had an average score of 6.48 and the colts had a score of 6.0. Compared to March foals, foals born in January and February were 6.8 kg lighter at 14 days of age. They remained smaller, by as much as 15.3 kg at 72 days of age, until about 9 months of age when they averaged about the same as the March foals. April and May foals were larger at 14 days of age than March foals, and remained slightly heavier until 6 months of age. Average daily gain among the four groups was similar until about 7 months of age. ADG averaged 1.5-1.7 kg/d during the first month and declined linearly to about 0.70-0.80 kg/d at 7 months of age. After 7 months of age, ADG tended to be more variable and by 12 months, ADG was very different among the different months of birth. Foal growth rates were reduced during the winter months regardless of when the foals were born and increased during April and May of the foal's yearling year. Growth rate in these yearlings was more a function of season of the year than age.

Introduction

Nutrient requirements for growing horses are usually based on age, body weight, mature body size and growth rate (average daily gain). For instance, the 1989 NRC calculates the digestible energy (DE) requirement of growing horses using a regression equation that incorporates age, body weight and average daily gain. Other nutrients are then calculated based on either the DE requirement, the foal's body weight, average daily gain or estimated dry matter intake which is based on body weight. Ideally, to accurately determine the nutrient requirements of an individual, its body weight and growth rate should be measured. Unfortunately, most young growing horses are not weighed on a regular basis and their body weights must be estimated based on their age and predicted mature body size.

Hintz *et al* (1979) summarized growth data from 1,992 Thoroughbred foals raised at a single Canadian farm over an 18 year period. The effect of age of dam, year and month of birth and sex of foal were evaluated. These data have been accepted universally as the typical growth patterns for Thoroughbred foals. It has not been adequately established, however, whether these growth rates are representative for Thoroughbred foals raised in other areas. Therefore, the following growth data were compiled for a large number of Thoroughbred foals raised under commercial conditions in Kentucky.

Methods

Over a three year period (1993, 1994, and 1995), a total of 350 Thoroughbred colts and 350 Thoroughbred fillies in Central Kentucky were weighed monthly on a portable electronic scale (Equimetrics, Inc., Redfield, Arizona) through 18 months of age. Wither height and condition score were also measured in about half of the foals. Condition score was based on the system developed by Henneke *et al* (1981) for mature horses using a scoring system of 1 through 9 to estimate fat deposition. In order to estimate mature body size in these horses, 472 brood mares were weighed 60 to 90 days after foaling. In addition, 25 Thoroughbred breeding stallions were also weighed.

Results and discussion

Growth rates of Kentucky colts and fillies are shown in table 1. Fillies were 1.6 kg lighter and 1 cm shorter than colts at 14 days of age. By 127 days of age fillies were on average 3.4 kg lighter and 0.2 cm shorter than the colts. By 350 days of age, colts averaged 14.0 kg heavier and 1.5 cm taller than fillies. By 490 days, the difference in body weight between colts and fillies in the present study had been reduced to 9.9 kg.

Condition score

The average condition score of the foals at 1-18 months of age is summarized in figure 1. Fillies tended to have higher condition scores throughout this time period.

Table 1. GROWTH RATES OF FILLIES AND COLTS IN CENTRAL KENTUCKY

Average days of age	Colts bw (kg)	Fillies bw (kg)	Colts adg (kg/d)	Fillies adg (kg/d)	Colts ht (cm)	Fillies ht (cm)	Colts condition score	Fillies condition score
14	77.7	76.1	--	--	107.3	106.3	5.7	6.0
43	116.3	115.1	1.38	1.34	115.7	115.5	6.2	6.4
72	149.5	148.5	1.20	1.19	122.6	121.8	6.2	6.3
99	182.1	178.6	1.14	1.11	127.3	127.1	6.0	6.5
127	208.8	207.9	1.01	1.01	129.8	130.3	5.8	5.9
155	233.6	230.2	0.89	0.84	133.5	132.5	5.5	5.7
183	255.9	250.7	0.80	0.75	135.8	134.7	5.4	5.6
212	277.1	271.0	0.75	0.71	138.2	137.4	5.5	5.5
240	295.1	287.3	0.68	0.60	140.0	139.4	5.4	5.5
267	309.1	300.6	0.55	0.48	141.8	140.7	5.4	5.4
296	322.0	311.0	0.43	0.40	144.2	142.5	5.3	5.4
323	335.1	322.5	0.40	0.35	145.4	144.0	5.4	5.4
350	349.2	335.2	0.43	0.39	147.0	145.5	5.3	5.4
378	362.5	350.1	0.45	0.51	148.3	146.7	5.4	5.5
406	378.9	367.9	0.52	0.60	150.2	148.2	5.5	5.7
435	396.2	388.9	0.62	0.65	150.8	149.6	5.5	5.8
462	414.2	407.9	0.59	0.60	152.5	151.5	5.6	5.8
490	427.8	418.0	0.55	0.54	153.4	151.8	5.7	5.8

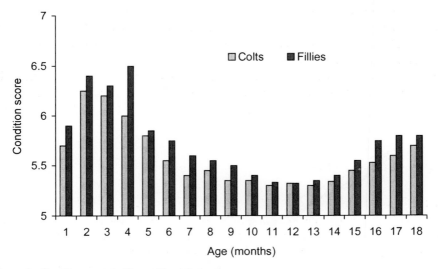

Figure 1. Condition score in Thoroughbred foals

The greatest difference in condition score between sexes occurred at four months of age when the fillies had an average score of 6.48 and the colts had a score of 6.0. These condition scores are considered moderate to fleshy according to the Henneke scoring system. By twelve months of age the condition scores of the colts and fillies had dropped to 5.3 and 5.4, respectively. Both sexes increased condition score slightly from 14 to 18 months.

Effect of month of birth

The foals were divided into 4 groups based on the month that they were born. These groups consisted of January and February foals (16.9%), March foals (35.7%), April foals (32.5%) and May and June foals (21.4%). Compared to March foals, foals born in January and February were 6.8 kg lighter at 14 days of age. They remained smaller, by as much as 15.3 kg at 72 days of age, until about 9 months of age when they averaged about the same as the March foals.

April and May foals were larger at 14 days of age than March foals, and remained slightly heavier until 6 months of age. Figure 2 summarizes average daily gain (kg/d) in the different groups as a function of age. Average daily gain among the four groups was similar until about 7 months of age. ADG averaged 1.5-1.7 kg/d during the first month and declined linearly to about 0.70-0.80 kg/d at 7 months of age. After 7 months of age, ADG tended to be more variable and by 12 months, ADG was very different among the different groups. This variability can be explained, however, by the season of the year in which each group reached a particular age. ADG has been regraphed in figure 3 as a function of the month in which a weight was taken rather than as a function of days of age. Foal growth rates were reduced during the winter months regardless of when the foals were born and increased during April and May of the foal's yearling year. Growth rates during these months were remarkably similar regardless of age. Each group of foals experienced their slowest growth during January, February and March. During the spring months of April and May, each group of foals increased their ADG with peak gains occurring in May.

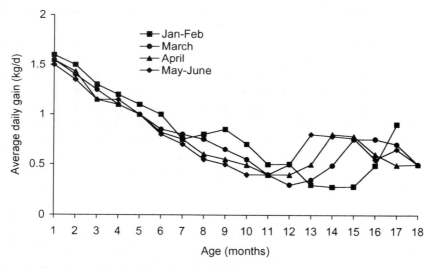

Figure 2. Growth rate of foals (effect of month of birth)

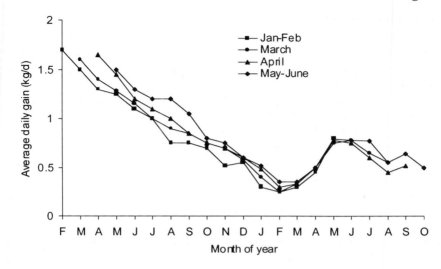

Figure 3. Growth rates of foals (effect of season)

These data clearly demonstrate that growth rate in these yearlings is more a function of season of the year than age. These changes in growth rate closely follow changes in temperature and pasture growth in Kentucky. Most foals in Kentucky are raised in large paddocks with a great deal of available forage. During April and May, pasture growth is quite rapid. Supplemental grain intake is generally not greatly reduced during this time and growth rate accelerates as a result of increased caloric intake from forage. Assuming that grain intake remains constant and pasture contains about 9.2 MJ DE/kg DM, then these yearlings would need to consume about 3.25 additional kg of pasture DM per day in May to increase their ADG from 0.35 kg during the winter to about 0.8 kg/d. This increase in dry matter intake would equal about 0.75%-1.0% of BW per day.

A comparison of body weight and height between Kentucky foals and Canadian foals born in March is shown in figures 4, 5 and 6. In figure 4 the Kentucky foals' weights and heights are shown as a percentage of the Canadian foals. Kentucky foals were slightly taller (101.2) and heavier (102.0 %) at 14 days of age. From 6 to 9 months of age, the Kentucky foals grew from 1.7 to 3.0 cm taller. These foals were also heavier from 4 to 10 months of age. At 6 months of age, the Kentucky foals averaged 107.2 % of the Canadian body weight. By 12 months of age, the two groups had similar heights and weights. The Kentucky foals became heavier at 15 and 16 months, the age that coincided with rapid spring pasture growth in Kentucky.

The difference in body weights seen between these two groups of March foals could be the result of several factors. First, the foals in Canada were weaned at 3 months of age while Kentucky foals are not usually weaned until they are 5-6 months old. These foals therefore had access to milk as well as grain and pasture for a longer period of time. At 6 months of age, March foals in Kentucky have access to high quality fall pasture. This forage remained lush and abundant until November when the foals are 10 months of age. Fall pasture in Ontario is not as abundant and temperatures begin to drop much earlier than in Kentucky.

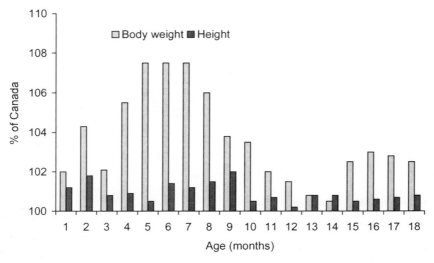

Figure 4. Comparison of body weight and height of Kentucky and Canadian foals (as a % of Canadian average)

Mature body weights

The average body weight of 472 brood mares 70 days post foaling equaled 570 kg. The average weight of 25 breeding stallions equaled 580 kg. From these data, an average mature weight of 575 kg seems reasonable. The 1989 NRC provides tables of nutrient requirements for horses with 500 and 600 kg mature body weights. Interpolating between these tables, weanlings with a mature BW of 575 kg would be expected to weigh 194 and 238 kg at 4 and 6 months of age, respectively. Four month old foals are expected to gain 0.96 kg/d and 6 month old foals are expected to gain between 0.725 kg/d and 0.925 kg/d. The Kentucky foals averaged 7 kg heavier (201 kg) and gained 1.0 kg/d at 4 months of age and weighed 12 kg more (250 kg) and gained 0.77 kg/d at 6 months of age. Thus, ADG was similar to values given by the NRC while body weight was 3-5% heavier.

At 12 and 18 months of age, the NRC would estimate that yearlings with a mature BW of 575 kg would equal 362.5 kg and 456 kg, respectively. These yearlings would be expected to gain between 0.62-0.71 kg/d at 12 months and 0.42 kg/d at 18 months of age. Kentucky yearlings weighed an average of 348 kg and had an ADG of 0.41 kg/d at 12 months and weighed 445 kg and gained an average of 0.425 kg/d at 18 months of age. The Kentucky yearlings were 96% and 98% of the weights estimated by the NRC for 12 and 18 month yearlings and their 12 month ADG was only about 61% of that estimated by the NRC. It should be noted, however, that 12 months of age was before the average age at which rapid growth occurred in response to spring pasture growth. During this time (at about 14 months of age), ADG equaled about 0.75 kg/d.

Conclusion

Thoroughbred foals raised in Kentucky grew faster from 4 to 9 months of age than foals raised in Ontario, Canada. These differences in growth were probably related to a later weaning time and abundant fall pasture in Kentucky compared to Canada. By 12 months of age, height and weight differences between the two groups had disappeared. Since rapid growth and excess body weight have been implicated as possible causes of skeletal disorders in foals, this extra growth in the Kentucky foals during the fall months is probably not desirable. Extra weight gain could be controlled by earlier weaning and by reducing supplemental grain intake as pasture becomes more available. Monthly weight monitoring can be used to signal the onset of this excessive weight gain. Average daily gain in yearlings was affected more by season than age. All of the foals experienced accelerated growth in the spring as pasture growth increased. Again, this accelerated growth can be identified by regular weighing and controlled by reductions in supplemental grain intake.

The weights and growth rates used by the NRC to calculate nutrient requirements for foals are generally accurate for Thoroughbred foals when seasonal variations in growth rate are taken into consideration.

References

Henneke, D.R., G.D. Potter and J.L. Kreider. 1981. A condition score relationship to body fat content of mares during gestation and lactation. In: Proc. 7th ENPS, Warrenton, Va pp 105-110.

Hintz, H.F., R.L. Hintz, and L.D. Van Vleck. 1979. Growth rate of Thoroughbreds: Effect of age of dam, year and month of birth, and sex of foal. J. Anim. Sci. 48:480.

NRC. 1989. Nutrient Requirements of Horses (5th Revised Ed.)

Nutrient Requirements of Domestic Animals. National Research Council. National Academy Press. Washington, D.C.

This paper was first published in "Focus on Equine Nutrition," Proceedings for the 1996 Short Course for Feed Manufacturers

THE EFFECT OF WEANING AGE ON FOAL GROWTH AND BONE DENSITY

L.K. WARREN, L.M. LAWRENCE, A.S. GRIFFIN, A.L. PARKER,
T. BARNES AND D. WRIGHT
University of Kentucky, Lexington, Kentucky, USA

Weaning can be one of the most stressful events in a foal's life, often resulting in a decreased growth rate, increased susceptibility to infectious disease and an increased risk of self-induced injury. Foals may take several weeks to resume their rapid growth following weaning, which may lead to a competitive disadvantage in foals intended for show or sale in late summer and early fall. More importantly, loss of the mare's milk may reduce the nutrients available for bone formation during the postweaning period. The purpose of this study was to assess the effect of weaning and weaning age on foal growth and bone density. Weaning ages of 4.5 and 6.0 months were chosen because they represented ages commonly used in the industry. Foals weaned at 6.0 months should be relying less on the dam's milk and more on solid feed for their nutrients at the time of weaning. Therefore, we hypothesized that the growth and bone density of foals weaned at 6.0 months should be affected less by weaning compared to foals weaned at 4.5 months.

Seven foals (4 Quarter Horses (QH), 3 Thoroughbreds (TB)) were weaned at 140 days of age (4.5 months) and 8 foals (4 QH, 4 TB) were weaned at 182 days of age (6.0 months). Foals were weaned under identical management conditions, beginning in late June and continuing through mid-October. Body weight (BW), withers height (WH) and cannon circumference (CC) measurements were obtained from each foal at 3 week intervals before and after weaning. Measurements were collected from 119 days of age through 224 days of age in foals weaned at 4.5 months and through 266 days of age in foals weaned at 6.0 months. Additional BW measurements were obtained from all foals at 1 week postweaning. Dorsopalmar radiographs of the right and left third metacarpals (MCIII) were also obtained at 3 week intervals for the determination of radiographic bone density.

Foals gained 0.83 ± 0.06 kg/d during the 3 week interval prior to weaning. Average daily gain (ADG) decreased (P<0.01) to 0.13 ± 0.17 kg in the first week postweaning and remained lower than the preweaning ADG (P<0.01) through 3 week postweaning (0.57 ± 0.07 kg). The decline between pre- and postweaning ADG was similar between foals weaned at 4.5 months and foals weaned at 6.0 months, indicating a similar reduction in ADG in response to weaning. When compared at the same age intervals, BW was similar between weaning groups (Figure 1). The gain in WH was similar before and after weaning (P>0.05); thus, weaning did not appear to affect the rate of growth at the withers. Furthermore, no differences in WH were observed between foals weaned at 4.5 months and foals weaned at 6.0 months when compared at similar ages. Therefore, weaning age did not appear to affect WH growth. The postweaning gain in CC was less than the preweaning gain in foals weaned at 4.5 months (P<0.05), but not in foals weaned at 6.0 months. As a result, foals weaned at 4.5 months had smaller CC at 161 days (P<0.05) and 182 days (P<0.10) than foals weaned at 6.0 months (Figure 2). Thus, it appears that weaning may result in growth depression of CC in younger foals. The densities of the medial, medullary and lateral areas of the right and left MCIII continued to increase after weaning (P<0.05), indicating that weaning did not affect bone density. Medial bone density was greater at 140 days of age (P<0.05) in foals weaned at 6.0 months than in foals weaned at 4.5 months; however, there were no differences in medial density between weaning groups at any age beyond 140 days (Table 1). No differences were observed in medullary bone density between weaning groups (Table 1). However, lateral bone density was greater at 140 days and 161 days of age in foals weaned at 6.0 months (P<0.05) compared to foals weaned at 4.5 months (Table 1). Because differences in bone density were noted before any of the foals had been weaned (i.e., the differences observed at 140 days of age), it is difficult to determine if weaning age influenced changes in bone density in response to weaning. In conclusion, weaning at 6.0 months of age may provide little growth advantage over weaning at 4.5 months of age.

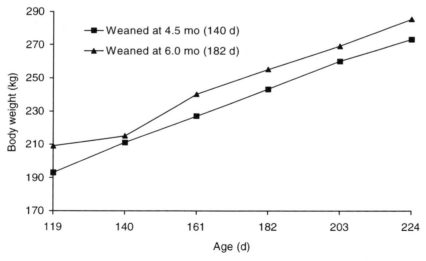

Figure 1. Comparison of body weight between foals weaned at 4.5 months and foals weaned at 6.0 months of age.

Table 1. COMPARISON OF MEDIAL, MEDULLARY AND LATERAL RADIOGRAPHIC BONE DENSITY (MM AL) (±SE) BETWEEN FOALS WEANED AT 4.5 MONTHS (140 DAYS) AND FOALS WEANED AT 6.0 MONTHS (182 DAYS) OF AGE[a].

Age (d)	Medial 4.5	Medial 6.0	Medullary 4.5	Medullary 6.0	Lateral 4.5	Lateral 6.0
119	18.9±0.4	19.0±0.5	14.7±0.3	14.7±0.5	18.8±0.5	17.9±0.6
140	20.1±0.2[a]	21.2±0.5[b]	15.1±0.3	15.2±0.4	18.9±0.5[b]	0.0±0.6[c]
161	**21.5±0.4**	22.0±0.6	**16.4±0.4**	16.4±0.5	**20.0±0.5[b]**	**1.5±0.5[c]**
182	**21.8±0.3**	21.8±0.6	**17.1±0.3**	16.5±0.4	**20.2±0.3**	**20.3±0.5**
203	**23.0±0.4**	**22.5±0.4**	**17.7±0.4**	**16.8±0.4**	**21.1±0.6**	**21.0±0.5**
224	**23.5±0.4**	**23.5±0.4**	**18.1±0.4**	**18.2±0.3**	**21.3±0.5**	**22.2±0.4**

[a] Variables highlighted in bold type are those observed postweaning.
[b,c] Means of the same variable in the same row with different superscripts differ P<0.05).

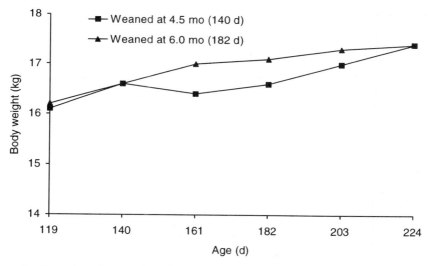

Figure 2. Comparison of cannon circumference of the left MCIII between foals weaned at 4.5 months and foals weaned at 6.0 months.

This paper was first published in Proceedings, Kentucky Equine Research 1997 Equine Nutrition Conference

INVESTIGATION OF FARM WIDE INCIDENCE OF BONE FORMATION PROBLEMS IN THE HORSE

L.R. BRAMLAGE

Rood and Riddle Equine Hospital and The Ohio State University, Ohio, USA

The first step in identification of a herd problem is to determine if the individual occurrences of disturbed bone formation have anything in common. The clinical signs may be different, but the problem may be the same because the same disturbance will affect different sites at different ages under different circumstances.

The investigation of a herd problem begins by examination of the individual problems. Identification of any common factors among individual cases, and retrospective identification of where in the growth process the bone formation problems are occurring, is most likely to result in help with a farm wide problem. Concurrent ration analysis should also occur and be reviewed by a competent nutritionist. Marginal deficiencies can often lend clues as to where the bone formation disturbance is occurring. Integration of ration analysis information, bone formation disturbance data and management schedules are the best clues to the cause of a herd problem, if one exists.

Normal bone formation

The normal development of equine bone is a multi-phase two-step process occurring as a continuum of activity resulting in calcification of degenerating physeal cartilage, reabsorption, and redeposition as trabecular bone. The process takes place at the metaphyseal side of the physis and circumferentially around the ossification fronts of all epiphyses and cuboidal bones simultaneously. The growth process requires the formation of cartilage which causes the increase in size or length. The cartilage degenerates in an orderly fashion, as its inter-cellular matrix is calcified (step 1). This calcified cartilage must be reabsorbed and bone must be redeposited as trabeculae, oriented against the lines of stress and deposited in sufficient numbers and size, to handle the load applied to the bone (step 2). It is not until trabeculae are deposited that "ossification" has occurred. If either of these two steps is disturbed or interrupted, one of the syndromes we generally refer to as developmental orthopedic disease results.

Developmental orthopedic disease (DOD)

The conditions referred to as developmental orthopedic disease are those which result from a disturbance in the change from the cartilage precursor of the skeleton into functional bone. Clinical manifestations include, but are not limited to, physitis, osteochondritis dissecans (OCD), and some angular limb deformities.

Since acquired contracted flexor tendons can develop as a sequela to the pain resulting from these diseases, they are generally included as a part of the syndrome (Knight, *et al.*, 1985). Histologic changes in the cervical vertebrae of horses diagnosed as having cervical vertebral malformation have been reported and recently incriminated as a form of developmental orthopedic disease (Stewart, Reed and Weisbrode, 1991). Some articular bone cysts and juvenile arthritis, due to malformation of articular surfaces and cuboidal bones, especially of the distal tarsal joints and interphalangeal joints are probably manifestations of this same disease complex.

Physeal disturbances

Defective or slowed conversion of the calcified cartilage into mature (trabecular) bone results in a weakened metaphyseal component of the growth plate complex. This weakened bone leads to structural overload, microfracture and inflammation. The response to the microfractures is inflammation and callus formation leading to the enlargement of the physis. Physitis in the long bones, which results from a disturbance in the ossification of the calcified cartilage (step 2) on the metaphyseal side of the physis, is largely reversible because the physeal plate is a temporary structure, which is remodeling continuously and which disappears at skeletal maturity. A disturbance in ossification (step 2) of calcified physeal growth cartilage is seen most commonly clinically. A disturbance in the physeal cartilage degeneration and calcification (step 1) results in retention of cartilage and a much more severe structural deficit, which is more difficult to overcome but is fortunately less frequently seen clinically. The initial clinical signs are similar but the cause is a different process.

Epiphyseal disturbances

When either of these two disturbances involves the subarticular epiphyseal growth surfaces, the articular surface becomes involved and may permanently affect the pain free function of the joint. In the epiphysis, defective formation of the subchondral bone results in a poorly supported articular surface. Increasing weight and activity levels which result from advancing maturity overload the poorly formed joint surfaces. The articular cartilage, undermined by abnormal bone formation, fractures, becomes detached or loosened (osteochondritis dissecans), and results in signs of arthritis.

Osteochondritis dissecans is often the underlying cause of secondary degenerative joint disease (osteoarthritis) in the young horse. Though bone formation problems and their clinical manifestations differ depending on the site of the disturbance, similar types of problems can yield a clue as to where to look in the process of bone formation for the cause of the disturbance.

Evaluation of a herd problem

Some horses have more than one manifestation of developmental orthopedic disease simultaneously and often many horses are affected on the same farm. On some farms, the problem recurs annually. Though developmental orthopedic disease is multifactorial, clinical impression suggests that one variable needing investigation in most large scale multi-horse manifestations of the disease is the diet. The diet is also the only easily manipulated factor. Though diet changes are often helpful, they can not prevent the disease completely, because it is caused by many factors. Genetics and management are two additional major factors (Knight, *et al.*, 1985). Since genetics is a major contributor, elimination of all genetically predisposed animals would solve much of the problem. However, even if we could manage to identify all carrier animals it is doubtful if a purge would occur since many of the producers of offspring with bone formation problems are also producers of talented athletes, and therefore we persist in breeding them in spite of their possible genetic flaws.

Management factors

Management of the growth of a foal consists primarily of controlling diet and exercise. Therefore, we will consider them together in the evaluation of possible sites of bone formation disturbance. The formation of functional bone requires the delivery of 1) the right material; 2) in the right proportions; 3) with the right cofactors; 4) at the proper rate; 5) for the right stimulus. If any of the factors are disturbed, the possibility of poorly formed or malformed bone exists.

Delivery of "the right materials" indicates that the three major components of bone, calcium, phosphorus, and protein must be made available at the site of bone formation. A severe or prolonged Ca^{++} or PO_4 deficiency can limit the availability of these mineral substrates of bone. The bone protein, osteoid, is manufactured at the site of bone formation, so unless deprivation is severe, it is rarely a cause of depression of osteoid formation. A more frequent cause of malformation of bone due to Ca^{++}, PO_4, or protein deficiency at the site of bone formation, is an interruption of the delivery of these nutrients due to disruption of the blood supply. This interruption may result from traumatic, infectious, and possibly even metabolic causes. It is usually localized and therefore creates a localized disruption of bone formation. Any obstruction of the tenuous vascular supply to the growing bone will result in the lack of transformation of the degenerating cartilage to calcified cartilage and eventually to bone. Vascular obstruction can result in the interruption of bone formation locally even though the bodywide supplies of Ca++, PO_4 and protein may be plentiful. The most common localized vascular obstruction is fibrous tissue left behind after resolution of an infectious process. A hematogenous shower of bacteria, as is frequent in a foal, can create multiple potential sites of disturbed bone formation simultaneously. Trauma can also strike at any site or in multiple sites.

The delivery of the Ca++ and PO_4 in reasonably "the right proportions" is necessary for the hydroxyapatite crystal to be formed and deposited within the osteoid matrix. The crystal $Ca(10)\{PO_4\}(6)\{OH\}(2)$ requires the delivery of calcium and phosphorus at about 1.7 to 1 to form bone. The body can fine tune needs as long as reasonable proportions and quantities are fed. The most well known disparity in Ca++ and PO_4 balance is secondary nutritional hyperparathyroidism caused by feeding excess phosphorus and deficiencies of calcium. The resultant robbing of the skeleton of the calcium necessary for the more critical metabolic needs results in an inability to reform the hydroxyapatite crystal after routine bone remodeling. This gradually reduces skeletal content of hydroxyapatite leaving the osteoid without mineral to stiffen its structure. The more rapid remodeling in the flat bones make the clinical signs apparent in the jaw ("rubber jaw") first, but in the growing animal OCD can also result. Due to current owner awareness, nutritional secondary hyperparathyroidism is unusual.

What is occasionally seen in the current management systems is absolute calcium deficiency due to a relatively low level of both nutrients. Absolute deficiencies in calcium in the presence of normal phosphorus in foals is most common and will result in poor bone strength seen as an increase in fractures of the more trabecular sesamoid and third phalangeal bones as well as physitis at the most active, most vulnerable physes at the time. Therefore, clinical signs referable to deficiencies in structural integrity of cancellous bone should cause the available levels of Ca++ and PO_4 to be examined.

"The correct cofactors" for bone formation are still largely speculative. Vitamins A, C and D, copper and zinc are proven cofactors, but manganese and others may be needed in small amounts. Horsemen are very aware of the need for vitamins, but are unaware, in most instances, of the horse's ability to provide these vitamins when supplied with sunshine and pigmented roughage.

Relatively recently, the trace minerals copper and zinc have seen increased attention (Knight, *et al.*, 1985; Knight, *et al.*, 1990). Their supplementation appears to help protect the quality of newly formed bone in the foal. In our experience, copper supplementation is most effective when trying to prevent the formation of poor quality bone (step 2) such as with physitis and less effective with retarded cartilage mineralization (step 1).

"At the correct rate" recognizes the spectacular coordination, among the many physeal functions, which must result in growth to a body size of 5 times the human in about 1/10th the time, must result in limb straightening of any angular limb deformity, and must bear a body weight increase of 2 to 3 lbs per day. Slowed bone formation, resulting in inferior bone quality, can occur if deficiencies or imbalances exist. However, the most frequent bone formation rate derangement encountered is the addition of body weight faster than the natural or even accelerated bone growth rate can accommodate. The juvenile physis is wide, made up of a thick layer of the growth cartilage. It gradually thins to decrease the vulnerability to trauma as the stress, a result of body size and activity, increases with age. The more distal the growth plate the less the soft tissue protection by muscles and tendons, and therefore the more vulnerable the physis. As a result, the distal physes close earlier than the more proximal physes.

Human intervention to alter development and form of an appealing halter horse often results in an oversized body on normal sized limbs. Since the maturation of the physis is primarily time dependent, acceleration of the body growth can overload the physes which are normally mature and closed prior to attainment of a particular body size. Even though bone formation may be normal, the signs are the same as poor quality bone. Normal activity of the horse then becomes traumatic to the growing bone due to the body size. Injury to the growing bone can result in pain, structural damage and OCD if the traumatic insult results in interruption of vascular ingrowth at a localized epiphyseal bone formation site.

Pharmacologic alterations in bone formation rates may also be possible. We have correlated extended Dexamethasone use with the occurrence of OCD in our practice. Though speculative, the catabolic effects of corticosteroids may affect the anabolic process of new bone formation. These effects are generally body wide but clinical signs become apparent only in the rapid bone formation sites.

The "correct stimulus" for bone formation is the exercise which the newly formed bone is expected to withstand. The gradual increase in body size combined with the gradual increase in strength and activity causes the bone to be gradually "trained" to accept the load to be applied. Danger appears when this gradually increasing load, which results in gradual adaptation, is interrupted.

Stress, a product of body load and activity, dictates the size and number of trabeculae produced to withstand the stress applied. Since growth occurs at such a rapid rate in the foal, stress is a continual necessity to dictate proper bone formation. Deprivation of exercise due to illness of the mare or foal, or other influences such as weather or management practices, can leave the foal's newly formed bone inadequate when normal exercise is resumed. A few days is generally of little consequence, but a few weeks can result in a significant amount of structurally inferior bone. When exercise is resumed the now larger foal's normal activity can change stress to trauma on the poorly prepared bone. The injury to the bone can disturb bone formation to the point that physitis and OCD can be created. If exercise is curtailed for a prolonged period, it must be resumed gradually to circumvent the risk of disturbed bone formation. If the return to exercise is accompanied by signs of cancellous bone overload (most evident at the rapidly growing physes as inflammation and lameness) then the quantity of daily exercise must be reduced until the inflammation subsides and then exercise can be gradually increased. Conformation flaws are another way of increasing the load (stress) on a physis. Angular deformities have a very marked propensity for increasing the load in a localized area of the physis. If this load magnification, combined with exercise, creates physitis, either the angular deformity must be corrected or the exercise curtailed until the physis matures or compensates for the overload.

Summary

There is little doubt that multiple factors are involved in the development of developmental orthopedic disease in young horses. Some are identifiable, some are as yet unknown. Genetic predisposition, conformation, lack of exercise and nutrition have been said to contribute to the etiology of these disease states. Of all the factors, nutrition has received the most attention in recent years because it is the only factor under direct control of the management.

Results of the recent study at Ohio State (Knight, *et al.*, 1985; Gabel, et al., 1987) indicate that there is a strong inverse relationship between ration and farm problems. It appeared likely in that study that calcium, phosphorus, copper and zinc deficiencies were involved in the development of epiphysitis, contracted tendons and OCD lesions in yearlings. Since protein and energy levels were similar on all farms in the study, it is unlikely that they are directly involved in this disease process. In fact, farms with the most problems (highest scores) had the lowest protein levels in the study. From the data collected in the survey, it is apparent that the quality of nutrition, rather than the quantity, plays a significant role in the development of metabolic bone disease.

In addition to proper nutrition, proper management practices are part of the development of a normal foal. Any variation from the original ecological niche of the horse presents a potential for disruption. Extreme variations from normal management practices should be looked at most closely. The integration of nutrition and management is the art of raising a horse.

In the investigation of a "herd" problem the bone formation disturbances of the individual must be identified and investigated. The same herd wide insult causes different clinical signs when different anatomic sites are involved and vary in severity and signs when different aged individuals are involved. It is only by identifying the commonalities of a herd situation that causes and eventually therapy can be identified.

References

Gabel A.A., D.A. Knight, S.M. Reed, *et al*: Comparison of incidence and severity of developmental orthopedic disease on 17 farms before and after adjustment of ration. Proc Am Assoc Equine Pract 33:163, 1987.

Knight D.A., A.A. Gabel, S.M. Reed, *et al*: Correlation of dietary mineral to incidence and severity of metabolic bone disease in Ohio and Kentucky. Proc Am Assoc Equine Pract 31:445, 1985.

Knight D.A., S.E. Weisbrode, L.M. Schmall, S.M. Reed, A.A. Gabel, L.R. Bramlage, and W.J. Tyznik: The effects of copper supplementation on the prevalance of cartilage lesions in foals. Eq Vet J 22 (6) 425, 1990.

Stewart R.H., S.M. Reed and S.E. Weisbrode: Frequency and severity of osteochondrosis in horses with cervical stenotic myelopathy. Am J Vet Res. 52: (8) 873, 1991.

This paper was first published in "Feeding the Performance Horse," Proceedings for the 1993 Short Course for Feed Manufacturers

THE INCIDENCE OF DEVELOPMENTAL ORTHOPEDIC DISEASE (DOD) ON A KENTUCKY THOROUGHBRED FARM

JOE D. PAGAN

Kentucky Equine Research, Inc., Versailles, Kentucky, USA

Summary

The incidence of developmental orthopedic disease on a commercial Thoroughbred farm was studied over a four year period. A total of 271 foals were monitored. DOD was diagnosed in 10% of the foals. Fetlock OCDs tended to occur before 180 days of age while hock, shoulder and stifle OCDs occurred around 300-350 days of age. Foals that developed hock and stifle OCDs as yearlings tended to be large foals at birth that grew rapidly from 3 to 8 months. These foals were heavier than the average population as weanlings. Foals that developed fetlock OCDs before 6 months of age were born early in the year (January, February or March). The results of this study suggest that growth rate and management may affect the incidence of certain types of DOD.

Introduction

Developmental orthopedic disease (DOD) is a term used to describe a group of diseases that affect the skeleton of growing horses. These include physitis, osteochondrosis, osteochondritis dissecans (OCD), wobbler syndrome and acquired flexural deformities. Although not a new problem, DOD captured the attention of horse breeders in 1985 when a survey conducted by Ohio State University suggested that many of the orthopedic problems in young horses were the result of nutrient deficiencies or imbalances (Knight, *et al.*, 1985). Major changes were made in the way most horse feeds were formulated, with much higher levels of trace mineral fortification added to the diets of pregnant mares and young growing horses. There seemed to be a reduction in certain types of DOD with these dietary changes, but the problem did not go completely away. Why has trace mineral supplementation not proven to be the panacea that breeders had once hoped it would be? What other factors play a role in DOD? This paper will summarize the incidence of DOD on a large Thoroughbred farm over a four year period, evaluating various factors which may play a role in the DOD syndrome.

Materials and methods

Over a four year period (1991-1994), the incidence of developmental orthopedic disease was monitored on a single large commercial Thoroughbred farm in Kentucky. During this period, the farm produced a total of 271 foals. Foals were weighed on a portable electronic scale monthly.   For the purpose of this study, developmental orthopedic disease was defined as osteochondrotic lesions occurring in either the fetlock, hock, shoulder or stifle. Lesions were initially diagnosed radiographically after a foal displayed either lameness or joint effusion. Often this diagnosis was confirmed by arthroscopy. Other manifestations of DOD such as physitis, acquired contracted flexor tendons and angular limb deformities were not included in this study since they were more difficult to quantify. No foals were diagnosed as wobblers during this four year period.

This farm used a single grain mix for brood mares, weanlings and yearlings. This grain mix consisted of oats, molasses and a protein/vitamin/mineral supplement pellet. The grain mix contained 15.5% protein, 1.0% Ca, 0.81% P, 144 ppm Zn, 59 ppm Cu and 0.5 ppm Se. Brood mares were fed 3-5 kg of the grain mix during pregnancy and 4-6 kg during lactation. Foals were first offered grain starting at 90 to 120 days of age. From 90 days until weaning (at 5 months), the foals received grain at a level of intake equal to 0.5 kg per month of age. At weaning, the foal's grain intake was increased to 3 kg/day. Grain intake for the weanlings and yearlings was then adjusted based on growth rate and body weight, but averaged between 3 and 5 kg/day until the yearlings were sold or sent away for training. In certain instances, a weanling's or yearling's grain intake might fall below 3 kg/day. When this happened, the protein/vitamin/mineral pellet was supplemented at a level equal to 0.33 kg of pellet for each 1 kg of grain intake below 3 kgs.

Mares with foals born before April 15 were kept in box stalls from 15:00 in the afternoon until 8:00 the following morning. During the day, the mares and foals were housed in small grass paddocks (1-2 hectares).   After April 15, mares with foals older than 4 weeks stayed out during the night in large grass paddocks (25-50 hectares) and were kept in box stalls between 8:00 and 15:00. The mares were fed their grain in two meals while in their box stalls. The paddocks housing the mares and foals were well drained and level, but the ground could become quite hard during dry weather or when frozen.

During the winter months, the mares and foals received a grass/legume hay free choice both outside and while in their stalls. During the spring, summer and fall months, the majority of the horses' forage intake came from pasture. Table 1 contains the average composition of the supplement pellet, grain, hay and pasture from this farm.

Table 1. NUTRIENT COMPOSITION OF GRAIN, HAY AND PASTURE.

Nutrient	Supplement[1] pellet	Grain[1] mix	Mixed[1] hay	Fall[2] pasture	Spring[2] pasture
Crude protein (%)	25.00	15.50	12.10	16.00	16.50
DE (MJ/kg)	11.68	11.95	8.27	9.20	10.11
Calcium (%)	2.57	1.00	0.82	0.55	0.48
Phosphorus (%)	1.73	0.81	0.20	0.30	0.43
Zinc (ppm)	360.00	144.00	24.00	35.00	28.00
Copper (ppm)	143.00	59.00	9.00	12.00	15.00
Manganese (ppm)	228.00	105.00	75.00	70.00	75.00

[1] as fed basis
[2] 100% DM basis

Results

Tables 2 and 3 summarize the frequency of DOD as a function of sex, month and year of birth, age and lesion location. 30% of the foals in this study were born in January or February and 30% were born in March. 23% of the foals were born in April and 17% of the foals were born in May or June. DOD was divided into four categories based on the location of the lesion and the age at diagnosis. Lesions in the fetlock were divided into early lesions (102 ± 48 days) and late lesions (379 ± 140 days), while lesions of the stifle and shoulder were grouped together. Hock lesions were grouped separately.

Table2. FREQUENCY OF DOD (NUMBER AND PERCENTAGE OF TOTAL FOALS BORN EACH MONTH)

Birth Month	Total foals	Total No. DOD	% DOD	Early fetlock (total)	Early fetlock (%)	Late fetlock (total)	Late fetlock (%)	Stifle & shoulder (total)	Stifle & shoulder (%)	Hock (total)	Hock (%)
Jan-Feb	81	9	11.0 %	3	3.7 %	1	1.2 %	1	1.2 %	4	4.9 %
March	81	11	11.1 %	3	3.7 %	2	2.5 %	4	4.9 %	2	2.5 %
April	62	2	3.2 %	0	0 %	0	0 %	0	0%	2	3.2 %
May-June	47	5	10.3 %	0	0 %	0	0 %	1	2.1 %	4	8.5 %
TOTAL	271	27	10.0 %	6	2.2 %	3	1.1 %	6	2.2 %	12	4.4 %
Colts	136	13	48.1 %	1	16.6 %	2	66.6 %	4	66.6 %	6	50 %
Fillies	135	14	51.9 %	5	83.3 %	1	33.3 %	2	33.3 %	6	50 %

A total of 10% of the foals in this study suffered one of these types of lesions. The incidence of total lesions was evenly distributed between January-February, March and May-June foals. April foals had a lower incidence of total lesions (3.2%) (p<0.05) and all of these lesions were confined to the hock. Fetlock lesions only occurred in January-February and March foals. Early fetlock lesions occurred in more than one joint 83.3% of the time. Stifle, shoulder and hock lesions tended to occur most often in a single joint.

Table 3. AGE OF DIAGNOSIS, NUMBER OF JOINTS AFFECTED, AND DISTRIBUTION BY YEAR

	Early fetlock	*Late fetlock*	*Stifle and shoulder*	*Hock*
Age of diagnosis				
days (mean ± SD)	102 ± 48	379 ± 140	335 ± 102	304 ± 100
Single joint (%)	16.7 %	66.6 %	83.3 %	75 %
Both joints (%)	83.3 %	33.3 %	16.7 %	25 %
1991 (number)	1	0	0	1
1992 (number)	1	1	3	5
1993 (number)	1	2	1	4
1994 (number)	3	0	2	2

The body weights of the affected foals are graphed relative to the Kentucky average in figure 1. Foals with early fetlock lesions tended to be of average size and their growth rates were similar to the average of a large population of Thoroughbred foals raised in Kentucky (Pagan, *et al.*, 1996). Foals that were diagnosed with fetlock lesions at a later age tended to be of normal size during the first 120 days, but grew heavier than the Kentucky average after weaning. Those foals that developed hock OCDs averaged 5 kg heavier than the Kentucky average at 25 days of age. By 240 days, these foals were 14 kg heavier than the population average. Foals that developed stifle or shoulder lesions averaged 5.5 kg heavier than the Kentucky average at 25 days of age and 17 kg heavier at 120 days of age. By 300 days of age, these foals were 12 kg heavier than the Kentucky average.

Discussion

The nutrition program on this farm was carefully monitored and both pregnant mares and growing foals received adequate quantities of both macro and micro minerals throughout the year (Table 1). In spite of this, this farm still experienced a 10% incidence of DOD. Therefore, other factors besides mineral intake must have played a role in the development of skeletal lesions in these foals.

Dr. Roy Pool, a pathologist from the University of California at Davis veterinary school, has recently addressed the question of what is the primary cause of skeletal lesions in growing horses (Pool, 1995; 1993). His conclusions may explain why dietary changes have not totally eliminated DOD from horses.

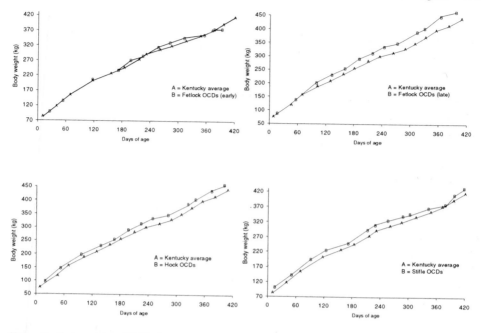

Figure 1. Body weights of DOD foals compared to Kentucky average

Dr. Pool maintains that early explanations of DOD in horses were based on studies in other animals such as swine and poultry. In these animals, osteochondrosis is a systemic disease affecting joints scattered throughout the body. It is largely genetic and can be enhanced or suppressed through nutritional manipulation. These are not the "typical" types of lesions seen in horses. In horses, lesions usually occur in specific joints such as the stifle, shoulder, hock and fetlock. Usually, only one or two joints are affected and if two are affected, they normally occur bilaterally in the same joint. For instance, one stifle may have a large lesion causing lameness while another smaller, asymptomatic lesion may be found in the other stifle. This was the pattern of lesions seen in the foals on this farm.

Dr. Pool maintains that these types of lesions are most likely the result of excessive biomechanical forces exerted on otherwise normal cartilage. These forces disrupt the blood supply to the cartilage and prevent its conversion to bone. There are several possible reasons why normal cartilage could not withstand these forces:

1) Specific joints have "windows of vulnerability" when they are particularly susceptible to damage. At this point in development, perhaps there is not adequate underlying bone to support the weight and force exerted on the joint. For example, stifles and hocks seem to be most vulnerable at 6 to 8 months of age. At this point, excessive force may damage the underlying bone and vascular supply to the cartilage. The cartilage does not ossify and

a lesion forms. The clinical expression of the lesion may not occur until later when the lesion becomes severe enough to cause lameness or swelling.

The average ages of diagnosis of hock and stifle lesions in this study were 304 days and 335 days, respectively. These foals grew faster and were heavier than the Kentucky average. Perhaps this extra weight caused excessive forces on otherwise normal cartilage leading to the development of a lesion. Kentucky foals born early in the year enter this 6 to 8 month age period at a time when pasture quantity and quality increase during the months of September and October. Increased intake of high quality pasture may have contributed to the rapid growth rates seen in these large foals.

2)   Foals with genetic potential for rapid skeletal and muscle development may simply develop more muscle mass than the rapidly growing bone can support. Again, the foals that developed hock and stifle lesions may have fit this category.

3)   Foals that don't have the genetic potential for rapid growth become fat because of excessive energy intake and overload the joint. This was probably not the case in the present study, since each foal's body condition was regularly evaluated and individuals that were deemed too fat had their grain intake restricted.

4)   A conformation defect creates an uneven distribution of force upon the joint surface. No records were kept of conformation defects, so this factor cannot be adequately addressed in the present study.

5)   Foals that have been confined due to illness do not develop enough subchondral bone to support their weight. When they are finally returned to the herd, the bone is too weak to support a normal amount of exercise and the joint cartilage collapses.

6)   Rapid changes in management that greatly alter the foal's exercise patterns may overload the joint. For instance, foals born early in the year are kept inside for up to 16 hours per day. When the weather improves in April, they are turned out all night with their dams. Often, mares run their foals for long periods in the paddock and the foal becomes fatigued. At this point, joints may be more vulnerable to injury. This may have been a factor in the foals which developed early fetlock lesions. All of the foals that developed early fetlock lesions were born in January, February and March. These foals were all housed indoors at night until mid April. Perhaps these foals did not develop adequate subchondral bone to withstand the forces placed on it once they were allowed greater amounts of exercise as the weather improved.

Osteochondrosis involving the cervical vertebra often affects multiple sites randomly and may be considered an "atypical" type according to Dr. Pool. This type of lesion is often responsible for "wobbles" in foals and it may result from a mineral deficiency or imbalance. None of the horses in the present study were diagnosed with this type of OCD lesion, suggesting that macro and micro mineral intake were adequate.

Conclusions

The etiology of developmental orthopedic disease is almost certainly multifactorial. A primary focus of much of the research concerning DOD has been on mineral intake and balance. While minerals are certainly important for skeletal development, mineral deficiencies or imbalances are not the only cause of DOD. In the present study where mineral intake was carefully monitored, 10% of the foals still developed DOD.

A major factor to consider in the etiology of DOD is whether the lesion develops because of a failure in proper cartilage formation and maturation or whether the lesion develops in normal cartilage. The types of lesions seen in the present study may have been the result of excessive biomechanical forces exerted on otherwise normal cartilage. Early fetlock OCDs may have resulted from inadequate subchondral bone formation due to restricted activity in foals born early in the year and housed indoors at night. Hock and stifle lesions may have occurred in heavy foals that grew rapidly after weaning.

The present study raises several intriguing questions about which factors are involved in the development of orthopedic disease under commercial management conditions. Controlled research is necessary to determine if management of growth rate and exercise can reduce the incidence of developmental orthopedic disease in horses.

References

Knight, D.A., A.A. Gabel, S.M. Reed, L.R. Bramlage, W.J. Tyznik, and R.M. Embertson (1985) Correlation of dietary mineral to incidence and severity of metabolic bone disease in Ohio and Kentucky. In: Proc. 31st Annu. Conv. Am. Assoc. Eq. Pract., F.J. Milne, ed., Lexington, Ky.

Pagan, J.D., S.G. Jackson, and S. Caddel (1996) A Summary of Growth Rates of Thoroughbreds in Kentucky. In: Proc: 2nd European Conference on Equine Nutrition (1996)

Pool, R.R. (1995) Nutritional Insignificance as it relates to developmental orthopedic disease. In: Proc. 14th ENPS, Ontario, CA. pp. 344-352.

Pool, R.R. (1993) Difficulties in definition of equine osteochondrosis; differentiation of developmental and acquired lesions. Equine vet J. Suppl. 16, pp. 5-12.

This paper was first published in "Focus on Equine Nutrition," Proceedings for the 1996 Short Course for Feed Manufacturers

PATHOLOGICAL CONDITIONS

NUTRITION RELATED PATHOLOGICAL CONDITIONS OF THE PERFORMANCE HORSE

STEPHEN G. JACKSON

Kentucky Equine Research Inc., Versailles, Kentucky, USA

Introduction

The athletic horse is subjected to a variety of stresses ranging from extreme work bouts to exposure to sometimes pathological levels of environmental pollutants. Due to the taxing nature of exercise and training regimes horses may develop any number of potentially career ending or compromising pathological situations. Many of the problems associated with the athletic horse are thought to have nutritional components while others appear to have no association at all to nutrition, or at least not to the feeding program in use at the time the problems surface. It will be the goal of this paper to categorize ailments of the performance horse into three categories:

1) those problems with direct nutritional implications

2) those problems that may or may not have nutritional variables in their etiology and

3) problems with no reasonable nutritional explanation.

Obviously it is the tendency in many instances to blame nutrition if no other reasonable explanation exists. This attitude does nothing to move us forward, toward actually diminishing injury to the athletic horse and the resultant financial loss. Only those conditions with probable nutritional causes will be discussed in this paper.

Exertional rhabdomyolysis (ER)

Tying-up, also know as exertional rhabdomyolysis, azoturia, myositis, set-fast, paralytic myoglobinuria, and Monday morning sickness, is a disease that has been around for as long as horses have done work for man. Early reference to the disease was in draft horses that after having not worked over a weekend, while on full ration, tied-up on Monday morning when put in harness and asked to work. The disease affects the muscle and may vary widely in severity, clinical signs and prognosis for recovery. Horses that develop myositis may show any one or a combination of the clinical signs listed in Table 1.

Table 1. CLINICAL SIGNS ASSOCIATED WITH EXERTIONAL RHABDOMYOLYSIS

• Stiff and abnormal gait	• Increased body temperature
• Reluctance to move	• Profuse sweating
• Increased heart and respiratory rate	• May become recumbent
• Muscles painful to touch	• Myoglobinuria

The prognosis for recovery of affected horses is in general related to the severity of the episode and the quality of medical care they receive during the chronic stage of the disease. Although all ages and sexes of horses are affected, the incidence appears to be greater in fillies and mares than in geldings or stallions. This suggests a possible endocrine relationship, but efforts to confirm a direct relationship between estrogen and the occurrence of the problem have not been fruitful.

For as long as the condition has been documented, efforts have been made to elucidate the cause and to develop strategies to prevent the problem. The result of these efforts has been the realization that the etiology of the disease is multifactorial and includes nutrition, genetics, environmental and endocrine factors. To ignore familial tendencies toward tying-up would be to defy conventional wisdom and the experience of trainers having trained several generations of a line of horses. It is common to find, in researching a case of myositis, that one or both of the parents of an affected horse were known to have tied-up. Besides the previously mentioned possible role of steroid hormones, thyroid hormone has been mentioned as a possible factor which initiates the disorder. Hypothyroid, heavily stressed horses, have been know to develop chronic muscle problems and some have benefitted from thyroxine supplementation. An in depth discussion of the biochemistry of all of the possible causes of this disease is beyond the scope of this paper; however, I would be remiss if non-nutritional contributing causes were not at least mentioned. The nutritional connection to myositis revolves around two major areas:

1) management of grain intake and muscle glycogen status and

2) maintaining proper electrolyte and pH balance in the working muscle.

The most classic example of tying-up is in response to full grain feeding during periods of inactivity (usually a day or two) followed by a return to training. This cause may really be one of nutritional and training mismanagement rather than being strictly dietary. Nonetheless, when horses are to be rested it is prudent to drastically reduce the amount of grain that is being fed.

In some instances selenium and vitamin E supplementation have been reported to be effective in the treatment/management of the disease. In many cases adequate levels of vitamin E and selenium have neither prevented nor been effective in preventing the reoccurrence of the disease. Even so, field experience has resulted in the practice of dietary fortification with both selenium and vitamin E.

Recently there has been increased interest in potassium concentration shifts or in lowered intracellular potassium as a possible cause of exertional rhabdomyolysis. In many cases RBC or intracellular potassium concentrations are lower than normal in affected horses and when the problem is corrected using potassium chloride, there is a decrease in the incidence of ER.

Anhydrosis

Anhydrosis is the inability to sweat in response to work output or increases in body temperature. The condition may also be referred to as "dry coated." The condition may develop gradually with normal sweat output associated with exercise followed by decreased sweat output with successive exercise bouts, or may be precipitated by one bout of exercise. Most "dry coated" horses are athletic horses though frequently the condition appears in pastured horses not being ridden. Anhydrosis most commonly occurs when both temperature and humidity are high as in the southern US or in sub-tropical areas such as Brunei, Jamaica or Singapore. Horses reared in temperate regions and then transported to hot climates are most prone to develop the condition, but even "hot climate acclimated" horses are seemingly at risk.

The exact cause of anhydrosis is not well elucidated. Clinical signs include inability to sweat, increased respiratory rate, elevated body temperature and decreased exercise tolerance. Due to heat stress, affected horses will go off feed, lose weight and show signs of depression. These are inconsistent signs with respect to histological findings in skin but alteration of sweat glands is a common occurrence. The condition almost always requires a combination of high temperature and high humidity for its development and the most effective treatment is moving the affected horses to a cooler climate. Resumption of normal sweating is frequently observed on horses moved to more favorable environments, but the prognosis is guarded in horses not moved. Some success has been achieved by placing horses in air conditioned stalls, but work intolerance may persist when the affected horses are worked outside. Anhydrotic horses are prone to suffer from heat stroke (usually fatal) and other forms of heat stress and as such are not suitable for athletic events if recovery is not achieved.

From a nutritional standpoint, electrolyte imbalances or inadequacies are the most frequently indicted causes of anhydrosis. Inadequate sodium, chloride or potassium in the diet coupled with extreme electrolyte loss in the sweat has been thought to precipitate the condition and hyponatremia and hypochloremia are frequently seen in anhydrotic horses. Nonetheless, a great many horses are not helped by electrolyte therapy nor does the condition seem to be prevented by prophylactic electrolyte administration. Even so, it is wise to consider electrolyte supplementation in "at risk" horses. Any number of drug therapies from ACTH to calcium-pantothenate administration have been tried with limited to variable success, so exact cause and manner of dietary interaction remain unclear.

Synchronous diaphragmatic flutter (thumps)

Synchronous Diaphragmatic Flutter (SDF), also referred to as "thumps," is characterized by contraction of the diaphragm in synchrony with the heart beat. Affected horses are observed to have a noticeable twitch or spasm in the flank which may be pronounced enough to cause an audible thumping sound which is where the common name of the condition came from.

SDF is most commonly seen in electrolyte depleted/exhausted horses. Other anomalies associated with SDF include dehydration, decreased plasma volume, gut stasis (lack of gastro-intestinal mobility), and metabolic alkalosis. Consistent findings include lowered plasma chloride, calcium, sodium and magnesium concentrations, and aggressive electrolyte therapy is both preventive and of therapeutic value. There is some indication that horses on excessive calcium intake may be very susceptible due to their inability to mobilize calcium rapidly enough to meet exercise induced requirements.

Heaves

Heaves, also called chronic obstructive pulmonary disease (COPD), has been associated with "winded" horses. COPD is a hyperallergenic response of the respiratory system similar to that seen in human asthma. Affected horses may cough, develop a nasal discharge and have excessive tearing of the eyes. Respiratory rate is increased, and lung elasticity diminished, and in some cases a characteristic "heave" line develops due to muscular hypertrophy associated with the increased expiratory effort needed. Additionally expiration may become biphasic.

The most important aspect of treatment is recognition of its cause: exposure to dust, mold spores and respiratory irritants such as ammonia. Horses affected with COPD are best kept outside and managed in pastures rather than in stalls. When this is not possible, horses should be bedded on dust free bedding such as shredded paper or on rubber mats rather than on straw, hay or wood shavings. Horses would be removed from the barn during management procedures likely to increase the amount of dust in the air (cleaning and re-bedding of stalls, sweeping the aisle, filling or cleaning hay lofts).

Particularly challenging is continuing to meet the horse's fiber requirement while minimizing exposure to causative agents. Frequently the problem can be controlled by wetting hay before feeding it which reduces particulate matter such as dust and mold spores and as such the irritation of the respiratory tract. Many times alternative fiber sources such as grass cubes, soaked oaten or wheaten chaff have been used effectively to manage horses with COPD but particularly effective has been the use of diets containing shredded beet pulp as the predominant fiber source. These diets are characteristically up to 30% beet pulp and 20% molasses.

Affected horses may also respond favorably to the use of expectorants to reduce coughing and to the use of bronchodilators to reduce respiratory rate and airway resistance.

Degenerative joint disease (DJD)

Degenerative joint disease (DJD) is second only to tendinitis as a cause of removing race horses from training. Though there is no specific evidence to suggest that DJD is the result of nutritional disorders at the time at which clinical signs appear, one must wonder if early nutritional mistakes might not subsequently precipitate the appearance of the disease. DJD consists of a multitude of clinical manifestations including degeneration of articular cartilage, subchondral bone, and other bone comprising both the articular and periarticular aspects of the joints. Cartilage/bone anomalies are most frequently described in the joints distal to the radius in the foreleg and femur in the hindleg. Suggested causes include repeated trauma (wear and tear), conformation faults (straight pasterns, stifles, etc.), joint septicemia, traumatic joint injury, subchondral bone defects (OCD lesions) and intra-articular glucocorticoid administrations to name a few of the more common ones.

It is beyond the scope of this paper to describe in full the relationship thought to exist between developmental orthopedic disease (DOD) and DJD which might then occur. However, some workers suggest that OCD and other defects (subchondral bone cyst) associated with DOD are the primary causes of catastrophic breakdown of race horses as well as traumatic, but equally important injuries, including carpitis, synovitis, sesamoiditis and various manifestations of DJD. As such, early nutritional management has a rather marked and serious effect on potential performance of the horse and the prevention of at least some of the pathological conditions of the athletic horse.

The use of methyl sulfonyl methane (MSM) in the treatment of arthritic disease in the horse has received some attention and varying degrees of support among both equine veterinarians and horsemen. There are no real data from controlled experiments to suggest that MSM (closely related to dimethyl sulfoxide - DMSO) has therapeutic or prophylactic value but the clinical experience of some veterinarians suggests it may be helpful. One could postulate that as a source of sulfur, MSM may contribute to the maintenance of the articular cartilage matrix; however critical research needs to be conducted before any conclusion can be reached regarding the effect or lack of effect of using MSM (or perhaps other sulfur sources) on the prevention or treatment of cartilage/synovia disorders of the performance horse.

This paper was first published in "Feeding the Performance Horse," Proceedings for the 1992 Short Course for Feed Manufacturers

COLIC

MIKE BEYER

Hagyard-Davidson-McGee Veterinary Clinic, Lexington, Kentucky, USA

Colic is any abdominal pain. The causes are numerous and many unidentified, but in general they are related to the anatomy of the horse's gastro-intestinal tract (GI) and the balance of bacterial flora in the gut. From a veterinarian's viewpoint the nutritionally-related causes lie in the disruption of the bacterial flora in the gut and its consequences. Two scenarios can lead to an abrupt change in the bacterial flora: first, feeding improper ratios of forage and grain; second, feeding tainted forage or grain (moldy hay or grain).

To better appreciate the mechanism of colic keep in mind the anatomy of the horse's GI tract; they are hindgut fermenters, more like a rabbit than a dog. The path of ingesta through the horse's GI tract is oropharynx, esophagus, stomach, small intestine, cecum, large colon, small colon, rectum. The cecum and large colon are large segments of the tract which allow for fermentation and absorption of nutrients after partial digestion in the stomach and small intestine. These large segments are prone to malfunctions in position, absorption, and motility, all of which can be nutritionally related.

The first category, an improper position, can sometimes potentially be attributed to diet. A change in diet which causes increased gas production can cause part of the intestinal tract to become buoyant as well as create abnormal motility which in turn leads to a change in position. Displacement or torsion is most common in the large colon. The large colon forms two horseshoe shaped loops (one on top of the other) on the floor of the abdomen with little tissue attachment and can thus almost be free-floating. Being displaced with gas buildup is one potential cause of large colon displacements, torsions, and nephrosplenic entrapments. Some simple displacements can be corrected without surgery whereas other lesions including torsions must be corrected surgically.

The second category, malfunctions of motility, can be due to the feed consistency and content. We will often see impactions or increased transit time due to lack of moisture or too much coarse material. Referrals in our practice show a 30-50:1 ratio of impactions in confined horses versus farm horses. Common sites of impaction include the pelvic flexure of the large colon, the transverse colon, and the cecum. All three sites are areas of abrupt change in the diameter of the colon.

The third category of causes of colic are those due to abnormality in absorption. If, for example, a horse is suddenly fed a large amount of grain, the time the ingesta spends in the stomach and small intestine is significantly decreased because of the decrease in the amount of fiber in the diet. The hindgut, the cecum, and colon receive a large volume of highly digestible foodstuff, bacteria rapidly break the ingesta down, and the pH of the hindgut decreases. The bacteria produce a large volume of gas and can in turn have a large increase in numbers and subsequent die-off in bacteria leading to endotoxin release and mucosal damage. Mucosal damage reduces absorption and less fluid is absorbed. In this scenario both a faster transit time through the gut and a decrease in the amount of absorption can lead to spasmodic gut activity, colic, and even diarrhea.

Treatment of the cases of colic associated with diarrhea consists of compensating the horse for its fluid losses, treating potential secondary complications, and attempting to reverse the process which led to the diarrhea. Fluid replacement is accomplished through aggressive IV fluid therapy.

Secondary complications include laminitis, endotoxemia, and peritonitis if the bowel is compromised to the point of leaking.

Once the horse is maintained through the acute phase of diarrhea, we attempt to improve absorption by repopulating the gut with normal bacterial flora and secondarily by slowing or altering the transit time of ingesta. The tactic for slowing the transit time consists of feeding a ration high in dry matter and fiber in an attempt to pull some of the excess fluid in the gut into a foodstuff that is not readily broken down and stays in the hindgut for a longer period of time. One such foodstuff that we recommend is beet pulp, especially in chronic diarrheas. Any feed that is high in fiber, low moisture, and relatively absorptive or hygroscopic will meet this need.

The interplay of increased transit time through the gut and mucosal damage especially to portions of the hindgut explains why the most significant complication of diarrhea is laminitis. With compromised GI mucosa, the toxins in the gut and endotoxins released from the breakdown of gram negative bacteria cell walls can readily enter the systemic circulation leading to toxemia and endotoxemia. Endotoxic horses suffer from numerous pathological responses to the systemic insult.

In diarrhea cases treatment is directed towards ameliorating some of the effects of endotoxin and consequently indirectly addressing the potential for laminitis. Endotoxins in the systemic circulation lead to vasoconstriction especially in some of the smaller peripheral vascular beds, release of tumor necrosis factor, elaboration of clotting factors, and increased tendency to form microthrombi in small vessels. To oversimplify: because there is an insult to the body systemically blood supply is preserved to the vital, major organs and sacrificed to the peripheral, less essential vascular beds. One of these beds is that of the laminae of the hoof wall.

Endotoxemia is treated through fluid therapy, use of nonsteroidal anti-inflammatory drugs, use of rheologic drugs to decrease blood viscosity, and use of peripheral vasodilators to preserve blood supply to the peripheral vascular beds. The most commonly used drugs at our clinic are flunixin meglumine, pentoxifylline, and occasionally aspirin to help decrease the likelihood of microthrombi.

The most common presentations of feed-related colic and diarrhea at this practice are middle-aged adult horses who have either had an abrupt change in diet, have recently been shipped (deprived of free access to water and have become impacted) or have recently been on a course of antibiotics which alter the gut flora. Correction lies in providing digestible fiber to the hindgut and repopulation of the gut with normal bacterial flora. We have little we can offer with feed and basically rely on natural repopulation of the gut. It is questionable whether any live bacterial cultures reach the hindgut and survive the acidity of the stomach, but we will sometimes use yogurt to attempt to replace bacteria in the gut.

Many colic disturbances may be able to be traced back to changes in GI motility or bacterial flora. The horse was designed to be a grazer continually ingesting small quantities of forage all of the time. In our attempts to feed the highest quality rations for maximum performance we cannot overlook the potential complications caused with different feeding regimes.

Laminitis

Laminitis by definition is any inflammation of the laminae that interdigitate between the hoof wall and P-3. These laminae can become inflamed in any generalized systemic condition which can affect peripheral circulation such as endotoxemia, septicemia, severe dehydration, and cardiovascular shock. Experimentally induced laminitis models are those caused by carbohydrate overload and black walnut induced toxicity (Praase, 1990 and Galey, 1991). Other causes include mechanical stress, endocrine disease, steroids, and some predisposition as seen in some ponies (Byars, 1995).

By far the most common cases of laminitis we see in the clinic situation are those that occur secondarily to diarrhea, especially colitis which compromises the gut mucosa and allows for absorption of endotoxins from the GI tract. As these toxins are absorbed into the circulation, the blood supply to the foot changes and the small laminae are compromised through poor circulation and ischemia (or deprivation of oxygen) to their tissues. Once signs of laminitis are obvious, the pathological process of ischemia and vessel endothelial damage due to venoconstriction or microthrombosis is already in effect. In practice the most successful intervention we can offer is a prophylactic one aimed at preventing the onset of the process.

Any therapies directed towards abating the effects of inflammatory mediators and circulatory changes have a therapeutic potential. Primarily used are anti-inflammatories such as flunixin meglumine (Banamine) or phenylbutazone (Bute), vasodilators such as acepromazine for short term or isoxsuprine for long term therapy, anticoagulants such as heparin, and pentoxifylline which blocks the production of tumor necrosis factor and decreases the viscosity of the blood. In cases of diarrhea/colitis with laminitis as a sequela, the prevention of absorption of endotoxins from the gut may address the potential cause. Experimentally, however, sublethal doses of endotoxin have not been shown to induce laminitis.

Clinically the most successful treatment occurs very early in the disease process or even prophylactically. Medically we can effect decreased blood viscosity, vasodilation, and decreased systemic inflammation. Nutritionally we have to effect a decreased absorption of endotoxin from the GI tract, repopulation of the bacterial flora of the gut, and increased transit time of ingesta through the hindgut via increased fiber content and less acidic pH in the colon.

Once the laminae are affected to the point of partial separation between the hoof laminae and those of P-3, the prognosis of an athletically sound horse decreases (Stick in Kobluk, 1995).

In practice we rarely see laminitis in neonates, seldom see it in weanlings, and commonly see it in adults. Ponies are prone to laminitis as are heavily muscled stallions, obese horses and endotoxic adults. Nutrition can play a role both in initiating laminitis either through precipitating an abrupt change in bacterial flora and releasing an endotoxic shower or directly through a carbohydrate overload. It is also necessary to nutritionally manage the laminitic horse to reduce the numbers of endotoxin-producing bacteria and increase hindgut fermentation. The myriad of treatments we have to implement for laminitis indicate the limited success of any one treatment modality.

Ulcers

Gastric ulcers were first recognized as a serious clinical entity by Rebhun in 1982. Since then, however, they have become widely recognized as a clinical problem in young adults as well due to the decrease in performance among racehorses.

Two regions of the stomach can be ulcerated. The nonglandular portion or the squamous epithelial portion is primarily ulcerated due to increased gastric acidity whereas ulceration of the mucosal glandular portion is due to a compromise in mucosal protection. Prostaglandin E is required for normal gastric mucus production. Non-steroidal anti-inflammatory drugs inhibit the production of prostaglandin E and hence the maintenance of the protective mucosal barrier of the glandular portion of the stomach.

In racehorses in training usually 2-5 years of age we see ulceration of the non-glandular portion of the stomach more frequently. This portion is also the most readily visible portion with the endoscope. The causes for gastric ulceration are numerous. In the young racehorse it is thought to be related to increased stress and feeding regimes. Most often these horses are being fed large quantities of grain with reduced quantities of hay and in 2 or 3 large feedings per day. Studies have shown that horses fed grain increase gastric acid production in the stomach as compared to those fed hay (Murray, 1994).

Adults with gastric ulcers usually present as having mild colic signs sometimes associated with eating, unthriftiness, and poor performance. Murray suggests that the activity of eating small amounts, often, decreases the acidity of the stomach. Conversely acidity is greatest in horses that are held off of feed altogether through increased gastrin production. Therefore feeding a large quantity of grain 2-3x/day may exacerbate the tendency of horses in training to have hyperacidic stomachs and thus leads to the increased incidence among this group of horses. Again the diet best suited to prevention is one which has more forage than grain.

Our treatment for this group of horses consists of altering the feeding regime as much as is practical and instituting anti-ulcer medication with sucralfate and H2 antagonists. The H2 antagonists are cimetidine (Tagamet), ranitidine (Zantac), and famotidine (Pepcid). We commonly use ranitidine or cimetidine in the adult. An effective but expensive drug currently available is omeprazole (Prilosec). As a proton pump inhibitor it is especially effective against both squamous and mucosal ulceration.

Foals are prone to gastric ulceration, yet it is generally considered stress-induced hyperacidity that leads to both gastric and duodenal ulceration in foals. Foals affected are often not weaned and whose diet consists primarily of the mare's milk. It is therefore questionable whether diet is a factor. There is, however, a positive association of Rotavirus and other causes of diarrhea with the incidence of gastric ulcers in foals.

Foals are also treated with H2 antagonists (usually ranitidine) and sucralfate if ulcers are thought to already be present. Clinically affected foals can show signs including bruxism, excess salivation, colic after nursing, dorsal recumbency, diarrhea, weight loss, and pot-bellied appearance.

In general clinically significant ulceration has decreased in foals in this area probably as a result of widespread anti-ulcer use on farms. Ulceration in adults, however, is a more frequently diagnosed problem often as a reason for poor performance in training. Feeding regimes and perhaps feeds that would reduce the acidity of the stomach may be helpful in decreasing the incidence among young adults.

References

Allen, D., and J.N. Moore. Equine Acute Laminitis. Veterinary Learning Systems, Inc., 1995.

Byars, T.D., R.J. Hunt and P.S.C. Hagyard-Davidson-McGee. 4250 Iron Works Pike, Lexington, KY USA, 40511.

Byars T.D. Proceedings 17th Bain-Fallon Memorial Lectures, 1995:27-33.

Hunt R.J., D. Allen and J.N. Moore. Effect of Endotoxin Administration on Equine Digital Hemodynamics and Starling Forces. Am J Vet Res, 1990:51(11);1103-1707.

Murray M.J. Gastric Ulcers in Adult Horses. Comp Cont Educ, 1994:16(6);792-794.

Rebhun W.C., S.G. Dill and H.T. Power. Gastric Ulcers in Foals. J Am Vet Med Assoc, 1982:180(4);404-407.

Stick J.S. The Horse, Diseases and Clinical Management. Kobluk CN *et al*, eds. W.B. Saunders Company, 1995.

Swerczek T.W. Toxicoinfectious Botulism in Foal and Adult Horses. Am J Vet Res, 1980:176(3);217-220.

This paper was first published in "Recent Advances in Equine Nutrition," Proceedings for the 1995 Short Course for Feed Manufacturers

NUTRITION AND PRODUCTIVITY: PRACTICAL PROBLEMS RELATED TO NUTRITION

STEPHEN G. JACKSON

Kentucky Equine Research, Inc., Versailles, Kentucky, USA

If you really can't figure out the problem it must be the feed. Many of us in the nutrition and feed manufacturing business have felt the frustration of having our formulas and our feed blamed for a myriad of problems on the horse farm and in the training stable. Many people engaged in the production of horses attribute miraculous healing and preventative qualities to feed and/or feeding management. This is all too easy to understand as the easiest change to make in response to a problem is to change the feed. The old saying goes, 'if it ain't broke, don't fix it.' It seems that the second part of the saying is: 'If it is broke, fix it.' Even if you don't know what's broke, fix it by changing the feed! Certainly much of the overall success of a breeding farm or racing stable can be attributed to accurate feeding programs and good feed management systems. This alone is why we as feed manufacturers and horse nutritionists have jobs. However to attribute all or a majority of the problems on a farm to nutrition is foolish. It will be the purpose of this paper to try to identify areas of production that are nutrition responsive and to try to explain the manner in which nutrition may be related to various problems that exist on the farm or in the training barn. Obviously time and space do not permit a thorough discussion of all of the various problems that may have a nutritional variable but we will try to discuss some of the more important ones. Problems of the performance horse were discussed in the 1992 proceedings of this course. A discussion of myositis, thumps, anhidrosis, COPD, and degenerative joint disease will be found in that publication. The problems and conditions below are still only a partial list of the problems that may have a nutritional origin or the manner in which nutrition is thought to influence productivity on the horse operation.

Nutrition and the broodmare

It is a common occurrence for people to erroneously attribute many fertility problems in the brood mare to vitamin deficiencies and to neglect to consider the single most important nutritional variable in reproductive efficiency - energy balance. More progress can be made in terms of increasing conception rates by insuring appropriate body condition than by using any other nutritional tool. This is not to say that meeting vitamin, mineral and protein requirements is not important but from a practical standpoint energy balance tends to be more a concern. There is really no reason to assume that any species of animal is designed to conceive, carry a pregnancy to term and re-breed while in a negative energy balance. It is surprising that energy intake should be a major problem as it is really one of the easiest nutrients to assess.

Broodmares should be kept in reasonable flesh throughout the year. I would ask clients to try to practice what I would refer to as straight line broodmare nutrition. By this I mean that an optimum condition should be established for each mare and appropriate adjustments made in the feeding program to maintain this condition. This means that coming into the last trimester of pregnancy the mare should begin receiving more feed in preparation for lactation and that during lactation, feed intake should be increased to support the production of milk without excessive loss of body condition. During the final half of lactation the energy intake of the mare should be adjusted depending on condition at that point in time and on forage availability, again in hopes of maintaining optimum condition. Once a foal is weaned and the mare "dries up," an assessment of condition should be made and this period should be used to adjust the mare's condition back to optimal. This means that for the heavy milking mare that has gone through a tough lactation, we may want to continue to feed her at pre-weaning levels of feed intake and allow her to gain condition and for the mare that is fat we may want to not feed any feed and allow her to meet needs on good quality forage alone. Work at Texas A&M would indicate that mares that are a little too fat are far more reproductively efficient than are mares that are too thin.

For barren and maiden mares, plane of nutrition should be increased as the mares come into the breeding season. It makes good sense to increase nutrient intake when mares are put under lights so that an increase in condition is achieved at the same time as an increase in day length. This practice is referred to as nutritional flushing and from experience is effective in shortening the transitional period and increasing conception rates. This practice, done on mares to be bred in February and March, would mimic what would occur in nature when the spring flush of grass would result in mares increasing in body fat stores.

Dr. Walter Zent, considered one of the better reproduction practitioners, once remarked that if he were limited to one practice to increase conception rates in mares it would be "suturing" the mare. However, he added that poor conformation of the external genitalia of the mare is often as much a function of body condition as anything else. Thin mares are especially more prone to sunken vulvas that are apt to result in fecal contamination or wind sucking (pneumovagina). Especially in older mares, adding body weight may improve conformation and hence reproductive performance. Like Dr. Zent, as a nutritionist if I could do but one thing to the broodmare from a nutritional point of view it would be to insure energy intake to insure optimum body condition.

Another nutrient that I am always looking at in terms of reproduction is selenium. Maylin at Cornell reported that mares receiving inadequate selenium were much more prone to reproductive problems than were mares receiving adequate selenium. I try to insure that selenium intake in the mare is from 2 -3 mg/day.

Developmental orthopedic disease

Developmental orthopedic disease (DOD), also referred to in some circles as metabolic bone disease, consists not of a singular but of several related disorders affecting the young horse during the critical developmental stage. Included in the disease are: Epiphysitis (Physitis), Osteochondrosis (OC), Osteochondritis Dissecans (OCD), Wobbler Syndrome and acquired flexural deformity. At the outset it must be understood that all of these conditions are multifactorial in cause and are, for the most part, a related set of diseases. Furthermore, it is important that one realize that there is a strong genetic component which must not be disregarded. Whether the genetic component is a specific gene, or several genes that do not behave in a normal fashion, or simply as a result of selection pressure for one trait that resulted in the increase in the incidence of the problem, is not well understood. Certainly it is known that faster growing, earlier maturing, larger horses exhibit a greater tendency toward the disease than do their slower growing, smaller counterparts. The selection for early and rapid growth along with speed has seemed to bring with it an increased tendency to develop DOD and a greater need for understanding the problem. In other species, the problem has been diminished by eliminating offending individuals from the gene pool and from the standpoint of the purist this is not a bad idea. However, this approach is not feasible in most horse breeds. Those breeds that have put selection pressure on elimination of the problem have had some success yet this is the exception rather than the rule. The solution to the problem rests in an understanding of the possible causes, a realization of the genetic component and the establishment of management and feeding techniques that minimize the expression of these potentially catastrophic disease states.

Physitis

Actually the term epiphysitis is in itself a misnomer. The condition should more appropriately be referred to as physitis or metaphysitis. Defined simply, physitis is an inflammation of the physis (epiphyseal plate) which exist as a centers of ossification or growth in the bones of all of the mammalian species. Epiphyseal plates are found both at the proximal and distal ends of all of the long bones and are the means by which longitudinal growth occurs. The epiphyseal cartilage is dynamic and new cartilage is being formed as old cartilage cells are converted to bone. Physitis occurs when the cartilage growth plates become inflamed or when normal maturation of cartilage to form bone is disrupted. Although any growth plate can be affected, those most commonly thought of in relation to the disease are at the distal ends of the metacarpal bones, the metatarsal bones, radius and tibia. The incidence of the problem seems also to be in the order in which the sites were listed.

The "lesion" appears as a bony enlargement at the level of the metaphysis and is more frequently seen on the medial rather than lateral side. Epiphysitis may be accompanied by palpable amounts of heat in the affected areas and in some cases by lameness, though many young horses show varying degrees of clinical epiphysitis without exhibiting lameness. Causes of epiphysitis include but are not limited to:

Angular limb deformity	Very rapid growth
Nutritional deficiencies	Injury
Nutrient excess	Nutrient imbalance
Concussional damage	Genetic predisposition

One must be sure to understand those changes in joint architecture that are normal and distinguish between normal changes and physitis that is potentially threatening to development. It is entirely possible that subtle changes in the shape of joints is in the realm of what is normal in the developmental process and should not be misconstrued to be a real threat. It is also entirely possible that some mild physitis is a normal process or at least that what some people might be calling physitis is not outside the normal range of what is acceptable.

Treatment of physitis is varied depending on the severity and the cause (if one can be determined). In most instances it is advisable to reduce caloric intake such that the rate of growth of the affected horse is slowed. One of the most critical errors that is commonly made is to slow growth excessively and not only reduce the intake of energy but also of other nutrients critical to bone growth. It is far more prudent to try to continue to meet the horse's requirement for protein, minerals and vitamins than to simply quit feeding the affected horse. One of the ways in which this can be nicely done is by utilizing a protein, vitamin, mineral supplement fed at approximately 2 lbs.(1 kg.) per day. This feeding rate will of course depend upon the type of product that is available and how it is formulated. In addition to this "supplement" good quality hay should be offered ad-libitum. Once feed intake has been reduced, a professional assessment of the diet should be obtained. Nutrients of critical concern in doing a ration evaluation for young horses include protein, calcium, phosphorus, copper and zinc. If, after evaluation of the ration, one can find no reason from a nutritional standpoint that a problem should exist then other causes of the problem should be considered such as angular limb deformities and so on (see above). Even if the ration appears to be balanced in all respects it is probably best to proceed conservatively in terms of feeding rates until the problem is resolved. Many times it seems that mild physitis goes away in 60 days if it is treated and 2 months if it is not. In the final analysis it is not particularly alarming to see some inflammation of the physes just prior to closure. The major concern about physitis is that it may be the visual indicator that a more serious metabolic problem such as osteochondrosis exists.

Osteochondrosis

One of the more serious aspects of the DOD complex is osteochondrosis. Unlike physitis, osteochondrosis may result in a debilitating lameness in many instances reducing or eliminating any chance of an athletic career. Osteochondrosis is a disorder involving the maturation of joint cartilage. Aberrant cartilage formation results in the separation of cartilage from the subchondral bone resulting in the formation of subchondral cysts and cartilaginous flaps. When these lesions are observed, usually by taking X-rays, the condition is referred to as osteochondritis dissecans (OCD). It is most frequently seen in the ankle, hock and stifle joints. The lesions may involve the articular or non-articular surfaces, with the former posing the greatest immediate risk of lameness. Articular lesions which become detached from the subchondral bone may be surgically removed with variable degrees of success.

A number of causes of OC have been proposed, yet the specific etiology of the disease is far from understood. Interest in OC has been generated by a perceived increase in the incidence of the condition and a report from Ohio State University which suggests that the occurrence of OC may be the result of mineral deficiencies or imbalances. It is difficult to determine if indeed the incidence of the problem has increased or if the condition is being diagnosed more frequently due to superior radiographic techniques and equipment. With respect to the micro-mineral theory, careful balancing of rations containing liberal concentrations of copper and zinc have resulted in only a slight alteration in the occurrence of OC, emphasizing the multifactorial cause of the problem. Other factors currently under consideration include hypercalcitoninism as a result of high calcium intake in mares and hyperthyroxemia due to excessive carbohydrate intake. It is likely that genetic, nutritional and endocrine components contribute to the etiology and to obtain a decrease in incidence all must be considered.

Until the cause of OC is better elucidated it is appropriate to take a conservative approach to the nutritional management of affected populations of horses. Rations should be designed that meet but do not significantly exceed the horse's requirements for all nutrients, with specific emphasis on copper, zinc, manganese, calcium and phosphorus. Once formulated the ration should be fed in a manner that results in moderate growth rates and maximizes the forage rather than the grain part of the diet.

Wobbler syndrome

One of the earliest accounts of the wobbler syndrome was written in 1939 by members of the Department of Veterinary Science at the University of Kentucky. They described 47 cases which had occurred in central Kentucky between 1937 and 1939. Cases occurred particularly among Thoroughbreds and Saddlebreds, breeds which have long necks. Foals around weaning developed a lack of coordination in the hindlimbs, which progressed to include the forelimbs, eventually causing the animal to stumble and fall. Well grown weanling and yearling colts seemed particularly prone, with three colts affected to every one filly. As a result of necropsy studies, it was suggested the condition was related to abnormalities of the vertebrae of the neck, which caused damage to the spinal cord. These observations were confirmed some 20 years later by Dr. James Rooney, also from the University of Kentucky, who identified more precisely the sites and nature of the lesions in the cervical vertebrae. Rooney suggested the overgrowth of the articular processes on which vertebrae move upon each other causes distortion and narrowing of the spinal canal and results in pressure and damage to the cord. The most frequent sites of lesions are between cervical vertebrae C3 and C7, although the presence of lesions does not always result in clinical signs of wobbler disease. When the neck is flexed, the lesions may cause pressure to be exerted on the spinal cord.

Clinical signs associated with wobblers may be related to other causes including trauma, parasitic infection of the spinal cord, and infection with equine rhinopneumonitis virus. In terms of prognosis it is therefore important to differentiate and establish an accurate diagnosis. Currently a true wobbler, the condition of which has recently been given the name cervical vertebral malformation (CVM), is confirmed by taking X-rays of the neck region. To do this, the horse must receive a general anaesthetic so that a technique know as myelography can be performed. This involves the injection into the spinal canal of a contrast fluid so that the space between the cord and the surrounding bony mass of the vertebra can be readily visualized. Narrowing of this space due to lesions of CVM can then be located. The procedure is not without its hazards and should only be undertaken by those who are experienced with the technique and its interpretation. Two types of lesions have been identified. The first typically affects horses from 4 to 12 months of age and occurs most frequently between vertebrae C3 and C4, and C4 and C5. It causes pinching of the cord only when the neck is flexed. The second affects horses between 12 and 36 months of age and occurs between vertebrae C5 and C6, and C6 and C7. Compression of the spinal cord is not relieved or exacerbated by flexion or extension in this region. Injury to the cord results from pressure which interferes with blood flow, causing damage to the cells comprising the cord. It is this injury which results in signs of incoordination, the severity of which are related to the extent and site of damage.

In the young horse destined to become a wobbler, osteochondrosis intervenes, allowing cartilage within the vertebra to develop in the absence of bone formation. The blood supply becomes inadequate leading to death of the surrounding tissue and the subsequent development of chronic joint lesions between the cervical vertebrae. What triggers these pathological changes at this critical growing period is still a matter of considerable debate. The initial suggestion that wobbler syndrome was an inherited condition linked to certain families has not been proven, although genetic influence has not been eliminated. By breeding two wobbler parents it has not been possible to increase the incidence of wobblers in their offspring. It was noted, however, that the incidence of other bone deformities was increased.

It is interesting to compare the development of similar bone lesions, including spinal deformities, in other species, particularly in poultry and pigs, both of which have been subjected to intensive genetic selection and high planes of nutrition to improve growth rate and feed conversion. It is apparent that within these populations, genetic selection has contributed to an overall increase in skeletal problems. A similar situation may well have evolved in the Thoroughbred, with the current commercial incentive to produce a well-grown but nevertheless skeletally immature yearling in time for the summer and autumn (fall) sales. Foals and yearlings which receive a diet high in protein and energy have a critical demand for the correct balance of vitamins and minerals. This feeding level occurs at a time when the skeleton is still not capable of bearing increased muscle mass, nor is it able to respond to the strains and pressures imposed upon it. As a consequence, lesions of osteochondrosis may develop, causing CVM.

The prognosis for a wobbler has always been poor because of the progressive nature of the condition. However, within the last ten years a number of wobblers have been treated surgically. It has been reported that clinical improvement does occur in some cases but there is still considerable concern as to whether such animals should be allowed to participate in athletic competition. An alternative but less dramatic approach is to try to eliminate factors which might promote the wobbler condition, primarily by reducing the level of nutrition in the young horse.

Research workers at the New Bolton Center, Pennsylvania, have developed criteria for the early recognition of 'potential' wobblers using radiographic techniques devised by Mayhew of the Animal Health Trust, Newmarket. Treatment of the 'suspect' horses includes complete stall rest and a level of nutrition only slightly in excess of maintenance requirements. Horses on this program with which the author has had contact appear neurologically normal after completion of the treatment regime and by late in their two-year old year have achieved growth similar to that of their contemporaries.

Acquired flexural deformities

Acquired flexural deformities, also acquired contracted flexor tendons, appear frequently as a sequel to DOD. Rapidly growing horses that are erect in their pasterns are at most risk. The exact cause and an effective treatment remain elusive. Reducing growth rate, bandaging, surgery and tetracycline therapy have all been tried with varying degrees of success. The incidence of acquired contractures is high among horses that have been on a restricted diet and are then fed more liberally, a trend observed among horses in the USA and UK.

Fescue toxicity

Fescue toxicity is a condition primarily affecting pregnant mares grazing endophyte infected tall fescue pastures. Fescue (*festuca arundinacea*) is a cool season grass found in the central and northern regions of the United States that has desirable agronomic properties such as drought resistance, resistance to over grazing and insect damage and yields greater than most pasture species. However, mares grazing endophyte infected pastures exhibit a variety of reproductive problems that make the grass unsuitable for use for that class of horses. Symptoms of toxicity include prolonged gestations, tough thick and rubbery placentas, agalactia, premature placental separation and small weak foals. The causative agent in the toxicity is thought to be the endophyte (*acremonium coenophialum*) which inhabits the tissue of the fescue plant.

The endophyte is a potent vasoconstrictor and a strong prolactin antagonist, an antagonism which may be mediated via the prolactin antagonist melatonin. The entire mechanism by which the endophyte exerts its effect is not clearly understood. However, human placenta deprived of vascular supply shows the same tendency to become thickened and lose its characteristic fragility at parturition. This mechanism may explain the toughened placenta in mares grazing affected pastures. The depressed prolactin levels in affected mares would account for both the prolonged gestations and agalactia. At this time, the best recommendations for preventing the problem is to graze pregnant mares on pastures other than fescue. If fescue is the only pasture species available, mares should receive the predominant amount of their feed intake in the form of a good quality concentrate and properly cured non-fescue hay. This is particularly important in the last 90 days of gestation. If mares do not begin to make a significant udder within 10 days of their due date a toxicity problem should be suspected and the mares immediately removed from the pasture and fed liberal quantities of grain and a high quality legume hay as the condition of the mare allows. Because one of the major causes of foal loss due to the problem is neonatal asphyxia, a foaling attendant should be present at all births to assist the foal in breaking through the placenta. A ready supply of colostrum and a high quality milk replacer should be available in case the mare does not produce any milk. Many times affected mares will begin to produce adequate quantities of milk for the foal several days post-partum, but in the interim the foals' nutrient needs must be met using another source.

Nutritional secondary hyperparathyroidism

Nutritional Secondary Hyperparathyroidism (NSH), also known as millers disease, bran disease and big head disease, is caused by excessive mobilization of calcium from the bone under the influence of parathyroid hormone. The maintenance of blood calcium homeostasis is critical to the function of the muscular and nervous systems and is therefore under close regulation of the hormones parathormone and calcitonin. When blood calcium levels fall below normal, calcium is resorbed from the bone under influence of parathormone in order to re-establish normal blood levels. If this occurs over an extended period of time, the bones become depleted of calcium, and lose their structural integrity resulting in lameness. The facial bones, depleted of calcium, become fibrotic and enlarged, hence the name big head disease. The condition occurs due to a dietary calcium deficiency, excess levels of phosphorus, an inverted calcium:phosphorus ratio in the total diet and high levels of oxalates in forages which interfere with digestion and absorption of calcium. In early times, millers fed the horses they used to work their mills the wheat bran that was a by-product of the mill. Bran is very high in phosphorus and low in calcium and many of the millers' horses developed this condition, thus the name millers disease or bran disease. In modern times the problem is most prevalent in instances when high levels of grain are being fed without calcium supplementation or adequate intake of good quality forage or when horses are grazing pasture high in oxalate content. Due to the strong homeostatic mechanism controlling blood calcium, analysis of the blood for calcium is not very valuable as a diagnostic tool. Instead the most accurate method of determining if this problem exists is by evaluation of the ration. The calcium intake of the horse should be determined and compared with the requirement of the specific class of horse in question. Additionally feed phosphorus should be determined to make sure that its level is not greater than that of calcium. Provided that an inverted calcium:phosphorus ratio is not being fed and that calcium levels are adequate this problem should then be limited to areas in which there are high levels of oxalates. Horses respond very nicely to supplemental calcium in the form of calcium carbonate and as such the problem of NSH should not be of concern on the well managed stud feeding a properly formulated diet.

Blister beetles

Blister beetle poisoning is confined to horses eating hay produced in the southwest where blister beetles are found in large concentrations. The toxin responsible for the expression of toxicity is cantharidin, which is present in the beetle and relatively stable over extended periods of storage. It takes only a few blister beetles, when ingested by the horse, to be fatal. Beetles are baled with hay, transported to the horse and then eaten inadvertently resulting in severe illness or death. The problem of blister beetles has become more pronounced since the replacement of the sickle bar mower with mower conditioners that crush the beetles rather than allowing them to crawl from the windrow as was the case for the older method of cutting hay.

Cantharidin, the toxin in blister beetles, is an extreme irritant to the digestive tract causing necrosis of the gut mucosa, the gastric mucosa and the lining of the esophagus as well as irritation to the urinary tract. Affected horses usually show severe colic and discomfort, an elevated respiratory and heart rate, diarrhea and dehydration. Death usually occurs within 48-72 hours after ingestion of the beetles. The only treatment is that which reduces insult to the gut and includes tubing with mineral oil, fluid therapy and the use of analgesics such as butazolidin. The best way to control the problem is to feed hay produced in areas where blister beetles are not found or that produced from certified blister beetle free fields.

Colic

It is beyond the scope or intent of this paper to cover colic in its entirety. However, some mention of colic with respect to nutrition related causes is warranted. Since the advent of modern anthelmintics (dewormers), the most important cause of colic in horses is nutritional mismanagement. Nutritionally induced colic can be grouped into two categories: 1) improper forage:grain ratios or inadequate amounts of forage and 2) the use of tainted feedstuffs.

Far and away the more important of these two is the former. The horse is a wandering herbivore, a continuous grazer and has an absolute requirement for long stem hay or pasture. Failure to realize this simple fact probably results in more colics than any other single cause. The fact that hay or pasture is limited in some instances is made worse by the fact that in many of these cases the horses are on a high level of grain intake as well. On high grain diets rate of passage of ingesta is increased allowing more readily fermentable carbohydrate to reach the hind gut. Fermentation of this material many times results in a decrease in cecal and colonic pH under the influence of the lactic acid that is produced. This decrease in gut pH causes a shift in the microflora of the hindgut, which may result in the release of toxins and subsequent clinical colic. Additionally, in this type of etiology there is frequently an increase in the gas production in the hind gut that may lead to a flatulence and subsequent colic. The most effective way to reduce the incidence of colic on the farm or on the race track is to feed liberal quantities of good quality forage, limit grain intake to that necessary to maintain acceptable body condition and feed the grain portion of the daily ration in small meals and as frequently as is practical. Additionally it is a good idea to have hay available to mares even in the spring or other times when pasture growth is lush. In many instances there is simply not enough 'gut-scratch' factor in young lush growth. This combined with the increased rate of passage associated with a low dry matter feed leads to the appearance of more soluble forage constituents in the hind gut which again can lead to gas build-up and abdominal discomfort. There are very few if any instances when over feeding dry hay can lead to a problem, but there are numerous problems that can develop if hay is limited.

Although everyone is taught of the perils of feeding moldy hay to horses, this practice is not nearly as important a cause of colic as is under feeding forage.

Nonetheless we would be remiss in not mentioning the potential for problems of the gut if tainted or moldy feedstuffs are fed. The horse has a much lower threshold of pain than do cattle and as such can not tolerate GI tract insult inflicted by certain molds or the toxins they produce. Moldy hay and/or grain should not be fed to horses as certainly the risk of colic is increased. It is common in some parts of the world to see large round bales of hay and/or silage fed to horses. Although many times this is done successfully one must realize that there is an increased risk of gastric upset when either of these practices is used. Horses generally will not ingest moldy feedstuffs if given a choice, but moldy hay or spoiled silage can be deadly if the horse is forced to eat either. High quality forage products should be fed to horses. Feedstuffs fed to horses should be free of mold and other foreign debris, be of a forage species appropriate for the horse and should be properly cured and stored in a manner that will prevent their contamination.

Black walnut toxicity

The use of wood shavings from various species of trees is becoming more commonplace as labor cost of keeping horses becomes a greater concern. In most instances the use of shavings or saw dust provides an economical alternative to the use of wheat or rye straw or hay. The time necessary to clean stalls bedded in shavings is less than that required for straw and generally it is less expensive to use. Many soft woods and hardwoods alike are appropriate for use as a bedding material for horses. One type of shavings that should not be used for bedding is black walnut as severe founder (laminitis) has resulted from bedding horses on these shavings. Although the exact toxin has not been identified, it is probably the compound juglone in the walnut shavings that is the culprit.

Cystitis

Cystitis is an inflammation of the urinary tract that may be caused by the consumption of certain sudangrass and sudan-sorghum hybrids. Cystitis is characterized by an increase in urination or a dribbling of urine, incoordination and continuous estrus behavior in mares. The problem is most severe when horses are allowed to graze pastures that have been stressed. Drought, freezing temperatures and injury to the plant such as by trampling seem to increase the danger of these pastures when grazed by horses. Cystitis is caused when a glycoside in the plant is converted to prussic acid in the gut. Besides cystitis, prussic acid poisoning may cause muscle tremors, nervousness, respiratory distress and ultimately respiratory failure and death. Symptoms of prussic acid poisoning are also seen when wilted wild cherry leaves are ingested (hydrocyanic acid poisoning).

To prevent this problem one should not allow horses to graze sudan or sudan-sorghum pastures such as sudex. Hays made from these pastures appear not to be toxic to the horse, but they generally are stemmy and of poor quality when compared to hays traditionally fed to horses. If one is forced to use sudangrass or sudan-sorghum pastures every attempt should be made to discontinue their use in periods of stress such as during a drought or immediately following a freeze.

Enteroliths

Enteroliths, also called stones or calculi, may form in the intestine of the horse when several criteria are met. Generally they require the presence of a foreign object such as a nail, stone, ball of hair, or other piece of debris. These objects serve as centers for the formation of the enterolith which is composed primarily of salts. Stones found in the gastrointestinal tract of the horse usually consist of magnesium ammonium phosphate.

The enterolith may cause symptoms ranging from weight loss and mild abdominal discomfort to an obstruction requiring surgical intervention. Size of the stone can range between the size of a pea to larger than a bowling ball. Smaller stones may be passed by the horse and cause no symptoms, but larger ones tend to cause an obstruction at the pelvic flexure of the large intestine or at the interface of the large and small colons. An affected horse may have only one enterolith or may have a large number of enteroliths of variable size.

The exact cause of the development of the stones remains uncertain and no specific dietary cause has been identified. The problem appears to be of the greatest magnitude in areas where access to fresh forage is somewhat limited rather than in areas where horses have access to an abundant supply of good quality forage. Some have indicted wheat bran, alfalfa hay and diets very high in iron as possible causes of the stones, yet no experimental evidence exists to corroborate that feeling. H.F. Hintz of Cornell University has suggested that feeding of vinegar, acetic acid, may reduce the occurrence and severity of the problem.

Wood chewing

The exact cause of wood chewing is not known. Horses that chew wood should be distinguished from the classical cribber in that they actually eat wood from fences, barns and other wooden structures rather than grabbing hold and sucking in air. Wood chewing may result from boredom, as in a stabled horse, from the learned habit, or possibly from a nutritional inadequacy. Experience suggests that frequent and vigorous exercise of stalled horses will minimize this behavior if it is boredom induced. Isolation of horses that chew wood from the rest of the herd in a paddock lined with electric fence will both reduce the behavior in the offending horse and prevent other horses from picking up the habit. Although the two causes discussed above account for a fair percentage of horses that chew wood, the majority of horses that eat fences, trees and other wooden objects do so for other, less obvious reasons. Some of the more reasonable explanations are presented below.

Horses have an absolute requirement for long stem hay or fiber. When they are deprived of this requirement the frequency of wood chewing increases. Horses in the stall that are allowed minimal hay intake and horses in areas where fibrous feeds are in short supply due to inadequate rainfall or expense of importation are most inclined to begin chewing wood. In these instances the obvious and many times effective remedy is allowing for more fiber intake. As this will decrease the incidence of both colic and wood chewing it is probably most economical in the long run. Work at the University of Kentucky by Willard and others has shown a direct relationship between wood chewing and amount of fiber in the diet. Horses that were fed a concentrate diet low in fiber ate significantly more wood than horses allowed more hay. The class of horses that chew wood which are the most difficult to understand are horses on abundant, high quality pasture. These horses have access to plenty of fiber, are not in a stall most of the time and get plenty of exercise. So why do they chew wood and even more intriguing why does this behavior seem to be somewhat season related? Horses are most apt to exhibit wood chewing behavior in the times of the year when forage growth is rapid and lush grass is available. When this occurs the dry matter content of the forage is low, the crude fibre content is low, and the rate of passage is high. It is the author's opinion that the pH of the gut is decreased during this time due to a greater amount of soluble sugars in the forage reaching the hind gut. Additionally, the fiber content of the forage is so low that the effective fiber is inadequate to meet the horse's requirement for long stem fiber. In an attempt to increase the amount of effective fiber in the diet the horse eats fences, tree bark and other wooden objects. One way in which one can reduce the frequency of wood chewing in pastured horses is to continue to provide long hay to the horses during the period when rapid growth of low dry matter forage occurs. It is surprising how much hay horses will continue to eat when there is an abundance of lush pasture growth available. In addition to reducing the wood chewing problem it has been the author's observation that flatulence colic associated with horses grazing these lush pastures is reduced as well when hay is offered free-choice during extreme pasture growth phases.

Urea toxicity

Urea and biuret are non-protein nitrogen sources commonly used in the diets of ruminant animals. These feed ingredients provide nitrogen to the intestinal (ruminal) microflora for use in the synthesis of microbial protein which may then be used to meet a significant portion of the ruminants' protein requirement. The arrangement of the horse's gastrointestinal tract makes the use of urea questionable in terms of contributing to their nitrogen requirements. Studies conducted at universities in the US indicate that the horse receiving marginal protein intake can benefit from urea, especially mature horses on a forage diet. However, urea may also be toxic to the horse.

Contrary to popular belief, horses are not extremely sensitive to urea and in fact show greater tolerance to urea than do ruminant animals. Urea is generally broken down in the stomach and small intestine of the horse, absorbed and excreted via the kidneys prior to the time it arrives in the cecum. Therefore, urea is not broken down to form carbon dioxide and ammonia, the latter of which causes the toxicity to occur in the ruminant animal. This does not mean that urea is not potentially toxic to the horse. Hintz and co-workers fed ponies a diet which consisted of twenty-five percent urea and resulted in the death of the ponies to which it was fed. The classical symptoms attributed to urea toxicity in the horse are incoordination, wandering and head-pressing (horses will stand pressing their heads against solid objects). Although it is generally not recommended, horses are tolerant of urea-containing ruminant diets and indeed older horses may make use of some of the non-protein nitrogen. Urea should not be fed to young horses at all. A note: feeding rations designed for one class of livestock to another class of livestock for which it is not intended is never a good idea. For instance, even though horses can tolerate the NPN levels practical in ruminant diets, they are intolerant of ionophores which might be present in those diets.

Ionophores

Ionophores are antibiotic-like compounds used in ruminant diets to alter rumen fermentation. These compounds cause a shift in the volatile fatty acid (VFA) ratio that favors the production of propionate and reduces the molar percentage of acetic acid. The net result of the action of ionophores in ruminant diets is greater feed efficiency. The two most common ionophores used are MONENSIN SODIUM (rumensin) and LASALOSID (bovatec). Both of these ionophores are extremely toxic to the horse. As such feeds containing ionophores should never be fed to horses. There have been several instances in the US when ionophores have mistakenly gotten into horse feed and have resulted in the death of horses. Litigation in these cases is ongoing.

Levels of rumensin as low as 1 mg/kg of body weight have resulted in the death of horses. However the LD-50 (level at which 50 % of horses would be expected to die) is reported to be 2-3 mg/kg of body weight. This means that 50% of horses that consumed 1,000 mg of rumensin would be expected to die. The normal inclusion rate of rumensin in cattle feed is 3 -5 grams per ton (3.3 - 5.5 ppm). This means that a 500 kg horse would have to eat from 300 -500 kg of a feedlot cattle ration for it to be toxic. These feeds should not result in toxicity. The real hazard with ionophores is errors by feed manufacturers, or with horses consuming pasture cattle supplements or poultry feed which could contain 400 and 100 ppm ionophore respectively. Affected horses show restlessness, colic, sweating, and incoordination and generally die within 12-36 hours of the onset of toxicity symptoms. Post-mortem examination shows severe damage to the cardiac (heart) muscle. In horses that have shown signs but recovered, cardiac damage is frequently evident such that a return to athletic performance is questionable.

Rumensin and other ionophores are frequently used in cattle feed as a coccidiostat, especially in the diets of replacement dairy heifers. Additionally, ionophores are used in poultry feeds to control coccidiosis. These facts and the extreme toxicity of ionophores to horses make feeding cattle feed or poultry feed to the horse risky. Many feed mills that make a significant amount of horse feed will not make ionophore containing feed due to the possibility of contaminating horse feeds and the potential for liability that exists.

Heaves

CHRONIC OBSTRUCTIVE PULMONARY DISEASE

Heaves has long been associated with horses not sound of wind. It is characterized by hyper-reactive airways, and an allergic response similar to asthma in humans. Affected horses show coughing, forced expiration of air and a heave line in the region of the base of the ribs associated with muscular hypertrophy caused by effort of expelling air from the lungs. Horses with this condition frequently have a nasal discharge. The lungs lose their elasticity, which results in a heightened respiratory distress. Affected horses tend to be very hard keepers and their athletic ability is impaired, especially in events where maximal effort is required.

The exact cause of heaves is not clearly understood, nor is there an effective cure. Hence, management of the disease is the sole way in which it can be coped with. Most of the time horses with heaves are best kept outside in the pasture rather than in a barn. Keeping the horses' environment as free from dust and mold spores as possible is the most effective way to treat the disease. Heavey horses should be bedded on paper, clean wood shavings or even on a rubber mat in preference to bedding on straw or hay. Hay should be wet prior to feeding. This practice minimizes the extent of dust, mold spores and other airborne particulate matter. Frequently the use of fiber sources other than long hay can minimize allergic reactions. Cubed grass or lucerne hay, shredded beet pulp, and mashes made with oaten or wheaten chaff are alternatives to long hay.

In addition to nutritional management, several other things can be done to reduce the problem of the disease to affected horses. Never clean the barn with a heavey horse inside. Sweeping, dusting, moving hay into and out of the loft, and other activity in the barn increases the amount of airborne particulate matter which results in an increase in allergenic response of affected horses. Provide for good ventilation in the barn. Airflow increases the fresh air available to the horse and helps to dissipate the ammonia in the stall. Ammonia, like dust, can serve as a severe respiratory irritant and as such pose a problem for the horse with hyper-reactive airways. Chronic, heavey horses may also benefit from the use of expectorants to reduce coughing and of bronchodilators to allow for eased breathing. When possible, do not restrict the heavey horse to the stall. Horses maintained in pastures are less likely to develop heaves, and are better able to cope with the disease once affected.

Goiter and iodine deficiency

Goiter, an enlargement of the thyroid gland, may occur in response to deficient (hypo-iodine goiter) or toxic (hyper-iodine goiter) levels of iodine in the diet. Iodine is a component of the hormone thyroxin produced by the thyroid gland. When iodine levels in the diet are inadequate to meet the horse's requirement the thyroid gland becomes enlarged, which is indicative of thyroid disfunction. Thyroxine is responsible for regulation of metabolic rate and as such hypothyroid horses may exhibit slowed skeletal growth, rough hair coat, delayed shedding of hair and muscular weakness. Foals born to thyroid hormone, iodine deficient, mares are frequently dysmature appearing and lack hair and may or may not exhibit an enlarged thyroid gland. Supplementation of horses with iodized salt is generally adequate to meet iodine requirements, although most modern diets contain levels of iodine higher than those that would be obtained from consuming iodized salt alone.

If goiter appears in the presence of what appears to be adequate levels of iodine in the diet, then an iodine toxicity must be suspected. Workers at Cornell University in the US have reported goiter in foals born to mares consuming high levels of a supplement containing kelp, a seaweed high in iodine. Levels of iodine intake as low as 50 mg/day by pregnant mares have resulted in goitrous foals. As such random supplementation of mares with high iodine supplements is not a good practice and the iodine provided from these supplements should be considered in assessing the iodine status of the horse's diet. The symptoms of hyper-iodine goiter are very similar to those seen in instances of hypo-iodine goiter and as such evaluation of the diet is the first diagnostic tool to use in determining the cause of the problem. The current NRC publication, Nutrient Requirements of Horses, suggests the iodine requirement of the young growing horse is 0.1 mg/kg of diet while 5 mg/kg of diet is thought to be the potentially toxic level of dietary iodine.

Goiter may also be caused by goitrogenic substances in the diet that exhibit an antithyroid activity. Feedstuffs known to exhibit antithyroid activity include uncooked soybeans, cabbage, kale and mustard. The enzyme responsible for the antithyroid effect is inactivated by heating and cooking and as such properly prepared soybean meal is safe to feed. The goitrogenic effect of these feeds is not effectively inhibited by supplemental iodine, suggesting that, with the exception of properly heated soybean meal, they should be avoided in equine diets.

Selenium deficiency and white muscle disease

In areas of the world where selenium levels in the soil and forages are inadequate, selenium supplementation is necessary to prevent the appearance of selenium deficiency. Although the current NRC requirements suggest that the selenium level of the diet be 0.1 ppm, most well formulated equine diets contain a level of from 0.2-0.4 ppm. The most common manner in which selenium supplementation is achieved is by adding sodium selenite to the grain mix.

Selenium deficiency is characterized by white muscle disease in foals. The skeletal muscle is pale to white in color due to degeneration of the muscle cells. The cardiac muscle is also affected. Foals exhibiting white muscle disease are frequently weak at birth, suffer from respiratory distress and have difficulty nursing. Due to the loss of muscle integrity respiration is impaired and foals often die of respiratory failure. The serum selenium level and plasma glutathione peroxidase (a selenium dependent enzyme) concentration of mares has been effectively used as a predictive diagnostic tool in averting the incidence of white muscle disease in foals produced by mares grazing selenium deficient pastures. The expected normal range of serum selenium in selenium adequate mares is from 0.06 to 0.15 ppm (mg/100ml), although mares at the lower end of the expected range have been known to produce foals with white muscle disease. Plasma glutathione peroxidase concentrations of less than 20 units are indicative of marginal selenium status and horses with this low value should be treated by either addition of dietary selenium or by injection of selenium. It is worth noting that Se-E injections have resulted in anaphylactic shock on occasion and as such should be administered with care.

Myositis or tying-up

Myositis, or tying up, is an exertional myopathy common to performance horses. Another condition with much the same etiology and effect is azoturia. Some would disagree with grouping, for purposes of discussion, myositis and azoturia. However in practice these two conditions appear to be a continuous progression of muscle dysfunction rather than distinctly different disease entities. Symptoms common to the two conditions are an elevated level of the muscle enzymes AAT (aspartate amino transferase) and CPK (creatine phosphokinase), decreased muscle pH, stiffness over the loin and back, an unwillingness to move, and some degree of myoglobinuria (myoglobin is a muscle pigment which appears in the urine after damage of the muscle membrane and muscle fibers). The urine of affected horse takes on a characteristic coffee color indicating the presence of myoglobin in the urine. The exact cause of these conditions is not known.

Myositis or tying-up occurs most frequently in athletic horses of light horse breeds. It may occur at any time from the beginning of an exercise bout to several hours post-exercise. Most frequently there is an obvious change in the horse's gait which rapidly progresses to a reluctance to move at all. Affected horses should not be forced to move as this makes the damage to the already compromised muscle worse. Definitive data that would clearly elucidate the mechanism for this muscle problem are lacking but clinical evidence suggests that affected horses may benefit from Se-Vitamin E injections. The dual roles of these two nutrients in maintaining muscle membrane integrity and preventing tissue peroxidation suggest that they may be involved in the problem. Elevated levels of AAT and CPK characteristic of horses having been through a bout of tying up are indicative of muscle membrane damage and leakage of these two enzymes into the circulation and it stands to reason that selenium and vitamin E therapy in horses prone to tie-up is probably warranted. Even though some horses respond to supplementation, others do not. Myositis is a management related problem in many instances. Failure to allow a horse to warm up properly, intake of high carbohydrate diets in conjunction with irregular and inappropriate exercise programs and asking a horse to do more than it is fit enough to do all contribute to the occurrence of tying-up syndrome. Additionally nervous fillies are more inclined to develop the problem than are colts and once afflicted, horses are much more inclined to tie up again. As a general rule the following management practices should reduce to an absolute minimum the incidence of tying-up.

1. On days that a horse is not to be worked cut the feed allowed by one-half and allow at least some exercise even if it is only 10-15 minutes on a longe line or 20 minutes of hand walking.

2. Try to meet at least 50% of the horse's requirement for DE using fibrous feeds.

3. Allow for adequate time to properly warm up and cool down the horse. An effectively managed cooling down period allows for the muscle to return to resting state more rapidly, encourages the lactic acid in the muscle to diffuse into the blood more quickly which in turn decreases muscle acidity and will effectively prevent some of the muscle soreness associated with intense exercise.

4. Use training techniques that minimize physical and psychological stress while allowing the horse to get fit enough to perform the task for which it is intended.

This paper was first published in "Feeding the Performance Horse," Proceedings for the 1994 Short Course for Feed Manufacturers

EXERTIONAL RHABDOMYOLYSIS IN THE HORSE

STEPHANIE J. VALBERG

Department of Clinical and Population Sciences, College of Veterinary Medicine, University of Minnesota, St Paul, Minnesota, USA

The term "tying-up" has been applied to describe horses that develop firm hard gluteal and lumbar muscles and the inability to move the hind quarters after exercise. Other terms for this syndrome include azoturia, Monday Morning Disease, exertional rhabdomyolysis and chronic intermittent rhabdomyolysis. It has been implied or assumed that all horses which show evidence of muscle pain and cramping following exercise have the same disease. As a result, a great deal of controversy and confusion has developed regarding the cause and approach to treatment of this condition. Exertional rhabdomyolysis likely represents a pathological description of a number of muscle diseases which have common clinical signs. Recently by applying clinical protocols that include muscle biopsies and exercise testing a number of specific disorders have been identified.

Two general syndromes are apparent from a clinical standpoint: 1) sporadic rhabdomyolysis following exercise in horses that have a previous history of satisfactory performance, and 2) recurrent exertional rhabdomyolysis.

Sporadic exertional rhabdomyolysis

CLINICAL SIGNS

Signs of exertional rhabdomyolysis can range in severity from mild stiffness following exercise to recumbency. During exercise, horses develop a short stiff stride, sweat profusely, and have an elevated respiratory rate. Upon stopping horses are reluctant to move, males frequently posture to urinate and in severe cases myoglobinuria may be apparent. Physical examination reveals painful muscle cramps especially in the gluteal area. Scintigraphic evaluation of horses with rhabdomyolysis following exercise shows symmetrical damage to the gluteal, semitendinosus and semimembranosus muscles. Some horses may be extremely painful which could be confused with colic. Muscle pain usually persist for several hours. Endurance horses often show other signs of exhaustion including a rapid heart rate, dehydration, hyperthermia, synchronous diaphragmatic flutter and collapse.

DIAGNOSIS

A diagnosis of exertional rhabdomyolysis is made on the basis of a history of muscle cramping and stiffness following exercise and moderate to marked elevations in serum myoglobin, creatine kinase (CK), lactate dehydrogenase (LDH) and aspartate aminotransferase (AST). These serum proteins are listed in the order of their rate of increase in the blood and in reverse of their rate of clearance from serum.

TREATMENT

The objective of treatment is to relieve anxiety and muscle pain, correct fluid and acid base deficits and prevent renal compromise. The hydration status of horses with myoglobinuria should be assessed immediately. Oral and/or intravenous fluid therapy is a first-order priority in dehydrated horses prior to the administration of nonsteroidal anti-inflammatory drugs (NSAID).

Acepromazine, an alpha-adrenergic antagonist, is helpful in relieving anxiety and may increase muscle blood flow. Its use is contraindicated in dehydrated horses. In extremely painful horses, detomidine provides better sedation and analgesia. Nonsteroidal anti-inflammatory drugs at relatively high doses provide pain relief. Intravenous dimethyl sulfoxide (as a < 20% solution) and corticosteroid administration have also been advocated in the acute stage. Muscle relaxants such as methocarbamol seem to produce variable results.

Rest with hand walking once the initial stiffness has abated is of prime importance. At this time the diet should be changed to good quality hay with little grain supplementation. The amount of rest a horse should receive is controversial. Horses with recurrent problems with rhabdomyolysis appear to benefit from an early return to a regular exercise schedule. Horses that appear to have damaged their muscles from over-exertion may benefit from a longer rest period with regular access to a paddock. Training should be resumed gradually and a regular exercise schedule, which will match the degree of exertion to the horses underlying state of training, should be established. Endurance horses should be encouraged to drink electrolyte supplemented water during an endurance ride and monitored particularly closely during hot humid conditions.

PATHOPHYSIOLOGY OF ACUTE RHABDOMYOLYSIS

The most common cause of exertional rhabdomyolysis is exercise that exceeds the horse's underlying state of training. This includes both exercise at speed as well as endurance riding. Tears in the junctions between intracellular myofilaments (Z lines) are a common cause of post-exercise muscle soreness in humans. The incidence of muscle stiffness and exertional rhabdomyolysis has been observed to increase during an outbreak of respiratory disease. Both equine herpes virus 1 and equine influenza virus have been implicated as causative agents. Mild muscle stiffness with concurrent viral infections is likely the result of the release of endogenous pyrogens. More severe rhabdomyolysis may be due to exertion during a concurrent systemic infection and/or viral replication in muscle tissue. Since the inciting cause is usually temporary, most horses respond to rest and a gradual increase in training. This may also account for the myriad of treatments guaranteed to cure tying-up in horses.

REPAIR OF SKELETAL MUSCLE

Skeletal muscle shows remarkable ability to regenerate following injury. Following exertional complete repair of muscle tissue is possible within 4 - 8 weeks.

Recurrent exertional rhabdomyolysis

A number of horses, predominantly fillies, will have recurrent episodes of rhabdomyolysis even with light exercise. Recurrent exertional rhabdomyolysis (RER) is seen in many breeds of horses including Quarter Horses, American Paint Horses, Appaloosas, Thoroughbreds, Arabians, Standardbreds and Morgans. A wide variety of causes for RER have been proposed including electrolyte imbalances, hormonal imbalances, lactic acidosis vitamin E and selenium deficiencies. Most recently, however, some specific causes of RER have been identified in the horse. These include a disorder of muscle contractility or excitation contraction-coupling (chronic intermittent rhabdomyolysis) and a disorder in carbohydrate storage and utilization (polysaccharide storage myopathy).

CHRONIC INTERMITTENT RHABDOMYOLYSIS

RER is a common occurrence in Arabian, Standardbred and Thoroughbred horses. It most commonly occurs in young fillies with a nervous disposition. About 5 % of Thoroughbred race horses develop RER during the racing season, often when they trained at a gallop but held back from full racing speeds. Some highly susceptible individuals have repeated episodes resulting in persistent elevations in serum AST and poor performance. Many of these fillies are retired as brood mares. In other susceptible horses, episodes may be very intermittent and as a result the term chronic intermittent rhabdomyolysis has been used to describe this syndrome. Stress and a period of stall rest preceding exercise appear to trigger RER in susceptible horses. Studies of equine lymphocyte antigens provide some support for a familial basis for

RER in Standardbred horses and a much higher prevalence of ER has been noted in the offspring of one of two Thoroughbred stallions bred and trained at the same farm. A diagnosis of chronic intermittent rhabdomyolysis is based on the history and clinical signs as well as documented elevations in serum AST and CK. Muscle biopsy findings in affected horses include varying stages of muscle necrosis and regeneration with centrally located myonuclei.

Lactic acidosis was previously believed to cause RER and many treatments still used today are directed at resolving a lactic acidosis (lactinase, DMG, sodium bicarbonate). Research has shown, however, that RER occurs most commonly with aerobic exercise and that during an episode affected horses have low muscle lactate concentrations and a metabolic alkalosis. In England, a dietary deficiency of sodium or a low calcium: phosphorus ratio based on urine creatinine clearance ratios was suggested to contribute to RER. Subsequent studies showed that many of the Thoroughbred racehorses with chronic intermittent rhabdomyolysis had normal electrolyte ratios. Most recently an abnormality in excitation-contraction coupling has been identified in Standardbred and Thoroughbred horses with RER. The altered relaxation of muscle following a contractile twitch in affected horses suggests that abnormal intracellular calcium regulation is the cause of this form of RER. In addition a recent study showed elevated myoplasmic calcium concentrations in horses with acute RER.

Prevention of further episodes of RER in susceptible horses should include standardized daily routines and an environment that minimizes stress. The diet should be adjusted to include a balanced vitamin and mineral supplement, high quality hay and a minimum of carbohydrates such as grain and sweet feed. Dietary fat supplements may help to maintain weight in nervous fillies without providing excessive carbohydrates. The use of low doses of acepromazine before exercise in excitable horses is believed to help some horses. Daily exercise is essential, whether in the form of turn-out, longeing or riding. In the past, horses have been box stall rested for several weeks following an episode of RER. It is the author's opinion that this is counterproductive and increases the likelihood that the horses will develop RER when put back into training. The initial muscle pain usually subsides within 24 hours of acute RER and daily turn-out in a small paddock can be provided at this time. Subsequently, a gradual return to performance is recommended once serum CK is within normal range. Dantrolene (2mg/kg PO) given 1 hour before exercise is believed to be effective in preventing RER in some horses. Dantrolene is used to prevent malignant hyperthermia in humans and swine by decreasing the release of calcium from the calcium release channel. Phenytoin (1.4-2.7 mg/kg PO BID), has also been advocated as a treatment for horses with RER. Therapeutic levels vary, so oral doses are adjusted by monitoring serum levels to achieve 8 ug/ml and not exceed 12 ug/ml. Phenytoin acts on a number of ion channels within muscle and nerves including sodium and calcium channels. Unfortunately long-term treatment with dantrolene or phenytoin is expensive.

POLYSACCHARIDE STORAGE MYOPATHY (PSSM)

A subset of horses with recurrent exertional rhabdomyolysis (ER) have been found to have a glycogen storage disorder characterized by the accumulation of a nonbioavailable polysaccharide in their muscle. To date Quarter Horses, Paint, Appaloosa, Draft, Draft crossbreds, warmbloods and a few Thoroughbreds have been identified with PSSM. Horses with PSSM often have a calm and sedate demeanor. Most horses have a history of numerous episodes of ER beginning with the commencement of training; however, mildly affected horses have only one or two episodes/year. Exercise intolerance, muscle atrophy, renal failure or respiratory distress are less common presenting complaints. Elevations in muscle enzymes are usually found if blood samples are obtained and muscle enzymes may remain elevated for long periods even when rested. The severity of episodes of rhabdomyolysis can range from mild stiffness to severe pain resembling colic. Several horses have been euthanized due to the severity of muscle damage. A diagnosis is based on examination of muscle biopsies. The distinctive features of these muscle biopsies are subsarcolemmal vacuoles, glycogen storage and abnormal PAS positive inclusions in fast twitch fibers. Muscle glycogen concentrations are often 1.5 - 4 X normal. Serum CK activities are often increased by 1000 U/L or more 4 hours after 15 minutes of exercise at a trot.

While histological and biochemical studies identify PSSM as a glycogen storage disorder, the exact metabolic defect in glycolysis or glycogen synthesis has not been identified. Muscle cramping and damage with exercise has been attributed to the inability of glycolysis to generate ATP for mechanical work and maintenance of chemical gradients. Treatment of horses with polysaccharide storage myopathy is based on increasing the oxidative capacity of skeletal muscle through gradual training and providing a high fat diet. Most PSSM horses have competed successfully as pleasure and hunter horses when their diets are switched to good quality grass hay, no grain or sweet feed and a fat supplement. Rice bran consisting of 20 % fat, corn oil, or spray dried fat supplements can be used. Daily longeing or riding as well as pasture access are essential. Box stall rest for more than 12 hours per day appears to increase the incidence of rhabdomyolysis.

A familial basis for this disorder has been identified in Quarter Horse-related breeds. Currently breeding trials are underway at the University of Minnesota to determine if this is a heritable condition. A few young Quarter Horses (8months-2 yrs) have recently been identified with polysaccharide storage myopathy that developed moderate to severe rhabdomyolysis without any associated exercise. These young halter horses were on a high grain diet and serum CK normalized when switched to a lower carbohydrate ration.

References

Beech J., S. Lindborg, J.E. Fletcher *et al.*: Caffeine contractures, twitch characteristics and the threshold for Ca^{2+}-induced Ca^{2+} release in skeletal muscle from horses with chronic intermittent rhabdomyolysis. Res Vet Sci 54:110, 1993.

Valberg S.J., L. Jonsson, N. Holmgren and A. Lindholm: Muscle histopathology and plasma aspartate aminotransferase, creatine kinase and myoglobin changes with exercise in horses with recurrent exertional rhabdomyolysis. Equine Vet J, 1993;25:11.

Valberg S.J., J. Häggendal and A. Lindholm: Blood chemistry and skeletal muscle metabolic responses to exercise in horses with recurrent exertional rhabdomyolysis. Equine Vet J 1993;25:17.

Valberg S.J., G.H. Cardinet III, G.P. Carlson and S. DiMauro: Polysaccharide storage myopathy associated with exertional rhabdomyolysis in the horse. Neuromusc. Disord 1992;2:351.

Valberg S.J.: Exertional rhabdomyolysis and polysaccharide storage myopathy in Quarter Horses. Proceedings American Association of Equine Practitioners. 1995;228.

Valberg S.J., C.J. Geyer, S. Sorum and G.H. Cardinet III: Familial basis of polysaccharide storage myopathy and exertional rhabdomyolysis in Quarter Horses and related breeds. Am J Vet Res 1996;57:286.

This paper was first published in Proceedings, Kentucky Equine Research 1997 Equine Nutrition Conference

TIED UP WITH ELECTROLYTES - OR NOT?

PAT HARRIS

Waltham Centre For Equine Nutrition and Care, Leicestershire, UK

Background information

A. DEFINITIONS

1. Electrolytes are substances which exist as positively or negatively charged particles in aqueous solution.

    The elements that form part of the ash produced by combustion of food material/body tissues, etc. at high temperatures (from which impurities have been removed) are known as minerals or inorganic elements.

    Therefore, not all electrolytes are minerals, e.g. the proteins, organic acids.

2. Minerals can be classified in a number of ways, but practically and most usefully as either Macro-, Micro-, or Trace Elements (according to amounts required and amounts present in animal tissues) or Essential, Probably Essential or Function Unclear.

The essential elements include calcium, sodium, potassium, magnesium (cations - positively charged i.e. Ca^{2+}, Na^+, K^+, Mg^{2+} respectively) and chloride plus phosphate (anions -negatively charged ie Cl^-, PO_4^{3-} respectively). These are also known as macrominerals as they are required in several gram quantities by animals per day. These six elements will be discussed in more detail below.

B. FUNCTIONS AND STORES

The main functions of the various minerals include:

1. Muscle and nerve function.
2. Formation of skeletal tissue.
3. Maintenance of homeostasis of internal fluids.
4. Maintenance of cell membrane equilibrium.

5.   Activation of biochemical reactions by action on enzyme systems.

6.   Direct or indirect effects on the function of the endocrine glands.

7.   Effect on the symbiotic microflora of the gastrointestinal tract (GIT).

Calcium makes up about 35% of bone structure and the skeleton represents 99% of total body stores. Approximately 85% of total body phosphorus is present in the bones and teeth. Bone contains about 60-70% of the body stores of magnesium with the remaining 30-35% found in body fluids and soft tissues. 50-75% of the body's sodium is contained in the ECF. Most of the rest is found in bone. 85% of the total body store of potassium is intracellular.

C. INTERACTIONS

Due the relative ease by which minerals tend to form bonds, they are much more liable to interact than are other nutrient substances. Minerals may interact with:

1. Each other

2. Other nutrient factors

3. Non-nutritive factors

These interactions may be:

1. Synergistic

2. Antagonistic

The interactions may occur:

1. In the feed

2. In the GIT

3. During tissue and cell metabolism

Few of the possible interactions have been thoroughly investigated in the horse and in practice only a few of the possible interactive effects require practical measures to avoid adverse consequences.

D. METHODS TO STUDY ABSORPTION AND RETENTION OF MINERALS

The three most common ways used are:

1. Material balance

    i.e.:   M feed - M faeces = absorption

    M feed - (M faeces + M urine) = retention

where M is the concentration of a particular mineral, but these are only relative figures as the faeces not only contain the non-assimilated minerals from the dietary intake, but also the so-called endogenous component (and any unassimilated "extra" mineral from soil or other contamination.)

   The endogenous component reflects the amount of each element that comes into the GIT from the animal's body rather than via the diet (i.e. expelled into the GIT either in the various digestive juices or directly across the intestinal wall or via unavoidable losses due to sloughed GIT cells.)

   Ways of overcoming the interference of endogenous losses have been investigated; for example, the apparent digestibilities for a range of nutrient intakes have been determined and plotted against the corresponding level of intake. The slope of the regression line can then be taken to represent the estimated true digestibility for that nutrient.

2. Use of inert substances

This method is based on the use of poorly assimilatable substances which are uniformly distributed in the feed. Chromium is often used, but not considered by everyone to be ideal.

Calculation:

% absorption = 100 x (1 - ([M:label] in faeces or chyme/[M:label] in the feed)).

3. Radioactive indicators

Preferable to introduce two radioisotopes at the same time, one intravenously and the other *per os*. The percentage of the mineral absorbed is calculated from the ratio between the content of the radioisotope introduced per os to the content of the intravenously introduced radioisotope in the urine. NB (Expensive)

E. CA, P, MG, NA, K, CL GIT ABSORPTION.

Calcium

•   Bound in plants with protein and organic acid anions.

•   Most of the calcium compounds ingested (apart from oxalates) are converted by the gastric juices (HCl) to CaCl which is almost completely dissociated into ions.

- Ionic calcium is the principal form that is absorbed from the duodenum (and possibly the stomach). There is apparently active transport of calcium as well as passive or facilitated diffusion. The possible role of the Vitamin D responsive calcium binding protein in the horse is not clear, although it has been identified in the duodenum of the horse.

- When anions which bind or precipitate calcium are present in excess, they may interfere with the absorption of calcium ie: oxalates, phytates, phosphates and possibly sulphates.

- As the soluble calcium compounds pass along the GIT, many of them are converted back into the low solubility phosphates and carbonates and into almost insoluble compounds with the higher fatty acids (palmitic, stearic and oleic acids).

- The bile salts form complex compounds with calcium salts of unsaturated fatty acids. These micelles (3-10 mm diameter) are highly dispersed in an aqueous medium and enhance the dissolution and absorption of some calcium salts.

- Most of the active Ca absorption occurs in the duodenum: as the ingesta passes along the GIT the mechanism of micellar transfer becomes more prominent.

- Post absorption passed via the portal vein to the liver where complexes break down and new compounds form (often with proteins). Like other cations, it remains some time in the liver so that the rate of release into the blood is relatively uniform.

- High intakes of calcium, at least in other species, have been shown to influence zinc, magnesium, iron, sulphur and fluorine utilization.

- Individual variation in the ability to absorb calcium has been suggested.

Magnesium

- Forms part of chlorophyll. Some bound as proteinates, carbonates or phosphates. Magnesium fertilizers tend to result in increased concentration of the mobile Mg fractions in plants whereas potassium fertilizers tend to cause the opposite.

- Mg is partly converted into its ionized form by HCl. It is predominantly absorbed in the upper part of the small intestine by ordinary and facilitated diffusion. An active transport mechanism is believed to exist.

- As the dissociated Mg ions pass through the GIT, they are converted to the poorly soluble carbonates, phosphates and the insoluble Mg salts of the fatty acids.

- In other species at least excess fat, calcium, sulphate, phosphates (especially when potassium is in excess), phytic acid and oxalates are believed to decrease absorption.

Phosphorus

- Enters as the mono-, di-, or tri- substituted inorganic phosphates plus the organic compounds: phytates, phospholipids and phosphoproteins.

- Acid gastric juice dissolves the soluble and also some of the insoluble phosphates. Digestive juice phosphatases (especially alkaline phosphatase) split phosphoric acid from organic compounds. Phytates (especially calcium and magnesium) are not well digested but some hydrolysis due to the action of bacterial phytases.

- Soluble phosphates coming from the stomach and those formed in the intestine are readily absorbed (mainly end of small intestine and large intestine, in particular dorsal large colon and the small colon).

- ? an active mechanism present. The secondary and tertiary calcium phosphates are partly absorbed after reacting with fatty acids and forming diffusing chelates.

- At least in other species, excessive iron, aluminum, lead, magnesium and calcium impair absorption of phosphorus due to formation of insoluble phosphates. In the horse, there is little evidence that moderate excesses of dietary calcium have any deleterious effects on phosphorus utilization providing intake is adequate, although it is suggested that an excessive dietary concentration of phosphorus with a low dietary Ca:P ratio of less than 1 will depress calcium absorption.

- Important as a buffer for the volatile fatty acids produced by microfloral fermentation.

Potassium

- Commonly found as carbonates, chlorides and with organic acids.
- Tend to be readily soluble and readily extracted from feed stuffs.
- Absorption mainly by diffusion throughout the GIT but mainly in the proximal small intestine.
- May be very important in the caecum/LI (as per the rumen to buffer the fluids and maintain moisture levels so as to produce an optimum medium for bacterial fermentation) and has been as is considered to be indispensable for normal microbial activities.

Sodium and chloride

- Sodium is not considered to be essential for plants.

- The sodium salts of animal/vegetable feeds and mineral supplements are readily absorbed.

- Na absorption possibly predominantly active. Cl possibly a combination of movement along electric and concentration gradients once the minimum threshold of concentration attained. Predominant site of Cl absorption is the distal small intestine.

- Large amounts of water and, in particular, Na and Cl enter the SI via the saliva, stomach juices, pancreatic juice and bile. Only about 50% water, 35% Na and 80% Cl will be absorbed by the end of the SI. Therefore, a large ileocaecal flow of water and Na (and to a lesser extent, Cl) takes place. Most of the water and Na/Cl which enters the large intestine will be absorbed.

Summary

Along the entire length of the GIT, intensive excretion of minerals takes place at the same time as absorption. The intensity of the various processes will vary at different sites.

F. PRINCIPAL NATURAL SOURCES

Ca:	leafy forages, particularly legumes
P:	cereal grains and their by-products
Mg:	legume forages, sugar beet pulp and sugar beet molasses
K:	leafy forages, sugar beet molasses and milk products
Na and Cl:	common salt, milk products and sugar beet molasses

G. HOMEOSTASIS IMPOSSIBLE TO GO INTO DETAIL BUT MAIN POINTS ARE AS FOLLOWS.

Calcium and phosphorus

A number of hormones affect calcium status, principally parathyroid, calcitonin and vitamin D but also the adrenal corticosteroids, estrogens, thyroid hormones and glucagon.

PTH principally acts when blood Ca levels fall in order to increase blood Ca concentrations and at the same time decrease the P levels. Acts via effects on the urinary excretion of P and Ca and the rate of skeletal remodeling and bone resorption.

Calcitonin interacts primarily on bone and kidney and to a lesser extent, the intestine. Calcitonin acts to lower blood calcium concentration. Vitamin D's role in the horse is not extremely clear but it acts, at least in other species, to increase Ca and P absorption from the intestine, but also has an effect on the bone where small amounts are believed to be necessary to allow the osteolytic cells to respond to PTH.

The renal excretion of calcium has been reported to be directly related to the amount of absorbed calcium, the phosphorus level of the diet and the anion-cation balance of the diet (it has been shown that in the horse, high sodium diets do not affect calcium urinary excretion). The major route of excretion for calcium is via the kidney.

Magnesium

Homeostasis occurs mainly via a balance between absorption from the GIT and excretion via the kidney.

No primary hormonal control but influenced by adrenal and thyroid hormones plus PTH. Mg has a similar effect on PTH as Ca but not equipotent.

Hypermagnasaemia or very severe hypomagnasaemia may result in a decrease in PTH whilst moderate hypomagnasemia may cause an increase in PTH. PTH causes an increase in plasma Mg by increasing intestinal absorption, increasing renal tubular resorption and increasing bone resorption. But PTH needs Mg ions for activation of adenylate cyclase in bone and kidney.

Aldosterone increases result in lowering of the plasma Mg and an increase in urinary Mg excretion (and vice versa) although Mg has no effect on aldosterone levels. (In other species, low dietary levels of Na which produce increased levels of aldosterone result in increased Mg excretion and a negative Mg balance.) Increased thyroid activity results in a decrease in plasma Mg.

Sodium, potassium, chloride

The major excretory pathway for these three electrolytes in the resting animal is via the kidney. The homeostasis of these electrolytes is largely controlled by the hormone aldosterone (plus the renin-angotensin system).

The amount of Na excreted in the urine is determined by the ratio between urinary filtration and resorption. This ratio in turn depends on Na/water levels in diet and so on.

Effect of age and other factors

The efficiency of absorption of the various minerals can be affected by age and dietary intake level eg. calcium efficiency increases as dietary intake decreases. Calcium absorption has been said to decrease with age. Phosphorus absorption may be decreased with age although older animals may be able to decrease urinary losses better. Increasing magnesium intake may significantly increase magnesium absorption and retention.

Dietary cation-anion balance

As Na and K are often absorbed from the GIT in exchange for a proton and Cl is absorbed in exchange for a bicarbonate ion, the relative balance of these cations and anions in the diet can affect acid-base balance and the metabolism of other electrolytes.

Dietary cation-anion balance (DCAB) is defined as meq(Na + K)-Cl/kg dietary DM.

Many equine diets with a high percentage of grain or corn based concentrate may be highly anionic with a low DCAB.

- Low DCAB associated with low urine and blood pH.
- Urinary excretion of Ca and Cl said to significantly increase with decreasing DCAB.
- Mixed effects reported on Na, Mg, P and K excretion. More work needed.
- Faecal, urine and blood pH found to decrease when a high starch diet was fed with increased urinary clearance of Ca and P unrelated to changes in DCAB.

H. REQUIREMENTS

Need to take into account unavoidable losses, and availability from feedstuffs plus any requirements for growth, exercise, lactation, etc. plus individual differences. Many assumptions still have to be made in order to arrive at a "guide figure."

Maintenance requirements

Table 1. BASED ON A VARIETY OF PAPERS (AS REPORTED IN HARRIS, *et al.,* 1995).

			Maintenance	
Element	Unavoidable losses (mg/kg BW/day)[a]	Availability %[b]	mg/kg BW/day	g/500 kg
Ca[c]	30	60 (36-82)*	50	25
P	12	40 (30-55)*	30	15
Mg	5	35(-61)	15	7.5
Na	18 (15-20)*	90 (45-90)*	20	10
K	40	80	50	25
Cl	5-10	100	80	40

* range in literature
^a With a low sodium or potassium intake, the Na/K losses said to be substantially reduced to less than 10 for Na and around 5 for K. The same is not believed to be true for Cl.
^b The availability will vary with type of feed, presence of interfering substances, the individual animal and the amount supplied.
^c After a prolonged period of inactivity, calcium and phosphorus supply should be increased about 20% above recommended figures to compensate for the losses from the skeleton during inactivity.

Table 2. BASED ON *IN VIVO* WORK BY PAGAN (1994).

Element	Unavoidable losses g/day	Availability*	Maintenance g/500 kg
Ca	17.4	74.7	23.3
P	4.7	25.2	18.5
Mg	2.2	51.8	4.2

*very similar values

Requirements for exercise

The total requirement of electrolytes for the exercising horse depends largely on the amount of sweat produced and its composition.

Sweat losses

Electrolytes are continually lost from the body via the kidney, gut and from the skin in sweat. Sweat electrolyte losses are therefore an important factor to consider in mineral nutrition of the exercising horse, which can lose large amounts of sweat.

The amount of sweat produced depends on the environmental conditions, nature of the work (this in turn will depend on the rider's ability and the terrain), and the animal's fitness. Under favorable climate conditions, sweat loss can be in the order of 7-8 liters per hour in long distance rides. In hot, humid conditions where sweating is partially ineffective, production can be as high as 10-15 litres/hour. This means an endurance horse may lose 25-30 litres or more if conditions are unfavorable. Under average conditions a race horse performing at high speeds even for a short period of time can lose between 1-5 litres. Sweat production seems to only decrease after extreme water loss. When the sweat loss is low, much of the loss can be made up by absorption of water contained in the large intestine and no disastrous effects are seen. But if water losses are between 3-4% of body weight, a decrease in circulatory volume as well as a loss of skin elasticity occurs. This will occur after about 3 hours of exercise with moderate sweating, but much sooner at rates of 10-15 litres/hour.

Sweat composition

There is some controversy over sweat composition due primarily to difficulties in collection. Newer methods are currently being explored which may answer some of these concerns.

Sweat however is believed to contain low concentrations of calcium, magnesium and phosphate but relatively high concentrations of sodium, potassium and chloride. Some workers have suggested that the potassium and chloride concentration decreases after the first hour. A decrease in magnesium concentration has also been shown to occur. Whatever the exact sweat composition turns out to be, a heavily sweating horse may rapidly develop a negative water and electrolyte balance as sweat is accompanied by an obligatory loss of electrolytes. The exhausted horse syndrome is believed to reflect a combination of fluid and electrolyte losses, depletion of energy stores and extremes of environmental conditions. Affected animals appear severely depressed, dehydrated, unwilling to eat or drink, with elevated temperatures, pulses and respiration rates. Laminitis and synchronous diaphragmatic flutter may be found. Metabolic acidosis with a paradoxical aciduria, hypokalemia, hyponatraemia and hypochloraemia with elevated CK, AST and LDH activities tend to be found (Carlson 1987). Horses can die from this condition.

Estimated/approximate sweat composition

Na	3.1 g/l
K	1.6 g/l
Cl	5.5 g/l
Ca	0.12 g/l
Mg	0.05 g/l
P	<10 mg/l

Focus on Na requirements for the exercising horse

Endogenous losses given as 15-20 mg/kg BW/day in a non-sweating horse. Availability reported as varying from 45-90%.

Therefore requirements for a mature 500 kg non-exercising horse as fed would vary from 8-22 grams of sodium a day.

For a sweating horse doing moderate work with sweat loss of around 10 liters, the theoretical required Na intake would vary from 42 - 91 g/day. Very few horses would be fed or eat or need 91 g Na (approx. 8 oz. of NaCl)!!

Some factors to be considered

a.   Content of the gastrointestinal tract may provide an important reservoir for sodium during hard work.

b.   Electrolyte losses that occur with heavy sweating do not need to be restored all at once.

c.   We need to know availabilities for exercising horses - currently unknown.

d.   Need to have a better knowledge of sweat composition.

Practical evaluation of electrolyte status (Harris 1988, Harris and Gray 1992)

Whole body electrolyte content may be a reliable and accurate estimate of whole body status, but it is not practical. There are difficulties with methods involving whole body calcium composition, bone biopsies, mineral content of hair and random analysis of saliva samples. Sweat collection can be problematical and significant alterations in sweat electrolyte content may not be seen until severe electrolyte depletion has occurred. Faecal electrolyte content may not reliably reflect dietary intake or body status. Muscle electrolyte content is not practical for regular monitoring and does not seem to be very sensitive to mild alterations in electrolyte intake. Serum or plasma concentrations cannot be used reliably to indicate electrolyte imbalances due to efficient homeostatic mechanisms which maintain normal blood concentrations despite body depletion. Normal daily requirements for a horse are affected by a number of factors including age, body weight, exercise and environmental conditions. Dietary analysis alone may not reflect the electrolyte status of the horse because the availability varies, especially between individual animals and there are many interactions.

ESTIMATION OF EXCHANGEABLE CATION LOSS

Based on work by Carlson, an estimation of exchangeable cation loss following exercise can be obtained if pre and post exercise plasma Na concentrations and body weights are known and the following formulas applied.

A.   water deficit (WD) = weight loss x 0.9

B.   pre-exercise total body water (TBWPre) = 66% of pre-exercise body weight

C.   post exercise total body water (TBWPo) = TBWPre - WD

D.   plasma sodium concentration (Na)p x TBW = exchangeable cations (Na and K) therefore:

Pre(Na)p x TBWpre = A meg
Post(Na)p x TBWpo = B meg

Total deficit of exchangeable cations = A - B = C mg.

Assume that 70% of the total exchangeable cation loss is Na and 30% is K

Then   Na loss is 70% x C = D
        K loss is 30% x C = E

e.g. :   if
          Pre (Na)p = 138
          Post (Na)p = 142
          Pre BW = 613
          Weight loss= 27
          WD= 243
          TBWpre= 405
          TBWpost= 381

Then exchangeable cations   pre (A) = 55890
                                 post (B) = 54102 mmol

        Na loss (D) = 1252 mmol
        K loss (E) = 536 mmol
But many assumptions are made and not all proven.

FRACTIONAL ELECTROLYTE EXCRETION TEST

Electrolyte homeostasis is mediated primarily by the kidney. Simple measurements of urinary electrolyte concentrations are unreliable due to variations in urine volume and 24 hour urine collections rely on the accurate collection, timing and measurement of urine volumes. A more practical alternative, which removes the need for accurate urine volume measurements, compares the excretion of an electrolyte to that of a control substance. The control substance ideally has an excretion rate which reflects the glomerular filtration rate and is not secreted or re-absorbed by the renal tubules. Inulin is an ideal compound that fulfills these criteria. However, the measurement of the exogenous inulin clearance is not practical. Measurement of the exogenous creatinine clearance is a more applicable alternative, although less ideal. The renal excretion of an electrolyte can then be compared with the creatinine excretion or clearance. The ratio of these two excretion values has been referred to as the urinary fractional excretion of an electrolyte (X) CrCl i.e. the FE X (fractional excretion index) or the % creatinine clearance ration %CrCl X i.e:

clearance of an electrolyte (X) x 100

_____

clearance of creatinine (Cr)

$$\frac{\dfrac{(X)_u}{(X)_p} \times \text{volume of urine time period kg body weight}}{\dfrac{(Cr)_u}{(Cr)_p} \times \text{volume of urine time period kg body weight}} = \frac{(X)_u}{(X)_p} \times \frac{(Cr)_p}{(Cr)_u} \times 100 = FEX$$

u = urinary concentration   p = plasma concentration

PRACTICAL ISSUES TO BE CONSIDERED

1.   Freely-voided urine samples are preferred - often not possible to obtain these.

   a) Use a urine collection harness (Harris, 1988b)

   b) First thing in the morning, take horse out of the stable (if stabled) and walk slowly around at the horse's pace whilst stable is mucked out so returns to clean straw or shavings, etc.

   c) In females only, catheterized samples may be acceptable, but the fillies/ mares should first be bled and then given a short brisk trot before urine sample is collected. Post-exercise samples are not reliable.

2.   No significant differences in the FE values for Na, K, PO^4 or Cl results have been found with samples collected at the start, middle or end of a urine stream. Differences in calcium content have however been found and it is adviseable to collect all of a voided urine sample.

3.   There may be a delay in the analysis of samples at a laboratory. Very little alteration in urinary or plasma concentration of Na, K or Cl occurs with storage at 18, 4 or -20°C. However, there are considerable changes in the Ca, PO^4 and Cr concentrations, particularly when samples are stored at 18°C although the extent of changes varies between samples. In urine, this may be linked to the pH and degree of bacterial contamination. Plasma and urine samples should therefore be transported in capped, sterile containers and although short term storage in the refrigerator may be adequate, longer storage should be at -20°C.

Samples should ideally be analyzed as soon as possible for Ca, Cr and PO^4 i.e. within 4 days.

4.   Samples should not be collected for the determination of base line electrolyte status during or soon after an episode of the equine rhabdomyolysis syndrome (ERS) because circulatory disturbances and increased plasma myoglobin concentrations may affect renal function and result in unrepresentative FE values.

5.   Before analysis all urines should be checked and those with:

a. pH of 6 or below

b. positive for glucose

c. more than 0.3g protein per litre

d. positive for blood or myoglobin/haemoglobin should not be considered normal.

6.   If a sample has a Cr concentration of < 9,000 mmol/L (AHT Laboratories, Newmarket) need to check that:

a. no contamination of the sample has occurred

b. excessive salt has not been given to cause polydipsea

c. no signs of polydipsea/polyuria

(It has been suggested that Cr may be significantly lowered when sugar beet pulp is fed.) Usually, if such a value is found, one needs to repeat the test. The test should not be interpreted as an indication of electrolyte status if the sample has a low urinary creatinine concentration. But, problems arise in young animals less than 18 months old which often have low urinary creatinine concentrations.

7.   Urinary Ca determinations should be carried out using a flame atomic absorption spectrophotometer because colormetric methods used for serum/plasma have been shown to be unsuitable. Samples must be very well mixed.

8.   Cannot use the FE test to monitor low phosphate intakes. (Raised % FE PO^4 values tend to represent a Ca:P imbalance.)

9.   Decreased urinary Mg and Ca concentrations have been found shortly before and after feeding with maximum values 4-8 hours after feeding. (Myer, *et al.*, 1989)

10. Watch out for low blood potassium values which will 'falsely' elevate the % FE values for K. These low levels seem to occur in animals rested for a period of time, around the time of hay ingestion, etc. Usually advisable to repeat before interpreting further. (Can use a more "acceptable" plasma level

to provide an adjusted %FEK). High plasma values may occur with even slight haemolysis. *Collect blood sample pre-exercise/prefeeding ideally and remove plasma as soon as possible.

CALCIUM

It has been suggested that the precipitation of calcium as crystals or salts in the bladder means that urinary calcium concentrations may not reflect calcium status adequately because an unpredictable amount of this precipitate may be voided at any one time. However, Meyer, *et al.*, 1989 reported that a low calcium intake could be confirmed by analysis, although when the calcium intake was above requirement, the renal calcium excretion was not closely correlated with the calcium intake. Magnesium, which does not tend to precipitate out, may be used to give additional information on calcium status.

The anion-cation balance has been shown to affect calcium urinary excretion and may falsely affect the interpretation of the Fe Ca values.

PRACTICAL ADVICE

a. Do not interpret an FE test if the urinary pH is 6 or below.

b. High Ca/Mg excretion values are difficult to determine. If the diet is known and does not appear to be providing excessive Ca/Mg intakes, then anion-cation balance of the diet should be examined further.

c. Use the FE test more to detect low % FE Ca/Mg values rather than high values (low % FE Ca can be false due to sedimentation, etc.), but a low FE Ca with a concomitantly low % Fe Mg most probably indicates a Ca (and possible Mg) imbalance.

INTERPRETATION

Always have the dietary information available. The expected "reference" ranges for the % Fe values will vary with the diet.

There are diurnal variations in urinary electrolyte (and Cr) concentrations. 24 hour collections are more reliable (and have fairly consistent Cr excretion values) but not as practical. However although the single sample may not be accurate it may be sufficiently representative to enable certain metabolic abnormalitites to be detected.

Table 3. EXPECTED "REFERENCE RANGES" FOR % FE VALUES

Grain based[1]		*Typical compound cube and hay "balanced" diet reference range[2]*
	Ca	>7
	Mg	>15
0.02 - 1	Na	0.04 - 0.52
15 - 65	K	35 - 80
0.04 - 1.6	Cl	0.7 - 2.1
0 - 0.5	PO$_4$	0 - 0.2

[1] Traver, *et al.,* 1976 [2] Harris 1988, Harris and Snow, 1991

USE IN THE EQUINE RHABDOMYOLYSIS SYNDROME (TYING-UP)

Animals without renal disease that have abnormal FE values whilst being fed a diet containing an adequate and balanced electrolyte content may have an individual absorption/utilization problem. Such abnormalities have been found in horses suffering from ERS. Restoration of the FE values to within the expected reference range for the type of diet fed may result in clinical improvement (Harris and Colles 1988, Harris and Snow 1991). Abnormal FE values in horses with rhabdomyolysis are complicated by the fact that many diets of horse are low or imbalanced with respect to their electrolyte and vitamin content. Ideally affected animals should be sampled while being fed their regular diet (on which they had suffered attacks) and then after a period on a diet balanced with respect to its electrolyte content. For practical and financial reasons, this may not be possible. A compromise therefore is to feed the animal a diet believed to provide an adequate and balanced diet for at least 2 weeks before collection of appropriate blood and urine samples. The appropriate supplementation could then be given and the level of supplementation altered accordingly following a monitoring. If an FE abnormality was not detected on this 'balanced diet', the animal could then be kept on the diet with the knowledge that the electrolyte intake would remain fairly constant and any further attacks would be unlikely to be related to electrolyte imbalances (as detected by the FE test). However because of the increased requirements of certain electrolytes with exercise, the test should be repeated when the horse is in full work on full feed.

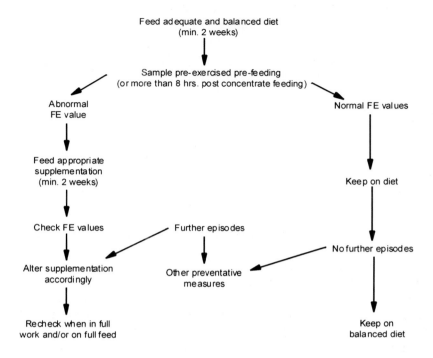

References

Carlson, G.P. 1987. The Exhausted Horse Syndrome. In Robinson N.E. (ed) Current Therapy in Equine Medicine. W.B. Saunders, Philadelphia pp. 482-485.

Harris, P.A. 1988. Aspects of the Equine Rhabdomyolysis Syndrome. Ph.D. Thesis, University of Cambridge.

Harris, P.A. 1988b. Collection of Urine. Equine Veterinary Journal Vol. 20 pp 86-88.

Harris, P.A. and Colles C. 1988. The Use of Creatinine Clearance Ratios in the Prevention of Equine Rhabdomyolysis. Equine Vet. Jrnl. Vol. 20 pp 454-463.

Harris, P.A. and Snow, D.H. 1991. Role of Electrolyte Imbalances in the Pathophysiology of the Equine Rhabdomyolysis Syndrome. Equine Exercise Physiology 3 Eds. SGB Persson, A. Lindholm and L.B. Jeffcott. ICEEP, Davis, Calyomea pp. 435 - 442.

Harris, P.A. and Gray, J. 1992. The Use of the Urinary Fractional Electrolyte Excretion Test to Assess Electrolyte Status in the Horse. Equine Vet. Educ. 4(4) 162-166.

Harris, P.A., Lucas, D., Frape, D. and Meyer, H. 1995. Equine Nutrition and Metabolic Diseases. In: The Equine Manual - Eds. A.J. Higgins and I. Wright.

Meyer, H., Heilmann, M., Perez, H., and Gomda, Y. 1989. Investigations on the Post Prandial Renal Ca, P and Mg Excretion in Resting and Exercised Horses. in Proceedings. 11th ENPS, Oklahoma pp. 133-138.

Pagan, J. 1994. In: Feedstuffs, May 23, 1994.

Traver, D.S., Coffman et al 1976. Urine Clearance Ratios as a Diagnostic Aid in Equine Metabolic Disease. In Proceedings. Am. Ass. Equine Pract. 22 pp. 177-183.

This paper was first published in "Recent Advances in Equine Nutrition," Proceedings for the 1995 Short Course for Feed Manufacturers

MYCOTOXINS
A NATIONWIDE PROBLEM

JOHN C. REAGOR

Texas A&M University, College Station, Texas, USA

Toxic fungal metabolites are chemically diverse and occur in a wide variety of feeds and foods. They impair human health and cause economic losses in livestock through disease and reduced production efficiency.

The fungal organisms that produce mycotoxins can invade the feed supply, grow, and produce toxins when conditions are proper. This can occur during production in the field, transportation, processing, or storage. Some are produced on the farm in feed mixers or in feed bunks. The three major genera of mycotoxin-producing fungi are *Aspergillus, Fusarium* and *Penicillium*. Several factors which influence mycotoxin production are: strain of fungus, substrate, moisture, humidity, temperature, pH, growth of other fungi or microbes, and stresses such as drought. The major crops affected in the United States are corn, peanuts and cotton.

The aflatoxins, the most important group of mycotoxin discovered to date, are produced primarily by *Aspergillus flavus* and *A. parasiticus*. Sterigmatocystin is a precursor in the biosynthesis of aflatoxins but can also be produced as an end product by several species of *Aspergillus*. The large family of mycotoxins known as trichothecenes (T-2, the most notable) are produced by *Fusarium*. Zearalenone is produced by *F. graminearum*. The ochratoxins are produced by *A. ochraceus* and several *Penicillium spp*. Some species of *Penicillium* and *Aspergillus* are capable of producing either citrinin, citreovirdin, or cyclopiazonic acid. Fumonisins (the newest described mycotoxins) are produced by *F. moniliforme* and *F. proliferatum*. Tremorgens (literally 'tremor producing') are produced by species of *Penicillium, Aspergillus, Claviceps*, and *Acremonium*.

The toxicity of mycotoxins to animals ranges from acute death to chronic disease and interference with reproductive efficiency. Aflatoxins (notably B1 and its metabolite M1) can cause liver damage or cancer, decreased rate of gain, decreased milk and egg production, reduced feed efficiency, abortion and immune suppression. The young are most susceptible to the effects of aflatoxins, which may be expressed as gastrointestinal disturbances, anemia, jaundice, and reduced feed intake and efficiency. Nursing animals may be affected by exposure to aflatoxin metabolites secreted in milk.

The trichothecenes primarily cause necrosis and hemorrhage throughout the gastrointestinal tract, depression of blood regenerative processes in the bone marrow and spleen, and changes in the reproductive organs. Signs of disease include: weight loss, reduced feed consumption and utilization, vomiting, diarrhea, abortion and death. Immune suppression may also be important in trichothecene affected animals.

Ochratoxin A causes kidney damage and renal fibrosis at concentrations usually found in feeds. However, higher concentrations may cause liver damage, as well as intestinal necrosis and hemorrhage. This mycotoxin is also immunosuppressive and carcinogenic. It does not seem to be a common problem across the United States.

Zearalenone is an estrogenic fungal metabolite which induces feminization in swine at dietary concentrations of less than 1 ppm. Higher concentrations can interfere with conception, ovulation, implantation, fetal development and the viability of newborn.

The fumonisins cause a wide variety of problems depending upon the species. Affected horses may have leukoencephalomalacia and/or liver damage while swine may have pulmonary edema and/or liver damage.

A wide variety of other effects in animals have been attributed to mycotoxins, including embryonic death, inhibition of fetal development, and abortions attributed to aflatoxins, zearalenone, rubratoxin, and ergot toxins. Teratogenicity has been described for aflatoxins, ochratoxin, T-2, zearalenone, sterigmatocystin and rubratoxin. Nervous system function is adversely altered by at least nine mycotoxins, including the tremorgenic mycotoxins. Clinical signs include tremors, uncoordinated movements, weakness in the legs, staggering and sudden muscular collapse. The neurological signs may be complicated with seizures, hemorrhage, diarrhea, profuse salivation, feed refusal and gangrene of the extremities.

Human mycotoxicoses are documented for relatively few of the many mycotoxins. Of considerable importance are those mycotoxins such as aflatoxins, that are potentially carcinogenic to humans. Major epidemiological studies regarding the aflatoxins have been conducted, primarily in Asia and Africa. Some have shown a positive association, while others have indicated a lack of positive association, between exposure of aflatoxins and disease outcome. Major criticism of many of these studies surrounds the role of hepatitis B virus as an agent for liver cell cancer in the populations studied. Therefore, the exact relationship of aflatoxins with liver cell cancer in humans has not been fully established. Nevertheless, in 1988, the International Agency for Research on Cancer placed aflatoxin B1 on their list of human carcinogens.

Unlike Africa and Asia, the incidence of liver cell cancer in the United States is relatively low as is the exposure to aflatoxins. Although there have been no complete investigations conducted in the United States, a limited retrospective population study demonstrated no apparent association between consumption of aflatoxins and liver cell cancer. New epidemiology studies in the United States, utilizing recently developed techniques, could provide a better determination of the extent of exposure to populations. They also would have the potential to aid in clarifying the role of aflatoxins in liver cell cancer and other disease states in the relative absence of alternate risk factors. However, conduct of these studies may not be practical. The liver cell cancer incidence in the United States is so low that such studies would require undeniably large numbers of participants to yield meaningful statistics. In contrast, cases of acute aflatoxicosis leading to death or disease involving gastrointestinal disturbances, hemorrhage, vomiting and hepatic changes have been well documented in humans.

Mycotoxins can contaminate crops before harvest, in transport and in storage. Thus, raw or processed foods and feeds can become contaminated. With the exception of the aflatoxins, the frequency of contamination by mycotoxins is unknown. The aflatoxins are frequently detected in a variety of feeds and foods produced in the United States, as well as in imported commodities and products. Contamination of milk, eggs and meat can result from animal consumption of mycotoxin contaminated feed. Aflatoxins, ochratoxin and some trichothecenes have been given considerable attention, because they are either carcinogenic or of economic concern in animal health.

Additional mycotoxins produced by various *Aspergillus, Penicillium, Fusarium* and other fungal genera can contaminate foods; however their importance to animal and human health has not been established.

The economic losses due to mycotoxins are multifaceted involving direct crop and livestock losses through reduced health and production efficiency, regulatory programs, processing and diagnostic expenses. The incidence of mycotoxins varies among commodities, climatic conditions and regions. For these reasons, the economic importance of mycotoxins is difficult to quantify. Product losses likely occur, but except for certain corn and peanut products, milk, and eggs, there is no documentation. Increased costs resulting from mycotoxin-contaminated commodities are likely passed on to the buyer or consumer. Such costs have significant direct or indirect effects on the control of mycotoxins and international trade of commodities and processed feeds and foods.

Because mycotoxins are unavoidable, naturally occurring compounds, regulations provide an important means to control the quality of the food and feed in which they may occur. Presently, in the United States, only the aflatoxins are regulated. To accomplish such controls, the concentration of mycotoxins in foods and feeds must be accurately assessed. Such accuracy involves adequate sampling of the food or feed, chemical extraction, cleanup and quantitative analysis of the mycotoxins. Although most of the procedures are developed for the laboratory and often utilize sophisticated equipment, field-practical screening tests are available for rapid detection of selected mycotoxins in certain commodities.

Regardless of our best efforts to control the occurrence of mycotoxins in commodities, they do occur, and therefore strategies have been developed to decontaminate or detoxify the commodity. Presently, this is true primarily for the aflatoxins. These methods for decontamination/detoxification include physical separation, thermal inactivation, irradiation, microbial degradation and chemical treatment. Ammoniation has been safely and effectively used for aflatoxins in some commodities used for animal feed, but has not yet been sanctioned by the U.S. Food and Drug Administration. A new approach using selective adsorption of aflatoxins by dietary compounds has resulted in reducing or preventing some adverse effects of aflatoxins. Continued efforts are needed to establish these kinds of methods to practically, safely, and effectively control mycotoxins in foods and feeds.

This paper was first published in "Feeding the Performance Horse," Proceedings for the 1994 Short Course for Feed Manufacturers

IMPLICATIONS OF MYCOTOXINS

JOHN C. REAGOR

Texas A & M University, College Station, Texas, USA

This paper will cover the most important mycotoxins which affect cattle and horses with emphasis on the newly discovered fumonisins. Many adult horses have consumed moldy feed or forage. In most instances, these fungal contaminated materials are consumed without harm. Feeds which contain a significant concentration of a mycotoxin can and do cause severe problems.

Aflatoxins, the most studied mycotoxins, were first discovered some 30 years ago after the death of thousands of birds in England. The most abundant and most toxic of the group is aflatoxin B1. This and its metabolite, aflatoxin M1, are the compounds most commonly referred to when aflatoxicosis is discussed. Livestock are usually poisoned when the toxins contaminate corn, peanut or cottonseed products, as these commodities may support toxin production in the field prior to harvest. These, as well as other high energy feedstuffs, may support fungal growth and toxin production by improper storage or handling. We have seen significant aflatoxin production occur in feed mixer wagons and bunks where wet feed was fed to dairy cows. The equipment was not cleaned on a regular basis and a moldy layer allowed toxins to form over a period of a few days to weeks. Aflatoxin levels can increase dramatically in harvested corn (16-18% moisture) that is allowed to stay in the wagon overnight at harvest.

Aflatoxin production requires a suitable substrate, a toxigenic strain of *Aspergillus*, the proper temperature (80-110° F), adequate moisture (14-22%) and the correct relative humidity (62-99%). Widespread aflatoxin problems (like those occurring in corn from Texas, Florida and Georgia) are the result of adverse growing conditions.

Problems with aflatoxin have been far more severe on corn and peanuts when drought stress prevailed during the latter part of the growing season. Under such conditions, factors favoring infestation are ideal because temperatures are high, relative humidities around kernels are high and the kernel moisture lowered enough for infestation to occur. High grain moisture (22 to 30%) is not conducive to the infection process for this fungus. The fungus that produces aflatoxin also has less competition from other organisms when drought stress conditions prevail.

Confusion often arises when one thinks of production and storage conditions at the same time. Those oriented toward considering the aflatoxin problem to be a harvesting and storage problem find it difficult to see how drought stress (low moisture) can cause a problem considered to be related to high moisture at harvest time. Corn, for example, is vulnerable when it reaches the dough stage when the moisture usually is too high for infection by *Aspergillus*. If severe drought stress is present, however, kernel moisture is lowered to the point where infection can occur.

Numerous field studies have documented infection of corn kernels by aflatoxin-producing fungi. Corn silks protruding from shucks are readily invaded by these fungi. Germ tubes rapidly grow down these tubes to the kernel surface where they lie until late in the development of kernels. Once the kernel reaches a moisture content of approximately 32%, the fungus enters the kernel. *Aspergillus favus* is capable of direct penetration in the absence of insect injury even though the latter may enhance the chances for organism development. It is rare indeed to find a corn ear that is not infected with a corn ear worm larva.

Extensive research shows that corn kernels may be preconditioned by a multitude of factors that may interact to influence the amount of aflatoxin that may occur in a given field at harvest. These include the potential for harvest cracks in kernels and holding high moisture corn on transport equipment an excessive period before drying.

Silage production from drought-stressed corn may also contain sufficient levels of aflatoxin to be of concern to livestock producers and dairymen. Therefore, it is advisable to evaluate the potential aflatoxin content in drought-stressed crops before harvesting for "green-chop" or silage production.

The most significant effect of aflatoxins to dairy cattle is the contamination of milk by aflatoxin M1. Of the over 200 mycotoxins identified, aflatoxin is of major concern to dairymen. The maximum level of aflatoxin allowed in dairy feed is 20 ppb (parts per billion). When aflatoxin is consumed by lactating cows, it not only can be toxic to the cow but also appears in the milk within 24 hours. Since aflatoxins also affect humans, a maximum level of 0.5 ppb of the aflatoxin is permitted in bulk tank milk. A general conversion factor of 100 to 200X reduction in the aflatoxin fed to that appearing in the milk or 0.91% of the aflatoxin consumed in the feed appearing in the milk is used. For both rules of thumb, the aflatoxin metabolite appearing in milk would be 0.1 to 0.2 ppb if feed containing 20 ppb aflatoxin is fed. Generally, levels of 50 ppb or greater in the feed produce metabolite levels over 0.5 ppb. Once the affected feed is removed, aflatoxin levels in the milk will disappear in 48 to 72 hours.

While ruminant animals, such as dairy cows, are more resistant to aflatoxins, toxicity does occur with disastrous results. Calves are particularly sensitive and exhibit reduced growth rate. The target sites of action of mycotoxins are organs such as liver, heart, kidney and adrenal. Aflatoxins are particularly damaging to the liver with noticeable reduction in milk production and appetite. Diarrhea, internal hemorrhaging, abortion and weight loss may also occur.

When we know aflatoxin problems are common to an area, it is extremely important that feeds–particularly corn, whole cottonseed and cottonseed meal–be checked for mycotoxins. This is important both for the short term and long term, with the short term being for the protection of milk supplies. Long-term consequences can be devastating, as aflatoxins may permanently reduce productive capacity due to organ damage. This is particularly significant since contaminated corn supplies are often fed to heifers as a means of saving the commodity without regard to the long-term effects.

The federal allowable level for aflatoxin in corn for beef cattle is quite acceptable. Young calves, under 200 lb., should not receive feed containing over 20 ppb. Beef cows should not receive over 100 ppb, while finishing feedlot cattle can tolerate up to 300 ppb.

Immunosuppression occurs when cattle rations exceed 200 ppb and severe health problems (chronic liver damage, reduced growth and feed efficiency) can result from the continued intake of 600 to 700 ppb aflatoxin in the feed of 450-pound cattle.

Kidney damage, anemia, interference with the body's immune system, greater susceptibility to bruising and interference with normal protein and fat metabolism have all been reported with varying levels of intake. In acute cases, those below the level that lead to sudden death in cattle, the following signs may occur: depression, lack of appetite, nervousness, abdominal pain (animals may stretch or kick at their abdomen), diarrhea and rectal prolapse. Death of steers has been reported from an intake of 1,000 ppb of aflatoxin in feed during a 59-day trial.

The tremorgens produced in bermudagrass and on seedheads infected with *Claviceps spp.* can be a significant problem in cattle. Ergot-infected dallisgrass, rye, ryegrass, bahiagrass and other native *Paspalum spp.* seedheads can cause staggers, abortion and death in cattle or horses which consume large amounts. Most cases occur when animals are moved to a pasture that contains mature seed or when round bales containing mature plants are fed. The ergot bodies are retained in the round bales and are not lost in the feeding process, as is usually the case with small square bales.

Tall fescue grass, other than pastures planted with endophyte-free seed, contains the fungus *Acremonium coenophialum*. Cattle grazing contaminated fescue develop fescue toxicity which results in lower feed intake, reduced grazing time, lower animal performance (for example, gain, milk production, reproductive performance) and sometimes the extreme toxicity called "fescue foot" where animals develop lameness and sometimes lose portions of their feet and tails from the restricted blood circulation caused by the disease. Mares that graze contaminated stands often abort, produce stillborn foals, retain placentas and have reduced milk production

The fungus is transmitted by seed and does not affect the growth or appearance of the grass. Hence it requires a laboratory test to detect its presence. Prevention measures include planting fungus-free seed in newly established pastures or destroying old pastures before seed formation and replanting with fungus-free seed. Interseeding pastures with clover or other cool season grasses helps dilute the effect of the fungus.

Equine leukoencephalomalacia (ELEM) or moldy corn poisoning in horses has been recognized since the turn of the century. The disease has been associated with *Fusarium moniliforme* and was experimentally reproduced with *F. moniliforme* culture material in 1971. Fumonisin B1 was identified and reported to cause a similar condition following IV injection in 1988. Oral administration of purified Fumonisin B was reported to produce ELEM in 1989.

A large amount of effort has been placed on fumonisin recently. There are now assay procedures for the mycotoxin and many samples associated with ELEM have been analyzed.

ELEM may be clinically characterized by a sudden onset of one or more of the following signs: depression, aimless circling, head pressing, paresis, ataxia, blindness, hypersensitivity and frenzy. Some animals are found dead where they have run through a fence. Diagnosis has been based on the classical brain lesions. There is liquefactive necrosis of the white matter of the cerebral hemispheres. These lesions may also include the gray matter and may be located in the midbrain or brain stem. With the advent of chemical analysis of feed for fumonisin, some cases are being diagnosed where the only brain lesions are areas of hemorrhage and the "impression of edema."

ELEM is not an acute mycotoxin poisoning. Typically, affected animals have consumed toxic feed for at least 14 days and often as long as 60 days. The morbidity rarely exceeds 50% but the mortality is high.

Fumonisin appears to be limited to corn or corn products. Most cases involve horses which were consuming feed that was composed of, at least in part, corn screenings. Based on field cases, animals must consume a feed which contains at least 10 ppm fumonisin B1 for ELEM to occur.

Very high levels of fumonisin have been seen in corn which was down and had extensive water damage prior to harvest. We have seen some selected, damaged kernels that contained over 700 ppm (parts per million) fumonisin. This is an extremely high mycotoxin concentration considering that most mycotoxins are reported as ppb.

There was a significant number of ELEM cases from the 1989 corn harvest. It was not uncommon for corn screenings from export elevators in Louisiana to contain 40 to 50 ppm fumonisin B1. This was from corn which originated from the Corn Belt.

Fumonisin may well become one of the most significant mycotoxins. Unlike many of the newly discovered fungal metabolites or mycotoxins, there is no need to look for a clinical disease associated with this one. In addition to ELEM, this toxin can cause liver damage in horses and pigs as well as pulmonary edema in swine. It is also a strong tumor promoter in rats.

Much of the corn in the United States appears to be contaminated with at least 0.5 to 1 ppm fumonisin. If this is the case, the screenings from this corn could poison horses if it were fed at a high level. Horse feed should not contain corn screenings!

This paper was first published in "Feeding the Performance Horse," Proceedings for the 1994 Short Course for Feed Manufacturers

SMALL AIRWAY DISEASE AND EQUINE RESPIRATORY HEALTH

SUSAN L. RAYMOND AND ANDREW F. CLARKE
Equine Research Centre, Guelph, Ontario, Canada

The focus of this paper is lower airway disease and its relationship to poor air quality. We will take a journey through the horse's lungs and examine their various challenges. There have been several exciting developments recently which have changed our understanding of and approaches to dealing with respiratory problems in horses. On the broader front, there is a clear emergence in veterinary and indeed human medicine which sees a change away from treating disease to maintaining health. This approach focuses on providing knowledge which will empower those involved in the day-to-day care of horses to maintain their horse's health. In the context of the respiratory system, this approach can also have direct benefits for people who care for horses.

This article begins with a description of the journey air takes to reach the lungs. The costs and demands placed on the lung are then reviewed, followed by a description of the most common problems of airways. Practical husbandry and management procedures which can help maintain the horse's respiratory health are then described. Finally there is a description of some of the pharmacological approaches your veterinarian may use in treating a respiratory problem.

The respiratory system

Air enters the nostrils and is warmed and humidified by the turbinates (blood rich scrolls of bone) prior to entering the trachea. Larger particles in the air are also trapped by the turbinates as a first line of defence of the lungs. From the trachea, the air travels along an ever increasing number of initially larger airways (bronchi) to small airways (bronchioles). In the horse, the airways are lined by cilia which act as an escalator to move mucus and particles up from the lungs. As well as cilia, there are mucus-producing cells in the linings of the airways. Indeed, the cilia normally beat in a thin layer of mucus which is moved up the airways. However, in disease states, such as with infection, the nature of the mucus can become tenacious. This is an important consideration later in the section on pharmaceuticals. Groups of lymphoid cells are scattered throughout the airways. They form and maintain the lung's immunity to many infectious agents.

The inward journey of air through the airways comes to an end at the alveolar sacs. It is within these sacs and across a very fine membrane, known as the alveolar membrane, that gas exchange occurs. Oxygen passes across the membrane into the red blood cells and carbon dioxide passes back across the other way. Oxygen is necessary for the survival of the tissues and carbon dioxide is a by-product of energy production. The journey of this stale air back out of the lungs then commences as the horse exhales.

A final defence barrier exists in the alveoli. Tiny inhaled particles which get passed through the turbinates and airways land in the air sacs and are cleaned up by cells called macrophages. These cells engulf material ranging from tiny particles of dust to bacteria. However, they can be overloaded. For example, heavy burdens of dust can decrease the ability of those cells to fight infectious agents such as bacteria. A horse in a dusty environment will therefore be more prone to infection than a horse in a cleaner environment.

The lung evolved to deal with air. To maintain a healthy lung, it is important to minimize pollutants it is exposed to.

THE COSTS AND DEMANDS OF RESPIRATORY FUNCTION

Athletic performance puts extra demands on the respiratory system. At rest, an average horse takes in approximately five litres of air with each breath. It takes 12 breaths per minute and has a heart rate of approximately 32 beats per minute. Therefore, at rest, our average horse will inhale and exhale approximately 60 litres of air per minute. However, during competition, the horse will increase the volume of air per breath to between 12 and 15 litres taking over 150 breaths per minute. The lungs now have to move over 2,250 litres of air per minute, with less than half a second for each breath. The breathing patterns of equine athletes are closely linked with locomotion. The cantering and galloping horse has respiration and locomotion locked into a 1:1 phase. With each stride the horse will be taking a breath. This action aids in respiration, as it allows the large body mass of the abdominal organs to act like a piston. The galloping horse takes over 150 breaths per minute. This is in contrast to a Standardbred which takes upwards of 70 breaths per minute with between 20 and 25 litres of air per breath. Thus, the galloping horse takes shallower and more frequent breaths than the Standardbred. However, both athletes have to move large volumes of air efficiently to compete successfully. The equine athlete has to move large volumes of air in a very short period of time. Even a small increase in the amounts of mucus in the airways and minor degrees of airway spasm or thickening of the lining of the airways will adversely affect performance.

The demands of athletic exertion are not without their costs on the horse's lungs. Training, strenuous exercise and the stress of transport affect one of the lungs' main defence mechanisms, i.e. macrophages (clean up cells). Such changes are believed to be important in explaining the increased incidence of respiratory diseases in horses exposed to these conditions. Air quality is a concern for air transport. Research by Dr. Des Leadon has shown that one of the most critical factors is the time the airplane spends on the ground. This is when the level of airborne pathogens can be highest. Hence, it is important to minimize the time it takes to load and unload horses and avoid delays at take off and sitting on the tarmac.

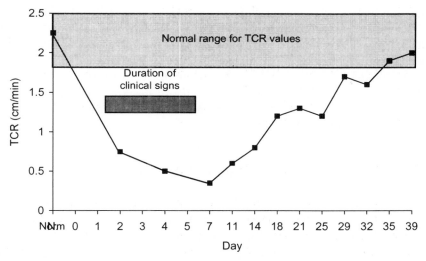

Figure 1: Summary of the average tracheal clearance rate (TCR) that occurred in seven horses before and following experimental infection with equine influenza (flu) virus on Day 0. The stippled area of the graph represents the normal range for TCR. For the 32 days between the pre-exposure (NORM) TCR to a return of TCR to the normal range at Day 35, the TCR values were significantly decreased. Note that the overall average TCR remained significantly decreased for more than four weeks after clinical signs had disappeared. (Willoughby *et al.*, 1990).

Horses involved in most forms of athletic exertion suffer exercise-induced pulmonary hemorrhage (EIPH). While only a small percentage of horses show blood at the nostrils, a much higher percentage will have a small amount of blood present in the airways after their competition. This hemorrhage originates from the upper back corner of the horse's lung. Previously, it was believed that underlying airway disease (inflammation) led to EIPH. However, it has also been shown that blood in the lung causes inflammation. This new knowledge will change our approaches to tackling EIPH. The latest research focus has been on the vascular system and blood pressure changes during exercise. Although the cause is not clear, on a day-to-day management basis we must remember that this hemorrhage occurs commonly and the site of hemorrhage makes an ideal location for secondary infection.

Inflammation of the small airways

The focus of this article is on small airway disease in horses. The best known is Chronic Obstructive Pulmonary Disease (COPD or "heaves"). This is a full-blown allergic disease. Horses suffering from COPD show obvious symptoms while at rest. These include a chronic cough, flared nostrils and forced abdominal breathing. This characteristic abdominal breathing occurs as the horse contracts its stomach muscles to force air through obstructed airways. The obstruction is caused by inflammation, increased mucus production and bronchospasm. COPD arises from what is believed to be a full-blown allergic response, usually to dust from the horse's feed and bedding. It is comparable to a person with severe asthma. A horse suffering with this condition would not be capable of moderate exercise without becoming severely distressed. COPD can manifest in many degrees of severity.

At the other end of the scale is a lower airway disease described as Lower Respiratory Tract Inflammation (LRTI) or Small Airway Disease (SAD). While it is not a full blown allergy as in the case of heaves, it is an inflammatory process. It usually becomes apparent when the horse is put under extreme exertion. This inflammation may not become apparent in the horse that is used for pleasure although the disease can become more severe with time until even light exercise becomes distressing.

The question arises: "Is small airway disease significant to the apparently healthy athlete?" The answer is, unfortunately, a resounding "yes!". Minor degrees of airway inflammation and small increases in mucus production quickly take their toll on the equine athlete attempting to take 150 breaths per minute, as is the case with horses in competition. Another complicating factor is that horses do not have a sensitive cough reflex. There can be quite a lot of mucus in the horse's airways without it coughing. This is in sharp contrast to humans and dogs. An endoscopic examination of the airways can reveal large amounts of mucus in a horse with no history of coughing. A horse with respiratory disease does not necessarily cough.

If a sample of mucus material is collected from the lungs, large numbers of neutrophils (pus cells) are usually found. Significant bacterial infections can be found when the samples are taken to the microbiology laboratory. These bacteria can be the primary cause of the problem, or they can be a secondary complicating issue following a viral infection. These secondary infections can increase the horse's recovery time.

COMMON CAUSES OF SMALL AIRWAY DISEASE

There are three common causes of small airway disease:

1. Infectious agents (including bacteria and viruses).

2. Airborne dust. Mould spores are the most common constituents and causes for concern in the air of stables. When inhaled in large enough numbers, these spores can cause inflammation and irritation of the small airways in horses which do not suffer allergy.

3. Noxious gases. The most common is ammonia.

It should always be highlighted that the above causes can interact in many ways. For example, dust can increase a horse's susceptibility to infection. Equally, a horse suffering a respiratory tract infection in a dusty environment will take a lot longer to recover than if it was breathing fresher air.

Another way these factors can interact has been demonstrated using nuclear medicine studies at the Equine Research Centre. These studies showed that it takes a month for the cilia lining the airways to recover their function following a bout of influenza. So, while the horse looks sick for only a few days, its lungs will take up to a month to recover (Figure 1). At this time, the lungs will also be very sensitive to the inhalation of airborne pollutants.

With the motto of "prevention being the best cure," emphasis should be placed on providing fresh air. Both the provision of fresh air, and therapeutic agents, will be discussed in this article as the latter can be particularly beneficial to getting horses back to full health and fitness to meet their true athletic potential.

Environment

The successful environmental control of disease involves maintaining the horse's level of exposure to irritants below that which induces disease. This critical level is called the Threshold Limiting Value (TLV). Unfortunately, the TLV for stable irritants is unknown. The level of irritants which can affect horses varies within and between individuals. The best approach lies in minimizing the horse's exposure to such contaminants at all times. The simplest management method is to turn the horse out for as many hours in the day as possible. This can facilitated by use of a run-in shed. When horses cannot be turned out in this way managing the indoor air quality becomes critical. There are two main sources of dust in the stable: the first is the horse's feed and the second is the bedding.

Forage

Hay is the single most common source of mould spores for the horse. All hay will have some mould spores present. There are many types of mould living on the hay as it grows in the field. These spores come from what are typically referred to as "field fungi" and are usually large and do not have a good chance of getting into the lower airways. The dust spores that are more dangerous are small (respirable). The highest exposures to dust are associated with hay that has been baled damp, as can happen after a rainy summer. The high moisture content influences the microflora in the bales and metabolic activity of the organisms causes the bales to heat. The moulds that thrive in this high moisture and heat are very prolific. The spores from these moulds are very small and when inhaled can reach deep into the lungs.

The soaking of hay is a time-proven method of minimizing the horse's exposure to mould spores. However, feeding soaked, poor quality hay to horses cannot be condoned. As hay which falls to the floor dries, the spores can again become airborne to be inhaled by the horse. Furthermore, even though the spores are not inhaled from soaked hay, they are still ingested along with any toxins present. Moulds produce secondary metabolites called mycotoxins which if present in large enough amounts can cause health problems. Mycotoxins may contribute to reproductive, immunological, respiratory, gastrointestinal and other disorders in livestock, including the horse. Preliminary studies at the Equine Research Centre have shown the presence of potentially significant levels of mycotoxins in hay being fed to horses. This was in hay that owners were happy with, based on visual inspection. In addition, in heavily moulded hay the nutritional content can be changed.

Alternatives to hay such as alfalfa cubes or haylage can be fed whenever the hay quality is in question (Figure 2). Silage and haylages are increasingly being successfully used as alternatives to hay. Haylage is mature grass or legume that is baled with a high moisture content but sealed in airtight plastic bags. As fermentation occurs the pH becomes lower. These acidic conditions inhibit mould growth. As long as the bags are airtight then there should be no mould growth. When the bags are opened to feed, they should be fed within two to three days as this product moulds very quickly once it has been exposed to air. Broken or damaged bags should not be used. There have been some deaths due to botulism associated primarily with big-bale silage. In this context, silage which smells of ammonia or contains dirt should be avoided.

Treated chaffed hay and straw and complete cubed diets also offer alternatives to feeding hay. These products are convenient and usually effective in minimizing respiratory disease.

Mycotoxins

"Mouldy" forage can contribute to a range of disorders in the horse. Inhaled fungal and actinomycete spores can cause primary allergic and inflammatory respiratory disease, as well as influencing the incidence, severity and duration of episodes of infectious respiratory disease. However, moulds may also produce toxic secondary metabolites called mycotoxins. Mycotoxins may contribute to reproductive, immunological, respiratory, gastrointestinal and other disorders in livestock including

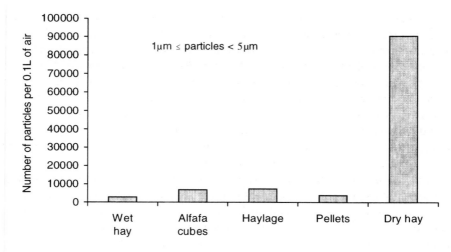

Figure 2. Dust particles associated with five forage products during feeding

the horse. Mycotoxins can behave as immunosuppressants thus having the possibility to contribute to secondary disorders. Mould and subsequent mycotoxin contamination of a forage can increase in extreme environmental conditions such as droughts or rain, followed by cold weather, or from mechanical damage to the forage.

Fusarium mycotoxins include vomitoxin (deoxynivalenol or DON), zearalenone, fumonisins, moniliformin and fusarin C. There is evidence of synergism between mycotoxins, one example being between vomitoxin and fusaric acid (a phytotoxin). Symptoms are induced at much lower levels of exposure when these two toxins are ingested together than when ingested separately.

Fumonisin B1 is associated with mouldy corn poisoning in horses (ELEM or Equine leukoencephalomacia). Animals must consume a feed which contains at least 10 ppm fumonisin B1 for ELEM to occur. Fumonisin B1 can also cause liver damage and pulmonary edema in horses and swine. Combined levels of fumonisin B1 and fumonisin B2 as low as 5 ppm have been associated with ELEM whereas swine were unaffected at those levels. Zearalenone is an estrogenic toxin. Toxicity can lead to reproductive problems including hyperestrogenism. Disorders seen in swine and horses include uterine enlargement and inflammation and atrophy of the ovaries. It has not been shown to cause abortions. Vomitoxin belongs to a group of mycotoxins called tricothecenes which have been associated with loss of appetite, vomiting, lesions of the intestinal tract, immunosuppression, lethargy and ataxia in domestic animals and man.

Preliminary studies at the Equine Research Centre have shown the presence of potentially significant levels of vomitoxin in hay being fed to horses. This was in hay that owners were happy with, based on visual inspection. Vomitoxin is among the most frequent tricothecene contaminant found on cereal crops in the United States. FDA levels of concern for vomitoxin for wheat are 2 ppm for wheat entering the milling process for humans and 1 ppm for the finished product for humans. The level for wheat for livestock is 4 ppm. As a comparison, the levels found in this study could potentially have an influence on the health of horses consuming such hay. The threshold of significant biological activity is unknown for the horse; however, chronic exposure to lower levels rather than acute exposure to high levels may contribute to a wide range of disorders.

Bedding

Even the cleanest of straw contains significantly more small, respirable fungal spores than alternative beddings, such as wood shavings, paper, peat or the new synthetic beddings. However, in poorly ventilated stables or where deep litter is allowed to accumulate, significant moulding of the plant-based beddings can occur. Deep litter management systems have the added disadvantage of allowing build-ups of bacteria, the larvae of gastro-intestinal parasites and noxious gases such as ammonia.

Ammonia

Ammonia is a recognized concern of stable management. The source of ammonia is the horse's urine and feces. Ammonia is released by the action of bacteria that degrade organic matter. Ammonia inhibits the movement of the cilia in the airways, consequently affecting these defence mechanisms' ability to remove particles from the lung. Ammonia can also increase mucus production. Aerial ammonia is highly soluble in water so much of it is absorbed in the upper airways. Ammonia can also be absorbed by hygroscopic dust particles. The ammonia can be released from these particles in the lung. Ammonia can be particularly high when stalls are being mucked out (Figure 3). If the horse is left in the stall during mucking, it will be subjected to high levels of ammonia and high levels of dust.

Management practises will affect the levels of ammonia that are found in a horse barn. Ammonia is water soluble so manure pits, wooden walls, bedding with high moisture contents and humid air can hold ammonia. Ammonia levels in barns increase with increasing temperatures and humidities. Methods which lower ammonia levels include a well drained floor, high ventilation rate, frequent mucking out and dry bedding with some commercially available control products.

Ventilation

A well-ventilated stable will help to minimize the horse's exposure to a wide range of environmental contaminants. These include fungal spores, bacteria, and noxious gases.

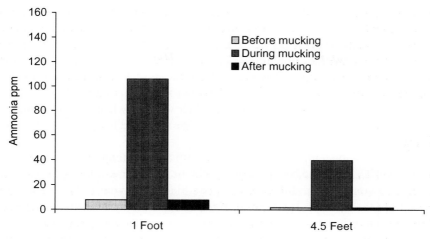

Figure 3. Ammonia levels measured at two heights above floor level in stalls with straw bedding

However, significant levels of fungal spores can be inhaled in well-ventilated stables when contaminated feeds and beddings are present. The horse is inquisitive; it sniffs at its bedding. When the horse lies down, its nostrils are positioned for maximum uptake of spores released from its bedding. Indeed, a horse given mouldy hay in the field (the ultimate of natural ventilation) can still come down with airway problems.

The importance of ventilation in stalls even where clean feeds or beddings are used cannot be over-emphasized (Figure 4). Ventilation will help to overcome condensation, prevent moulding of bedding material *in situ* and minimize the levels of all airborne contaminants to which the horse may be exposed.

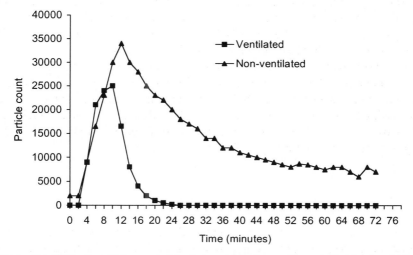

Figure 4. The effects of ventilation on dust levels in a stable after mucking out. Dust levels quickly drop in the well-ventilated stable

To ensure adequate ventilation when designing new or altering existing horse accommodation, openings must be positioned or mechanical ventilators used to allow six to eight air changes per hour. Proper mixing of air throughout the whole building is critical, the latter being particularly important with barns. Louvres or Netlon can be used to prevent draughts at horse height. In warmer weather, barn doors and windows are usually left open. Ventilation systems should be designed to achieve sufficient air changes in the barn in colder weather when these openings are closed. The ideal ventilation system must provide adequate fresh air and distribute it uniformly without causing drafts.

Horses have a wide temperature tolerance, with an ideal temperature range being between 10-30°C. In a cold barn without drafts the only horses likely to experience cold stress are young foals. It is better to put a blanket on your horse and to allow some air flow then to shut the barn up tight. If extra heat is needed there are a number of infrared heaters on the market that are very suitable for stables.

Insulation

During the winter many people make the mistake of trying to keep the barn warm by severely reducing ventilation. The result is that moisture cannot escape and a cold, clammy, damp environment is produced. Insulation allows you to maintain a tolerable temperature inside the stable, even though a constant air exchange is occurring. In the winter insulation conserves heat and reduces condensation and in the summer it helps to keep the barn cooler. In the spring and fall, insulation helps to maintain a stable environment inside while there are temperature fluctuations outside caused by warm days and cold nights. The vents in a well insulated barn can be smaller than in a non-insulated barn.

Condensation occurs when warm moist air contacts a cold inside wall (Figure 5). If the surface temperature of the inside wall is below the dew point (55°F or 13°C), air next to the surface becomes saturated and moisture condenses to water. When the surface temperature is below freezing, frost occurs. Water stains on the ceiling of a barn or stable are tell-tale signs of moisture and/or ventilation problems.

If the inside wall is warmer then the outside wall (close to 55°F or 13°C, the dewpoint) then condensation will not occur (Figure 6). However, the air will cool as it passes between the two walls and condense on the outside wall. To solve this problem, a vapour barrier on the warm wall can also help prevent condensation in the insulation. Wet insulation is not as effective and condensation could lead to rotting of the barn structure.

Sunlight

Sunlight is one useful natural resource often overlooked with horse housing. A skylight of clear perspex in the roof allows light, including the UV rays, into the stable. The UV rays are a strong and inexpensive natural killer of bacteria and viruses. A general guide is 10% of the roof area used for skylights.

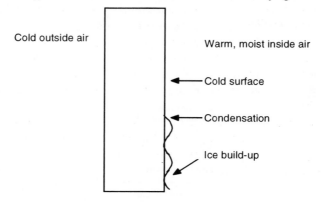

Figure 5. No insulation

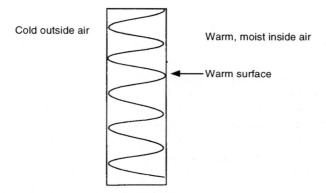

Figure 6. Insulation

Prophylactic and therapeutic approaches to non-infectious lower respiratory tract diseases

An overview of prophylactic and therapeutic approaches to LRTI and COPD will be provided in this section. These conditions share some common pathophysiological changes. However, there are facets of both conditions that are unique in terms of therapeutic approaches and some situations where pharmaceuticals used in treating one condition are inappropriate when dealing with the other. Even more seriously pharmaceuticals appropriate for the treatment of one condition could be life threatening in the other.

Figure 7 presents a step-wise progression up a pyramid for the treatment and alleviation of COPD. Therapy starts at the bottom of the pyramid and if symptoms persist or worsen each tier is added in turn until satisfactory control occurs. Once the horse is stabilized, the pyramid can be descended as tiers are progressively removed.

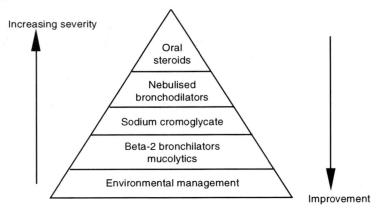

Figure 7. COPD therapy objectives (Clarke, *et al.*, 1995)

STEP 1: ENVIRONMENTAL MANAGEMENT

This is the most important component of treating and preventing COPD. Failure to properly attend to air hygiene is the primary reason for failure of therapeutic regimens. Poor air quality is also an important causative factor associated with LRTI. Inhaled mould spores can induce a primary inflammatory response without an allergic reaction occurring. However, it must also be remembered that infectious agents including viruses, bacteria and mycoplasms are involved in many episodes of LRTI. Even when these pathogens are involved, attention to air hygiene is important in decreasing the severity of symptoms in individual cases and also in hastening the recovery from an infection.

The principles involved in the environmental management in relation to air hygiene of stables have been reviewed previously in this article. The critical factors include:

a)   the provision of adequate ventilation and appropriate drainage within stables,

b)   the use of alternatives to straw for bedding,

c)   the avoidance of deep litter bedding and

d)   the provision of forage using the than traditionally made hay.

STEP 2: BRONCHODILATORS AND MUCOLYTICS

Bronchodilators, mucus accumulation and the increased production of thick tenacious mucus are common pathophysiological changes associated with diseases of the lower airways. The B2-agonist clenbuterol (Ventipulmin, Boehringer Ingelheim) is the most widely used bronchodilator in equine practice. Anticholinergics e.g. atropine though effective as bronchodilators can have unwanted systemic side effects. Xanthene derivatives including theophylline and aminophylline are bronchodilators, but have short durations of action and side effects including tachycardia and sweating which are frequently seen due to their narrow therapeutic margin. The mucolytic agent dembrexine is often used in combination with a beta2-agonist to alleviate symptoms associated with accumulators of mucus. Mucolytic agents help to decrease the viscosity of thick tenacious mucus while the beta2 agonist will stimulate mucociliary clearance enhancing the removal of mucus from the lungs.

STEP 3: SODIUM CROMOGLYCATE

The administration of sodium cromoglycate by nebulizer one a day for 5 days can provide up to 1 month of prophylaxis to asymptomatic COPD horses exposed to poor air hygiene. There does appear to be individual variation in responsiveness to sodium cromoglycate. Sodium cromoglycate is known as a mast cell stabilizer. There may be another mechanism by which it induces protection to inhaled allergens.

STEP 4: NEBULIZED BRONCHODILATORS

Nebulization of clenbuterol has been shown to be effective in inducing bronchodilation in horses which are non-responsive to intravenous or oral clenbuterol. Ipratropium bromide is an atropinic agent which induces bronchodilation when administered by nebulization. One advantage of nebulization is that it can be used to avoid unwanted side effects associated with systemic administration of pharmaceuticals; however, there is added inconvenience and cost associated with the use of nebulization. While there are unlikely to be a lot of new drugs to treat respiratory disease in the future, there will be new technologies such as inhalers which will facilitate the delivery of pharmaceuticals directly into the lung.

STEP 5: ORAL CORTICOSTEROIDS

Corticosteroids are used to treat COPD a lot more frequently in North America than in Great Britain. Laminitis is one steroid-induced side effect that is cause for concern.

Care should also be taken in administering corticosteroids to horses which may have a respiratory tract infection. These risks can be minimized by careful choice of dose and frequency of administration. Dosage should be decreased as the horse's condition improves. Another strategy involves the simultaneous use of a corticosteroid with a beta2-agonist.

Conclusion

Considerable short and long term demands are placed on the equine athlete's lungs. Special attention must be paid to the quality of the air which our horses breathe. Respiratory tract infections are practically unavoidable with competing athletes, even with the most up-to-date vaccines. Pharmaceuticals will continue to have an important role in these and in other respiratory problems of horses. As to respiratory disease of horses, the two main messages suggested are firstly, that prevention is better than cure, and secondly, the earlier treatment is commenced, the sooner the horse will recover.

FOR CONSIDERATION IN EVERYDAY STABLE MANAGEMENT:

- wet all hay that is fed indoors and feed it on ground level
- sprinkle the barn aisle with water when sweeping
- remove the horse from the barn when the stalls are being mucked or swept
- turnout for as long as possible
- use a low dust bedding with a daily mucking out
- consider ventilation during all seasons
- up to date vaccination program
- exercise horses regularly

References

Barnett D.T., R.A. Mowery, W.M. Hagler, D.G. Bristol and R.A. Mansmann: The correlation of selected mycotoxins to the incidence of colic in horses. Proceedings of the Fourteenth Equine Nutrition and Physiology Symposium. 242-247, 1995.

Casteel S.W., G.E. Rottinghaus, G.C. Johnson and D.T. Wicklow: Liver disease in cattle induced by consumption of moldy hay. Vet. Human Toxicol. 37(3): 248-251, 1995.

Clarke A.F.: Stable dust-threshold limiting values, exposure variables and host risk factors. Eq. Vet. J. 25(3): 172-174, 1993.

Clarke A.F., P.M. Dixon and J.D. Slater: The Lower Respiratory Tract in *The Equine Manual.* Higgins A,J. and I.M.Wright (ed). 355-379, 1995.

Gimeno A. and J.A. Quintanilla: Analytical and mycological study of a natural outbreak of zearalenone mycotoxicosis in horses. Proceedings of the International Symposium of Mycotoxins. 387-392, 1983.

Hintz H.F.: Moldy corn, megacolon and hyperlipidemia. Eq. Prac. 13(5): 23-24, 1991.

Lacey J.: Potential hazards to animals and man from microorganisms in fodders and grain. Trans. Br. Mycol. Soc. 65(2): 171-184, 1975.

Mills P.C., D.J. Marlin, E. Demoncheaux, C. Scott, I. Casas, N.C. Smith and T. Higenbottam: Nitric oxide and exercise in the horse. J. Physiol. 495(3): 863-874, 1996.

Robinson N.E., F.J. Derksen, M.A. Olszewski and V.A. Buechner-Maxwell: The pathogenesis of chronic obstructive pulmonary disease of horses. Br. Vet. J. 152(3): 283-306, 1996.

Smith B.L., J.H. Jones, W.J. Hornof, J.A. Miles, K.E. Longworth and N.H. Willits: Effects of road transport on indices of stress in horses. Eq. Vet. J. 28(6): 446-454, 1996.

Smith T.K. and I.R. Seddon: The effect of feeding *fusarium* mycotoxins, individually and in combinations, on animal health and performance. Proceedings of the fifth international symposium on animal nutrition. 103-117, 1996.

Smith T.K.: Recent advances in the understanding of *Fusarium* trichothecene mycotoxicoses.J. Anim. Sci. 70: 3989-3993, 1992.

Wood G.E.: Mycotoxins in foods and feeds in the United States. J. Anim. Sci. 70:3941-3949, 1992.

This paper was first published in Proceedings, Kentucky Equine Research 1997 Equine Nutrition Conference

INDEX

A

acid detergent fiber (ADF) 16
acid detergent insoluble nitrogen 16
acquired angular limb deformities 387
acquired flexural deformities 495
Acremonium coenophialum 537
adenosine triphosphate (ATP) 141
aflatoxins 531, 535
age of weaning 457
ammonia 546
angular limb deformities 390, 403
anhydrosis 479
antioxidants 195
arsenic 245
aspartate amino-transferase (AST) 299
Australia
    feeding practices 331

B

B-vitamins 194
    effect of exercise 259
barley 63
bee pollen 192
beet pulp 35, 308
big head disease 51
biomechanics 127
biotin
    hoof condition 253
black walnut
    toxicity 499
blister beetles 497
blood
    analysis 167

blood flow 153, 251
    effect of exercise 151
    effect of feeding 151
blood glucose 93
blood spavin 136
blood tests
    interpretations 173
    to evaluate nutritional status 172
    various parameters 174
body weight 105
    estimation 107
body weights
    mature Thoroughbreds 454
bog spavin 136
bone density 458
bone disease
    in the athletic horse 405
bone spavin 137
bowed tendons 137
bran mashes 307
broodmare
    nutrition 489
bufotenine 245

C

Ca:P ratio 52
caffeine 246
calcium 515, 527
    growing horses 423
    recommended intake
        Sweden 348
    requirements
        growing horses 53
        lactating mares 53

maintenance 52
pregnant mares 53
calcium:oxalate ratio 25
capped hocks 137
carbohydrate
digestibility 31
cardiac output 152
cardiovascular system 127
carnitine 192
cation-anion balance 520
cecal pH 6, 7, 8
cereal grains 57
chaff 322, 337
chloride 517
choke 311
chromium 40, 211
effect on performance 263
chronic obstructive pulmonary disease
(COPD) 503, 542
cocaine 247
coenzyme Q10 192
colic 483, 498
concentrates
Australia and New Zealand 334
condition score 109, 450
conformation 129
balance 129
muscling 131
copper 212
growing horses 423
requirements 53
weanlings 53
coprophagy 315
corn 60
cortisol 265, 284
cotinine/trans-3-hydroxycotinine 246
creatine kinase (CK) 299
creatinine 169
crimped oats
vs whole 312
cuboidal bone abnormalities 387
cuboidal bone malformation 391
curb 137
cystitis 499

D

degenerative joint disease (DJD) 481
developmental orthopedic disease (DOD)
386, 461, 469, 491
and body weight 473
fetlock 472
frequency 471
hock 472
shoulder and stifle 472
dexamethasone 465
digestibility
extruded 5
in ponies 322
pellets 5
prececal 32
starch 33
protein 43
starch 4
textured 5
digestible energy (DE) 71, 72
content
feed ingredients 74
from chemical composition 73
requirements
exercise 355
digestive function 13
digestive system 149
dimethyl sulfoxide (DMSO) 244
dimethylglycine (DMG) 275
dressage horse
feeding 319
drugs
testing 229

E

effect of feeding
glucose and glycogen response 293
electrolyte requirements
function of exercise intensity 203
function of sweat loss 201
electrolyte status 523
electrolytes 201, 358
and rhabdomyolysis 202

chloride 201
magnesium 201
potassium 201
requirements for exercise 521
sodium 201
supplementing 203
sweat losses 521
ELISA tests 233
endogenous losses 52, 79, 81
endurance
  effect of feeding 297
endurance horse
  calcium 346
  fatty acids and glycerol 344
  feeding 341, 351
  insulin 345

  magnesium
    deficiency 347
  potassium 342
  protein
    excess 344
  sodium 342
energy
  performance horse 141
  requirements
    growing horses 407
energy requirements
  lactating mares 415
  suckling foals 415
enteroliths 500
enzymes 10
epiphyseal disturbances 462
equine digestive tract
  pH 3
equine leukoencephalomalacia (ELEM)
  537
ergogenic aids 191
exchangeable cation loss 523
exercise
  aerobic 185
  anaerobic 186
  and gut function 153
exercise performance

effect of warming up 303
exercise-induced pulmonary hemorrhage
  (EIPH) 541
exertional rhabdomyolysis 507
  acute 508
  recurrent 509
  sporadic 507
    diagnosis 508
    treatment 508

F

fat 40, 146, 356
  body condition
    athletic ability 256
  digestibility 254
  feeding
    for performance 253
feed
  expected consumption 27, 115
  processing 66
    extrusion 69
    grinding 66
    micronizing 66
    pelleting 68
    popping 66
    roasting 67
    steam flaking 67
feed processing
  effect on digestion 3
feeding
  behavior 38
  halter horses 365
  sales horses 365
  weanlings 365
  yearlings 443
feeding fat
  long term effects 281
feeding frequency
  effect on digestibility 85
  effects on behavior 89
feeding management
  endurance
    forage 359

grain 360
feeding recommendations
  high intensity, short duration exercise 157
  low intensity, long duration exercise 158
  moderate intensity, moderate duration exercise 157
fescue
  toxicity 496
fiber 147, 357
  fermentable 40
fistula 137
flexural deformities 387
forage 13
  analysis 15
    acid detergent fiber (ADF) 16
    crude fat 16
    crude fiber 17
    dry matter 15
    lignin 17
    neutral detergent fiber (NDF) 17
    protein 15
  composition 14, 21
  digestibility
    effects of silica and lignin 24
  intake 26
  quality 19
  time of feeding 33
forage composition 14
forage quality
  factors affecting
    inhibitory substances 23
    latitude 23
    species 19
    stage of maturity 21
forging 137
founder (laminitis) 137
fractional electrolyte excretion test 524
free choice minerals 314
Fusarium 531, 545
futurity weanlings 440

G

glucose 284, 290
  blood 39
glycemic response
  effect of added fat 93
glycogen
  utilization
    function of speed 142
glycolysis 142
goiter 504
gross energy 71
  values 72
growth rate
  effect of month of birth 452
  effect of season of year 453
growth rates
  colts 451
  fillies 451
  Thoroughbreds 449

H

halter and sales horses
  feeding 365
halter yearlings 443
hay
  coastal bermuda 317
  first cutting 316
  new 315
hay grades 20
haylage 321
hays
  selecting 26
heart rate 268
heat of combustion 71
heating feed 309
heaves 503
hematinics 195
hordenine 243
hormones
  resting levels 282
hydrocortisone 247
hyperglycemia 39

I

insulin 265, 284, 294
  resistance 39
iodine 210
ionophores 502
iron 196, 205
  deficiency
    performance horses 196

J

juvenile osteoarthritis 387

L

lactate 265, 291
laminitis 137, 485
Lucas test 80
lupins 337
lysine requirements 411
lysine:DE ratio 411

M

magnesium 516
  deficiency 347

  recommended intake
    Sweden 348
magnesium deficiency 347
manganese 207
micronized feeds 320
MicroSteed™ 122
mineral absorption
  effect of age 519
mineral requirements 51, 83
  calcium 83
  copper 54, 83
  magnesium 83
  manganese 83
  phosphorus 83
  zinc 54, 83
molasses
  colic 310
molasses, cane 30, 36

moldy corn poisoning 537
morphine 244
muscle fiber types 354
muscle glycogen
  concentrations 295
mycotoxins 531, 535, 544
myths and wives' tales 307

N

navicular disease 137
neutral detergent fiber (NDF) 17
New Zealand
  feeding practices 331
niacin
  supplementation
    exercise 271
nicotine 246
non-structural carbohydrates (NSC)
  29, 35
  fructose 30
  glucose 30
  starch 30
  sucrose 30
nutrient
  interactions 82
  requirements 82, 112
    digestible energy (DE) 113, 114
    minerals 83
nutrient composition 36
  barley 63
  cereal grains 36
    digestible energy 74, 116
  corn 60
  hay
    digestible energy 74, 116
  hays 36
  oats 62
  pasture
    digestible energy 116
  wheat products 65
nutrient digestibility 77, 79
  apparent 79
  true 79
nutrient requirements

growing horses 424
protein
  performance horses 161
weanlings 424
yearlings 425
nutritional secondary hyperparathyroid-
    ism (NSH) 24, 464, 496

O

oats 61
osteochondritis dissecans (OCD)
    390, 394
  hock 397
    treatment 397
  shoulder 400
  stifle 395
    treatment 396
osteochondrosis 53, 386, 389, 493
  causative factors 391
    endocrine factors 393
    exercise 394
    genetic predisposition 391
    growth and body size 392
    mechanical stress and trauma 392
    mineral imbalances 393
    nutrition 392
    site vulnerability 394
osteoporosis 51
oxalate 23, 24, 25, 52
oxidative phosphorylation 142

P

pasture
  intake 117
pastures
  Australia and New Zealand 331
pathological conditions
  performance horse 477
    anhydrosis 479
    degenerative joint disease (DJD) 481
    thumps 480
    tying-up 477
peas 337
phosphorus 517

growing horses 423
requirements 53
  growing horses 53
  lactating mares 53
physeal disturbances 462
physitis 387, 390, 405, 491
  and copper 464
  treatment 405
phytate 23
plasma cortisol 267
plasma glucose 266, 294
plasma insulin 266
plasma lactate 267
plasma triglycerides 268
plasma volume 35
polysaccharide storage myopathy
    (PSSM) 511
pot bellies 312
potassium 517
protein 146, 358
  behavior 308
  DOD 314
  excess
    adverse effects 164
  quality 44
  requirements
    broodmares 47
    growing horses 45, 407
    performance horses 48, 161
protein supplements
  Australia and New Zealand 335
protein to energy ratio 45

R

rate of intake 5
requirements
  protein 43
respiratory system 126, 539
rhabdomyolysis 202, 477, 507, 528
  chronic intermittent 509
ringbone 138
roughage
  Australia and New Zealand 332

S

sales weanlings 442
sales yearlings 444
salicylate 243
scopolamine 244
selenium 97, 208
  deficiency 505
  functions of 99
  injectable Se/vitamin E products 101
  reference values 100
  status
    assessment of 99
  toxicity 101
serotonin 39
sidebone 138
skeleton 383
sodium 517
sodium bicarbonate 196, 242
soy hulls 35
soybean meal 58
soybean oil 93
splint 138
standardized step-wise exercise test
    (STEP) 283
starch 32, 145, 356
  processing 33
  sources 31
structural carbohydrates (cell wall) 29
subchondral cystic lesions 387, 390, 400
suckling foal
  supplemental energy 418
suckling foals 408
sunflower seeds 337
supplements
  Australia and New Zealand 335
sweat composition
  electrolytes 522
sweeney 138

T

T^4/T^3 ratio 278
testosterone 247
theobromine 246

three-day event horse
  feeding 319
thumps 480
thyroid hormone
  effect of feeding 277
thyroxine 345
tick beans 337
time of feeding 360
  before competition 37
  effect on exercise 289
total digestible nutrients (TDN) 73
total plasma protein (TPP) 35
trace mineral salt 313
trace minerals
  performance horses 205
training
  endurance 187
  speed 188
trimethylglycine (TMG)
  effect on performance 275
two year olds 410
tying up 39, 505
  electrolytes 513

U

ulcers 486
urea toxicity 501
urine fractional excretion, FE 169

V

V^{200} 283
vitamin A 216
  dietary sources
    natural 217
    synthetic 217
  forms
    active 216
    inactive 216
  functions 216
  requirement 217
    maintenance 217
  toxicity 218
vitamin D 219
  forms
    plant and animal 219

functions 219
performance 221
toxicity 221
vitamin E
  dietary sources 222
  forms
    natural 222
    synthetic 222
  functions 221
  performance 261
  requirements
    maintenance 225
    performance 225
  toxicity 225
vitamin K
  added to feed 225
  forms
    microbial 224
    plant 224
    synthetic 224
  functions 224
  requirements
    maintenance 225
    performance 225
  sources
    natural 224
  toxicity 225
V^{LA4} 283
volatile fatty acids (VFA) 6
vomitoxin 545

W

water 358
weanling 457
  foal growth 457
  nutrition evaluation 119
weanlings 409
  futurity 440
  sales 442
western performance horse
  feeding 373
wheat 64
  bran 64
  middlings 64
  mill run 64
white muscle disease 505
wobbler syndrome 493
wood chewing 500

Y

yearlings 410
yeast culture 9, 24, 447
  growth of foals 447

Z

zearalenone 531, 545
zinc 212
  growing horses 423

CONTRIBUTING AUTHORS

Beyer, Mike, D.V.M.
Hagyard-Davidson-McGee Veterinary Clinic, USA

Bramlage, L.R., D.V.M., M.S., Diplomate ACVS
Rood and Riddle Equine Hospital, USA

Breuer, Les, Ph.D.
L.H. Breuer & Associates, USA

Brewster-Barnes, Tammy, M.S.
University of Kentucky, USA

Clarke, Andrew F., Ph.D., B.V.Sc., MRCVS
Equine Research Centre, Canada

Crandell, Kathleen, Ph.D.
Kentucky Equine Research, Ind., USA

Danielsen, Kristin, Ph.D.
Halsetreina 17, Trondheim, Norway

Duren, Stephen E., Ph.D.
Kentucky Equine Research, Inc., USA

Fahrenholz, Charles, Ph.D.
SmithKline Beecham, USA

Gill, Amy, M.S.
University of Kentucky, USA

Griffin, Ashley S., M.S.
University of Kentucky, USA

Harris, Pat, Ph.D., B.V.Sc.
Waltham Centre for Pet Nutrition, England

Hintz, Harold, Ph.D.
Cornell University, USA

Hollands, Teresa, M.Sc.
Dodson and Horrell, UK

Huntington, Peter, B.V.Sc. (Hons), MACVSc, MRCVS
Rhone-Poulenc Animal Nutrition, Australia

Jackson, Stephen G., Ph.D.
Kentucky Equine Research, Inc., USA

Lawrence, Laurie, Ph.D.
University of Kentucky, USA

McIlwraith, C. Wayne, B.V.Sc., Ph.D., Diplomate ACVS, FRCVS
Colorado State University, USA

Pagan, Joe D., Ph.D.
Kentucky Equine Research, Inc., USA

Parker, Amy L., M.S.
University of Kentucky, USA

Powell, Debbie, M.S.
University of Kentucky, USA

Raymond, Susan L.
Equine Research Center, Canada

Reagor, John, Ph.D.
Texas A&M University, USA

Rokuroda, S., M.S.
University of Kentucky, USA

Siciliano, P.D., Ph.D.
University of Kentucky, USA

Spangfors, Per, D.V.M.
Euro-VETS AB, Sweden

Tobin, Thomas, M.V.B., Ph.D.
University of Kentucky, USA

Valberg, Stephanie, D.V.M., Ph.D.
University of Minnesota, USA

Warren, Lori K., M.S.
University of Kentucky, USA

KENTUCKY EQUINE RESEARCH
TEAM MEMBERS

AUSTRALIA

New South Wales:
  Pryde's Feed
  Gunnedah, NSW
Queensland:
  Jenco Feeds
  Allora, QLD
South Australia:
  Hy Gain Feeds
  Officer, VIC
Tasmania:
  Pivot, Ltd.
  Launceston, TAS
Victoria:
  Hy Gain Feeds
  Officer, VIC
West Australia:
  Hy Gain Feeds
  Officer, VIC

CANADA

Alberta:
  Landmark Feed
  Clare's Home, ALB
British Columbia:
  Otter Co-Op
  Aldergrove, BC
Ontario:
  Brooks' Feed
  Port Perry, ONT
  Tottenham
  Feed Services
  Tottenham, ONT
Quebec:
  Nutribec, Ltd.
  St. Hyacinthe

COLOMBIA

  Solla
  Medellin

IRELAND

  M. Kelliher
  & Sons, Ltd.
  Tralee, Co. Kerry

NEW ZEALAND

  NRM
  Auckland

PUERTO RICO

  Molinos de
  Puerto Rico
  San Juan, PR

SWITZERLAND

  AllPharm Ag
  Pfeffingen

UNITED KINGDOM

  Dodson &
  Horrell, Ltd.
  Ringstead, Kettering

UNITED STATES

Arizona:
  Lakin Milling Co.
  Avondale, AZ

California:
Farmers
Warehouse Co.
Keyes, CA

Florida:
Lakeland Cash Feeds
Lakeland, FL

Georgia:
Flint River Mills
Bainbridge, GA

Indiana:
Farmers Grain Co.
Pershing, IN

Kentucky:
Bagdad Roller Mills,Inc.
Bagdad, KY
Burkmann Mills
Danville, KY
Brumfield Hay
& Grain
Lexington, KY
Farmer's Feed Mill
Lexington, KY
Producer Feeds
Louisville, KY
Woodford Feed
Versailles, KY

Michigan:
Armada Grain Co.
Armada, MI
Hamilton Farm Bureau
Hamilton, MI

Minnesota:
Hubbard Feeds, Inc.
Mankato, MN

Nebraska:
Nutrition Services, inc.
York, NB

North Carolina:
Bartlett Milling Co.
Statesville, NC

Ohio:
Premier Feeds
Wilmington, OH

Pennsylvania:
Brandt's Mill
Lebanon, PA
Pennfield Corp.
Lancaster, PA

South Carolina:
Banks Mill
Aiken, SC

Texas:
PM Ag Products
Fort Worth, TX
Postive Feed, Inc.
Sealy, TX

Utah:
Cache Commodities
Ogden, Utah

Vermont:
Poulin Grain, Inc.
Newport, VT

Virginia:
Culpeper Farmers
Co-op.
Culpeper, VA

Washington:
LMF Feeds Incorporated
Deer Park, WA
Aslin-Finch Wholesale
Spokane, WA
Otter Co-op
Sumas, WA

Wisconsin:
Burlington
Consumers Co-op
Burlington, WI

WEST INDIES

Master Blend Feeds
St. Catherine, Jamaica